Literary Geography

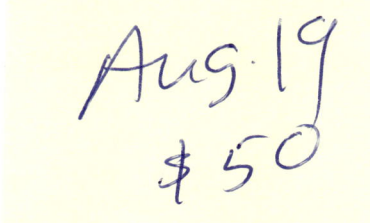

Literary Geography

An Encyclopedia of Real and Imagined Settings

Lynn Marie Houston, Editor

GREENWOOD

An Imprint of ABC-CLIO, LLC
Santa Barbara, California • Denver, Colorado

Copyright © 2019 by ABC-CLIO, LLC

All rights reserved. No part of this publication may be reproduced, stored in a retrieval system, or transmitted, in any form or by any means, electronic, mechanical, photocopying, recording, or otherwise, except for the inclusion of brief quotations in a review, without prior permission in writing from the publisher.

Library of Congress Cataloging-in-Publication Data

Names: Houston, Lynn Marie, editor.
Title: Literary geography : an encyclopedia of real and imagined settings / Lynn Marie Houston, editor.
Description: Santa Barbara, California : Greenwood, 2019. | Includes bibliographical references and index.
Identifiers: LCCN 2019003287 (print) | LCCN 2019004372 (ebook) | ISBN 9781440842559 (ebook) | ISBN 9781440842542 (hardback : alk. paper)
Subjects: LCSH: Setting (Literature) | Literary landmarks. | Literature—Encyclopedias.
Classification: LCC PN56.S48 (ebook) | LCC PN56.S48 L58 2019 (print) | DDC 809/.922—dc23
LC record available at https://lccn.loc.gov/2019003287

ISBN: 978-1-4408-4254-2 (print)
     978-1-4408-4255-9 (ebook)

23 22 21 20 19   1 2 3 4 5

This book is also available as an eBook.

Greenwood
An Imprint of ABC-CLIO, LLC

ABC-CLIO, LLC
147 Castilian Drive
Santa Barbara, California 93117
www.abc-clio.com

This book is printed on acid-free paper ∞

Manufactured in the United States of America

Contents

Acknowledgments ix

Introduction xi

Place in Poetry xvii

Place in Prose xxi

A–Z Entries
Absalom, Absalom! 1
Adventures of Huckleberry Finn 4
Adventures of Sherlock Holmes 7
All Quiet on the Western Front 10
All the Pretty Horses 14
Almanac of the Dead 17
Antigone 20
Anzaldúa, Gloria 22
Arthurian Tales 25
As I Lay Dying 28
Awakening, The 30
Beloved 34
Berry, Wendell 37
Billy Budd 39
Bishop, Elizabeth 42
Bless Me, Ultima 45
Book Thief, The 47
Brave New World 50
Brideshead Revisited 52
Call of the Wild, The 56
Catcher in the Rye, The 59

Ceremony 61
Crime and Punishment 64
Crucible, The 66
Daisy Miller 70
Death of a Salesman 73
Dickinson, Emily 75
Dispatches 79
Dracula 83
Ender's Game 86
Enemy of the People, An 88
Extremely Loud & Incredibly Close 90
"Fall of the House of Usher, The" 94
Fear and Loathing in Las Vegas 97
Frankenstein 100
Frost, Robert 102
Glass Menagerie, The 105
Grapes of Wrath, The 107
Great Expectations 111
Great Gatsby, The 114
Gulliver's Travels 117
Hamlet 120
Handmaid's Tale, The 122
Harry Potter Series, The 127
Hass, Robert 130
Heaney, Seamus 132
Heart of Darkness 135
Hitchhiker's Guide to the Galaxy, The 138
House on Mango Street, The 140
Hughes, Langston 143
Hugo, Richard 146
Hunger Games, The 147
Irving, Washington 150
Jane Eyre 153
Jungle, The 156
King Lear 160
Kite Runner, The 163
Last of the Mohicans, The 166

Contents

Long Day's Journey into Night 168
Lord of the Flies 171
Lord of the Rings 174
Macbeth 177
"*Metamorphosis, The*" 179
Midsummer Night's Dream, A 181
Moby Dick 184
My Àntonia 187
Nineteen Eighty-Four 192
No Country for Old Men 194
Odyssey, The 197
Oedipus Rex 200
Of Mice and Men 203
Old Man and the Sea, The 205
Oliver, Mary 208
Oliver Twist 211
On the Road 214
One Flew Over the Cuckoo's Nest 217
One Hundred Years of Solitude 220
Plague, The 223
Poe, Edgar Allan 225
Poisonwood Bible, The 230
Pride and Prejudice 234
Raisin in the Sun, A 238
Red Badge of Courage, The 240
Robinson Crusoe 242
Romeo and Juliet 247
Scarlet Letter, The 252
Slaughterhouse-Five 255
Snyder, Gary 258
Sound and the Fury, The 260
Stevens, Wallace 264
Streetcar Named Desire, A 266
Sula 268
Sun Also Rises, The 272
Their Eyes Were Watching God 275
Things They Carried, The 277

To Kill a Mockingbird 280
Uncle Tom's Cabin 283
Waiting for Godot 288
Walcott, Derek 290
Whitman, Walt 293
Williams, William Carlos 296
Wizard of Oz, The 299
Wordsworth, William 302
Wuthering Heights 304
"Yellow Wallpaper, The" 309

Appendix: Literary Landscapes and Capital Cities 315
Bibliography 335
About the Editor and Contributors 339
Index 345

Acknowledgments

Two things happened nearly simultaneously during one week in October 2014: I signed the contract for this book and I was interviewed by phone for a teaching job that I wanted very much. Green Mountain College in Vermont was hiring a poetry teacher whose duties were to include teaching an introductory class on the environment, pretty much my dream class. I had a long list of ideas ready for that course, which I would have taught as "geography and place in poetry": I was ready with readings I would have included, assignments I would have offered, and outdoor activities we would have done. I was sure that in signing the contract for this book, I was all but guaranteeing that I would be offered the position. I'd had a long history as a poetry scholar and an award-winning start to my creative writing career once I started publishing poetry regularly. I even had a long history as an environmentalist: from my teenage years as a counselor in training at the New York State Department of Environmental Conservation summer camp named Camp Debruce, to a recent stint of four years during which I conducted my own transcendentalist experiment by living in an Airstream camper that I hooked up to solar panels and in which I installed a waterless, composting toilet.

Well, I didn't get the job at Green Mountain College. They hired a more established poet, opting to emphasize the poetry portion of the job description over the environmental component. And there I was with this long, involved book to edit and write. I had already imagined myself consulting colleagues in Vermont for input, writing it next to a cozy fire at a campus coffee shop while snow confettied the mountains around us. I stewed about it for a few months, and then I got to work. I decided that I was looking at things the wrong way: the real win was the opportunity to write and publish this book. As I've grown older, I've discovered that the real prize is always the work itself.

Life has brought me many other surprises during the nearly five years I've worked on this project, and the work was there with me through it all, a steady friend. I'm feeling a little sad to let it go now so that it can do its work in the wider world. This manuscript was my companion through a couple of romances, celebrations for poetry prizes I've won, the passing of friends and relatives, and moves to three different states, including this last one, which has taken me out of the halls of academia and into an entirely new career field: overseeing the production of technical manuals for avionics systems and writing about military history. Since then, Green Mountain College has announced that it will close its doors in May 2019.

Acknowledgments

With that news and my new career, it feels like the end of an era. I finished the last sections of this book with the urgent feeling that I wanted to record on paper everything I had learned from discussing many of these works with students over the nearly 20 years I taught college English. I'm incredibly grateful to the federal government for their flexibility in offering a wide range of work schedules so that I had enough large blocks of free time to complete this work.

My life now is very different than what I imagined it would be when I daydreamed about a poetry position at Green Mountain College. However, over the years, reflections on my failure to get that job have prompted me to change this book in positive ways: for instance, when I first began working with my editor on the table of contents, we did not have a single poet in it. It finally dawned on me—how can we say this book is a reference work for geography in "literature" when we are missing coverage of one of the major genres in the field? Including poetry made this work different from almost any other book like it. My former mentor, Bob Bensen, helped too, in submitting what I thought was going to be cursory coverage of the genre through a single short essay: he did such a good job that my editor agreed we needed to revise the table of contents to include the work of key poets. I thank Dr. Bensen, and on that note, I have a few other expressions of gratitude to include here:

First and foremost, to Julie Dunbar, my editor—thank you for being clear in your feedback, and for having enough faith in me to let me work undisturbed for long periods of time, but most of all, thank you for being a cheerleader on the days when I didn't think I was going to be able to bring this work to completion in a timely manner.

Contributing authors—I am grateful for your areas of expertise and your writing skills. This book is of better quality than a single-authored book because of the varied perspectives and interdisciplinary methodologies we were able to capture with a collaborative effort. Thank you for being a good team and for being good sports regarding my requests for revisions.

Allison Opitz (now, Buettner!)—thank you for offering your expert editing and citation skills.

Other writers, mentors, family members, fans, and neighbors—thank you for supporting me, checking in on me during this process, or just offering me a hug, a glass of wine, and some quality downtime. This goes out especially to John and Sandy Houston, Mary Lou Emanuel, Dennis Rothermel, Vivian Shipley, Pat Mottola, Mary Jane Miller, Sharon Reddick, Rich and Lisa Fasano, and John Glass.

Most of all, I'd like to thank my parents and my brother: Tom, Sylvia, and Paul Houston. My folks got near-daily calls during the entire writing of this book, often with updates on its progress. Thanks for listening, and thanks for loving me.

Lynn Marie Houston
Aberdeen, Maryland
November 2018

Introduction

HOW THIS BOOK CAME ABOUT

I probably first became interested in the interrelationship between place and writing when, as a preteen, I attended an educational summer camp sponsored by the Department of Environmental Conservation. Before meals in the mess hall and at night around a campfire, the counselors would quote passages from writers who were highly attentive to place: John Burroughs, Aldo Leopold, Henry David Thoreau, Rachel Carson, John McPhee, and so on. The beauty of those ideas, shared under a canopy of green, to the music of crackling wood, was one of the reasons I majored in literature as an undergraduate.

After that, a highlight of my postgraduate career was when I hosted the acclaimed urban theorist Dr. Ayona Datta, a friend from graduate courses at Arizona State, who was presenting at the Association of American Geographers (AAG) conference held in New Orleans, just across the lake from where I was living in Louisiana at the time. I ended up having to navigate French Quarter streets during parade time on Mardi Gras day to get to her conference hotel, and decided I was too frazzled to drive back, so I stayed and attended the conference. The panels I attended changed the way I think about place and how it is studied.

And now I've crisscrossed the country as an academic, taking with me a growing appreciation of the beautiful and varied geography of the United States—from my New York home, to Arizona for my doctoral work, to Louisiana for a visiting assistant professorship while I finished my dissertation, Northern California for my first tenure-track position, back to New York to teach at the community college in my hometown, and then to Connecticut to complete my MFA in poetry while teaching various writing classes and two sections of a course called "The City in Literature."

On summer breaks, I have traveled around the country for short-term employment (Kentucky and Missouri) and writing residencies (Vermont, Tennessee, and Nebraska). I've even lived abroad: four years in Geneva, Switzerland, as a Fulbright Fellow. In moving around so much, I've come to crave a deeper knowledge of place, which means that I often turn to others' experiences of it, stories from people who have sat a long time under the same tree or who have been able to return, season after season, to their favorite fishing hole. Although this book was physically in production for over four years, it has taken a lifetime to write in another sense—perhaps even multiple lifetimes if we combine my years with those of the interdisciplinary team of scholars who contributed to it.

WHAT IS INCLUDED IN THIS BOOK

What you will find in this book are thoughts on the role of place in literary works from people who have been teaching and studying them, sometimes for their entire careers. We selected the literary works for inclusion in this reference guide by reviewing syllabi and researching the most popularly taught selections in high school and college, which we then cross-referenced with the most cited works in databases of scholarly articles. I also made sure that most of the texts that have shown up in the last 10 years on the advanced placement exam in English literature (the exam that determines whether high school students receive college credit for their AP English course) are included within these pages, especially if the essay question that year related to concerns about setting, landscape, nature, or cultural and/or human geography. The works covered in this book represent the texts at the forefront of our current educational curriculum, and the information presented will be useful for students and teachers at the high school and college levels. Moreover, we did not restrict ourselves to what are considered the "classics," but made sure that more "popular" works were included, as many teachers are working hard to show how teaching more contemporary, popular readings benefits students in terms of achieving important skills in reading, comprehending, and building arguments that analyze written works. The analyses of literary works included here make use of interdisciplinary techniques that blend the study of literary texts with an attention to both physical and cultural geography. Also known as "literary geography," this field has enjoyed an increasing popularity and renewed interest among contemporary scholars.

One of my most important contributions to this collective endeavor has been the inclusion of a hearty selection of poetry. Most of the other reference guides on this topic stop at fiction and drama (some include select works of literary nonfiction, as we have done in including a few texts that skirt the line between journalism and fiction). However, anyone who was taken a basic literary genre course knows that (even with the inclusion of literary nonfiction) such a list is incomplete because it leaves off the genre of poetry. Because I was writing part of this book while going back to school for an MFA in poetry, I felt committed to making sure that the genre was well represented in this collection. Among all the genres, poetry often seems considered the elite domain of "specialists." It has been my pleasure to record in these pages the work of poets whom I have been teaching for years, works by poets who are also regularly studied in terms of their relationship to place and that are regularly anthologized in textbooks used to teach such courses at high school and college levels. We also consulted former U.S. poet laureate Billy Collins's "Poetry 180" project, available online at the Library of Congress website, which offers online educational resources for instructors to teach a poem a day in American high schools. If space had permitted, we would have included in this book more of the contemporary poets from Collins's project. A number of works (both poetry and prose) central to understanding narrative representations of place in the history of literature are not included in this book because our selection criteria involved how frequently the work is taught in high school and college. As an example, an old favorite of mine, *Don Quixote,* a work in which the spatial imaginary drives the plot and the character development in magical ways, had to be excluded because it is rarely taught anymore.

What we have not included in this book is any peripheral issue that has become its own field of study. Food, for example, is an important element of place and cultural geography. However, food studies is now a discipline of its own, with many reference guides specifically treating the role of food and agricultural production in literature. Instead, we offer a more global overview regarding the study of place. Another topic of study has cropped up recently and is called "literary tourism." This area of study, which involves traveling to sites of literary importance, is also not a specific focus of this collection. Although studies of this nature can have a high relevance to studies of maps and geography, the field of study is also interested in travel guides and concerns related to tourist economies, which are outside the scope of this book. The Appendix to this book comes closest to issues of literary tourism; in it, we discuss the major cities and regions where writers have congregated or that have inspired them to produce their works. Finally, we focus exclusively on written texts, meaning that television or film adaptations, if addressed at all, are only mentioned briefly.

HOW TO USE THIS BOOK

The entries in this book—over 100 of the most popularly taught literary texts dealing with issues of space, place, landscape, and/or regional cultures—have been written so as to remind readers of the whole context of the work by providing a brief summary, and then the entries focus in on the most important topics related to physical and cultural geography. In offering brief summaries of the literary works, this book is ideal for high school classes and introductory college-level courses where readers might not be as familiar with analyzing the messages authors craft through literary devices. In this respect, it is also ideal for use in general education classes where readers might be new to approaching literature as an art form. More advanced students will appreciate the more sophisticated and in-depth analyses in each entry of topics related to the field of geography. Such analyses make this book an ideal reference material for a themed approach to literature, such as courses on "Literature and the Environment," "Literature of the Borderlands," "Animals in Literature," "Writing from Combat Zones," "Place in Science Fiction," "Agriculture and the Great Depression," "Offshore Narratives," "The Pastoral Tradition," "Homecomings in Literature," "Regional Authors," themed classes on literature of specific regions within the United States or abroad (see Appendix for a succinct and informative overview of "Literary Landscapes and Capital Cities"), or classes that focus on literary movements to which place is central (the Gothic, Romanticism, Modernism, the American Renaissance, the Harlem Renaissance, and so on). The Further Reading sections will help high school students develop into more avid readers, while the Bibliography sections provide useful lists of the most important recent scholarship on each work that would assist even graduate students or junior faculty in their research.

For students, we recommend using this book as a resource only after an initial reading (or multiple readings) of the literary work. The summaries provided here do not provide minor details that might help them make an argument (or that might run counter to an argument they are trying to make), and cannot replace reading the actual text. To cite any of the words or ideas in this book, follow the latest guidelines for "a multiauthor anthology" in the relevant discipline's citation style. The format of this book is modeled after an encyclopedia so that we can provide broad coverage of literary works and so that students' attention doesn't fade from long chapters or from the inclusion of information that might not be relevant to the scholarly process that brought them to this work.

WHAT IS LITERARY GEOGRAPHY?

This book takes the position that setting in literature is more than just backdrop, that important insight into literary texts can be made by paying close attention to how authors craft place, as well as to how place functions in a narrative. The authors included in this reference work engage deeply with either real or imagined geographies. They care about how human decisions have shaped landscapes and how landscapes have shaped human practices and values. Some of the best writing is highly vivid, employing the language of the senses, because this is the primary means through which humans know physical space.

Literature can offer valuable perspectives on physical and cultural geography. Unlike scientific reports, a literary narrative can provide the emotional component missing from the scientific record. In human experience, geographical places have a spiritual or emotional component in addition to and as part of a physical layout and topography. This emotional component, although subjective, is no less "real" than a surveyor's map. Human consciousness of place is experienced in a multimodal manner. Histories of places live on in many forms, one of which is the human memory or imagination.

Both real and imaginary landscapes provide insight into the human experience of place. The pursuit of such a topic speaks to the valuable knowledge produced from bridging disciplines and combining material from both the arts and the sciences to better understand the human condition. The perspectives that most concern cultural geographers are often those regarding movement and migration, cultivation of natural resources, and organization of space. The latter two reflect concerns of the built environment, a topic shared with the field of architectural study. Many of these concerns are also reflected in work sociologists do. Scholars from literary studies can contribute an aesthetic dimension to what might otherwise be a purely ideological approach.

Literature can bring together material that spans different branches of science. For example, a literary description of place may involve not only the environment and geography but the noises and quality of light, or how people from different races or classes can experience the same place in different ways linked to those racial or class disparities. Literary texts can also account for the way in which absence—of other people, animals, and so on—affects a human observer or inhabitant. Both literary and scientific approaches to place are necessary, working in unison, to achieve a complete record of an environment. It is important to note that the interdisciplinary nature of this work teaches us that landscapes are not static, that they are not unchanged by human culture. At least part of their identity derives from the people who inhabit them and from the way space can alter and inspire human perspective. The intersection of scientific and literary expression that happens in the study of literary geography is of prime importance due to the complexity of the personal and political ways that humans experience place.

THEORISTS OF PLACE

Yi-Fu Tuan's theoretical studies in "human geography" have become necessary reading for scholars approaching any aspect of spatial studies. A geographer by training, Tuan's work broadens its scope to include the emotional connections that people feel to space (the term *topophilia,* in other words the "love of place"); he especially is interested in how people become aware of local places that form their concept of "home" and interact with nation-state spaces that help form their civic or religious identities. In *Space and Place* (1977), he divides his approach into separate categories of space: the sacred, the mythical, the architectural, and experiential, to name a few. He also addresses how time affects human knowledge of space.

Prior to Tuan, Gaston Bachelard had laid down a beginning framework to this area of study in his *Poetics of Space* (1958). His work brings the philosophical study of ways of being into the realm of the built environment. Focusing on studies of literature and daily life, Bachelard encourages architects to factor in the emotional experience of space rather than its mere functionality. His theories result from his reading of poems and the way in which domestic spaces and furnishings function in them. He then turns his analysis around and meditates on the poetry of real interior spaces, the symbolism of the spaces we experience daily. His "topoanalysis," a study of the meanings we make from the "home" spaces of our lives, is ultimately a way to better understand human psychology.

More recently, and bridging the domains of ecocriticism, literature, and geography, is the work of Lawrence Buell. In *The Environmental Imagination,* he uses Thoreau's *Walden* as a representative text to make larger claims about the Western cultural beliefs associated with the pastoral writing tradition. He extends his claims to an analysis of literary representations of nature as a character with agency and subjectivity. Although more rooted in literary study than Tuan, Bachelard, or most other spatial theorists, Buell's work only deals with nonurban spaces and mainly with the representation of nonhuman characters. His conclusions establish a direction for "ecocentric" scholarship, which places land at the center of our understanding of the history of human activities and thought, and which prompts us to question the goals of technological developments and notions of progress.

A numerous and ever-growing list of theorists across many disciplines work in scholarly analyses of space, which might sometimes be referred to as geocriticism, literary cartography, or by other names not yet as fashionable in intellectual communities. As an addition to those theorists mentioned previously, we recommend that interested scholars further investigate the contributions of the following to the field of spatial studies: Michel de Certeau, Michel Foucault, David Harvey, Hsuan L. Hsu, Fredric Jameson, Annette Kolodny, Henri Lefebvre, Edward Said, Edward D. Soja, and Raymond Williams.

This book includes ideas inspired by these theorists, as well as many other leading thinkers in the fields related to the study of place, space, and urban and rural landscapes. In addition, the analyses of literary works provided in this collection employ ideas found in ecocriticism, feminist ecocriticism, feminist geography, postcolonialism, and race and gender studies.

DEDICATION

I did much of the intense writing for this book during the summer of 2017, at a writing residency on the Art Farm in Marquette, Nebraska. I had randomly applied to the residency program, not knowing anyone who had attended, but having been disillusioned about another residency program I had attended in the South. I was determined to find a better destination for my summer breaks from university teaching. Indeed, I found a home away from home.

Prior to June 2017, I had never visited the Midwest. When I arrived, the landscape surrounding the small town of Marquette, Nebraska, was a complete shock to me: cornfields as far as the eye could see and a sky that made me feel small and vulnerable, almost dizzy from the spread-wide horizon. I lived and wrote there in the attic of a falling-down farmhouse that was like a Willa Cather description come to life. I was assisting a crew with a roof remodel on the house, working a couple of hours every morning and waking up to get buckets and towels when nighttime storms passed through before we had the roof sealed. In the cool and quiet of early mornings, I would take a cup of tea to the landing outside my room and walk among open rafters, looking up at tree leaves and sky. I had mixed feelings after tar-papering the entire roof one afternoon as a storm threatened on the horizon: I was glad my stuff would stay dry, but sad that my large skylight was gone. I lived there for seven weeks, and with a week to go before leaving, I found out that a few miles away lived people who were related to me through my father's brother's marriage. This was my Aunt Sandy's brother, his wife, and kids. Traveling 1,500 miles and randomly discovering new members of my extended family changed my ideas about home and about the nature of place. American life in the 21st-century often requires us to travel far distances (either geographically or electronically) to find a sense of belonging. Unfortunately, the solar eclipse party held at their house was the first and only time I got to meet Roy, my uncle by marriage. He passed nine months later from an aggressive cancer that was only discovered a few weeks before his death.

I dedicate this book to the memory of Roy Emanuel; to his widow, Mary Lou; and to the director of the Art Farm, Ed Dadey, who brought me to Nebraska. Inviting me to the Art Farm's writing residency helped me to discover that the place of home transcends regional geography, is more of a network than a single point on a map, and that, also, I carry it with me wherever I go.

Lynn Marie Houston

Place in Poetry

Place is our notion of where things are and where things, as we say, *take place*. Poetry takes place in time. It also takes place *into* itself, composes place in its lines, and makes a place of itself. Just as we inhabit the world, we inhabit poems—John Donne wrote that his love will "build in sonnets pretty rooms"—and we roam the terrain of poetry from pole to imaginary pole. Poetry enacts the mystery of being in a certain place, at a certain time. It deploys the image-making power of words to imitate the world as it appears and as we experience it. With poetry, we can draw the sensible surface of things, as well as draw out what we sense is hidden there. The earliest natural histories in verse read the "book of nature" for what is revealed therein of divine purpose (and science still does so, in its own terms, to discover the laws of nature).

Words have creative force. Wallace Stevens (1879–1955) wrote that "what we said of it became / A part of what it is" ("A Postcard from the Volcano"). The creative power of the word begins in our earliest stories and experiences, both as individuals and as a human race. The mansion-house in Stevens's poem is shuttered and abandoned, and those long gone who lived there: "Children picking up our bones / Will never know that these were once / As quick as foxes on the hill." The place keeps what they left behind: the "look of things" and "what we felt / At what we saw" and "what we said of it. . . ." What we said and what we felt at what we saw might start to define the poetry of place. The need to speak our feelings about the place we inhabit led Seamus Heaney (1939–2013) to say that the writer "stands in some directly expressive or interpretative relationship to the milieu. He or she becomes a voice of the spirit of the region [. . .]. [Place] is sensed as a distinctive element in the work" ("The Place of Writing"). Place in Stevens's "A Postcard from the Volcano" is given voice through the speaker, who is one of those who used to live in the house. The poetry ("what we said") prompted by what they saw and felt changed the house in its very being by becoming part of it.

GEOGRAPHY AND THE IMAGINATION: THE WORD AND THE WORLD

Poetry lives in the reciprocal creative force between word and world. The biblical book of John reads, "In the beginning was the Word." In Genesis, utterance of the word *light* made light, and divine imperatives named and separated the elements, bringing form out of chaos. From the Judeo-Christian-Muslim creation story and the Greco-Roman creation story (as in Ovid's *Metamorphoses),* the Word gave form to the elements in shaping the world, and passed to human speech the power to name, create, and discover. That words have the power to create gives poets power that has always been associated with divinity. William Shakespeare wrote that the poet "gives to airy nothing/A local habitation and a name" *(A Midsummer Night's Dream).*

The place of geography in poetry begins with shaping the poetic line, the line of vision that looks out on the world and connects the poet to it. Use of the line by two contemporary 19th-century poets Walt Whitman (1819–1892) and Emily Dickinson (1830–1886) could hardly be more extreme in their differences. On the one hand are Whitman's long lines expressing a continent-wide song of the American self:

From the peaks gigantic, from the great sierras and the high plateaus,
From the mine and from the gully, from the hunting trail we come [. . .].
("Pioneers! O Pioneers!")

On the other, Dickinson's lines pace inside her stanza's room, a hymnody of sprung clocks, dashed to syntactic pieces, until she breaks free and plunges:

And then a Plank in Reason, broke,
And I dropped down, and down—
And hit a World, at every plunge,
And Finished knowing—then—

("I felt a Funeral, in my Brain")

Contrast Whitman's full-throated "barbaric yawp" (as he called it) across cities and mountains and plains versus Dickinson's closeted intimacies, from her room looking over the church graveyard. In both we discover the relation of geography to personal space and lives. When geography is superhuman-sized, the effect is sublime, instilling humility and awe at grandeur. When place is a tight fit, though we were, as Hamlet said, "bounded in a nutshell," our minds are monarchs "of infinite space."

Modern poetry inhabits a world that originates in the Romantic tradition of William Wordsworth's praise for the pristine natural world where, as in "Ode: Intimations of Immortality," he wrote that "meadow, grove, and stream / The earth, and every common sight, / To me did seem / Apparell'd in celestial light." For Wordsworth, the nature of every person originated in the ethereal innocence of childhood, while nature itself hearkened back to the age of innocence in the mythic golden age and the biblical Garden of Eden. His poetry asserted the paradisal state of nature against the dehumanizing effects of the Industrial Revolution and the reductive effects of the age of reason and the Enlightenment. But innocence in the foundation stories gave way to experience, the age of gold turned to iron, and the humans made of clay and divine breath fell from grace. The child who came to earth "trailing clouds of glory," in the later crises of warfare and inhumanity, became the man anxious, alienated from his own countrymen and women, and came to feel himself to be an "uninvited guest" at life's feast *(The Prelude).*

As human beings come from and return to earth, they are made of the place their lives take place upon. And so the geography of poetry is the story of our origin and end, from original glory, through trials and struggles, to faith in the redemptive, instructive, restorative experience of time. Such is the pattern of life graphed on Earth, inseparably from Earth, of which poets write to remind us of our truest selves. The ancient poetry of Greece, in particular Homer's *Odyssey,* dramatizes the dichotomy inherent in the human relation to Earth as home and as exile. The hero Odysseus, having offended the god Neptune, is condemned to wander the Earth for 10 years, unable to return home to Ithaca. The geography of the Mediterranean world is integral to the trials he undergoes. Shipwrecked on the island of Calypso, a beautiful, tropical paradise where all his wants are supplied but one, Odysseus spends his days weeping and gazing homeward out to sea. His exile strengthens his desire for his homeland and his family, as he shuns the promise of immortality and love from the goddess of the island, Calypso.

Elaborating on the Homeric theme over two millennia later, John Milton in *Paradise Lost* (1667, 1674) depicts Earth as paradise created in the likeness of heaven, so that "That Earth now / Seemd like to Heav'n, a seat where Gods might dwell, / Or wander with delight, and love to haunt / Her sacred shades." The Garden is not static, but fecund and tending to overgrowth, and so requires the labors of the couple to keep fruitful and prepare for the lives of their children to come. This promised course is disrupted at the Fall, and the Earth itself injured physically, when Eve:

Forth reaching to the fruit, she plucked, she ate:
Earth felt the wound, and Nature from her seat
Sighing through all her Works gave signs of woe,
That all was lost

(IX. 781–4)

That Milton built into his poems, cosmic and terrestrial geography a relation to the lives of the inhabitants, in a moral as well as a physical dimension, influenced the relations of later poets to their worlds ever since. All was not lost, though the narrator thought so. Earth would rediscover its paradisal nature in human life, subject to the rhythm of creation and destruction, of the world as home and the world as place of exile and estrangement.

Consider the sense of place in four poets, justly celebrated, all in the poetic lineage of Homer, Milton, and Wordsworth, all of the same literary age (the Modernist later 20th-century), all influential on contemporary and younger poets, all strongly identified with their geographies, and all with bodies of poetry that have a pervasive engagement with their places of origin, of exile, and travel. Derek Walcott, a Caribbean writer whose personal geography takes him from the paradisal island of his birth to the metropolitan countries and home again, was estranged from his native Saint Lucia by exile in the metropolitan countries to pursue his craft, like many West Indian writers of his generation. Walcott won the Nobel Prize for Literature in 1992; his friend Seamus Heaney won in 1995. Heaney, the greatest Irish poet since Yeats, expressed his Gaelic sensibility through the English tongue to rescue vestiges of ancient Éire in spite of the current time of Troubles. Elizabeth Bishop (1911–1979), born in Massachusetts, lived along the Eastern Seaboard of the Western Hemisphere, from Nova Scotia to Florida to Brazil. Some biographers say that her poetry embodies the search in those places for a home that was denied her in early childhood, by the early loss of her parents. From the opposite side of the country, a poet of the vast American West, Richard Hugo (1923–1982) expresses the spirit of the region in which place is often sheer space, sparsely peopled, and studded with abandoned mines and ghost towns. Geographic space is, for Hugo, metaphor and condition for the space between people that the poem itself seeks to overcome. His poems delve into the troubled past of conquest and dispossession, which is lively in his imagination with the Native American peoples who named the places of desolation where his poems dwell.

Lines of poetry on the page can simultaneously make magical both the subject space (the geography that is being written about) and the reader space (the geography inhabited by the reader), the latter being a space that was a mystery to the writer at the time of writing. Poetic images, in being free from the requirements of narration, can evoke a sense of place unfettered by the restraints of historical time, which is the time of traditional narrative (first this happened, then this). Of all genres, poetry is involved with the invention and eternal recreation of the language of place through sensory images.

Robert R. Bensen

Place in Prose

Virginia Woolf states in her essay "A Room of One's Own" that "a woman must have money and a room of her own if she is to write fiction." The money she refers to represents independence, and the room, of course, is an architectural metaphor for privacy. One can have the money without freedom and the room without the ability to write. Take, for example, the fictional character of Bertha Mason in *Jane Eyre,* who resembles the autobiographical narrator of Charlotte Perkins Gilman's "The Yellow Wallpaper" and a host of other real and imagined "madwomen in the attic" (per Sandra Gilbert and Susan Gubar). Bertha came from a family of wealthy Caribbean plantation owners, so she had money. After she married the wrong man, she found herself labeled as insane and confined to a room by herself. It is clearly not just the solitude of a single-occupant room that Woolf refers to in her essay. It is the emotional, not architectural, space that provides the proper conditions for emerging women writers. Space matters to writers, and space matters in their works. Domestic space can cut both ways for women. For instance, kitchens have historically been a site of a kind of imprisonment for women, keeping them busy with things other than writing. On the other hand, the space of the kitchen has shaped the writing of some women. Many can trace their beginnings as writers to the education in voice and narrative style they received from listening to women talk to each other at the kitchen table (see fiction writer Paule Marshall's essay "From the Poets in the Kitchen"). Space resonates in personal and political ways for writers, and this translates into the emotional complexity of their settings.

Prose accounts for novels, plays, short stories, creative nonfiction, and literary journalism, basically anything that is not poetry. This means that prose writers often have more space than poets in which to craft their stories and invent their characters. Descriptions of place in prose can leave the symbolic realm and become more realistic, even if the settings are imaginary. By allowing for more details of place, prose writers can help readers more readily enter their world; they can use sensory images to make readers feel present in a place.

A writer's reasons for wanting readers to feel present in a given place have changed over the history of prose genres. Ancient playwrights, like Aeschylus, Sophocles, and Euripides, wanted to draw readers' attention to issues that threatened the Greek democracy. Place in their plays often involved a city-state in peril because of a conflict between human will and the fate decreed by gods. In this case, physical earthly spaces took on a political and spiritual significance.

> One's destination is never a place, but rather a new way of looking at things.
> **Henry Miller, *Big Sur and the Oranges of Hieronymus Bosch* (1957)**

By the time Shakespeare wrote his first play, the role of place in playwriting had become more subtle. Settings no longer operated as venues for larger concerns of the city-state, but were more personal expressions. Spaces in Shakespeare become highly intimate, and much less focused on larger governmental concerns in favor of truths about the daily wins and losses of our human attachments to each other—Hamlet's library, for instance, becomes his space of deep reflection over his feelings of grief and inadequacy. The aesthetic his plays captured have continued on well into the present era.

Some of the earliest forms of the novel in the 17th century manifested as adventure novels. In these, concerns of place housed the conflict between man and nature. Think of Daniel Defoe's Robison Crusoe stranded on his island, a hostile space that he learns to dominate. In adventure novels and travelogues, place—whether real or imagined—functions as part of an ethnographic representation of otherness that ultimately serves to reinforce the protagonist's cultural values.

Shipwrecks and failures of technology bring us into the realm of the Gothic, of science fiction, and of dystopian works. Place in these prose works often serves the writers' goals of critiquing dangerous human inclinations, such as the temptations of medical doctors to play God, as Dr. Frankenstein does when he creates his monster. Settings in these works, even if they are imaginary, are venues to explore the realities that scare us, our darker propensities.

Once novelists and essayists begin to critique modern technologies, prose works begin to feature reactions against industrial development. Such works use place to draw attention to a growing urban-rural divide and celebrate the natural world being lost to such innovations as the railroad and assembly-line manufacturing. Works in the pastoral tradition mourn the loss of a previous, simpler way of life, and glorify older agricultural traditions and the sense of community created in smaller localities. Herman Melville's "Bartleby, the Scrivener" is a great example of a work of fiction that explores the office place as a space of dehumanization. Bartleby is asked to be a human copy machine; when he refuses, Melville shows readers how his very existence is caught up in an all-invasive capitalist machine that relies on private ownership of property and a self-gratifying moral pursuit by property holders.

By the time we enter the literary period of modernism, prose works craft places where people feel alienated from others and where they suffer from a fragmented sense of self. Many of the works by writers associated with existentialism, nihilism, or theater of the absurd offer settings that are stagnant, where no resolution of the plot conflict can happen. Samuel Beckett's play *Waiting for Godot* does this, as do Jean-Paul Sartre's and Tom Stoppard's respective plays *No Exit* and *Rosencrantz and Guildenstern Are Dead*. Faulkner's novels and stories are other wonderful examples as he features Southern towns that decay and rot as families hold on to past traditions that no longer serve them.

Immigrants writing prose works based on their lives is a major feature of 20th-century American literary history. Concerns of place in these works are often concerns for freedom and safety from tyranny, monopoly, and capitalist greed. Upton Sinclair's work *The Jungle* is considered a novel, but it was based on the real-life stories of people he interviewed. In it, he exposed the shocking conditions of immigrants working in Chicago's stockyards and slaughterhouses. This kind of social critique also characterizes the concerns of prose works in the 21st century, where issues of race, class, and gender are at the forefront of many narratives, and settings emphasize the search for access to equality and justice for the marginalized and oppressed.

In reading and analyzing works of prose for what they say about place, it is important to interrogate the works in terms of the distinctive features of geographical space that they represent, just as it is important to analyze the cultural and ideological settings. Characters in prose can be identified or shaped through the use of regional dialect, which is a linguistic feature of place, and place can further impact characters through their acceptance or rejection of a place. Geographical features often stand in for symbols of human decision making, just as the physical description of a room in a house often reflects what a character is feeling internally. The status of the land affects the human bodies that live on it, not just in terms of the agricultural production but in terms of its toxicity from waste. Certain settings resonate deeply with the search for one's identity, such as the concept of home. Other spaces dictate the terms of interpersonal relationships between characters, or reveal interpersonal politics and social inequalities.

The history of place in works of prose is a varied one. What is perhaps more interesting is what happens after a reader closes the book and returns to daily life. How does the setting of the novel they were just reading affect the reader's experience of the real places they occupy in the world? If the writer was successful, the geography the reader inhabits will be more alive with meaning, more apt to be remembered, and more likely to factor into decisions that the reader makes about the rights and uses associated with those spaces. If works of literature teach us anything about place, they teach us about our interconnectedness: that decisions one makes about "a room of one's own" never happen in isolation from what happens to the neighboring rooms that other people inhabit.

Lynn Marie Houston

A

Absalom, Absalom!

In William Faulkner's 1936 novel *Absalom, Absalom!*, several characters from Jefferson, Mississippi—located in the fictional Yoknapatawpha County—narrate the story of Thomas Sutpen, a stranger who arrives in town to build a plantation he calls Sutpen's Hundred. He fathers two children, Judith and Henry, with his new wife, but after many years, Sutpen's mixed-race son Charles Bon arrives in Mississippi, revealing the patriarch's hidden past as an overseer in the French colony of Saint-Domingue (present-day Haiti). The lethal violence between Sutpen's first and second families ultimately destroys the future of this planter dynasty, and the book's title refers to the Bible verse 2 Samuel 19:4, in which King David mourns the death of his son Absalom, after Absalom was killed fighting in a rebellion against his own father. Ultimately, Sutpen's repressed past, which is tied to the South's history as part of the Caribbean, brings about his undoing, and also disrupts the cultural geography of Faulkner's Mississippi.

THE CULTURAL GEOGRAPHY OF MISSISSIPPI

The geography of *Absalom, Absalom!* is indeed cultural, as the novel takes the narrative of history, which supposedly moves backward and forward in time, and instead flattens it across the space of the region's terrain. For example, before the main action of the novel, Sutpen spends his early adulthood in Saint-Domingue, and when one narrator suggests that Sutpen moves directly from the Haitian Revolution (which happened in the 1790s) to Mississippi in 1833, one starts to think this stranger might also be a time traveler. He disturbs other white people in Mississippi, furthermore, because he brings the region's Caribbean identity in the 18th century face-to-face with Mississippi's assumed identity as an Anglo-Saxon territory-state in the 19th century.

The South's image of itself as an Anglo-Saxon stronghold was indeed an assumed one because, starting in the colonial era, American colonies from the Chesapeake on down were considered part of the West Indies, as they shared a tropical climate and a dependence upon African slavery to produce profitable cash crops. Major island colonies changed hands between European powers, and so too did the colonies surrounding the Gulf, and indeed, the region now recognized as the U.S. state of Mississippi was originally part of colonial Louisiana and Spanish Florida. The Mississippi Territory was finally established as part of the United States in 1798, and granted statehood in 1817. This incorporation into the antebellum U.S. South brought about a major cultural shift in terms of language, religion, and attitudes about racial mixing. Like Britain and the United States, French and Spanish colonizers placed genealogically "white" males at the top of the social order, but there also existed subtle and complex distinctions between different *gens* (for the French) or *castas* (for the Spanish) based upon racial mixture, wealth, and one's status as enslaved or free. Racial mixing, or "miscegenation" as racists described it, was an ever-present reality in the Mississippi Territory, but by the early 19th century the Anglo-American South imagined itself as a region defined by strict racial separatism, and instead projected onto the Caribbean. In this context, Sutpen's sudden arrival directly from Haiti and the familiarity he shows with the francophone slaves he brings with him reminds white inhabitants of the area that "Mississippi" was for many years part of the extended Caribbean, and not a constituency of the Anglo-American imperial project.

MISSISSIPPI AND NEW ORLEANS

Ironically, when Sutpen journeys to Mississippi, he arrives in a town called "Jefferson," a name that invokes the hierarchical violence and racial separatism of the Anglo-American South. Because they are ruled by such social divisions, everyone in the town pretends that desire—between opposite sexes, between people of the same sex, between people of different races, between people of the same family—only really exists in New Orleans, a city that retains its connections to the Caribbean and to European colonialism. Charles Bon actually has a home in New Orleans, and the novel does not say what kinds of intimacies take place in that city between Charles and his half brother Henry. All is well as long as it is contained in the Creole city of New Orleans. When Charles announces his intentions to marry his own half sister Judith, in Mississippi, however, his presence cannot be suborned. The match would shatter Jefferson's delusions about being a segregated society, and it would disrupt the white-supremacist patriarchy that places Thomas Sutpen at the top of the social order. The sudden eruption of the South's Caribbean past, as embodied in the figure of Charles, thus lays bare the hypocrisy within Southern culture and within individual Southerners such as Thomas and Henry Sutpen. Henry responds to this crisis with horrific violence, murdering his half brother before the marriage to Judith can take place, but the suffering that ensues afterward shows that the South cannot escape its past.

Amanda Louise Johnson

Further Reading

If you liked *Absalom, Absalom!*, then you might like *Look Homeward, Angel* by Thomas Wolfe: the story line follows Eugene Grant, a young man who struggles to find himself within his turbulent family. Another work that similarly captures the longing to find oneself is Cormac McCarthy's *Suttree,* which features a wealthy young man who gives up a life of privilege to live on a run-down houseboat. Another good recommendation is *The Adventures of Augie March* by Saul Bellow because it explores Augie March's search for himself in Chicago during the Great Depression.

Bibliography

Aiken, Charles. "Faulkner's Yoknapatawpha County: Geographical Fact into Fiction." *Geographical Review* 67, no. 1 (1977): 1–21. doi:10.2307/213600.

Allister, Mark, ed. *Eco-Man: New Perspectives on Masculinity and Nature.* Charlottesville: University of Virginia Press, 2004.

Andersen, Jill. "'God Gave Women a Sign When Something Has Happened Bad': An Ecofeminist Reading of William Faulkner's 'As I Lay Dying.'" In *Forces of Nature: Natural(-izing) Gender and Gender(-ing) Nature in the Discourses of Western Culture,* edited by Bernadette Hyner and Precious Mckenzie Stearns, 88–111. Newcastle upon Tyne: Cambridge Scholars Publishing, 2009.

Baldwin, Marc. "Faulkner's Cartographic Method: Producing the 'Land' through Cognitive Mapping." *The Faulkner Journal* 7, no. 1 (1991): 193.

Bone, Martyn. *The Postsouthern Sense of Place in Contemporary Fiction.* Baton Rouge: Louisiana State University Press, 2005.

Brown, Calvin S. "Faulkner's Geography and Topography." *PMLA* 77, no. 5 (1962): 652–59. doi:10.2307/460414.

Garver, Ashley. "'I Don't. I Don't! I Don't Hate It! I Don't Hate It!' The Function of Place in William Faulkner's *Absalom, Absalom!*" Master's thesis, Lake Forest College, 2016.

Glissant, Edouard. *Faulkner, Mississippi.* Translated by Barbara Lewis and Thomas C. Spear. Chicago: University of Chicago Press, 2000.

Kartiganer, Donald, and Ann Abadie, eds. *Faulkner and the Natural World: Faulkner and Yoknapatawpha, 1996.* Jackson: University Press of Mississippi, 1999.

Kohler, Dayton. "William Faulkner and the Social Conscience." *College English* 11, no. 3 (1949): 119–27. doi:10.2307/585974.

Miner, Ward. *The World of William Faulkner.* New York: Cooper Square Publishers, Inc., 1963.

Mitchell, Dennis J. *A New History of Mississippi.* Jackson: University Press of Mississippi, 2014.

Mize, Brendan. "Acolyte of Nature: Spirituality in Faulkner's Wilderness." Master's thesis, Appalachian State University, 2018.

Moon, Michael. "Wherein the South Differs from the North: Naming Persons, Naming Places, and the Need for Visionary Geographies." *Southern Spaces,* May 16, 2008. southernspaces.org/2008/wherein-south-differs-north-naming-persons-naming-places-and-need-visionary-geographies.

Owens, Margaret R. "Faulknerian Social Strata Meridians in Yoknapatawpha County: A Study in Literary Geography." Honors thesis, University of North Georgia, 2018.

Pocock, Douglas C. D., ed. *Humanistic Geography and Literature (RLE Social & Cultural Geography): Essays on the Experience of Place.* New York: Routledge, 2014.

Putzel, Max. *Genius of Place, William Faulkner's Triumphant Beginnings.* Baton Rouge: Louisiana State University Press, 1985.

Railey, Kevin. *Natural Aristocracy: History, Ideology, and the Production of William Faulkner.* Tuscaloosa: University of Alabama Press, 1999.

Ross, Patricia. *The Spell Cast by Remains: The Myth of Wilderness in Modern American Literature.* New York: Routledge, 2006.

Ryden, Kent. *Mapping the Invisible Landscape: Folklore, Writing, and the Sense of Place.* Iowa City: University of Iowa Press, 1993.

Saikku, Mikko. "A True Ecological Complex." In *This Delta, This Land: An Environmental History of the Yazoo-Mississippi Floodplain.* Athens: University of Georgia Press, 2005.

Simon, Julia. "Property in *Absalom, Absalom!:* Rousseau's Legacy in Faulkner." *The Faulkner Journal* 28, no. 2 (2014): 3–24, 97.

Smith, Lindsey. *Indians, Environment, and Identity on the Borders of American Literature.* New York: Palgrave Macmillan, 2008.

Sweet, Timothy. "Projecting Early American Environmental Writing." *American Literary History* 22, no. 2 (2010): 419–31.

Williams, Michael. *Americans and Their Forests: A Historical Geography.* Cambridge, UK: Cambridge University Press, 1989.

Wittenburg, Judith. "Go Down, Moses and the Discourse of Environmentalism." In *New Essays on Go Down, Moses,* edited by Linda Wagner-Martin, 49–72. Cambridge, UK: Cambridge University Press, 1996.

Adventures of Huckleberry Finn

Since publication, Mark Twain's *Adventures of Huckleberry Finn* has been the subject of controversy. It has been variously vilified and celebrated, banned outright, and made required reading. The heart of the controversy comes from the fact that the story is told from the perspective of a young lower-class white boy from Missouri who travels down the Mississippi River with an escaped slave named Jim, and modern readers find offensive the attitudes that Huck and the other characters around him express as well as the use of the pejorative term for African Americans, although appropriate in the context of the time period. The story treats Jim as a fully fledged character with faults and virtues who believes himself justified in escaping slavery, which society now characterizes as an evil institution but which, at the time the story was written, had ended less than two decades before and, in the story's setting, is still an established practice. In modern works that depict slavery, the slaves are always victims and the slave owners are perpetrators of crime and most often shown as violent, sadistic, and almost inhuman in their capacity to harm others. *Huckleberry Finn* does not necessarily agree with this view. The little old lady, Miss Watson, who Jim escapes from is not an evil person although Jim believes she intends to sell him to a plantation in New Orleans where he will have to endure the indignities of a cruel master. The farther south Huck and Jim travel, the more perilous their journey and the more likelihood of Jim finding himself in a more dour position than the one from which he escaped.

NATURE VERSUS CIVILIZATION

The novel begins with Huck chafing under the guardianship of Miss Watson's sister, the widow Douglas, who is trying to civilize him in St. Petersburg, Missouri. Huck feels that this environment is oppressive as he is used to running about the town without any form of supervision and left to his own devices. Huck is accustomed to sleeping in the forest and climbing trees, so he is more comfortable out in nature than in the whitewashed wood homes of civilization. This conflict is resolved by Huck's being kidnapped and held hostage by his drunken father who intends to steal Huck's money. Pop Finn keeps Huck in a dirty shack on the shore of a river. It is closer to the nature Huck is used to, but subverted for an immoral purpose. In turn, this conflict is resolved by Huck staging his own murder and

Everett Henry's 1959 map sketches scenes from the *Adventures of Huckleberry Finn*. The depiction of the Mississippi River follows Mark Twain's narrative from Hannibal, Missouri, to Pikesville, Mississippi. (Library of Congress)

taking a raft down the Mississippi River with Jim. He is reaffirmed that he is better off under his own authority and out in nature. Even though Jim is an adult, Huck does not see him as having authority over a white child and takes command. Missouri is a slave state, and it is Jim's intention to make his way down to Illinois, a free state in which he can build a life and acquire enough funds to free his wife and children. Unfortunately, that plan is subverted and they have to continue down the Mississippi.

In this situation, both Huck and Jim find that they are safest when they are on the raft and on the river. As long as they are on the water, Huck feels in charge and is best able to continue his journey and protect Jim. At one point, the two are waylaid by a passing group of white men who are hunting escaped slaves. Huck, being the figure of authority in his party, is able to convince them that the only person with him is his father who is sick with pox, and encourages the men to help them. In so doing, he ensures the men beg off and go away. Here Huck feels in control, and this sense of power keeps Jim free and himself away from danger. On their own, the two are safe. It is when they make contact with the external, civilized world that they find themselves in peril.

RACISM

Most of their journey is spent rafting down this river with periodic stops to get supplies or earn some money. With each mile that Huck and Jim travel down the

Mississippi, the more difficult the journey is for Huck. He has been taught his entire life that slaves are property and not people. Yet what he witnesses in the criminality is counter to the idea that a black man is inferior to a white one. While in Kentucky, Huck befriends a young boy around his own age named Buck. Despite the fact that they live in the same area and are the same race and same faith, Buck's family is in a blood feud with a neighbor. The close proximity of the two families in terms of location and personality should make it easier to resolve the conflict, but rather, on the occasion of a union between Buck's sister and a member of the enemy, the two families commence with murdering one another. He also sees an attempted mob lynching and two men who swindle money from a town before trying to con an inheritance out of young orphans, and who eventually sell Jim to a family who will in turn give him back to Miss Watson for a financial reward. Huck's voyage is one through a physical landscape, but also one through the symbolic landscape of human racial bias.

THE MORAL LAW OF THE RIVER

At first, Huck believes it is sinful to help Jim escape, that it is wrong morally and legally. By the novel's end, he is determined to help Jim even if it means sending his soul to hell. He is still not convinced that it is the right thing to do in any accepted meaning of the word, but he does feel that it is the thing he must do. While on the river, they had become something of equals, a state not echoed once they land their raft, that is to say, when they are confronted with the rule of white man.

Rachelanne Smith

Further Reading

If you liked *Adventures of Huckleberry Finn*, then you might like *Little Britches: Father and I Were Ranchers* by Ralph Moody, because it is also a coming-of-age story told through the eyes of an eight-year-old boy on a Colorado ranch in 1906. A work that similarly explores the way a community's worldview is shaped by place is Steinbeck's *Cannery Row*, which provides a vignette of life in the cannery district of Monterey, California. Another good recommendation is *Absalom, Absalom!* by William Faulkner, the story of a young man's search for his identity.

Bibliography

Alvarez, Joseph A. *Mark Twain's Geographical Imagination.* Newcastle upon Tyne: Cambridge Scholars Publishing, 2009.

Berry, Wendell. "Writer and Region." *The Hudson Review* 40, no. 1 (1987): 15–30.

Eckstein, Barbara. "Child's Play: Nature-Deficit Disorder and Mark Twain's Mississippi River Youth." *American Literary History* 24, no. 1 (2012): 16–33.

Jackson, Robert. "The Emergence of Mark Twain's Missouri: Regional Theory and 'Adventures of Huckleberry Finn.'" *The Southern Literary Journal* 35, no. 1 (2002): 47–69. www.jstor.org/stable/20078349.

Jenn, Ronald. "Transferring the Mississippi: Lexical, Literary, and Cultural Aspects in Translations of Adventures of Huckleberry Finn." *Revue française d'études américaines* 4, no. 98 (2003): 57–68.

Miller, E. Joan. "Mark Twain in the Geography Classroom: Should We Invite Him In?" *Journal of Geography* 88, no. 2 (1989): 46–49. doi:10.1080/00221348908979806.

Miller, Michael G. "Geography and Structure in 'Huckleberry Finn.'" *Studies in the Novel* 12, no. 3 (1980): 192–209. www.jstor.org/stable/29532049.

Myers, Jeffrey. *Converging Stories: Race, Ecology, and Environmental Justice in American Literature.* Athens: University of Georgia Press, 2005.

Rulon, Curt M. "Geographical Delimitation of the Dialect Areas in *The Adventures of Huckleberry Finn*." *Mark Twain Journal* 14, no. 1 (1967): 9–12. www.jstor.org/stable/41999971.

Adventures of Sherlock Holmes

Between 1887 and 1927, British writer Sir Arthur Conan Doyle wrote 4 novels and 56 short stories, the latter collected in 5 volumes, about the fictional "consulting detective" Sherlock Holmes. In many ways, the works are a mirror of their times, reflecting a period during which Britain represented a force for peace and order in a changing world. Holmes himself plays a similar role in the lives of the private individuals and government officials seeking his help, and he uses the latest scientific advances in criminology—often of his own devising—to help him solve the mysteries brought to his attention. The novels and stories featuring him take a variety of settings, from London and its environs to the counties of Britain and, in some cases, the nations beyond. As the late 19th and early 20th centuries were times of increasingly frequent and rapid movement, various forms of transportation—horse-drawn cabs, bicycles, trains, and London's underground railway—are mentioned regularly.

IN LONDON

During the period in which the Sherlock Holmes stories are set, London was the nerve center of the vast British Empire, a teeming metropolis inhabited by more than six million people. Holmes's rooms, which he shared for a time with Dr. John

---

"Sir Charles lay on his face, his arms out, his fingers dug into the ground, and his features convulsed with some strong emotion to such an extent that I could hardly have sworn to his identity. There was certainly no physical injury of any kind. But one false statement was made by Barrymore at the inquest. He said that there were no traces upon the ground round the body. He did not observe any. But I did—some little distance off, but fresh and clear."

"Footprints?"

"Footprints."

"A man's or a woman's?"

Dr. Mortimer looked strangely at us for an instant, and his voice sank almost to a whisper as he answered:—

"Mr. Holmes, they were the footprints of a gigantic hound!"

Sir Arthur Conan Doyle, *The Adventures of Sherlock Holmes* (1902)

Watson (the narrator of most of the stories), lay on a short thoroughfare in the borough of St. Marylebone in the city's West End. The specific address, 221b Baker Street, would have been on an upper floor, with Holmes's landlady, Mrs. Hudson, living on the ground floor. Holmes remained at the address after Watson married and moved out, and Holmes's brother Mycroft, reputedly more brilliant than Holmes himself, maintained them during Holmes's absence. The address is probably the most famous in London—but in fact it does not exist. Baker Street itself is real, having been laid out in the late 18th century, and Doyle's descriptions of the location are realistic, but there is not a building on the street with the number 221.

Doyle introduced Holmes and Watson, along with many of the secondary characters of the series, in the 1887 novel *A Study in Scarlet*. Besides establishing its London setting in detail, the novel makes clear Holmes's various eccentricities and his methods of detection, the latter of which seem to Watson to verge on the miraculous. The novel also includes a complicated background story involving members of the Church of Jesus Christ of Latter-day Saints, or Mormons, in what is today the state of Utah—a subject about which Doyle had no firsthand knowledge.

Doyle's second novel, *The Sign of the Four,* has a similar structure and features the Baker Street address and various sections of London and its suburbs. It, too, includes a backstory—in this case, one involving India and the Andaman Islands, an archipelago east of India in the Bay of Bengal whose inhabitants are noted for their small stature. Once again, Doyle had no personal experience of the region, but he may have seen the skeleton of an Andaman Islander at the Royal College of Surgeons in Edinburgh, Scotland, during his years of medical study in that city. If so, it would explain his choice of such an individual to play a key role in the novel.

THE DETECTIVE ABROAD

Doyle refers to Holmes's travels in Tibet, Persia (Iran), Sudan, and what are today Ukraine and Saudi Arabia, as well as a period of study in southern France. Doyle suggests that Holmes was in the African country of Sudan helping the British government during an insurrection against occupying British forces in 1884, but does not develop the reference. In one crucial case, however, Doyle describes Holmes's direct involvement abroad—in a country that the writer himself had visited.

Doyle had traveled twice to Switzerland with his wife in 1893, and he set the conclusion of what he expected would be his final Holmes story, "The Adventure of the Final Problem," in that country. The story suggests that Holmes and his archnemesis, Professor James Moriarty, both perished in a fall over Reichenbach Falls near the village of Meiringen. The story appeared in British and American magazines in late 1893, and was published in book form with other stories the following year.

HOLMES IN SOUTHERN ENGLAND

Public dismay at Holmes's apparent death forced Doyle to revive his creation, leading to two more Holmes novels and enough stories to fill three more collections. In *The Hound of the Baskervilles,* by general agreement the best novel in the series, Doyle made generous use of a British locale with which he was very familiar. He had worked as a doctor in the port of Plymouth on the coast of the county of Devon in 1882, and went on to visit the county repeatedly. In *The Hound of the Baskervilles,* he deals with a family apparently cursed by a gigantic, seemingly supernatural dog. The family's ancestral home is in Dartmoor, a desolate, sparsely populated region of Devon known for its tors (hills topped with outcroppings of rock), heather-covered moors, and dangerous bogs.

Another English county is the setting of two stories about Holmes. In one, "His Last Bow," the detective has retired to the county of Sussex in southeast England to raise bees. Uncharacteristically, the story is told in the third person rather than being narrated by Watson. Another Sussex story, "The Adventure of the Lion's Mane," is one of only two stories in the entire series narrated directly by Holmes himself. Doyle had moved to the southern county in 1908, and lived there until his death in 1930.

SPACE AS MYSTERY

In the scenes in which Sherlock Holmes has to solve some mystery, space becomes a puzzle to be solved. What Doyle does to our everyday rooms and streets is to write a layer of spirituality into them—to admit that trace evidence lingers after we have been present in a room may speak to some lingering presence after death. On another level, Doyle picks up a trend toward many of the surveillance techniques of the 21st century.

Some of the tragic nature that Doyle explores in Holmes as a hero is that he has to forsake other experiences of space, such as engaging more fully with it and the other people in it, to produce such masterful results. Yet, his ability to read the effects that actions have had on a localized place make him capable of sustaining such long-lasting admiration from readers.

Grove Koger

Further Reading
Other works from the time period of the early detective story include E. W. Hornung's *The Collected Raffles Stories,* Emmuska Orczy's *The Old Man in the Corner: Twelve Mysteries,* and Sax Rohmer's *The Insidious Dr. Fu-Manchu.*

Bibliography
Agathocleous, Tanya. "London Mysteries and International Conspiracies: James, Doyle, and the Aesthetics of Cosmopolitanism." *Nineteenth-Century Contexts: An Interdisciplinary Journal* 26, no. 2 (2004): 125–48. doi:10.1080/0890549042000242759.

Battista, Kathy, Brandon LaBelle, Barbara Penner, Steve Pile, and Jane Rendell. "Exploring 'An Area of Outstanding Unnatural Beauty': A Treasure Hunt around King's Cross, London." *Cultural Geographies* 12, no. 4 (2005): 429–62. doi:10.1191/1474474005eu345oa.

Broughton, Mark. "From Ham House to the Pineapples of Groombridge Place: Locating the Draughtsman's Contract." Paper presented at the Art and Landscape: Interdisciplinary Perspectives, Reading, United Kingdom, May 2010.

Cranfield, Jonathan L. "Sherlock's Slums: The Periodical as an Environmental Form." *Textual Practice* 28, no. 2 (2014): 215–41. doi:10.1080/0950236X.2013.848926.

Duncan, Alistair. *No Better Place: Arthur Conan Doyle, Windlesham and Communication with the Other Side (1907–1930)*. London: MX Publishing, 2015.

Fitzpatrick, Rob W. "Nature, Distribution, and Origin of Soil Materials in the Forensic Comparison of Soils." In *Soil Analysis in Forensic Taphonomy: Chemical and Biological Effects of Buried Human Remains,* edited by Mark Tibbett and David O. Carter. Boca Raton, FL: CRC Press, 2008. doi:10.1201/9781420069921.ch1.

Gates, Samantha. "'Romantic Realities': Sherlock Holmes and Urban Imagination." Honors thesis, Bucknell University, 2016.

McLaughlin, David. "The Game's Afoot: Walking as Practice in Sherlockian Literary Geographies." *Literary Geographies* 2, no. 2 (2016): 144–63.

McLaughlin, Joseph. *Writing the Urban Jungle: Reading Empire in London from Doyle to Eliot*. Charlottesville: University of Virginia Press, 2000.

Passey, Joan. "'Imagined Ghosts on Unfrequented Roads': Gothic Tourism in Nineteenth-Century Cornwall." In *Virtual Dark Tourism: Ghost Roads*, edited by Kathryn N. McDaniel, 41–61. Cham, Switzerland: Palgrave Macmillan, 2018.

Robbins, Lauren. "Science and the Lost World: Sir Arthur Conan Doyle's Reworking of the Vernian Adventure Novel." Honors thesis, Mount Holyoke College, 2010.

All Quiet on the Western Front

All Quiet on the Western Front, written by German author Erich Maria Remarque, is a novel set in World War I. Most of the action in the story takes place on the German line of the Western Front. Several years after Remarque fought with the German army on the Western Front, he wrote and published this novel based on his own experiences, garnering international fame.

The novel is narrated by the character of Paul Bäumer, a 19-year-old who, along with his classmates, enlists in the army and is sent to war. The young men have been pressured to join the war by their schoolteacher, Kantorek, who inspires them with lofty nationalist rhetoric and paints war as romantic and heroic. The brutal landscape of war, which defies human logic and compassion, contrasts sharply with the empty but beautiful rhetoric that encouraged the young men to fight.

The narrative opens as Paul Bäumer and the 80 remaining members of Second Company (originally comprised of 150 men) are rotated off the front lines and sent to rest. The men have spent the past two weeks in trench warfare. No longer a student in school, Bäumer as a soldier has no interest or time for the things he once admired, like writing poetry and plays. The impact of war begins to hit him, and Paul feels a distance from his former self, as war seems to have robbed him of his capacity for joy and filled him with an emptiness that prompts a new cynical outlook on life. Paul, along with others from his school, starts to remember distastefully the people from home who suggested that they join the war effort. The young men at the novel's opening have already become disillusioned with the clichés that glorify war, as well as the ideals of patriotism and nationalism. They bitterly blame the older generation for deceiving them about the true horrors of battle and decry the hypocrisy of those with authority who preach the virtues of sacrifice while sending other men to fight on the battlefield.

The thought of finding glory on the battlefield is a distant memory as Paul is forced to watch many of his friends die. For example, as one of his former classmates, Kemmerich, lies dying from the gangrene that has already taken his leg, Müller, another classmate, requests the dying man's boots. His request and the fact that it is granted reflect the brutal necessity of thinking clearly, without sentimentality, as a means to survive war, as survival at any cost is the only goal. In another vivid moment, the company is attacked and forced to take cover in a cemetery, where shells throw dead bodies into the air to mix with those of both the living and dying. Moments like these in Remarque's construction of battlefield geography show war as a kind of hell on Earth, a meeting place between the two worlds shared by the living and the dead.

Reinforcements arrive, but they are mere teenagers. Paul and his friends, already jaded, begin to understand that they are now hardened veterans. As a way to bridge the distance between the new arrivals and the established unit, an older soldier, Kat, gives some beans to one of the young men. He explains to him that the cook can be bribed with tobacco.

On their way back to the front lines, the men pass a schoolhouse that has been destroyed by mortar fire. In the yard outside are freshly made coffins. Suspecting that the coffins may have been made for them, the soldiers joke around and engage in horseplay to gather courage. At the front, they realize that men and heavy artillery reinforce the enemy's lines. The men begin to lose hope. They have nothing to compete against the superior technology of British tanks.

The new recruits are quickly killed in action. Paul thinks about how he and his comrades have to rely on their animal instincts to survive. As this battle concludes, Second Company is reduced to 32 men. They are given a short reprieve, during which the soldiers swim and cook sausages, which attracts a group of French girls because they have no food and are hungry.

Paul returns to his hometown on leave and finds that his mother is dying from cancer. His father wants to hear his stories about war, which illustrates the detachment that war creates between veterans and civilians. Paul wants to escape the reality he has been living, while his father cannot hear enough about it. The patriotism of the townspeople, including Paul's own father, and their ignorance of the horrors of trench warfare annoy Paul while causing him to also feel that he is lost. This "lost generation" theme is also developed in Paul's and the other men's inability to think of life after the war, having no jobs or wives to return to and being too psychologically scarred to return to civilian life. Paul visits Kemmerich's mother and comforts her with a lie: he says that her son died peacefully without pain.

Paul is sent for more training at a prisoner of war (POW) camp. There, he encounters Russian prisoners, and they are unexpectedly humanized in his eyes. He shares some of the food his mother prepared for him and contemplates how war turns innocent people against each other.

Once again at the front, Paul and the other men prepare for the next battle. As the unit marches onward into battle, Paul is separated from the others and is forced to use a shell hole for protection as the French army advances. While Paul is waiting for the attack to end, a retreating French soldier falls into the hole with him. Paul reflexively stabs the man, but the man does not die right away. For the next few days, Paul comforts him while feeling regret and realizing that soldiers sent to fight on battlefield are not enemies, but simply other people just like him. This affects Paul, and when he meets back up with the men in his company, they attempt to console him.

Paul and his unit are sent to evacuate a Russian village. Paul, Kropp, and others are wounded in the process and are sent to a Catholic hospital. Paul's leg is put in a cast, and Kropp ends up having his leg amputated. Once he is able to walk again, Paul returns to the front. As resources dwindle, morale is diminished and the men are fatigued. Paul's friends are steadily dying on the battlefield. Detering tries to desert but is caught in his hometown and court-martialed. Müller is shot at close range and dies. Kat is shot and wounded in the leg, and Paul carries him to camp. Along the way, he realizes Kat has been shot in the head while being carried. Eventually, Paul is the last among his group of friends. He prays for the fighting to be over, but contemplates if he could ever be "normal" again after his experiences.

By the end of the novel, all of the classmates have met grim fates, some going crazy, many killed, and one captured after an attempted escape. In the closing scene, narrated in third person, on an otherwise quiet day when a report is made that "all [is] quiet on the Western Front," Paul is shot dead, his face bearing an expression of relief.

WAR AND THE PHYSICAL GEOGRAPHY OF MORTALITY

Remarque's novel portrays the stark realities of war, and that involves the brutal devastation done to human bodies. Fought from 1914 to 1918, World War I is considered the first modern war—fought with mechanized killing machines, poison gas, and armored tanks in the brutal and fetid conditions of trench warfare. Death and the threat of death pervade every page, which makes the frailty of the human body front and center in this novel. The proximity of death heightens the narrator's and other character's senses.

Despite the carnage and the risk of death, the soldiers must continue to live. This means that they must continue to eat. Despite various shortages, Paul is amazed by Kat's ability to barter for or find additional provisions. Through the character Kat, Remarque explores how soldiers have to make the most of life on the front, especially because they could lose their lives at any minute. There are many poignant scenes in the novel involving food. Eating together still brings with it a sense of community, even if it provides a contrast to shared meals at home during peacetime. For example, when the men share their food with the starving French women, Paul wishes it was under different circumstances, for fun and enjoyment, rather than tinged with the desperation of survival. Later, sharing food with others is an ultimate reinforcement of bonds between people and a recognition of a common humanity: Paul shares some of his mother's cooking with Russian prisoners of war. Later, she sends him off with homemade potato cakes, and he saves the best ones to give to his friends.

Beyond the sounds of war and the necessity of eating, which becomes a burden at times, other key moments highlight the continued life in these soldiers through the way they interact with their locale. During his training in the POW camp, Paul has more downtime than when he was at war. He begins to find joy in his natural

This photo shows German soldiers taking a break in a trench near St. Michel, France, circa 1915. German author Erich Maria Remarque fought in the trenches of World War I and draws on his experiences as inspiration for his novel. (Library of Congress)

surroundings, noting the crispness of fall air and the sound of wind through juniper and birch trees. He even revels in the feeling of the sand under his boots. Such heightened senses are key to an experience where soldiers are constantly reminded of the body's frail mortality.

Lacar Musgrove and Lynn Marie Houston

Further Reading

If you enjoyed *All Quiet on the Western Front,* you might like to read *Goodbye to All That* by Robert Graves, a memoir that provides an account of the social changes in British society following the war. You may also like *The Price of Glory,* the second book in a trilogy by Alistair Horne, which tells of the historical rivalry between France and Germany. Other novels set during World War I include *A Farewell to Arms* by Ernest Hemingway, *The Guns of August* by Barbara W. Tuchman, and *Birdsong* by Sebastian Faulks.

Bibliography

Higonnet, Margaret R. "Authenticity and Art in Trauma Narratives of World War I." *Modernism/modernity* 9, no. 1 (2002): 91–107.

Liulevicius, Vejas Gabriel. *War Land on the Eastern Front: Culture, National Identity and German Occupation in World War I.* Cambridge, UK: Cambridge University Press, 2005.

Saunders, Nicholas J. "Bodies of Metal, Shells of Memory: 'Trench Art,' and the Great War Re-cycled." *Journal of Material Culture* 5, no. 1 (2000): 43–67.

Smith-Casanueva, Brent M. "Nation in Remarque's *All Quiet on the Western Front* and Eastwood's Flags of Our Father." *CICweb: Comparative Literature & Culture* 14, no. 1 (March 2012): 1–9.

Ulbrich, David J. "A Male-Conscious Critique of Erich Maria Remarque's *All Quiet on the Western Front*." *The Journal of Men's Studies* 3, no. 3 (1995): 229–40.

All the Pretty Horses

All the Pretty Horses is a 1992 novel by the American author Cormac McCarthy, which won the National Book Award for Fiction and the National Book Critics Circle Award for Fiction. The title comes from a lullaby in which the caretaker promises a sleeping baby that he will have all the pretty horses when he wakes up. The poetic voice is a slave woman lamenting that she is taking care of the master's baby and not her own. The novel is the first installment of the Border Trilogy, with *The Crossing* (1994) and *Cities of the Plain* (1998). *All the Pretty Horses* is an anachronistic Western set in 1949 in which a 16-year-old cowboy, John Grady Cole, and his friend, Lacey Rawlins, ride by horse from San Angelo, Texas, to the Nuestra Señora de la Purísima ranch in Cuatro Ciénagas, Coahuila. This is a 390-mile ride by car in modern times. When they are crossing the border, they meet a 13-year-old boy (who claims to be older) who rides an extraordinary bay horse and owns an old Colt pistol. He tells Cole and Rawlins that his name is Jimmy Blevins. Cole will later learn that the name Jimmy Blevins belongs to a popular radio evangelist. Cole and Rawlins get work at the ranch, and soon Cole is in charge of training horses and breeding mares. He becomes the most important cowboy on the ranch. Concurrent with the narrative set at the ranch, Blevins shoots three men at La Encantada, Coahuila, and he is taken to the *prisión* Castelar in Saltillo with Cole and Rawlins. During the trip, Blevins is summarily executed. Cole is a modern Don Quixote, idealistic in his quest to recuperate the loss of cowboy culture in Texas and Mexico. He is always ready to help those in distress, like Blevins, and doing it without considering the (fatal) consequences of his actions. Rawlins, Cole's squire, is the voice of reason; he will blindly follow his buddy in spite of his apprehensions.

THE GEOGRAPHY OF PLACE

McCarthy's geography puts together geology and biology, economic and social forces, and historical change and desire. Set during a time of cultural shifts, the novel features characters who are skeptical of maps because they cannot fully represent reality. At the beginning of the novel, the narrator depicts Cole riding his horse by the Concho River (a name of Spanish European origin, meaning "shell"),

---

"Where is your country?" he said.

"I don't know," said John Grady. "I don't know where it is. I don't know what happens to country."

Cormac McCarthy, *All the Pretty Horses* (1992)

moving from what used to be Comanche territory and entering Kiowa country. The Comanches and the Kiowas were displaced tribes. Cole is riding on what used to be a war trail in a ranch of Anglo-European origin. Barbed wire, that by the 1880s had compartmentalized the countryside, prevents Cole's free rides and reminds the characters and readers of the privatization of land. The presence of the train is also used as a reminder of modernity and its changes.

The protagonists strip off to cross the Rio Grande like a baptism. Once in Mexico, they pass by dry scrublands, a barren wind gap in the mountains, grassland, and desert. The Mexican landscape is lacking modern features like vehicles, radios, and paved roads. The country is wild and raw, and during the night the cowboys can hear the overwhelming howling of wolves. They reach La Purísima, a 27,500-acre ranch with 1,000 head of cattle and hundreds of wild horses; the protagonists compare it to a Big Rock Candy Mountain. La Purísima Ranch is dotted by many bodies of water that look like enchanted islands by the Sierra de Anteojo with all its natural springs, marshes, shallow lakes, and lagunas. Cole falls in love with the aristocratic Alejandra, daughter of Don Héctor Rocha, owner of the ranch and patriarch of an old family who can trace its roots to Toledo, Spain. The erotic encounter between the young lovers happens in a pastoral, that is a laguna surrounded by sedge, willow, and wild plum.

The betrayal of their confidence in Cole, combined with Blevins's crimes, take Cole and Rawlins to the prison of Saltillo, capital of Coahuila. The prison follows the topoi of Mexican inferno, a place of human depravation where Rawlins is presumably sodomized, and Cole is scarred and has to kill a fellow inmate, a *cuchillero,* to survive. Alejandra's aunt, who holds the medieval name of Dueña Alfonsa, indicating the feudal relationship of the ranch, rescues the young cowboys by bribing the corrupt authorities. Rawlins returns by bus to Nuevo Laredo, and Cole travels south to Zacatecas to meet Alejandra one last time. Here he realizes the impossibility of his love quest and his journey to find the lost arcadia of free cowboys. When Cole returns to Texas, he crosses the Rio Grande at Langtry, Texas, moving from one historical place to another. Cole will travel all over Texas trying to find the true owner of Blevins's horse. He goes to Ozona, Texas, where his horses are impounded and, after a hearing, he recuperates them. From there he goes to Del Rio, Texas, to meet with the real Jimmy Blevins, the radio preacher. Cole briefly returns to San Angelo to attend his *abuela*'s funeral in the Mexican cemetery of Knickerbocker, Texas. The novel finishes with Cole driving farther west.

POLYGLOSSIA

The U.S./Mexico border is presented as a "contact zone" as defined by Mary Louise Pratt, where disparate cultures meet and asymmetrically try to come to terms with each other. The presence of conversations, toponyms, geological, and botanic vocabulary in Spanish contest the centrality of Anglo culture to explain the Southwest of the United States and the border. This concept is reinforced by the ways in which the novel makes reference to texts from earlier time periods in Spanish literary history, such as *Don Quixote*.

Salvador Oropesa

Further Reading

If you liked *All the Pretty Horses,* then you might like Wright Morris's *Plains Song,* which tells the story of women on the Nebraska plains in the late 19th century. Another work is Conrad Richter's *The Waters of Kronos,* which traces a young man's cross-country return to his hometown only to discover the town has been destroyed after being submerged by a lake for a hydroelectric dam. Also consider *Ten North Frederick* by John O'Hara, which shows multiple perspectives of three generations of a wealthy family living in Gibbsville, Pennsylvania.

Bibliography

Berk, Figen. "An Ecocritical Approach to Cormac McCarthy's *The Road.*" *RSIRJLE: Research Scholar—An International Refereed Journal of Literary Explorations* 2, no. 3 (2014): 62–76.

Berry, K. Wesley. "The Lay of the Land in Cormac McCarthy's *The Orchard Keeper* and *Child of God.*" *Southern Quarterly* 38, no. 4 (2000): 61.

Cella, Matthew J. C. "The Ecosomatic Paradigm in Literature: Merging Disability Studies and Ecocriticism." *ISLE: Interdisciplinary Studies in Literature and Environment* 20, no. 3 (2013): 574–96.

Cheuse, Alan. "A Note on Landscape in *All the Pretty Horses.*" *Southern Quarterly* 30, no. 4 (1992): 140.

Datema, Jessica, and Diane Krumrey, eds. *Wretched Refuge: Immigrants and Itinerants in the Postmodern.* Newcastle upon Tyne: Cambridge Scholars Publishing, 2010.

Eklund, Lovisa. "Shut in or Exposed—Inhospitable Landscapes in Joseph Conrad's *Heart of Darkness* and Cormac McCarthy's *Blood Meridian.*" Bachelor's thesis, Lund University, 2013.

Godfrey, Laura G. "'The World He'd Lost': Geography and 'Green' Memory in Cormac McCarthy's *The Road.*" *Critique: Studies in Contemporary Fiction* 52, no. 2 (2011): 163–75.

Godfrey, Laura G. "Hemingway, the Preservation Impulse, and Cultural Geography." In *Hemingway's Geographies: Intimacy, Materiality, and Memory.* New York: Palgrave Macmillan, 2016. doi: 10.1057/978-1-137-58175-4.

Jillet, Louise, ed. *Cormac McCarthy's Borders and Landscapes.* New York: Bloomsbury Publishing, Inc., 2016.

Keller Estes, Andrew. *Cormac McCarthy and the Writing of American Spaces.* Amsterdam: Rodopi, 2013.

Kunsa, Ashley. "'Maps of the World in Its Becoming': Post-Apocalyptic Naming in Cormac McCarthy's *The Road.*" *Journal of Modern Literature* 33, no. 1 (2009): 57–74. doi:10.2979/jml.2009.33.1.57.

Latshaw, Skyler. "Burning on the Shore of an Unknowable Void: Nature as Mystical Reality in the Fiction of Cormac McCarthy." Master's thesis, Grand Valley State University, 2013.

McFarland, Ron. "Mapping Cormac McCarthy's *No Country for Old Men.*" *The Midwest Quarterly* 58, no. 4 (2017): 347–48, 433–53.

McGilchrist, M. *The Western Landscape in Cormac McCarthy and Wallace Stegner.* New York: Routledge, 2009.

Morton, Adam D. "The Warp of the World: Geographies of Space and Time in the Border Trilogy by Cormac McCarthy." *Environment and Planning D: Society and Space* 33, no. 5 (2015): 831–49.

Rudzitis, Gundars. "Nonmetropolitan Geography: Migration, Sense of Place, and the American West." *Urban Geography* 14, no. 6 (1993): 574–85. doi:10.2747/0272-3638.14.6.574.

Short, Stacy K. "Borders, Barriers, and Crossings: Cormac McCarthy's *All the Pretty Horses* and *The Crossing.*" Master's thesis, Texas Woman's University, 2009.

Soto, Isabel. "The Border Paradigm in Cormac McCarthy's *The Crossing.*" In *Literature and Ethnicity in the Cultural Borderlands,* edited by Jesus Benito and Ana Maria Manzanas, 51–62. Amsterdam: Rodopi, 2002.

Warde, Anthony. "'Justified in the World': Spatial Values and Sensuous Geographies in Cormac McCarthy's *The Road.*" In *Writing America into the Twenty-First Century: Essays on the American Novel,* edited by Elizabeth Boyle and Anne-Marie Evans. Newcastle upon Tyne: Cambridge Scholars Publishing, 2010.

Weiss, Daniel. "Cormac McCarthy, Violence, and Borders: The Map as Code for What Is Not Contained." *The Cormac McCarthy Journal* 8, no. 1 (2010): 73–89. www.jstor.org/stable/42909411.

Almanac of the Dead

Leslie Marmon Silko's epic novel *Almanac of the Dead* seeks to reimagine the 500-year history of conflict between native and Anglo Americans. In it, Silko conceives of a possible future brought about by the uprising of marginalized peoples. Set in the American Southwest, including Arizona, Mexico, and the borderlands, this narrative is told through multiple points of view and contains at least 70 characters. In six parts, *Almanac of the Dead* tells a story from the point of view of the conquered rather than the conquerors. In this way, Silko endeavors to reimagine the history of the American Southwest in contrast to traditional white colonial representations. The landscape of the Southwest plays a prominent role in inspiring the details of Silko's vision for racial and social equality.

The individual narratives that make up the novel are told from the point of view of a wide cast of characters of various ethnic and socioeconomic backgrounds, while moving between different settings and time periods. The characters represent groups that are usually marginalized both in the real world and in literature—including indigenous peoples, the homeless, and the disabled. This structure, which reverses the tendency in Western literature to speak from the point of view of the conquerors, mimics that of Maya almanacs, including the one from which Silko has taken her title, the *Almanac of the Dead.* This form allows Silko to employ these multiple narratives told in different voices. The novel lacks a definable linear plot or singular protagonist and is a fragmentary collection of dreams, maps, lists, and prophecies of various characters, both major and minor, whose worlds eventually intersect. Readers can sometimes experience these seemingly rapid shifts into scenes and moments as random and lacking transition, but they are part of Silko's strategy to push against what she sees as the linguistic and narrative power structures of Anglo culture.

In Native American culture, history is experienced through storytelling. The Maya, as they watched their culture being lost to that of the Spanish and Portuguese conquerors, worked frantically to preserve their stories recorded in glyphs carved into stone as well as stored in their collective memories. Their *Almanac of the Dead* includes lengthy flashbacks tied to this mythos and indigenous knowledge, which are woven into Silko's plot. The plot is not simply chaotic, as some readers might be tempted to conclude. Silko's circular story arc demands that time not be deciphered linearly because Native Americans believe time to be circular.

The nonlinearity and fragmentation of the structure are also reflective of a major theme of a world thrown into chaos, particularly as the borderlands have become a place of violence and ecological devastation. This chaos is expressed through transmutations in which crime families or human networks for weapons, drugs, and organ smuggling and pornography have replaced the traditional bonds of family and other nurturing relationships; sexuality has become an instrument of torture; women are excluded from the reproductive process; and scientific advancements, rather than providing for comfort and better quality of life for humans, have become perverted in the service of trafficking human organs on the black market. Silko traces a lineage between the contemporary violence in the Southwest, what she calls the "Days of the Death-Eye Dog," and its history of colonization.

By the end of the novel, the story lines begin to converge in and around Tucson, Arizona, to form a whole as the characters and their world and stories come into sharper focus. All of the seemingly disconnected mini-plots lead to a finale that speaks to alliance and coalition building. The central narrative of the novel culminates in various indigenous groups planning to overthrow the government of the European conquerors, that of the United States. Veterans are squatting in expensive homes, preparing to take over U.S. military bases; two brothers are leading a group of revolutionaries toward the U.S. border through Mexico; hackers are preparing to shut down the power grid of the United States; and ecoterrorists have taken explosives to a dam, where they are prepared to detonate them. These groups form a jumbled and fragmented alliance in an effort to deliver a message about how a revolutionary new future might be brought, even as it seems that Silko remains somewhat critical of violence as a means to achieve independence and freedom from oppression.

THE GEOGRAPHY OF THE SOUTHWEST

The first page of this novel is a map of the Southwest, which features Tucson as a kind of capital city of the new, alternative space of power that Silko imagines for oppressed peoples. However, the locations of action in the novel or the places that shape Silko's characters are not limited to the United States: the work makes reference to Africa, Colombia, El Salvador, Haiti, Honduras, and Panama. This multiplicity of diverse places as central to character formation and plot emphasizes the political and social realities of transnationalism—a worldview that transcends the confines of national boundaries. Although references to larger countries and continents represent the global view in Silko's novel, she cultivates an awareness of local place through her concern for and descriptions of Laguna Puebla land, especially areas of the reservation in New Mexico. This concept of the local, inspired by Native American belief, emphasizes that stories/histories live in the geography of a place and that the categories of "human" and "nature" are not separate entities, except from a colonialist standpoint that dehumanizes other races by describing them as "subhuman" and a part of nature. Silko's novel reminds us that all humans are part of the natural world. In fact, one of her characters, Calabazas, voices stories about indigenous figures who outsmarted European colonizers because of the latter's inability to recognize differences between tribes and also differences in the landscape. Marks or traces on the land, such as what would be left by passage there, were invisible to most of the would-be captors, allowing fugitives (such as Geronimo) to escape capture. First and foremost in the novel is a concern for environmental justice and also an awareness of how the plight of the land is linked to the plight of the people living on the land. In this novel, Silko seems to argue that the only cure for the violent destruction of people and landscapes is a turn toward a spirituality inspired by place.

Lacar Musgrove and Lynn Marie Houston

Further Reading

Leslie Marmon Silko's work has much in common with that of other indigenous female writers who seek to draw attention to the legacy of violence in the Americas. Such writers include Paula Gunn Allen, Louise Erdrich, Joy Harjo, and Linda Hogan. Specifically, Harjo has written a collection of poems entitled *In Mad Love and War* that reminds us that history often ignores the beauty of the civilizations that were conquered. Another work that similarly questions the status and perspective of history is *Fools Crow* by James Welch, which tells a Blackfeet Indian's story of transition into manhood while white invasion looms. Another good recommendation is Paula Gunn Allen's *The Sacred Hoop: Recovering the Feminine in American Indian Traditions* because it documents the role of women in American Indian traditions.

Bibliography

Brigham, Ann. "Productions of Geographic Scale and Capitalist-Colonialist Enterprise in Leslie Marmon Silko's *Almanac of the Dead*." *Modern Fiction Studies* 50, no. 2 (2004): 303–31.

Delgado, Francisco. "Trespassing the U.S.-Mexico Border in Leslie Marmon Silko's *Almanac of the Dead* and Karen Tei Yamashita's *Tropic of Orange*." *CEA Critic*, 79, no. 2 (2017): 149–66.

Griffith, Jane. "Law, Literature, and Leslie Marmon Silko: Competing Narratives of Water." *Studies in American Indian Literatures* 29, no. 2 (Summer 2017): 26–48.

Hunt, Alex. "The Radical Geography of Silko's *Almanac of the Dead*." *Western American Literature* 39, no. 3 (2004): 256–78.

O'Meara, Bridget. "The Ecological Politics of Leslie Silko's *Almanac of the Dead*." *Wicazo Sa Review* 15, no. 2 (2000): 63–73.

Reed, T. V. "Toxic Colonialism, Environmental Justice, and Native Resistance in Silko's *Almanac of the Dead*." *Melus* 34, no. 2 (2009): 25–42.

Romero, Channette. "Envisioning a 'Network of Tribal Coalitions': Leslie Marmon Silko's *Almanac of the Dead*." *American Indian Quarterly* 26, no. 4 (Fall 2002): 623–40.

Spurgeon, Sara L. "Sanctioned Narratives and the (Non)Innocent Triumph of the Savage War: Mythic Co-Dependence in Leslie Marmon Silko's *Almanac of the Dead*." In *Exploding the Western: Myths of Empire on the Postmodern Frontier*. College Station: Texas A&M University Press, 2005.

Tillett, Rebecca. *Afterword. Almanac: Reading Its Story Maps after Twenty Years: An Interview with Leslie Marmon Silko*. Tucson: University of Arizona Press, 2014.

Antigone

Using the Theban civil war as a backdrop, the play *Antigone* highlights the destructive landscape of war and its negative impact on families and communities. It is the third in Sophocles's trilogy of Theban plays, after *Oedipus Rex* and *Oedipus at Colonus*. The plot begins as Polynices and Eteocles, both sons of Oedipus (and also his half brothers), are killed on the field of battle, where they were fighting over who would be the king of Thebes.

After Eteocles failed to cede his rule to Polynices, as they had agreed, the latter had invaded. Thebes' new king, Creon, their uncle, has decided to honor Eteocles with proper burial rights; however, he decides to leave Polynices's body unburied, as he believes that the invasion was a crime against the city. This is an incredible dishonor, as the Greeks believed that proper burial rituals aided the soul's journey into the afterlife. Burying their dead also reflected well on the rest of the family because reverence and proper respect of the dead were considered key duties of familial ties. They believed that the gods would curse them if they did not enact the proper rituals when caring for the dead.

Antigone and Ismene, sisters of the fallen, find themselves at the heart of the play's conflict. They have to decide to either bury their brother or follow the edict of their new king. They must choose between loyalty to their family or to the throne. Antigone cannot relinquish her loyalty to her family and seeks her sister's help in burying their brother. Fearing they will be put to death, Ismene refuses to assist Antigone.

Learning that Polynices has been buried, Creon orders a search for those responsible. Antigone is brought before him, but the king does not believe she acted alone. Assuming that her sister must have conspired with her, he orders them both to be imprisoned. Antigone stands firm in her conviction that burying her brother was the right thing to do and that Ismene had nothing to do with her actions, even though the latter, out of guilt, has given a false confession.

Creon has a change of heart and frees Ismene, but he buries Antigone alive in a cave. Haemon, Antigone's fiancé and son of the king, arrives to talk to his father. He attempts to convince Creon to spare Antigone, but the conversation devolves and Haemon declares he will never see his father again.

Tiresias, a blind prophet, warns Creon that the gods side with Antigone. He informs Creon that because of his actions, one of his children will die for the crimes of leaving Polynices unburied and for subsequently punishing Antigone. The chorus of elders convinces Creon to heed their advice. Creon sets out to right his wrong by agreeing with the elders to bury Polynices and free Antigone.

However, Antigone has already taken her own life by hanging. Finding his fiancé has killed herself, Haemon decides to join her and kills himself, too. When Creon's wife, Eurydice, learns of her son's death, she is overtaken with sorrow and also commits suicide.

At the end of the play, as Creon holds his son's body, he is told of his wife's death. Sophocles leaves his audience with this image of a broken family. Creon may be king of Greece, but his family members are all dead. The last words of the play are from the chorus of elders, who sum up the plot by saying that although the gods punish the proud, punishment brings wisdom.

DISTANCE OF TIME AND PLACE

Although Sophocles sets the play in ancient times and in the city of Thebes, he was writing in the fifth century in Athens. One of the reasons critics think that he distanced the time and place of the play *Antigone* was to be able to put into a dramatic situation some current social politics that would have been too difficult for audiences to deal with had they been presented in a more familiar time and place. For example, Athenian women were beginning to push against the strict gender roles in their society and to demand greater freedom. Antigone's resistance to her male family member and to the king might have helped their cause. However, Antigone's position is complicated: in one respect, she dies as a martyr for female empowerment, and in another contradictory respect, she dies because she is trying to "do a woman's duty" by honoring a deceased male family member and placing his well-being before her own.

THE PLACE AND VALUES OF THE POLIS

The conflict of Antigone centers around the Greek notion of *polis,* the city-state, which emphasizes the communal concerns over those of the individual. At the beginning of the play, Sophocles places Antigone and Ismene into a scene where they are located outside of the home, whispering in the dark. By placing these two female characters in a setting outside the home at night, many critics argue that Sophocles begins the play by casting audience suspicion on the two women. Audiences at the time this was written would have suspected the characters of plotting against the polis, as they were in a location they should not have been at night. However, the two women stand up for a morality that is ultimately recognized as correct. They stand in opposition to the villain of the play, King Creon, as he develops into a character that Athenians would have despised. Their strong belief in democracy, a form of government that promoted the polis, would have augmented the message of the play about the negative consequences when a ruler does not listen to the voice of his people.

THE GEOGRAPHY OF BURIAL

It was common practice in ancient Greece to allow even the losing side of a war to bury their dead. Regular breaks in fighting, called burial truces, were taken to allow for this. There was little precedent for refusing to bury the body of an enemy. The *Iliad,* for instance, opens with anxiety over burying all those who died in the Trojan War. The narrator does not want any of the bodies, even those from the other side, to go without proper burial. Achilles angers the gods by dragging one of the bodies, that of Hector (who had killed Achilles's best friend), in the dirt, but he finally relinquishes the body for burial.

In *Antigone,* scholars note that she actually buries her brother's body twice. Many debate why this would have been necessary beyond the conventions of plot—in other words, so that she could be caught in the act and punished. They cite Greek custom and note that the first time she sprinkled dirt on his body, even if it was removed later, would have been enough for his soul to find peace in the afterlife.

Some scholars look into the nature of Antigone's character and state that Sophocles developed her as singularly focused on performing the funeral rights that were denied. Her obsession, then, may have been why Sophocles writes the second burial, which leads to the many deaths in this tragic play. Both Antigone and Creon, in this respect, come off as characters diametrically opposed by their obsessions.

The play is one of the only plays in the Theban trilogy to focus on the space between life and death. Polynices is dead, but his body is unburied. Antigone, when she is put in the cave, is buried but not yet dead. Much of the plot conflict is generated from the desire to allow what is dead to be buried and trying to save what is buried from death.

Lynn Marie Houston

Further Reading
Other ancient and classic Greek playwrights who wrote tragedies include Aeschylus, Euripedes, and Seneca. Aristophanes was also an ancient playwright from Athens, but he wrote only comedies.

Bibliography
Budelmann, Felix. *The Language of Sophocles: Communality, Communication and Involvement.* Cambridge, UK: Cambridge University Press, 2006.
Dillon, Matthew P. J. "The Ecology of the Greek Sanctuary." *Zeitschrift für Papyrologie und Epigraphik* (1997): 113–27.
Heirman, Jo, and Jacqueline Klooster. *The Ideologies of Lived Space in Literary Texts, Ancient and Modern.* Ghent, Belgium: Academia Press, 2014.
Hughes, J. Donald. "Ecology in Ancient Greece." *Inquiry* 18, no. 2 (1975): 115–25.
Janssens, David. "Locus Tragicus: The Problem of Place in Greek Tragedy." In *The Locus of Tragedy,* edited by Arthur Cools, Thomas Crombez, Rosa Slegers, and Johan Taels, 7–28. Leiden, Netherlands: Brill, 2008.
Neyrat, Frédéric. "Planetary Antigones: The Environmental Situation and the Wandering Condition." *Qui Parle: Critical Humanities and Social Sciences* 25, no. 1–2 (2016): 35–64.
Rodighiero, Andrea. "The Sense of Place: Oedipus at Colonus, 'Political' Geography, and the Defence of a Way of Life." In *Crisis on Stage: Tragedy and Comedy in Late Fifth-Century Athens,* edited by Andreas Markantonatos and Bernhard Zimmermann, 55–80. Berlin: De Gruyter, 2012.

Anzaldúa, Gloria

Gloria Anzaldúa writes in both English and Spanish. Most of her work fluctuates back and forth between the two languages. Her poetry also often shifts into sections that are more like prose. This mixing of languages and genres is part of Anzaldúa's plan to create a form that matches the function of her writing. Having grown up along the Texas-Mexico border, Anzaldúa often writes about the ways in which our borderlands, and the people who inhabit them, are controlled. She represents that space as one where bodies and identities are heavily surveilled, but also as a space capable of great possibility.

HYBRIDITY AND THE BORDER

Anzaldúa's landmark book of poetry is *Borderlands/La Frontera: The New Mestiza*. The book is divided into two parts: the first section is a mix of poetry and feminist theory, and the second is a collection of poems. This work by Anzaldúa expresses a philosophical notion that was important to her, which is hybridity, a mixing of various elements. She mixes languages and genres for a new effect, which parallels the ways in which she has had to create a new identity for herself in a space in between cultures. The notion of hybridity is very important to understanding Anzaldúa's depictions of life along the border as a crossroads space where cultures meet and often clash. In "To Live in the Borderlands," she describes that space as a "battleground" where nonwhite and nonheterosexual people live as ghosts, invisible, as their identities are not accepted by the hierarchical power structures that favor whiteness and heterosexuality. She closes this poem by arguing that to survive a space like the borderlands, you have to be fluid in the way you think about identity—like the ways elements (natural elements, for instance) cross the border, no matter how much it is patrolled. Essentially as a person, you have to internalize and become a human crossroads or a place where many different languages, cultures, and identities meet.

In a couple of stanzas in her poem "El otro Mexico," she points out ocean waves that pound against the border fence, making a hole. The intrusion of the sea into this artifact of containment draws attention to the permeable nature of the border between San Diego and Tijuana. In the same poem, she also shows how capricious this dividing line of the border really is, capturing a scene of Mexican children playing soccer and running over the border to get the ball when it is kicked too hard.

Her speakers often identify their own bodies with the land separated by the border, talking about the walls and fences there as a "wound" that does physical violence, capturing in that symbol all of the violence done to bodies in those regions throughout the history of conquest and imperialism.

CHICANA THIRD SPACE FEMINISM

Beyond the physical and geographical border diving the United States and Mexico, Anzaldúa's *Borderlands/La Frontera* draws attention to the invisible boundaries between people. She argues for the inherent value of personal accounts from threshold spaces and subjectivities. In other words, she fights for the literary and cultural merit of testimonies from people who are "marginal" to mainstream power structures in the United States. The reference to a "third space" is a way to invoke a desire to exist outside a two-entity system (in other words, a binary system or a dichotomy) of the empowered versus the disempowered. Anzaldúa imagines a third space from which these power relationships can be critiqued and thwarted.

The concept of the "third space" comes out of what she imagines is a "third country" positioned between the United States and Mexico: the borderlands, which have their own culture, language, and history. Key to Anzaldúa's idea of Chicana third space feminism is that the land and the people along the border retain or develop a unique emotional resonance. The power dynamics of the conflict between cultures is most apparent in the emotional lives of Chicana women.

Lynn Marie Houston

Further Reading

Cherríe Moraga was Gloria Anzaldúa's co-editor for the groundbreaking anthology *This Bridge Called My Back: Writings by Radical Women of Color* (1981). Moraga is primarily a playwright, but her writing works toward the same political ends as Anzaldúa's. Other authors who write about Chicano/a and Native American culture and the boundaries between them and white mainstream culture are Helena Maria Viramontes, Leslie Marmon Silko, Rudolfo Anaya, and N. Scott Momaday.

Bibliography

Blend, Benay. "Intersections of Nature and the Self in Chicana Writing." *Bucknell Review* 44, no. 1 (2000): 56.

Boon, Sonja, Lesley Butler, and Daze Jefferies. "Place: Re/mapping." In *Autoethnography and Feminist Theory at the Water's Edge,* 75–80. Cham, Switzerland: Palgrave Macmillan, 2018.

Brady, Mary Pat. *Extinct Lands, Temporal Geographies: Chicana Literature and the Urgency of Space.* Durham, NC: Duke University Press, 2002.

Cantú, Norma Elia. "Sitio y lengua: Chicana Third Space Feminist Theory." In *Landscapes of Writing in Chicano Literature,* 173–87. New York: Palgrave Macmillan, 2013.

Cocola, Jim. *Places in the Making: A Cultural Geography of American Poetry.* Iowa City: University of Iowa Press, 2016.

Concannon, Kevin. "The Contemporary Space of the Border: Gloria Anzaldúa's Borderlands and William Gibson's *Neuromancer.*" *Textual Practice* 12, no. 3 (1998): 429–42.

Friedman, Susan Stanford. *Mappings: Feminism and the Cultural Geographies of Encounter.* Princeton, NJ: Princeton University Press, 1998.

Gil, Isabel Capeloa, and João Ferreira Duarte. "Introduction: Modernity's Fluid Cartographies." *Journal of Romance Studies* 11, no. 1 (2011): 1–9.

Keating, AnaLouise. "From Borderlands and New Mestizas to Nepantlas and Nepantleras: Anzaldúan Theories for Social Change." *Human Architecture: Journal of the Sociology of Self-Knowledge* 4, no. 3 (2006): 3.

Kirby, Kathleen M. "Thinking through the Boundary: The Politics of Location, Subjects, and Space." *Boundary* 220, no. 2 (1993): 173–89.

McDowell, Linda, and Joanne Sharp. *Space, Gender, Knowledge: Feminist Readings: Feminist Readings.* New York: Routledge, 2016.

Mermann-Jozwiak, Elisabeth. "Cartographies of Resistance: Poetics and Politics of Space in Chicano/a Writing." *MFS Modern Fiction Studies* 50, no. 2 (2004): 469–76.

Oliver-Rotger, Maria Antònia. *Battlegrounds and Crossroads: Social and Imaginary Space in Writings by Chicanas.* New York: Rodopi, 2003.

Orozco-Mendoza, Elva Fabiola. "Borderlands Theory: Producing Border Epistemologies with Gloria Anzaldúa." PhD diss., Virginia Tech, 2008.

Price-Chalita, Patricia. "Spatial Metaphor and the Politics of Empowerment: Mapping a Place for Feminism and Postmodernism in Geography?" *Antipode* 26, no. 3 (1994): 236–54.

Prieto, Eric. "Geocriticism, Geopoetics, Geophilosophy, and Beyond." In *Geocritical Explorations,* edited by Robert T. Tally Jr., 13–27. New York: Palgrave Macmillan, 2011.

Prieto, Eric. *Literature, Geography, and the Postmodern Poetics of Place*. New York: Palgrave Macmillan, 2012.

Zygadło, Grażyna. "*Landscapes of Writing in Chicano Literature* ed. by Imelda Martin-Junquera" (review). *Canadian Review of Comparative Literature/Revue Canadienne de Littérature Comparée* 44, no. 2 (2017): 346–51.

Arthurian Tales

The Arthurian tales are stories revolving around the character of King Arthur and his Knights of the Round Table. There are numerous versions of the Arthurian tales throughout art and literature, for the tales are open to a number of different interpretations. One of the most celebrated accounts of King Arthur and his knights is Thomas Malory's 15th century work, *Le Morte d'Arthur*. This is a compilation of Arthurian tales taken from both English and French sources. In general, the Arthurian tales are stories concerned with supernatural adventure, courtly romance and tragic love, issues of kingship, questions of morality and chivalry, and the conflict between love and duty. The Arthurian tales form an important part of the national mythology of Great Britain and Ireland and are also deep rooted in French culture. Indeed, though often considered synonymous with Great Britain, King Arthur has international roots. For instance, one of the most famous chroniclers of Arthurian tales was the 12th-century French poet Chrétien de Troyes who is generally considered to have originated the character of Sir Lancelot in works such *Le Chevalier de la Charrette (The Knight of the Cart)*.

BRITISH GEOGRAPHY

The geography and settings that appear in the Arthurian tales offer a rich blend of the real and the fantastical that successive writers and various literary traditions have shaped and revised. Though the Arthurian tales are fantasies, the tales are set within the landscape of the real British Isles and refer to actual places in Britain such as Carlisle in northern England and Cardiff in Wales. Other locations that occur in the Arthurian tales, such as Camelot and Avalon, are fictional though they may be based on actual places. That the tales take place against a backdrop of real geography is significant for it shows that the writers wished to give the tales added political and cultural significance. Moreover, the writers of the tales, who came from royal courts located in various parts of Britain, found that setting the tales within actual British geography endorsed the royal courts to which they belonged. Also, by setting the fantastical tales of King Arthur and his knights in real Britain, writers were able to add a level of plausibility to the tales, meaning that people reading or listening to the tales took more notice of them. It was important that people believed in the Arthurian tales because to a certain degree, they were morality tales intended to convey to their audience that humankind must fight the forces of evil to overcome the powers of darkness and therefore make the world a better place—a world where duty, moral goodness, love, honor, and justice prevail.

By employing realistic geography and topography in the Arthurian tales, writers made King Arthur's kingdom, and by association Britain, a land in which all men and women wanted to reside. In doing so, the writers of the Arthurian tales cast Britain as a sort of paradise that was symbolic of a world in which virtue was rewarded. Throughout the Arthurian tales, the people writing them adapted and transformed the landscape and geography of Britain to thereby enhance the symbolism of the tales. To a certain extent this makes the geography of Arthur's kingdom seem confused, but conversely the disordered topography of King Arthur's realm helped to create a mythical world that functions as a sort of Arthurian universe exhibiting its own internal logic where physical geography, symbolism, and emotion are interwoven. For this reason, some critics in recent times have pointed to the fact that some Arthurian tales, such as *Sir Gawain and the Green Knight,* display an inverted reality that makes the natural realm seem more real than the apparently historical courts inhabited by King Arthur's court, despite the fact that the courtly society of the Arthurian tales is described in a way that mimics the terms used to describe contemporary feudal Norman French courts. Supernatural and otherworldly forces govern the natural realm that is the backdrop to many of the Arthurian tales, and humans are immersed into this world of the supernatural. As humans are only part of this otherworldly realm, they are unable to control or understand it fully. This feeling of being powerless against nature is exemplified in the tale of *Sir Gawain and the Green Knight,* in which the perils of the landscape and inclement weather are seen as far more dangerous to the knight than monstrous supernatural beings.

Victoria Williams

This 1893 Art Nouveau illustration by Aubrey Beardsley depicts the Lady of the Lake telling King Arthur about the sword Excalibur. The details of the trees and river suggest a real woodland setting, but the ornate decorations framing the scene capture the enchanted nature of the tale. (Culture Club/Getty Images)

Further Reading

If you enjoyed the Arthurian tales, you might like to read the *Mabinogion,* a medieval collection of stories interweaving Celtic folklore with history that features King Arthur and his knights. Alternatively, many writers working in the 19th century based works on the Arthurian tales. For example, the poem "The Lady of Shalott" by Alfred, Lord Tennyson employs an Arthurian setting and Arthurian characters, including Sir Lancelot.

Tennyson also reworked the Arthurian tales as the *Idylls of the King,* a cycle of 12 narrative poems. The Arthurian tales are also the inspiration for more recent works, such as *The Once and Future King* by T. H. White. You may also like to read the fairy tales of the Brothers Grimm, which, like the Arthurian tales, are set among enchanted forests, where knights and kings embark on heroic quests while finding romance and fighting supernatural entities.

Bibliography

Armstrong, Dorsey. "Mapping Malory's 'Morte': The (Physical) Place and (Narrative) Space of Cornwall." In *Mapping Malory,* edited by Dorsey Armstrong and Kenneth Hodges. New York: Palgrave Macmillan, 2014. doi: 10.1057/97811374 43274_2.

Armstrong, Dorsey. "Conclusion: Malory's Questing Beast and the Geography of the Arthurian World." In *Mapping Malory,* edited by Dorsey Armstrong and Kenneth Hodges. New York: Palgrave Macmillan, 2014. doi: 10.1057/9781137443274_7.

Bender, Barbara. "Time and Landscape." *Current Anthropology* 43, no. S4 (2002): S103–S112. doi: 10.1086/339561.

Carman, Justice Neale. *A Study of the Pseudo-Map Cycle of Arthurian Romance, to Investigate Its Historico-Geographic Background and to Provide a Hypothesis as to Its Fabrication.* Lawrence: University Press of Kansas, 1973.

Kelly, Kathleen Coyne. "The Eco-Tourist, English Heritage, and Arthurian Legend: Walking with Thoreau." *Arthuriana* 23, no. 1 (2013): 20–39.

Lacy, Norris J., Geoffrey Ashe, and Debra N. Mancoff. *The Arthurian Handbook: Second Edition.* New York: Garland Publishing Inc., 1997.

Lane, Belden C. "Fantasy and the Geography of Faith." *Theology Today* 50, no. 3 (1993): 397–408. doi: 10.1177/004057369305000306.

Lavezzo, Kathy. *Angels on the Edge of the World: Geography, Literature, and English Community, 1000–1534.* Ithaca, NY: Cornell University Press, 2006.

Lilley, Keith. *Mapping Medieval Geographies: Geographical Encounters in the Latin West and Beyond, 300–1600.* Cambridge, UK: Cambridge University Press, 2013.

Murrieta-Flores, Patricia, and Naomi Howell. "Towards the Spatial Analysis of Vague and Imaginary Place and Space: Evolving the Spatial Humanities through Medieval Romance." *Journal of Map & Geography Libraries* 13, no. 1 (2017): 29–57. doi: 10.1080/15420353.2017.1307302.

Rouse, Robert Allen, and Cory James Rushton. "Arthurian Geography." In *The Cambridge Companion to the Arthurian Legend,* edited by Elizabeth Archibald and Ad Putter. Cambridge, UK: Cambridge University Press, 2009.

Rouse, Robert Allen. "What Lies Between?: Thinking through Medieval Narrative Spatiality." In *Literary Cartographies: Spatiality, Representation, and Narrative,* edited by Robert T. Tally Jr. New York: Palgrave Macmillan, 2014. doi: 10.1057/9781137449375_2.

Rudd, Gillian. "'The Wilderness of Wirral' in *Sir Gawain and the Green Knight.*" *Arthuriana* 23, no. 1 (2013): 52–65. doi: 10.1353/art.2013.0005.

Siewers, Alfred K. "The Green Otherworlds of Early Medieval Literature." In *The Cambridge Companion to Literature and the Environment,* edited by Louise Westling, 31–44. New York: Cambridge University Press, 2014.

Solopova, Elizabeth, and Stuart D. Lee. *Key Concepts in Medieval Literature.* Hampshire, UK: Palgrave Macmillan, 2007.

Vermette, Rosalie. "Terrae Incantatae: The Symbolic Geography of Twelfth-Century Arthurian Romance." In *Geography and Literature: A Meeting of the Disciplines,* edited by William E. Mallory and Paul Simpson-Housley, 145–60. Syracuse, NY: Syracuse University Press, 1987.

As I Lay Dying

As I Lay Dying, a novel by American author and Nobel laureate William Faulkner, begins with Addie—a frail, elderly African American woman—on the verge of death. Her dying wish is to be buried in her hometown of Jefferson, Mississippi. This necessitates a difficult journey, whose perils consume the rest of *As I Lay Dying.*

Some readers find the incessant series of monologues that make up the work a distraction, whereas others note the innovative use of the technique known as stream of consciousness, whereby an author seeks to give readers free access to all the thoughts in a character's mind. Although Irish writer James Joyce pioneered the technique, William Faulkner was a worthy imitator.

THE PHYSICAL AND CULTURAL GEOGRAPHY OF MISSISSIPPI

As I Lay Dying is an archetypal novel because Faulkner placed it, as with much of his fiction, in Yoknapatawpha County, Mississippi. The county is fictional but bears strong resemblances to Faulkner's home county. Yoknapatawpha County has its own mythology, but one that treats the historical reality of place with great care. The original inhabitants of the county were Chickasaw Amerindians, but by the time of *As I Lay Dying,* they are no longer present. Faulkner never says what happened to them, but the answer must be rooted in the result of European conquest, which was the genocide of Native American peoples. Yoknapatawpha County may not have existed outside Faulkner's mind, but the historical geography is accurate. After the Civil War, whites could no longer compel the labor of African Americans, but after generations of slavery, African Americans were so poor that the family that gathers around Addie has very little money, the legacy of a bankrupt South.

In *As I Lay Dying,* readers encounter long and often grammatically incorrect sequences of thought. The thoughts of the characters appear in inchoate form. Logic and any semblance of rationality lie very much at the margins. Readers may struggle to make sense of long fragments of thought, long attempts at thought. Faulkner seems to be saying that the characters in *As I Lay Dying* are not only poor but also ill-educated. This insight was true not just of Mississippi but also of large parts of the South, where all-white legislatures gave money to the white schools but very little to African American schools. Faulkner wrote at a time when "separate but equal" was the law, but separate and unequal the reality. The challenge in *As I Lay Dying,* as in so much of Faulkner's fiction, is to construct meaning from inarticulate characters, and in the process, to empathize with them.

THE GEOGRAPHY OF DEATH AND DECAY

At its core, *As I Lay Dying* wrestles with a woman's last days and the aftermath of her death. Traditionally in the Christian West, the geography of death is not of this world. The soul goes to one of two places: heaven for the blessed and hell for the damned. Yet this geography does not permeate *As I Lay Dying*. This could be the case because Faulkner, like most sensitive artists or intellectuals of the time, developed a resistance to Christian ideals in the wake of the German philosopher Friedrich Nietzsche's proclamation a generation earlier that "God was dead" and the subsequent importance of that proclamation to the philosophy of existentialism, which many grappled with during Faulkner's time.

Instead of the geography of death, Faulkner supplies the geography of decay. The family cannot afford to hire a mortician to embalm Addie's body. Instead, from the moment of her death, she begins to rot. The process is purely biological and inexorable. In the case of Addie, her death during the heat of summer only hastens her decay. Her decomposition casts a macabre spell over *As I Lay Dying*. Her body is taking the route of all life, the path that all the dead must travel. But the stench of her decay is a source of displeasure to the family. After an awful journey, the family reaches Jefferson. The husband borrows several spades. He and other men dig a grave and deposit what remains of Addie in the spot where she wished to be buried. This victory, if one may call it that, alleviates the pessimism that weighs down the earlier parts of the novel. One has a sense of finality that Addie is where she had wished to be. However, Faulkner withholds any true resolution: whether she has an immortal soul that can seek the geography of heaven is not for us to know.

Christopher Cumo

Further Reading

If you liked *As I Lay Dying*, consider James T. Farrell's *Studs Lonigan* trilogy, a story about a family's journey through figurative and literal rough terrain that tells an adolescent's coming-of-age story in Chicago in the early 20th century. Another work that similarly explores family members' legacies is *The Violent Bear It Away* by Flannery O'Connor, which tells an orphan's story as he struggles to reconcile his own identity with his dead uncle's own plans for him. Another good recommendation is *Nostromo* by Joseph Conrad, because it challenges us to consider the legacy we leave behind after death.

Bibliography

Aiken, Charles. *William Faulkner and the Southern Landscape: A Geography of Faulkner's Mississippi*. Athens: University of Georgia Press, 2009.

Atkinson, Ted. *Faulkner and the Great Depression: Aesthetics, Ideology, and Cultural Politics*. Athens: University of Georgia Press, 2005.

Baldwin, Marc. "Faulkner's Cartographic Method: Producing the 'Land' through Cognitive Mapping." *The Faulkner Journal* 7, no. 1 (1991): 193.

Brown, Calvin S. "Faulkner's Geography and Topography." *PMLA* 77, no. 5 (1962): 652–59. doi:10.2307/460414.

Doyle, Don Harrison. *Faulkner's County: The Historical Roots of Yoknapatawpha*. Chapel Hill: University of North Carolina Press, 2001.

Hamblin, Robert W., and Charles A. Peek, eds. *A William Faulkner Encyclopedia*. Westport, CT: Greenwood Press, 1999.

Owens, Margaret R. "Faulknerian Social Strata Meridians in Yoknapatawpha County: A Study in Literary Geography." Honors thesis, University of North Georgia, 2018.

Peek, Charles A. *A Companion to Faulkner Studies*. Westport, CT: Greenwood Publishing Group, 2004.

Putzel, Max. *Genius of Place: William Faulkner's Triumphant Beginnings*. Baton Rouge: Louisiana State University Press, 1985.

Spillers, Hortense J. "Topographical Topics: Faulknerian Space." *Mississippi Quarterly* (2004): 535–68.

Stewart, George C. *Yoknapatawpha, Images and Voices: A Photographic Study of Faulkner's County, with Passages from Classic William Faulkner Texts*. Columbia: University of South Carolina Press, 2009.

Urgo, Joseph R. "The Yoknapatawpha Project: The Map of a Deeper Existence." *The Mississippi Quarterly* 57, no. 4 (2004): 639–55.

The Awakening

Kate Chopin's novel *The Awakening* (1899) is set in southeastern Louisiana and involves the increasing desperation of its main character, Edna Pontellier, as she tries, unsuccessfully, to find a life that makes her happy. The novel begins at the popular tourist destination of Grand Isle: Edna, her husband, and their two children are on vacation at the shore with other families. While there, Edna begins to doubt that she is fulfilled by being a mother and wife and subsequently falls in love with a young man, Robert, who departs for a business venture in Mexico rather than risk beginning a relationship with a married woman. Edna tries to return to her normal life back in New Orleans, but while her husband is away on business, she moves next door into a small cottage where she plans to set up a painting studio. She also forms an intimate relationship with Alcée Arobin, a man with a reputation for having low morals. Robert returns from Mexico and admits his feelings for Edna, but leaves because he doesn't want to ruin her reputation. Edna returns to Grand Isle, where she first felt the desire for a different life, and devoid of any hope for the kind of happiness she wants, she drowns herself in the ocean.

NEW ORLEANS, ESPLANADE AVENUE

The primary residence of Edna and her husband is located in a wealthy section of New Orleans, the Esplanade. The tension of the novel focuses on the unspoken rules of life for upper-class people as Edna begins to discover that she is unhappy with their proscriptive values. She begins to understand that she would have been happier as an artist than as a mother and a wife.

Various characters in the work attempt to caution Edna and those around her by voicing the gendered value system of the upper class: that a woman is to be faithful to her husband, even though her husband is not expected to be, that a woman's highest importance is as a mother, and that a woman serves her family by maintaining social connections that require attendance at social calls and parties. Despite these warnings, Edna continues to assert that upper-class life is too restrictive, and she begins to rebel against all of these conventions. However, when she does, she realizes that there is no place where she can live how she wants to, not inside her husband's house and not in the little painting cottage she tries to move into. The judgments of social class are too deeply ingrained in everyone around her that she cannot achieve the freedom she wants. She discovers this unhappy truth during a conversation with Robert, the man she loves. He admits that he also has feelings for Edna and that he wants to be with her. However, because he is a product of the rules of the upper class, he can only imagine being with her through marriage. Edna is determined not to submit herself again to an institution she finds restrictive of her freedom and that makes her the property of her husband. She understands then that she is very much alone in the world in wanting a kind of freedom that doesn't exist for women. Edna has a few different layers of awakening in the novel: one of those is becoming aware of what she wants when she had never been taught to think about herself and her own desires. Her final awakening is a devastating one: understanding that she can never step outside of the rules that govern her social class, she realizes that she can never live the carefree life of an artist that she desires. The end result of her series of awakenings is that Edna realizes that, for her, the empty upper-class life she is stuck in is not worth living.

THE REPRESSIVE SPACE OF DOMESTIC LIFE

For Edna, the home she shares with her husband and children in New Orleans is repressive and dull. It is significant that her first moment of awakening occurs when they are on vacation, staying in a rented cottage in a rural area near the ocean. This vacation home brings new freedom into Edna's life and gives her a taste of the life she wishes she could have. On the first night that she willfully defies her husband, she is swinging in a hammock located outside the cottage on its porch. She refuses to enter the interior space of the cottage until she is ready, and she is enjoying the cool night air and the time with her own thoughts. The basis for Edna's later decisions is firmly set during this time in a rural area: she is empowered by learning how to swim and by going off with Robert to an island under the pretension of attending religious service. Instead, Edna takes a long nap in another cottage there, symbolizing the toll her awakening has taken on her. Robert revives her and has her eat some freshly caught fish, prepared simply. This time in a more natural setting away from her family home in the city serves as a harsh contrast for their return to a life where Edna feels imprisoned by expectations for her behavior. Once back home, she is bored and saddened by a life of superficial party gossip and her husband's complaints about their servants. Madame Ratignolle, a character in the novel who represents a completely selfless and devoted mother and wife, serves as a mouthpiece for societal expectations and tells Edna that above all, she should "remember the children" and comport herself accordingly so as not to bring shame on them. Edna admits to herself that she does not much enjoy being a mother.

WATER AND AIR AS SYMBOLS OF FREEDOM

Edna's awakening is very much connected to the natural landscape of Grand Isle. There, she learns to swim and embraces water as a symbol of her renewal. Additionally, given the composition of coastal lands predominantly as sea and sky, the latter also becomes a symbol of freedom. In particular, birds recur as symbols for Edna's imprisonment and failure to find freedom. Chopin, in choosing these natural elements as symbols of Edna's new desires, creates an implicit critique of upper-class culture as "unnatural." In wanting a freedom associated with water and air, Edna only wants what is natural, what is permitted men, and what is in abundance in the wetlands and coastal areas of southeastern Louisiana.

Mademoiselle Reisz, a pianist who has never married, gives advice to Edna, saying "the bird that would soar above the level of plain tradition and prejudice must have strong wings." Mademoiselle Reisz understands that not every woman can live with the isolation that comes with rebelling against the prevailing class conventions, especially for a woman who has children. Edna has lived an easy life, first being taken care of by her father and now by her husband. She admits that she is a reluctant mother, and Chopin reveals that her failure to properly fulfill her role as a mother, more than anything, is what elicits such harsh judgment from those around her. Mademoiselle Reisz's words foreshadow the consequence of Edna's awakening: that there is no place for her to have the life that she wants. The story ends with Edna's suicide by drowning in the ocean where she had learned to swim while on vacation. The setting for her suicide is highly symbolic: she dies under the two natural symbols of the freedom she couldn't achieve.

Lynn Marie Houston

Further Reading
Other short stories by Kate Chopin that tell about women's dysfunctional and oppressive experiences of marriage are "The Story of an Hour" and "Desiree's Baby." Charlotte Perkins Gilman was also writing in the 19th century. In "The Yellow Wallpaper," she wrote about a woman being literally trapped inside her own home by her husband as part of a "rest cure" for her postpartum depression. A work set in Europe that similarly has a female protagonist who thinks outside of societal conventions is *Daisy Miller* by Henry James.

Bibliography
Bonner, Thomas, Jr., and Judith H. Bonner. "Kate Chopin's New Orleans: A Visual Essay." *Southern Quarterly* 37, no. 3–4 (1999): 53–64.

Ewell, Barbara. "Placing the City: Kate Chopin's Fiction and New Orleans." *Southern Studies* 8, no. 1–2 (1997): 99–110.

Fox, Heather. "Mapping Spatial Consciousness in Kate Chopin's *Bayou Folk* Stories." *South: A Scholarly Journal* 48, no. 1 (2015): 108–28. http://www.jstor.org/stable/24721802.

George, Jessica Bridget. "'The Whole Island Seems Changed': A Bioregional Approach to Kate Chopin's Fiction." *The Journal of the Midwest Modern Language Association* 49, no. 1 (2016): 25–51. www.jstor.org/stable/44134675.

Higonnet, Margaret R., and Joan Templeton, eds. *Reconfigured Spheres: Feminist Explorations of Literary Space.* Amherst: University of Massachusetts Press, 1994.

Jones, Suzanne W. "Place, Perception and Identity in *The Awakening.*" *Southern Quarterly* 25, no. 2 (1987): 108–19.

Levin, Jessica. "The Feminine Voyage: Travel and Feminine Space in Chopin's *The Awakening,* Wharton's *The House of Mirth,* and Larsen's *Passing.*" Master's thesis, Seton Hall University, 2001.

Meyers Skredsvig, Kari. "Mapping Gender: Feminist Cartographies in Kate Chopin's 'Regionalist' Stories." *Filología y Lingüística* 23, no.1 (2003): 85–101.

Nelles, William. "Edna Pontellier's Revolt against Nature." *American Literary Realism* 32.1 (1999): 43–50.

Rainwater, Catherine. "The Fauna and Flora of Her Species: Nature and Southern Womanhood in Glasgow and Chopin." *Ellen Glasgow Newsletter* 41 (1998): 9–11.

Ryu, Chung-Eun. "Nature and Sexuality in the Fiction of Kate Chopin." *Journal of English Language and Literature* 35, no. 1 (1989): 131–47.

Skredsvig, Kari Meyers. "Mapping Gender: Feminist Cartographies in Kate Chopin's 'Regionalist' Stories." *Filología y Lingüística* XXIX, no. 1 (2003): 85–101.

Taylor, Helen. "Walking through New Orleans: Kate Chopin and the Female Flâneur." *Southern Quarterly* 37, no. 3–4 (1999): 21–29.

Thompson, Rachael Lynne. *"Somewhere and Not Anywhere": A Place-Conscious Study of Literature Set in the City of New Orleans.* Master's thesis, Wake Forest University Graduate School of Arts and Sciences, 2013.

Toth, Emily. *Unveiling Kate Chopin.* Jackson: University Press of Mississippi, 1999.

Warren, Robin O. "The Physical and Cultural Geography of Kate Chopin's Cane River Fiction." *Southern Studies* 7, no. 2–3 (1996): 91–110.

Williams, Mina Gwen. "The Sense of Place in Southern Fiction." PhD diss., Louisiana State University and Agricultural & Mechanical College, 1973.

B

Beloved

Toni Morrison's 1988 Pulitzer Prize–winning novel *Beloved* brought to light for a contemporary literary audience the collective trauma of American slavery and its dehumanization of African Americans. Place, as a concept in the novel, joins together with traumatic memory to reveal that the way to reclaim a sense of home is through family, the power of community, and the strength of interpersonal relationships.

The main setting of the novel is 1870s Cincinnati. At the novel's opening, Sethe, a former slave, is living with her mother-in-law, Baby Suggs, and Sethe's 18-year-old daughter, Denver. Sethe has escaped slavery in Kentucky while pregnant with Denver, along with her three older children. Sethe's two sons, Howard and Buglar, have both run away from home before the age of 13 to escape the presence of a "baby ghost," whose haunting includes objects being thrown around the room. Baby Suggs dies soon after the book's opening, and a former slave named Paul D arrives on Sethe's front porch in Cincinnati and chases this baby ghost away. Soon after Paul D's arrival, however, a young woman calling herself "Beloved" appears on Sethe's front porch.

The second plane of time is presented through flashbacks from the point of view of different characters. Twenty years before, Sethe and Paul D live on a farm in Kentucky called Sweet Home. The master who originally brought Sethe to Sweet Home, Mr. Garner, is humane, but he dies and is replaced by

Novelist Toni Morrison (in an image from 1988 above) often writes about how American geography is haunted by the legacy of slavery. She has won numerous awards for her work, including the Nobel Prize and Pulitzer Prize. (Ron Galella, Ltd./WireImage)

Mrs. Garner's brother. This new master, known only as "schoolteacher," is a sadistic, vicious racist, and the conditions at Sweet Home become so terrible that four slaves—Sethe, her husband Halle, Sixo, and Paul D—try to escape. The pregnant Sethe sends her three children ahead to her mother-in-law's in Cincinnati. The adults are captured, and two nephews of schoolteacher rape Sethe in a barn while Halle looks on from the loft. Sethe manages to run away again and gives birth in a forest with the help of a young white woman named Amy Denver, after whom she named her baby.

After Sethe makes it to Cincinnati, schoolteacher arrives to take them back to Kentucky. Sethe attempts to kill her three older children to prevent them being taken back. Only one, the two-year-old daughter, dies, her throat slit with a handsaw. Sethe has her gravestone marked with one word, "Beloved." Sethe and Denver are locked up by the sheriff, but then are freed again by a group of abolitionists and remain at Baby Suggs'. Because of Sethe's infanticide, the entire household is shunned by the community.

Back in the present day of the narrative, Sethe becomes convinced that "Beloved," the woman who arrives on their porch, is the embodied spirit of her dead daughter and becomes very attached and indulgent toward her. As Beloved becomes increasingly demanding, abusive, and manipulative, Sethe deteriorates. Paul D, on learning that Sethe killed her daughter, is horrified and leaves the household but remains nearby sleeping in a shed.

Finally, Denver goes to seek help from the community to exorcise Beloved, and a woman named Ella organizes a community effort. The women descend upon the house with charms, while singing songs, in an attempt to banish the malignant spirit of Beloved. When Mr. Bodwin, a white man, arrives at the home to escort Denver to a new job, Sethe in her madness mistakes him for schoolteacher and runs at him with an ice pick. In the confusion and Sethe's delirium, Beloved vanishes and is never seen again. Denver gets a job and rejoins the community. At the novel's conclusion, Sethe retreats to Baby Suggs' bed, supposedly to die of her continued grieving for Beloved, but Paul D returns to reconcile with her and give her encouragement.

THE GHOSTLY GEOGRAPHY OF TRAUMA

Sweet Home's name is highly ironic as it is a place of great suffering for Sethe, her family, and many others. However, the rest of this novel is about how the past comes back to haunt those who have been traumatized by slavery, and how they can overcome the limitations of such a history to lay claim to a place they call home. The place of home in *Beloved* is not so much an architectural structure—Paul D's character certainly finds comfortable places to sleep in rather paltry circumstances (a rocking chair and then a storeroom, for instance)—but it is the particular group of people, the community, that can see a person's pain and empathize with it. Even Denver's name, which would ordinarily signify a place, is actually a reference to a person. In terms of interpersonal relationships, Paul D is the first character to find and meet Sethe where her pain lives, but by the end of the story, the entire local African American community has become involved, crossing the threshold between what is private and what is public.

The ghost of Beloved occupies a space between worlds and between past and present, which highlights the postmodernity of this novel. The ghost is symbolic of a disturbance of both time and space, a historical trauma that is localized in space, but is larger than just the one place that her death occurred. It is also a physical embodiment of the constant fear Sethe lives in that she or her children will be recaptured by the men from Sweet Home. The setting of that death links to what happened in the previous setting of Kentucky, creating a nexus of suffering that transcends time and place, the very kind of unnamable pain that exists in in-between spaces that traditionally birth ghosts, especially to haunt someone like Sethe who has never been able to make peace with her past and still occupies a space where the time of the past is still very much present. The events of the novel *Beloved* collapse both space and time and show how the violence of slavery creates a painful history that is difficult to escape from in order to find peace and a sense of rootedness in a community. This is representative of more recent trends in postcolonial studies and in psychology to talk about the complexity of trauma, its ripples over generations and the ways it infects distant places, as it has the ability to trigger in the present the same amount of shame and anger as the initial incident in the past. Individuals, like Sethe, can think themselves crazy until they start to tell their stories and realize that others can relate to them, too. When trauma is perceived (and its healing pursued) as a communal experience, then it can be overcome. This is the hope that Morrison expresses in her novel.

The house at 124 Bluestone Road is the main setting for Morrison's psychological exploration of how a former slave's grief over feeling powerless, over being forced to participate in a cycle of violence in which victim becomes perpetrator, ends up pulling a family apart and pushing them out of their house. However, stepping out of the interior of their home and into the light of public acknowledgement of this pain saves them.

Lacar Musgrove and Lynn Marie Houston

Further Reading

If you liked *Beloved*, then you might like *The Black Book* by Middleton A. Harris, a collection of primary sources documenting the role Africans have played in Western culture, capturing their collective perseverance and strength. Particularly appropriate for pairing with *Beloved*, this book includes an article from 1856 entitled "A Visit to the Slave Mother Who Killed Her Child." Another good recommendation is *Possessing the Secret of Joy* by Alice Walker, because it tells the story of a tribal African woman's struggle to find healing after being genitally mutilated as a young woman.

Bibliography

Askeland, Lori. "Remodeling the Model Home in *Uncle Tom's Cabin* and *Beloved*." *American Literature* 64, no. 4 (1992): 785–805.

Bashirahishize, Leon. "Going Home or Going in Exile: The Conception of Home in TM's Dichotomy North-South Reflected in Beloved." *The Achievers Journal: Journal of English Language, Literature and Culture* 3, no. 2 (2017).

Bonnet, Michele. "'To take the sin out of slicing trees . . .': The Law of the Tree in *Beloved*." *African American Review* 31, no. 1 (1997): 41–54.

Hall, Alice. "No Place Like Home: Journeying in Toni Morrison's *Song of Solomon* and *Beloved*." www.americanstudies.ro/libs/docs/1354384353-84353.pdf.

Jones, Carolyn M. "Southern Landscape as Psychic Landscape in Toni Morrison's Fiction." *Studies in the Literary Imagination* 31, no. 2 (1998): 37.

Miller, J. Hillis. "Boundaries in *Beloved*." *symplokē* 15, no. 1/2 (2007): 24–39.

Minor, Lisa Graves. "'Sweet Home': Spirit of Place, Memory, and Rememory in Toni Morrison's *Beloved*." In *NAAAS Conference Proceedings,* 1244. National Association of African American Studies, 2006.

Ng, Andrew Hock Soon. "Toni Morrison's *Beloved:* Space, Architecture, Trauma." *symplokē* 19, no. 1–2 (2011): 231–45.

Noxolo, Pat, Parvati Raghuram, and Clare Madge. "'Geography Is Pregnant' and 'Geography's Milk Is Flowing': Metaphors for a Postcolonial Discipline?" *Environment and Planning D: Society and Space* 26, no. 1 (2008): 146–68.

Pearce, Richard. "Geography Lessons." *Novel: A Forum on Fiction* 32, no. 3 (1999): 449–52.

Russell, Danielle. *Between the Angle and the Curve: Mapping Gender, Race, Space, and Identity in Willa Cather and Toni Morrison*. New York: Taylor & Francis, 2006.

Sandy, Mark. "'Cut by Rainbow': Tales, Tellers, and Reimagining Wordsworth's Pastoral Poetics in Toni Morrison's *Beloved* and *A Mercy*." *MELUS* 36, no. 2 (2011): 35–51.

Scruggs, Charles. "The Invisible City in Toni Morrison's *Beloved*." *Arizona Quarterly: A Journal of American Literature, Culture, and Theory* 48, no. 3 (1992): 95–132.

Wallace, Kathleen R., and Karla Armbruster. "The Novels of Toni Morrison: 'Wild Wilderness Where There Was None.'" In *Beyond Nature Writing: Expanding the Boundaries of Ecocriticism*, edited by Karla Armbruster and Kathleen R. Wallace, 211–30. Charlottesville: University Press of Virginia, 2001.

Berry, Wendell

Wendell Berry's verse is often situated in his home state of Kentucky and its rural landscape, where he searches for, and often finds, a gateway to the sacred. As developed societies distance themselves from agricultural production by use of machine technology, the relationship that farmers once had with the land becomes a nostalgic sentiment. His written work continues the tradition of pastoral poetry as it responds to what Berry perceives is the increasing damage done to the environment by capitalist values.

Berry writes fiction and nonfiction in addition to poetry. In a few of his essays, like "The Long-Legged House," he talks about being taught by his father how to farm, but subsequently seeing that way of life destroyed by the influx of industrial practices.

Berry's poetry often takes a didactic approach, teaching others about how to value the land. In his poem "History," he talks about wanting to retrain his desires, which have been made vulgar by consumer culture. He wants to direct his "wants" back to the land, to not need anything that is not local or done through work he considers ethical, which has the land's needs in mind, as much as those of the humans who live on it. He feels that one of the most important messages he can convey to readers, through any of the genres of his writing, is about how to heal ourselves and the land from the greed and waste encouraged by capitalist culture.

SCARRED GEOGRAPHY

Berry writes often about the need for humans to help heal the land that we have injured through our industrial agricultural practices. In a few poems, like in "XI" from his collection *This Day,* he writes about the number of years it will take for the land to be healthy again, for overused farmland to return to its natural state as a forest. His perspective here is multigenerational, and it views the encroaching forest as a covenant that restores the relationship between humans and the landscape, setting things right again between the two parties and bringing a sense of balance to our lives.

In another poem, "2008, XI," he uses the illness and injury of the land as a way to gauge the quality of human life. He argues that human don't fully live the life that is possible for us if we are in disconnect from the land. In his plain-speaking style of writing, he indicts our capitalist economies that are often founded on elaborate stock prospects rather than anything tangible. The terms he uses in this poem are apocalyptic and hellish: a consuming fire, darkness, and burning. Berry seems to feel that what is at stake in how we treat the land is the status of our souls in the afterlife but also the quality of our lives here on Earth.

SACRED GEOGRAPHY

In other poems, he turns away from such indictments and shows us that communion with nature can be heaven on Earth. With wonder and gratitude, he points out the small miracles in his daily life. In his poem called "History" and in other works, he often invokes a rather Eastern philosophy of presence in the moment, what he calls "the art of being here." He feels that we have lost touch with things that sustained our ancestors in the past, such as a true sense of community and a connection to others. By living close to the land, Berry documents how he is in touch with all of the lives that intersect with it: "All the lives this place / has had, I have" ("History"). In eating the crops he grows, he takes into himself the history of the land and it becomes a part of him. He encourages others to find community as he has done: in a life lived close to the land, so that healing it becomes a way to heal oneself. In engaging with others who live this way, he ensures that his individual journey connects with a wider network and also with larger natural history.

Berry connects with the longer history of pastoral poetry by praising an agrarian life. However, he differs from traditional pastoral works because his farms are not mythological and imaginary; they are real. In *The Farm,* Berry presents a complete cycle of the seasons with down-to-earth advice about daily farm life. He is joyful in his depiction of the work, but he is realistic about it. Although Berry and his family farm the land as their jobs, he encourages people to turn away from producing as a goal and to live more in harmony with the natural cycles, which means sometimes doing what is right for the ecosystem rather than what makes a profit.

Lynn Marie Houston

Further Reading

The poetry of Wendell Berry is often compared to that of Robert Frost. They both write about similar themes: the life of people who work the land. Because Berry often writes about agricultural practices that pre-date industrial technology, he is often writing about techniques similar to those described in Frost's poetry, even though Frost is writing a century before Berry. Many of Berry's poems also capture the same idea found in poems by Walt Whitman and Mary Oliver, his contemporary: speakers who "loaf" in nature as a way to celebrate being alive. Henry David Thoreau is also a natural comparison because of the similarity of *Walden,* a nonfiction work, to many of Berry's projects.

Bibliography

Bryson, J. Scott. *The West Side of Any Mountain: Place, Space, and Ecopoetry.* Iowa City: University of Iowa Press, 2005.

Castellano, Katey. "Romantic Conservatism in Burke, Wordsworth, and Wendell Berry." *SubStance* 40, no. 2 (2011): 73–91.

Louv, Richard. *The Nature Principle: Human Restoration and the End of Nature-Deficit Disorder.* Chapel Hill, NC: Algonquin Books, 2011.

McClintock, James I. *Nature's Kindred Spirits: Aldo Leopold, Joseph Wood Krutch, Edward Abbey, Annie Dillard, and Gary Snyder.* Madison: University of Wisconsin Press, 1994.

Morgan, Speer. "Wendell Berry: A Fatal Singing." *The Southern Review* 10, no. 4 (1974): 865.

Robinson, David M. "Wilderness and the Agrarian Principle: Gary Snyder, Wendell Berry, and the Ethical Definition of the 'Wild.'" *Interdisciplinary Studies in Literature and Environment* 6, no. 1 (1999): 15–27.

Scigaj, Leonard M. *Sustainable Poetry: Four American Ecopoets.* Lexington: University Press of Kentucky, 2015.

Slovic, Scott. *Seeking Awareness in American Nature Writing: Henry Thoreau, Annie Dillard, Edward Abbey, Wendell Berry, Barry Lopez.* Salt Lake City: University of Utah Press, 1992.

Smith, Kimberly K. *Wendell Berry and the Agrarian Tradition.* Lawrence: University Press of Kansas, 2003.

Snauwaert, Dale T. "Wendell Berry, Liberalism, and Democratic Theory: Implications for the Rural School." *Peabody Journal of Education* 67, no. 4 (1990): 118–30.

Billy Budd

Herman Melville began the manuscript for the novella *Billy Budd* in 1888, but it was unfinished at the time of his death in 1891. His widow, Elizabeth, worked on the manuscript after his death before storing it with his other literary papers in a tin box, where it remained undiscovered for the next 28 years, until 1919. In this respect, *Billy Budd* is considered a "mediated" text, a manuscript with many notes that was revised by others for publication. Various versions of the novella exist, having been published first in 1924, then in 1948 and 1962 by different editors who interpreted Melville's purpose differently. The first editor, Raymond Weaver, was also Melville's first biographer. His 1924 version is considered by critics to be marred by Weaver's misinterpretation, including mistaking Elizabeth's writing for Melville's. The 1962 version, edited by Harrison Hayford and Merton M. Sealts Jr. is considered the best transcription and critical reading. The setting of the story—a British naval ship on the Atlantic Ocean—emphasizes the tension between the characters, as they have limited space in which to negotiate their differences of opinion.

MUTINY AND OCEAN TRAVEL

The novella takes place starting in 1797 aboard the HMS *Bellipotent*. The protagonist is a handsome young sailor named Billy Budd. He is a "foundling" who never knew his parents and is characterized as both very likable and innocent to the malice of others. His one flaw is that he has a stutter that becomes pronounced when he is excited or troubled. He goes to work on a merchant ship called *The Rights of Man* but is soon "pressed" onto a British warship (called *Indomitable* in earlier versions but changed to *Bellipotent* in later ones, according to notations in the manuscript indicating Melville's intent to change it). Billy takes his impressment in good spirit and quickly becomes popular with the crew and highly valued by the ship's captain, Captain Vere.

One of the crew, however, the master-at-arms named John Claggart, despises Billy. Claggart is supposedly possessed of "elemental evil," which he usually hides behind a demeanor of reasonableness. He envies Billy for his good looks, popularity, and innocence, and because he knows he can never attain Billy's natural goodness. The conflict between Billy and Claggart is viewed by critics as representative of the central conflict in the novella—the struggle between good and evil. Claggart's hatred becomes obsessive until he accuses Billy of plotting mutiny. Billy is outraged by the accusation but, unable to get out the words due to his stutter, he lashes out and strikes Claggart with his fist, killing the other man immediately.

Melville was aware of numerous examples of mutiny during his lifetime. In 1797, for instance, there were two famous Royal Navy mutinies: at the port of Spithead (near Portsmouth), sailors on board 16 ships staged a successful mutiny for better working conditions, and at the port of Nore (on the Thames estuary), a handful of ships attempted a similar coup about a month later, but failed to achieve their objective. Many of the instigators were punished or put to death.

MAPPING THE MORALITY OF CHANCE

Billy is court-martialed by the ship's officers, who reluctantly convict him according to the Mutiny Act and the Articles of War, and sentence him to death by hanging at dawn. Captain Vere, an intellectual but rigidly conservative man, believes in Billy's moral innocence but feels compelled to uphold the strict letter of military law lest he be perceived as weak and more trouble stirs among the British fleet. In Captain Vere's view, Billy struck an officer in a time of war, and for that the penalty was death. This outcome expresses a central theme of the novella, that innocence ultimately cannot survive in the context of war and the military.

Billy accepts his fate without protest, and as the rope is slipped around his neck the next morning, he declares, "God bless Captain Vere!" His story becomes a legend among sailors and the subject of a ballad called "Billy in the Darbies."

The novella's subtitle, "An inside narrative," presents an opportunity for reflection on the spatial layout of an ocean vessel, in this case a "man-of-war" (a cannon-armed warship). While traveling on the ocean, the ship is a confined space; there is technically no "outside," as the ship narrows the world of the sailors to its borders. Although the broader "outside" contexts of naval codes and martial law apply, the plot develops in such a way that the situation is highly irregular: the ship's captain has to condemn to death a young man he knows is innocent to keep from losing his power over the sailors on the ship. This is an "inside narrative" because it is about a peculiar application of law that makes no sense on land; it only makes sense in the confined space of a ship, where the captain's hold on his power is tenuous given the difference in number between him and the men he governs.

THE CULTURAL SPACE OF CAPITAL PUNISHMENT

Melville was writing *Billy Budd* during a time when New York State, where he was living, was considering the legal and cultural ramifications of capital punishment. The political debates surrounding this issue drew national and international attention, and many scholars believe that Melville's plot is a response to that cultural context. In 1890, a vote by the New York Assembly proposed to abolish capital punishment, but the State Senate did not back it. Later that same year, William Kemmler was the first criminal to be put to death via the electric chair. Melville's choice to have Billy strike Claggart in the head echoes the details of Kemmler's case as the latter was convicted of murdering his common-law wife with a hatchet blow to the head. Both fatal injuries are to the same part of the body, and both victims are well known by their assailants. However, while Kemmler was well known for violent alcoholism, Billy is known for his moral goodness. Melville frames Billy's "crime" and his punishment as if asking readers to question which of these deaths is truly murder. The conditions surrounding Claggart's death suggest that Billy was acting in self-defense and that it was an accident: he had not intended to kill Claggart. On the contrary, the captain and his crew spend time deliberating about how Billy is to be punished: when he is killed, it is premeditated and sanctioned by law. It seems Melville uses the text of his novella to express some doubts about the ethics of state-sanctioned killing.

Lacar Musgrove and Lynn Marie Houston

Further Reading

Readers of Melville's *Billy Budd* often enjoy the works of other 19th-century American authors who write about the tension between an individual and the collective, in particular *The Scarlet Letter* by Nathaniel Hawthorne, *Daisy Miller* by Henry James, and *The Call of the Wild* by Jack London.

Bibliography

Bersohn, Leora. "Melville's England." PhD diss., Columbia University, 2011.

Carlson, Patricia Ann, ed. *Literature and Lore of the Sea*. Amsterdam: Rodopi, 1986.

Casarino, Cesare. *Modernity at Sea: Melville, Marx, Conrad in Crisis*. Minneapolis: University of Minnesota Press, 2002.

Greiman, Jennifer. "Circles upon Circles: Tautology, Form, and the Shape of Democracy in Tocqueville and Melville." *J19: The Journal of Nineteenth-Century Americanists* 1, no. 1 (2013): 121–46.

Jonik, Michael. *Herman Melville and the Politics of the Inhuman*. Cambridge, UK: Cambridge University Press, 2018.

Kelley, Wyn. *Melville's City: Literary and Urban Form in Nineteenth-Century New York.* Cambridge, UK: Cambridge University Press, 1996.

Leroux, Jean-François. "The End of America: Geology and Cartography in Herman Melville's Pierre and Victor-Lévy Beaulieu's Voyageries." *Canadian Review of American Studies* 27, no. 1 (1997): 93–118.

Manning, Susan. "Mapping the Language: A Scottish-American Stylistics of Consciousness." In *Fragments of Union,* 241–88. London: Palgrave Macmillan, 2002.

Pritchard, Gregory R. "Econstruction: The Nature/Culture Opposition in Texts about Whales and Whaling." PhD diss., Deakin University, 2004.

Schirmeister, Pamela. *The Consolations of Space: The Place of Romance in Hawthorne, Melville, and James.* Redwood City, CA: Stanford University Press, 1990.

Schultz, Elizabeth. "From 'Sea of Grass' to 'Wire and Rail': Melville's Evolving Perspective on the Prairies." *American Studies* 52, no. 1 (2012): 31–47.

Uphaus, Maxwell. "The Sea Has Many Voices: British Modernism and the Maritime Historical Imagination." PhD diss., Columbia University, 2015.

Bishop, Elizabeth

THE GEOGRAPHY OF TRAVEL: ELIZABETH BISHOP'S NORTH AND SOUTH AMERICA

For the American poet Elizabeth Bishop (1911–1979), the geography of places she visits, both in fact and in imagination, preoccupies her imagination and work. Geographic depiction is inextricable from her travel, and it is inherent to her poems as travelogues, whether they move expansively through a country or more narrowly through a doctor's waiting room or a pasture. Her techniques for description of geophysical forms imply as much as render the life that finds the place hospitable enough to thrive or just survive. Her book titles show her obsession: *North & South* (1946), *A Cold Spring* (1955), *Questions of Travel* (1965), *Geography III* (1976), and her poems follow suit: "The Map," "Casablanca," "North Haven," "Santarém," "From the Country to the City," "Paris, 7 A.M.," "Quai d'Orléans," "Seascape," "Cape Breton," "Arrival at Santos," "First Death in Nova Scotia," "Florida," and "Varick Street." In these and many others, place-names and locations situate the poet's voice in a wealth of sensual, emotional, descriptive, and narrative detail, that deepen readers' understanding of the relation of geography to human and creaturely life.

Her poem "Over 2,000 Illustrations and a Complete Concordance" recollects poring over the family Bible as a child, with its pictures of the Seven Wonders of the World and "innumerable" other scenes from places near and far. The poem is filled with intimations of her childhood desire for the variety of places and cultures of her later poems. The vignettes of the exotic and familiar that the poem animates excited her young imagination being formed in the world of her "family with pets" where she "looked and looked [her] infant sight away." The child's hunger for the world's lands and people is translated into the journeying through her volumes of poetry. In this nostalgic poem, the compass of her poetry began to point, as her first book is entitled, north and south, along which many of these poems find their locus plotted following the movements of her life.

Many of her northern poems concern Nova Scotia, where she lived and visited from age 9 until about 30 years of age. Her "Cape Breton" begins rather as a letter home by an impressionable tourist, sharing some witty observations about the exotic auks and puffins on the "bird islands," then more mundanely, the sheep that "go 'Baaa, baaa'" there, and comically (and in coy parentheses) fall into the sea when an airplane startles and stampedes them. After tuning up her imaginative eye, the poem moves to the mainland, its gorges and valleys and the "ghosts of glaciers" in the forest. She follows the road inland to the landscape she has heard about but never seen, the deep lakes, rock mountains, forests, and features of sublime magnitude that dwarf human scale. Just as the poem ranges toward the impenetrable and inaccessible, a little bus emerges crammed with people on Sunday, surprisingly reasserting human presence and ordering of time and space. The drama of the poem has been clarified, residing in the landscape itself as utterance, following its own life scarcely touched by wildlife, especially the birds that make their music throughout the poem, much less touched by people, who go about their Sunday business soundlessly, in the coastal fringe permitted it by the overwhelming magnitude of the land. The sole humanly sourced sound, a passing motorboat, is dissolved in mist. Creature sounds of sundry birds, a calf's bawl, and the sheep predominate, but are rendered almost as ephemeral as the silent people by the enduring, "admirable scriptures made on stones by stones," however little, Bishop wrote, the region has to say to the observing poet.

Poet Elizabeth Bishop (in an image from 1954) had homes in Nova Scotia and Florida, spent time in Boston, and lived for almost two decades in Brazil. In her poems, human emotions drive descriptions of place. (Library of Congress)

As with many poems on North America, her poems of South America are replete with imagery of the geography that is steeped in the history of place. In "Brazil, January 1, 1502," for instance, Bishop imagines the first encounter between the Portuguese invaders and indigenous Brazilians. She immerses the poem in imagery of a lush natural world that she imagines to be unchanged from that which first Europeans found. Successive lines magnify more and more detail. The discoverer/invader Europeans translate what they find novel and strange into familiar categories.

The indigenous women occupy the place differently, with knowledge and intelligence. Bishop imagines the women warning each other in voices mimicking birds, to confuse the men, and turn their identity with the place from that of victim to, if not victor, at least survivor. Being *of* the place, the women understood that their knowledge could protect them. That Bishop projects her sexual and cultural sympathies onto this encounter with wishful thinking only enhances the artistry of the poem, which plays out the 450 years of colonial history that devolved from the mindscape of invader and the mental resourcefulness of native women.

A companion poem in the same volume, "Questions of Travel," has the poet confronting her own desire to be elsewhere, to discover, to be the foreigner in an alien land where the excesses of natural beauty oppress more than delight her northern sensibilities: "There are too many waterfalls here . . . / the mountains look like the hulls of capsized ships, / slime-hung and barnacled." But she wins her argument with herself (Yeats defined poetry as the argument with oneself) by reflecting on the world of experience versus imagination, and the drive each supplies the other. The poem's final gesture questions these questions of travel, offhandedly wondering if she could have located that most elusive of places for the wanderer. In doubt about where home may have been for her, the poems themselves invite readers to experience the varieties of the world that drew her all her life, from north to south and back ever again.

Robert R. Bensen

Further Reading

Elizabeth Bishop was friends with Marianne Moore, another Modernist poet who mentored her, tuning her poetic eye to the sharp imagery for which she became known. Bishop was also close to Robert Lowell. Although he is considered a Modernist, he writes in a much more narrative fashion than Bishop; however, the two poets often wrote in a kind of conversation with one another.

Bibliography

Ellis, Jonathan. "From Maps to Monuments: Elizabeth Bishop's Shoreline Poems." *Mosaic: An Interdisciplinary Critical Journal* 36, no. 4 (2003): 103–19. www.jstor.org/stable/44029998.

Gordon, Jan B. "Days and Distances: The Cartographic Imagination of Elizabeth Bishop." *Salmagundi*, no. 22/23 (1973): 294–305. www.jstor.org/stable/40546786.

Haft, Adele J. "The Poet as Map-Maker: The Cartographic Inspiration and Influence of Elizabeth Bishop's 'The Map.'" *Cartographic Perspectives* no. 38 (2001). doi:10.14714/CP38.794.

Haft, Adele J. "'The Map Shows Me Where It Is You Are': Gloria Oden Responds to Elizabeth Bishop across National Geographic and Rand McNally World Maps." *Cartographic Perspectives* no. 61 (2008).

Huong, Irish Shu-O. "Landscapes, Animals and Human Beings: Elizabeth Bishop's Poetry and Ecocentrism." *Intergrams* 10 (2010).

Mills, Rebecca. "The Elegiac Tradition and the Imagined Geography of the Sea and the Shore." *Interdisciplinary Literary Studies* 17, no. 4 (2015): 493–516. doi:10.5325/intelitestud.17.4.0493.

Paton, Priscilla M. "Landscape and Female Desire: Elizabeth Bishop's 'Closet' Tactics." *Mosaic: An Interdisciplinary Critical Journal* 31, no. 3 (1998): 133–51. www.jstor.org/stable/44029814.

Spiegelman, Willard. "Landscape and Knowledge." In *Imaginative Transcripts: Selected Literary Essays.* Oxford Scholarship Online, 2011. doi:10.1093/acprof:oso/9780 195368130.003.0007.

Bless Me, Ultima

Set in rural eastern New Mexico at the end of the Second World War, Rudolfo Anaya's best-selling novel *Bless Me, Ultima* (1972) traces the bond that develops between the narrative's protagonist, a six-year-old child named Antonio Márez y Luna, and Ultima, an elderly *curandera* (healer) who is invited by Antonio's family to leave the isolated plains village of Las Pasturas, where she is its last remaining resident, and live with them nearer to the neighboring river town of Guadalupe. A *bildungsroman* or novel of education, *Bless Me, Ultima* traces Antonio's maturation process over the course of two years. The narrative's central conflict is whether the boy will choose to become a *vaquero* (cowboy) like his father once was, a farmer like his mother's father and brothers are, or whether he will reject both potential life paths to fulfill his mother's ambition for him to enter the priesthood—which she also associates with the quiet, rooted existence her family has led for generations. Anaya binds the question of how and where Antonio will decide to live his adult life to a larger question of faith: does he choose Catholicism, which is associated with town life and a legacy of Spanish conquest, or does he embrace a pagan or pantheistic spirituality associated with indigenousness and the natural landscape of the *llano* (plain)?

THE CHICANO MOVEMENT

Bless Me, Ultima is considered a foundational contribution to the body of literature produced during the Chicano movement; however, a number of scholars have criticized the work, charging Anaya's representation of identity conflict as so rooted in a personal, familial context that the narrative seems divorced from "larger social and identity issues at the heart of the Chicano movement of the 1960s and early 1970s—a movement that strove to construct and celebrate an ethnic identity on the basis of *mestizaje* ('hybridity') and the recovery of an indigenous past" (Caminero-Santangelo 2004, 115). Anaya's novel is not associated with the ideological frankness common in other literary texts written by Chicanos during *el movimiento*. Yet, considering Ultima's and Antonio's interactions with the New Mexican landscape enables readers to perceive the ways that environment shapes the people who live there as well as better to understand how the text engages a key movement concern in circulation at the time of the novel's publication.

THE LAND AS A SOURCE OF HEALING

Ultima reflects on a critical movement impulse to recuperate an Amerindian heritage that the novel presents in terms of her practically mystical connection to the natural landscape of rural New Mexico, a connection she fosters in Antonio. Under Ultima's tutelage, Antonio too becomes conscious "of a new world opening up and taking shape": he learns from her "the names of plants and flowers, of trees and bushes, of birds and animals," and of herbs and roots native to the *llano* and that are the raw materials for the medicines she makes. He learns to identify and gather "yerba del manso [to] cure burns, sores, piles, colic in babies, bleeding dysentery and even rheumatism. . . . orégano . . . for coughs and fever," and "oshá . . . like la yerba del manso, a cure for everything." In short, Ultima provides Antonio with a practical education in the ways of *curanderismo,* of healing through traditional folk medicine. Some townspeople vilify Ultima's work as *brujería* or *hechicería* (witchcraft or sorcery), even as many of them have benefitted from her services (or know other community members who have). Antonio, however, comes to recognize that her power stems from a deep knowledge of the life-sustaining resources the *llano* may provide those who have the appropriate repository of cultural memory from which to draw or coax that "magic harvest" from the land. Through Ultima's teachings, Antonio begins to connect with an indigenous past.

Furthermore, as Antonio becomes a de facto apprentice to Ultima, she encourages in him a reverential attitude toward the land, for she believes that "even plants had a spirit." Until Ultima helps Antonio to understand that his "spirit shared in the spirit of all things," he is afraid of the *"presence"* he feels by the river near his home and in the llano's hills. Joseph Morales observes that changing religious practices often mark sites of protest. In the 1960s and 1970s, many Mexican Americans struggled to reject the assimilatory pressures exerted upon them by dominant U.S. culture in the present and by the legacy of Spanish and Mexican colonization in the American Southwest, the mythical geography of Aztlán. That contemporary social struggle is dramatized in the novel through Antonio's fear that acknowledging a pantheistic spiritual presence is blasphemy against God. He recalls, "I was still trying to hold on to God. . . . I did not want to give Him up." But ultimately he realizes that from "the llano and the river valley, the moon and the sea, God and the golden carp . . . a new religion [can] be made." In that moment, the novel offers both a resolution to Antonio's existential struggles and a tacit call to readers to remember an occluded Amerindian heritage that undergirds contemporary Chicano life and that may be a source of strength for Chicanos. Consequently, although religious or cultural syncretism may be new concepts for Anaya's young protagonist, for many Mexican Americans, they are fundamental means for individual and communal self-definition and autonomy.

Marci L. Carrasquillo

Further Reading

For other classic readings about the pressures of assimilation and the impact of place on the construction of individual and communal Mexican American identity see, for instance, José Antonio Villarreal's *Pocho;* Tomás Rivera's *. . . y no se lo tragó la tierra / And the Earth Did Not Part;* or Anaya's second novel, *Heart of Aztlán,* in which he expands the scope of his narrative vision to depict New Mexican Chicanos in urban as well as rural settings.

Bibliography

Alvarez, Robert R., Jr. "The Mexican-US Border: The Making of an Anthropology of Borderlands." *Annual Review of Anthropology* 24, no. 1 (1995): 447–70.

Caminero-Santangelo, Marta. "'Jasón's Indian': Mexican Americans and the Denial of Indigenous Ethnicity in Rudolfo Anaya's *Bless Me, Ultima.*" *Critique* 45, no. 2 (2004): 115–28.

Cochran, Stuart. "The Ethnic Implications of Stories, Spirits, and the Land in Native American Pueblo and Aztlán Writing." *MELUS* 20, no. 2 (1995): 69–91. doi:10.2307/467623.

Davis-Undiano, Robert C. "Land, the Southwest, and Rudolfo Anaya." In *The Forked Juniper: Critical Perspectives on Rudolfo Anaya,* edited by Roberto Cantú. Norman: University of Oklahoma Press, 2016.

Hamilton, Patrick L. *Of Space and Mind: Cognitive Mappings of Contemporary Chicano/a Fiction.* Austin: University of Texas Press, 2011.

Hunt, Alex. "In Search of Anaya's Carp: Mapping Ecological Consciousness and Chicano Myth." *Interdisciplinary Studies in Literature and Environment* 12, no. 2 (2005): 179–206. www.jstor.org/stable/44086436.

Junquera, Carmen Flys. "Shifting Borders and Intersecting Territories: Rudolfo Anaya." In *Literature and Ethnicity in the Cultural Borderlands,* edited by Jesus Benito, Ana Maria Manzanas, and Ana María Manzanas Calvo. Amsterdam: Rodopi, 2002.

McCormick, Peter J. "Re-Imagining New Mexico: Geography, Literature, and Rudolfo Anaya." PhD diss., University of Oklahoma, 1999.

Morales, Joseph. "Quinto Sol's Chicano Archive: Reading Anaya's *Bless Me, Ultima* through Romano's *Don Pedrito Jaramillo:* The Emergence of a Mexican-American Folk Saint." *CiberLetras: Revista de crítica literaria y cultura / Journal of Literary Criticism and Culture* 34 (2015).

The Book Thief

The Book Thief, by Australian author Markus Zusak, is a story set in Nazi Germany during the Holocaust. Some parts of the book are narrated by death himself, who comes for the souls of those who have died and who admits that he has more work than he cares for during wartime. The novel features the residents of Himmel Street, a poor section of a town named Molching, located in southern Germany, just outside of Munich. It chronicles the lives of Liesel Meminger, her adopted parents, and their neighbors as the Nazi Party comes to power and begins to terrorize Jewish citizens by rounding them up and sending them to concentration camps. Primarily a coming-of-age story about a young girl's relationship with books and writing, the setting of the novel underscores the brutality of war in its effects on those in the lower socioeconomic classes. Despite all of the suffering, the book's characters manage to find beauty in their lives and struggles and power in the art of storytelling.

THE GEOGRAPHY OF FASCISM

The book is set in the imaginary town of Molching, inspired by the existing town named Olching, also situated outside of Munich in the direction of Dachau. Jewish prisoners would have marched through Olching on their way to the Dachau concentration camp, as is described in the book. Also, the book's characters often visit the Amper River, which borders the real town of Olching, making it highly likely that this is the location the author had in mind. In fact, a poorer neighborhood in Olching was decimated in bomb attacks during World War II and rebuilt in the 1950s. Markus Zusak has indicated in various interviews that the plot of *The Book Thief* is based loosely around stories his parents told him about surviving as children and young adults in Germany and Austria before they moved to Australia.

European cities involved in the war are only vaguely referenced as the plot is centered around Himmel Street, an ironic name that means "heaven street," although it is one of the poorest areas in the town. Two main streets comprise the bulk of Liesel's activities in Molching: Himmel Street and Munich Street. The first is where she lives and the second is the main commercial street. The narrator of the book, death, briefly mentions his work in other places: other cities in Germany, and also cities in Poland and Russia. Death tolls were high in these areas during that time.

Munich plays an important role as a secondary place in the novel. It is the nearest city and is known for being the birthplace of Nazism. Rosa and Hans Hubermann's daughter, Trudy, is a live-in nanny for a wealthy family in Munich. Both she and her brother, Hans Junior, are supportive of Hitler's Third Reich, whereas their parents in the smaller village of Molching are not. Munich is also the hub for travel in and out of Molching, just as it would be for the real-life town of Olching. While traveling on the train to Molching with her mother, Liesel's brother dies just before they stop in Munich. Additionally, the Jewish man they hide in their basement, Max, comes to the Hubermanns' on a train that passes through Munich. Hans Hubermann sends Max a map of Molching that includes Munich, along with directions that detail the trip he would have to make on foot from the Pasing train station (just northwest of Munich) to the front door of 33 Himmel Street, Hans' home (Olching is about a three-hour walk from Pasing). To get to where they are going, the characters all have to pass through Munich, a hotbed of Nazi fanaticism. This dangerous situation allows place to function as a device that creates suspense and also serves as a means to test the strength of the characters. The author drew his research from the municipal archives of Munich as well as from research he did in various museums.

In fact, Munich and Molching can be discussed in terms of the parent-child relationship that plays out in the book. Munich is the parent to Molching. It is the larger city that has spawned settlement in its suburbs. When Munich is bombed, the residents of Molching suffer. The first few times it is bombed, they receive air raid notifications over the radio and seek shelter. However, when it is bombed on October 2nd, Himmel Street is decimated. Located on the outskirts of the bombs' true target, the residents are collateral damage of the Allied attack. Just as Molching suffers for the beliefs of its parent, Munich, the heartland of the Nazi Party, so does Liesel, who must enter the care of strangers because of her parents were being persecuted for their communist beliefs.

The specter of concentration camps haunts the protagonist and the story. Although never shown, the camps are frequently present in the consciousness of the main character. For example, Liesel, Rudy, and other townspeople watch as Jews are marched along the roads on their way to Dachau. Liesel also hears that her biological father was taken to a camp for being a communist and suspects this was also the likely fate of her mother as well. After Hans is whipped for helping a Jewish prisoner marching to a camp, Max flees the Hubermanns' for his safety, as they suspect that the Third Reich will be coming to search the house or worse. After Max leaves, whenever the Nazis march Jews through Molching, Liesel runs to see if he is among the prisoners. One day he is, and the time he spends in the Dachau camp is not described. His story resumes again only with his liberation and reunion with Liesel.

THE SKY

Much of the devastation resulting from World War II came from the sky. Although it was a war fought by land, sea, and sky, new technologies allowed aircraft to become deadlier than they had been in previous wars. By 1943, both Germany and the United States implemented new guided munitions into their attacks, meaning bombs that could be released from planes and whose tail fins could be controlled to send it to a desired location. This changed the nature of the sky as a landscape in war. Just like the narrator in *The Book Thief* who seems to fly through the air and who has a bird's-eye view of human struggles, in World War II death often came from above.

THEFT AND THE LANDSCAPE

Class changes characters' relationship to the landscape in *The Book Thief*. As food rations get smaller, Liesel and Rudy begin to steal from orchards, farms, grocery stores, and even bike delivery boys. As winter turns to spring each year, the two keep watch for fruit trees to harvest. Backyards and farms become opportunities to supplement their diet. For Liesel, houses in town are also places that might yield books for her to steal. Although the two are nearly captured numerous times, the novel makes no judgment against them morally for these thefts. In fact, once when the grocer catches Rudy trying to steal the largest potato in his store, the other customers speak up on his behalf, citing that he has a large family and lives on Himmel Street. That location is enough for the grocer to let him go. The extreme poverty of Liesel and her neighbors is addressed with humor and by focusing on the positive aspects of their lives, such as music and familial bonds.

BASEMENTS AS SHELTERS

Basements are the most important places in the novel. They are where people hide during air raids, and it is ultimately because Liesel is in a basement writing her life's story that she is spared from the air raid that decimates Himmel Street: writing literally saves her life. Throughout the novel, reading and writing are shown to have great impact on Liesel's life, but her relationship with language is cultivated primarily in the space of the basement, symbolizing the "underground" nature of what she is doing, learning to speak truth to power. In the basement of 33 Himmel Street, Hans Hubermann teaches Liesel the alphabet by painting it on the wall. There, she also engages in other creative acts, such as bringing in snow from the outside to construct a snowman. She and Max bond in the basement of their house, where he hides from the Nazis. During the time he lives in the Hubermanns' basement, he often dreams of fistfighting with the Führer, and writes down his story for Liesel to read. He also writes a story about Liesel and the power of language, referring to her as the "word shaker." When everyone from the street gathers in the Fiedlers' basement during the air raids, Liesel takes to reading while they are there to calm everyone. Basements are key to the plot and to the character development in *The Book Thief.*

Lynn Marie Houston

Further Reading

A book to read in conjunction with *The Book Thief* would be *Anne Frank: The Diary of a Young Girl.* Anne Frank, who was Jewish, kept her diary while she spent two years hiding from the Germans. Her letters are a testament to the fear and courage of those persecuted during the Nazi occupation of World War II. Another young female hero of World War II is featured in the novel *Code Name Verity* by Elizabeth E. Wein.

Bibliography

Adams, Jenni. "Cities Under a Sky of Mud: Landscapes of Mourning in Holocaust Texts." *Spatial Practices* no. 13 (2012): 141–63.

Jilovsky, Esther. *Remembering the Holocaust: Generations, Witnessing and Place.* London: Bloomsbury Academic, 2015.

Kirk, Bryannie. "Spaces of the Holocaust: Alternative Narrative Forms in *Briar Rose, The Boy in the Striped Pajamas,* and *The Book Thief.*" Master's thesis, University of British Columbia (Vancouver), 2010.

Brave New World

Aldous Huxley's *Brave New World* explores an unpleasant future through the lens of science and technology. It focuses on a world in which some people are engineered to be superior, others mediocre, and yet others deficient. It is a world in which humans seem less humane. They have limited capacities for real intimacy and tend to view one another as objects, but this may be less science fantasy than the reality of capitalism, which treats people as objects, as widgets, units of production. *Brave New World* is a novel of suicide and sorrow that offers a dismal look at the experience of living in the spaces of our economic and political systems.

THE LANDSCAPE OF DYSTOPIA

Brave New World gives readers a glimpse of a *dystopia,* a word that derives meaning in opposition to utopia. English author and government servant Thomas Moore coined the term *utopia* in his work of the same name to describe an ideal community. Moore was not alone in his quest for a better society. Long before him, Greek philosopher Plato sought to create an ideal political community in *The Republic.* Plato must have envisioned his community as ideal for all. Certainly the philosopher kings who governed this community would have viewed it as ideal, but the masses appear to have had little freedom or opportunity for advancement. In the *Communist Manifesto*, German English economist Friedrich Engels and German economist Karl Marx are more idealistic, conceiving of a mass revolution that overthrows a corrupt political and economic system, ushering in a stateless society in which workers control their own destiny. Governments that claim to be communistic have never achieved anything close to this vision.

A dystopia shunts aside any hope for a bright future. The future instead is full of horrible events. Although it ends well, much of the book of Revelation in the New Testament is a dystopia full of suffering and death. It provides a landscape of nightmares. *Brave New World* is much less hyperbolic, but it too is a dystopia and one that seems vaguely plausible. It is not difficult to imagine an incubation and baby factory that creates mentally deficient people by depriving the brain of oxygen. Whereas Revelation is hysterical at times, *Brave New World* is coldly rational. By increments it reveals a world of deprivation and loss of true aspirations.

SCIENCE AND TECHNOLOGY

It is not surprising that Aldous Huxley turned to science and technology as the forces behind *Brave New World*. His lineage and siblings provide examples of people who excelled in science and medicine. His ancestor Thomas Henry Huxley was in the 19th century one of the strongest defenders of Darwinism. People like Thomas Huxley prized science for what it could achieve. Aldous Huxley, however, pinpoints the weaknesses of what to him must have been the amoral, even immoral, use of science. If humans invented science, they are its victims in *Brave New World*. Science assumes sinister hues and apparently has escaped human control or at least the control of compassionate humans. Perhaps here is a link to *Frankenstein,* in which scientist Victor Frankenstein unleashes a monster on the world. In *Brave New World,* science itself is the monster. Huxley wrote *Brave New World* before physicists created the atomic bomb, which the United States used to destroy two Japanese cities to end World War II. In this sense, *Brave New World* seems prophetic but one-sided. Science has never produced just destruction. It has yielded vaccines, antibiotics, and better varieties of many crops. Used properly, science can be a ramp that elevates humans and improves their living standards. It is this science that *Brave New World* overlooks.

THE LANDSCAPE OF TOTALITARIANISM

Like British author George Orwell in *Nineteen Eighty-Four,* Aldous Huxley in *Brave New World* is at his sharpest in attempting to deflate the evils of totalitarianism. Huxley wrote *Brave New World* at a crucial moment in history. In the excesses of zealotry, the communist takeover of Russia caused enormous suffering. The dislocation of agriculture caused millions of peasants to starve. If the czar's regime had been horrible, Russian communism might have been worse. None of Marx and Engel's predictions of a stateless society came true. Instead, communism had become a version of totalitarianism. In Germany, Adolf Hitler was consolidating all power into his own hands and seeking to absorb his neighbors. In Italy, dictator Benito Mussolini wished to revive the Roman Empire and was already at war in Africa. Against this backdrop, Huxley shows readers how damaging a totalitarian state could be. In this sense, *Brave New World* may have been a polemic against communism, Nazism, and fascism. If *Brave New World* is fiction, it is a kind of fiction that lays bare the truth of human societies and their destructive capacities. Perhaps in this sense *Brave New World* prophesied much of the 20th century, among the most inhumane periods in human history. If events in western Asia are predictive, the 21st century might not turn out much better. It may be here that the science of the human brain and tragedy conjoin. Scientists understand that the most primitive parts of the human brain are part of our reptilian past. They are a source of unchecked aggression and savagery. It is this brain that *Brave New World* featured as the centerpiece of the future.

Christopher Cumo

Further Reading

If you liked *Brave New World,* then you might like *The Penultimate Truth* by Philip K. Dick, because it is also a story about elite oppression in which millions of people live underground thinking World War III is raging, only to find out that there is peace on Earth's surface. Another work that similarly explores rigid control of the public is *Red Rising* by Pierce Brown, which is about a hierarchical society organized into arbitrary colors and the exploitation of the lowest caste. Yet another good recommendation is Arthur Koestler's *Darkness at Noon,* a story about an imprisoned revolutionary in the Soviet Union.

Bibliography

Castree, Noel, Catherine Nash, Neil Badmington, Bruce Braun, Jonathan Murdoch, and Sarah Whatmore. "Mapping Posthumanism: An Exchange." *Environment and Planning A* 36 (2004): 1341–63.

Firchow, Peter. "Science and Conscience in Huxley's *Brave New World.*" *Contemporary Literature* 16, no. 3 (1975): 301–16.

Firchow, Peter Edgerly. *The End of Utopia: A Study of Aldous Huxley's* Brave New World. Lewisburg, PA: Bucknell University Press, 1984.

Meckier, Jerome. "Aldous Huxley's Americanization of the *Brave New World* Typescript." *Twentieth Century Literature* 48, no. 4 (2002): 427–60.

Meckier, Jerome. "'My Hypothetical Islanders': The Role of Islands in Aldous Huxley's *Brave New World* and *Island.*" In *Brave New World: Contexts and Legacies,* edited by Jonathan Greenberg and Nathan Waddell. London: Palgrave Macmillan, 2016.

Parrinder, Patrick. *Utopian Literature and Science: From the Scientific Revolution to* Brave New World *and Beyond.* London: Palgrave Macmillan, 2015.

Pepper, David. "Utopianism and Environmentalism." *Environmental Politics* 14, no. 1 (2005): 3–22. doi:10.1080/0964401042000310150.

Theis, Mary E. "The Geography of Postmodern Meta-Utopian Spaces: 'Last Call for a Revolution?'" In *Landscape, Seascape, and the Eco-Spatial Imagination,* edited by Simon C. Estok, Jonathan White, and I-Chun Wong. New York: Routledge, 2016.

Brideshead Revisited

Evelyn Waugh wrote *Brideshead Revisited* in 1944, while on leave from his regiment in the British army during World War II. Published the following year, the

> We drove on and in the early afternoon came to our destination: wrought-iron gates and twin, classical lodges on a village green, an avenue, more gates, open parkland, a turn in the drive; and suddenly a new and secret landscape opened before us. We were at the head of a valley and below us, half a mile distant, prone in the sunlight, grey and gold amid a screen of boskage, shone the dome and columns of an old house.
> "Well?" said Sebastian, stopping the car. Beyond the dome lay receding steps of water and round it, guarding and hiding it, stood the soft hills.
> "Well?"
> "What a place to live in!" I said.
>
> **Evelyn Waugh, *Brideshead Revisited* (1945)**

novel is narrated by Charles Ryder and centers on the Flyte family—Lord and Lady Marchmain, their sons "Bridey" and Sebastian, and their daughters Julia and Cordelia. As the novel opens, Ryder himself is serving in a unit of the army, and he and his men have been quartered in the Flytes' ancestral home of Brideshead, a grand country house that Ryder had grown to love as a young man years before. Other British settings include Ryder's college at Oxford and the country's capital city of London. Episodes also take place in Venice, Italy; a transatlantic liner; New York City; and Fez, French Morocco. With the exception of Fez, the settings lie within the privileged world of Britain's high society.

TWO IDYLLIC SETTINGS

Waugh himself attended the University of Oxford, and his description of the school in *Brideshead Revisited* makes clear his love for it and the centuries of tradition that it represents. As presented in his novel, Oxford is an arena for the discovery of new ideas about art, literature, and life. But the freedom it offers is also an opportunity for idleness and drunkenness, and proves to be a dangerous place for Sebastian, who has what grows into a debilitating weakness for alcohol.

Brought up in less luxurious surroundings, Ryder is awed by Brideshead and its extensive grounds when Sebastian takes him to meet his aging nanny. He has another, more extended opportunity when he stays with Sebastian while the latter recovers from an injured ankle. At this time, Ryder is able to study and admire the house's many spacious rooms, its ceilings decorated with fanciful classical scenes, its pillared halls, and its gardens. It is also at this time that he discovers his vocation for architectural painting and meets Sebastian's sister Julia, whom he will fall in love with much later.

The Flytes are Roman Catholics and maintain a small chapel, elaborately decorated in the conservative Arts and Crafts style of the late 19th century. The element of religious belief is at the core of *Brideshead Revisited,* but on his first extended visit, Ryder gives religion little thought. He does, however, think of the house as an "enchanted palace."

REAL AND FICTIONAL GEOGRAPHY

In an author's note preceding the text of *Brideshead Revisited,* Waugh wrote that "I am not I; thou art not he or she; they are not they." Behind this puzzling assertion lies the fact that the novel and the house it describes had close counterparts in Waugh's own experience. Waugh based Brideshead on a large country house and a charming but troubled household that he had become familiar with in the 1930s.

Waugh was drawing upon his experiences with the Lygon family, whose members had virtually adopted the young novelist in the early 1930s. The Lygons lived at Madresfield Court in the parish of Malvern in the English county of Worcestershire, West Midlands, and one of the younger members of the household had been Waugh's close friend at Oxford. Although seemingly idyllic, the lives of the Lygons had been blighted when rumors of homosexuality forced the head of the family to leave the country and his wife to divorce him. Despite these events, however, the Lygons continued to live in luxury.

In writing his novel, Waugh changed the location of the house to the county of Wiltshire in southwest England, although he does not emphasize the geographical details. He also changed the nature of the scandal that besets the Flytes, depicting Lady Marchmain as a stiflingly manipulative woman who has alienated her husband, now living in Venice with his mistress, and is driving her son to alcoholism.

Besides its treatment of Brideshead and the Flyte family, Waugh's novel deals with the nature of faith—a theme that becomes more prominent as the story progresses. Fearing what he referred to as the "Chaos" that seemed to be descending on Europe, Waugh had converted to Roman Catholicism in 1930, becoming one of a number of prominent British writers to do so. This took place at about the same time that he became familiar with the Lygons and Madresfield Court, and the novel intertwines and fictionalizes various aspects of these events. Ryder once believed that he was "very near heaven" at Brideshead, but as he learns more about the Flytes, he realizes that the distance is much greater. After the death of Lady Marchmain, her husband returns to Brideshead to die, and accepts the last rites from a Catholic priest. But the same faith leads Julia, who has made an unhappy marriage, to tell Ryder that in good conscience as a Catholic she cannot marry him or live with him, as to do so would be refusing God's mercy.

A RICH TRADITION

English literature has a rich tradition of country house novels, ranging from the books of Henry Fielding and Jane Austen through *Brideshead Revisited* and on to the present day. The great popularity of the television series *Downton Abbey* (2010–2015) illustrates the continuing appeal of the tradition.

To many readers on both sides of the Atlantic, the English country house represents a benign world in which aristocratic families preserve the best of England: great architecture and art, refined manners, care of the land, and a concern for the well-being of those living on that land. However, most examples of the genre utilize the setting to reveal a more complicated reality.

Grove Koger

Further Reading

If you liked *Brideshead Revisited,* then you might like Samuel Butler's *The Way of All Flesh,* because it is also a story about deteriorating privilege and that chronicles Butler's own upbringing in the early 20th century as 19th-century ideals were brought into question. A work that similarly explores the decline of the golden age is *Appointment in Samarra* by John O'Hara, a story about a wealthy man's totally preventable downfall. Another good recommendation is Arnold Bennett's *The Old Wives' Tale,* the story of two sisters' lives over the course of half a century.

Bibliography

Chard, Chloe. *Pleasure and Guilt on the Grand Tour: Travel Writing and Imaginative Geography 1600–1830.* Manchester: Manchester University Press, 1999.

Cosgrove, Denis. "The Myth and the Stones of Venice: An Historical Geography of a Symbolic Landscape." In *Culture and Society: Critical Essays in Human Geography,* edited by Nuala C. Johnson. London: Routledge, 2008.

Eliot, T. S. "Isolation and Community in Evelyn Waugh's *Brideshead Revisited.*" *Twentieth Century Literature in English* 1 (1996): 109.

Faulstick, Dustin. "A Pilgrimage to Passion: Charles Ryder's Emotional Conversion in *Brideshead Revisited.*" *Religion and the Arts* 15, no. 201 (2011): 1.

Miles, Peter. "The Writer at the Takutu River: Nature, Art, and Modernist Discourse in Evelyn Waugh's Travel Writing." *Studies in Travel Writing* 8, no. 1 (2004): 65–87. doi:10.1080/13645145.2004.9634951.

Moran, Joe. "A Cultural History of the New Nature Writing." *Literature & History* 23, no. 1 (2014): 49–63.

Otis, Harrison. "Finding the Lush Place: Waugh's Moral Vision in *Scoop.*" *Evelyn Waugh Studies* (2015): 13.

Rauchbauer, Otto. "The Presentation and Function of Space in Evelyn Waugh's *Brideshead Revisited.*" In *A Yearbook of Studies in English Language and Literature* 78 (1981): 61–77.

Reilly, Mary Kate. "Place & Space in Waugh's *A Handful of Dust.*" *Evelyn Waugh Studies* 45, no. 2 (2014): 15–21.

Schönberg, Ulf. "Architecture and Environment in Evelyn Waugh's *Brideshead Revisited.*" *Orbis Litterarum* 45, no. 1 (1990): 84–95.

Williams, Annabel. "'Vagabond-Language Scrawled on Gate-Posts': Locating Home in Evelyn Waugh's Travel Writing." *Textual Practice* 32, no. 1 (2018): 41–58. doi:10.1080/0950236X.2016.1238003.

C

The Call of the Wild

The Call of the Wild is an adventure novel by Jack London told in the third person but focused mostly on the point of view of a dog named Buck. The story is set in the 1890s, beginning briefly in California but primarily set in Alaska and the Klondike region of Canada. The setting is a brutal landscape often imprisoned by a cold that makes survival difficult.

THE GEOGRAPHY OF MUSHING

An increased demand for powerful sled dogs in the Klondike region during the gold rush spawned a new criminal enterprise: the theft of dogs and subsequent sale of them to traders. People who use dogs to pull sleds are often known as "mushers" because the French commonly used this as a mode of transportation when settling areas of Canada. They would call out to the dogs to "marche," which means "go" or "move." This French word was adapted in English as "mush."

At the opening of the novel, the protagonist, a large Saint Bernard–sheepdog mix named Buck, lives as the pampered pet of Judge Miller in warm, comfortable Santa Clara, California. The gardener, needing to settle gambling debts, kidnaps Buck and sells him. Buck is sent to the north, where he is sold as a sled dog. Upon his arrival in Alaska, Buck's new friend Curly is attacked and killed by a group of huskies and vows not to fall to the same fate. Survival becomes his only imperative. The narrative arc takes us through Buck's transition from a pampered dog of civilization to a wild beast, a transformation that links his present time to the older world of his ancestors, which Buck connects to through mystical visions.

Buck's first new owners in Alaska are a pair of French mail carriers for the Canadian government, Perrault and Francois. As Buck adjusts to his new life of sleeping under the snow, scavenging for food, and fighting for survival, he begins to rediscover the instincts of his wild ancestors and gradually trades the order of civilization for the rules of the wild. Buck develops a rivalry with the vicious lead

---

Deep in the forest a call was sounding, and as often as he heard this call, mysteriously thrilling and luring, he felt compelled to turn his back upon the fire and the beaten earth around it, and to plunge into the forest, and on and on, he knew not where or why; nor did he wonder where or why, the call sounding imperiously, deep in the forest.

Jack London, *The Call of the Wild* (1903)

This drawing of a pack of wolves appeared as an illustration in Jack London's novel *The Call of the Wild*. His writing often depicts the brutality of winters in Canada and the Pacific Northwest. (DEA Picture Library/Getty Images)

dog, Spitz, whom he eventually defeats in a fight. Spitz is subsequently killed by the pack, and Buck becomes their leader. In contrast to Spitz's leadership style of siding with the strongest dogs, Buck identifies with the weaker, more marginalized dogs, a character trait that he learned from his former master back in civilization, Judge Miller.

The team is turned over to a Scottish mail carrier who makes the dogs carry heavier loads, leading to the death of one of the dogs, Dave. The team then goes to a trio of inexperienced American gold prospectors, Hal, Charles, and Mercedes, who beat the dogs, overload the sled, and plan poorly. They run out of food halfway through their journey and wind up at the camp of a man named John Thornton, with most of the dogs dead from starvation. An experienced outdoorsman, Thornton warns the American trio of danger of melting ice ahead. Disregarding this warning, they try to force Buck to lead the team across the ice, but he refuses, lying down in the snow. When Hal starts beating Buck, Thornton intervenes, cuts Buck loose from the team, and takes him. The trio goes on ahead, where they fall through the melting ice, drowning everyone—a fate that is a consequence of their ignorance and disrespect for the rules of the wild.

Buck becomes fiercely loyal to Thornton and wins the man a great deal of money in a wager by pulling a 1,000-pound load. Buck, Thornton, and two friends push farther into the forest in search of a lost gold mine. Buck leaves the camp every day to socialize with a timber wolf from a local pack but returns to Thornton's camp every night. One night, Buck returns to find the three men murdered by Yeehat Indians. Buck finds the natives and kills some of them. In his final shedding of the thin veneer of modern civilization, Buck joins the timber wolf pack, eventually becoming its leader and fathering many cubs. He becomes a legend among the Yeehat as a terrifying "Ghost Dog" who returns yearly to mourn Thornton at the camp where he was killed.

THE CULTURAL BORDER BETWEEN CIVILIZATION AND WILDERNESS

The native Yeehat people exist in London's fiction as troubled figures. Although they are the villains in one respect, having killed a master Buck loved, they are also the catalyst that allows him to complete his transition from a civilized disposition to a wild one, which is seen as the more "natural" state. However, the fact that Buck returns to the site of Thornton's death speaks to the way in which a fondness for human culture lingers on in Buck.

As the central character, Buck represents a transitional figure bridging civilization and the wilderness. The space in between is one that he navigates with sorrow because he did not choose his fate. London often creates out of the snowy tundra a schoolhouse of sorts because his characters learn tough lessons that form them or that push them into some understanding of their own identity, especially as something wild rather than civilized. However, just as Buck at the end of the story vacillates between the wilderness and the camps of men, the two exist as a kind of perpetual tug-of-war on the spirit.

Lacar Musgrove and Lynn Marie Houston

Further Reading

London wrote other stories, like *White Fang,* that deal with human-animal relationships and the human tendency to underestimate the brutality of the natural world. The setup of his short story "To Build a Fire" is very similar to the scene in *The Call of the Wild* where the men fall through ice trying to navigate in the snow. The legend of *Tarzan* as written by Edgar Rice Burroughs or Rudyard Kipling's *The Jungle Book* may also pique the curiosity of readers interested in humans living in close proximity to animals in the natural world. Other authors have also written young adult classics involving famous dog figures: such as *Old Yeller,* by Fred Gipson, and *Where the Red Fern Grows,* by Wilson Rawls. Like Jack London, Bret Harte also writes about the wilderness of Northern California and the Pacific Northwest at the time of the gold rush.

Bibliography

Auerbach, Jonathan. *Male Call: Becoming Jack London.* Durham, NC: Duke University Press, 1996.

Harper, Pamela Evans. "Shared Spaces: The Human and the Animal in the Works of Zora Neale Hurston, Mark Twain, and Jack London." PhD diss., University of North Texas, 2008.

Harris, W. C. "Undifferentiated Bunnies: Setting Psychic Boundaries in the Animal Stories of Beatrix Potter, Jack London, and Ernest Seton." *Victorian Review* (1997): 62–113.

Hogan, Maureen P., and Timothy Pursell. "The 'Real Alaskan' Nostalgia and Rural Masculinity in the 'Last Frontier.'" *Men and Masculinities* 11, no. 1 (2008): 63–85.

Jones, Karen. "Writing the Wolf: Canine Tales and North American Environmental-Literary Tradition." *Environment and History* 17, no. 2 (2011): 201–28.

Klaver, Coran. *Victorian Dogs, Victorian Men: Affect and Animals in Nineteenth-Century Literature and Culture.* Columbus: Ohio State University Press, 2018, 1–3.

Labor, Earle. "Jack London's Symbolic Wilderness: Four Versions." *Nineteenth-Century Fiction* 17, no. 2 (1962): 149–61.

Ratelle, Amy. "Contact Zones, Becoming and the Wild Animal Body." In *Animality and Children's Literature and Film,* 41–64. London: Palgrave Macmillan, 2015.

Reesman, Jeanne Campbell. "'Never Travel Alone': Naturalism, Jack London, and the White Silence." *American Literary Realism, 1870–1910* 29, no. 2 (1997): 33–49.

Shortridge, James R. "The Concept of the Place-Defining Novel in American Popular Culture." *The Professional Geographer* 43, no. 3 (1991): 280–91.

Wiener, Gary, ed. *Wildness in Jack London's* The Call of the Wild. Farmington Hills, MI: Greenhaven Publishing LLC, 2014.

Wöll, Steffen. "Inertia and Movement: The Spatialization of the Native Northland in Jack London's Short Stories." *GeoHumanities* 3, no. 1 (2017): 65–87.

The Catcher in the Rye

J. D. Salinger's *The Catcher in the Rye* was first published in 1951; it is still one of the canonical pieces of American fiction. The novel gained Salinger instant and widespread fame, in which Salinger had no interest and after which he retreated into a life of near solitude. The title of the novel comes from a Robert Burns poem, which protagonist Holden Caulfield initially misinterprets. Believing that the poem reads, "If a body catch a body comin' though the rye," Holden tells his younger sister Phoebe, named after and servicing as a bit of an oracle, that all he wants to do in life is catch kids playing in a field of rye who are in danger of falling off "some crazy cliff." He tells Phoebe, "I know it's crazy, but it's the only thing I'd like to be." Although Holden ultimately changes his mind by the close of the novel, this desire gives the novel its name. Though criticism on the novel continues to be mixed, Holden's *bildungsroman* is a direct result of his journey through and interaction with the inhabitants of New York City.

THE CITY

The Catcher in the Rye very specifically takes place in New York City where teenaged Holden seeks out authenticity in a landscape of phonies. The novel's action occurs post-World War II, and more importantly post-Great Depression, and revolves around a privileged young man who comes from a wealthy family. Holden feels the general sense of ennui felt by someone who has never truly had to struggle. Holden's struggles are more existential, concerning his own existence and the motivations of others. Irony exists in the postmodern New York setting of Holden's odyssey; postmodern New York featured architecture and structures that existed for entirely superficial reasons. It's no surprise, then, that Holden feels a sense of fraudulence in the midst of a fraudulent town, but that same place is

> I live in New York, and I was thinking about the lagoon in Central Park, down near Central Park South. I was wondering if it would be frozen over when I got home, and if it was, where did the ducks go? I was wondering where the ducks went when the lagoon got all icy and frozen over. I wondered if some guy came in a truck and took them away to a zoo or something. Or if they just flew away.
>
> **J. D. Salinger, *Catcher in the Rye* (1951)**

perhaps not the best place to find sincerity. New York is often seen as inherently depraved and amoral, inhabited by phonies, fakes, criminals, and otherwise generally unsavory people.

SEX, NUNS, AND THE CITY

But New York also gives Holden the opportunity to encounter others from diverse walks of life, the most dichotomous of which are the prostitute and the nuns. About halfway through the novel, Holden agrees to invite a prostitute to his hotel room "for a throw." Ironically, Holden lies about his age to the prostitute's handler, and lies to her about why he cannot engage in sex—recent surgery on his "clavichord." He lies about his age as well, making him a phony right along with the prostitute, whose occupation requires a certain sense of phoniness to get by. Holden also proves himself in a way phony when he expects her to adhere to social norms, something he's refused to do since one of his first scenes in which he wears his iconic red hunting hat backward. Even more ironically, when the woman begins to act more like a prostitute and less like a date, that is, when she lets go of her phony act, Holden has even more problems with her, feeling peculiar, depressed, and uneasy. Instead of the typical 16-year-old's marveling at a woman who has just taken off her dress in front of him, he contemplates when and where she bought the dress, and how the salesman could not have known where she would wear it. Although Holden often seems young and naive, in this moment, he is almost too empathetic for his own good. He eventually offers her money, in spite of not receiving her services, and sits alone and miserable in the hotel. For one who is superficially so against the institution of norms and rules, Holden is very uncomfortable with a situation that blatantly ignores those rules. For all his chastising of phonies, some level of phoniness is comforting.

Likewise, the nuns that Holden encounters at the train station reveal his simultaneous search for the sincere and his own phony behavior. When Holden sees them, he remarks that their suitcases are shabby and look cheap. He naively offers them ten dollars, later regretting that he did not give more. The nuns' worn-out suitcases make Holden pity them. He later tells Phoebe that the nuns were "collecting dough" in their ratty baskets; he has already rewritten the situation for himself, imagining that he has in some way helped the nuns who, in fact, have not asked him for any help. Like his pity for the prostitute and his presumed saving her from a night of less savory activities, Holden believes that he has helped these nuns, but due to his own expectation of adherence to social norms, it is a phony act. Holden's search for authenticity is fraudulent. That fraudulence is only highlighted and exaggerated by the fact that his search occurs in New York, a crowded area, often seen as superficial in itself.

CENTRAL PARK EPIPHANY

New York's Central Park carousel provides the location for Holden's epiphany, the climax of his *bildungsroman*. Through his encounters with his schoolmates, his sister, the prostitute, and the nuns, Holden continues to search for something authentic, and he continues to try to save people who do not need to be saved. His assertion to his sister that the "only thing [he]'d like to be" is the savior of kids playing in a field about to fall off "some crazy cliff" asserts Holden's place as a would-be savior. However, Holden's heroic intentions are misplaced in an antiheroic world, and he realizes this before it is too late. While watching his sister ride the carousel in Central Park, Holden reaches an epiphany that makes Holden's previous intention ambiguous. Unlike his previous dream of being the catcher of children, Holden now realizes that he has to let the children fall. If his sister wants to reach for the gold ring on the carousel, he has to let her, "and not say anything. If [kids] fall off, they fall off, but it's bad if you say anything to them." Just as the congestion and crowding of the city allows Holden to encounter a great diversity of different people, thereby allowing us to examine his interactions with them, Central Park provides the opposite. Although it's in the middle of New York, Central Park offers Holden a place where he can finally have some quiet reflection. He is not bombarded by sounds, imagines, or new people. Finally, he is able to feel something authentic, unconcerned with his own or others' adherence to norms. Central Park allows Holden to truly not be a phony.

Andrea Laurencell Sheridan

Further Reading

If you liked *The Catcher in the Rye,* then you might like Capote's *Breakfast at Tiffany's,* because the relationship between Holly Golightly and her companion Fred similarly explores Holden Caulfield's search for belonging and connection. Another work about teenage angst and rebellion is *The Outsiders* by S. E. Hinton, which in addition to exploring the gap between rich and poor, demonstrates the need for connection and the destructive nature of feeling like an outsider. Another good recommendation is F. Scott Fitzgerald's romance *Tender Is the Night,* which explores loneliness even in love.

Bibliography

Baer, Leonard D., and Wilbert M. Gesler. "Reconsidering the Concept of Therapeutic Landscapes in J. D. Salinger's *The Catcher in the Rye*." *Area* 36, no. 4 (2004): 404–13.

Ghasemi, Parvin, and Masoud Ghafoori. "Holden in Search of Identity: Recreating the Picture of the Flâneur." *English Studies* 91, no. 1 (2010): 74–88.

Tang, Junhong, and Wei Zhang. "The Hard but Holly Life of the Eco-Warrior of Holden." *Advances in Literary Study* 1, no. 4 (2013): 31–33. doi:10.4236/als.2013.14008.

Thomas, Ebony Elizabeth. "Landscapes of City and Self: Place and Identity in Urban Young Adult Literature." *The ALAN Review* 38, no. 2 (2011): 13–22.

Wang, Cui, and Xiaofen Zhang. "Returning to Youth and Nature—*The Catcher in the Rye* in Ecocriticism." *Journal of Language Teaching and Research* 1, no. 3 (2010): 269–73.

Whitfield, Stephen J. "Cherished and Cursed: Toward a Social History of *The Catcher in the Rye*." *The New England Quarterly* 70, no. 4 (1997): 567–600.

Ceremony

Ceremony, by Leslie Marmon Silko, is the story of a Tayo, a half-white, half-Laguna Pueblo man who returns to his people's reservation in New Mexico after fighting in the Philippines in World War II. The main time period of the story is in the aftermath of WWII, but additional historical times are woven throughout the narrative. *Ceremony* is about the perils of forgetting tradition, as contact with the white man has caused the Laguna to abandon and forget their traditional farming practices and stories in favor of a white worldview.

WAR AND HOMECOMING

After a long period in a veterans' hospital attempting to recover from battle fatigue, Tayo goes to stay with his grandmother, his aunt, and her husband, Robert. He is constantly nauseous, vomiting in bright light, has weak muscles, and is plagued by nightmares of the death of his cousin Rocky in the Bataan Death March and also by thinking he saw his now deceased uncle's face in the visage of a Japanese soldier he faced as part of a firing squad. His people are suffering from a terrible drought, which Tayo believes he has brought on by saying a prayer against the rain while in the Philippines. Here, we see Silko infusing into the narrative a native belief in the connectedness of places: Tayo's prayer is so powerful that it risks extending beyond nation-state boundaries and following him home. The trauma he suffered abroad also follows him home, and this is obviously the greater curse and the greater illness that infects his life as he attempts to return to it after war.

THE GEOGRAPHY OF RECOVERY

Tayo's grandmother takes him to a medicine man called Ku'oosh to pursue a cure for his illness. Ku'oosh performs a ceremony for warriors who have killed in battle. The ceremony helps Tayo but does not cure him, as Ku'oosh knows nothing of the modern world of war. Tayo then goes to Betonie, a Navajo medicine man who integrates knowledge of the modern world into his practice. Tayo learns from Betonie that he must complete a ceremony, one that goes beyond his personal troubles to defeat the "destroyers" and the "witchery" in order to protect the Pueblo peoples in the future.

As part of his ceremony, Tayo sets off to retrieve his Uncle Josiah's cattle, a special spotted type of Mexican cattle that he had promised to help take care of before the war, but that had wandered off to the south and cannot be found. On his way there, he meets a woman named Ts'eh, who offers him food and clothing and becomes his lover. Tayo finds the cattle on the ranch of a rich white man and cuts the fence to free them. With the help of Ts'eh, Tayo manages finally to round up the cattle and returns them to the reservation.

The quest for the cattle is symbolic as Tayo is really searching for the connection he has lost to his tribe. In many ways, the cattle are the other indigenous people who wander away from the traditional life and have to be brought back. Tayo comes to understand that he can serve as a role model for this return.

When Tayo returns to Ku'oosh and tells him about Ts'eh, Ku'oosh believes her to be a spirit woman, possibly the Reed Woman from the ancient stories. Rain soon comes to the Pueblo, the cattle thrive, and everything becomes green again. Silko ends the novel with a restoration of balance and prosperity. Acts of caring and love triumph over killing to show Tayo and others how life can continue after traumatic events.

Rediscovering the ancient stories of his people allows Tayo to see that others before him have lived his experience and shows him there is always hope for recovery. By returning to the traditional native stories and embracing the natural rhythms of nature, Tayo is able to overcome his trauma and bring the rain back to his people.

Lacar Musgrove and Lynn Marie Houston

Further Reading
If you liked *Ceremony,* then you might like *The Way to Rainy Mountain* by N. Scott Momaday, a memoir written by a member of the Kiowa tribe that collects stories previously only captured in the oral tradition. Another work that similarly explores the healing of despair and search for identity is James Welch's *Winter in the Blood,* in which the narrator's tribe struggles with the effects of federal government oversight prior to the United States bicentennial. Another good recommendation is *Waterlily* by Ella Cara Deloria, a story about a Sioux woman's coming-of-age around the time when the first settlers landed in what would become the United States.

Bibliography
Bomberry, Victoria. "Constructing the Imagined Space of Native America: Leslie Silko, Joy Harjo, and Lucy Tapahonso." *Native Americas* (1994): 128.
Garcia, Reyes. "Senses of Place in *Ceremony.*" *Melus* 10, no. 4 (1983): 37–48.
Hokanson, Robert O'Brien. "Crossing Cultural Boundaries with Leslie Marmon Silko's *Ceremony.*" *Rethinking American Literature* (1997): 115–27.
Holm, Sharon. "The 'Lie' of the Land: Native Sovereignty, Indian Literary Nationalism, and Early Indigenism in Leslie Marmon Silko's *Ceremony.*" *American Indian Quarterly* 32, no. 3 (2008): 243–74.
Karem, Jeff. "Keeping the Native on the Reservation: The Struggle for Leslie Marmon Silko's *Ceremony.*" *American Indian Culture and Research Journal* 25, no. 4 (2001): 21–34.
Nelson, Robert M. "Place and Vision: The Function of Landscape in *Ceremony.*" *Journal of the Southwest* (1988): 281–316.
Orr, Lisa. "Theorizing the Earth: Feminist Approaches to Nature and Leslie Marmon Silko's *Ceremony.*" *American Indian Culture and Research Journal* 18, no. 2 (1994): 145–57.
Piper, Karen. "Police Zones: Territory and Identity in Leslie Marmon Silko's *Ceremony.*" *American Indian Quarterly* 21, no. 3 (1997): 483–97.
Rice, David A. "Witchery, Indigenous Resistance, and Urban Space in Leslie Marmon Silko's *Ceremony.*" *Studies in American Indian Literatures* 17, no. 4 (2005): 114–43.
Satterlee, Michelle. "Landscape Imagery and Memory in the Narrative of Trauma: A Closer Look at Leslie Marmon Silko's *Ceremony.*" *Interdisciplinary Studies in Literature and Environment* (2006): 73–92.
Swan, Edith. "Laguna Symbolic Geography and Silko's *Ceremony.*" *American Indian Quarterly* (1988): 229–49.

Teorey, Matthew. "William Wordsworth and Leslie Marmon Silko: Toward an Ecofeminist Future." *Interdisciplinary Studies in Literature and Environment* (2004): 31–56.

Walter, Roland Gerhard Mike. "Unwriting Manifest Borders: On Culture and Nature in Leslie Marmon Silko, James Welch and Linda Hogan." *Acta Scientiarum. Human and Social Sciences* 28, no. 1 (2006).

Crime and Punishment

Russian novelist and short story writer Fyodor Dostoyevsky was already an accomplished and skillful author when he turned to *Crime and Punishment,* the first of the four stunning novels to elevate him to the status of being the world's greatest novelist according to French author and Nobel laureate André Gide. *Crime and Punishment,* like Dostoyevsky's other works, was a novel of ideas. The content was philosophical, theological, and psychological. It is part murder mystery, though not in the traditional sense because readers know early the identity of the murderer. The suspense comes from not quite knowing until toward the end whether he will be caught. Within these parameters, Dostoyevsky wrestles with questions about whether murder can ever be justified, whether Christian morality can operate in a nihilistic world, and whether a killer can ever experience redemption.

THE GEOGRAPHY OF ATHEISM

Dostoyevsky set *Crime and Punishment* in Saint Petersburg, Russia, an important location because Czar Peter the Great had founded it centuries earlier as his Window to the West. Czar Peter aimed to align Russia with western Europe and thereby to advance the cause of scientific and technological progress. In the process, Europe gave Russia a core of ideas. The 19th century in which Dostoyevsky wrote was crucial in this regard because, among other ideas and movements, Europe was enmeshed in a debate over atheism versus traditional theism. Christianity had become a target of intellectuals. German economist Karl Marx and German British economist Friedrich Engels had in the *Communist Manifesto* taken an atheistic stance in denouncing religion as the "opiate of the masses." German philosophers Arthur Schopenhauer and even more strongly Friedrich Nietzsche, both near contemporaries of Dostoyevsky, turned sharply toward atheism. Nietzsche scandalized many Europeans by arguing that Christianity was not only false but its morality weakened humankind and so was an impediment to progress, if such a thing were still possible.

Dostoyevsky absorbed all these ideas in what must have been a painful process because he still retained the Orthodox Christianity that had defined Russia for centuries. *Crime and Punishment,* like his other great novels, is not so much an exploration of atheism as an exploration of the effects of atheism in the context of Christian morality. Dostoyevsky articulated the dilemma best in *The Brothers Karamazov,* in which he asserted that if God were dead, then everything is permissible. This is the intellectual landscape of *Crime and Punishment,* in which Dostoyevsky articulates an idea close to that of Nietzsche. One might term it the great man thesis. The protagonist Raskolnikov is a former student and impoverished man barely able to subsist. He fancies himself a brilliant, bold, courageous man, one for whom the norms of Christianity no longer apply. Christianity sets the agenda for the meek and weak. It is the herd mentality, the morality that keeps sheep in a state of docile acquiescence. This is not the morality of a heroic figure like Raskolnikov. In this method of thinking, he determines that he is justified in killing and robbing an old woman, a pawnbroker who he repeatedly calls a "louse" for sucking the money from her customers. She is greedy and base, whereas he is noble and heroic. Accordingly, he kills her with an ax, an ugly crime, only to be surprised by her half sister. What began as murder becomes double homicide.

THE GEOGRAPHY OF GUILT

These events so shake Raskolnikov that he manages to steal only a few items. Within a short time guilt begins to consume him, causing him to sleep poorly and act strangely during the day. The ideas of Marx, Engels, Schopenhauer, and Nietzsche did not account for guilt, at least not in this context, and Raskolnikov did not expect it either. Yet for Dostoyevsky, guilt was the only possible reaction against two horrific murders and marked the reaction of Christian morality against savagery.

A novel that had begun as a study of the effects of atheism turns into a drama of Christian morality. Raskolnikov manifests this guilt in many ways, the most striking of which is his habit of repeatedly ringing the doorbell of the apartment the two women had once shared. Police and the prosecutor begin to suspect him as the killer, and the tension builds. Will he be caught? Will he confess as his guilt mounts?

At this point Raskolnikov meets Sonya, a saintly woman who herself is in desperation. She is poor and her family has next to nothing. To support herself and her family, she has turned to prostitution, a horrible way to make a living, whereby she must let men repeatedly violate her. Yet her Christian faith is never in doubt. Attracted to her beauty and her faith, Raskolnikov confesses the murders to her. Sonya does not reject him but instead begins to deepen her connection to him. She wants him to confess his guilt to the police and prosecutor so he may seek redemption for his crimes. She gives him a necklace with a cross as a symbol of Jesus' forgiveness.

Raskolnikov capitulates and is sentenced to labor in a Siberian penal colony, exactly the penalty Dostoyevsky received as a young man when convicted of supporting the overthrow of the government. The charge was probably untrue though Dostoyevsky had engaged in radical politics that alarmed authorities. Sonya moves to Siberia to be near Raskolnikov so the two may be together once his term ends. Christian morality has triumphed over atheism.

Christopher Cumo

Further Reading

If you liked *Crime and Punishment,* then you might like *Fathers and Sons* by Ivan Turgenev, because it is also a story about alienation from social society that tells the story of a young man's struggle with his elders during social change across 19th-century Russia.

Another work that similarly offers depictions of Russian life in the premodern world is Anton Chekhov's *Selected Stories,* which is a collection of short stories that transforms the seemingly mundane aspects of daily life into vignettes about what it means to exist. Also consider *The Doll* by Boleslaw Prus, a story about social and personal conflict in 1870s Warsaw.

Bibliography
Alter, Robert. *Imagined Cities: Urban Experience and the Language of the Novel.* New Haven, CT: Yale University Press, 2005.
Boym, Svetlana. "From the Russian Soul to Post-Communist Nostalgia." *Representations* 49 (1995): 133–66. doi:10.2307/2928753.
Budrewicz-Beratan, Aleksandra. "The Urban River in Dickens, Dostoevsky and Prus." *Prace Filologiczne. Literaturoznawstwo* no. 5 (2015): 407–25.
Halpin, Eamon G. "Seen and Unseen Cities: Embodied Worlds in Epic and the Novel." PhD diss., Louisiana State University and Agricultural & Mechanical College, 1995.
Moran, Dominique, Judith Pallot, and Laura Piacentini. "The Geography of Crime and Punishment in the Russian Federation." *Eurasian Geography and Economics* 52, no. 1 (2011): 79–104. doi: 10.2747/1539-7216.52.1.79.
Platonov, Rachel S. "Remapping Arcadia: 'Pastoral Space' in Nineteenth-Century Russian Prose." *The Modern Language Review* 102, no. 4 (2007): 1105–21. doi:10.2307/20467553.

The Crucible

The Crucible is a play written by Arthur Miller in the 1950s, during the McCarthy era, when social dissent was regarded as dangerous for the country and paranoia ran high over the idea that communists were infiltrating America. Many careers were ruined during this time by accusations that people were secret communist agents. This play is understood to be Miller's commentary on McCarthyism as a phenomenon similar to what happened during the Salem witch trials, in which fear overcame reason and people wielded the religious hysteria as a weapon against their enemies. One of the settings symbolic to this play is the forest as a place of "evil" outside of the Puritan settlement; however, what the plot of Miller's play reveals is that the real evil is in the hearts of the men and women in town, who use beliefs of the Puritan religion to kill off their rivals.

TOWN VERSUS FOREST IN THE BATTLE FOR SOULS

Based on real historical events, *The Crucible* is set in 16th-century Salem, Massachusetts, in a puritanical society where the strict religious law is law of the land. Hysteria breaks out when members of the community start accusing each other of consorting with the devil and practicing witchcraft. These events are set into motion when Reverend Parris discovers a group of girls dancing in the woods with Tituba, his African slave servant. The girls include Parris's daughter, Betty, and his niece and ward, Abigail. After this incident, Betty falls into a state of unconsciousness and rumors of witchcraft begin.

In literature referencing Puritan society, a forest setting typically reflects the Puritan fear of the wild spaces of nature that they do not control. These spaces would have been inhabited by Native Americans, whom the Puritans considered "heathens" and devil worshippers. They were suspicious of anyone who did not believe the way they did, including immigrants from other places with other religious backgrounds, such as Africans living in the Americas who practiced non-Christian religious traditions prior to contact with European missionaries and/or slave traders. The forest represents a place of "wildness" feared by Puritans. They find comfort in their towns and feel that it is part of their God-ordained duty in America to conquer and settle the natural landscape. Nathaniel Hawthorne's "Young Goodman Brown" is another example of the woods as a place where, in the Puritan worldview, the devil tempts the faithful. Miller's play situates the real temptation to do evil among the supposed "civilized" townspeople; the play's title refers to a small container used in labs to heat up various materials to test them.

THE GEOGRAPHY OF HYPOCRISY: PURITAN GREED AND INFIDELITY

Abigail, the ringleader of this group of girls, insists that the girls were only dancing in the woods and instructs the others to admit nothing. When a farmer named John Proctor comes to talk to her, Abigail makes a sexual advance, and we learn that the two had an affair while she was working for him as a maid. Although this might make Proctor seem like the villain of the story, that would be a complicated argument to make. Miller shows that Proctor accepts his shortcomings and is willing to own them publicly—in the end, showing that Proctor is a kind of martyr, willing to die for what is right. On the other hand, he shows that Abigail is willing to lie and hurt others to act on base desire, with hopes of winning Proctor back after he broke off their affair and after he admits that he does not want to resume it.

When Betty finally wakes up, she is disturbed and agitated. This prompts the crowd that has gathered in the house to debate whether she's been the victim of witchcraft. Meanwhile, an argument breaks out between Parris, Proctor, and two other men, Giles Corey and a wealthy man named Thomas Putnam. Reverend Hale arrives to examine Betty. When Parris and Hale question Tituba, she confesses to consorting with the devil and hysterically accuses other townspeople of doing the same. Abigail and Betty join her in these accusations, and soon the whole town is embroiled in accusations of witchcraft.

Back at their farmhouse, Proctor's wife Elizabeth tries to convince him to denounce Abigail's claims as fraudulent, but he refuses. As they argue, their maid, Mary Warren, arrives with the news that Elizabeth has been accused of witchcraft, and then two men arrive from town with the news that their wives have been arrested. Elizabeth is arrested by two officers of the court and taken away.

Proctor then convinces Mary to come to town and testify that Abigail and the other girls are lying. Mary is allowed to testify in front of Judge Danforth, but the other girls accuse Mary of witchcraft, feigning that they are being bewitched. Proctor confesses his affair with Abigail in an effort to save Elizabeth, arguing that

Abigail's false accusations are motivated by jealousy. But Elizabeth denies the affair under questioning, wishing to save her husband's honor. The other girls again act as if Mary is bewitching them, and Mary accuses Proctor of witchcraft. Proctor is then arrested. Abigail's plan to instigate accusations against Proctor's wife so that she could be with him has backfired as hysteria grows to the level of a religious Crusade, as the religious leaders and other townspeople see this as an opportunity to do away with rivals, including those who own farmland they covet.

As the witch trials continue into the fall, the wealthy Thomas Putnam uses accusations of witchcraft to pursue old grudges and acquire land. The Putnams accuse a woman named Rebecca Nurse of using witchcraft to kill Ann Putnam's babies, all but one of whom died shortly after birth. The surviving child is Ruth, one of the girls caught dancing in the woods.

Reverend Hale tries to convince the accused to confess to witchcraft to save themselves. Elizabeth initially manages to talk her husband into confession, but then he learns that he must incriminate others and confess publicly. He changes his mind and instead goes to the gallows with the others, who have also refused to confess.

Lacar Musgrove and Lynn Marie Houston

Further Reading

A more modern tale involving allegations regarding whether or not witnesses can be believed and what their motivations might be is the play *Doubt: A Parable,* written by John Patrick Shanley. This tells the story of a Catholic nun, who like many of the accusers in *The Crucible,* seems to have her own agenda in investigating the truth. Another literary work that involves unearthing underlying reality through what seems initially to be lies is in the heated conversation between a male college professor and his female student in David Mamet's play *Oleanna*. Of course, Nathaniel Hawthorne's novel *The Scarlet Letter* is set in colonial New England and also deals with confronting the hypocrisy of Puritan values.

Bibliography

Adler, Thomas P. "Conscience and Community in *An Enemy of the People* and *The Crucible*." In *Arthur Miller's* The Crucible, edited by Harold Bloom, 69–82. New York: Bloom's Literary Criticism, 2008.

Aziz, Aamir. "Using the Past to Intervene in the Present: Spectacular Framing in Arthur Miller's *The Crucible*." *New Theatre Quarterly* 32, no. 2 (2016): 169–80.

Bonnet, Jean-Marie. "Society vs. the Individual in Arthur Miller's *The Crucible*." *English Studies* 63, no. 1 (1982): 32–36.

Brater, Enoch, ed. *Arthur Miller's America: Theater and Culture in a Time of Change*. Ann Arbor: University of Michigan Press, 2010.

Brater, Enoch, ed. *Arthur Miller's Global Theater*. Ann Arbor: University of Michigan Press, 2007.

Hooti, Noorbakhsh. "The Quest for Identity in Arthur Miller's *The Crucible*." *International Journal of English and Literature* 2, no. 3 (2011): 68–74.

Mason, Jeffrey Daniel. *Stone Tower: The Political Theater of Arthur Miller*. Ann Arbor: University of Michigan Press, 2008.

Morgan, Edmund S. "Arthur Miller's *The Crucible* and the Salem Witch Trials: A Historian's View." In *Arthur Miller's* The Crucible, edited by H. Bloom, 41–53. New York: Bloom's Literary Criticism, 2008.

O'Neal, Michael J. "History, Myth, and Name Magic in Arthur Miller's *The Crucible*." *Clio* 12 (1983): 111–22.

Pearson, Michelle. "John Proctor and the Crucible of Individuation in Arthur Miller's *The Crucible*." *Studies in American Drama, 1945 to Present* 6, no. 1 (1991): 15–27.

Popkin, Henry. "Arthur Miller: The Strange Encounter." *The Sewanee Review* 68, no. 1 (1960): 34–60.

D

Daisy Miller

This 1878 novella by Henry James takes place in two European cities, following Frederick Winterbourne as he encounters Daisy and her family on their European travels. Daisy and Frederick first meet in Vevey, Switzerland, and then again in Rome. In both cities, Daisy comes into conflict with a number of the wealthy elite because she does not behave the way they think a young lady should. In fact, they take issue with her family because they are "new money" and don't maintain enough distance from the servants or follow rigid formalities. Frederick has feelings for her and attempts to pursue her but is put off by her frankness, flirtatiousness, and lack of decorum, the same reasons his aunt and other members of the elite circle of American expatriates reject her. At the Roman Colosseum, he confronts Giovanelli, another of Daisy's suitors, and admonishes him for having Daisy out at night where she could catch malaria. Daisy dies shortly thereafter from a terrible fever. When Winterbourne talks with her grieving family and acquaintances, he finds out that Daisy was merely a headstrong young woman, not immoral, and that she had genuine feelings for him.

THE GEOGRAPHY OF FLIRTATION

James's story testifies to how, at the time it was written, the European landscape was converted in summers to a place that drew tourists from around the world, especially America, and served as a location where young singles could meet. The initial description of the little lakeshore town north of Geneva emphasizes that the young people who come there wear their most stylish clothes and engage in dancing and conversation. In fact, the narrator continues, visitors who don't know better might start to suspect that they are in Newport or Saratoga, except for the excellence of the European service, diversity of international visitors, and tidy landscape itself. Vevey boasts the ruins of a castle that Winterbourne and Daisy visit; the trip puzzles Winterbourne as Daisy agrees to go off with him without a chaperone. During his interactions with her, he spends much time trying to determine whether she is an innocent flirt or something more sinister. When he tells Daisy that he must return to Geneva, she seems upset at the thought of his departure and makes him promise to visit her when she is with her family in Italy.

Winterbourne's aunt is in Rome at the same time as the Millers and lets Winterbourne know that Daisy is sightseeing and attending parties with a handful of what she calls "third-rate" Italian men. Winterbourne, still trying to decipher Daisy Miller's character, ends up accompanying her on a walk with one of her Italian suitors, Mr. Giovanelli. Both men are disappointed to be sharing her attention in this manner, and Winterbourne's appreciation of Daisy suffers for it: he decides that she cannot tell the difference between a true gentleman and one merely pretending to be one. For her part, Daisy constantly tells him that he is "too stiff," as a way to suggest that he puts too much value in doing what is "proper" rather than having fun. Winterbourne finally informs Daisy that flirting and teasing are not the custom among polite society in Europe. She is judged by him and by the rest of society because she finds joy in the company of others and is not looking to enrich her status by an advantageous marriage, as a similar European lady of her age and wealth would do. The Colosseum of ancient Rome becomes the scene of Winterbourne's transition from extreme appreciation of Daisy's beauty to his decision that she is not worthy of him. However, when he learns that she is ill with the Roman fever, which he had tried to prevent by telling her not walk around Rome after sunset, he is distraught, revealing that he maintained feelings for her despite concluding that she was "improper."

THE FIGURE OF THE EXPATRIATE

Even though he is from America originally, Frederick Winterbourne has trouble deciphering Daisy's behavior because it has been some time since he has interacted with other Americans or visited the United States. His aunt warns him that he lacks perspective on his interactions with Daisy: "You have lived too long out of the country." In Winterbourne, whose name depicts the frosty disposition that comes to symbolize his interactions with almost everyone around him, Henry James has created a character who is incapable of appreciating Daisy's beauty because of his keen awareness of others' judgment and his lack of confidence in his own instincts. Winterbourne misses out on the vitality and freshness that Daisy represents, symbolizing a springtime of flowers to his icy winter. Instead, he lets the opinions of others influence him. The status of the expatriate in this work is a very lonely space between cultures and continents, where Winterbourne belongs neither to one nor the other. He has lost touch with his homeland in America, and the social circles he inhabits in Europe are cruel and misguided, leaving him to a lonely existence.

CONTRASTS BETWEEN EUROPEAN AND AMERICAN CULTURE

One of the driving criticisms that Henry James puts forth in this novella is of the falseness of proper European social customs. Writing in the 19th century, Miller was aware that, as transportation options across the Atlantic increased, more Americans were traveling to Europe on vacation or "European tours," which were seen as a formative part of a young person's education if he or she were of the upper class. Daisy fully enjoys her time sightseeing in Europe, unlike the Europeans who live there, who don't seem to know how to embrace the monument of their history with the exuberance that Daisy does. And she is the only American in her party who is not sick from Europe's climate: her mother suffers from indigestion and her brother's teeth are falling out. Ultimately, this novella reveals how arbitrary and superficial European notions of exclusivity are, and through the tragedy of Daisy Miller, reveals James's project to be one of encouraging frankness and openness, which in the story is seen as a more natural way of being, rather than the changing tastes of fashionable society. When Daisy dies, she doesn't die so much of a preventable fever from being exposed to mosquitoes carrying disease, she dies of the rejection and exclusion she faced by rigid members of the European upper class.

Lynn Marie Houston

Further Reading

In Edith Wharton's "Roman Fever and Other Stories," the title story also deals with young American women visiting Europe. Many of Wharton's stories deal with her characters' anxiety over acceptance into upper-class society and the pitfalls of marriage. French writer Honoré de Balzac takes a more passionate and devious approach to his tale of social exclusion and romantic jealousy in the novel *Cousin Bette*.

Bibliography

Anderson, Charles. *Person, Place, and Thing in Henry James's Novels*. Durham, NC: Duke University Press, 1977.

Buitenhuis, Peter. "Henry James and American Culture." In *Challenges in American Culture,* edited by Ray B. Browne et al. Bowling Green, OH: Bowling Green University Popular Press, 1970.

Despotopoulou, Anna. "'Terrible Traps to Memory': National Monuments, Collective Memory, and Women in Henry James." *MFS Modern Fiction Studies* 63, no. 3 (2017): 429–51. doi:10.1353/mfs.2017.0031.

Falcus, Sarah, and Katsura Sako. "'I Must Learn to Grow Old before I Die': Women, Ageing and Travels to Italy." *Women: A Cultural Review* 25, no. 2 (2014): 194–214. doi:10.1080/09574042.2014.944413.

Goble, Mark. "Wired Love: Pleasure at a Distance in Henry James and Others." *ELH* 74, no. 2 (2007): 397–427.

Jones, Granville H. *Henry James's Psychology of Experience: Innocence, Responsibility, and Renunciation in the Fiction of Henry James*. The Hague: Mouton, 1975.

Mariani, Umberto. "The Italian Experience of Henry James." *Nineteenth-Century Fiction* 19, no. 3 (1964): 237–54.

Oltean, Roxana. "Colonial Hysteria, the American, and James's Paris." *The Henry James Review* 24 (2003): 269–80.

Oltean, Roxana. *Spaces of Utopia in the Writings of Henry James*. Bucuresti: Editura Universitatii din Bucuresti, 2005.

Pana-Oltean, Roxana. "'The Extravagant Curve of the Globe': Refractions of Europe in Henry James's *An International Episode* and *The Ambassadors*." *The Henry James Review* 22, no. 2 (2001): 180–99. doi:10.1353/hjr.2001.0015.

Pana-Oltean, Roxana. "From Grand Tour to a Space of Detour: Henry James's Europe." *The Henry James Review* 31, no. 1 (2010): 46–53.

Rix, Alicia. "Transport in Henry James." PhD diss., University College London, 2014.

Salmon, Richard. *Henry James and the Culture of Publicity*. Cambridge: Cambridge University Press, 1997.

Schloss, Dietmar. *Culture and Criticism in Henry James*. Tübingen: Gunter Narr Verlag, 1992.

Short, R. W. "Henry James's World of Images." *PMLA* 68, no. 5 (1953): 943–60.

Death of a Salesman

This 1949 play by Arthur Miller opens with the main character's return from a business trip. Willy Loman has been a traveling salesman for most of his life but has never achieved the kind of success he wanted. His wife, Linda, has been loyal and supportive as they eked out an existence and are nearing the final mortgage payments on their modest home. However, Willy is becoming increasingly delusional, hallucinating scenes from the past, and has gotten into a car accident. Linda encourages Willy to go see his boss to ask for a job closer to home, so he won't have to travel as much, but the outcome of that tense meeting is that Willy is fired. Afterward, he goes out to dinner with his two sons, Biff and Happy, who are home visiting, and the men end up fighting. Willy wants his sons to be highly successful businessmen, but neither of them is living up to the image Willy has for them in his mind. Biff went to meet with a former employer to ask about starting a new business and when he is turned down, he steals a pen from the man's desk. Happy, although he has a job in sales, is unhappy with his life and engages in unethical behavior, such as lying, womanizing, and taking bribes. In high school, Biff had been a star football player with a scholarship for college, but after discovering that his father was having an affair, he never finished the summer course he needed to graduate. Willy still blames himself for Biff's failure to be successful and ends up killing himself so that his wife can use his life insurance money to pay off their house.

SHIFTING MODES OF CAPITALISM

Willy Loman was first inspired to pursue a career in sales by observing Dave Singleman, a wealthy salesman who was very popular with his clients. However, the corny jokes that were at one time impressive to office staff of a previous generation are no longer what help business professionals be successful. In addition, Willy Loman's attempts at humor do not seem organic; they seem desperate. Even when Willy sleeps with a receptionist who works at the office of one of his clients, his attempt only comes off as sad—he gifts his mistress new stockings, which causes him to become angry whenever he sees his wife darning her old ones, and he is caught in the act by his son, Biff, who loses all respect for his father. The world of business has changed drastically during Willy Loman's life, and what was once a burgeoning industry that rewarded entrepreneurs with a lot of personality has shifted now into valuing more highly skilled and trained laborers. It's no longer possible for Willy to make good money merely on charm alone. However, he has not yet figured this out. Nor has he figured out that his personality was never that stellar anyway, that he was never the "great man" he thought he was. Willy is caught in an older paradigm, where a pioneering spirit, like that of his brother Ben, is guaranteed to strike it rich. Those days passed and Willy has still been trying to prove himself as some kind of pioneer. His flashbacks into history help illustrate that even when he was younger, he was trying too hard to follow in his brother's footsteps, never quite the man that Ben was. Willy is a tragic hero because he cannot accept that he is simply an ordinary man—he is always working the next angle as to how he's going to "make it," when a life of drudgery is all he was ever destined for. Miller, in creating a character that cannot accept his own reality, crafts a tragic antihero who will never find happiness.

LAND AND THE AMERICAN DREAM

Owning land is essential to Willy Loman's idea of a successful life. However, because he and his wife have only a small lot with a modest home, around which have been built numerous high-rise apartment complexes, he constantly feels frustrated by his lack of connection to the land. He claims to have taught his sons to hunt, but in the semi-urban area where he lives, game is sparse. They even attempt to build a porch on their house, but the exercise turns into one of the moments where Willy is encouraging his sons to do something immoral in the name of pursuing their goals: Willy tells Biff to steal the lumber they need from a nearby construction site. Willy acts like he is part of the Wild West, where anything goes, and where people will overlook societal transgressions if they are done in an effort to improve one's situation. Even if that mythic version of the West did exist in some form at one point, Willy's historical time period and geographical setting—Brooklyn of the late 1940s—are far removed. He operates from the standpoint of a fantasy that has caused him and his family deep unhappiness and problems in their relationships.

THE CULTURAL LANDSCAPE OF MASCULINITY

Not only is his idea of success attached to land ownership, but so is his concept of masculinity. Trying to teach his sons to hunt, shoot, and build things is a very superficial take on the idea of being a "good" man, one that chooses physical brawn over intelligence or ethics. This is seen throughout the play in the way Willy makes fun of Bernard, his neighbor's son. In high school, Bernard was a nerd, a bookworm, and although highly intelligent, he was looked down on by Willy and his family because he was not "popular" in the way that Biff was as a football star. And yet, years later, Willy finds out that Bernard is a highly successful lawyer with a wife and son. Bernard has achieved wealth and popularity by being true to himself and cultivating his talents. Miller reveals a critique of the hypermasculine in the play, asking his audience to see the shortcomings of men who attempt to define themselves through their relationship to the body—sports, hunting, and working the land—rather than the mind.

Willy holds on to an outdated notion of masculinity, which he teaches to his sons, Biff and Happy, neither of whom are happy with their lives or prepared for success in the new realities of the world in which they live.

Lynn Marie Houston

Further Reading

If you liked *Death of a Salesman,* then you might like *The Iceman Cometh* by Eugene O'Neill, because it is also a story about reflection of what could have been that takes place in a bar whose patrons eagerly await the arrival of a traveling businessman who inspires them to actually do something with their lives, if only to go back to their old ways. Another work that similarly questions long-held values is *The Goat, or Who Is Sylvia?* by Edward Albee, which is about a family that must respond to an unforeseen event. Another good recommendation is Thornton Wilder's *Our Town,* a play about absorbing everything life has to offer, even the parts that don't seem much worth absorbing.

Bibliography

Bigsby, Christopher W. E. *Arthur Miller: A Critical Study.* Cambridge, UK: Cambridge University Press, 2005.

Centola, Steven R. "Family Values in *Death of a Salesman.*" *CLA Journal* 37, no. 1 (1993): 29–41.

Ferguson, Alfred R. "The Tragedy of the American Dream in *Death of a Salesman.*" *Thought: Fordham University Quarterly* 53, no. 1 (1978): 83–98. doi:10.5840/thought19785318.

Gros, Camille. "The Myths of the Self-Made Man: Cowboys, Salesmen and Pirates in Tennessee Williams' the *Glass Menagerie* and Arthur Miller's *Death of a Salesman.*" Master's thesis, Georgia State University, 2009.

Ribkoff, Fred. "Shame, Guilt, Empathy, and the Search of Identity in Arthur Miller's *Death of a Salesman.*" *Modern Drama* 43, no. 1 (2000): 48–55.

Savran, David. *Communists, Cowboys, and Queers: The Politics of Masculinity in the Work of Arthur Miller and Tennessee Williams.* Minneapolis: University of Minnesota Press, 1992.

Thomieres, Daniel. "All Is Not Gold: Fatherhood and Identity in Arthur Miller's *Death of a Salesman.*" *PsyArt,* no. 20 (2016): 1–23.

Dickinson, Emily

Nineteenth-century poet Emily Dickinson lived in the town of Amherst, Massachusetts, where she was a local legend, even during her lifetime. Many literary critics foster an understanding of her in terms of a reclusive figure, but historical documents indicate that, although she spent a lot of time in her bedroom writing poetry, she had an emotionally complex family life and a robust correspondence with friends, whom she also visited in her travels. Many of her poems were circulated to friends and family in letters. Dickinson often wrote to her acquaintances about the seasonal flora of New England. Her love of botany also comes across clearly in many of her poems, where trees and flowers are identified by name. Her family house was surrounded by well-kept gardens, and she cultivated plants in their greenhouse. In addition to an intense and educated interest in the natural landscape, one of the elements common to many of Dickinson's poems is a speaker who tells her story from the first-person perspective. The location of this speaker is central to his or her worldview and, therefore, to the meanings Dickinson conveys through her work.

DICKINSON'S PASTORAL

Emily Dickinson is not readily talked about by scholars in terms of the pastoral tradition, which is the literature since ancient times that praises the beauty and simplicity of a life spent outside working in a rural setting. Dickinson's higher-class status kept her from the necessity of doing any manual labor, and the family house was located within walking distance of the town center in a populated area. However, she tended her gardens and took her work there seriously, so much so that she grew plants year-round with the help of a greenhouse. These concerns for planting and growing make their way into her poetry and align her with the pastoral tradition. In one poem, Dickinson refers to the land of her gardens as her "farm," writing about an occasional harvest that exceeds her modest expectations: "The Products of my Farm are these / Sufficient for my Own / And here and there a Benefit / Unto a Neighbor's Bin." However, Dickinson often writes about an abstract "nature" that fails to provide. In this seeming rejection of the pastoral tradition (which saw nature as abundant and generous to humans, rewarding their work), Dickinson is separating out the global concept from its local manifestation. Although nature in general may not be something one can count on to be kind in the worldview represented in her poetry, specific instances of it often do present her speakers with hope and a reason to believe in the beauty of one's surroundings. In those specific instances of the larger natural world, she often finds moments for meditation that bring her a feeling of having connected with the Divine. Through her gardens and references to plants in her poems, Dickinson charts one of the paths through which she comes to know God, and to understand the connections that exist between living things. These are also one of the many ways she plays with the notion between interior and exterior locations, between private and public space. Being outside in the yard to weed and harvest her gardens would have been one of the ways that Dickinson puts herself in the public eye. Her work often suggests that any descriptions of space should be highly attentive to the different emotional registers of private spaces versus public ones.

MAPPING THE AFTERLIFE

The space of death interested her greatly, and often exhibits this same attentiveness regarding how private and public space resonate differently. The house in Amherst where Dickinson lived when she was younger was located next to a cemetery, so it may not be surprising to find that many of her poems are related to death, or feature voices that speak to us from beyond the grave. Dickinson does not give us the standard Christian interpretation of the afterlife, but instead imagines a spiritual consciousness that lasts for some time after death. Some of her poems in which speakers narrate to readers from in or beyond the grave are "Because I Could Not Stop for Death," "I Heard a Fly Buzz—When I Died," and "I Died for Beauty."

Death is often a physical place in Dickinson's poems, such as the grave or tomb. Although she might represent it as a quiet resting space, she does not describe it in typical Christian terms, such as the kind implied by the overused phrase "gone to his final resting place." She imbues that space of the grave with a consciousness that continues after death.

For Dickinson's speakers, the grave is a deeply private space, a chance to finally be alone with one's thoughts. Her work does not indulge in any grand imaginings in the style of Dante's *Inferno*. The space of the grave in her poems is simply an extension of life. She fails to imagine a transcendent vision where there is something "more than" or beyond human in the space we occupy after death. Her idea of peace in the afterlife was a quiet solitude, much like she lived her life. One of her poems claims, "This World is not conclusion."

THE ARCHITECTURE AND GEOGRAPHY OF THE HUMAN MIND

Similar to how Dickinson's work views death as being continuous with the space of human life, therefore representing it as "unlimited," she also feels that the human mind is unlimited. Often her attempts to encompass it cause her to acknowledge the way such a task is bound to fail. In contrast to the popular metaphor in Western culture for the heart as the seat of emotions, for Dickinson, the brain is the physical location where she explores intense feelings. In her poem "I Felt a Funeral, in my Brain," she uses the metaphor of a funeral, of a ritual for something that is dead, to talk about what seems to be the mental process of letting go of an old conception in favor of a new one. She talks about the process as one in which "Sense was breaking through" and which finishes with "Knowing," as if her speaker is mourning some idea she used to cling to but has since had to change her mind as new information comes to light. In this poem, the mind is the ground on which this ritual of mourning occurs, linking in one poem her fascination with death and the ways in which she tries to map out the human mind and its processes.

In her poem "There's a Certain Slant of Light," she positions human suffering as a result of perceiving a message in the landscape about death that creates an "internal difference—/ Where the Meanings, are." Conceiving of our own mortality is one of the most difficult things human beings grapple with, and here, Dickinson's speaker confronts the idea of mortality through the lesser light of winter, as the sun strikes the Earth as a smaller angle. Fall and winter in literature are traditionally associated with death. Dickinson features an attention to outdoor light in other poems, as well. These works contribute to how she tends to take emotional states and embody them in the natural world. Places for Dickinson, both interior and exterior, are emotional epicenters.

One of the ways her poems create a map of a mental landscape is through her repeated references to taking large concepts and localizing them into smaller bodies or spaces. In doing this, Dickinson often captures something poignant about the human struggle to confront mortality because often smaller vessels in her poetry fail to encapsulate the full idea: the remainder—what's left over, the gap—is often likened to a space of death or to eternity. An example of one of the ways she represents through spatial metaphors the human mind's desire for philosophical pursuit is in the poem "Perhaps I asked too large": "My Basket holds—just—Firmaments—/ Those—dangle easy—on my arm, / But smaller bundles—Cram." Here, the speaker's basket could be a symbol for the mind and the difficulty of perceiving particulars as opposed to notions that are larger and vaster. In fact, this poem names the "firmaments," which are skies, and skies are often referenced as thought in her some of her poems. She writes "The Brain—is wider than the sky— / For—put them side by side— / The one the other will contain." The sky is normally a symbol for eternity, but here it is the human brain that is fashioned as limitless.

With scientific precision, Dickinson attempts to map the mind and to trace or document its interactions with the exterior world. In doing so, she often erases boundary line between this world and the next.

THE EYE IS A WINDOW . . .

Visual perception is very important to how her speakers are able to make sense of the world, whether they are outside in natural spaces or in interior architectural ones. Often in her works, the house interior represents a mindscape. Dickinson made an important contribution to the history of women's literary production because she helped readers understand the domestic sphere as an important geography that was not just for feelings but for thoughts. During the 19th century, women were known to conceive of the home as a space that celebrated their feelings of love for their husband and children. Important to Dickinson's contribution is the architectural element of the window that allows her to be physically inside but visually outside. She writes as the first line of one poem, "By my Window have I for Scenery. . . ." In this way, the interior space of her house could be comforting but not limiting to her experiences.

Lynn Marie Houston

Further Reading

Emily Dickinson's poetry is often compared to that of Walt Whitman, although in her letters she expressed some discomfort at the comparison. Walt Whitman's poetry is much more free-ranging in its themes and unified by political purposes, such as his project to reclaim the divinity of the body. However, they are two of the strongest voices in 19th-century American poetry. Edna St. Vincent Millay's style is close to Dickinson's in terms of form. Additionally, Dickinson is often cited as inspiration for later confessional poets like Sylvia Plath, Anne Carson, and Robert Lowell. These poets found that Dickinson's exploration of her personal feelings and her disclosure of intimate thoughts fueled the kind of authenticity they were interested in capturing in their poetry.

Bibliography

Anderson, Douglas. "Presence and Place in Emily Dickinson's Poetry." *The New England Quarterly* 57, no. 2 (1984): 205–24.

Barker, Wendy. *Lunacy of Light: Emily Dickinson and the Experience of Metaphor.* Carbondale: Southern Illinois University Press, 1987.

Freeman, Margaret H. "Grounded Spaces: Deictic Self Anaphors in the Poetry of Emily Dickinson." *Language and Literature* 6, no. 1 (1997): 7–28.

Freeman, Margaret H. "Metaphor Making Meaning: Dickinson's Conceptual Universe." *Journal of Pragmatics* 24, no. 6 (1995): 643–66.

Gerhardt, Christine. *A Place for Humility: Whitman, Dickinson, and the Natural World.* Iowa City: University of Iowa Press, 2014.

Gerhardt, Christine. "'Often seen-but seldom felt': Emily Dickinson's Reluctant Ecology of Place." *The Emily Dickinson Journal* 15, no. 1 (2006): 56–78.

Giles, Paul. "'The Earth Reversed Her Hemispheres': Dickinson's Global Antipodality." *The Emily Dickinson Journal* 20, no. 1 (2011): 1–21.

Guthrie, James R. "'A Revolution in Locality': Astronomical Tropes in Emily Dickinson's Poetry." *The Midwest Quarterly* 37, no. 4 (1996): 365.

Juhasz, Suzanne. *The Undiscovered Continent: Emily Dickinson and the Space of the Mind.* Bloomington: Indiana University Press, 1983.

O'Donnell, Patrick. "Zones of the Soul: Emily Dickinson's Geographical Imagery." *CLA Journal* 21, no. 1 (1977): 62–73.

Dispatches

Written by journalist Michael Herr (1940–2016), *Dispatches* was published in 1977, as a memoir of his personal experience during the Vietnam War, and is considered by critics to be the definitive account of that war. Hailed as a masterpiece when it was published, it was ranked by the *Guardian* in 2017 as ninth on a list of the 100 best nonfiction books of all time. In *Dispatches*, Herr writes about the real Vietnam War, one told from the perspective of men on the frontline, rather than from politicians and daytime commanders far removed from the battlefield. Herr spent a year following the Marines and Army in Vietnam, witnessing firsthand the experiences of combat soldiers. Herr was originally sent to Vietnam on a special assignment for *Esquire*. He wrote the book from New York after returning from Vietnam, and parts of the book were first published as articles in *Esquire, Rolling Stone,* and *New American Review*. These articles were combined and revised to form the core of the narrative of *Dispatches*. In Herr's work, the land and culture of Vietnam are full of contradictions. He uses motion picture techniques to redraw a map of Vietnam after the changes brought about by war.

WAR AND CHAOS

Although the book was originally published as nonfiction, Herr later admitted in a 1990 interview with the *Los Angeles Times* that two of the main characters, Day Tripper and Mayhew, are fictional composite characters and that parts of the book are fiction. Herr's book is considered an example of the "new journalism" pioneered in the 1960s by such writers as Tom Wolfe and Joan Didion that emphasizes "truth over facts," and in which the writer acknowledges the subjectivity of the observer rather than claiming an objective account written by an impassive observer. Instead of being removed from the reported events, the writer and his personal voice are integral to the story.

Dispatches is an effort to report the experience of war "the way it was," capturing the experience of American soldiers in combat through impressions of their emotional reactions, including fear, courage, anger, confusion, and a pervasive sense of both compassion and violence. Rather than a chronological account, the book is organized as a series of thematically connected vignettes, presented without context or background, mimicking the way that a typical soldier was dropped into the chaos of war. The nonlinear structure is not a narrative but rather a montage of poetry, prose, images, stories, and dialogues taken from Herr's memories after his return from Vietnam. Each story builds on and contrasts with the other in a manner that is disjointed and formless. The effect is disorienting, but it also creates a vivid immediacy.

NEW JOURNALISM

During the 1960s and '70s, journalists writing for major magazines such as *Esquire, Harper's,* and the *New Yorker* began experimenting with new ways to investigate and write about newsworthy events. The essence of traditional journalism is the collection and representation of facts. To achieve this, journalists must try never to let their personal experiences and judgments cloud their observations of events. Third-person narrative, which establishes a distant viewpoint by usually relying on facts collected from go-betweens—police, government, witness or an expert, is the conventional voice for writing. New Journalists valued facts but they also sought "truth." This made their work subjective because truth always depends on personal beliefs and vision. They immersed themselves into a situation or community and wrote in a literary style favoring the first-person narrative. This drew readers into the immediacy of the action or event. Some of the most famous works of New Journalism are Truman Capote's *In Cold Blood* (1966), Hunter S. Thompson's *Hell's Angels* (1966), and Joan Didion's *Slouching towards Bethlehem* (1968).

In *Dispatches,* Herr constructed a new language appropriate for representing his vision of the Vietnam War—history's first televised war. He aimed to capture a clear picture of war after tragedy had burned away anything extraneous and left only the essential. For Herr, the extraneous included fact-ridden information, patriotic platitudes, and excessively optimistic statements, which he called "communications pudding" dished out by the military marketing machine and fed to the American public by wide-eyed mass media. He figured the "dripping, laughing death-face" alive "in back of every column of print you read about Vietnam" could be captured in a book that included multiple perspectives, composite characters, offbeat punctuation, snazzy discourse, and slick rhythms.

WAR AND WITNESS

Herr arrived in Vietnam as a young journalist wholly unprepared (by his own admission) for the complexities and horrors of war in Southeast Asia as well as the extent of his involvement. He was keenly aware of his role as a voluntary participant among soldiers who had been drafted. In attempting to grapple with this difference, Herr expresses his belief that he is responsible not only for everything he does but also everything he sees, and embraces what he feels was his call to bear witness.

Although he attempts to address and understand the politics and history of the war, Herr takes no political position, and overall the politics of the war is of minor interest. Instead, Herr is concerned with the experience of the common solider, whom he neither romanticizes nor condemns but rather shows in all his honest humanity.

AT THE MOVIES

Herr co-wrote the screenplays for two Oscar-nominated films about the war in Vietnam: *Apocalypse Now* (1979) and *Full Metal Jacket* (1987). Scenes in each movie show TV reporters and camera crews filming soldiers in the midst of battle and even directing them to not look into the camera as battle unfolds. The scenes point to the unprecedented synergy that existed between Americans fighting the war and the perception of "being on camera." To begin with, Herr lays bare the animosity that the "grunts" held toward journalists who *chose* to come to the hell that was Vietnam and who were exploiting the bloodletting. Herr was able to gain deeper impressions of the war because the young soldiers seemed to confide in him. He noticed early on how they would frame their experiences in terms of motion pictures. Their sense of war came only from the big screen.

Herr's nonfiction novel itself unfolds like a screenplay. In fact, the structure and style of his writing correspond with interplay between war and cinema that he finds in Vietnam. He intentionally adopts cinematic techniques such as montage, and even incorporates a rock-and-roll "soundtrack" by referring to songs and artists. Moreover, he writes in a prose style that mimics the panning of a motion-picture camera. He knew readers would easily relate to his mode of expression because war-as-(war) movie was not far removed from life as movie.

THE VIETNAM LANDSCAPE

Herr rides "choppers" (helicopters) like they were taxis. When he lands in a place, perhaps Saigon, Khe Sanh, or Hue, he begins his vignettes by setting the scene or, as they say in motion-picture parlance, composing the "establishing shot." He does so with a smart eye for landscape features such as barracks, jungle, and perimeters. This gives readers a clear view of spatial relations before they move on to the action at hand. In *Dispatches,* Herr is constructing a predominantly visual experience—the backbone of geographical knowledge.

"Geography is facts" promised an early European explorer. Such facts are best captured through a god's-eye view of the world—on the map. *Dispatches* opens with Herr describing a map on a wall in his Saigon (Ho Chi Minh City) hotel room. However, the map no longer represented the reality of the country. Herr doesn't go into details, but he does mention the map was made in Paris, which would have probably meant the map was a celebration of French conquests in Indochina, a token of its imperialism. In other words, the map was likely a French celebration of their colonial holdings. The French were eventually ousted from Vietnam, and then Americans stepped in during the war to defend the people in the south against communist forces in the northern half of their country, drawing a dividing line between them. More than the changing names and shapes of territories, however, Herr is referencing how the land changed drastically due to bombing and use of Agent Orange, a harsh chemical, to destroy crops that might feed the enemy and defoliate trees so that the U.S. troops could have a better aerial view of battlegrounds. He talks about how the map represents the uselessness of most of the information they have, and how land tells different stories to different audiences. The map, a tool of science, reduces and simplifies the landscape. Herr draws a new geography by immersing himself in place. His map could only be a personal response to an unknown people—American soldiers and reporters—in an obscure land. Ultimately, he concludes that the war is the only country that exists anymore in Vietnam because it is the only reality that the people in that country know.

Later in the chapter, Herr talks about his thoughts as he was flying in a helicopter over jungles, exchanges he has with pilots who would discuss the contradictory aspects of a war that had a supposedly humanitarian mission. Vietnam was the first war in which helicopters played such a crucial role. Herr describes the sheer beauty of flying in a helicopter and covering so much ground in a day. For Herr, interacting with the Vietnam landscape while flying over it at great speeds was the perfect metaphor for the war: beauty and brutality living just seconds apart from one another. He gives the oft spoken "spookiness" of the Vietnamese landscape an intensely real vitality unavailable on conventional maps or in traditional reporting.

Ken Whalen, Dalilah Nabilah Laidin, Lacar Musgrove, and Lynn Marie Houston

Further Reading

Any of Tim O'Brien's works from Vietnam would be good to read along with *Dispatches*. These would include *The Things They Carried, If I Die in a Combat Zone,* and *Going After Cacciatto*. Philip Caputo also has a memoir of his service in Vietnam called *A Rumor of War*.

Many critics have detailed the ways in which Herr's work compares to Joseph Conrad's classic take on imperialism in Africa. Other works that envision the U.S. entry into Vietnam as if it were a voyage into "the heart of darkness" are *No Bugles, No Drums* by Charles Durden, *Fields of Fire* by James Webb, and *Meditations in Green* by Stephen Wright.

Bibliography

Armstrong, John. "Haunted Jungles of Horror and Trauma: Elements of the Gothic in Vietnamese and American War Fiction." In *War Gothic in Literature and Culture*, edited by Steffen Hantke and Agnieszka Soltysik Monnet. New York: Routledge, 2015.

Bleakney, Julia. *Revisiting Vietnam*. New York: Routledge, 2013.

Bowen, Claire, and Catherine Hoffmann. *Representing Wars from 1860 to the Present: Fields of Action, Fields of Vision*. Leiden, Netherlands: Brill, 2018.

Carman, John. "Paradox in Places: Twentieth-Century Battlefield Sites in Long-Term Perspective." In *Matériel Culture: The Archaeology of Twentieth-Century Conflict*, edited by Colleen M. Beck, William Gray Johnson, and John Schofield, 29–41. New York: Routledge, 2003.

Cruz, Juan José. "Vietnam as 'Frontier': Some Literary Responses." *Revista de Filología de la Universidad de La Laguna* 10 (1991): 95–108.

Der Derian, James. *Virtuous War: Mapping the Military-Industrial-Media-Entertainment-Network*. New York: Routledge, 2009.

Gordon, Maggie. "Appropriation of Generic Convention: Film as Paradigm in Michael Herr's *Dispatches*." *Literature/Film Quarterly* 28.1 (2000): 16–28.

Harrison, Rachel V. "Up the Congo River into Cambodia: Literary and Cinematic Journeys to the Dark." *Asian Affairs* 43, no. 1 (2012): 49–60.

Musiaà, Aleksandra. "Outside the World: Vietnam as a Mythic Landscape in Michael Herr's *Dispatches*." In *War and Words: Representations of Military Conflict in*

Literature and the Media, edited by Wojciech Drąg, Jakub Krogulec, and Mateusz Marecki, 45. Newcastle upon Tyne, UK: Cambridge Scholars Publishing, 2016.

Naito, Hiroaki. "Vietnam Fought and Imagined: The Images of the Mythic Frontier in American Vietnam War Literature." PhD diss., University of Glasgow, 2014.

Poremba, Timothy F. "Killer Trees and Homicidal Grass: The Anthropomorphic Landscape in the American Prose Narrative of the Vietnam War." Master's thesis, Eastern Illinois University, 1991.

Schlund-Vials, Cathy J. "Ecological Imaginations, the Vietnam War, and Vietnamese American Literature." In *Asian American Literature and the Environment,* edited by Lorna Fitzsimmons, Youngsuk Chae, and Bella Adams, 135–49. New York: Routledge, 2014.

Dracula

Dracula is a supernatural novel by Anglo-Irish writer and theatrical agent Bram Stoker. Although not the first literary work about vampires—undead human beings who subsist on the blood of the living—it established many of the themes that have since become common in stories and novels about them. By the time *Dracula* was published in 1897, readers were familiar with adventure novels in which a hero ventures out into a distant and dangerous part of the world. In the case of *Dracula,* however, the situation is more complex. One of Stoker's main characters *does* travel to an unfamiliar part of the world where he undergoes a frightening ordeal, but then, in a reversal of the pattern, a representative of that unfamiliar land ventures into Harker's own country to threaten his friends and loved ones.

ABROAD AND AT HOME

Told through diaries, letters, and newspaper articles, *Dracula* utilizes three primary settings. The first is Transylvania, where the opening and closing sections of the novel take place. Today, Transylvania is a part of the nation of Romania, but in Stoker's day it was a remote and little-known province of the Austro-Hungarian Empire. Stoker's character Jonathan Harker, an English lawyer, is visiting the region

---

What I saw was the Count's head coming out from the window. I did not see the face, but I knew the man by the neck and the movement of his back and arms. In any case I could not mistake the hands which I had had some many opportunities of studying. I was at first interested and somewhat amused, for it is wonderful how small a matter will interest and amuse a man when he is a prisoner. But my very feelings changed to repulsion and terror when I saw the whole man slowly emerge from the window and begin to crawl down the castle wall over the dreadful abyss, face down with his cloak spreading out around him like great wings. At first I could not believe my eyes. I thought it was some trick of the moonlight, some weird effect of shadow, but I kept looking, and it could be no delusion. I saw the fingers and toes grasp the corners of the stones, worn clear of the mortar by the stress of years, and by thus using every projection and inequality move downwards with considerable speed, just as a lizard moves along a wall.

Bram Stoker, *Dracula* (1897)

to help Count Dracula purchase property in England. As Harker describes it, Transylvania is heavily forested and mysterious, its inhabitants fearful and superstitious. Much to his dismay, he discovers the nature of the Transylvanian's fears when he finds himself imprisoned in Dracula's castle.

The second setting is London, the capital of Britain and the nerve center of the British Empire. It is here that Harker's fiancée Mina Murray, lives, and it was here that Stoker himself lived while working for famed English actor Henry Irving as business manager of the Lyceum Theatre. He also served as Irving's secretary, traveling with him on tours. Irving was a notably commanding and charismatic figure, and Stoker gave the sinister Count Dracula the actor's overpowering, hypnotic personality.

The third setting is the small British port of Whitby, where Stoker and his family vacationed in 1890. Here the writer started making notes for *Dracula*. What is more, the port supplied a key incident to the novel's plot. According to a story that Stoker heard and subsequently researched in the local newspaper, a Russian sailing ship named the *Dmitry* had run aground at the port in 1885. Happily, the ship's crew all survived, but in *Dracula,* the only passengers are a huge dog—the evil count in another form—that leaps ashore, and a dead man roped to the ship's wheel.

CREATING A TRANSYLVANIAN MONSTER

Bram Stoker spent seven years writing *Dracula,* and besides drawing key elements from his own life and from his travels, he did extensive research in a wide range of books. At first, he planned to set many of his novel's scenes in Styria. Then a province of Austria (and today divided between that country and Slovenia), Styria is the setting of J. Sheridan Le Fanu's short vampire novel *Carmilla* (1872), which Stoker had read. In time, however, he transferred Dracula's castle farther east, to Transylvania. This locale may have been suggested by the writings of Emily Gerard—an 1885 article, "Transylvanian Superstitions," which appeared in a popular British periodical, and an 1888 book, *The Land beyond the Forest.* (The book's title is a literal translation of the name Transylvania.)

Another of Stoker's sources, which by good luck he discovered in the public library at Whitby, was the 1820 book *An Account of the Principalities of Wallachia and Moldavia,* by William Wilkinson, who had been a British consul in the region. Besides describing Transylvania, which shares borders with the two principalities, the book actually gave Stoker his evil character's name, at one point explaining that "Dracula in the Wallachian language means Devil."

Originally, however, the name Dracula had no supernatural significance. Fifteenth-century Wallachian nobleman Vlad II adopted the designation Dracul as a reference to his membership in the Order of the Dragon, a chivalric order charged with defending Christianity and fighting the infidel Turks. His son Vlad III added an "a" to the name, signifying simply that he was the son of Dracul. Due to his notoriously excessive cruelty, Vlad III was remembered after his death as Vlad Ţepeş, meaning Vlad the Impaler. Due to this association, the name Dracula took on the meaning of devil. Combining the name he found in Wilkinson's book with details about vampires from the writings of Gerard and others, Stoker created a monster.

A THREAT TO THE EMPIRE

In describing the manner in which groups reject those who are different, literary critics use the term "the Other." Britain had long feared invasion, but by the time that Stoker wrote *Dracula*, the country had amassed a vast empire, and there was growing concern with threats to that empire from within and without. Some of these threats were real, but the British rejection of the unusual and foreign—the Other—contributed to the concern. This attitude was intensified, although probably unintentionally, by Stoker and writers like him.

"Orientalism" is a related concept that is useful in thinking about the impact of *Dracula*. The term refers to the way western Europeans think of the lands and peoples to the east ("Orient" means "East") and south as being not only exotic and alluring but also, at the same time, "primitive" and frightening. Considered in these terms, *Dracula* is a psychologically acute dramatization of the threat from the Other and from the Orient, and its appeal—then and now—is a testament to some of humankind's most basic fears.

Grove Koger

Further Reading

If you liked *Dracula*, then you might like J. Sheridan Le Fanu's *Carmilla*, which inspired Bram Stoker's later interpretation of the vampire concept. Another work preceding *Dracula* is *Melmoth the Wanderer* by Charles Robert Maturin, the macabre story of a diabolical main character who enters a bargain with the devil to exchange his soul for immortality. Another recommendation from the Gothic classics is Edgar Allan Poe's *Spirits of the Dead: Tales and Other Poems*.

Bibliography

Bibeau, Paul. *Sundays with Vlad: From Pennsylvania to Transylvania, One Man's Quest to Live in the World of the Undead*. New York: Three Rivers Press, 2007.

Bollen, Katrien, and Raphael Ingelbien. "An Intertext that Counts? *Dracula, The Woman in White,* and Victorian Imaginations of the Foreign Other." *English Studies* 90, no. 4 (2009): 403–20. doi:10.1080/00138380902990226.

Converse, Joshua Patrick. "Of Fangs and Phonographs: The Past as Un-Dead in Bram Stoker's *Dracula*." Master's thesis, San Francisco State University, 2016. http://hdl.handle.net/10211.3/162913.

Cristina, Artenie. "Transylvania and Romania in Scholarly Editions of Bram Stoker's *Dracula*." PhD diss., Université Laval, 2015. http://hdl.handle.net/20.500.11794/26404.

Dittmer, Jason. "Teaching the Social Construction of Regions in Regional Geography Courses; or, Why Do Vampires Come from Eastern Europe?" *Journal of Geography in Higher Education* 30, no. 2 (2006): 49–61. doi:10.1080/03098260500499618.

Generani, Gustavo. "Bram Stoker's *Dracula*: Breaking the Imperial-Anthropological Time." *Horror Studies* 9, no. 1 (2018): 119–39. doi:10.1386/host.9.1.119_1.

Glover, David. *Vampires, Mummies, and Liberals: Bram Stoker and the Politics of Popular Fiction*. Durham, NC: Duke University Press, 1996.

Valente, Joseph. *Dracula's Crypt: Bram Stoker, Irishness, and the Question of Blood*. Urbana: University of Illinois Press, 2002.

E

Ender's Game

Ender's Game is a science fiction story set in a distant future in which humans must fight off the invasion of an insectlike alien species called "buggers." The protagonist, a young boy named Ender Wiggin, is chosen for Battle School, where the brightest kids on Earth are being prepared to fight in anticipation of an alien invasion. As the plot unfolds, readers of Orson Scott Card's popular novel come to understand that the space of the school acts as a metaphor for the process by which the military makes men and women into warriors by breaking down their civilian identities and rebuilding them according to a worldview of "us versus them."

THE ARCHITECTURE OF SURVEILLANCE

The novel imagines a planet Earth on the brink of fascism. National governments have started limiting reproduction to curtail overpopulation and scarcity of resources, and they also control the flow of communication between people.

The protagonist is bullied by children at home and at school; he begins embracing violence as a means to defend himself. After Colonel Graff transports Ender to Battle School, which is on a ship far from Earth, the military commanders take special notice of his intelligence and exceptional abilities. Unknown to the students, they are being observed at all times. Being noticed or watched is important to the culture of Battle School, as is who has access to information, given that some information is manufactured for political ends.

Ender gets in a fight with one of the kids at school who attacks him. He easily defeats the kid and, although he doesn't know at the time, kills him. He is promoted from the new recruit group to the Salamander Army, which is made up of kids much older than Ender who have displayed superior leadership skills.

Ender gets into a disagreement with an army commander in the Salamander Army named Bonzo Madrid, who has always disliked Ender. Although Ender ignored Madrid's command, Ender's decision allows his unit to win the battle. Ender then is traded to the Rat Army, where he grows in skill. The military leadership is impressed when Ender is jumped by four boys and injures all of them. The teachers know that he is being attacked but continue to allow him to fend for himself. Their surveillance of Ender and the other children is part of how they exert control in creating warriors who are more focused on survival than on individual freedoms.

THE CULTURAL GEOGRAPHY OF
THE MILITARY-INDUSTRIAL COMPLEX

The students are educated in an institution that values conflict and competition. Ender eventually joins the army that Petra leads, the Phoenix Army, as a platoon leader under Petra's command, before being made commander of Dragon Army. Leadership intentionally sends him into battle with small and ill-prepared armies who have very little chance of winning due to advantages of his opponents, but he always wins. After he conquers Bonzo's army, the humiliated Bonzo attacks Ender in the shower room, and Ender defeats him, learning only later that Bonzo died of his injuries. Ender is promoted to Command School. Orson Scott Card reveals a military command that ironically rewards brutality under the guise of building soldiers who can keep the rest of the population safe.

Ender travels with Colonel Graff to Eros, the location of the International Fleet command, and meets Mazer Rackham. Rackham is considered a hero who saved mankind in the second bugger invasion. He tells Ender all about the buggers, sophisticated insectlike beings whose attacks are highly coordinated because they can all communicate directly with their queen. Ender is put to the task of fighting the buggers in small simulated battles, which he wins, but with many casualties. He soon starts having nightmares about the buggers. Here, Card depicts the cultural issue of post-traumatic stress disorder (PTSD) as an outcome of the way that the military command pushes soldiers to commit acts that have negative psychological effects.

Orson Scott Card includes a twist in the narrative to offer commentary on how soldiers sometimes feel betrayed by officers' wartime decisions, which may not always take individual soldiers into account. In the military, this situation can happen because of the way in which details of operations are considered "need to know," meaning that only certain people are deemed worthy of certain information. This is done to achieve certain strategic outcomes because increasing the amount of people who know information about a battle strategy, for instance, increases the chance that this information could fall into the wrong hands.

Ender is sent into a large and highly complex battle that all the officers watch. When he wins, destroying the buggers, the commanders then reveal that the battles with the buggers were real the whole time, and that Ender has nearly wiped out the bugger race. They explain that they pretended it was just a game so he would not be hampered in his decisions by the loss of life, and also that they needed a child to lead the battle because his empathy would help him understand the enemy, how they operate. Ender and his teachers realize that he has been used by the commanders. Moreover, the latter have manufactured the war against the buggers to keep people united against a common enemy and to maintain control.

Orson Scott Card concludes his novel on a hopeful note, however, setting out his vision for peace and reconciliation. Ender and his sister decide to go in search of surviving buggers. When they find some, they realize they can communicate with them telepathically, and that the buggers had been monitoring Ender's mind the whole time, knowing he would defeat them. Ender and his sister learn that the creatures never wanted to attack humans, but that the governments of the world were starting wars with them to go after their resources. The military's "us versus them" mentality could not conceive that this other race wanted to live peacefully with them. He decides to help a "queen bugger" find a new planet to populate with her race. His choice to help the defeated buggers rebuild is one that suggests the need for reparation and cooperation after the devastation of war.

Lacar Musgrove and Lynn Marie Houston

Further Reading

The Hunger Games, by Suzanne Collins, is a series of novels that also imagines children and young adults pitted against each other for survival, and a society controlled by a fascist government. A similar scenario is imagined in the *Divergent* series by Veronica Roth. J. K. Rowling's *Harry Potter,* of course, seems to be a common inspiration for all of these works. Although *Ender's Game* and the others novels mentioned here have no "magic" in them, they feature various technological devices that seem magical.

Bibliography

Blackmore, Tim. "Ender's Beginning: Battling the Military in Orson Scott Card's *Ender's Game*." *Extrapolation* 32, no. 2 (1991): 124–42.

Collings, Michael R. *In the Image of God: Theme, Characterization, and Landscape in the Fiction of Orson Scott Card.* Westport, CT: Greenwood Publishing Group, 1990.

Day, Sara K. "Liars and Cheats: Crossing the Lines of Childhood, Adulthood, and Morality in *Ender's Game*." *ESC: English Studies in Canada* 38, no. 3 (2012): 207–25.

Doyle, Christine, and Susan Louise Stewart. "*Ender's Game* and *Ender's Shadow:* Orson Scott Card's Postmodern School Stories." *The Lion and the Unicorn* 28, no. 2 (2004): 186–202.

Hantke, Steffen. "Surgical Strikes and Prosthetic Warriors: The Soldier's Body in Contemporary Science Fiction." *Science Fiction Studies* (1998): 495–509.

Heidkamp, Bernie. "Responses to the Alien Mother in Post-Maternal Cultures: CJ Cherryh and Orson Scott Card." *Science Fiction Studies* (1996): 339–54.

Langford, Jonathan D. "In the Image of God: Theme, Characterization, and Landscape in the Fiction of Orson Scott Card." *Contributions to the Study of Science Fiction and Fantasy,* 42 (1992): 210–15.

Malmgren, Carl D. "Self and Other in SF: Alien Encounters." *Science Fiction Studies* (1993): 15–33.

Newcomb, Erin Wyble. "Orson Scott Card's *Ender's Game*." In *The Gothic Fairy Tale in Young Adult Literature: Essays on Stories from Grimm to Gaiman,* edited by Joseph Abbruscato and Tanya Jones, 47. Jefferson, NC: McFarland & Co., 2014.

An Enemy of the People

Written in Dano-Norwegian with the title *En folkefiende* (1882), Henrik Ibsen's play explores a conflict between economic profit and environmental safety. The main character, Dr. Stockmann, discovers that the natural springs baths about to open up in the town are polluted and will cause health issues to anyone who uses them. His news is ill received by his brother, the town's mayor, because the baths were a huge financial investment and are expected to bring much-needed tourism to the area. Many characters, including his father-in-law, Morten Kiil, try to talk Stockmann out of going public with this information and even threaten him and his family. Thwarted by the newspaper in his attempt to publish an article announcing the contamination of the springs, Dr. Stockmann organizes a town meeting instead. He gets frustrated at the meeting and launches into a tirade against "the authorities" and "the majority." The townspeople present are greatly insulted and call him "an enemy of the people." They threaten to vandalize his house, but Stockmann continues, even telling his father-in-law that his tannery is contributing to the polluted waters. The next day, the price of stocks in the baths falls, and the town has turned against Stockmann: his windows have been smashed by rocks, he loses his job, his daughter is kicked out of school, and he finds out that he is being evicted and that no one in town will hire him in a new position. Morten Kiil arrives to tell them that he has invested all of the family's inheritance money in the baths to keep Stockmann from exposing the contamination. Ibsen ends the play on a bleak note: Stockmann has had to give up everything he has worked for to do what he believes is the right thing.

POLLUTION OF LAND AND POLITICS: THE ROLE OF SCIENCE

In *An Enemy of the People,* Ibsen uses the pollution of the baths as a symbol of a corrupt political system. At first, the reporters at the newspaper agree to publish Stockmann's article because they have been waging a campaign against the "backdoor deals" of the town's political elite. However, they change their minds because of the harm the news will do to everyone in town, not just the authorities. By the end of the play, Stockmann realizes that complacency of the masses is the real pollution in his society, the fact that people are so willing to just go along with the status quo instead of taking a moral stand, like Stockmann does. None of them seem to take seriously the damage that has been caused and that will be further caused by remaining silent about the water pollution.

The play takes up a moment in Norway's history when it is having an awkward time of transitioning out of its agrarian past and into a modern, industrial present. Stockmann has unwittingly become a part of that past in marrying his wife, as her family has been in the tanning business for at least three generations. The process of tanning animal hides to make leather takes a high environmental toll. Even this source of revenue, although enriching Morten Kiil, has failed to save the family or the town. Ibsen may want readers to ask, in terms of the human geography in this play, who should feel more isolated—Stockmann, the sole proponent of environmental cleanup whose purpose is community-minded, or the upper-class members of the community whose morality has been compromised by the pursuit of profits that cannot save their town or future generations.

At a larger level, the play asks questions about the ethics of science. When a scientist discovers a problem, is it right to report it at all costs? This play draws attention to how facts can and do get used for the agenda of the person who knows and controls them.

Lynn Marie Houston

Further Reading

Other European playwrights writing in the 19th century whose plays dealt with realistic social issues are August Strindberg and Anton Chekhov. Together with Ibsen, these three writers are known for bringing the literary movement of modernism to European theater.

Bibliography

Adler, Thomas P. "Conscience and Community in *An Enemy of the People* and *The Crucible*." In *Arthur Miller's* The Crucible, edited by Harold Bloom, 69–82. New York: Bloom's Literary Criticism, 2008.

Cless, Downing. *Ecology and Environment in European Drama.* New York: Routledge, 2010.

Garaventa, Eugene. "*An Enemy of the People,* by Henrik Ibsen: The Politics of Whistle-Blowing." *Journal of Management Inquiry* 3.4 (1994): 369–74.

Holledge, Julie, Jonathan Bollen, Frode Helland, and Joanne Tompkins. "Mapping the Early Noras." In *A Global Doll's House.* London: Palgrave Macmillan, 2016.

Lindholdt, Paul. "Greening the Dramatic Canon: Henrik Ibsen's *An Enemy of the People.*" *Interdisciplinary Literary Studies* 3, no. 1 (2001): 53–65.

Rees, Ellen. "Problems of Landscape and Representation in Ibsen's 'Når vi døde vågner.'" *Ibsen Studies* 10, no. 1 (2010): 37–61. doi:10.1080/15021866.2010.495533.

Sweeting, Adam, and Thomac C. Crochunis. "Performing the Wild: Rethinking Wilderness and Theater Spaces." In *Beyond Nature Writing: Expanding the Boundaries of Ecocriticism,* edited by Karla Armbruster and Kathleen R. Wallace. Charlottesville: University Press of Virginia, 2001.

Torrissen, Wenche. "Geographies of Superstition, Myths, Freedom: Ibsen and Northern Norway." *Hjem* 34 (2015). doi:10.7557/13.3366.

Varley, Peter, and Tristan Semple. "Nordic Slow Adventure: Explorations in Time and Nature." *Scandinavian Journal of Hospitality and Tourism* 15, no. 1–2 (2015): 73–90. doi:10.1080/15022250.2015.1028142.

Extremely Loud & Incredibly Close

Jonathan Safran Foer, popularly deemed a "wunderkind," published his second novel, *Extremely Loud & Incredibly Close* in 2005, just three years after his first highly acclaimed novel, *Everything Is Illuminated* (2002). He was only 25 when *Everything Is Illuminated* was published; he wrote the novel as an undergraduate at Princeton, working closely with Joyce Carol Oates. Both novels are set with a backdrop of a significant world tragedy: *Everything Is Illuminated* occurs in the shadow of the Holocaust, while *Extremely Loud & Incredibly Close* is set during and shortly after the terrorist attacks on 9/11, with some flashbacks to the World War II Dresden bombings and bombings of Hiroshima. Foer's depiction of post-9/11 New York City is incredibly and poignantly told through the perspective of a precocious nine-year-old, Oskar Schell, son of 9/11 victim Thomas Schell. New York in the immediate wake of 9/11 is a geographically, socially, and culturally unique landscape that Foer reveals humanistically through his child narrator.

THE CITY: BEFORE AND AFTER 9/11

The fractured narrative structure of the book mimetically represents the fracturing of New York following the 9/11 attacks. The novel opens with the book's chronologically last moment, but the book itself does not seem to follow a prescribed plot structure. However, the book alternates between chapters from Oskar's perspective two years after the 9/11 attacks, depicting the events during and immediately following. Even in reflection, Oskar is prodigiously precocious, observing events around him with great astuteness. Oskar recalls "reconnaissance expeditions" that his father sent him on, asking him to find artifacts around the city based on obscure and sometime abstract clues. After Thomas Schell dies, Oskar finds what he believes to be a clue: a key, labeled "Black," at the bottom of a vase in the top of his closet. The novel follows Oskar's search, at least superficially, for the lock that fits the key. On a deeper level, though, Oskar is in fact searching for a connection to his father and to community.

The geographical and physical landscape of New York City changed drastically following 9/11. Not only were the mammoth landmarks of the twin towers no longer present in the Lower Manhattan sky, but many New Yorkers, including Oskar, felt that they could no longer trust the subways, the mode of transportation that had always functioned as a lifeline of the city, connecting uptown to downtown, borough to borough. After the attacks, though, the subway lines were fractured. No longer could one travel seamlessly from point to point. Oskar's apparent trauma following his father's death leads him to be afraid of the subways as well as elevators and upper floors of buildings. Oskar's search for the owner of the key, therefore, must occur entirely aboveground, but not *too* far above. Seeing the key labeled "Black," Oskar determines that the key must belong to someone named Black. Although he has experience searching geographically with the clues that his father gave him, Oskar's search is no longer geographically logical; rather than search for Blacks by borough or neighborhood, he searches alphabetically, often crossing or crisscrossing large parts of the city in a day. Without his father's guidance, Oskar's formerly familiar landscape is defamiliarized.

THE PLACE OF FAMILY

In the same way that Oskar's father was the center of his world, the twin towers were, for many New Yorkers, at center of the world. The towers and Thomas are simultaneously destroyed on 9/11, leaving Oskar, like many New Yorkers and Americans, searching. Oskar must now search for some connection to his father in the same way that New Yorkers must search for meaning in the disaster. On the most literal level, Oskar is searching for a lock that fits a key. Though his search seems hopeless, he does eventually find its owner, but the owner is not what he expects. So on the most literal level, Oskar's search is a success: he has found the lock that fits the key. On a more figurative, yet still tangible, level, Oskar is searching for a connection to his father. He hopes that the key will unlock something that will make sense of his father's death for him, or at least make sense of some part of his father's life. When the key turns out to be something that his father did not even know that he had, Oskar's search seems to fail on this level. He has not found what he set out to find.

On the deepest level, Oskar is on a search for meaning, rebuilding, and community. And on this level, the search is a success. Although Oskar has not found what he initially wants, he has found what he needs. His search begins alone, sneaking out of his apartment and concealing his activities from his mother, or so he thinks. After visiting a few Blacks on his own, he teams up with Mr. A. R. Black, the first Black he visits. He also befriends many other Blacks, many of whom attend his school play, where he plays Yorick, a disembodied skull, in an elementary school production of *Hamlet*. Oskar is also able to provide closure for William Black, the son of the key's owner and husband of Abby Black, to whom Oskar makes his second visit. At the end of his journey, Oskar discovers that he hasn't been alone on his journey; his mother has been a step ahead of him the entire time. So although Oskar cannot recover his father, he can find something valuable nonetheless. He has found a community with his mother, his mother's friend Ron, and the city full of Blacks. Though he initially butts heads with his mother because he disagrees with how she mourns his father, by the end of the novel, he confesses, "I don't believe in God, but I believe that things are extremely complicated, and her looking over me was as complicated as anything ever could be. But it was also incredibly simple. In my only life, she was my mom, and I was her son."

POST-POSTMODERN REDEMPTION

In early postmodernism, searches were relatively typical plot devices, but they highlighted nihilism, emptiness, and games. The postmodern searches were marked by fraudulent searches for something that was never there to begin with, such as Holden Caulfield's search for authenticity in J. D. Salinger's *The Catcher in the Rye*, and Oedipa Maas's search for the meaning of the Trystero system in Thomas Pynchon's *The Crying of Lot 49*. Although on the surface, Oskar's search may seem fruitless, he finds a community at which he is now center. He does not need his father to center his world; he now centers his own, exemplifying the redemptive nature the late-postmodern novel.

Andrea Laurencell Sheridan

Further Reading

Other novels about the September 11 tragedy that approach the aftermath in the lives of ordinary New Yorkers include Don DeLillo's *Falling Man,* Jay McInerney's *The Good Life,* Amy Waldman's *The Submission.*

Bibliography

Brandt, Stefan L. "The City as Liminal Space: Urban Visuality and Aesthetic Experience in Postmodern U.S. Literature and Cinema." *Amerikastudien/American Studies* 54, no. 4 (2009): 553–81. www.jstor.org/stable/41158465.

Fitzgerald, Andrew Robert. "Millennial Fiction and the Emergence of Posthuman Cosmopolitanism." PhD diss., University of Washington, 2011.

Lynn, Marie Elizabeth. "The Place of Story and the Story of Place: How the Convergence of Text and Image Marks the Opening of a New Literary Frontier." Master's thesis, Montana State University, 2007.

Robertson Wojcik, Pamela. *Fantasies of Neglect: Imagining the Urban Child in American Film and Fiction.* New Brunswick, NJ: Rutgers University Press, 2016.

Snyman, Adalet. "Complex Urban Identities: An Investigation into the Everyday Lived Realities of Cities as Reflected in Selected Postmodern Texts." Master's thesis, University of Stellenbosch, 2010.

Tsiokou, Katerina. "Reading the Cityscape in Post-9/11 Fiction: Urban Manifestations of Trauma and National Identity in Don DeLillo's *Falling Man* and Joseph O'Neill's *Netherland*." Master's thesis, Aristotle University of Thessaloniki, 2017.

Turner, Kathleen Marie. "'My Life Story Was Spaces': Marginalized Women Maneuvering Urban Environments in Literature and Film." PhD diss., Northern Illinois University, 2013.

F

"The Fall of the House of Usher"

Nineteenth-century American author Edgar Allan Poe managed to transcend a troubled life to write among the most iconic fiction and poetry in American letters. He often protested that he was not a fiction specialist, but his stories make clear the effort and energy he took to structure them for maximum horrific effect. Among the best known, and there are many, is "The Fall of the House of Usher." In it, Poe used a technique he perfected in "The Tell-Tale Heart" of the unnamed and almost unknown narrator. The narrator of "The Fall of the House of Usher" is a man who as a child was friends with another boy, Roderick Usher. This is nearly all that Poe tells readers about the narrator. The story begins with the narrator, having received a letter from his onetime friend, on his way to visit Roderick. The experience is unpleasant and his initial meeting with Roderick is not reassuring because the man has become too thin and is ill. The narrator briefly glimpses Roderick's sister Madeline. She too is emaciated and ill. The suggestion here is that the Usher family line is not long for this world; however, much mystery surrounds its demise.

THE GEOGRAPHY OF PLACE

Part of the appeal of "The Fall of the House of Usher" is Poe's decision not to reveal too much about where the Ushers live. One gains from the narrator a sense that the land is desolate, barren, and devoid of anything that might have cheered his soul. Perhaps one might guess a setting in a semiarid region, but this supposition does not appear to accord with the storm that the narrator and Roderick experience in the ancient mansion. To be sure, there is nothing lush about the region, ruling out the tropics or subtropics. This accords with the experiences of Poe, who lived his life in the temperate zone. A temperate zone setting thus seems plausible, but one devoid of anything healthful or beautiful. One gathers that the narrator must travel far on horseback, day after day, through a bleak landscape to reach the Ushers. Poe wrote the story only about a decade after the invention of the railroad locomotive, so it is not surprising that he did not feature a more rapid means of transport. One might suppose that a quick trek through the country would have weakened the effect that Poe attempted to create, though later in the 19th century, Irish author Bram Stoker used the train skillfully to bring the lawyer Jonathan Harker to Transylvania in the novel *Dracula*.

THE GEOGRAPHY OF THE HOUSE OF USHER

Poe used the phrase "house of Usher" in two ways. First, he wished to convey the family of Usher, of which nothing remained but brother and sister. Second, and perhaps more obvious, Poe meant the house, the physical structure in which Roderick and Madeline resided. In one sense, Poe, like his description of the geography of place, is not as precise as one might wish. One does not know, for example, how many stories the house contains, though one has the impression that it is large. One does not know how old the house is, though again the impression is obvious enough for one to assert great antiquity. Even though readers do not know all the details, the narrator makes clear that the house has an entranceway that leads to what one might call the first floor. Living quarters are upstairs, though the number of upper floors and rooms is unclear. In addition, the house contains what might be called a basement, though a subterranean chamber might better convey its attributes.

Although the narrator first glimpses Madeline Usher on the first floor, most of the action takes place above and below this level. Madeline is as inscrutable as the narrator, perhaps more so because she never utters a word. The narrator remarks that she is beautiful, but one does not know whether he lusts after her. Madeline is typical of the women who populate Poe's stories and poems: white, brunette, and too slender. Like the other women, Madeline is doomed. Roderick confides to his friend that Madeline is susceptible to cataleptic states in which she is so still and her breathing so shallow that she appears to be dead, even though she is not. This confession will become significant even though it does not appear to resonate with the narrator at the moment.

One day Roderick tells the narrator that Madeline has died. Presumably this occurred in an upper room, but the geography of action now descends to the subterranean chamber. The place must be dark and dank and easy to conceive as a source of evil. That is, one has entered the geography of evil. With the narrator's help, Roderick places Madeline in an aboveground crypt. In other words, she is not interred. Such a choice should be satisfactory, but Roderick and the narrator go one step too far. They screw down the lid on her coffin. If she were dead, why would such action be necessary? Here, it is puzzling that the narrator makes no comment about the wisdom of this action. Can he not have known that Madeline was alive by this action and nonetheless have chosen to restrict her? He knew she was cataleptic

This drawing by Arthur Rackham illustrates the arrival of Poe's narrator at the house of Roderick and Madeline Usher. He captures the decay of the architectural structure before it sinks into the bog, signifying the end of the Usher lineage. (Culture Club/Getty Images)

yet appears not to have considered the fact that she might have swooned rather than actually died. Perhaps the narrator did know and wanted Madeline dead as much as Roderick did. Whatever the conjectures and answers, it seems clear that the entombment of Madeline marks the nadir in this geography of malevolence.

This task accomplished, the narrator and Roderick retire to their upstairs bedrooms. Neither can sleep. The narrator attributes his restlessness to the approach of a storm, though guilt may be the real cause. He enters Roderick's room to find him agitated and the windows open. The narrator attempts to restore calm by reading an old story to Roderick. The violence of its actions mirrors the situation in the subterranean chamber. Madeline awakens to find herself entombed. One might expect that such a frail woman of ill health would die of fright or exhaustion, but she summons the ferocity to break free from her crypt. Knowing what Roderick and the narrator have done, she exacts revenge, pulling Roderick to the ground when she reaches him. The narrator comments that he is dead, but morally he has been dead the entire story. The geography of evil ends in the geography of death, the final destination of us all. The narrator escapes though nothing can expiate his culpability.

Christopher Cumo

Further Reading

Bram Stoker has a story about the unexpected evil that can happen when a student rents an old dilapidated house for some peace and quiet. "The Judge's House" picks up the same theme of how the fates of past tenants linger on in a house and affect those who inhabit it afterward. Henry James's novella *The Beast in the Jungle* explores a similar tale of a woman who loves a man who feels he is doomed by fate. Ultimately, this is a more realistic story, lacking the theatrics of Poe's story of doomed siblings in "The Fall of the House of Usher."

Bibliography

Baym, Nina, Ronald Gottesman, Laurence B. Holland, Francis Murphy, Hershel Parker, William B. Pritchard, and David Kalstone. *The Norton Anthology of American Literature,* 2nd ed. New York: W. W. Norton, 1986.

Bowers, Katherine. "Haunted Ice, Fearful Sounds, and the Arctic Sublime: Exploring Nineteenth-Century Polar Gothic Space." *Gothic Studies* 19, no. 2 (2017): 71–84. doi:10.7227/GS.0030.

Davenport, Guy. *The Geography of the Imagination: Forty Essays.* Boston: David R. Godine, 1954.

Forbes, Erin E. "Edgar Allan Poe and the Great Dismal Swamp: Reading Race and Environment after the Aesthetic Turn." *Modern Philology* 114, no. 2 (2016): 359–87. doi:10.1086/687366.

Garcia, Patricia. "The Architectural Void: Space as Transgression in Postmodern Short Fiction of the Fantastic (1974–2010)." PhD diss., Dublin City University, 2013.

Hsu, Hsuan L. *Geography and the Production of Space in Nineteenth-Century American Literature.* Cambridge, UK: Cambridge University Press, 2010.

Lutwack, Leonard. *The Role of Place in Literature.* Syracuse, NY: Syracuse University Press, 1984.

Monahan, Peter Friedrich. "The American Wild Man: The Science and Theatricality of Nondescription in the Works of Edgar Allan Poe, Jack London, and Djuna Barnes." PhD diss., Washington University, 2008.

Redding, Arthur. "Burial Grounds and Dead Lovers: Places of Interment in the Gothic Modernism of the American South." *AVANT* 8, no. 2 (2017).
Silverman, Kenneth. *Edgar A. Poe: Mournful and Never-Ending Remembrance.* New York: HarperPerennial, 1991.
Tuan, Yi-Fu. *Romantic Geography: In Search of the Sublime Landscape.* Madison: University of Wisconsin Press, 2013.
Varnado, S. L. *Haunted Presence: The Numinous in Gothic Fiction.* Tuscaloosa: University of Alabama Press, 1987.
Wirth-Nesher, Hana. "Impartial Maps: Reading and Writing Cities." In *Handbook of Urban Studies,* edited by Ronan Paddison. London: SAGE Publications, 2001.

Fear and Loathing in Las Vegas

Hunter S. Thompson published *Fear and Loathing in Las Vegas* as a serial story in *Rolling Stone* magazine in 1971 before publishing it as a book the following year. The story narrates a trip to Las Vegas taken by Raoul Duke and his attorney, Dr. Gonzo, the purpose of which is ostensibly to cover the Mint 400 motorcycle race for a news outlet. However, their journey turns into a surreal drug binge, during which they search for the American dream.

LAS VEGAS AS A SYMBOL FOR AMERICA

Las Vegas is the site where the top members of the national press convene to cover the Mint 400, but instead of acting as "professionals," in Thompson's story the journalists are drinking heavily, carousing, and generally availing themselves of all the pleasures Las Vegas has to offer. The activities of the other members of the press legitimize Raoul Duke's behavior, but they also call attention to a culture that views a work assignment as a pretext for excess, and that pits some kind of agents of control (the people running the Mint 400, the staff members of hotels, or law enforcement) against citizens who constantly seek greater excesses of pleasure. Raoul and Dr. Gonzo goad each other into increased consumption under the pretense of "needing" it to do the job.

As Raoul engages in heavy drug and alcohol use during the race, he starts to question how to cover the events of the race in a news story. Essentially, what is revealed is that the job is a mere pretense for the consumption. Raoul and Dr. Gonzo do so many drugs that they drive over curbs and have to hold each other up to walk. They invent stories about this to avoid suspicion—they often cite needing the drugs

---

San Francisco in the middle sixties was a very special time and place to be a part of. Maybe it meant something. Maybe not, in the long run ... but no explanation, no mix of words or music or memories can touch that sense of knowing that you were there and alive in that corner of time and the world. Whatever it meant ...
Hunter S. Thompson, *Fear and Loathing in Las Vegas* (1972)

as "medicine" for heart conditions, or they claim to know someone famous as a way to avoid trouble. Las Vegas helps to camouflage them—a pair of staggering buddies might be in town to celebrate a wedding. However, the two visit the Circus-Circus Hotel while on an ether trip and their relationship to Las Vegas changes. Raoul claims that the bizarre scenes in that hotel could freak out even any regular acid user. It's as if the scenes of Las Vegas are more bizarre than any hallucination that can be conjured by drugs. The indictment here to American culture is that we always seek to escape our daily lives by any means possible.

The absence of any notion of limits here underscores an American exceptionalism and points to troubled practices of consumption. The text also offers commentary on American moral consciousness. It upends a Puritan-inspired notion that good things happen to people who comport themselves with dignity and righteousness. Raoul Duke and Dr. Gonzo get away with scamming the system, taking a free trip to Vegas, and indulging whatever drug-inspired whim they have. Nothing and no one can keep them in check, except their own sense of boundaries, which are few. In this way, they explore the contours of the American dream. They do whatever they can simply because they can, not because it is particularly enjoyable, but because they feel compelled to seek pleasure at all times and at all costs. With references to a top-of-the-line motorcycle, the Vincent Black Shadow, and lies about being close personal friends of celebrities, the two intimidate those who threaten to expose them as high or who get between them and their intake of illegal substances.

ROAD TRAVEL AND SETTLEMENT OF THE WEST

Fear and Loathing in Las Vegas begins with preparations in Los Angeles. Raoul is drinking with his attorney when he gets the call offering him the job, for which the news outlet will pay his expenses in Las Vegas and also give him a cash advance. The two use the cash to purchase the necessary items for their trip: convertible rental car, drugs, alcohol, recording equipment, and Hawaiian shirts. Some of the first drug-fueled hallucinations are while they are driving through the desert to get to Nevada. Raoul pulls over after he has to swerve the car to avoid bats that his attorney does not appear to see. They pick up a hitchhiker and it is unclear from the narrative exactly what is said aloud versus what are unspoken thoughts in the main character's mind, but the result is that the hitchhiker appears extremely scared of the duo, so much so that he jumps out of the car when they stop to do more drugs. This opening section of the book includes some reflections about the American car culture, especially the American love of large automobiles. The two drive through the desert at high speed, alternating between worries of getting stopped by law enforcement and anxiety over not making it to the press check-in on time. During much of their time in the car, whether on the drive there or on the streets of Las Vegas, the duo do drugs and play loud music. They are a danger and nuisance to others. The notion of the automobile as an extension of one's public persona and as a site of entertainment, rather than functionality, is underscored by the convertible in which the travel.

THE SURREAL LANDSCAPE OF HALLUCINOGENIC DRUGS

The desert scenery blends with the urban setting of Las Vegas in the drug hallucinations of Raoul and Dr. Gonzo. The nature of their imaginative visions pick up desert motifs: during the press registration at the hotel and their arrival at their hotel room, they imagine reptiles and snakes in the place of the people and infrastructure that exists. The desert becomes the inspiration for their pursuit of excess, just as it was a blank slate for the businessmen who built Las Vegas as a tourist destination for travelers.

Las Vegas thrives on the loss of inhibitions. By giving free drinks to gamblers, the casinos try to ensure that they feel less inhibited about spending money. This is ultimately what the long drug binge in *Fear and Loathing in Las Vegas* draws our attention to: the duo is able to get away with their shenanigans because consumer culture is already so bizarre and yet we're taught that it's completely normal. Two guys who are high on almost every conceivable mix of hallucinogenic drugs don't even stand out in a crowd.

Lynn Marie Houston

Further Reading

If you liked *Fear and Loathing in Las Vegas,* then you might like Hubert Selby Jr.'s *Requiem for a Dream;* it is also a story about lives severely affected by drugs and depicts a family's spiral into impending tragedy. A work that similarly signals the end of American innocence in the 1960s is *The Electric Kool-Aid Acid Test* by Tom Wolfe, a nonfiction book about the inception of the hippie movement. Another good recommendation is *Dispatches* by Michael Herr, a New Journalism book about a war correspondent's experience in Vietnam.

Bibliography

Anleu, Sharyn R., Bill Martin, and Maria Zadoroznyi. "Editor's Introduction to the Special Issue: 'Fear and Loathing in the New Century.'" *Journal of Sociology* 40, no. 4 (2004): 315–19.

Banco, Lindsey M. "Trafficking Trips: Drugs and the Anti-Tourist Novels of Hunter S. Thompson and Alex Garland." *Studies in Travel Writing* 11, no. 2 (2007): 127–53. doi:10.1080/13645145.2007.9634825.

Brandt, Stefan L. "The City as Liminal Space: Urban Visuality and Aesthetic Experience in Postmodern U.S. Literature and Cinema." *Amerikastudien/American Studies* 54, no. 4 (2009): 553–81. www.jstor.org/stable/41158465.

Hellmann, John. "Corporate Fiction, Private Fable, and Hunter S. Thompson's Fear and Loathing: On the Campaign Trail '72." *Critique* 21, no. 1 (1979): 16–31.

Self, Will. *Psychogeography: Disentangling the Modern Conundrum of Psyche and Place.* New York: Bloomsbury USA, 2007.

Sims, Norman. "Tourist in a Strange Land: Tom Wolfe and the New Journalists." In *True Stories: A Century of Literary Journalism.* Evanston: Northwestern University Press, 2007.

Weber, Ronald, ed. *Reporter as Artist: A Look at the New Journalism Controversy.* New York: Hastings House, 1974.

Weingarten, Marc. *The Gang that Wouldn't Write Straight: Wolfe, Thompson, Didion, and the New Journalism Revolution.* New York: Crown, 2006.

Wolfe, Tom, and E. W. Johnson. *The New Journalism.* New York: Harper & Row, 1973.

Frankenstein

To correct the most common inaccuracy about the novel *Frankenstein*, the title does not refer to any sort of monster or dangerous creation. The title refers to the last name of scientist Victor Frankenstein, who arranged and then animated this creature of fear. If the scientist is a monster because of his actions, then one might revive the monster hypothesis but not in its original form. Author Mary Wollstonecraft Shelley meant *Frankenstein* to be a horror story. If it succeeds in this ambition, then science emerges as the culprit, or perhaps one should say the "sciences" because many types of scientists pursue different avenues of research. In this instance, the sciences and more particularly scientists deserve blame for hubris, for tinkering with the membrane that separates life and death and for daring to create life out of death. In this sense, *Frankenstein* is a warning, a cautionary tale about the mistake of placing too much faith in the sciences. If this is true, *Frankenstein* opposes the 18th-century Enlightenment in its faith in scientific and technological progress. Shelley's position seems to be that progress comes at a cost.

THE GEOGRAPHY OF PLACE

Frankenstein opens on a ship trapped in ice in what must have been Arctic waters. This setting captures the reality of life in Europe in 1816, the year Shelley conceived her novel. Mount Tambora on an Indonesian island had erupted in April 1815, spewing a thick layer of ash into the atmosphere. This ash spread throughout the air, blocking some of the sun's rays from reaching Earth. The entire globe suffered as temperatures dropped and crops failed. Snow fell in July and August in parts of Canada, the northern United States, and Europe. Consequently, Shelley and her friends Lord Byron and John William Polidori, a physician turned author, experienced 1816 as the "year without a summer." It was as though a brief ice age had recaptured Earth and inspired Shelley to create throughout *Frankenstein* an atmosphere pervaded by cold, anguish, and chills. The novel reflected the reality of the time.

SCIENCE AND THE LITERARY LANDSCAPE

The 19th century confronted Mary Shelley and everyone else in Europe with a series of scientific breakthroughs. British naturalist Charles Darwin forever changed the relationship between humans and all other life. He seemed as well to have altered the relationship between humanity and its god. This is one way of saying that the sciences unleashed revolutionary ideas in Europe. Perhaps the greatest excitement celebrated what seemed to be the new phenomenon of electricity. In retrospect, it is clear that the ancient Greeks knew—at a minimum—of static electricity, and some advances were made in the 18th century. But the 19th century seemed to offer the greatest promise. British physicist Michael Faraday invented an electric motor. Particularly intriguing were those scientists who sought the vital forces of life in electricity. A number of physicists and experimenters, the Italian physicists Luigi Galvani and Alessandro Volta deserve the most credit, demonstrated that an electrode touched to the nerves of a severed frog's leg caused the leg to leap repeatedly as though revivified. Grander experiments were conceived in which dead men, usually executed criminals, sat up, opened their eyes, and seemed almost alive when probed with electrodes. The correct conclusion was drawn that life, including humans, is an electrochemical machine. The additional conclusion that electricity was the phenomenon that animated life is more difficult to substantiate.

But in the 19th century, Mary Shelley responded to the lifelike properties of electricity. Her protagonist Victor Frankenstein performed all the requisite experiments to attempt to reanimate a corpse. He combined parts of one corpse with those of another. In short, he assumed the role of God in arranging and creating life. The Genesis account made clear that only God could create life, but Frankenstein inhabited a world in which this story was poetry not reality. He succeeded in his endeavor, and his monster quickly displayed superhuman strength and other uncommon abilities. The monster left Frankenstein's laboratory with the desire to obey no one but himself. The science of electricity, coupled with Frankenstein's hubris, created a demon that ruined the lives of others, including an innocent girl condemned to death for a crime he committed.

THE GEOGRAPHY OF HORROR

Many literary scholars agree that horror is a difficult state to induce in readers. That summer of 1816 Mary Shelley, Lord Byron, and Polidori had agreed that each would write a horror story. Mary was alone in completing the task, at least on a sufficient scale, though Polidori may have written the first vampire tale. She succeeded because she was attuned to the immediate weather, or perhaps one should say aberration, and to the dangers of the sciences. Why she picked on physics and the physics of electricity, in particular, is not entirely clear, but she saw the danger of trying to induce life among the dead. American author Edgar Allan Poe played upon this theme in "The Premature Burial," but *Frankenstein* existed on another plane in which it was possible for the sciences to wreck humanity. In this sense, *Frankenstein* is perhaps a cautionary tale that might resonate among those who pursue artificial intelligence, for there is no guarantee that a machine capable of cognition will decide to obey humans. Just as Frankenstein's monster defied and destroyed humans, intelligent machines might do the same. This is the horror of modern life that Shelley intuited in 1816. That is, *Frankenstein* depicts a horror that is still with us and may be inextricably part of the human condition.

Christopher Cumo

Further Reading

If you liked *Frankenstein*, then you might like Matthew Lewis' *The Monk* as a story that also scrutinizes human morality about one man's quest for gratification that leads to the ruin of innocent others. A more modern work that similarly questions humanity's role in nature is *Monster* by Dave Zeltserman, in which a man seeks vengeance after awakening on a lab table after being unwillingly mutilated and transformed into a gruesome monster. Another good recommendation is Sarah Maria Griffin's *Spare and Found*

Parts, which is about a society destroyed by an epidemic and a young woman's experiment to create her own companion out of artificial technology.

Bibliography

Dobson, Teresa, and Rebecca Luce-Kapler. "Stitching Texts: Gender and Geography in *Frankenstein* and *Patchwork Girl.*" *Changing English* 12, no. 2 (2005): 265–77. doi:10.1080/13586840500164540.

Hindle, Maurice. *Mary Shelley, Frankenstein, or, the Modern Prometheus.* London: Penguin Books, 1994.

Knellwolf King, Christa. "Geographic Boundaries and Inner Space: Frankenstein, Scientific Explorations and the Quest for the Absolute." In *Mary Shelley: Frankenstein,* edited by J. Paul Hunter. Norton Critical Editions, 2012.

Mehtonen, P. M., and Matti Savolainen, eds. *Gothic Topographies: Language, Nation Building and "Race."* London: Routledge, 2016.

Parui, Avishek. "Masculinity, Monstrosity, and Sustainability in Mary Shelley's *Frankenstein.*" In *Romantic Sustainability: Endurance and the Natural World, 1780–1830,* edited by Ben P. Robertson. Lanham: Lexington Books, 2016.

Rigby, Kate. *Topographies of the Sacred: The Poetics of Place in European Romanticism.* Charlottesville: University of Virginia Press, 2004.

Seed, David. *A Companion to Science Fiction.* Malden, MA: Blackwell Publishing, 2005.

Shoene-Harwood, Berthold. *Mary Shelley, Frankenstein.* New York: Columbia University Press, 2000.

Willis, Alexander J. "Boundless Explorations: Global Spaces and Travel in the Literature of William Wordsworth, Percy Shelley, and Mary Shelley." PhD diss., University of Toronto, 2011. http://hdl.handle.net/1807/29908.

Frost, Robert

Robert Frost never graduated from college, but he received many honorary degrees and successfully made a career out of both writing and teaching. Well read in both literature and philosophy, he was one of the most celebrated poets of his time and was awarded four Pulitzer Prizes, among many other honors. Although he spent his childhood in California and his early adulthood in England, once he moved to New Hampshire, his poetry became known for speakers who have intimate knowledge of the New England landscape they inhabit. Settings in his poetry are mainly natural ones and alternate between being beautiful and cruel. In the poetry of Robert Frost, geographical features are often a metaphor for states of being.

TRADITION AND THE CHANGING LANDSCAPE

In "Mending Wall," the space where the speaker's yard meets his neighbor's becomes a litmus test for how both men think about human relations, history, and cultural change. The neighbor wants to repair the stone wall at the border between their two yards, but the speaker questions why they still bother with such an activity. The purpose of the stone wall, he reminds his neighbor, was to keep livestock confined to their owner's land, but neither one of them keeps livestock. The practice is from a previous time period, when the land was used for agricultural purposes. However, the neighbor doesn't care about how the land use has changed; he believes in the value of tradition and unthinkingly accepts the aphorism that "good fences make good neighbors."

SELF-IDENTITY

"The Road Not Taken" features a crossroads that is symbolic of life decisions that become integral to how we tell the story of who we are. The speaker walks along a path in the woods and then must decide which of the two branches to follow. Although he wishes he could take both, and he admits that both roads were about the same, he makes a choice of one, but seems to reflect wistfully about the one he did not take. At the end of the poem, the speaker promises that no matter what happens, he will point to that decision in his life and make some meaning from it when he is telling the story of how he become the person he is. The poem employs the human interaction with place as metaphor for how small decisions in our lives can be transformed into significant events when we have to account for the effects our life experiences have had on us as people.

Robert Frost is pictured on his visit to poet Wilfrid Gibson in England around 1914. Although Frost traveled to many different places during his life, his poetry was firmly entrenched in the language and traditions of rural New England. (Library of Congress)

EARTH AND DEATH

Poems like "Stopping by Woods on a Snowy Evening" and "Birches" draw attention to a natural landscape that mediates life and death. The speaker in this poem stops his sleigh in a winter landscape to contemplate death but is called back to the business of life by remembering the commitments he has to other people. In "Birches," a speaker imagines that birch trees bent by an ice storm were instead bent by a boy playing on them, but by the end the poem becomes a meditation on the how death releases us from the weariness of life and provides, perhaps, a needed renewal. It is the image of the birch tree that becomes the passageway between the worlds of life and death. In the end, the speaker reaffirms the primacy of Earth's sensual beauty for the purpose of human delight. Frost may have agreed with the Modernist sense of alienation and isolation from fellow man, but ultimately, he feels the Romantic connection to nature as a source of strength, healing, and compassion that makes the human experience bearable.

NEW ENGLAND

Robert Frost's poems are filled with the activities and images of daily life in rural New England: piles of stacked firewood, mown hay, freshly picked apples, mud-caked boots, horse-drawn sleighs, and the solitude of the countryside heightened by a stoic culture. His speakers, when they work the land, are not out-of-date anachronisms, but realistic working-class people who could better witness the beauty of Earth's sensuality as well as its brutality. Frost straddles the Romanticism of the 19th century, where nature represents renewal and salvation, and 20th-century Modernism, in which renewal and salvation are viewed as false, impossible pursuits. The resulting effect in his work is a matter-of-fact acceptance of the harsh realities of life and people's shortcomings, along with a cheeky tone of someone who peeks behind the curtain of rural life and witnesses the joy of living close to the land and the cycle of seasons.

Lynn Marie Houston

Further Reading

Other American poets who write about the beauty of rural life and the agricultural landscape are Ralph Waldo Emerson, Walt Whitman, Wendell Berry, and Gary Snyder.

Bibliography

Kates, Robert W. "The Human Environment: The Road Not Taken, the Road Still Beckoning." *Annals of the Association of American Geographers* 77, no. 4 (1987): 525–34.

Levin, Phillip S., and Leif E. Anderson. "When Good Fences Make Bad Neighbors: Overcoming Disciplinary Barriers to Improve Natural Resource Management." *Coastal Management* 44, no. 5 (2016): 370–79.

Miller, Andrew. "Taking Fire from the Bucolic: The Pastoral Tradition in Seven American War Poems." *Amerikastudien/American Studies* (2013): 101–19.

Moore, Bryan L. "Jeffers's Inheritors: 'Transhuman Magnificence' in Late-Twentieth Century American Poetry." In *Ecological Literature and the Critique of Anthropocentrism*, 169–85. Cham, Switzerland: Palgrave Macmillan, 2017.

Mulder, William. "Seeing 'New Englandly': Planes of Perception in Emily Dickinson and Robert Frost." *New England Quarterly* (1979): 550–59.

Regan, Stephen. "North of Boston: Models of Identity, Subjectivity and Place in the Poems of Robert Frost." *Romanticism and Victorianism on the Net* 51 (2008). doi:10.7202/019262ar.

Stenning, Anna. "'What to Make of a Diminished Thing': Nature and Home in the Poetry of Edward Thomas and Robert Frost 1912–1917." PhD diss., University of Worcester, 2014.

Winchell, Mark Royden. "The Southernness of Robert Frost." *The Sewanee Review* 119, no. 1 (2011): 91–106.

G

The Glass Menagerie

The Glass Menagerie lifted American playwright Thomas Lanier (better known as Tennessee) Williams, from obscurity. One of the themes in American literature, viewed through the works of American dramatist Eugene O'Neill and American novelist and short story writer William Faulkner, is the decline of the family. *The Glass Menagerie* is about such a decline. The mother Amanda Wingfield lives primarily in the past, when she was an attractive, affluent girl with plenty of boys who adored her. The son, Tom, aspires to write poetry but his work at a factory leaves him little time and energy. Of this leisure time, he appears to spend little of it writing. Instead he patronizes the movie theater. Perhaps this is his way of coping with an unpleasant life in which he is sacrificing his existence for his mother and sister. The sister, Laura, suffered from polio as a child and walks with a limp. She is emotionally fragile and shy. Her mother wishes to see her married to a devoted husband with money, but nothing of the sort happens in this play.

THE LITERARY LANDSCAPE OF MEMORY

Tennessee Williams does not narrate *The Glass Menagerie* through omniscient third-person narration in the present, in which readers can follow events as they occur. Rather the action in this play occurred in the past and is now in the memory of Tom. Tom shares these memories with the readers, though he admits that not all details may be accurate. The idea of recitation through recollection is not new to Williams. More than 2,000 years ago, Greek philosopher Plato framed the *Phaedo,* an account of Socrates' last days, around the conversation of two men, one of whom is recalling these past events.

Both Plato and Tennessee Williams use a device that leaves readers dependent on the narrator, without whose memories it is impossible to reconstruct events. One learns at the end of the play that Tom abandoned his mother and sister, leading to the suspicion that his memories may not be edifying if he had the heartlessness to leave his family without a source of income. Even so, one comes to care about Amanda and Laura even though Tom makes no attempt to conceal their flaws.

THE GEOGRAPHY OF PLACE

As he would do later in *A Streetcar Named Desire* and *Cat on a Hot Tin Roof,* Williams sets *The Glass Menagerie* in the American South. The location is both vague and precise. It is vague because Amanda, without specifying the details of her upbringing, references the South and her status as a southern belle repeatedly. This is a South in which she was a girl of leisure and gaiety. She had friends and boys who liked her. She was presumably at the top of the social pyramid and was both girl and lady. Amanda's recollection of her status and the South that she inhabited is a series of memories within Tom's memories. Again Plato embedded memories within memories long before Williams did.

If Amanda does not give readers precision, Tom does by referring to the apartment they once shared in St. Louis, Missouri. The city and state have a tenuous relationship to the South. To be sure, Missouri is a southern state but it did not leave the Union during the Civil War. It thus never suffered from the baggage of having been part of the failed Confederacy. Missouri is also more peripheral to the South than is, say, Mississippi because Missouri points the way west. In fact, Meriwether Lewis and William Clark of the Lewis and Clark expedition began their trek west from St. Louis, which ever since has been known as the Gateway to the West. The setting in St. Louis is also important because it demonstrates that the family is already in decline. The members do not inhabit a fine home but a small, dingy apartment. This decline in status probably triggered Amanda's unconscious decision to live in the past. The reality of the present may be too much for her to bear.

THE FRAGILE LANDSCAPE OF LAURA'S PSYCHE

When Amanda inhabits the present, her focus turns to Laura. Amanda is disappointed with Laura, a high school dropout who failed even to earn a secretary's certificate at some career center or school. Laura appears to have no friends and to be too shy to make new ones. Her sense of inferiority only further isolates her. Amanda fears that Laura is incapable of taking care of herself and very much wants to attract a stable, financially secure man to marry her. Through Amanda's persistence, Tom invites Jim, a colleague, home to dinner. Laura and Jim recognize one another from high school, when Laura had a crush on him. Laura shows Jim her collection of small glass figurines of animals. Jim asks her to dance on the spot. Conscious of her limp, Laura wishes to decline, but Jim will not accept a rebuff. During their awkward dance, they brush against the figurines. The unicorn falls and breaks. But it is really Laura's heart, not the unicorn, that has broken because Jim confesses that he has a girlfriend and cannot see Laura again. Laura is confused and hurt and seems to retreat further into her own world of introspection and isolation.

Christopher Cumo

Further Reading

If you liked *The Glass Menagerie,* then you may also like *Our Town* by Thornton Wilder, a classic play about family dynamics that traces an American family over the course of 14 years, exploring themes of love, marriage, and death. A play that similarly explores family coping skills is *Long Day's Journey into Night* by Eugene O'Neill, which shows the life of a misfortune-filled Connecticut family over the course of one day in 1912. Another good recommendation is Anton Chekhov's *The Cherry Orchard,* a play about a family torn by history and society, which brings into question our own modern social climate.

Bibliography

Click, Patricia C. "The Uncertain Universe of *The Glass Menagerie*: The Influence of the New Physics on Tennessee Williams." *Journal of American Culture* 12, no. 1 (1989): 41–45.

Durán Manso, Valeriano. "Evocation of the Old South in Film Adaptations of Tennessee Williams: The Space as a Narrative Element." *Revista de Comunicación de la SEECI* 20, no. 41 (2016).

Fleche, Anne. "The Space of Madness and Desire: Tennessee Williams and Streetcar." *Modern Drama* 38, no. 4 (1995): 496–509.

Fleche, Anne. "When a Door Is a Jar, or Out in the Theatre: Tennessee Williams and Queer Space." *Theatre Journal* 47, no. 2 (1995): 253–67.

Gros, Camille. "The Myths of the Self-Made Man: Cowboys, Salesmen and Pirates in Tennessee Williams' *The Glass Menagerie* and Arthur Miller's *Death of a Salesman*." Master's thesis, Georgia State University, 2009.

Hovis, George. "'Fifty Percent Illusion': The Mask of the Southern Belle in Tennessee Williams's *A Streetcar Named Desire, The Glass Menagerie,* and *Portrait of a Madonna*." In *Tennessee Williams*, edited by Harold Bloom. New York: Bloom's Literary Criticisms, 2007.

Kolin, Philip C., ed. *The Undiscovered Country: The Later Plays of Tennessee Williams.* New York: Peter Lang, 2002.

Leal, Sandra. "A Jewel Box in Bloom: Translating Tennessee Williams's Scientific Knowledge into Art in *The Glass Menagerie* and *Suddenly Last Summer*." *Southern Quarterly* 48, no. 4 (2011): 40.

O'Connor, Jacqueline. "Moving into the Rooming House: Interiority and Stage Space in Tennessee Williams's *Fugitive Kind* and *Vieux Carre*." *Southern Quarterly* 42, no. 2 (2004): 19.

Savran, David. *Communists, Cowboys, and Queers: The Politics of Masculinity in the Work of Arthur Miller and Tennessee Williams.* Minneapolis: University of Minnesota Press, 1992.

Single, Lori Leathers. "Flying the Jolly Roger: Images of Escape and Selfhood in Tennessee Williams's *The Glass Menagerie*." *Tennessee Williams Annual Review* 2 (1999): 69–85.

Woźniakowska, A. 2016. "Romantic Representation of the City in Selected Plays by Tennessee Williams." *University of Bucharest Review: Literary & Cultural Studies Series* 6 (1).

The Grapes of Wrath

John Steinbeck's novel opens as one of the main characters, Tom Joad, is returning home to his family's farm after spending the last four years in prison. On his way, he meets Jim Casy, an unorthodox former preacher who embraces aspects of life that are typically thought to be sinful. Tom convinces Casy to travel with him to his family's farm, but when they get there, they discover that all the local farms, including his, are deserted. The agricultural crisis that prompted this exodus, known as the Dust Bowl, is the tragedy that inspires this novel about a family's bleak migration west during the 1930s to search for viable land and work. Steinbeck's novel is lauded as a realistic depiction of the hardships suffered during this historical time period.

DUST STORMS AND THE GEOGRAPHY OF AN ECOLOGICAL DISASTER

The phenomenon known as the Dust Bowl references both an event and a geographical location. The effects of the Dust Bowl were felt in North and South Dakota, Texas, Kansas, Oklahoma, Colorado, Nebraska, and New Mexico, the worst of it being in the last five states. A small percentage of farmers in Arkansas and Missouri were also negatively impacted. Altogether, these states represented at least 20 to 30 percent of all Americans at the time who lived off income from farming.

The Dust Bowl was primarily a man-made disaster, which was made worse by an intense drought. It was both influenced by and then contributed to the Great Depression. In response to falling prices for crops, farmers began to mechanize their labor so that they could work more land and increase production (and be able to afford the cost of their new machinery). The growth in farmland removed almost all of the grasslands, which began a significant and dangerous process of erosion. Plowed-up, overfarmed, and overgrazed land was brutalized by several periods of drought beginning in 1930 and continuing periodically until 1940. Crops like wheat did not help the soil retain nutrients and moisture like the natural grasses did. Farmland dried up and blew away, making deserts out of what was once prairies.

In the beginning of Steinbeck's *Grapes of Wrath,* when Tom Joad and Jim Casy first arrive to the place where Tom's family farm used to be, they encounter Muley Graves, an old neighbor, who informs them that everyone has been

This photo from 1936 depicts the struggle of people in the Dust Bowl during the Great Depression. Steinbeck's novel *The Grapes of Wrath* is set in the wake of this ecological disaster and tells the story of a family forced to leave their farm to seek work in California. (Library of Congress)

"tractored off" the land. What Graves means by this is the previously described process, where the land owners switched to using tractors to do the work of farming and thus, no longer needed as many tenants to work the fields with horses. This dynamic was exacerbated at the start of the Dust Bowl as crops began to fail due to drought and the subsequent erosion. Farm owners would also be "tractored off" the land if they were forced to sell their farms to wealthier neighbors (who could afford tractors) because they were unable to make payments on their debt once crops began to fail.

By the middle of the decade, almost 100 million acres of land were ruined by the Dust Bowl. The people trying to live on that land experienced the effects of wind erosion, which caused sand blows that collected like dunes on a beach. It also caused Black Blizzards when the wind blew off the top, rich layer of soil, causing blackouts with zero visibility for hours at a time. Given the massive ecological changes, some areas experienced plagues of insects. Health problems also resulted for people living in affected areas: "dust pneumonia," for instance, was a potentially fatal condition in which the lungs clogged with dirt. The dust storms were so bad that farm equipment and even some houses were buried.

MAPPING MIGRATION DURING THE "DIRTY THIRTIES"

In Steinbeck's novel, Tom Joad's homecoming is ruined when he discovers that his family has had to leave their farm. He catches up with them at his uncle's house, where they are making preparations to sell their belongings and move to California in search of work. Many migrants at this time, like the Joads, saw California as a "promised land." During the Dust Bowl, one of the heaviest migrations of people in American history, up to an estimated 500 million people moved away from the High Plains. Most went to California because the state's climate allowed for a longer growing season, with a nearly continuous cycle of planting and harvesting throughout the year and a greater variety of crops, which translated into more work. Most of these migrants traveled along Highway 66, now known as the historic Route 66. Temporary camps were set up to house and care for migrants as they worked in agricultural areas, partly to protect them from local residents who were often ready to discriminate against the newcomers. In fact, Arizona and Oregon tasked law enforcement personnel with monitoring the state borders to keep out unwanted migrants. The name "Okie" derives from this period as a derogatory way to refer to these Dust Bowl refugees as many of them were from Oklahoma.

All of these historical realities are reflected in *The Grapes of Wrath*. The Joad family journeys to California in a run-down truck along Route 66, which is littered with broken vehicles, some weighed down with people's last remaining possessions. Along the way, the Joads meet Ivy and Sairy Wilson, who are experiencing car troubles. They travel with the family after they acquire at a junkyard the part they need to fix the car. At that point, they encounter a man returning from California, who tells them there is no work available. Their first days in California are difficult as the family tries to stay together despite lacking food and work. Noah, the oldest of the Joad children, soon abandons the family, as does Connie, Tom's brother-in-law, who abandons Tom's pregnant sister, Rose of Sharon.

They lose a number of other friends and family, as well, during their arduous journey. Grampa Joad, who did not want to leave his home, dies on the road shortly after the trip begins. Just before the California border, Sairy Wilson becomes too sick to continue the journey. Lastly, the grandmother dies, but Ma Joad conceals her death to avoid an inspection of their vehicle by police, saying that the grandmother is in desperate need of medical assistance.

However, California is not the paradise they had hoped it would be. Life in the camps is full of conflict and violence. Work is hard to find, the locals are harassing, and the pay is so meager that a meal costs more than the wages received for a full day's work.

The novel represents the historical reality of migrants being harassed by law enforcement officers on behalf of wealthy landowners. In one incident in the novel, the family is staying in a camp called "Hooverville" when Tom and several men get into an altercation with a sheriff's deputy over the formation of a workers union. Tom and Casy knock out an officer, and Casy takes the sole blame to prevent Tom from going back to jail. Next, the family moves to a government-run camp, but they still encounter problems with law enforcement. Tom learns that the police are trying to shut down the camp by faking a riot. After that is thwarted, Tom uncovers a police plot to embed agitators who will start trouble at the dance that weekend. Tom and others work to save the camp.

The family then journeys to Hooper Ranch to harvest peaches, where they find that Jim Casy has organized a strike. One of the strikebreakers murders Casy in a fight, and then Tom kills Casy's murderer. The family has to flee to avoid the police. Over the course of Steinbeck's action-packed plot, the Joads cover a large portion of the state of California.

At the end of the novel, in an ironic twist of fate (because drought was partly responsible for sending them on their journey), the Joads are caught in a dangerous flood when Rose of Sharon goes into labor. After she delivers a stillborn baby, the family seeks shelter in a barn where they find a man dying of starvation. Rose of Sharon offers the man her breast milk to keep him alive. This powerful image at the end of the novel speaks to one of the main themes throughout Steinbeck's book, which is that disadvantaged people can often only count on other disadvantaged people to help them. Class warfare and existing governmental structures may have failed these farmers, but they still retain their agrarian values and a recognition of the importance of community service.

Lynn Marie Houston

Further Reading

If you enjoyed *The Grapes of Wrath,* you might enjoy the work of Willa Cather, who also writes about the Great Plains. She documents the lives of working-class people there in her Prairie Trilogy: *O Pioneers!, The Song of the Lark,* and *My Antonia.* Like Cather, Upton Sinclair writes about life at the turn of the century, which is a few decades earlier than the Dust Bowl crisis Steinbeck documented, but in *The Jungle,* Sinclair captures a similar level of despair surrounding the conditions of people producing our food. He presents in journalistic style the ways that owners of slaughterhouses and factories cheated and abused immigrants seeking jobs in Chicago. Another Dust Bowl novel to consider is

Whose Names are Unknown by Sanora Babb, which, like Steinbeck's classic, tells the story of migrant workers during the Great Depression.

Similarly, in *The Octopus: A Story of California,* Frank Norris portrays the conflict between wheat farmers and the railroad company during the 1880s in California as the railroad makes incursions into farmland. His story is based on the Mussel Slough Tragedy, where ranchers fought law enforcement officers who were protecting the interests of the Southern Pacific Railroad.

Bibliography

Cassuto, David N. "Turning Wine into Water: Water as Privileged Signifier in *The Grapes of Wrath*." *Pace Law Faculty Publications* (1993): 458.

Cruz, Frank Eugene. "'In Between a Past and Future Town': Home, the Unhomely, and *The Grapes of Wrath*." *Steinbeck Review* 4, no. 2 (2007): 53–75.

DeLucia, Laura. "Positioning Steinbeck's Automobiles: Class and Cars in *The Grapes of Wrath*." *The Steinbeck Review* 11, no. 2 (2014): 138–54.

Fine, David. "Running Out of Space: Vanishing Landscapes in California Novels." *Western American Literature* 26, no. 3 (1991): 209–18.

Griffin, Robert J., and William A. Freedman. "Machines and Animals: Pervasive Motifs in *The Grapes of Wrath*." *The Journal of English and Germanic Philology* 62, no. 3 (1963): 569–80.

Keane, Kiely. "Matriarchy, Patriarchy, and Community: Moving from 'I to We' in Steinbeck's *The Grapes of Wrath*." *Languages and Literature Undergraduate Theses* 30 (1996).

Kopecký, Petr. "Czeching American Nature Images in the Work of Robinson Jeffers and John Steinbeck." *Studies in Environmental Humanities* 5 (2018): 139.

Levy, Josephine. "Biological and Animal Imagery in John Steinbeck's Migrant Agricultural Novels: A Re-evaluation." *Between the Species* 10, no. 1 (1993): 15.

Marshall, Richard D. "*The Grapes of Wrath:* John Steinbeck's Cognitive Landscapes as Commentary on 1930s Industrialization." Master's thesis, Saint Louis University, 2009.

Rice, Rodney. "Circles in the Forest: John Steinbeck and the Deep Ecology of *To a God Unknown*." *Steinbeck Review* 8, no. 2 (2011): 31–52.

Sackman, Douglas Cazaux. *Orange Empire: California and the Fruits of Eden*. Berkeley: University of California Press, 2005.

Salter, Christopher L. "John Steinbeck's *The Grapes of Wrath* as a Primer of Cultural Geography." *Humanistic Geography and Literature: Essays on the Experience of Place* (1981): 142–58.

Thompson, Paul B. "Agriculture and Working-Class Political Culture: A Lesson from *The Grapes of Wrath*." *Agriculture and Human Values* 24, no. 2 (2007): 165–77.

Trianawati, Diah. "The American Social Life in John Steinbeck's *The Grapes of Wrath*." Master's thesis, University of North Sumatera, 2009.

Williamson, Jenn. "'His Home Is Not the Land': Caretaking, Domesticity, and Gender in *The Grapes of Wrath*." *Modern Language Studies* (2011): 38–57.

Great Expectations

Great Expectations by Charles Dickens examines the personal development of orphaned Pip alongside the issues of morality and social mobility in England during the early part of the 19th-century era. The novel looks at the distinctions between rich and poor at a time when the advent of the Industrial Revolution meant that people from the manufacturing classes were able to become rich, and social class was not totally determined by the circumstances of a person's birth. To show that Pip, the novel's narrator, grows through his various adventures and experiences, Dickens established his novel within the bildungsroman genre, a type of episodic novel depicting the maturation of the book's main character as they journey from childhood (or young adulthood) through life's trials toward adulthood and achievement. This type of novel was very popular during the 19th century.

THE BRITISH COUNTRYSIDE VERSUS LONDON

The events of *Great Expectations* occur in a limited geography that encompasses a small village on the North Kent marshes, as well as Satis House, the home of Miss Havisham that is located in a market town, and the metropolis of London, England's capital city. Very generally speaking, the rural marshes represent Pip's childhood, while urban London is synonymous with Pip's adolescence. Pip leaves the marshes when he is a very young teenager to travel to the city, a journey that represents his journey toward adult maturity. Through the course of the novel, Pip becomes a grown-up by overcoming the conflict between his social aspirations and his personal morality, for only then can he acquire a sense of himself and act as an adult. Pip spends most of his childhood in the marsh village though he is also a frequent visitor to Satis House. Then after inheriting money, Pip moves to London to learn how to be a gentleman. Throughout *Great Expectations,* Pip travels between these locations as he moves toward adulthood.

Great Expectations begins on the menacing Kentish marshes, a place that though home to Pip, also provides an intimidating and confusing wilderness that makes the boy feel isolated and fearful. Therefore, though the marshes are Pip's home, they are nonetheless a place of dread. Pip's sense of anxiety is heightened when he visits the bleak marsh graveyard in which his parents and siblings are buried only to encounter the convict Magwitch who has escaped from captivity and asks Pip for help. More than likely, when writing this section of the novel, Dickens drew on his own childhood experiences of growing up in the southern English county of Kent. Indeed, some academics suggest that one of the most interesting aspects of *Great Expectations* is that Dickens draws on places important to him for the inspiration for the novel's settings. At the same time as providing an autobiographical element to Pip's story, by depicting the marshes as menacing, Dickens suggests that the landscape is an outer expression of Pip's internal fears and feelings of alienation. Only at the end of the novel when Pip has matured and returns to the marsh region hoping to marry Biddy does he feel at peace there and is able to appreciate the landscape's natural beauty. The marshes are such an important element of who Pip is that even when he is living elsewhere, the marshes continue to loom over his story. This is demonstrated by the fact that the sense of menace that Pip feels on the marshes continues when he begins to visit Satis House, the lair of disturbed and disturbing Miss Havisham, which like a Gothic or fairy-tale castle is sinister, mysterious, and impenetrable to strangers. At Satis House, Pip's childish imagination runs wild, and he first encounters Estella, the girl Miss Havisham has trained to break Pip's heart.

After a while, Pip leaves the marsh region and travels to London to become a gentleman. Dickens depicts London as the complete opposite of the sparsely populated, rural marsh area of Pip's childhood, for the London of *Great Expectations* is portrayed as a dark place teeming with people, and it is here that Pip believes he will be able to realize his ambitions. Much of Dickens's work, both fictional and journalistic, concerned London, and he seems to have never wearied of describing the city from which he drew inspiration. In *Great Expectations,* Dickens describes London so vividly and in such imaginative ways that readers have to remember that Pip is recalling events that occurred in his past. The fact that the London of *Great Expectations* is drawn from reality can be seen when Pip provides detailed information on the London locations of Jaggers's office near Smithfield and other London locations such as Estella's living in Richmond-upon-Thames and the Pockets' residing in Hammersmith, real London locations that still exist today. On the whole, however, the London that Pip describes is the city that Dickens remembered in the 1830s, which existed before the advent of the railways, sewer system, and embankments along the River Thames, and where luxury, grime, and poverty coexist. This dual-natured version of London is often referred to as Dickensian London because Dickens portrayed the city at this time in such an evocative manner. Although much of the London of *Great Expectations* draws on real life, Dickens at the same time embroidered reality and created places that never existed, such as Satis House and Wemmick's castle-like home in Walworth.

Victoria Williams

Further Reading

If you enjoyed reading *Great Expectations,* you might also like to read another of Dickens's bildungsroman novels such as *David Copperfield.* Alternatively, Charlotte Brontë's *Jane Eyre* is also a bildungsroman and, like *Great Expectations,* features many fairy-tale elements. If you would like to read an alternative examination of social mobility in 19th-century England, you could read William Makepeace Thackeray's *Vanity Fair.* Meanwhile, other novels by Dickens that center on events occurring at least in part against the backdrop of Victorian London include *Our Mutual Friend, Little Dorrit, Oliver Twist,* and *Bleak House.*

Bibliography

Avner, Jane. "A Medway Childhood: The Dickensian '*arrière-pays*'?" In *Dickens and the Imagined Child,* edited by Peter Merchant and Catherine Waters, 93–110. Farnham, UK: Ashgate, 2015.

Berard, Jane H. *Dickens and Landscape Discourse.* New York: Peter Lang Publishing, 2007.

Brantlinger, Patrick. "Empire, Place, and the Victorians." In *The Oxford Handbook of Victorian Literary Culture,* edited by Juliet John. Oxford, UK: Oxford University Press, 2016.

Budrewicz-Beratan, Aleksandra. "The Urban River in Dickens, Dostoevsky and Prus." *Prace Filologiczne. Literaturoznawstwo* no. 5 (2015): 407–25.

Chapman, Stephen. "Imagining the Thames: Conceptions and Functions of the River in the Fiction of Charles Dickens." PhD diss., University of Plymouth, 2012.

Hanson, Julienne. "Presentiment, Contrast and Ambiguity in Fictional Space: The London Novels of Charles Dickens and Peter Ackroyd." *JOSS: Journal of Space Syntax* 3, no. 1 (2012): 81–124.

Heady, Emily. "Lost on the Map: Distant Reading in the Travel Writings of Harriet Martineau and Charles Dickens." *Prose Studies* 34, no. 2 (2012): 101–14. doi:10.1080/01440357.2012.701074.

Kaufmann, Priscilla. "Urban Images of Nineteenth-Century London: The Literary Geography of Charles Dickens." Master's thesis, University of Nebraska: Omaha, 1987.

Liu, Chien-hang. "Mapping the Social Body in Charles Dickens's Novels." PhD diss., National Sun Yat-sen University, 2016.

Schlicke, Paul, ed. *The Oxford Companion to Charles Dickens* (Anniversary Edition). Oxford, UK: Oxford University Press, 2011.

Schweizer, Bernard, and Robert A. Segal, eds. *Critical Insights: The Hero's Quest*. Ipswich, MA: Salem Press, 2012.

Sipley, Tristan Hardy. "The Revenge of Swamp Thing: Wetlands, Industrial Capitalism, and the Ecological Contradiction of Great Expectations." *Journal of Ecocriticism* 3, no. 1 (2011): 17–28.

Sipley, Tristan Hardy. "Second Nature: Literature, Capital and the Built Environment, 1848–1938." PhD diss., University of Oregon, 2010. http://hdl.handle.net/1794/10911.

Tambling, Jeremy. *Lost in the American City: Dickens, James, and Kafka*. New York: Palgrave, 2001.

The Great Gatsby

The Great Gatsby, written by F. Scott Fitzgerald, was published in 1925 and is almost ironically named after its less-than-"great" eponymous protagonist, Jay Gatsby, née James Gatz. With Ernest Hemingway, Gertrude Stein, Cole Porter, Pablo Picasso, and others, Fitzgerald was a founding member of the post-World War I "Lost Generation." The novel is very specifically set in Roaring Twenties New York City and Long Island, specifically in East Egg and West Egg, fictional manifestations of Long Island's Great Neck and Little Neck, respectively. The novel is largely a commentary on the American dream and its manifestation in the elite 1920s party world, concerned with "old money" and "new money." Readers of *The Great Gatsby* can view the novel as an exploration of the changes taking place in America, particularly wealthy New York, at the beginning of the 20th century. The novel can also be read as a retelling—necessarily an updated one—of the classic and ubiquitous medieval quest for the Holy Grail. But this time, antiheroic Gatsby has no damsel in distress, and no holy or chivalrous quest. Gatsby's quest is ultimately one for wealth, and he does whatever he has to do to get it.

GEOGRAPHICAL LANDSCAPE

The events of the novel's present take place in Roaring Twenties New York. Fitzgerald creates fictionalized versions of Great Neck and Little Neck, as well as the "valley of ashes," the space that must be traversed to travel from East and West Eggs into Manhattan. Each geographical space provides fictional though specific geographical representation. At the novel's open, we find ourselves with narrator

Nick Carraway remembering "the man who gives his name to this book," and the summer that Nick spent living next door to Gatsby on West Egg. Although we do not get a glimpse of Gatsby himself until almost halfway through the novel, Nick provides thorough—though perhaps flawed—explanations of his geographical location as well as the social and cultural implications of that location. Gatsby throws many wild, lavish parties at his mansion, often not even making his presence known by his guests. Before we even encounter the parties, though, Nick provides a glimpse of East Egg: the old money. Residents of East Egg, Tom and Daisy Buchanan specifically, live lavishly and without regard for the money they spend. They are pretentious and belittling of anyone who is not in their similar financial class. Tom's old money, he feels, privileges him and his family. Because Nick is Tom's former college schoolmate and Daisy's cousin, Tom views him with some of that same privilege; their spontaneous, or at least seemingly so to Nick, jaunt into the city provides a first glimpse at the valley of ashes.

Much of *Gatsby*'s most iconic imagery comes from the valley of ashes and plot moments therein—the desolate, run-down region through which the East and West Eggers must go to enter the city. The valley of ashes represents the destruction of one for the success of another. The only people in the valley are George and Myrtle Wilson. George is the husband of Tom's mistress Myrtle; he works at and lives above his gas station, and both George and Myrtle eventually die due in part to Gatsby's unyielding fidelity to Daisy. Also present are the long-abandoned eyes of Dr. T. J. Eckleburg, whose billboard watches godlike over the valley and the characters' comings and goings. The transition from East Egg's old money, through West Egg's new (and, in Gatsby's case, corrupt) money intensifies with the transition through the valley of ashes. The physical decay is a tangible representation of the social and cultural decay of New York's elite that inevitably occurs as the characters make their way through the valley and into the city. In the city, Tom engages in a wild party of his own as an excuse to carouse with his mistress, Myrtle, and where we first learn of Gatsby's unsavory dealings with the likes of Meyer Wolfsheim to attain his wealth. His bootlegging is entirely to impress and eventually "save" Daisy from her life with Tom—a life from which she does not need nor even want saving.

THE FAILED DREAM

Although the novel's current action takes place in and around Long Island and New York City, the flashbacks into Gatsby and Daisy's past show them in Louisville when Gatsby was a moneyless soldier in World War I. In their past, and more importantly in Louisville, Daisy's innocence entices Gatsby, and the two hope to reunite when Gatsby is more worthy of Daisy, at least financially—a theme omnipresent in many of Fitzgerald's works. Once Gatsby and Daisy reappear in the East, in New York, their depravity overcomes their innocence, a problem often associated with relocation to amoral New York.

Rather than being the classic medieval knight in shining armor riding in on a white horse to save a damsel in distress, Gatsby attains his "new money" through shady dealings, and Daisy is no damsel. One of the most salient symbols of *Great Gatsby* is the green light at the end of Daisy's dock, across the bay from Gatsby's home. Nick often describes Gatsby keeping watch over Daisy via observation of the green light, attempting to protect her in her life from which she does not need protection. Whereas the medieval knight was constantly on his holy quest, heroically rescuing a worthy damsel from some worthy adversary, Gatsby is antiheroic due not only to his cultural moment, but also the geographical landscape in which he exists; New York is not the Midwest. The two are dichotomous.

THE ANTIHERO

Although Gatsby's intentions are heroic, he lives in a world marked by bootlegging, organized crime, adultery, emptiness, fraudulence, and frivolity. There is no room for the heroic quests of the medieval knight. Fitzgerald's contrast of the Midwest and New York is, in a way, representative of the difference between tradition and moral decay akin to the physical decay of the valley of ashes. *The Great Gatsby* is not the story of the attained American dream, but rather of its failures, resulting from America's failure to live up to its expectations.

Andrea Laurencell Sheridan

Further Reading

Many readers find that the character Holly Golightly, from Truman Capote's *Breakfast at Tiffany's*, resembles Daisy Buchanan from *The Great Gatsby*. This is probably the case because Capote's protagonist disdains the New York City 1940s high-class society she travels in and yearns for deeper connection. *Such Great Heights* by Chris Cole is also frequently compared to *The Great Gatsby*, as it is about how one young man spends a summer with the ultrarich and discovers that they often have to sacrifice freedom, happiness, and love to maintain their lifestyles. Gordon Korman offers a modern retelling of Gatsby, in his novel *Jake, Reinvented* about a popular new student in a high school with a mysterious past.

Bibliography

Beuka, Robert. *SuburbiaNation: Reading Suburban Landscape in Twentieth-Century American Fiction and Film.* New York: Palgrave Macmillan, 2004.

Frye, Charles Mitchell, III. "Country of Illusion: Imagined Geographies and Transnationoal Connections in F. Scott Fitzgerald's America." PhD diss., Louisiana State University and Agricultural and Mechanical College, 2012.

Reaves, Gerri. *Mapping the Private Geography: Autobiography, Identity, and America.* Jefferson, NC: McFarland & Company, Inc., 2001.

Sellers, Christopher. "Body, Place and the State: The Makings of an 'Environmentalist' Imaginary in the Post-World War II U.S." *Radical History Review* no. 74 (1999): 31–64. doi:10.1215/01636545-1999-74-31.

Tunc, Tanfer Emin, and Annessa Ann Babic, eds. *The Globetrotting Shopaholic: Consumer Spaces, Products, and Their Cultural Places.* Newcastle upon Tyne: Cambridge Scholars Publishing, 2008.

Vale, Thomas R. *The American Wilderness: Reflections on Nature Protection in the United States.* Charlottesville: University of Virginia Press, 2005.

Vince, Raymond M. "The Great Gatsby and the Transformations of Space-Time: Fitzgerald's Modernist Narrative and the New Physics of Einstein." *The F. Scott Fitzgerald Review* 5, no. 1 (2008). doi:10.1111/j.1755-6333.2006.tb00034.x.

Worster, Donald. *Shrinking the Earth: The Rise and Decline of American Abundance.* New York: Oxford University Press, 2016.

Gulliver's Travels

After 1492, as images of new lands in exotic places changed Europe's understanding of geography, literature, and philosophy, these provided a counterpoint to European convention and assumption. In the context of this discovery of already inhabited lands, *Gulliver's Travels* proved popular as soon as it was published in 1726. In almost four centuries, *Gulliver* has never been out of print.

THE GENRE OF THE TRAVEL NARRATIVE

Gulliver's Travels arrived in Europe within the context of many travel narratives that claimed to be factual, but often were nearly as fanciful as author Jonathan Swift's creations. Aside from religious works, accounts of travels, geography, and atlases were the best-selling reading matter during the reign of Queen Anne. Maps were in demand during Swift's time in Britain, and the first editions of *Gulliver's Travels* were subtitled *Travels into Several Remote Nations of the World*. The book contained maps for all four of Gulliver's voyages, copied from the work of some of Britain's best cartographers, but with some names changed, and some very liberal and sometimes contradictory geography.

Swift's work is an entertaining parody of both contemporary English society and its culture of "discovery"; the story is a travel narrative that imagines exotic societies at four locations around the world.

SEMIFICTONAL GEOGRAPHY AND ETHNOGRAPHY

Gulliver's Travels includes four voyages (with dates and maps) where the protagonist encounters four different societies. The first (May 4, 1699 to April 13, 1702) is to Lilliput, the miniature world. The second (June 20, 1702 to June 3, 1706) takes Gulliver to Brobdingnag, land of gentle giants. The third (August 5, 1706 to April 16, 1710) lands him on a rocky island near India, where he encounters the flying island of Laputa. The fourth (September 7, 1710 to December 5, 1715) is to the land of Houyhnhnms—wise, talking horses—as well as the Yahoos, humanity in its basest form.

Swift's Brobdingnag may have been inspired by the Pacific Northwest of North America. As of that date, no European had explored much of that area, leaving plenty to the imagination. In 1578, Sir Francis Drake had landed in Northern California, and in 1592, Juan de Fuca had passed the mouth of the strait that is named for him between present-day Washington State and Vancouver Island. Only in 1792 did George Vancouver and Peter Puget, who also left their names on the landscape, explore that area.

A map published in an early edition of the book locates Drake's landfall in "New Albion," an early name for California, with a peninsula to the north labeled Brobdingnag. Gulliver placed Brobdingnag at 44° north latitude and 143° west longitude, west of present-day Portland, Oregon. The area's imaginary society was made up of peaceful 70-foot-tall oafs and house cats three times the size of an English ox. Volcanoes studded the landscape (as they do in the Northwest). Although the book's map presents a Brobdingnag that is about the size of the Olympic Peninsula, the book says it is 6,000 by 4,000 miles, bigger than all of North America.

Locations described in the text rarely coincided with the maps, but even as Swift complained about these differences in some of his letters, he never called upon publishers to change them as *Gulliver's Travels* was reprinted. Swift may have reasoned that his work was fiction, and the existing maps were good enough because his geographical locations in the text were often inconsistent and sometimes contradictory anyway. It was clearly all a fantasy.

Geographical locations described in the various editions of *Gulliver's Travels* are incredibly sloppy by any measure, but they do provide a general idea that three of the four voyages were located near Australia, Sumatra, India, and Japan. On the maps, and in the text, Lilliput is shown to be close to the coast of Sumatra in some accounts, but off Tasmania (30.2° south) on others. Others lead readers to inland Australia. The land of the Houyhnhnms was described as having been between 41° and 49° south and between 110° and 117° east on a London meridian; that location is part of the Indian Ocean southeast of Australia, with no land nearby. The third voyage took Gulliver to Japan (its title says as much), between 26° and 34° north and between 150° and 162° east—several hundred very wet miles from any landmass, although Japan is closer than anything else. In the text, however, Swift places this location at 29° N and 140° E, a little closer to Japan, but still in the ocean.

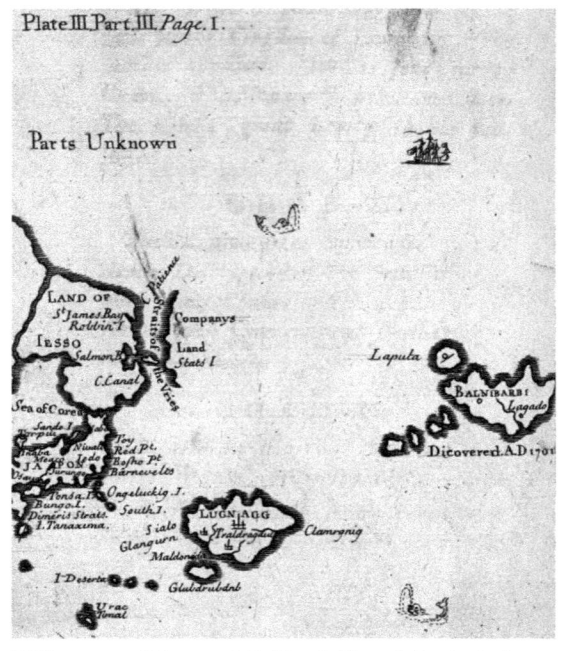

Different editions of *Gulliver's Travels* included variations on the maps that chart the hero's journey. In this one, fictional lands are mapped over real places. (British Library)

A CATALOG OF VIRTUE AND VICE

Regardless of exact locations, the main lessons of Swift's story have to do with the universal nature of human virtue and vice. No matter where Gulliver travels, he narrates similar events everywhere. Swift wrote that "The same vices and follies reign everywhere. If I had written of England alone, or of my century alone, my work would not deserve to be read." His work assembles between its covers a compendium of what it means to be human, including our difficulties with narrating stories of travel to foreign places.

Bruce E. Johansen

Further Reading

If you liked *Gulliver's Travels,* then you might like *The History of Rasselas, Prince of Abissinia* by Samuel Johnson, because it is also a story about the search for knowledge and happiness in which a prince seeks to understand what other fruits life can bear in other places. Another work that similarly desires to find personal identity in a foreign place is *Robinson Crusoe* by Daniel Defoe, which is about a shipwrecked Englishman's attempt at survival on an island. Another good recommendation is Henry Fielding's *Joseph Andrews,* an adventure across the English countryside in which characters must take control of their own happiness.

Bibliography

Bracher, Frederick. "The Maps in *Gulliver's Travels.*" *Huntington Library Quarterly* 8, no. 1 (1944): 59–74.

Engberg-Pedersen, Anders, ed. *Literature and Cartography: Theories, Histories, Genres.* Cambridge, MA: Massachusetts Institute of Technology, 2017.

Korn, Karen Abney. "Reading the Red Island: Travel Writing and Maps of Madagascar." Master's thesis, Indiana University, 1994.

McLeod, Bruce. *The Geography of Empire in English Literature, 1580–1745.* Cambridge, UK: Cambridge University Press, 1999.

Moore, John Robert. "Swift as Historian." *Studies in Philology* 49, no. 4 (1952): 583–604.

Moore, John Robert. "The Geography of *Gulliver's Travels.*" *The Journal of English and Germanic Philology* 40, no. 2 (1941): 214–28.

Neill, Anna. "Swift and the Geographers: Race, Space and Merchant Capital in *Gulliver's Travels.*" In *British Discovery Literature and the Rise of Global Commerce.* London: Palgrave Macmillan, 2002. doi:10.1057/9780230629226.

O'Sullivan, Emer. "Imagined Geography: Strange Places and People in Children's Literature." *The Wenshan Review of Literature and Culture* 10, no. 2 (2017): 1–32.

Pearl, Jason H. *Utopian Geographies and the Early English Novel.* Charlottesville: University of Virginia Press, 2014.

Savy, Guillaume. "A Vyrcanian Story: Materialising Alternate Histories and Geographies." Master's thesis, University of Melbourne, 2014.

Swift, Jonathan. *Gulliver's Travels: Complete Authoritative Text with Biographical and Historical Contexts, Critical History, and Essays from Five Contemporary Critical Perspectives.* Bedford Books of St. Martin's Press, 1995.

H

Hamlet

Scholars believe that Shakespeare wrote *The Tragedy of Hamlet, Prince of Denmark* between 1599 and 1601, but the play is set during an earlier time period, the 14th and 15th centuries. Shakespeare channels the intricacies of the castle architecture to increase the tension of the plot.

Shakespeare's *Hamlet* takes place after a regime change in Denmark. Claudius has married Queen Gertrude after his brother's death, and he has become king. In doing so, he has usurped Hamlet's claim to the throne. One night, Hamlet sees his father's ghost who lets him know that he was murdered by Claudius. Hamlet then sets out to avenge him, but doesn't know who he can trust. Although he appears to love Ophelia, his thoughts about women are tainted by suspicions of his mother's involvement in the murder, and he is preoccupied with his grief and thoughts of revenge. Meanwhile, various characters debate whether Hamlet is truly mad, and whether it is because of grief over his father or love of Ophelia. A troupe of actors visits the castle, and Hamlet instructs them to put on a play that reenacts his father's murder as he is hoping this will draw out the guilty party or parties. Later, he mistakes Polonius, Ophelia's father, for Claudius and mistakenly kills him, which drives Ophelia to her death. After the play, Claudius now knows that Hamlet suspects him, so he tasks Rosencrantz and Guildenstern with killing Hamlet. However, Hamlet finds out about the plan and has the two men killed instead. In the final scene, Hamlet and Laertes engage in a fencing match, which is rigged to kill the prince in one of two ways: if he is hit by Horatio's sword, he will die because the tip has been dipped in poison, and if he wins the match, he will die because poison has been placed in the cup of wine he will be given to drink. Hamlet is struck by the poisoned tip of Horatio's sword, which he then uses against Laertes. Hamlet's mother mistakenly drinks from his cup instead and dies. And when Hamlet realizes what is happening, he finally kills Claudius with his sword. Everyone dies, except Horatio, and the crown passes out of the family.

OUTSIDE THE WALLS OF ELSINORE

Travel is essential to the unfolding drama of Shakespeare's play. Hamlet is also sent away to England by Claudius, who arranges to have him murdered on the trip. Instead, the two would-be murderers, Horatio and Guildenstern, are put to death in a trick Hamlet plays on them. The fact that danger follows Hamlet abroad helps to reinforce the global nature of the drama. The fight over the throne has ramifications beyond the royal castle and the country of Denmark.

The majority of the action on stage takes place at the royal castle of Elsinore, Denmark, but a couple of key trips are narrated, such as when Hamlet travels to

England and the trip results in the deaths of Rosencrantz and Guildenstern, or when Ophelia dies by falling into the river. These plot points are not shown as action on stage, but are told to the audience in conversation by characters. When Hamlet returns from England, however, the play shows him outside of the castle, in the cemetery, where he muses on the remains of Yorick, the deceased court jester. He then encounters a funeral procession and discovers that Ophelia has passed away. Scenes are mainly within and around the castle, with the exception of the one scene in the cemetery.

THE INTRIGUE OF CASTLE ARCHITECTURE

The interior space of the castle plays an important role in the plot. Places in castles allow people to hide, like closets, curtains, and columns, and allow them to listen in on private conversations and produce subsequent plot twists based on the lack of privacy in that public space. One scene in particular relies heavily on the ability of a character to hide "in plain view." When Hamlet goes to speak to his mother in her room, he hears someone hiding behind a tapestry and assumes it is the king. He kills the person by stabbing his sword through the tapestry, only to discover that it was Polonius, not Claudius. The use of space to hide the identity of this character helps Shakespeare to emphasize the tragic nature of this situation, where grief piles on top of grief for everyone involved. Shakespeare develops a claustrophobic setting where the characters cannot seem to get out of one another's way, which accurately depicts the struggles of many aristocratic families at the time to gain and maintain power in the court system.

Although Shakespeare does not mention the name of the castle in which the play is set, the only royal castle in Elsinore, Denmark, is the Kronborg Castle, which has become a popular tourist destination because of the play. However, many other writers, filmmakers, and artists have resisted this notion to pin Hamlet down to a local place in Denmark. Instead, through adaptations of the story, Hamlet has gone global in his presence, having been adapted to fit cultures as diverse as Syria, China, Kuwait, Egypt, Tunisia, and Iran, among others. In one Egyptian performance, the ending of the play was changed so that Hamlet lives and receives the blessing of his father's spirit. Many cultures have been successful in adapting Shakespeare's play to their local context and to more contemporary time periods.

Lynn Marie Houston

Further Reading

The Spanish Tragedy by Thomas Kyd is often cited as one of the sources for Shakespeare's *Hamlet,* including its revenge theme. It was written a few years to a decade earlier. A modern work that tells the story of Hamlet's two friends who die in Shakespeare's play is *Rosencrantz and Guildenstern Are Dead* by Tom Stoppard. Lisa Klein has written a novel, *Ophelia,* that retells the story from this female character's perspective. *The Dead Father's Club* is a 2006 retelling of *Hamlet* by Matt Haig.

Bibliography

Beiswenger, April. "Of Sterile Promontory and Infinite Space: The Creation of the Scenic Design for Shakespeare's Hamlet." Master's thesis, West Virginia University, 2009.

Brown, Keith. "Hamlet's Place on the Map." *Shakespeare Studies* 4 (1968): 160.

Carpi, Daniela. "The Garden as the Law in the Renaissance: A Nature Metaphor in a Legal Setting." *Pólemos: Journal of Law, Literature, and Culture* 6, no. 1 (2012): 33–48.

Chaudhuri, Una. "Animal Geographies: Zooësis and the Space of Modern Drama." *Modern Drama* 46, no. 4 (2003): 646–62.

Cheang, Wai Fong. "Women and Visual Representations of Space in Two Chinese Film Adaptations of Hamlet." *Gender Studies* 13, no. 1 (2014): 1–21.

Cinpoes, Nicoleta. *Shakespeare's* Hamlet *in Romania 1778–2008: A Study in Translation, Performance, and Cultural Adaptation*. Lewiston, NY: Edwin Mellen Press, 2010.

Emmerichs, Sharon. "Inside-Out and Outside-In: Landscape and the Unnatural in Shakespeare's *Hamlet* and *Macbeth*." *The Upstart Crow* 23 (2003): 39.

Farabee, Darlene. "Narrative and Spatial Movement in *Hamlet*." In *Shakespeare's Staged Spaces and Playgoers' Perceptions*, 70–97. London: Palgrave Macmillan, 2014.

Freeman, John. "Holding up the Mirror to Mind's Nature: Reading 'Rosencrantz' 'Beyond Absurdity.'" *The Modern Language Review* (1996): 20–39.

Hiscock, Andrew. *The Uses of This World: Thinking Space in Shakespeare, Marlowe, Cary and Jonson*. Cardiff: University of Wales Press, 2004.

Ichikawa, Mariko. *The Shakespearean Stage Space*. Cambridge, UK: Cambridge University Press, 2013.

Madelaine, Richard. "'The dark and vicious place': The Location of Sexual Transgression and Its Punishment on the Early Modern English Stage." *Parergon* 22, no. 1 (2005): 159–83.

Pieldner, Judit. "Space Construction in Adaptations of *Hamlet*." *Acta Universitatis Sapientiae, Philologica* 4, no. 1 (2012): 43–58.

Poole, Kristen. *Supernatural Environments in Shakespeare's England: Spaces of Demonism, Divinity, and Drama*. Cambridge, UK: Cambridge University Press, 2011.

Raber, Karen. "Vermin and Parasites: Shakespeare's Animal Architectures." In *Ecocritical Shakespeare*, edited by Lynne Bruckner and Daniel Brayton, 37–56. London: Routledge, 2016.

Shaughnessy, Robert. "Stage, Screen, and Nation: Hamlet and the Space of History." *A Concise Companion to Shakespeare on Screen,* edited by Diana E. Henderson. Malden, MA: Blackwell Publishing Limited, 2006.

Shurgot, Michael. "'Get you a place': Staging the Mousetrap at the Globe Theatre." *Shakespeare Bulletin* 12, no. 3 (1994): 5–9.

Sillitoe, Peter. "'Thy state is the more gracious': Courtly Space and Social Mobility in Hamlet and Early Modern Culture." *Shakespeare* 9, no. 2 (2013): 204–19.

Speaight, Robert. *Nature in Shakespearian Tragedy*. New York: Collier Books, 1962.

Styan, John L. "Sight and Space: The Perception of Shakespeare on Stage and Screen." *Educational Theatre Journal* 29, no. 1 (1977): 18–28.

Tuan, Yi-Fu. *Space and Place: The Perspective of Experience*. Minneapolis: University of Minnesota Press, 1977.

Wood, Robert E. "Space and Scrutiny in *Hamlet*." *South Atlantic Review* 52, no. 1 (1987): 25–42.

Ziegler, Georgianna. "My Lady's Chamber: Female Space, Female Chastity in Shakespeare." *Textual Practice* 4, no. 1 (1990): 73–90.

The Handmaid's Tale

Margaret Atwood's dystopian novel about life in a new religious-based society was published in 1985, but has gained increasing relevancy during the culture wars of the early 21st century. Her novel spawned a popular television series of the same name, whose first season aired in 2017. The story is set in what was once the United States, now renamed the Republic of Gilead. The narrative unfolds after a Christian group kills the president and most of the political representatives, taking control of the government and killing anyone who resists or who doesn't fit into their belief system. They institute themselves as the ruling class and designate other classes in society by role, color-coding their clothing. The ruling class wives wear blue, handmaids wear red, and cooks (known as Marthas) wear green. A woman named Offred narrates the story from her perspective while serving as handmaid to a high-ranking official, called the Commander. "Aunts" are older women whose job is to "retrain" fertile women for their roles as handmaids, whose job is to produce babies for other couples. The geographical setting of the novel is in and around what was formerly Boston before the new regime stripped cities and roads of their names and began renaming them.

TOXICITY AND CHRISTIAN CULTURE

The founders of Gilead, known as the Sons of Jacob, use a biblical story to justify the use of handmaids to bear children for other families. The book of Genesis tells how Rachel, realizing she was infertile, gave her servant Bilhah to Jacob, her husband, to produce children. One of the stated purposes of the Sons of Jacob in taking over the government was their concern over declining birthrates. They traced increasing reproductive health problems, such as infertility and the inability to carry a healthy baby to term, to the toxic amount of chemicals being used in food production and also to improper disposal of industrial waste. They blame women for this, both in terms of biology and cultural values: the religious group wants to curtail women's rights (to read, to get an education, to work outside the home, and to have a say in government) so that they stay home and produce children. In Offred's time as a handmaid, she is finally able to get pregnant after she has sex with Nick, which suggests that the Commander might be sterile and that it is not his wife's fault that they have been unable to conceive children. The fear that women have been "tainted" by environmental hazards is what prompts the religious group to round up all of the women who have already given birth to healthy babies and force them into roles as handmaids. Prior to the revolution, in her former life with her husband, Offred had given birth to a daughter. Readers are given glimpses of this backstory in flashbacks detailing their lives as a family and their attempt to escape to Canada to avoid being separated. For most of the story, Offred does not know if her husband is alive or dead.

As the story develops and Offred is forced regularly to have sex with the Commander (with his wife present), he begins asking her to meet him in his study in the evening even though their contact is supposed to be limited to the "ritual." In the privacy of his study, he lets her indulge in items of contraband: a book, a fashion magazine, cosmetics, and finally lingerie. Then, he takes her to Jezebel's, a brothel sponsored by the government. She discovers that a friend from her former life, Moira, works there after escaping from the handmaid training facility. She was given a choice to either work as a prostitute or work in the Colonies where she would be forced, along with the other prisoners, to collect toxic waste.

The Colonies are not described in detail as a place in the narrative, only alluded to in conversation as a place of punishment for those who resist life in the new society.

As time passes and the Commander's wife, Serena Joy, grows increasingly desperate to have a child, she sets up a meeting between Offred and their driver, Nick, as she is afraid that her husband might be sterile. Because Offred agrees to do this, Serena Joy rewards her with a recent photo of her daughter. However, Offred and Nick begin to develop feelings for each other and start meeting regularly in secret. After Offred reveals to Nick that she is pregnant, the secret police come to take her away under guard. Nick tells her to trust him and that everything will be okay. It is possible that Nick has worked with the resistance, known as Mayday, to liberate Offred. In an epilogue, Offred tells us that the Republic of Gilead was overthrown and that women regained their rights.

THE GEOGRAPHY OF MISOGYNY

Offred's feelings about her forced role in the Commander's household articulates her lack of ownership over space and over her body as it occupies space in someone else's house. Offred has trouble calling the room she lives in "my room." She avoids, for the first part of the story, using the first-person pronoun of ownership because Gilead's social structure actively promotes her disenfranchisement by prohibiting her from owning anything or from forming any identity outside of the one given to her by her role as handmaid. Her room is laid out in a way meant to control her behavior. For instance, there is an empty fixture where a chandelier used to hang from the ceiling; it was removed so that Offred could not hang herself from it and commit suicide, like the previous handmaid did. She draws attention to small details that have been missed that suggest the difference between her past life and present, such as the throw pillows with embroidered words on them, given that women are no longer supposed to read or write. She has no privacy: the ruling class does not want her committing any subversive acts, so surveillance—or the threat of it—is key. She also has no bodily autonomy. Every month during the time when she is fertile, whether or not she wants to, she is forced to have sex with the Commander in the hopes of producing a baby for him and his wife.

Even though she feels that she has no claims to the interior space (the one bedroom where she lives), she is even more unwelcome in spaces outside the home. Her movement and travels are scripted and heavily surveilled. Armed guards patrol the streets, the access to public transportation, and the shopping areas. She has only few reasons to leave the house, such as getting groceries or attending a birth, and all of those trips happen in the company of other people, which has the benefit of protection but also the threat of surveillance. One of the reasons Offred does not feel "at home" in her room is that, like any interior space, it might be bugged. The forces controlling Gilead listen in on the handmaids and others to make sure they are complying with the rules and not forming a resistance movement. Even many of the green spaces outside the home are not welcoming to her. For instance, the wives maintain control over any gardens on their properties. In Offred's household, the Commander's wife takes her garden very seriously. Atwood perhaps wants us to understand that the character of Serena Joy nurtures her garden because she cannot have kids: instead, she directs motherly acts of nurturing toward the plants and flowers she cultivates. Serena Joy sometimes has a chair placed in the garden and sits there, fully occupying and owning that cultivated outdoor space. Other than this exception, however, the wives also do not have much ownership over public space. For instance, they do not walk on the streets; they are always driven in cars. This might appear like a privilege, but it is also a way of keeping them under surveillance and of controlling their movement. Space is dominated by the men who orchestrated the coup and who are now in charge.

Watching and being watched is an important element in the story. While in public, handmaids wear head gear that prevents others from seeing their faces. This is a complex symbol: for one, it is supposed to promote modesty and dissuade lust, but it also emphasizes that she is "owned" by a man and that she is his property and for his eyes only. There is a similar veiling that happens when handmaids receive medical treatment. They are not supposed to be unique individuals anymore, but vessels meant to serve a greater purpose beyond themselves. During medical examinations or during birthing, they drape sheets so that the doctors do not see their faces, just the lower part of their bodies. Women have ceased to be individual people and have become like machines to fulfill various functions. For the handmaids, that only function is to birth a baby, reducing a woman's identity to her reproductive system. The sex organs of the female body hold the greatest importance for this new society, undoing the gains women had made educationally and professionally.

THE GEOGRAPHY OF MEMORY AND RESISTANCE

The new society of Gilead orders its guards to paint over the names of shops, leaving only icons. They do the same to the food they produce, leaving language off the labels. Ostensibly, this is because they do not allow women to read; however, it reminds readers of how African slaves were not allowed to read in colonial America, because the plantation owners did not want them to form a resistance or, later, to know their rights. They also erase the names from streets, making it so that only a few in the know (with maps) can navigate travel. Even using public transportation becomes difficult when the streets lack names and the stops are not labeled. Removing the names of places serves to disempower the masses and helps keep them, quite literally, in their place. The new society uses the censorship of language and writing to disorient. The confusion of names goes even further to dehumanize the handmaids: their names refer to the name of the Commander to which they are assigned, preceded by the word "of" to indicate who owns them. In one example of the confusion these names generate by stripping these women of their individuality, when her friend is transferred, Offred asks the new girl who shows up to walk with her to the store where Ofglen is. The girl replies that she is Ofglen. The new handmaid belonging to Commander Glen has been assigned the same name as the last handmaid assigned to him. This prevents Offred, who never knew the previous handmaid by any other name, of getting information about her.

Beyond removing the names of places, in order to move society toward the new values they are imposing, the founders of Gilead have repurposed architectural structures to meet their needs. Churches have been turned into museums. Walls have been turned into canvases on which the new society displays what happens to those who break their laws: they hang the bodies of people they have killed so that everyone who walks by has to look at them.

One of the most powerful antidotes to oppressive fascism is the memory of a historical time when things were different. Atwood, through flashbacks, reveals the powerful pull of memories as our narrator remembers her life from before. Places often trigger these memories. For instance, one day when she is walking to the store, in a shopping area devoid of street names and store names, she is struck by the knowledge that an ice cream shop used to be situated on the street where she was. Although it is now gone, the memory lives on in her experience of place. Those personal memories cannot be erased by the new regime, and their powerful emotional ties fuel Offred's survival.

The garments and accessories of the characters in Atwood's dystopian novel are color-coded to identify their position in society: wives wear blue, while handmaids are in red. Just as societal roles are divvied up into distinct sects represented by these colors, the interior space of the home is divided up by gender. In every house, the wife maintains the sitting room, while the husband has an office. Each must knock and ask for entry before going in the other's space. These characters are keenly aware, as they move through space, of their place in Gilead's hierarchical structure. Toward the end of the novel, the Commander is hosting Offred in his office in the evenings, where she asks him to listen to the news on the radio. By inviting her into his space, he grants her access to privileged knowledge about the world that she would otherwise not have. Atwood creates a novel whose spatial layout draws attention to the power dynamics of oppression and resistance.

Lacar Musgrove and Lynn Marie Houston

Further Reading

Herland, by Charlotte Perkins Gilman, although written in 1915, much earlier than *The Handmaid's Tale,* is about a group of women discovering a remote women-only society. This discovery makes them question the role and responsibilities that women hold in their own society. Although Gilman's novel is utopian, meaning that it shows an ideal society, Atwood's *The Handmaid's Tale* is a cautionary tale, but both reveal women's oppression through the exploration of life in an imaginary society. Ursula K. Le Guin is generally considered one of the best science fiction authors who writes about the politics of gender. Any of her works would provide ample similarities with Atwood, but *The Birthday of the World and Other Stories* might be a particularly good choice given the inclusion of *Paradises Lost,* a novella about a group of humans traveling to a planet to create a new society.

Bibliography

Ahrentzen, Sherry. "The Meaning of Home Workplaces for Women." In *Thresholds in Feminist Geography: Difference, Methodology, Representation,* edited by John Paul Jones, Heidi J. Nast, Susan M. Roberts, 77–92. Lanham, MD: Rowman & Littlefield, 1997.

Atkinson, Jennifer. "Seeds of Change: The New Place of Gardens in Contemporary Utopia." *Utopian Studies* 18, no. 2 (2007): 237–60.

Díaz, Junot, ed. *Global Dystopias*. MIT Press, 2017.

Evans, Francis Eric Mark. "Margaret Atwood: Words and the Wilderness." PhD diss., University of Edinburgh, 1992.

Hatch, Ronald B. "Margaret Atwood, the Land, and Ecology." In *Margaret Atwood: Works and Impact,* edited by Reingard M. Nischik, 180–201. Rochester, NY: Camden House, 2000.

Howells, Coral Ann. "Atwood's Canadian Signature: From Surfacing and Survival to Wilderness Tips." In *Margaret Atwood,* 20–37. London: Palgrave, 1996.

Khan, Yasmeen Farooq, and Lily Want. "The Power and Promise of Ecofeminism: A Study of the Selected Novels of Margaret Atwood and Alice Walker." PhD diss., University of Kashmir, 2016.

Lamoureux, Cheryl. "History as Hysterectomy: The Writing of Women's History in *The Handmaid's Tale* and *Ana Historic.*" Master's thesis, University of Manitoba, 1998.

Lapointe, Annette. "The Machineries of Uncivilization: Technology and the Gendered Body in the Fiction of Margaret Atwood and William Gibson." PhD diss., University of Manitoba, 2011.

Ledyard, Margaret Dabney. "Metaphoric Landscape in the Novels of Virginia Woolf and Margaret Atwood." PhD diss., University of St. Andrews, 1994.

Mohammed, Arwa H., and Awfa H. Mohammed. "Margret Atwood: Social Brutality and Sexual Politics." *Journal of Surra Man Raa* 9, no. 35 (2013): 253–71.

Rule, Lauren A. "Not Fading into Another Landscape: Specters of American Empire in Margaret Atwood's Fiction." *MFS Modern Fiction Studies* 54, no. 4 (2008): 627–53.

Sturgess, Charlotte Jane. "A Politics of Location: Subjectivity and Origins in the Work of Mavis Gallant, Alice Munro and Margaret Atwood." PhD diss., Queen Mary University of London, 1993.

Vials, Chris. "Margaret Atwood's Dystopic Fiction and the Contradictions of Neoliberal Freedom." *Textual Practice* 29, no. 2 (2015): 235–54.

The *Harry Potter* Series

J. K. Rowling wrote the first Harry Potter novel, *Harry Potter and the Sorcerer's Stone* (published elsewhere as *Harry Potter and the Philosopher's Stone*) after being inspired while riding a train in her native England. She has stated that she had a vision of a young boy in a black robe and red scarf walking down the train's aisle. The train and the history of this old-fashioned form of travel informed the series as a whole with a mixture of modern society and the more ancient world associated with fantasy. In the seven novels in the series, the location of the characters has been a major factor in their adventures. Each of the books is about a year in the life of Harry Potter, with each volume extending the map of the fictional universe. However, each book also begins in the same way, with Harry Potter at a simple family home in the suburbs and reentering the magical world through physical travel, most often on the Hogwarts Express, a steam-powered train very much based on the one Rowling was traveling in when inspiration struck.

This photo of a British bookstore's window display shows a complete collection of all seven titles in the *Harry Potter* series. (Siempreverde22/Dreamstime.com)

THE THREE REALMS

The world of Harry Potter is expansive, encompassing much of England and Scotland particularly. Broken down into more simplistic characterizations for the sake of expediency, the Harry Potter books are divided into three essential realms. These are as follows: the nonmagical human or "muggle" realm; the world of magical education that includes Hogwarts School of Witchcraft and Wizardry, Diagon Alley, which is a secret street where young witches and wizards buy everything they need for success at school, and the train that takes students from the muggle King's Cross station to the school; and lastly, the larger wizarding world that encroaches on the other two realms, endangering their very existence.

The first location introduced in the series is the muggle realm. Harry lives most of the first 11 years of his life in an average middle-class home with his aunt and uncle. Although it is later ascertained that these two are aware of the magical world, they intentionally ignore anything connected to it because they are not able to take part in it. Uncle Vernon and Aunt Petunia suppress Harry's magical gifts as well as the truth about his parents while also treating him as a charity case in the vein of *Jane Eyre* or *Cinderella*. He lives in the house by their will and therefore they are welcome to mistreat him. As oppressed as Harry was in this home, it is stated repeatedly that it is also the place where he has been safest. Even once Voldemort— the major villain of the series—gains power, he cannot attack Harry while he resides in his uncle's house. It is explained that when sacrificing her life for his, Harry's mother cast a protective spell that continues in her sister's house because of their blood relation, and is renewed each year that Harry lives in that house, ensuring he returns each year. While at the Dursleys' home, he is also barred from doing any magic both by his relatives and the rules of the wizarding world. Harry is completely safe from the dangers of the magical world only when he takes no part in it.

On September 1st of each year, young witches and wizards leave London on their journey to Hogwarts in Scotland. In most books of the series, the only way of getting to Hogwarts is via this train. The exceptions are in *The Chamber of Secrets,* where Harry and best friend Ron are forced to take a sometimes invisible car to Hogwarts, and in *The Deathly Hallows,* wherein Harry and his two companions forgo attendance at Hogwarts and only enter the school in secrecy via a magical painting in Hogsmeade, the small village located just outside of Hogwarts. At the school, Harry learns the essential lessons needed to save the magical world. This education includes spell casting, potion making, flying on a broomstick, and learning how to defend himself against the dark arts. Without the teachers and the wisdom they impart, he would have died. At the same time, Harry faces his first real heroic challenges at Hogwarts. Despite the declaration of Hagrid, Hogwarts groundskeeper, that there is no safer place on Earth than Hogwarts, Harry faces potential death each and every year. In the first year alone, Harry has to save his friend Hermione from a troll, prevent Hagrid from raising a dangerous dragon, enter the Forbidden Forest, combat a series of obstacles to then face a possessed professor and kill him. The ability to perform these tasks is a combination of Harry's innate gifts and the education he receives. Each year the danger escalates as Harry's abilities improve, while still centered on this training ground. Only when Harry has mastered certain skills does Rowling allow him to enter the wider world and take up those challenges.

Once Harry has learned to combat obstacles in the former two realms, he is prepared to face the most dangerous enemies. In the final books of the series, Harry and his friends have to combat a multitude of crises, finally ending in an all-out battle with Voldemort and his acolytes. This war takes the trio all over England, including having to revisit locations wherein his younger self had already done battle and won, but alongside adults who were more skilled. At 16 and 17, Harry is asked to do combat against people more than two or three times his age and who, unlike the heroes, do not have a code prohibiting the use of torture or murder. They are also forced to forgo the comfort of home or the relative safety of Hogwarts, eventually unable to stay in any one place for long. The wider world is open to them at the same time they are hunted everywhere.

THE PLACE OF MAGIC IN GROWING UP

By comparing the three realms of the Harry Potter universe, one can see that the overreaching arc of the saga is reflected in the location the characters inhabit. While Harry's world was limited to the Dursley house, he was in no danger at all from mortal peril, although he did not fit in and was emotionally unfulfilled. As Harry's universe expanded, so did his knowledge of magic and so did the level of danger in equal measure. At the series' end, Harry is committed to a life of continued exploration in the magical world, which also means being perpetually involved in life-threatening situations.

Ultimately, the trials faced by Harry Potter and his friends represent metaphors for the tribulations of growing up and coming to terms with the shortfalls of one's family and teachers. These young characters grow up and learn to trust themselves and one another to solve problems that grown-ups cannot understand. They do so successfully over the course of a fantastical narrative that concludes when the protagonist learns his true place in the world.

Rachelanne Smith

Further Reading
If you liked *Harry Potter,* then you might like *The Lightning Thief* by Rick Riordan, because it also tells a story of the self-discovery and courage of Percy Jackson, who discovers his father is actually Poseidon, God of the Sea, and how he must use his own supernatural abilities to prevent a war between the gods. A novel trilogy that similarly explores adolescent identity is Suzanne Collins's *The Hunger Games*, in which a young woman who thought she was only meant to be a hunter and gatherer becomes the start of a revolution in a dystopian world. Another good recommendation is Madeleine L'Engle's *A Wrinkle in Time,* a story about courage, perseverance, and overcoming the battle between good and evil.

Bibliography
Baratta, Chris, ed. *Environmentalism in the Realm of Science Fiction and Fantasy Literature.* Newcastle upon Tyne: Cambridge Scholars Publishing, 2012.
Beauchamp, Michelle. "Sacred Places, Storied Places: Ancient Wisdom for a Modern World." PhD diss., University of Victoria, 2013.
Brooks-Gillies, Marilee. "Crafting Place: Rhetorical Practices of the Everyday." PhD diss., Michigan State University, 2013.
Carroll, Jane Suzanne. *Landscape in Children's Literature.* New York: Routledge, 2011.
Hameed, Alya Javed. "Drawing Resistance: The Unsettling and Provocative Influence of Maps in Children's Literature." Master's thesis, San Diego State University, 2014. http://hdl.handle.net/10211.3/127616.
Hochbruck, Wolfgang, Elmo Feiten, and Anja Tiedemann. "'Vulchanov! Volkov! Aaaaaaaaand Krum!': Joanne K. Rowling's 'Eastern' Europe." In *Facing the East in the West: Images of Eastern Europe in British Literature, Film and Culture,* edited by Barbara Korte, Eva Ulrike Pirker, and Sissy Helff. Amsterdam: Rodopi, 2010.
Lee, Christina. "'Have Magic, Will Travel': Tourism and Harry Potter's United (Magical) Kingdom." *Tourist Studies* 12, no. 1 (2012): 52–69.
Powell, Fred. "The Cultural Landscape of Childhood: Fairy Tales, Little People and Media Giants." *An Leanbh Óg* 8 (2014): 23–38.
Schult, Stefanie. *Subcreation: Fictional-World Construction from J. R. R. Tolkein to Terry Pratchett and Tad Williams.* Berlin: Logos Verlag, 2017.
Sundmark, Bjorn. "'Dragons Be Here': Teaching Children's Literature and Creative Writing with the Help of Maps." In *Thinking Through Children's Literature in the Classroom,* edited by Agustín Reyes-Torres, Luis S. Villacañas-de-Castro, and Betlem Soler-Pardo. Newcastle upon Tyne: Cambridge Scholars Publishing, 2014.

Hass, Robert

Since his first book *Field Guide* (1973), Robert Hass has grounded his poems in his home state of California and the way memories of place can bring comfort and healing to the emotional pain of life. The poems in *Field Guide* delve into the countryside and name the flora and fauna there. Hass tends to use place-names in his poem titles and to find answers to the private riddles of his speakers' lives within the landscape.

"Iowa City: Early April" is an obsessive chronicle of the animals he witnesses in his yard: cats, raccoons, woodchucks, cardinals, and so on. You might expect the long and lyrical list of animals sharing the landscape with him to end with some kind of moral, but Hass uses a light touch here. He points to some of the ways that humans and animals will never understand each other, and flips the perspective, imagining what it would be like to be a raccoon and have to come to terms with sharing your world with humans. He ends the poem with the idea that he doesn't even always know who he is himself, so it would be difficult for the raccoon to know him. The intersection of other lives with our own points to the inherent mystery of the self, whether animal or human.

"Meditation at Lagunitas" is another poem in which attention to the natural world reveals more mystery than it resolves. Images from nature are invoked here in a failed attempt to make meaning out of the details of the world we inhabit and point to the existence of certain symbols that take us into spaces of the memory, like the woman he recalls, whose body makes him remember a river he fished as a child. He concludes that we are often using the other lives close to ours as portals to memory, creating a disconnect between the concrete reality in front of us and the meanings it takes on.

In "San Pedro Road," the poem's speaker finds the lesson in nature for which his speakers had been searching. A fisherman casts from shore, and as he takes in the landscape he notices how hot it is, how the fish refuse to bite in the heat, and all the other creatures he observes are enjoying shade and cool water. He has an epiphany, abandons his fishing rod, and goes swimming in the cool water, communing with the creek as he becomes the fish he had been hoping to catch.

In much of Hass' work, he tackles the problems that language has to accurately represent the world that we see. Nowhere is that more clearly established than in his poem "The Problem of Describing Trees." In this poem, he eventually gives up trying to be poetic about how aspen move in the wind because nothing he says in words will truly capture the beauty of seeing it. Instead, he encourages his readers to live the moment with the tree when they see it. In this case, his writing calls attention to the presence of reality that words sometimes fail to adequately recapture.

However, sometimes this gap between the human experience in language and a wordless experience of the world is cause for some sorrow in Hass' work. "Misery and Splendor," for instance, captures that same desire to become animal that can be found in many other poems by Hass as well as the failure of language to fully articulate or make present again a physical connection with the natural landscape. In this poem, Hass describes that sorrow as a consciousness, that there is a world out there that humans cannot fully access, perhaps because of our own humanness, which implies pride and a turning away from the conditions of reality. Ultimately, it seems from the poem, it is the pursuit of human activities that might separate us from full involvement in the natural world around us. Hass seems to want the male and female characters in this poem to embrace their animal nature, something less refined, to access the "garden . . . to which they can never be admitted." Human relationships, in this poem and others, pale in comparison to the encounter one has to have with one's animal nature if one is to die in peace. Regarding romantic relationships, those are portrayed as fleeting in his work. The only fidelity worth pursuing in the universe his words build is that of the faithfulness of observation.

In many of Hass' poems, he seems to admit that the best way poetry can convey an experience of place and of the natural world is through mapping a speaker's private world onto the landscape. However, many of us can share those private moments as they are calling us to contemplation and self-reflection, as in "Measure," when a sunset prompts the speaker to assert ". . . I almost glimpse / what I was born to." By that, he means not necessarily the quality of light he admires from the sun setting behind the mountains, but in his struggle to write about it. This mirrors the emphasis Hass places on community and connectedness both in his poetry and in his activism. One of the common ways his speakers establish connection to place is through naming and through understanding the history of a place, both in terms of geology and human migration.

Politically, Hass advocates for conservationism and ecoliteracy. In line with the idea that living a moment is perhaps better than trying to describe it in poetry, Robert Hass cofounded a nonprofit organization called River of Words that is involved in various projects aiming to connect people to the environment. Hass has stated in various interviews that the attention to language and naming in poetry can help people pay better attention to places they inhabit.

Lynn Marie Houston

Further Reading
Other poets who write with a similar style about similar themes include Mark Doty, Brenda Hillman, Jane Hirschfield, and Charles Wright.

Bibliography
Gery, John. "Robert Hass and the Poetry of Nostalgia." *The Threepenny Review* 5 (1981): 6–7.

Hume, Angela. "Imagining Ecopoetics: An Interview with Robert Hass, Brenda Hillman, Evelyn Reilly, and Jonathan Skinner." *ISLE: Interdisciplinary Studies in Literature and Environment* 19, no. 4 (December 2012): 751–66. https://doi.org/10.1093/isle/iss104.

Terrence, Doody. "From Image to Sentence: The Spiritual Development of Robert Hass." *The American Poetry Review* 26, no. 2 (1997): 47–56.

Wilson, Edward O., and Robert Hass. *The Poetic Species: A Conversation with Edward O. Wilson and Robert Hass.* New York: Bellevue Literary Press, 2014.

Heaney, Seamus

THE GEOGRAPHY OF HOME: SEAMUS HEANEY'S IRELAND

Home for Nobel laureate (1995) Seamus Heaney was the north of Ireland, a country of ancient cultural continuities and a history of invasions and exiles, upheaval and disruption. Heaney's poetry is rooted in this ancestry and currency, as is his literary prose. These tensions are evident in his essay titles, which include "The Sense of Place," "Englands of the Mind," "The Place of Writing," "Place and Displacement," "The Placeless Heaven," "Through-Other Places, Through-Other Times: The Irish Poet and Britain," and other essays and reviews that consider the relation of place to the poets who write there. In one of those preoccupations in his first collection, *Preoccupations,* Heaney in "The Sense of Place" considers how specific Irish places have affected poets of the last century. He finds there are two ways that poets know and value places: it may be sensed either through a "shared oral inherited culture" or a "consciously savoured literary culture." Growing poetry in a land one belongs to is not unique to Heaney, but the urgency with which he pursues the relation in his work derives from the "fractures" of Irish history, north and south, and the possession and dispossession of both land and language. Heaney's poetry names, elicits, evokes, summons, or implies place in its fullest physical and spiritual presence, with a devotion and dexterity that animates the elegant economy of his line.

The first poem that Heaney said had "his feel" is "Digging," which establishes in a small, family tableau, the ancient connection between writing and plowing the earth, which is the literal sense of "geography," the writing in earth, or "earthwriting." The young man's father digging potatoes in the garden reminds him of his grandfather cutting turf, or peat, outside the room where Seamus is writing. Characteristically, Heaney's visceral language invokes the physical image, which prompts a paradoxical revelation that both distances him from and draws him closer to his ancestral occupations: the pen in his hand. The metaphoric pen as shovel evokes the ancient origin of writing in clay, the plowing and planting and harvesting of words. The Greek word for writing was *boustrophedon,* or "ox plowing a field." Many of the technical words in poetry originate in working the earth.

Heaney's poetic geography grew from that home garden to the wilds and bogs and cliffs and towns of Ireland now and of old. The poet-bard is the visionary one who sees into what others may not even see. In that way, Heaney's poetry strips the common from the commonplace, leaving the richest, deepest sense of place, cleansed of the dull obscurity of custom. Often a poem starts when his eye falls on what is at hand, such as a sandstone rock in "Sandstone Keepsake," which he picked up while wading in a river in the peninsula of Inishowen. A picturesque tourist destination, it was also the scene of murderous conflict during the Troubles (1968–1998). Heaney begins the poem with a quasi-scientific observation about a chunk of sandstone that tones down into the simple pleasure of hefting it. His literary imagination heats up, supposes it could be stone from the river of boiling blood in Dante's *Inferno,* or the heart of the murderer Guy de Montfort whom Dante consigned to the river. But he dismisses his imaginings and grounds us in the moment of being present with the stone "wet red stone in [his] hand."

One of the venerators, he says he was, possibly of the heart of de Montfort's victim, killed in 1271, which was kept in a casket and "long venerated." The poem's symmetry gives another object for his reverence: as he beholds the ordinary sandstone, he is checked as prey ("swooped on, then dropped") by predatory "trained binoculars" from a watchtower manned by one or another. The poet is hardly concerned. The trained lookout sizes him up, but is unable to see into his heart in sympathy with the murdered victims, and venerating as well the sandstone keepsake of the very rock that makes up Inishowen, that has endured, been injured, and fits his hand like a hurt heart.

Robert R. Bensen

Further Reading

Ted Hughes and Derek Walcott are poets whose works are often read in conjunction with Heaney's. Hughes and Heaney co-edited two poetry anthologies together: *The Rattle Bag* (1982) and *The School Bag* (1997). Similar to Heaney's, Walcott's poetry emphasizes metaphors related to space, especially the landscape and the built environment.

Bibliography

Alexander, Neal. "Contemporary British Poetry and the Senses of Place." *International Journal of Welsh Writing in English* 2 (2014): 1–27.

Alexander, Neal, and David Cooper, eds. *Poetry & Geography: Space & Place in Postwar Poetry.* Liverpool, UK: Liverpool University Press, 2013.

Butler, Toby. "A Walk of Art: The Potential of the Sound Walk as Practice in Cultural Geography." *Social & Cultural Geography* 7, no. 6 (2006): 889–908. doi:10.1080/14649360601055821.

Carruth, Allison. "On Bog Lands and Digital Markets: Seamus Heaney's Recent Poetry." *Pacific Coast Philology* 46, no. 2 (2011): 232–44. www.jstor.org/stable/41851027.

Coughlan, Patricia. "'Bog Queens': The Representation of Women in the Poetry of John Montague and Seamus Heaney." In *Seamus Heaney: Contemporary Critical Essays*, 185–205. London: Palgrave Macmillan, 1997.

Cronin, Nessa. "Lived and Learned Landscapes: Literary Geographies and the Irish Topographical Tradition." In *Irish Contemporary Landscapes in Literature and the Arts,* edited by Marie Mianowski. London: Palgrave Macmillan, 2012. doi:10.1057/9780230360297_9.

Garden, Alison. "'We Listen for What the Waves Intone': Intertextuality and the Circum-Atlantic Poetics of Seamus Heaney, Natasha Trethewey and Kwame Dawes." *Comparative American Studies: An International Journal* 14, no. 2 (2016): 91–108. doi:10.1080/14775700.2016.1242576.

Gladwin, Derek. *Contentious Terrains: Boglands in the Irish Postcolonial Gothic.* Cork, Ireland: Cork University Press, 2016.

He, Yaorong. "Allied and Alienated: Landscape in Seamus Heaney's Early Poetry." *English Language and Literature Studies* 4, no. 4 (2014): 79–85. doi:10.5539/ells.v4n4p79.

He, Yaorong. "Language and Landscape—Dinnshenchas in Seamus Heaney's Poetry." *Advances in Literary Study* 4, no. 1 (2016): 8–15. doi:10.4236/als.2016.41002.

Hong, Song Sook. "Utopia in Yeats's and Heaney's Poems." *The Yeats Journal of Korea* 45 (2014): 145–60.

Ingelbien, Raphaël. "Mapping the Misreadings: Ted Hughes, Seamus Heaney, and Nationhood." *Contemporary Literature* 40, no. 4 (1999): 627–58. doi:10.2307/1208797.

Kennedy-Andrews, Elmer. *Writing Home: Poetry and Place in Northern Ireland, 1968–2008.* Cambridge, UK: D. S. Brewer, 2008.

Lidström, Susanna. *Nature, Environment and Poetry: Ecocriticism and the Poetics of Seamus Heaney and Ted Hughes.* London: Routledge, 2015.

Lidström, Susanna, and Greg Garrard. "'Images Adequate to Our Predicament': Ecology, Environment and Ecopoetics." *Environmental Humanities* 5, no. 1 (2014): 35–53. doi:10.1215/22011919-3615406.

Malone, Christopher T. "Writing Home: Spatial Allegories in the Poetry of Seamus Heaney and Paul Muldoon." *ELH* 67, no. 4 (2000): 1083–109. www.jstor.org/stable/30031952.

McGinley, Christopher J. "'The Boundaries of the Land': Sectarian Division and the Politicization of Space in the Poetry of Seamus Heaney." *Colby Quarterly* 32, no. 2 (1996): 125–34.

McIntosh, Paul. "Poetics and Space: Developing a Reflective Landscape through Imagery and Human Geography." *Reflective Practice: International and Multidisciplinary Perspectives* 9, no. 1 (2008): 69–78. doi:10.1080/14623940701816667.

Nagnath, Mhamane Vijay. "An Exploration in the History, Maps and Landscape in the Selected Poems of Seamus Heaney." PhD diss., Solapur University, 2017. http://hdl.handle.net/10603/175887.

Nash, Catherine. "Remapping and Renaming: New Cartographies of Identity, Gender and Landscape in Ireland." *Feminist Review* 44, no. 1 (1993): 39–57.

Raez-Padilla, Juan. "Seamus Heaney's 'Elemental' Ecopoetics: Earth, Water, Air and Fire." *Journal of Ecocriticism* 1, no. 2 (2009): 21–30.

Ramazani, Jahan. "The Local Poem in a Global Age." *Critical Inquiry* 43, no. 3 (2017): 670–96.

Zirra, Oiana. "Re-Inscribing Irish History in the Language of Post-Colonial Geography." *University of Bucharest Review: A Journal of Literary and Cultural Studies* no. 1 (2007): 72–78.

Heart of Darkness

Joseph Conrad's 1899 novella is about European colonization of Africa. Narrated by the character Charles Marlow, the story follows his journey up the Congo River to find Kurtz, a man both feared and revered, as he has apparently achieved godlike status among the natives whose resources he is tasked with exploiting. Marlow's journey catalogs many of the injustices done to African natives by the encroaching European powers who seek to take ivory, among other natural resources. As Marlow continues on his quest to find Kurtz, he meets others who know him and who attempt to justify his brutal methods, of which Marlow sees evidence when he witnesses the native heads impaled on spikes surrounding one of the stations. Marlow finally reaches Kurtz and realizes that he is very sick. They get him aboard the steamship, but Kurtz leaves in the middle of the night, trying to get back to his settlement. They bring him back on board the ship, where he dies, uttering enigmatic last words that could be interpreted as a condemnation of his part in African imperialism. Marlow falls ill, too. When he recovers, he seeks out Kurtz's fiancée back in Europe and lies to her when she asks about his final moments, telling her instead that Kurtz was thinking of her at the end.

MAPPING AFRICA IN THE IMAGINATION OF COLONIZERS

Marlow admits that when he was young, he loved maps, and that this affinity led him to his current occupation, steamboat captain. He especially notes that he has a particular interest in the "blank places" that had not yet been detailed on maps. Marlow desires some "off grid" adventure, and this is what he finds in the Congo.

However, the description of this region in Africa moves from what Marlow was hoping to find—its blankness—with what he does find—its darkness. The two descriptions are not the same: the first suggests that the place is waiting for humans (Europeans) to make sense of it and to mark it as a place, fill in its contours. The second descriptor suggests a kind of evil. It's hard to know which of the many evils in the novella the word *darkness* references. For the thwarted colonizers, it is clearly the African natives themselves. However, at the end of the narrative, it might be argued that Marlow has come to understand the darkness of the European exploitation of Africa. Kurtz may be a god to the natives, but to Marlow he is a heavily flawed and failed man, whose inadequacies have to be ignored or rewritten by those who love him. The journey into "the heart of darkness" is also Marlow's journey from an innocent youth who craved travel and adventure to a worldly man who understands that one person's desire for trade routes is another person's experience of colonization and exploitation. When he was younger, Marlow wanted to make his mark on the world through discovery, but what he learns is that this is not the innocent or healthy enterprise he imagined it would be. It wasn't so much a space on the map that was blank at the outset of this story, but Marlow's understanding. He fills in that knowledge with the horrors of imperialism.

However, another instance of gazing on a map allows for a more nuanced interpretation: for Conrad, not all colonialism was to be treated equally. Before Marlow embarks on his voyage, Conrad positions him in front of another map, this one hanging in company headquarters. Here, Marlow takes in the different color-coding on the map, which marks the areas of different colonial rule in Africa. His commentary on the red, the British section, is that it represents "some real work" being done for the people in those areas. Colonialism, apparently, was only as good as the European power that conducted it. For Marlow, Britain's activities were worthy of praise, but not those by France, Germany, or Belgium.

THE MORAL LANDSCAPE OF COLONIALISM

Given that he had wanted to travel to Africa since he was a boy, one would expect that Marlow's descriptions of the scenery in his boat ride up the Congo would be particularly vivid and evocative. However, this is far from the truth. His descriptions of the landscape are often tentative and inexact. What does come across with certitude only has to do with the area's hostility and impenetrability. Marlow finds no beauty in what he views of the land, only darkness. The land he so desperately wanted to commune with, whose secrets he wanted to unravel, refuses to speak to him.

Kurtz appears to access more of Africa's secrets than Marlow does. He has a lover among the African natives who is devoted to him. He has been elevated to the status of a god among the locals. However, none of this matters, as the truth of the life he lived there is lost to history—both Kurtz's fiancée and Marlow traffic in lies (or half-truths) about him after his death, whitewashing his role in the subjugation and dehumanization of the Congolese natives.

Joseph Conrad traveled the Congo in 1890 and kept a diary as well as sent letters home. Yet much of what he witnessed there—efficient factories and sprawling plantations—was far more developed than the primitive and tentative footholds that

Marlow describes in his journey. Conrad writes to his family about feeling like a "white slave," while bankers back in Europe got rich off the work that traders like him were doing. Marlow becomes a mouthpiece for this worldview when one night he hears drumming from a nearby village and ponders how both he and the African people making that music are connected through a common humanity. Little glimpses of Conrad's disillusionment with the colonial enterprise make their way into the novella, which is not wholly unquestioning about the politics of imperialism. However, Marlow's brief philosophical musings about a common humanity are drowned out by the violence done to the African natives and the host of other characters who buy into the rhetoric of the Europeans' duty to bring civilization to these otherwise savage parts of the globe, which masked the theft of those regions' valuable natural resources. Confronting the ethics of such an endeavor—its heart of darkness—reveals European decadence and decline, as what was once thought to be "civilized" is now seen as barbaric.

Lynn Marie Houston

Further Reading

Although written 80 years later, V. S. Naipaul's *A Bend in the River* is often compared to Conrad's classic work. It involves an Indian protagonist who travels to and lives in an African society whose identity is in flux as it engages with its history of colonialism. Rudyard Kipling's novel *Kim* also captures a friendship between two men set against the backdrop of colonial considerations and involving a heroic quest. E. M. Forster's *A Passage to India* is also about India rather than Africa but many readers find that it captures the same conflict between colonialism and independence as Conrad's work.

Bibliography

Bulson, Eric. *Novels, Maps, Modernity: The Spatial Imagination, 1850–2000*. New York: Routledge, 2007.

Clemens, Florence. "Joseph Conrad as a Geographer." *The Scientific Monthly* 51, no. 5 (1940): 460–65. www.jstor.org/stable/17401.

Driver, F. "Geography's Empire: Histories of Geographical Knowledge." *Environment and Planning D: Society and Space* 10, no. 1 (1992): 23–40. doi:10.1068/d100023.

Eklund, Lovisa. "Shut In or Exposed—Inhospitable Landscapes in Joseph Conrad's *Heart of Darkness* and Cormac McCarthy's *Blood Meridian*." Bachelor's thesis, Lund University, 2013.

Frayn, Andrew. "'Now—Well, Look at the Chart': Mapping, Maps and Literature." In *Mapping Across Academia*, edited by Stanley D. Brunn and Martin Dodge. Dordrecht, Netherlands: Springer, 2017. doi:10.1007/978-94-024-1011-2_13.

Harpold, Terry. "Dark Continents: A Critique of Internet Metageographies." *Postmodern Culture* 9, no. 2 (1999).

Hudson, Brian J. "Geographical Education in the World of English Literature." *Journal of Geography* 86, no. 3 (1987): 109–13. doi:10.1080/00221348708979472.

Jarosz, Lucy. "Constructing the Dark Continent: Metaphor as Geographic Representation of Africa." *Geografiska Annaler: Series B, Human Geography* 74, no. 2 (1992): 105–15. doi:10.1080/04353684.1992.11879634.

Parrinder, Patrick. "'Heart of Darkness': Geography as Apocalypse." In *Fin de Siecle/Fin du Globe: Fears and Fantasies of the Late Nineteenth Century*, edited by John Stokes. London: Palgrave Macmillan, 1992. doi:10.1007/978-1-349-22421-0_6.

Phillips, Richard. *Mapping Men and Empire: A Geography of Adventure.* New York: Routledge, 1997.

Vivan, Itala. "Geography, Literature, and the African Territory: Some Observations on the Western Map and the Representation of Territory in the South African Literary Imagination." *Research in African Literatures* 31, no. 2 (2000): 49–70. www.jstor.org/stable/3821044.

West-Pavlov, Russell. "Maps and the Geography of Violence: Farah's *Maps* and Conrad's *Heart of Darkness.*" In *The New Violent Cartography: Geo-Analysis after the Aesthetic Turn,* edited by Samson Opondo and Michael J. Shapiro. London: Routledge, 2012.

The Hitchhiker's Guide to the Galaxy

Douglas Adams's *The Hitchhiker's Guide to the Galaxy* is an absurd and hilarious journey through the far reaches of space. It's an off-kilter odyssey in which the Prime Directive of *Star Trek* is, as a rule, repeatedly violated by a revolving door of characters. As the offspring of space opera and Monty Python, the story embodies the best of comedic sci-fi mixed with sociopolitical commentary.

Fictional geographies are central to *The Hitchhiker's Guide*. Modern Earth itself plays a somewhat minor role as a location. It exists—in the most literal sense of the word—only 25 or so pages before being demolished to build an intergalactic express route. During this sequence, readers are introduced to Arthur Dent, human, and Ford Prefect, extraterrestrial and traveling correspondent for the publication arm of the fictional Hitchhiker's Guide to the Galaxy. Ford's *Guide* entry on Earth is, like the planet, fleeting. "Mostly harmless" is the whole of the description.

EARTH AND ITS ANTECEDENTS

Though the Earth as we know it was not long a featured element in the story, there are instances in which variations of it do make an appearance. Arthur and Ford are saved by a starship called *The Heart of Gold,* integrating with the crew already aboard—the two of whom turn out to be a failed romantic conquest from Arthur's past as well as Ford's alien relative. The first task the group embarks on is locating Magrathea, a long-hibernating planet that at its cultural peak built planets for wealthy clientele. It turns out the recently destroyed Earth was one of these commissioned planets. This is where the author, in a particularly clever creation story and chronology, explains that the Earth was created to function as a living organic computer used to calculate the meaning of life. Moreover, the original commission to build Earth came from creatures known on Earth as laboratory mice, but which are actually sentient beings far more intelligent than *Homo sapiens.* After the destruction of the first Earth, a second is requested—again by some lab mice—and Magrathean civilization comes out of hibernation to complete the work.

In a different story thread, after a crash landing on a planet, there is a deep sense of geographic déjà vu, the sense of having been in the place before. The characters soon realize they have crashed on a prehistoric Earth. Many thousands of modern humans have survived the crash as well, and we soon realize that modern man is no more advanced than his prehistoric counterpart. The allegedly more sophisticated, modern humans are incapable of starting anew on this planet. Not only do the new inhabitants lack all practical and technical knowledge, they lack ethical principles as well. These new inhabitants continue to follow well-worn historical trajectories, declaring war on the first group of peaceful, prehistoric humanoids they meet. This is an interesting juxtaposition from a historical or anthropological viewpoint.

CHARACTERS AND PLACES

Throughout this book, the crew of the *Heart of Gold* encounter a staggering array of organisms and planets. A few of the more memorable include the Vogon, a disgusting, mean-spirited, and bureaucratic species, the Babel Fish, a benign creature that can be put in the ear canal and act as a translator for any language, the Ravenous Bugblatter Beast of Traal, and Marvin the Paranoid Android who works aboard the *Heart of Gold*. The *Hitchhiker's Guide* contains facts on most of these and their home planets, and readily dispenses wisdom on how to deal with those that an individual comes into contact with.

In the subsequent book in the series, *The Restaurant at the End of the Universe*, the crew travels to a restaurant at the edge of the universe, (almost) to the heart of the sun, a desolate, evil planet known as the Frogstar, and many more in addition. The distance they are able to travel is due to the Infinite Improbability Drive powering the *Heart of Gold,* which allows passage from one locational extreme to the other in an improbably short amount of time. At regular intervals, readers are treated to somewhat exhaustive and digressive planetary descriptions courtesy of the fictional *Hitchhiker's Guide*.

PERSPECTIVES

In *The Hitchhiker's Guide to the Galaxy,* there is no one central geography within which the story takes place. In fact, the closest the book comes to having a geographic center is the *Heart of Gold* ship. In this vessel, the crew spends most of its time traveling from one quasi-mission to the next. With the destruction of Earth, readers become hitchhikers as well, rousted from their home in the same way as Arthur Dent and Ford Prefect. The outsider perspective of readers—"hitchhikers"—provides a relatively unsullied view of the new geographies encountered. It is a way of observing without going native. Readers are meant to become comfortable with discomfort and uncertainty. For this reason, the *Guide* is emblazoned with the words "Don't Panic" on the cover.

In addition to the immeasurably large trove of facts the *Guide* contains, by its very nature readers are forced to contemplate geographic perspective and scale in the extreme. In the context of the *Guide* and the many worlds it contains, readers/hitchhikers realize that temporal and physical existence are fleeting and small. This is yet another reason to take seriously the *Guide*'s imperative slogan, "Don't Panic."

Chris Peters

Further Reading
Other writers whose works explore alternative worlds within the genre of science fiction are Isaac Asimov, Philip K. Dick, Frank Herbert, and H. G. Wells. Asimov and Dick often wrote about the human relationship with robotic technology, imagining possible futures for society here on Earth. Frank Herbert wrote the *Dune* saga, a series of novels about the political unrest and fragile ecology of a planet named Arrakis.

Bibliography
Kennedy, Barbara A. "On Outrageous Hypotheses in Geography." *Geography* 68, no. 4 (1983): 326–30.
Kirchner, James W. "The Gaia Hypothesis: Fact, Theory, and Wishful Thinking." *Climatic Change* 52, no. 4 (2002): 391–408.
Krylov, Anna I. "Equation-of-Motion Coupled-Cluster Methods for Open-Shell and Electronically Excited Species: The Hitchhiker's Guide to Fock Space." *Annual Review of Physical Chemistry* 59 (2008).
Wark, McKenzie. "Third Nature." *Cultural Studies* 8, no. 1 (1994): 115–32.

The House on Mango Street

Described variously as a bildungsroman (coming-of-age novel or novel of personal development), a *künstlerroman* (novel of artistic development), a novella composed of vignettes, a short story cycle, and as a collection of prose poems that may be read in or out of sequence, Sandra Cisneros's genre-busting text, *The House on Mango Street,* explores the relationship between place and (individual and communal) identity construction. Each of the text's 44 stories and character sketches are connected through adolescent Chicana narrator Esperanza Cordero, whose observations about her family's house and her Chicago neighborhood elucidate the ongoing disenfranchisement of minority communities in the United States, and, in particular, of Latinas who live in those communities. Esperanza witnesses neighborhood women and girls being confined to domestic roles in domestic spaces by their husbands, boyfriends, and fathers, which compels her to seek out a liberatory space that will facilitate, not foreclose, her personal agency.

ISSUES OF RACE AND CLASS

The collection's first vignette, "The House on Mango Street," begins with Esperanza listing the street names where her family rented apartments before buying the single-family property they now occupy: the list is long and eventually reaches a point where the narrator admits that she has forgotten a number of streets where she lived. She expresses gratitude for the house on Mango Street after such an itinerant life. Homeownership should signify the Cordero family's economic success and their rootedness in mainstream American life. Instead, the house is a metaphor for the ongoing political, social, and economic marginalization and containment of a minority community. The idealized suburban and middle-class home that her father dreamed of when he purchased a ticket for the lottery, that her mother spoke of wistfully in the stories she told her children before bed, and that Esperanza sees in television shows contrasts starkly with the house the Corderos actually are able to acquire.

The image of home that Esperanza's parents and dominant U.S. popular culture have presented to her as "real" (that is, legitimate and aspirational) has "a basement and at least three washrooms," is "white with trees around it, [and has] a great big yard and grass growing." Conversely, the Corderos' house is small, with red bricks that are eroding, and located on a very small piece of property. The family of six must all share one bathroom. By highlighting the discrepancy between the family's fantasy of owning a house like the ones they have dreamed about and the reality of homeownership in an impoverished urban environment, the text exposes the American dream as an exclusionary myth through the family's disappointment. In subsequent vignettes including "Those Who Don't," "Bums in the Attic," "Cathy Queen of Cats," and "Alicia & I Talking on Edna's Steps," Esperanza's disillusionment about her family's house evolves into a pointed commentary on a racist and classist ideology and attendant political structure that ignores the barrio's material conditions and that fuels white flight to racially homogenous suburban enclaves like those where Esperanza's father may work but never live.

THE BARRIO AS IDENTITY

The narrative's barrio setting reflects a critical shift in Chicano literature away from the natural environment in the 1960s and 1970s to houses and the built environment. In particular, as Monika Kaup and others have noted, many Chicana writers who rose to prominence during the 1980s, including Cisneros, sought to challenge the second-class status of women by using the image of the house as both a means to articulate sexual discrimination in Chicano culture and to imagine alternatives to women's marginalization due to gender subordination. Thus, even as Esperanza perceives the neighborhood to be an important site of communal belonging in racially, ethnically, and economically stratified Chicago—she feels safe in a neighborhood where everyone's skin color is like hers, but admits that she fears entering areas where she is in the minority—she also acknowledges the severe limitations Mango Street's gender hierarchy imposes on its female residents.

GENDER AND REPRESSION

The narrator's relative youth allows her to traverse the one-block perimeter of Mango Street, but most of the young Chicanas and Puertorriqueñas she knows are forced to occupy liminal spaces, like doorways and open windows, where they may observe, but not fully participate in, street life. For instance, Rafaela can only look out the window because her husband locks her inside their apartment because he worries that she will leave him. Another neighbor, Sally, endures violent beatings from her father if she does not come home immediately after school. Marin's, Rafaela's, and Sally's confinement stems from the community's phallocentric perception that young women who transgress the conventionally gendered boundary between masculine public and feminine private space are morally or sexually suspect. Observing the circumscribed lives her neighbors lead teaches Esperanza that she is unwilling to become like them. Consequently, the narrator rejects Mango Street's patriarchal value system by imagining her own space of feminist agency: a house that is her own and not one owned by a man. Esperanza's dream of having her own private physical space is, ultimately, a dream to dwell in an imaginative space that will foster the future storyteller's efforts at writing "her story," but not just for her own life: for the women in her community, as well.

Marci L. Carrasquillo

Further Reading

For further readings that foreground place and the construction of individual and communal Chicana/o identity, see, for instance, Norma Elia Cantú's *Canícula: Snapshots of a Girlhood en la Frontera;* Denise Chavez's *The Last of the Menu Girls;* Cisneros's collection of short stories, *Woman Hollering Creek and Other Stories,* or her novel, *Caramelo.*

Bibliography

Brady, Mary Pat. "The Contrapuntal Geographies of Woman Hollering Creek and Other Stories." *American Literature* 71, no. 1 (1999): 117–50. www.jstor.org/stable/2902591.

Comer, Krista. *Landscapes of the New West: Gender and Geography in Contemporary Women's Writing.* Chapel Hill: University of North Carolina Press, 1999.

Holmes, Christina. "Chicana Environmentalisms: Deterritorialization as a Practice of Decolonization." PhD diss., Ohio State University, 2010.

Holmes, Christina. *Ecological Borderlands: Body, Nature, and Spirit in Chicana Feminism.* Urbana: University of Illinois Press, 2016.

Jacobson, Kristin J. *Neodomestic American Fiction.* Columbus: The Ohio State University Press, 2010.

Kaup, Monika. "The Architecture of Ethnicity in Chicano Literature." *American Literature* 69, no. 2 (1997): 361–97.

Klahn, Norma. "Literary (Re)Mappings: Autobiographical (Dis)Placements by Chicana Writers." In *Chicana Feminisms: A Critical Reader,* edited by Gabriela F. Arredondo, Patricia Zavella, Aida Hurtado, Norma Klahn, and Olga Najera-Ramirez. Durham, NC: Duke University Press, 2003.

Lucksinger, Annette. "Ecopedagogy: Cultivating Environmental Consciousness through Sense of Place in Literature." *Pedagogy: Critical Approaches to Teaching Literature, Language, Composition, and Culture* 14, no. 2 (2014): 355–69. doi:10.1215/15314200-2400539.

Martin, Karen W. "The House (of Memory) on Mango Street: Sandra Cisneros's Counter-Poetics of Space." *South Atlantic Review* 73, no. 1 (2008): 50–67.

Mermann-Jozwiak, Elisabeth. "In the Corazón of the Capital: Globalization and Urban Design in Sandra Cisneros's *Caramelo.*" *Arizona Quarterly: A Journal of American Literature, Culture, and Theory* 74, no. 1 (2018): 93–117. doi:10.1353/arq.2018.0004.

Oliver-Rotger, Maria A. *Battlegrounds and Crossroads: Social and Imaginary Space in Writings by Chicanas.* New York: Rodopi, 2003.

Pérez, Lorna L. "Haunting the House on Mango Street: Sandra Cisneros's Radical Revisions." *CEA Critic* 74, no. 1 (2011): 80–98. www.jstor.org/stable/44378463.
Rodríguez, Rodrigo Joseph. "Whose House Is It Anyway?: Architects of the 'House' Leitmotif in the Literature from Mexican America." Master's thesis, University of Texas at Austin, 1999. http://hdl.handle.net/2152/14519.
Wickelson, Paul. "Shaking Awake the Memory: The Gothic Quest for Place in Sandra Cisneros's *Caramelo*." *Western American Literature* 48, no. 1 (2013): 90–114.

Hughes, Langston

Langston Hughes is known as one of the key figures in an African American literary movement known as the Harlem Renaissance. As the name implies, this movement was centered in the neighborhood of Harlem in the borough of Manhattan in New York City. This neighborhood became a kind of spiritual and cultural center for writers, artists, and musicians. Hughes was at the forefront of this movement that claimed legitimacy for forms of black cultural expression, which often included raising awareness of and encouraging resistance to institutions of white power. Scholars often consider the Harlem Renaissance to be an offshoot of an international literary modernism that was prevalent at the time; however, its inspiration was global in a unique way as it was tied to the African continent and to other countries around the world that house the African diaspora. The concept of diaspora is an important geographical element in Langston Hughes's poetry, as is the setting of Harlem.

THE GEOGRAPHY OF THE AFRICAN DIASPORA

In one of his most famous poems, "The Negro Speaks of Rivers," Hughes captures the spirit of the Harlem Renaissance as the emergence of a black identity as something to be championed over an American identity. The speaker of the poem narrates from the first-person perspective an existence that spans times and bridges distant places, becoming one voice for all African people who have come to the Americas. He uses rivers as the connection between these various lands, citing the Euphrates, the Congo, the Nile, and the Mississippi. By the end of the poem, rivers have become the blood of African people as the water branches out into a global diaspora, connected by a common blood to their ancient culture and lands. This connection with the land through its waterways is something that contributes to the richness of black culture in the poem; the speaker asserts that his "soul" is "deep like the rivers."

The poem "Brass Spittoons" offers a similar contemplation as the previously mentioned poem. In this poem, Hughes's speaker addresses a male figure who is cleaning spittoons in a number of named U.S. cities, which range from the East Coast, to the South, and the Midwest. Hughes compiles a verbal map of race and class exploitation, but the male character is meant to be all blacks and the individually named U.S. cities are meant to be all U.S. cities, a kind of African

American "everyman." The places and poor working conditions of the places in the poem speed by, and only slow down when Hughes delineates all of the bills this person has to pay. Although the male figure is repeatedly called "boy," readers realize from the bills he pays that the "boy" is actually a man, and the term is being used in a derogatory fashion. The male figure speaks in the first person in the second to last line of the poem, and Hughes betrays the kind of defeatist mentality he witnessed in people from the lower classes when faced with a system of racial oppression: the speaker seems to have bought into his own oppression, which Hughes shows is advanced in Christian terms, because he seems to feel grateful that he can clean spittoons for rich whites.

BLACK CULTURE IN HARLEM

Hughes was interested in portraying the reality of the black working class, not idealizing it. He writes poems about the difficult living situations people had in Harlem, their fights with landlords. Hughes borrowed his poetic cadence, the rhythm and repetition of his words, from the blues music popular in Harlem at the time that he as writing, a form of music that chronicled the difficulties and sorrows of the working class. On a larger level, Hughes writes about the failed promise of

This 1929 photo shows 130th Street in Harlem, New York, a few blocks from where Langston Hughes lived. Hughes was an important figure of the Harlem Renaissance movement in the 1920s. (Irving Browning/The New York Historical Society/Getty Images)

America, the failure of American democracy that promised freedom to everyone but only gave it to wealthy whites. This is the common theme of many of his famous poems, including "Let America be America Again" and "I, Too."

Perhaps his most famous poem of all time is "Harlem." Lorraine Hansberry used a line from this poem ("raisin in the sun") as the title of one of her plays. In this poem, Hughes poses the question: what is the result when someone has to give up on a "dream"? He lays out various scenarios, comparing the dream to various foodstuffs that go bad when they are no longer fresh. But in the final line of the poem, he suggests that the "dream deferred" goes off like a bomb. The suggestion of violence at the end of this poem is the inevitable outcome, Hughes seems to be saying, to the ways in which black Americans have been refused freedom and the pursuit of happiness. The Harlem Renaissance celebrated African American culture and called out racism in America.

Lynn Marie Houston

Further Reading
Some of Langston Hughes's poetic phrasings are inspired by Walt Whitman. Both of these poets had similar projects, to celebrate the American people and their work. Claude McKay and Countee Cullen were two other poets essential to the Harlem Renaissance movement.

Bibliography
Berry, Faith. *Langston Hughes: Before and Beyond Harlem*. New York: Citadel Press, 1992.

Davis, Arthur P. "The Harlem of Langston Hughes's Poetry." *Phylon (1940–1956)* 13, no. 4 (1952): 276–83.

Doyle, Laura, and Laura A. Winkiel, eds. *Geomodernisms*. Bloomington: Indiana University Press, 2005.

Dworkin, Ira. "'Near the Congo': Langston Hughes and the Geopolitics of Internationalist Poetry." *American Literary History* 24, no. 4 (2012): 631–57.

Edwards, Brent Hayes. "Langston Hughes and the Futures of Diaspora." *American Literary History* 19, no. 3 (2007): 689–711.

Farrell, Walter C., and Patricia A. Johnson. "Poetic Interpretations of Urban Black Folk Culture: Langston Hughes and the 'Bebop' Era." *MELUS* 8, no. 3 (1981): 57–72.

Kaup, Monika. "'Our America' That Is Not One: Transnational Black Atlantic Disclosures in Nicolás Guillén and Langston Hughes." *Discourse* 22, no. 3 (2000): 87–113.

Miller, W. Jason. *Langston Hughes and American Lynching Culture*. Gainesville: University Press of Florida, 2011.

Pike, Fredrick B. *The United States and Latin America: Myths and Stereotypes of Civilization and Nature*. Austin: University of Texas Press, 2010.

Rampersad, Arnold. "Langston Hughes and Approaches to Modernism in the Harlem Renaissance." *The Harlem Renaissance: Revaluations* 837 (1989): 49–71.

Taylor, Monique M. *Harlem: Between Heaven and Hell*. Minneapolis: University of Minnesota Press, 2002.

Watson, Steven. *The Harlem Renaissance: Hub of African-American Culture, 1920–1930*. New York: Pantheon Books, 1995.

Westover, Jeff. "Africa/America: Fragmentation and Diaspora in the Work of Langston Hughes." *Callaloo* 25, no. 4 (2002): 1–1223.

Hugo, Richard

THE GEOGRAPHY OF THEN AND NOW: RICHARD HUGO'S WEST

"If I painted, I'd paint landscapes," Richard Hugo wrote, but in fact land and its perception preoccupies his poetry ("Landscapes"). The human drama of Hugo's country is often human intimacy set off against the vastness of Western space: "The schoolbell rings and dies before / the first clang can reach the nearest farm" ("Camas Prairie School"). In "Indian Girl," he tells her "don't think I won't walk miles / of barren rails to touch you like a daughter." Hugo's country often is the American West and Midwest, Montana to Iowa and Michigan, though he also writes of Italy and his experience in World War II. He had flown many bombing missions there, and returned decades later to find what had become of the places and people ("*Ci Vediamo*," *The Triggering Town*).

The desire or need to look back at what happened is the trip wire to many of his poems. Hugo himself identifies place as the "trigger" for his poems. "Most places that trigger poems for me are places where little or nothing is happening" *(Triggering Town)*. He said that writing proceeds best if place is an active presence: "I find it hard to write unless I have a sense of where the speaker is. . . . When I'm not writing, I am a tourist, usually a foreign one" *(Triggering Town)*. Such connection of poem to place does not constrict the poem, but serves to "ignite [the] need for words."

Often that need is appeased in a summoning of the past, as in the Italian poems that emerged from war and long after. The Montana poems are grounded, literally, in the human relation to land. Hugo's engaging those aspects of poetry may place him among poets writing "ecopoetry," which foregrounds the relation of the human to nonhuman natural realms (see *The Ecopoetry Anthology*, edited by Fisher-Worth and Street). Hugo's sense of place is the assumption of a Native American ethos, as he wrote in a poem about his house in Missoula: "Better we think of spirits / as owning the land, and use it wisely" ("2433 Agnes, First Home, Last House in Missoula").

Hugo taught the Blackfeet writer James Welch (author of *Fools Crow*, the historical epic of the Blackfeet), and the Anishinaabe/Ojibwe writer Louise Erdrich (*Love Medicine* and other novels), both of whom began writing with Hugo as poets. The Hugo West is inhabited by Indians and ghosts of Indians ("Indian Graves at Jocko," "Pishkun," "A Map of Montana in Italy," "A Night at the Napi in Browning," "The Lady in Kicking Horse Reservoir," "Indian Girl," and others). In "Bear Paw," Hugo visits the site of a massacre that, lively in his imagination, took place and is still taking place at Bear Paw. Where little on the surface of the land stops the wind, the wind becomes the prime shaping force, and so Hugo builds his poem around that wind: "It still pours from the east / Like armies and it drains each day of hope." The poem defies our logics. Wind does not age, weather is not a god, surrender is defeat, not wisdom, and wisdom comes slowly, not of a sudden. But in its overarching knowledge, the poem proposes an antiverse, a turning against history as we have enacted it and written it, a history of death into a present of regret. The cloud raised by the historian is the cloud raised by armies from the east, or the

Indian horses, or the car from Indiana, named for people no longer there. Hugo's poetry emerges inseparably from the land, respectful of the original people of that land. He takes us not on a guilt trip but a quest for a vision that is larger than history, one that opens a poetry that encompasses the land, larger than the misbegotten story written there, but leaving no one behind and nothing out.

Robert R. Bensen

Further Reading

Other poets who have been influenced by Theodore Roethke and the culture of the West Coast are Robert Hass and Kim Addonizio.

Bibliography

Hanna, William Scott. "In Search of the Self, In Search of the Land: Toward a Contemporary American Poetics of Place." PhD diss., Indiana University of Pennsylvania, 2012. https://knowledge.library.iup.edu/etd/812.

Jacobs, Elliot. "Re(Place) Your Typical Writing Assignment: An Argument for Place-Based Writing." *The English Journal* 100, no. 3 (2011): 49–54. www.jstor.org/stable/25790061.

Pagh, Nancy. "On Sacred Ground: The Spirit of Place in Pacific Northwest Literature by Nicholas O'Connell (review)." *Western American Literature* 39, no. 2 (2004): 236–37. doi:10.1057/fr.1993.19.

The Hunger Games

Suzanne Collins's *The Hunger Games* is about Katniss Everdeen, a 16-year-old girl living in the most destitute part of a socially and economically stratified country. In the novel, Katniss is forced to literally fight for her life in a dystopian totalitarian state controlled by the dictator President Snow. After some unclear disaster, the United States has become Panem, a country divided into 13 numbered districts as well as the location simply known as "the Capitol," where all the wealthy elite of Panem reside, including the president. The geography of this fictional world is integral to the plot of the novel because the district people are born in defines them as people. Each district has a specified product that it provides to the other districts and the Capitol. The higher the number of the district, the more poverty exists and the greater the dependence of the populous on government subsidies in terms of food.

THE GAMES

When the novel begins, Panem is about to hold the 74th annual Hunger Games. Three quarters of a century ago, there was a war between the 13th district, who were tasked with the creation of weapons, and the Capitol—a rebellion soundly defeated by the Capitol forces. As punishment, each year the remaining 12 districts must sacrifice their children for the entertainment of the masses. All children in Panem, except those fortunate enough to have been born in the Capitol, are eligible for the Games. During the Hunger Games, two tributes from each of 12 districts are drawn at random, one female and one male between the ages of 12 and 18. The selected are taken to the Capitol and then put into the stadium where the 24 young people will fight to the death. Only one person will be left alive at Game's end. He or she is then heralded as the victor and given an annual income as well as a luxurious home. Each district has a Victor's Village where the victors live both as part of their home district but also separated permanently by economic advantage.

GEOGRAPHY AND WEALTH DISTRIBUTION

The poorest districts are 10, 11, and 12, which produce livestock, agricultural products, and coal, respectively. The people who live within these districts are extremely poor and often do not have enough food, despite the fact that two of them are food-producing districts. Most of the product is sent to the Capitol, and the people are forced to accept tesserae, which is a form of grain given by the government. However, to receive larger portions of the grain, the young people must agree to have their names placed in the lottery for the Hunger Games more than once, with exponential additions each year. The poorest families within each district, such as Katniss's family with a nonworking single mother and two children, thusly have more chances for participation and death in the Hunger Games. Being largely undernourished and possessing skills limited to those useful to cultivation of their assigned product also means that the tributes from these districts often die soonest in the Hunger Games. Tributes from wealthier districts, such as 1, 2, and 3, make luxury goods including gems, masonry, and technology. Most of the victors come from the first four districts of Panem; many of these are called Careers as they have the time and financial resources available to develop young people for the specific purpose of participation in the Games.

By keeping citizens within their realms, the government ensures that they are as divided as possible, both physically and politically. The intention is always to prevent the districts from feeling unified and always as the enemy, which prevents them from joining forces against the Capitol. Each district is separated from the next by a large open area that people are not permitted to enter, although some do. There are no cars or other usual means of longer transport except for a train that travels at high speeds, and this can only be used when on official Capitol business such as transporting tributes. Besides their encapsulation in districts, very few people are able to travel. Each area is surrounded by a barrier of some kind. District 12, for example, is surrounded by an electrified fence although it is very seldom turned on. The populous understands that besides the physical danger to themselves in crossing such a barrier, severe punishments await those caught violating the law of the Capitol. Everything the people in the districts know of the outside world is related through broadcasts from the Capitol. Everything is propagandized for the purpose of making each district and each person within feel isolated from the rest of the world. There are a few Capitol militants stationed in each district, called Peacekeepers, but they are perfunctory, some even indulging in illicit trade with the people. It is more akin to the Panopticon where the people have come to accept the idea that they are always being watched and always risk angering those in power so the majority do whatever they are told.

THE CHANGING GEOGRAPHY OF TOTALITARIANISM

Each Hunger Games has a unique arena designed by Capitol technicians and a Game Master. The designers have a digital map wherein whatever obstacles they place, full tangible versions appear in the Game. This can include both organic and inorganic matter as well as natural disasters such as fires. In this place, the geography of the landscape can be manipulated to force the tributes into contact. The first day in the arena, Katniss tries to stay as far away as possible from the other young people. The Gamemakers want conflict, and they create a fire to force her back into the interior of the arena, closer to her rivals. The physical space is modified for the specific purpose of bringing members of different districts together in the only permissible way, bloodshed. The Capitol uses the Games both as a reminder to the 12 districts of the failed rebellion, but more so to further alienate the districts from one another by forcing the children to murder and/or be murdered, and thus forcing people to root for their district to be victorious.

In the end, the concept of the Hunger Games is a metaphor for the ways in which totalitarian regimes attempt to appease the masses and keep them occupied while resources continue to be unevenly distributed. This series speaks to the political power of narrative—an unlikely hero, raised to the position of an icon, can break down barriers between people from different places and help them unite for the common good.

Rachelanne Smith

Further Reading

Lois Lowry wrote the young adult dystopian novel *The Giver,* which won the Newbery Medal in 1994 and which pits the individual against the collective. *Divergent* by Veronica Roth and *Maze Runner* by James Dashner both have a similar theme but are set in postapocalyptic worlds.

Bibliography

Bland, Janice. "The Hunger Games Trilogy: An Ecocritical Reading." *CLELEjournal* 2, no. 1 (2014): 22–43. doi:10.13140/2.1.3028.0329.

Burke, Brianna. "'Reaping' Environmental Justice through Compassion in *The Hunger Games.*" *ISLE: Interdisciplinary Studies in Literature and Environment* 22, no. 3 (2015): 544–67.

Burke, Brianna. "Teaching Environmental Justice through 'The Hunger Games'." *The ALAN Review* 43 (2013): 53.

Miller, Mary Catherine. "Restorying Dystopia: Exploring the Hunger Games Series through U.S. Cultural Geographies, Identities, and Fan Response." PhD diss., Ohio State University, 2017.

Narine, Anil. *Eco-Trauma Cinema.* New York: Routledge, 2014.

Stearns, Ami. "Censorship Citadels: Geography and the Social Control of Girls." PhD diss., University of Oklahoma, 2014. https://hdl.handle.net/11244/10377.

I

Irving, Washington

Washington Irving was an American short story and nonfiction writer who lived during the 19th century and was considered part of the American Renaissance movement, which included other writers such as James Fenimore Cooper, Herman Melville, Nathaniel Hawthorne, Ralph Waldo Emerson, Henry David Thoreau, and Edgar Allan Poe. He was born in New York City and lived most of his adult life traveling domestically and in Europe, until he settled in Tarrytown, New York, located in the southern Catskill Mountains on the eastern bank of the Hudson River. In Irving's short stories, the American landscape is populated by the ghosts of natives, explorers, and those who died in the Revolutionary War. The haunted nature of the natural world means that it is hostile to some while protecting others.

HAUNTED NATURAL SPACES

Both "Rip Van Winkle" and "The Legend of Sleepy Hollow" feature landscapes that are haunted by history. The supernatural elements in both stories are narrated with a suggestion to readers that the mysteries at the heart of each text are to be doubted, that they have been self-consciously invented. However, the effects of the landscape on the characters are meant to be taken seriously: in "The Legend of Sleepy Hollow" the townspeople and newcomers alike are transfixed by the beauty of the place, and in "Rip Van Winkle" the beauty of the Catskill Mountains provides solace from the tyrannous reign of both Britain and Rip's nagging wife.

The supernatural in both stories establishes a relationship between place and history that suggests the history of colonization leaves a presence on the land. In the case of "Rip Van Winkle," he encounters funny, little men during a stroll in the mountains to get away from his ill-tempered wife. When he drinks some of their liquor, he falls asleep and wakes up to a rusty gun, a long beard, and a missing dog. He is confused when he returns to the village, but he finally discerns that he was asleep for 20 years and missed the American Revolution. The townspeople tell him that the men he encountered are the ghosts of Henry Hudson's crew from the ship called the *Half Moon*. Whenever they hear thunder, they believe it is actually the ghosts playing a game of ninepins. The nature of the ghosts that haunt the Catskill Mountains in the story is important because Hudson would have been one of the first European explorers in that region. In 1611, after previously sailing to New York Harbor and up the river that was subsequently named after him, his crew mutinied and left him, his son, and a handful of loyal crew members in an area of Canada. They were never heard from again. That the townspeople's story would propose that their ghosts returned to that area of New York shows great pride in their locale. Looking for a Northwest Passage to China, Hudson had sailed the river from New York City to Albany, after which point the river becomes too shallow for large boats. However, the vast majority of the Catskill Mountain range is not accessible from the river.

In the story "The Legend of Sleepy Hollow," the ghost that chases Ichabod Crane out of town is supposedly the spirit of a Hessian mercenary killed in the Revolutionary War. This is particularly interesting because a Hessian would have been far from home with no stakes in the war except monetary profit, a soldier for hire fighting on the side of the British. The land is not his home. His spirit only belongs to the place because he died there, tragically, fighting someone else's war. Certain landscape markers are mentioned as part of the supernatural tale, which includes the information that the ghost cannot pass a bridge that leads out of town. It is very convenient that this should be the safety zone as the path of "safety" leads travelers out of and away from the village. However, readers are led to suspect that the story of the headless horseman is a fiction invented by the townspeople and put to use by Brom Bones in his attempts to fend off Ichabod Crane, a rival suitor for the affections of Katrina Van Tassel. In this way, the ghost of a foreigner serves to ward off other foreigners who attempt to gain access to the community, particularly the rich landholdings of the Van Tassel family, of which Ichabod states it would be his intention to sell off and then move west with the profits. This is an undesirable event for the community, to lose one of their own and then to have others coming in to purchase their best agricultural lands. Lastly, what is further interesting about the Headless Horseman's relationship to place is that, in being an outsider, he would have no power over those who know this place is theirs, but he can scare away anyone who is not deeply committed to putting down roots in the place, which is the same mistake the Hessian made when he decided to fight for the losing party in the war.

This illustration is from an edition of "Rip Van Winkle" and depicts the scene in which Rip drinks ale with the men he encounters in the mountains. Washington Irving's stories often include plots shaped by the history of settlement and development of the southern Catskill Mountains. (Library of Congress)

Lynn Marie Houston

Further Reading

Other stories that pick up the theme of haunted spaces in America are selections from the works of Nathaniel Hawthorne and Edgar Allan Poe. Hawthorne's "Young Goodman Brown" looks back at the Puritan legacy and uses elements of the supernatural to talk about religious hypocrisy. Poe's "Ligeia" is a story that imagines how one determined wife manipulates her will to leave the afterlife and return to her husband. Poe's short story "The Fall of the House of Usher" also uses the popular elements of haunted houses to symbolically narrate the fall of European aristocracy.

Bibliography

Apap, Christopher C. *The Genius of Place: The Geographic Imagination in the Early Republic*. Lebanon: University of New Hampshire Press, 2016.

Fetterley, Judith, and Marjorie Pryse. *Writing Out of Place: Regionalism, Women, and American Literary Culture*. Urbana: University of Illinois Press, 2003.

LeMenager, Stephanie. *Manifest and Other Destinies: Territorial Fictions of the Nineteenth-Century United States*. Lincoln: University of Nebraska Press, 2004.

Schuyler, David. *Sanctified Landscape: Writers, Artists, and the Hudson River Valley, 1820–1909*. Ithaca, NY: Cornell University Press, 2012.

Richardson, Judith. "The Ghosting of the Hudson Valley Dutch." In *Going Dutch: The Dutch Presence in American 1609–2009,* edited by Joyce Goodfriend, Benjamin Schmidt, and Annette Stott. Boston: Brill, 2008. doi:10.1163/ej.9789004163683.i-367.12.

Shortridge, James R. "The Concept of the Place-Defining Novel in American Popular Culture." *The Professional Geographer* 43, no. 3 (1991): 280–91.

J

Jane Eyre

Jane Eyre is Charlotte Brontë's short novel about a young woman who takes a position as governess at the estate of a wealthy landowner, Edward Rochester. Jane and Edward's relationship grows more intimate as events that are strange and seemingly supernatural take place in his home, suggesting that it is haunted.

Jane Eyre comes to the Rochester estate after a difficult upbringing—first, she was unwanted in the family of her uncle that raised her and bullied by the other children and her aunt; then she was deprived and subjected to brutal punishments in the Lowood girls' home where she was sent for an education.

Jane is happy at Thornfield Hall, as she enjoys tutoring his charge, Adele Varens. Even though Edward Rochester seems temperamental and difficult at the time, the two eventually grow close, sparking the strange events that occur in the house. One night, Jane finds Edward's bedroom in flames and pulls him out of the fire. Eventually, as Jane and Edward are about to marry, it is discovered that the "ghostly presence" in the house is really his wife, whom he keeps locked up in the attic because she is supposedly mentally unbalanced. Jane refuses to marry Edward when he already has a wife, and she runs away. Hungry and destitute, she is taken in by the Rivers family at Moor House and is eventually given a schoolhouse to run for the local children. She receives a marriage proposal from St. John Rivers, but under the condition that she accompany him to do missionary work in India. Jane knows that she does not love St. John and declines his offer. Meanwhile, the family discovers Jane has come into an inheritance and that the four of them are, in fact, related. Jane splits the money equally with her cousins and sets off in search of Rochester. She finds his estate burned down and he is living in a servant's cottage, having been blinded in the fire in an unsuccessful attempt to save his wife. Edward and Jane finally marry, and she takes care of him surrounded by a bounty of friends and family who adore her.

At the opening of the story, Jane Eyre is a young girl living with her aunt and cousins at Gateshead. Outside, the day is rainy and cold. We first see her as she is reading a book in a window seat. The book she has chosen is Bewick's *History of British Birds*. Jane tells us about passages that catch her attention, most of which are images of isolation. For instance, she notes that it comforted her to read about birds that lived alone on isolated cliffs. She is able to conjure up vivid images of these birds thanks to the illustrations on the pages of the book but also because she relates to their isolation, as she is cut off as a young girl from most positive human interaction, with the exception of Bessie, the maid, with whom she shares a minimal attachment. The rest of the novel documents Jane's coming-of-age, which is symbolically how she learns to be independent, a freedom akin to having wings like the birds she enjoys reading about in her favorite book.

BRITISH COLONIALISM

A number of critics have read Edward's imprisonment of his wife as an extension of British colonialism in the Caribbean. In *Wide Sargasso Sea*, Jean Rhys wrote the story of Bertha, Edward's wife, and elaborates with a backstory that posits Edward's marriage as a means to secure her plantation lands and income. In this story, the attic space of the Victorian house becomes the inevitable meeting place of England and its colonies, where natives are silenced and imprisoned due to their refusal to assimilate to British cultural customs. Edward's fist wife, Bertha, must trade the lush landscape of the Caribbean for what amounts to a prison cell in the stark climate of England.

THE HAUNTED SPACE OF THE GOTHIC MANOR

Edward Rochester's Thornfield Hall was likely modeled after North Lees Hall, a residence that Charlotte Brontë would have visited in about 1845. A number of ghostly events happen over the course of the novel, many of which rely on the darkness and gloominess of the sprawling manor, its long, shadow-filled hallways and many unused spaces.

THE BRITISH MOORS

Jane Eyre is especially sensitive to the distances she must travel in that region. The miles traveled by carriage and by foot are often specifically indicated. As she is poor, she does not have the proper attire to brave the elements. The severe weather of the area further impacts her. As a child, she is cold and hungry during the long winters. She narrates brutal depictions of the wind referenced in the title of the book. Although she relates that nature comes alive during spring, the joy is short-lived—rather than breeding new life, spring is the dying time, when the typhus fever sweeps through Lowood and claims the life of many of the girls, including her best friend, Helen Burns.

The landscape is also a scary place for Jane growing up because of regional folktales. Locals tell stories about various ghosts or specters that inhabit the moors. For example, when Jane first encounters Edward, it is evening and he is riding a horse. Given the dark hour, she wonders for a moment whether the figure approaching her might be the "Gytrash," a goblin that takes the shape of a horse or large dog.

THE CULTURAL GEOGRAPHY OF CLASS EQUALITY

Jane Eyre straddles the distinctions between social classes. Although she comes from a well-bred family and has an education, she has no money and little family left. Occupying the position of governess places her just one step higher than a house servant. Yet, this does not stop Jane from asserting herself as Rochester's equal during their conversations. This disdain for convention is part of what attracts Rochester to her.

Many of the moments in the text that elicit sympathy for Jane's class status happen during social gatherings when Mr. Rochester is entertaining guests at Thornfield Hall. Because he is secretly in love with her, Rochester invents all manner of reasons for Jane to be near at hand. This places her too close for the comfort of his distinguished guests who are very class conscious. One guest in particular, Blanche Ingram, fancies that Mr. Rochester is courting her, which he lets her believe, it seems, only to entice Jane into falling in love with him. Before that happens, however, Jane is subject to much derision from the guests who have a difficult time understanding even the marginal participation of a governess in their drawing room conversations. Jane Eyre is ultimately a fantasy about the fragility of a class system, which is brought down in the novel by sums of money that are gained and lost relatively quickly, and by true love.

Lynn Marie Houston

Further Reading

Other women writers in the 19th century that continued many of the themes in *Jane Eyre* are Charlotte's sisters Emily Brontë and Anne Brontë, and Jane Austen. A 20th-century British writer of Dominican descent, Jean Rhys, wrote a novel called *Wide Sargasso Sea* that tells the backstory of Rochester's first wife during her youth in Jamaica. Although Rochester names her Bertha in *Jane Eyre,* in *Wide Sargasso Sea* Rhys writes that the Creole heiress was originally named Antoinette Cosway.

Bibliography

Almutairi, Areej. "An Ecocritical Reading in *Wide Sargasso Sea.*" *Studies in Literature and Language* 7, no. 1 (2013). doi: 10.3968/n.

Bewell, Alan. "Jane Eyre and Victorian Medical Geography." *ELH* 63, no. 3 (1996): 773–808.

Carroll, Joseph. "The Ecology of Victorian Fiction." *Philosophy and Literature* 25, no. 2 (2001): 295–313.

D'Albertis, Deirdre. "Dark Nature: A Critical Return to Brontë Country." In *Victorian Writers and the Environment: Ecocritical Perspectives,* edited by Laurence W. Mazzeno and Ronald D. Morrison. London: Routledge, 2016.

Dowler, Lorraine, Josephine Carubia, and Bonj Szcygiel, eds. *Gender and Landscape: Renegotiating Morality and Space.* London: Routledge, 2005.

Duthie, Enid L. *The Brontës and Nature.* New York: St. Martin's Press, 1986.

Fuller, Jennifer D. "Seeking Wild Eyre: Victorian Attitudes towards Landscape and the Environment in Charlotte Brontë's *Jane Eyre.*" *Ecozone* 4, no. 2 (2013): 150–65.

Gold, Barri J. "Energy, Ecology, and Victorian Fiction." *Literature Compass* 9, no. 2 (2012): 213–24.

Henson, Eithne. *Landscape and Gender in the Novels of Charlotte Brontë, George Eliot, and Thomas Hardy: The Body of Nature.* Wensley, UK: Ashgate, 2011.

Kadish, Doris Y. *The Literature of Images: Narrative Landscape from Julie to Jane Eyre.* New Brunswick, NJ: Rutgers University Press, 1986.

Kennedy, Margaret. "Protecting the 'House Beautiful': Eco-Consciousness in the Victorian Novel." PhD diss., Stony Brook University, 2013. http://hdl.handle.net/11401/77567.

Nockolds, Peter. "Midsummer Moon: The Lunar Structure of Jane Eyre." *Brontë Studies* 29 (2004): 157–63.

Taylor, William M. *The Vital Landscape: Nature and the Built Environment in Nineteenth-Century Britain.* Aldershot, UK: Ashgate, 2004.

The Jungle

The Jungle (1906) by Upton Sinclair traces a family of immigrants as they try to make a life for themselves in the stockyards of Chicago. Jurgis Rudkus and his family travel from Lithuania to America for a better life, having believed some of the myths circulating about the abundance of wealth and opportunity in the country. Rudkus works in a slaughterhouse where workers are mistreated. He is fired after he is injured on the job. All the members of his family have industrial jobs in factories, even the small children and his elderly father. His wife, Ona, finally confesses to him that the only way she has been able to keep her job is by giving in to the demands for sexual favors from her boss. Rudkus attacks him and goes to jail. After he is released, Ona dies in childbirth, along with her child. After wandering around the country picking up migrant work, Rudkus realizes that workers in America have few opportunities. When he returns to Chicago, he is able to make a better life for himself by making friends with a group of socialists who give voice to Sinclair's distrust of the methods of capitalism.

THE CULTURAL GEOGRAPHY OF INDUSTRIAL PRODUCTION

Jurgis and his family are influenced by the American dream of equality and economic opportunity, which has communicated to them a false hope for a better life. They leave for America thinking they will become rich. This is far from the reality they find when they arrive. Their misperception is known as "imaginative geography," a term used to describe peoples' conceptions of space. In this case, the immigrants cling to success stories that they've heard other poor immigrants circulate. They end up living and working with other Lithuanian immigrants who were drawn to America by the same atypical stories of prosperity. Within just a few days in his new home, Jurgis realizes his mistake and admits that America is not what he expected. Still, he believes that if he works hard, he will be able to get ahead. What he finds is that the system in place is designed to use his strength and labor so that others can get rich.

One of Upton Sinclair's purposes in writing *The Jungle* was to expose the horrors of our industrial food system. A journalist by trade, Sinclair does that by giving readers a front-row seat to the horrors of mass-produced meat. Jurgis and many other newly arrived immigrants are sent by the police to Chicago's stockyards, where they witness firsthand on the assembly line of the slaughterhouse

This photo of the Chicago stockyards in 1944 shows the extensive facilities that employed immigrants like those portrayed in Upton Sinclair's *The Jungle*. Both humans and cattle had to negotiate the crowded conditions created by the meat industry's quest for profit. (Universal History Archive/UIG via Getty Images)

the unsanitary conditions of food production. Shortly after publication of *The Jungle*, President Roosevelt consulted with Sinclair, opened an investigation into the meatpacking industry, and passed the Pure Food and Drug Act, which imposed new safety regulations on food production. However, Sinclair was disappointed that Americans didn't relate what was happening to the animals we processed for food with the bodies of immigrants who were being sacrificed in that process. He famously quipped about the effect of his book that he had "aimed at the public's heart and by accident . . . hit it in the stomach," meaning that he had meant to build sympathy for better living and working conditions for immigrants.

THE HUMAN GEOGRAPHY OF THE IMMIGRANT EXPERIENCE

The domestic living spaces featured in the book are cramped and unsafe. Rudkus and his family sign a contract to purchase a house but it is in poor condition and the legal agreement contains hidden costs. The system that Sinclair was exposing implicates both employers and landlords—what immigrants were making in the factories and meatpacking plants at the start of the 20th century was not enough to survive with basic necessities. At one point, when one of the children in their family dies, the Rudkus family fails to feel grief because the child was another mouth to feed, and they could barely afford to eat.

Although the title of the book seems to invoke a natural space, the downfall of this immigrant family is set in the cramped quarters of an immigrant ghetto in Chicago, close to the factories in which they worked long hours. The symbolism of the book's title is that in the system of industrial production, immigrants were reduced to animals, struggling and fighting for survival among themselves.

Lynn Marie Houston

Further Reading

Another journalist known for his "muckraking" investigations is Samuel Hopkins Adams, who wrote a series of articles compiled into a book entitled *The Great American Fraud,* which, combined with Sinclair's *The Jungle,* emboldened Congress to pass the Pure Food and Drug Act of 1906. Adams's series of articles exposed the falsehoods told by quack doctors selling "patented" medicines that did not work.

Theodore Dreiser's novel *Sister Carrie* similarly explores the business of life in American cities, which suggests that the pursuit of the American dream leads to a soul weariness. Like Sinclair's immigrants, Carrie leaves her home (in rural Wisconsin) and travels to Chicago to make something of herself. She eventually moves to New York, and although she gains entry to high society, she finds her life unfulfilling.

Native Son, a novel by Richard Wright, is also set in Chicago just a couple of decades after *The Jungle.* In it, Wright suggests that the city's economy is tied into a system of racial discrimination as carried out by its justice system.

Finally, Stephen Crane wrote around the same time as Sinclair. His novella *Maggie: A Girl of the Streets* is about the poor conditions of immigrants in New York.

Bibliography

Adams, Whitney Elise. "Urban Solution from the Literary Examples of *Love in the Time of Cholera* and *The Jungle:* The Human Body and the Bios in Ethics, Politics, and the Biopolis." Master's thesis, University at Buffalo, State University of New York, 2013.

Bunthoff, Kathryn C. "Consuming Nature: Literature of the World that Feeds Us." PhD diss., University of Cincinnati, 2009. rave.ohiolink.edu/etdc/view?acc_num=ucin1241616520.

Fisher, Colin. "Nature in *The Jungle:* Ethnic Workers, Environmental Inequalities, and Subaltern Cultures of Nature in Chicago's Packingtown." *Resilience: A Journal of the Environmental Humanities* 3 (2016): 330–57. www.jstor.org/stable/10.5250/resilience.3.2016.0330.

Fitzgerald, A. "A Social History of the Slaughterhouse: From Inception to Contemporary Implications." *Human Ecology Review* 17, no. 1 (2010): 58–69.

Gilbert, Emily. "Naturalist Metaphors in the Literatures of Chicago, 1893–1925." *Journal of Historical Geography* 20, no. 3 (1994): 283–304.

Kneitz, Agnes. "'As If the River Was Not Meat and Drink to You!': Social Novels as a Means of Framing Nineteenth-Century Environmental Justice." *ISLE: Interdisciplinary Studies in Literature and Environment* 22, no. 1 (2015): 47–62. doi:10.1093/isle/isv006.

Nash, Roderick. *Wilderness and the American Mind: Fifth Edition.* New Haven, CT: Yale University Press, 2014.

Rosendale, Steven, ed. *The Greening of Literary Scholarship: Literature, Theory, and The Environment*. Iowa City: University of Iowa Press, 2002.

Sipley, Tristan. "Second Nature: Literature, Capital and the Built Environment, 1848–1938." PhD diss., University of Oregon, 2010.

Wald, Sarah D. "Visible Farmers/Invisible Workers: Locating Immigrant Labor in Food Studies." *Food Culture & Society: An International Journal of Multidisciplinary Research* 14, no. 4 (2011): 567–86. doi:10.2752/175174411X13046092851479.

K

King Lear

King Lear by William Shakespeare is a tragedy that depicts the gradual descent into madness of the play's titular character. Lear's madness is a consequence of the king losing his realm, having shared it between two of his three daughters. The play is concerned with issues such as the power of destiny, the nature of father-child relationships, reconciliation, forgiveness, questions of identity, metaphorical and physical blindness, madness, and justice. *King Lear* was written during the reign on Queen Elizabeth I, a time when English society was ranked according to social class, with the lower classes expected to obey the wealthy and powerful, particularly the aristocracy and royalty. This was also an era when children were supposed to obey their parents without question. *King Lear* shows how quickly obedience can turn to insubordination and, therefore, how society built on unearned respect is fragile and can crumble into chaos.

GEOGRAPHY AND IDENTITY

In *King Lear,* geography and identity are linked inextricably as is demonstrated by the way in which many of the characters share their names with real locations: Kent, Burgundy, Albany, Gloucester, Cornwall, and France. That said, the geography of *King Lear* is disorientated and confusing with only one location, Dover, named throughout the course of the play. The rest of the drama takes place at unidentified places such as unnamed castles, on a heath, and on an imaginary cliff. These settings exist within a fantasy, pre-Christian, ancient Britain that is populated by characters that believe the gods shape their destinies. The primitivism displayed by the play's characters is reflected by the elemental, wild locations that feature in *King Lear,* most notably the heath that is the location of the king's loss of reason.

WILDERNESS AND WILD WEATHER

The play begins at King Lear's palace, a location to which the play never returns—once the play starts, the action does not stop changing location until the play ends. At the beginning of the play, much of the action takes place indoors, in the palaces, courts, and castles owned by various characters. But as the play progresses, events occur with increasing frequency out of doors in locations such as the wild heath, a beach, and several military camps.

One of the most celebrated uses of location in *King Lear* occurs in Act 3, when the king rushes on to a heath during a fierce storm, having argued with his daughters. Both the wildness of this scene's setting and the violence of the weather symbolize the king's disordered emotions as well as the fury that will trigger his descent into madness. This is something the king acknowledges when he refers to the "tempest in my mind" (Act 3, Scene 4, Line 15), for he realizes that the literal storm on the wild heath echoes his disordered psychological state. Although the heath scene reflects Lear's inner turmoil, the wildness of the location and the disruptive weather also parallel the political turmoil into which Britain descends during the play. Furthermore, the wildness of the heath and the powerful forces of nature evident on the heath symbolize the fact that all humans, including royalty, are defenseless against the overwhelming power of nature.

BLINDNESS AND BORDERS

Another famous scene in *King Lear* occurs in Act 4, in which the Earl of Gloucester follows the king to the countryside near the coastal town of Dover. Edgar (disguised as Poor Tom) leads his father, the blinded Earl of Gloucester, to an imaginary cliff edge (actually a flat field) where Gloucester tries to commit suicide by jumping from the imaginary headland. The scene is important because it highlights another of the major themes of *King Lear,* blindness that is both physical and symbolic as well as the power of the gods to determine people's fates. A short while before Gloucester tries to jump to his death, he recognizes the power of the gods and prays that Edgar, whom he has disowned, will be safe. The scene is emotional, for Edgar does not reveal his true identity in the hope that this will allow Gloucester to continue on his journey of self-discovery. Instead Edgar continues in the guise of Poor Tom so that Gloucester can accept his blindness and vow to suffer until such time as the gods decide that he has endured enough.

Edgar's plan works, for eventually Gloucester is able to see that Edgar is the son that deserves his love rather Edmund. Dover is then an important location in *King Lear,* for it is not only the location for Gloucester's moment of self-realization but also because it is here that five of the play's main characters die. Moreover, all the play's characters, save the Fool, eventually end up at the coastal location (the Fool is said to be following the king and Gloucester to Dover but, for reasons unknown, never actually arrives). Dover serves as both the final location experienced by many of the play's characters and as the play's final setting, a place where many different plot endings converge. Furthermore, Dover is, both geographically and politically, the final bastion of King Lear's realm, for it is lies near the English Channel and is, therefore, extremely close to the coast of France. As a result of this geographical proximity to France, it is at Dover that the French military forces raised by Cordelia eventually land. In *King Lear,* Dover is then symbolic of termination, for the location represents both the boundary of a king's power and the limit of several characters' existence.

Victoria Williams

Further Reading

Shakespeare wrote many plays that feature royal characters. Some of these plays are known as history plays because they are named after real kings or royals—such as *Richard II* and *Henry V*—while others, like *King Lear, Cymbeline,* and *Hamlet* are based on legendary royal figures. If you enjoyed *King Lear,* another Shakespeare play that uses similar symbolism is *Macbeth,* in which storms are used to signal rebellion against a king as well as political turmoil. Shakespeare also wrote other plays that involve disguises and questions of identity, including *Twelfth Night* and *A Midsummer Night's Dream.*

Bibliography

Bozio, Andrew. "Embodied Thought and the Perception of Place in King Lear." *SEL Studies in English Literature 1500–1900* 55, no. 2 (2015): 263–84. doi:10.1353/sel.2015.0013.

Brayton, Daniel. *Shakespeare's Ocean: An Ecocritical Exploration.* Charlottesville: University of Virginia Press, 2012.

Brönnimann, Werner. "Thickets and Beaches: Evoking Place in the Stories of King Lear." In *Shakespeare and Space,* edited by Ina Habermann and Michelle Witen. London: Palgrave Macmillan, 2016. doi:10.1057/978-1-137-51835-4_4.

Emmerichs, Sharon. "'Thou Map of Woe': Mapping the Feminine in *Titus Andronicus* and *King Lear*." *English Studies* 97, no. 5 (2016): 546–67. doi:10.1080/0013838X.2016.1168647.

Eskew, Doug. "'Soldiers, Prisoners, Patrimony': King Lear and the Place of the Sovereign." *Cahiers Elisabethains: A Journal of English Renaissance Studies* 78, no. 1 (2010): 29–38. doi:10.7227/CE.78.1.4.

Estok, Simon C. "Doing Ecocriticism with Shakespeare: An Introduction." In *Ecocriticism and Shakespeare.* London: Palgrave Macmillan, 2011. doi:10.1057/9780230118744_1.

Estok, Simon C. "Shakespeare and Ecocriticism: An Analysis of 'Home' and 'Power' in King Lear." *Journal of the Australasian Universities Language and Literature Association* no. 103 (2005): 13–36. doi:10.1179/000127905805260537.

Flahiff, F. T. "Lear's Map." *Cahiers Elizabethains: A Journal of English Renaissance Studies* 30, no. 1 (1986): 17–33. doi:10.1177/018476788603000106.

Gillies, John. *Shakespeare and the Geography of Difference.* Cambridge, UK: Cambridge University Press, 1994.

Gillies, John, and Virginia Mason Vaughan, eds. *Playing the Globe: Genre and Geography in English Renaissance Drama.* London: Associated University Presses, 1998.

Gruber, Elizabeth D. "Nature on the Verge: Confronting 'Bare Life' in *Arden of Faversham* and *King Lear.*" *ISLE: Interdisciplinary Studies in Literature and Environment* 22, no. 1 (2015): 98–114. doi:10.1093/isle/isu128.

Halio, Jay L. *King Lear: A Guide to the Play.* Westport, CT: Greenwood Press, 2001.

Hanson, Susan, ed. *Ten Geographic Ideas that Changed the World.* New Brunswick, NJ: Rutgers University Press, 2001.

Hiscock, Andrew, and Lisa Hopkins, eds. *King Lear: A Critical Guide.* London, UK: Continuum, 2011.

Hollis, Gavin Russell. "Stage Directions: Shakespeare's Use of the Map." Master's thesis, University of Birmingham, 2000.

Laine, Tommi. "Shakespeare's Confines: Patriarchal and Natural Space in *King Lear* and *The Winter's Tale.*" Master's thesis, University of Helsinki, 2018. hdl.handle.net/10138/236146.

Roberts, Jeanne Addison. *The Shakespearean Wild: Geography, Genus and Gender.* Lincoln: University of Nebraska Press, 1991.

Rotherham, Ian D. "A Fear of Nature: Images and Perceptions of Heath, Moor, Bog and Fen in England." In *Between the Atlantic and the Mediterranean: Responses to*

Climate and Weather Conditions Throughout History, edited by Cristina Joanaz de Melo, Ana Isabel Queiroz, Luis Espinha da Silveira, and Ian D. Rotherham. Sheffield, UK: Wildtrack Publishing, 2013.

Sun, Emily. *Succeeding King Lear: Literature, Exposure, and the Possibility of Politics*. New York: Fordham University Press, 2010.

Waage, Frederick O. "Shakespeare Unearth'd." *Interdisciplinary Studies in Literature and Environment* 12, no. 2 (2005): 139–64. www.jstor.org/stable/44086434.

The Kite Runner

Afghan American author Khaled Hosseini's best-selling novel *The Kite Runner* is a story about a Pashtun boy Amir and his devoted servant, friend, and kite runner Hassan, an ethnic Hazara. Although Amir and Hassan are supposedly inseparable companions on the same kite team, inscribing their names on a pomegranate tree as "the Sultans of Kabul," their unequal social status eventually erodes their relationship. Hassan's presumed father Ali, a Shiite Hazara, works as a servant in Amir's home and shares his poor living quarters with his son while Amir lives in a grand mansion with his father, a wealthy Sunni Pashtun elite, fondly referred to in the book only as "Baba" (Dari for "Father"). Hassan and his father Ali are treated by Amir and Baba with much kindness, but never really as actual family. Social differences also affect the boys' individual roles in flying kites. Amir holds the glory role of fighter pilot by controlling the movements of the kite by pulling on the strings, while Hassan does all the behind-the-scenes grunt work, which mostly involves handling the spool of kite string and kite running. Hassan is never allowed to feel like a champion even though Amir could not possibly down a kite without his expertise.

During the grand kite tournament in 1975, just a few years before the invasion of Afghanistan by the Soviet Union and the ensuing Afghan civil war, Amir betrays his friend through an act of cowardice and selfishness that will haunt him for the rest of his life. This defining moment sets the stage for his later search for redemption, which he finds by rescuing Hassan's son from the Taliban regime two decades later. His long search for Hassan allows Amir to share with readers the beauty of the mountainous landscape of *Kabul jan*.

ETHNICITY

Kite fighting over Kabul is symbolic of the perpetual violence caused by ethnic and religious animosities that have plagued Afghanistan for a very long time and fueled its destruction. The Pashtun persecution of the Hazara (Pashtuns make up about 42 percent of the country's population, while the Hazara, 9 percent) is embodied by Assef, an older Pashtun boy, who emerges as Amir and Hassan's violent sociopathic nemesis. Assef believes that Afghanistan is "the land of Pashtuns" who are the "true, pure Afghans," and Hazaras are "garbage," "pollutants," "who dirty our blood." At one point in the book, Assef threatens to beat up Amir for associating with Hazaras, but Hassan protects Amir with his slingshot. Later, in a crucial part of the story, Assef brutally attacks Hassan while he is running a trophy kite for Amir. Amir stands by without helping Hassan but manages to save the kite so that Baba would be proud of his achievement. When they return home after this incident, Amir who is ashamed of what happened to Hassan and his role in it, tries to frame Hassan as a thief so that any evidence of his cowardice would be forever removed from his life-world. Although Baba still treats Hassan kindly even though Amir has framed him, Hassan and his father Ali leave the household. It is possible that the child Amir sensed that Hassan was indeed his half brother and was subconsciously ashamed of Baba "dirtying the blood," while at the same time jealous of the affection his Baba showed toward Hassan. Many years later, the guilt he feels from betraying his friend resurfaces, causing him to return to his homeland. Assef, in the meantime, has become a powerful Taliban leader and is ridding Afghanistan of pollutants. Hassan would be killed for defying the Taliban, but not before having two children of his own.

SENSE OF PLACE

In *The Kite Runner,* Hosseini cultivates a sense of place that is informed by his own experiences of growing up and later revisiting Afghanistan. Through his characters, he reveals his own deep attachment to the place of his childhood. Hosseini vividly describes physical landscapes and his emotional connection to them. He shows us the pomegranate tree where Amir reads stories to Hassan and on which they inscribe their claim to the throne of Kabul. We are taken to the springtime creek where the boys skip stones, the lake and mountains where Amir and Baba would picnic, and the "cypress trees and sugarcane fields" of Jalalabad where many Afghans spend their winter vacations. The street scenes as they are described offer access into a uniquely Kabuli landscape and way of life. Even the terrifying ride in a fuel truck through the rugged terrain of the Khyber Pass to seek refuge is a deeper experience of place that has changed the course of father and son's life.

When Amir returns to Kabul in 2001, he is shocked by the devastation of his homeland caused by Soviet carnage, Mujahideen civil war, and Taliban brutality. He sees fewer trees and more "rubble and beggars" in the streets, along with remnants of military hardware scattered about. A man tries to sell his prosthetic leg to Amir, hoping to find his way out of misery. For Amir, these encounters give rise to a sense of placelessness since the old associations with Kabul are hardly felt. His childhood home bares an emptiness that unsettles him. But, gradually, Kabul comes back into his life as he reminisces about his family's journey as Afghans. He admits that he was surprised to remember so much about the landscape of Afghanistan; this gives him hope that the land there remembered him, too.

Eventually, Amir and Baba become part of an Afghan immigrant community in California. There they, like others, attempt to re-create, to some degree, their homeland by imbuing the landscape with familiar meanings. At the San Jose flea market, for example, where Afghan families sell their secondhand goods, people greet each other with offerings of tea. The sounds of gossiping and political analysis mix with Afghan music. Festivities offer opportunities to reconnect to places linked to Afghan traditions, such as during Amir and Soraya's wedding, or at a gathering to celebrate the first day of spring they call Sawl-E-Nau (New Year). As Amir claims that, even if an Afghan leaves Paghman, Paghman never really leaves him. The gardens of Paghman, located in the hills just outside of Kabul is where Kabulis go to savor and share their love for their land.

Ken Whalen and Dalilah Nabilah Laidin

Further Reading

Another book about learning to make peace with one's past is Amy Tan's *The Bonesetter's Daughter*. Similar to *The Kite Runner,* the novel is about the global reach of memory from one's home country to impact one's new life America; this narrative is set in both San Francisco and China.

The Swallows of Kabul, by Mohammed Moulessehoul (writing under the pseudonym of Yasmina Khadra), is set in Afghanistan, the same country as *The Kite Runner*. It similarly explores the brutality of life there under the Taliban as well as the necessity and beauty of self-sacrifice. Many scholars also equate Moulessehoul's novel with Khaled Hossein's second novel, *A Thousand Splendid Suns*.

Bibliography

Agnello, Mary F., et al. "Afghanistan and Multiculturalism in Khaled Hosseini's Novels: Study of Place and Diversity." *Multicultural Education & Technology Journal* 3.2 (2009): 96–111.

Aubry, Timothy. "Afghanistan Meets the Amazon: Reading *The Kite Runner* in America." *PMLA* 124, no. 1 (2009): 25–43.

Jefferess, David. "To Be Good (Again): *The Kite Runner* as Allegory of Global Ethics." *Journal of Postcolonial Writing* 45, no. 4 (2009): 389–400.

Sarma, Mriganka Sekhar. "Masculinity, War and the Politics of Ethnic Identity: A Study of Khaled Hosseini's *The Kite Runner*." *Labyrinth: An International Refereed Journal of Postmodern Studies* 6, no. 4 (2015): 41–46.

Silvester, J. Dhivya. "Reconstruction of a Nation: A Reading of Khaled Hosseini's Fiction." *Language in India* 18, no. 6 (2018): 304–17.

L

The Last of the Mohicans

The Last of the Mohicans is a novel by James Fenimore Cooper set in central New York. Although written in the early 19th century, the story takes place during the mid-1700s, at the time of the French and Indian War. Cooper accurately captures in this historical novel the ways in which Native American tribes were pulled into the fight between the British and the French for control of territories in the American colonies. In this narrative, Cooper imagines the end of the Mohican tribe, and mourns the changes to the geographical and cultural landscape of a "pristine" America that has been corrupted by the invading colonial forces.

The Last of the Mohicans imagines a historical event that was part of the conflict at Fort William Henry between Colonel Munro and General Montcalm. Montcalm attacked the fort, situated on the shores of Lake George, in early August 1757. At about that same time, General Webb dispatched reinforcements. In the novel, Munro's daughters, Alice and Cora, travel with the troops on their way to join their father. When they reach him, he is greatly surprised that they were sent, as the situation is very dangerous. Without additional reinforcements, they will lose the fort to the French. Munro writes to Webb and explains the situation, but Webb refuses to send any more men, as they were trying to keep the French from getting to Albany. Montcalm intercepts Webb's message and takes it to Munro. After they surrender, Munro and his people march out in columns. However, they are attacked by some of the native allies of the French during their withdrawal. Because Cooper inserts the characters of Munro's daughters into the plot, they are present in his version of the massacre, which makes it much more melodramatic.

THE GEOGRAPHY OF UPSTATE NEW YORK

When Cora and Alice Munro leave Fort Edward for Fort William Henry, the detachment is guided by a Huron named Magua. Magua is bent on vengeance against Munro and wants to take his daughters captive. Telling them he wants to take a shortcut, he plans to lead them into an ambush set by the French-allied Hurons. However, during the trip, they encounter Hawkeye and two male members of the Mohican tribe, Chingachgook and Uncas, as they are hunting. The travelers save the women and Major Duncan Heyward from Magua and take them to Fort William Henry, which is about to fall into the hands of the French.

During the massacre on their withdrawal, Magua takes the two Munro sisters. Hawkeye, Heyward, the Mohicans, and Colonel Munro follow them to a Huron village and then into a mountainous area, where group has their final confrontation with Magua.

The geography and archeology of upstate New York provide numerous hiding places for the protagonists, especially for those who know how to track and read the land as a map as to who or what has passed there and how long ago. At one point, the group hides behind a waterfall. In another scene, they seek shelter in a burial ground. This deters the Hurons from pursuing because of their beliefs about desecrating such sites. There is a drawback, however, to navigating such a lush and majestic landscape: it sometimes overwhelms the characters and seems as if it consumes them, especially in the final scene of the novel, when three of the characters perish over a cliff.

Appearing in a 1910 publication of Cooper's *The Last of the Mohicans*, this image depicts the opening of Chapter 14 in the novel. Here, Hawkeye leads the group deeper into the woods in an attempt to escape Magua and the Huron, who are close on their trail. (Library of Congress)

THE LOSS OF INDIGENOUS LANDS AND THE SPACE OF INTERRACIAL RELATIONS

Cooper's story seems to express value of indigenous culture in the Americas by mourning their loss. However, he approaches such characters as "noble savages" typical in 19th-century literature: innocent, childlike figures to be revered from afar.

Additionally, a contested space exists between different races in Cooper's vision of America. For instance, although Hawkeye is Anglo, he adopts a Native American lifestyle. In befriending Chingachgook, Hawkeye has been able to master many skills for wilderness survival. Yet, Cooper chooses to have Hawkeye repeatedly assert his whiteness as a sign of his "purity of race." The figure of Hawkeye, also known in other Cooper novels as Natty Bumppo, is a troubling portrayal of an in-between character, who could operate as an empowering example of cultural hybridity (meaning, a mix of many cultures/races), but who ultimately fails to provide a meaningful message about diversity. Cooper concludes the novel with a message from the leader of the Delaware tribe, who says that native people in America must accept their subordinate role to white men.

Lynn Marie Houston

Further Reading

James Fenimore Cooper is known as part of the American Renaissance movement, a group of 19th-century authors who drew attention to the unique elements of the American landscape and culture, especially its geography, history, and native tribes. Other authors associated with this movement, whose works would be similar to those of Cooper, are Washington Irving, Herman Melville, and Nathaniel Hawthorne.

Bibliography

Bender, Thomas. "James Fenimore Cooper and the City." *New York History* 51, no. 3 (1970): 287–305.

Bevis, William W. "The Prairie: Cooper's Desert Ecology." *Environmental Review: ER* 10, no. 1 (1986): 3–15.

Cariou, Warren. "Haunted Prairie: Aboriginal 'Ghosts' and the Spectres of Settlement." *University of Toronto Quarterly* 75, no. 2 (2006): 727–34.

Crawford, James. "James Fenimore Cooper and the Art of the Erie Canal." *James Fenimore Cooper, His Country and His Art* 11 (1997): 32–38.

Erisman, Fred. "Western Fiction as an Ecological Parable." *Environmental Review* 2, no. 6 (1978): 14–23.

Flad, Harvey K. "The Parlor in the Wilderness: Domesticating an Iconic American Landscape." *Geographical Review* 99, no. 3 (2009): 356–76.

MacDougall, Hugh C. "'Their Waste Has Done It All': The Prairie as a Post-Apocalyptic Novel." *James Fenimore Cooper: His Country and His Art, Papers from the 2001 Cooper Seminar*, no. 13 (2001): 66–71.

Motley, Warren. *The American Abraham: James Fenimore Cooper and the Frontier Patriarch*. Cambridge, UK: Cambridge University Press, 1987.

Phair, Charles A. J. "Navigating the Transatlantic Threshold: James Fenimore Cooper and the Revolutionary Atlantic." PhD diss., University of Nottingham, 2010.

Ricci, Patricia Likos. "Natural Laws: The Literary and Artistic Roots of American Environmentalism." In *Cultural Landscapes*, edited by Gabriel R. Ricci, 47–64. Routledge, 2017.

Rosenberg, Bruce A. "James Fenimore Cooper's *The Spy* and the Neutral Ground." *ATQ* 6, no. 1 (1992): 5.

Shortridge, James R. "The Concept of the Place-Defining Novel in American Popular Culture." *The Professional Geographer* 43, no. 3 (1991): 280–91.

Shour, Nancy C. "Heirs to the Wild and Distant Past: Landscape and Historiography in James Fenimore Cooper's *The Pioneers*." *James Fenimore Cooper Society Miscellaneous Papers* 10 (1998): 17–23.

Tomc, Sandra. "'Clothes upon sticks': James Fenimore Cooper and the Flat Frontier." *Texas Studies in Literature and Language* 51, no. 2 (2009): 142–78.

Long Day's Journey into Night

Nobel laureates in literature tend to have produced their best work before the award and little afterward. This appears to have been the case for American novelists William Faulkner and Ernest Hemingway, but American dramatist Eugene

Gladstone O'Neill was a powerful exception. His masterpiece, *Long Day's Journey into Night,* came several years after the Nobel Prize. In many ways, it is not an easy work to summarize. Upon first reading, the play appears to be a display of unabated raw emotions full of tension. It is as though O'Neill put the id on overdrive. In addition, the play is autobiographical, and it is possible to grasp how intensely O'Neill poured himself and his dead parents and brother into the play. The action concerns a single family that O'Neill follows from morning to night. It is a literal journey, then, into night, as the title proclaims. But in a larger sense, it is a story about the inexorable movement from life to death that enmeshes us all.

The members of this family are James Tyrone—a double for Eugene's dead father James—Mary Tyrone—a re-creation of O'Neill's mother Ella Quinlan—and three sons, only two of whom are alive. The character named Eugene died as a child, and it is not easy to describe his relationship to the playwright. Of the surviving brothers, Edmund is representative of Eugene O'Neill as a young man, and Jamie of O'Neill's older brother of the same name. Although the play begins in good spirits during a pleasant morning, the descent thereafter is palpable in every line. In a sense, the Tyrones seem to lack volition because they appear unable to refrain from saying terrible things to one another and dredging up horrible memories. Try as she might to hide it, Mary is a morphine addict, but no matter how much of the drug she takes, she cannot expiate the memory of her dead child. In many ways, she is the central character because the husband and sons all respond to her words and actions. The three men reveal themselves to be alcoholics, as Eugene was for a time. Moreover, in real life, his brother Jamie drank himself to death. By night, Mary has taken so much morphine that she can barely function.

THE GEOGRAPHY OF PLACE

The Tyrones are wealthy because James, like Eugene's father, was a successful actor. Consequently, they have multiple geographies. At the moment the family is at a summer home in New England, a typical setting for many of O'Neill's plays. Mary early expresses frustration with this geography. The neighbors are banal. Worse, her husband is a spendthrift and will not invest any money in the home's upkeep. This is not to say that the home is unsuitable, only that it does not suit Mary. She feels uprooted in the sense of not having a real home to call her own, of not belonging to a real geography. Just as bad, Mary recalls how she hated living in a series of New York City hotels when the theater is in full swing, paralleling O'Neill's own mother's hatred of backstage life. In fact, Ella Quinlan O'Neill apparently began taking morphine to escape hotel life.

Mary seems to be alone in expressing these feelings. James appears to be content with their geography of place, and the sons do not whisper a word of dissent. Their acquiescence seems partly due to the fact that they like to frequent the local brothel. The geography of place thus becomes the geography of exploitation, for prostitution is nothing more than a way for men to exploit women.

Edmund, despite his amorousness with prostitutes, seems out of place. He seems to occupy not a set geography but a series of spaces. Readers learn that he spent years aboard a ship, traveling to various locales. Eugene O'Neill did much the same after his expulsion from Princeton University. Something in Edmund reacts against the summer home, for he contracts tuberculosis, an often fatal disease then. The parallel extends once more to Eugene, who contracted but recovered from tuberculosis. The physical disease of the character Edmund speaks to a *dis-ease* related to the setting in which this family falls apart.

THE GEOGRAPHY OF IDEAS

The play begins with a cataloging of the family study. James, Mary, Jamie, or Edmund must have been an avid reader because O'Neill lists a number of authors, among them German philosopher Friedrich Nietzsche. His ideas, particularly his atheism, resonate throughout the play, forming a geography of ideas or perhaps a geography of nothingness. Edmund and Jamie openly mock religion, to the father's horror. But in pushing him, the boys extract from James the admission that he, though raised Catholic, does not attend Mass. The father claims to pray daily but supplies no evidence of this habit. He says he has worn out the knees of his pants because of his devotion, but O'Neill supplies evidence of no such wear.

Nietzsche was able in his prose to capture the essence of nihilism and the finitude of existence, ideas that inform *Long Day's Journey into Night*. James and Mary recount ancestors who would not leave Ireland during the potato famine but stayed in their sod huts to die. Death by starvation is exceptionally painful and yet no one wept for them. They are dead and nothing more can be said about them because they inhabit the eternal silence of the grave.

In this way, the geography of ideas returns one to the geography of place because the Tyrones are not simply Americans. They are Irish Americans and their ancestors suffered in an Ireland that O'Neill portrays as a backward, primitive place. Perhaps this primitiveness infuses the Tyrones' actions, for the play does not exist on an elevated moral plane. It is visceral and raw, almost as though O'Neill intended to present a four-part stream of consciousness that unleashed the irrational. If Greek philosopher Aristotle defined humans as rational animals, O'Neill seems to be challenging this definition. Perhaps O'Neill substitutes realism for Aristotle's fiction.

Christopher Cumo

Further Reading

Many other American plays feature social and familial tensions stemming from characters with self-destructive tendencies that include excessive drug or alcohol use. If you liked O'Neill's portrayal of these themes, then you might like these dramatic works: *A Delicate Balance* by Edward Albee, *Buried Child* by Sam Shepard, and almost any play by Tennessee Williams, especially *Cat on a Hot Tin Roof* and *A Streetcar Named Desire*.

Bibliography

Allan, Cynthia. "Staging Place: The Geography of Modern Drama." *New England Theatre Journal* 7 (1996): 109–11.

Bloom, Steven F. "Empty Bottles, Empty Dreams: O'Neill's Use of Drinking and Alcoholism in *Long Day's Journey into Night*." *Critical Essays on Eugene O'Neill*, edited by James Martine, 159–77. Boston: GK Hall, 1984.

Bogard, Travis, and Eugene O'Neill. *Contour in Time: The Plays of Eugene O'Neill*. New York: Oxford University Press, 1988.
Fifer, Elizabeth. "Memory and Guilt: Parenting in Tracy Letts's *August: Osage County* and Eugene O'Neill's *Long Day's Journey into Night*." *The Eugene O'Neill Review* 34, no. 2 (2013): 183–97.
Grimm, Reinhold. "A Note on O'Neill, Nietzsche, and Naturalism: *Long Day's Journey into Night* in European Perspective." *Modern Drama* 26, no. 3 (1983): 331–34.
Hall, Ann C. *"A Kind of Alaska": Women in the Plays of O'Neill, Pinter, and Shepard*. Carbondale: Southern Illinois University Press, 1993.
Mann, Bruce J. "O'Neill's 'Presence' in *Long Day's Journey into Night*." *Theatre Annual* 43 (1988): 15–30.
Massey, Douglas S. "Long Day's Journey into Night: One Person's Reflections on International Migration." *Qualitative Sociology* 29, no. 1 (2006): 111–16.
McDonald, David. "The Phenomenology of the Glance in *Long Day's Journey into Night*." *Theatre Journal* 31, no. 3 (1979): 343–56.
Porter, Laurin R. "Modern and Postmodern Wastelands: *Long Day's Journey into Night* and Shepard's *Buried Child*." *The Eugene O'Neill Review* 17, no. 1/2 (1993): 106–19.
Raleigh, John Henrey. "Communal, Familial, and Personal Memories in O'Neill's *Long Day's Journey into Night*." *Modern Drama* 31, no. 1 (1988): 63–74.
Schvey, Hanry I. "The Master and His Double: Eugene O'Neill and Sam Shepard." *Journal of Dramatic Theory and Criticism* 5, no. 2 (1991): 49–62.
Shawcross, John. "The Road to Ruin: The Beginning of O'Neill's Long Day's Journey." *Modern Drama* 3, no. 3 (1960): 289–96.
Waith, Eugene M. "Eugene O'Neill: An Exercise in Unmasking." *Educational Theatre Journal* (1961): 182–91.

Lord of the Flies

Lord of the Flies, a novel by British author and Nobel laureate William Golding, derives its name from a rotting pig's head covered in flies that several boys erect on a stick to propitiate the monster that they believe to inhabit the island on which they reside. The monster is not some intangible presence but a manifestation of the boys and their descent into savagery. As such, the novel is partly the story of humanity's fall from grace, a theme that preoccupies the Genesis account of creation, and partly a commentary on "the state of nature," a construct of European intellectuals. Accordingly, one may read *Lord of the Flies* as an extended commentary about the Genesis story as well as a commentary about Europe's intellectual history. Although *Lord of the Flies* has been assigned in middle school or high school, it is not a children's book. Its themes are suited to readers of all ages.

THE GEOGRAPHY OF PLACE

The geography of place is difficult to pinpoint. After a series of events, a group of boys find themselves on an island in the Pacific Ocean. It appears to be uninhabited, though this does not mean that it cannot have been settled in the past, given that humans have colonized almost every island in the Pacific. The boys' accidental arrival on the island appears to coincide with or to follow closely some cataclysm, perhaps nuclear war. Whatever occurred does not appear to account for the fact that the boys found the island uninhabited. A nuclear blast on the island would have vaporized everyone, but then even the boys would have succumbed to radioactive fallout. Death by other means would have left corpses on the island, which the boys do not find. One might be tempted then, to view the island as a pristine sanctuary for the boys. The island has lush vegetation, which may or may not suggest a location in the tropics. Certainly when one thinks of islands in the Pacific, one is apt to select the Hawaiian Island or perhaps Tahiti. That is, one thinks of tropical islands. But Golding does not give us enough evidence to make this leap. An island in the temperate zone is also possible given sufficient rainfall to create a deciduous forest. Either way, a lush setting is possible so that the island must reside in some ill-defined geography rather than at some concrete latitude.

THE FALL FROM GRACE

Nonetheless, if one favors a tropical island in the Pacific, an interesting dynamic develops in which one might compare the tropical Pacific of Golding's imagination with the tropical Atlantic Ocean. In the West Indies, the Caribbean islands of the tropical Atlantic, Europeans found what appears to have been a pristine society of Amerindians in the late 15th century. Europeans, largely thanks to the diseases they carried, killed off all but a remnant of the Amerindians in the next generation or two. These depopulated islands needed workers to tend the new sugarcane estates that Europeans were planting. They solved the problem by importing African slaves to toil in the West Indies. In short, Europeans turned what might have been akin to a tropical paradise into hell.

The same dynamic operates in *Lord of the Flies*. The boys find a beautiful island only to despoil it and turn against one another. Golding does not give us the genocide that appears to have occurred in the Caribbean, but he narrates the killing of Piggy, a boy who bore a cruel name because he was overweight, out of shape, blind without his glasses, and asthmatic. Piggy was vulnerable because of his physical status as a weakling, just as the Amerindians had been vulnerable. In other words, Golding gives us a fall from grace that is as old as the story of Adam and Eve. In the Genesis account, the writer gives us the concrete sin of the couple's defiance of God. In *Lord of the Flies,* Golding gives readers the concrete abandonment of compassion and pity, traits without which a community must degenerate.

THE STATE OF NATURE

Another way to approach *Lord of the Flies* is through the lens of European intellectual history, particularly the changing concept of the state of nature. Although he was not the first to come to the idea, French Enlightenment intellectual and author Jean-Jacques Rousseau took an optimistic view of the state of nature, which was to have been a primordial condition of humanity before the establishment of laws, agriculture, and other economic activities. Rousseau held that in such a state, humans displayed nobility and pristine innocence. The state of nature was thus a condition free from corruption. Golding does not appear to hold this view. Rather, one must retreat to the time of English intellectual and author Thomas Hobbes, who thought of the state of nature as a time of unrestrained conflict and misery. Life was "nasty, brutish and short," and humans were engaged in a war of "all against all." The state of nature was thus one of primordial brutality, unchecked violence, and unrestrained id, to borrow from Austrian psychiatrist Sigmund Freud. This unpleasant vision seems to guide *Lord of the Flies*. Boys who should have been free from the contaminations of the world fail to establish anything akin to a utopia. Instead, they create a state of barbarism. Perhaps there exists a biological basis for depravity. Perhaps the reptilian portion of the human brain is selfish and cruel, and the boys, free from constraints, descend to these traits. Perfection and nobility do not exist in *Lord of the Flies,* only a rapid devolution into hell.

Christopher Cumo

Further Reading

As Golding's classic focuses on the fight for survival among a group of boys stranded on an island, other works that focus on representations of violence and youth would also explore similar themes. A list of such works might include *A Clockwork Orange* by Anthony Burgess, *Trainspotting* by Irvine Welsh, *The Hunger Games* by Suzanne Collins, and *Battle Royale* by Koushun Takami. Other classics about travel and adventure that would be similar to *Lord of the Flies* would be Daniel Defoe's *Robinson Crusoe* and Mark Twain's *The Adventures of Huckleberry Finn.*

Bibliography

Connell, John. "Island Dreaming: The Contemplation of Polynesian Paradise." *Journal of Historical Geography* 29, no. 4 (2003): 554–81.

Connor, Steven. "The Menagerie of the Senses." *The Senses and Society* 1, no. 1 (2006): 9–26.

Crawford, P. (2008). "Literature and Atrocity: *Lord of the Flies* and *The Inheritors*." In *William Golding's* Lord of the Flies, edited by Harold Bloom. New York: Bloom's Literary Criticism, 2008.

Dick, Bernard F. "'The Novelist Is a Displaced Person': An Interview with William Golding." *College English* 26, no. 6 (1965): 480–82.

Diken, Bülent, and Carsten Bagge Laustsen. "From War to War: Lord of the Flies as the Sociology of Spite." *Alternatives* 31, no. 4 (2006): 431–52.

Geertz, Clifford. "The Impact of the Concept of Culture on the Concept of Man." *Bulletin of the Atomic Scientists* 22, no. 4 (1966): 2–8.

Green, Martin. "The Robinson Crusoe Story." In *Imperialism and Juvenile Literature*. Manchester, UK: Manchester University Press, 2017.

Johnston, Arnold. *Of Earth and Darkness: The Novels of William Golding*. Columbia: University of Missouri Press, 1980.

Kneale, James. "Islands: Literary Geographies of Possession, Separation, and Transformation." In *The Routledge Handbook of Literature and Space,* edited by Robert T. Tally Jr. New York: Routledge, 2017.

Royle, Stephen A. *A Geography of Islands: Small Island Insularity*. London: Routledge, 2001.

Siegl, Karin. *The Robinsonade Tradition in Robert Michael Ballantyne's* The Coral Island *and William Golding's* Lord of the Flies. Lewiston, NY: E. Mellen Press, 1996.

Singh, Minnie. "The Government of Boys: Golding's *Lord of the Flies* and Ballantyne's *Coral Island*." *Children's Literature* 25, no. 1 (1997): 205–13.

Van Vuuren, Marijke. "Good Grief: *Lord of the Flies* as a Post-War Rewriting of Salvation History." *Literator: Journal of Literary Criticism, Comparative Linguistics and Literary Studies* 25, no. 2 (2004): 1–25.

White, Robert J. "Butterfly and Beast in *Lord of the Flies*." *Modern Fiction Studies* (1964): 163–70.

Lord of the Rings

The author of *The Lord of the Rings*, John Ronald Reuel Tolkien, was a renowned scholar, but the works that carry his name to the present are fantasy. Among these is *The Lord of the Rings*, a collection of three novels that follows his successful novel, *The Hobbit*. The language, characters and setting link *The Lord of the Rings* with *The Hobbit*. Humanlike creatures like wizards and hobbits inhabit *The Lord of the Rings*. Humans appear to be an afterthought. *The Lord of the Rings*, in simplest terms, is a morality tale in which good and evil are sharply drawn without room for ambiguity. At the center of the novels are a number of magical rings that are better destroyed than worn. These rings appear to derive from Norse mythology. Tolkien likely knew of German operatic titan Richard Wagner's use of Norse mythology and magical rings in the series of four operas unified under the title *The Ring of the Nibelung*. In this sense Tolkien appears to retrace old ground rather than carve out his own path.

THE GEOGRAPHY OF PLACE

The Lord of the Rings, like *The Hobbit,* is set in Middle-earth, apparently the main continent of earth during the time when the novels take place. Aside from characterizing it as a continent, it is hard to know what to make of Middle-earth. It does not appear to contain the lush vegetation that might mark it in the tropics or subtropics. Readers do not learn of the presence of ice or snow that would put it at high latitudes. There are mountains topped with enormous castles, so that we know that Middle-earth has topographical variations. In geological terms, the mountains point to a comparatively new continent, one in which the forces of uplift are still operating and in which gravity has not yet leveled the mountains into a wide plain. Middle-earth must therefore exist on a comparatively young earth, a place in which one might expect fanciful creatures and the telling of great deeds.

Some scholars believe that Middle-earth was part of a flat earth. Perhaps this notion turns to the Hebrew and Christian sources for support. The book of Revelation, for example mentions that earth has four corners. Such a configuration is possible only if earth were a rectangle or square or some quadrilateral in general. Such a setting is wildly fictitious. The ancient Greeks had been at pains to prove that earth is a globe. Since the Greeks, no educated person has clung to the fiction of a flat earth. If Tolkien held to a flat earth geography, the rationale is difficult to grasp. Perhaps he meant it simply as a fictional device to suggest intellectual impoverishment.

It is possible that Middle-earth might signify nothing more mysterious than the rural England that Tolkien knew as a child and to which he returned as an adult. It is an idealized English countryside of small cottages and sturdy hobbits. It is a source of goodness and purity.

TIME AND GEOGRAPHY

We noted earlier that the mountains often have grand castles. The castle was a feature of the Middle Ages, suggesting a medieval setting. This setting corresponds with the tendency of readers and critics to associate *The Lord of the Rings* with the Middle Ages. Tolkien romanticizes his medieval Middle-earth. The Middle Ages were a difficult time for Europeans. Mortality was high and life expectancy low. To be sure, difficulties face Middle-earth but so, too, do heroic deeds, magic, and quests for power and peace.

MORALITY AND MYTHOLOGY

The Lord of the Rings centers on a series of rings, one being the most powerful. Sauron, a figure of pure evil, perhaps tantamount to Satan, made the most powerful ring to control the other rings. This powerful ring makes anyone who wears it invisible and, over time, corrupts him, making him more like Sauron himself. Perhaps this scenario accords with the dictum that absolute power corrupts absolutely. The ring's evil must have come from Sauron, the source of evil. In the beginning Sauron possessed the ring but lost it in a violent struggle. For a time the ring was unknown, and aside from Sauron, no one knew its powers. Once rediscovered, the ring was the pretext for murder as the creature who took the name Gollum strangled the friend who had found the ring. The wearing of the ring conveyed an alchemical property on Gollum, as he grew very old without dying. If Gollum was now old and evil, he suffered the same fate as Sauron by losing the ring. By chance the hobbit Bilbo Baggins rediscovered the rings, the subject of *The Hobbit*. When he hands it to his cousin Frodo Baggins, *The Lord of the Rings* begins. The purpose of Frodo Baggins and everyone who helps him is to cast the ring to a pit of fire. The journey to this pit is full of danger, but the destruction of the ring symbolizes the destruction of evil.

In this context, Tolkien creates a morality without ambiguity. There is none of the ambiguity that one finds in Italian author Niccolò Machiavelli's *The Prince*. There is no mystery about who is evil and who is good. Similarly, though there are many moments of suspense, readers never doubt that good will triumph in the end. *The Lord of the Rings* thus affirms goodness, rewarding readers for their patience.

Christopher Cumo

Further Reading

Ursula K. LeGuin's *Earthsea Cycle* series shares the same intercultural message as *The Lord of the Rings,* along with its elements of magic. Other stories that offer these same kinds of themes, but that also narrate a classic hero's journey include C. S. Lewis's

The Chronicles of Narnia, J. K. Rowling's *Harry Potter* series, and George R. R. Martin's *A Game of Thrones.*

Bibliography

Brisbois, Michael J. "Tolkien's Imaginary Nature: An Analysis of the Structure of Middle-earth." *Tolkien Studies* 2 (2005): 197–216. doi:10.1353/tks.2005.0009.

Bushell, Sally. "Paratext or Imagetext? Interpreting the Fictional Map." *Word and Image, A Journal of Verbal/Visual Enquiry* 32, no. 2 (2016): 181–94. doi:10.1080/02666286.2016.1146513.

Dalby, Simon. "Challenging Cartographies of Enmity: Empire, War and Culture in Contemporary Militarization." In *Militarism and International Relations: Political Economy, Security and Theory,* edited by Anna Stavrianakis and Jan Selby. New York: Routledge, 2013.

Dawson, Deidre A. "Representations of Nature in Middle-earth (2016), edited by Martin Simonson" (book review). *Journal of Tolkien Research* 4, no. 1 (2017). scholar.valpo.edu/journaloftolkienresearch/vol4/iss1/5.

Ekman, Stefan. *Here Be Dragons: Exploring Fantasy Maps and Settings.* Middletown, CT: Wesleyan University Press, 2013.

Habermann, Ina, and Nikolaus Kuhn. "Sustainable Fictions—Geographical, Literary and Cultural Intersections in J. R. R. Tolkien's *The Lord of the Rings.*" *The Cartographic Journal: The World of Mapping* 48, no. 4 (2011): 263–73. doi:10.1179/1743277411Y.0000000024.

Higgins, Andrew. "Building Imaginary Worlds (2012) by Mark J.P. Wolf and Revisiting Imaginary World (2016) edited by Mark J. P. Wolf" (book review). *Journal of Tolkien Research* 4, no. 1 (2017). scholar.valpo.edu/journaloftolkienresearch/vol4/iss1/10.

Hynes, Gerard. "'Beneath the Earth's dark keel': Tolkien and Geology." *Tolkien Studies* 9 (2012): 21–36. doi:10.1353/tks.2012.0005.

King, Barry. "*The Lord of the Rings* as a Cultural Projection." In *Locating Migrating Media,* edited by Greg Elmer, Charles H. Davis, Janine Marchessault, and John McCullough. Lanham, MD: Lexington Books, 2010.

Lane, Belden C. "Fantasy and the Geography of Faith." *Theology Today* 50, no. 3 (1993): 397–408. doi:10.1177/004057369305000306.

Light, Rowan. "Destination Middle-earth: Hobbit Tourism and the Shaping of Postcolonial Spaces in Aotearoa New Zealand." *Melbourne Historical Journal* 45, no. 1 (2017): 39–68.

Page, John, Ann Brower, and Johannes Welsch. "The Curious Untidiness of Property & Ecosystem Services: A Hybrid Method of Measuring Place." *Pace Environmental Law Review* 32, no. 3 (2015): 756.

Peaslee, Robert Moses. "'There and back again,' but Where?: Tourism, *The Lord of the Rings,* and Media Power." PhD diss., University of Colorado, 2007.

Rosebury, Brian. "The Lord of the Rings: Imagining Middle-earth." In *Tolkien: A Cultural Phenomenon.* London: Palgrave Macmillan, 2003. doi:10.1057/9780230599987_2.

Sacknoff, Lance M. "Fantastic Ecosemiosis: An Analysis of Fantasy as Nature-Text in *The Lord of the Rings.*" Master's thesis, Iowa State University, 2014.

Werber, Niels. "Geo- and Biopolitics of Middle-Earth: A German Reading of Tolkien's *The Lord of the Rings.*" *New Literary History* 36, no. 2 (2005): 227–46. www.jstor.org/stable/20057890.

Wollen, Peter. "Mappings: Situationists and/or Conceptualists." In *Rewriting Conceptual Art,* edited by Michael Newman and Jon Bird. London: Reaktion Books Ltd., 1999.

M

Macbeth

English poet and playwright William Shakespeare wrote several types of plays, among them tragedies. *Macbeth* falls into this category and is, at its core, a play about murder, deception, and revenge. If Macbeth is the protagonist, he is also a murderer and usurper. Readers may have trouble empathizing with him and may feel satisfaction that he is killed in the end. In fact, Macbeth's death releases the tension that Shakespeare had built into the play.

THE GEOGRAPHY OF PLACE

Shakespeare set most of *Macbeth* in Scotland, apparently for two reasons. First he derived the characters of Macbeth and Duncan from a 16th-century history of Scotland. Macbeth and Duncan were apparently real people, both having been king of Scotland. As historical figures, the two do not seem to have been significant. They must have, however, caught Shakespeare's attention. As was often the case, Shakespeare modified the characters so that they became literary rather than historical figures. Given his tendency toward modification, Shakespeare did not, however, change the location. This leaves open the question of why Shakespeare was wedded to the geography of Scotland when he felt so free to change just about everything else. The second reason may help us. We must turn to informed conjecture for aid. Shakespeare wrote *Macbeth* during the reign of England's king James I. The king had been born in Scotland and was always proud of his Scottish ancestry and homeland. James was king of Scotland before he became king of England. When he became king of England, he did not renounce the Scottish throne but was thereafter king of both territories. With James an ardent Scotsman, Shakespeare may have set *Macbeth* in Scotland in hopes of interesting the king in his work. Any writer serious about his or her craft wants to be popular. Shakespeare may have set *Macbeth* in Scotland in a bid for popularity with the most influential audience in England.

THE GEOGRAPHY OF NIHILISM

Nihilism is literally a belief in nothing. The logician might retort that one cannot believe in nothing because such a claim amounts to a belief in something. Yet the term has value because it can speak to the immensity of despair and hopelessness beyond which humans cannot be redeemed, if such a thing were possible. In this sense nihilism goes beyond mere pessimism to assert a condition of eternal bleakness, a world indifferent to suffering and justice, and, in many cases, the longing for death. These strong words are usually associated with 19th-century German philosopher Friedrich Nietzsche, and much credit is due him in this regard. In fact, Nietzsche's understanding of nihilism informed existentialism in the 20th century. Indeed, one finds remnants of nihilism in some of the fiction of French novelist and art critic André Malraux and French Algerian author and Nobel laureate Albert Camus.

The real quest for the roots of nihilism does not begin in Germany or France, but in the Scotland that is the setting of *Macbeth*. Readers have no illusions about the protagonist. Early in the play, he murders King Duncan, falsely charges two servants with the deed, and then kills them. Macbeth is a liar, murderer, and likely a sociopath. By these evils, Macbeth usurps the throne of Scotland. As Shakespeare conceived him, a man of such malevolence must be a nihilist before the term was coined. A pivotal event in the play is Macbeth's encounter with three witches. They foretell the future, making clear that he will die for his crimes. Macbeth discounts their words as nonsense, but when, one by one, their predictions come true, Macbeth grasps that his end is near. Not given to much emotion throughout the play, Macbeth utters a short speech as he prepares for death. The tagline states that "It [Life] is a tale told by an idiot, full of sound and fury, signifying nothing." Here is the nothingness upon which Nietzsche would grasp three centuries later. It is a statement about the inherent meaninglessness of life, a meaninglessness that must have made it easy for Macbeth to kill as he did. With *Macbeth,* the assurances of the heaven of medieval Christianity seem remote. One has transgressed the bounds of religion as only a person devoid of faith can. One is at the nadir of despair, at the limits of one's tolerance for the indifference of the universe to human suffering and aspirations. One has become a nihilist in a Shakespearean landscape.

THE GENDERED LANDSCAPE OF WITCHCRAFT

Macbeth is not Shakespeare's only work to include references to witches. This penchant is not surprising given that Shakespeare lived at a time when Christian denominations were more certain than ever of the existence of witches and their capacity for evil. The witches in *Macbeth* are all women, which speaks to how embedded sexism was in early modern Europe. The figure of the witch was used to depict women in a host of unfair ways: women as wanton creatures who are willing to have sex with Satan or some demon to consummate their pact with him. Shakespeare's use of women as witches manifests a willingness to judge women as inherently sinful. Because of Shakespeare's derogatory references to witches, in *Macbeth* and *Hamlet* for example, it is possible to see a hint of misogyny in his attitudes toward women.

Christopher Cumo

Further Reading

It is hard to compete with Shakespeare, but some ancient Greek playwrights produced works that inspired the plot to *Macbeth:* the lengths to which someone will go to gain political power. The main character of Macbeth is doomed by fate, much like some of the heroes in the political dramas of ancient Greece, like *Antigone*. A more modern work that combines the world of the supernatural with a political coup is Isabel Allende's *The House of the Spirits.*

Bibliography

Ackroyd, Peter. *A Brief Guide to William Shakespeare.* Philadelphia: Running Press, 2010.

Barrett, Chris. "Shakespeare's Nature: From Cultivation to Culture." *Medieval & Renaissance Drama in England* 30 (2017): 239–41.

Berry, Ralph. *Shakespeare's Settings and a Sense of Place.* Cardiff, UK: University of Wales Press, 2016.

Brayton, Dan. "Sounding the Deep: Shakespeare and the Sea Revisited." *Forum for Modern Language Studies* 46, no. 2 (2010): 189–206. doi:10.1093/fmls/cqq006.

De Sousa, Geraldo U. *At Home in Shakespeare's Tragedies.* London: Routledge, 2010.

Dobbs-Buchanan, Allison M. "You Take the High Road, and I'll Take the Low Road: A Post-Colonial Analysis of Shakespeare's Macbeth." Master's thesis, Cleveland State University, 2013.

Estok, Simon C. "Doing Ecocriticism with Shakespeare: An Introduction." In *Ecocriticism and Shakespeare.* London: Palgrave Macmillan, 2011. doi:10.1057/9780230 118744_1.

Gleed, Paul. *Bloom's How to Write about Shakespeare's Tragedies.* New York: Bloom's Literary Criticism, 2011.

"The Metamorphosis"

The author of the short story "The Metamorphosis" was Czech writer Franz Kafka. He was almost unknown during his lifetime because he published so little of what he wrote. In this context, Kafka invites comparison with American author J. D. Salinger. During a life complicated and ultimately truncated by tuberculosis, a dangerous bacterial infection, Kafka worked as an attorney for an insurance company, being promoted thrice. As his life came to a close, Kafka admonished his friend Max Brod to burn all his work. Brod refused, giving the world the corpus of Kafka's work, including two celebrated novels, *The Trial* and *The Castle.* Thanks to these and other works, readers can appraise Kafka's gifts. In a strange, almost emotionless tone, Kafka narrated scenarios that are tantamount to nightmares in which ordinary people have no control over their fate and must suffer a horrible destiny despite their innocence. "The Metamorphosis" has all these qualities.

FREE WILL AND KAFKA'S LITERARY LANDSCAPE

"The Metamorphosis" focuses on Gregor Samsa, a traveling salesperson who appears to have done nothing wrong. Yet one morning he awakens in his bed to find himself no longer human but an insect. It is difficult to foresee a worse fate and to be conscious of it. Had Samsa any real volition, he would of course have chosen to remain human. But despite his desires, Samsa has no free will and cannot change himself back into a man. It seems, then, that Samsa—and, by extension, all of us—inhabits a universe bereft of free choices. Freedom must be an illusion or must be so circumscribed as to lack value. At the very least, one must admit that Samsa cannot change his fate. This admission speaks to our own plight. Here we seem to be close to the ideas of French mathematician and philosopher Blaise Pascal, who in some ways was a forerunner of existentialism. Pascal and Kafka understood that we are all thrown into the world without explanation or purpose. To make matters worse, we are all under that same death sentence. When sufficient time has passed, we too will die, all without ever understanding our purpose. Samsa live and dies without ever understanding any purpose to his existence.

THE LITERARY LANDSCAPE OF ALIENATION

As an insect, Gregor Samsa is alienated from himself. Obviously he is alienated from his former human body, which has suffered the transformation into something posthuman. Kafka has left him with sufficient cognition to realize his predicament but with no other human traits. He no longer has arms and legs in the traditional sense of what it means to be human. Instead, he has six legs that must have sensory abilities if he is a true insect. He no longer breathes through his nose and mouth, but through pores in the sides of his body. He no longer has bones in any real sense but rather the exoskeleton of an insect.

THE GEOGRAPHY OF PLACE

The transformation of Gregor Samsa into an insect occurs in his bed and must have happened during his sleep. If a bed is a safe haven in the domestic space, an impregnable place where one can retreat from the sorrows and demands of the world and rest, then Samsa's geography has betrayed him. The bedroom that once belonged to the real Gregor Samsa is now a prison cell. Samsa cannot leave his room for fear of what will befall him. He has become a convict, an outlaw. Samsa no longer feels safe anywhere. He has become an alien thrust outside the company of people. He is different and bears the stigma of being a repulsive insect. Through Samsa's ordeals, Kafka exposes the posthuman condition as a situation of alienation and imprisonment.

A CLOSET EXISTENTIALIST

Kafka is not normally grouped among the existentialists, though "The Metamorphosis" explores themes central to the movement. The inability to understand why Samsa has come to such a bad end, his sense of alienation, abandonment, and fear, his marginalization, and possibly the absence of free will may group Kafka with the existentialists, though French authors and Nobel laureates Jean-Paul Sartre and Albert Camus were fond of claiming that humans are condemned to be free. Kafka provides a dose of reality in circumscribing our putative freedom. Life's events intervene and narrow our choice in a way that Kafka appreciated more than Sartre and Camus. In the other previously cited examples, "The Metamorphosis" gives one a potent introduction to the kinds of ideas with which existentialism grappled.

Christopher Cumo

Further Reading
Life Is a Dream, a translation from the Spanish *La vida es sueño,* is a play by Pedro Calderon de la Barca that explores the confusion between reality and a dream state, which is much like the seeming supernatural element of Gregor's transformation. It also features a conflict between father and son, just as Gregor's relationship with his family, including his father, becomes strained. Nineteenth-century Russian author Fyodor Dostoyevsky in his *Notes from Underground* captures the same feeling of isolation that Gregor Samsa experiences.

Bibliography
Gerhardt, Christina. "The Ethics of Animals in Adorno and Kafka." *New German Critique* 97 (2006): 159–78.

Islam, Syed Manzurul. *The Ethics of Travel: From Marco Polo to Kafka.* Manchester, UK: Manchester University Press, 1996.

Král, Françoise. "Space, Discourse and Visibility: Towards a Phenomenology of Invisibility." In *Social Invisibility and Diasporas in Anglophone Literature and Culture.* London: Palgrave Macmillan, 2014. doi:10.1057/9781137401397_3.

Rhodes, Carl, and Robert Westwood. "The Limits of Generosity: Lessons on Ethics, Economy, and Reciprocity in Kafka's 'The Metamorphosis.'" *Journal of Business Ethics* 133, no. 2 (2016): 235–48.

Rowe, Michael. "Metamorphosis: Defending the Human." *Literature and Medicine* 21, no. 2 (2002): 264–80.

Ryan, Michael P. "Samsa and Samsara: Suffering, Death, and Rebirth in 'The Metamorphosis.'" *German Quarterly* (1999): 133–52.

Scholtmeijer, Marian. "What Is 'Human'?: Metaphysics and Zoontology in Flaubert and Kafka." In *Animal Acts: Configuring the Human in Western History,* edited by Jennifer Hamm and Matthew Senior, 138–55. New York: Routledge, 1997.

Sokel, Walter H. "Language and Truth in the Two Worlds of Franz Kafka." *The German Quarterly* 52, no. 3 (1979): 364–84.

Spilka, Mark. "Kafka's Sources for 'The Metamorphosis.'" *Comparative Literature* 11, no. 4 (1959): 289–307.

Sweeney, Kevin W. "Competing Theories of Identity in Kafka's 'The Metamorphosis.'" *Mosaic: An Interdisciplinary Critical Journal* 23, no. 4 (1990): 23–35.

Valk, Francina Cornelia. "Exclusion and Renewal: Identity and Jewishness in Franz Kafka's 'The Metamorphosis' and David Vogel's *Married Life.*" PhD diss., Leiden University, 2015.

Webster, Peter Dow. "Franz Kafka's 'Metamorphosis' as Death and Resurrection Fantasy." *American Imago* 16, no. 4 (1959): 349–365.

A Midsummer Night's Dream

A Midsummer Night's Dream is a fantasy comedy play written by William Shakespeare at some point between 1590 and 1597. The play consists of interconnected plots that follow events surrounding the marriage of the Duke of Athens, Theseus, and the Amazonian queen, Hippolyta, as well as the adventures of four young Athenian lovers—Demetrius, Lysander, Helena, and Hermia. Also involved are a group of six amateur actors (known as the mechanicals), who are manipulated by fairies led by Oberon and Titania. The fairies inhabit the forest in which most of *A Midsummer Night's Dream* is set.

A PLACE OF LAW AND ORDER

A Midsummer Night's Dream begins, however, in ancient Athens, a place of law and order. Here Theseus and Hippolyta are preparing for their wedding, and Hermia (who is in love with Lysander) does not wish to submit to her father's demand that she enter into an arranged marriage with Demetrius, who is loved by Helena. Hermia's father is enraged at his daughter's disobedience and invokes an ancient Athenian law that states a daughter must wed the suitor selected by her father or be killed. Ultimately, Hermia and Lysander opt to run away together to the Athenian forest that is inhabited by fairies. Unbeknownst to the many human characters that stumble into it, through the course of the play it becomes apparent that this forest is a world where magic, enchantment, and mischief are all-powerful and where the law and order of Athens hold no sway. Though they may be seeking the idyll of medieval romance, the humans soon discover that this forest is subversive, disordered, and crowded with myriad figures as are the forest of the Arthurian tales.

THE SETTING OF THE FOREST

The forest is the principal landscape in *A Midsummer Night's Dream* as well as a vital element of the play's dramatic structure. This forest differs, however, from the pastoral (if perilous) forest envisioned by Shakespeare in plays such as *The Two Gentlemen of Verona* or the forest as sanctuary as presented in *As You Like It*, because the forest in *A Midsummer Night's Dream* is dominated by the supernatural. That the forest is a place where the imagination runs free is reflected in the lines "in the night, imagining some fear, / How easy is a bush supposed a bear!" (Act 5, Scene 1, Lines 22–23).

The forest of *A Midsummer Night's Dream* is also a bewildering place in which people lose both their identities and their grasp on reality as certainties are undermined. Such inconsistency is highlighted by Hermia when, abandoned by Lysander, she exclaims "Since night you loved me; yet since night you left me" (Act 3, Scene 2, Lines 275–76). The identity confusion experienced by characters such as Bottom extends to the forest itself, for although supposedly located close to Athens, the forest setting of *A Midsummer Night's Dream* is by its magical nature really representative of the forests of England which, in the popular imagination of the time, were places of supernatural intrigue and mischief. That Shakespeare depicts the forest as a locus for uncertainty, confusion, and supernatural mischief is unsurprising, for this reflects the belief in fairies that people living in rural England up until the end of the 18th century commonly held. These were not the cuddly fairies of modern times, however, but rather mischievous, temperamental, supernatural beings that could cause as much harm as good. Indeed, there was a strong belief throughout rural England at this time that fairies stole human babies and left fairy babies, so-called changelings, in the human babies' place. Moreover, Puck is a traditional character from English folklore, something of which Titania speaks in the lines: "Are not you he / That frights the maidens of the villagery" (Act 2, Scene 1,

Lines 34–35). Furthermore, in the forest of *A Midsummer Night's Dream,* there is no sureness or fixed morality, and authority is questioned, thereby hinting at Elizabethan concerns that disorder and tragedy are always near.

Ultimately, however, the human characters of *A Midsummer Night's Dream* cannot make a permanent home in the enchanted forest, as it is not the world to which they belong. Instead, by the end of the play, all the humans must return to Athens. Once all the humans have returned to Theseus in Athens, the setting starts to resemble an Elizabethan nobleman's estate rather than a palace of ancient Greece. Indeed, after their lavish wedding, Theseus and Hippolyta enjoy courtly entertainments of the kind that Elizabethan nobles would experience after their weddings.

MYTHOLOGY AND FOLKLORE

In *A Midsummer Night's Dream,* ancient Greek mythology, rural England, and English folklore combine to create a landscape that is redolent of adventure, love, and surprise. The interconnectedness of the fairy realm and ancient Athens compels the audience to trust their imagination. Moreover, by setting the play principally within an enchanted forest, Shakespeare compels the audience to believe in something that does not exist in reality. The blending of worlds also allows the audience not only to believe in the magic that allows love to occur but also makes the audience itself believe in love, something that can only truly exist and flourish among the groves of the forest.

Victoria Williams

Further Reading

If you enjoyed *A Midsummer Night's Dream,* you may like to read the other Shakespeare plays that employ of a forest setting, especially *As You Like It, The Two Gentlemen of Verona,* and *Titus Andronicus.* Alternatively you could read *The Faerie Queene,* an epic, 16th-century, allegorical poem by Edmund Spenser, in which the titular character is a descendant of Titania. You might also like to read *Grimms' Fairy Tales,* in which the enchanted forest combines with reality to create a believable setting in which the incredible can occur. Another work in which supernatural beings interact with humans in a forest setting is Christina Rossetti's 19th-century narrative poem, "Goblin Market," which also features enchantment, loss of identity, and the depiction of true love, though in this case the love is familial rather than necessarily romantic.

Bibliography

Addison Roberts, Jeanne. *The Shakespearean Wild: Geography, Genus and Gender.* Lincoln: University of Nebraska Press. 1991.

Cless, Downing. *Ecology and Environment in European Drama.* New York: Routledge, 2010.

Daley, A. Stuart. "Where Are the Woods in *As You Like It*?" *Shakespeare Quarterly* 34, no. 2 (1983): 172–80. doi:10.2307/2869832.

De Sousa, Geraldo U. *Shakespeare's Cross-Cultural Encounters.* New York: Palgrave Macmillan, 1999.

Fox, Rachel. "Locating Fantastika." *Foundation* 44, no. 122 (2015): 80–83.

Hall, Kim F. *Things of Darkness: Economies of Race and Gender in Early Modern England.* Ithaca, NY: Cornell University Press, 1995.

Hendricks, Margo. "'Obscured by Dreams': Race, Empire, and Shakespeare's *A Midsummer Night's Dream.*" *Shakespeare Quarterly* 47, no. 1 (1996): 37–60. doi:10.2307/2871058.

Roberts, Jeanne Addison. *The Shakespearean Wild: Geography, Genus and Gender.* Lincoln: University of Nebraska Press, 1991.

Sanders, Julie. *The Cambridge Introduction to Early Modern Drama, 1576–1642.* Cambridge, UK: Cambridge University Press, 2013.

Saunders, Corinne J. *The Forest of Medieval Romance: Avernus, Broceliande, Arden.* Suffolk, UK: D. S. Brewer, 1993.

Scott, Charlotte. "Dark Matter: Shakespeare's Foul Dens and Forests." *Shakespeare Survey,* edited by Peter Holland. Cambridge, UK: Cambridge University Press, 2011.

Siewers, Alfred K. "Pre-Modern Ecosemiotics: The Green World as Literary Ecology." In *The Space of Culture—the Place of Nature in Estonia and Beyond,* edited by Tiina Peil. Tartu, Estonia: Tartu University Press, 2011.

Moby Dick

During his lifetime, American author Herman Melville was known as a storyteller, as someone who could describe the romance of tropical islands and imbue them with a sense of adventure. His greatest work, *Moby Dick,* departed from the charm and simplicity of his early works, and readers quickly tired of it. By Melville's death, the novel was out of print but has enjoyed a renaissance since then. Almost every notable author and literary critic has affirmed its greatness. American author and Nobel laureate William Faulkner once admitted that he wished he had written it. *Moby Dick* defies easy summation. From the simple opening line, the novel expands into the kind of gigantic story one finds in the works of Russian novelist and short story writer Fyodor Dostoyevsky. The comparison seems apt because both *Moby Dick* and Dostoyevsky's novels grapple with consequential issues and are full of philosophy, theology, psychology, and drama. They are all novels of ideas.

THE GEOGRAPHY OF PLACE

Here one comes at once to the subtlety that Melville displayed in *Moby Dick.* Readers prepare for a story set in New England, a tiny corner in North America, a speck on the globe. But the geography rapidly expands as Captain Ahab and his crew sail into the ocean. They do not confine themselves to the Atlantic but circle the watery globe in an act of circumnavigation that had become almost the norm

---

Queequeg was a native of Kokovoko, an island far away to the West and South. It is not down in any map; true places never are.

Herman Melville, *Moby Dick or, The Whale* (1851)

THE CRUISE OF THE *Pequod*

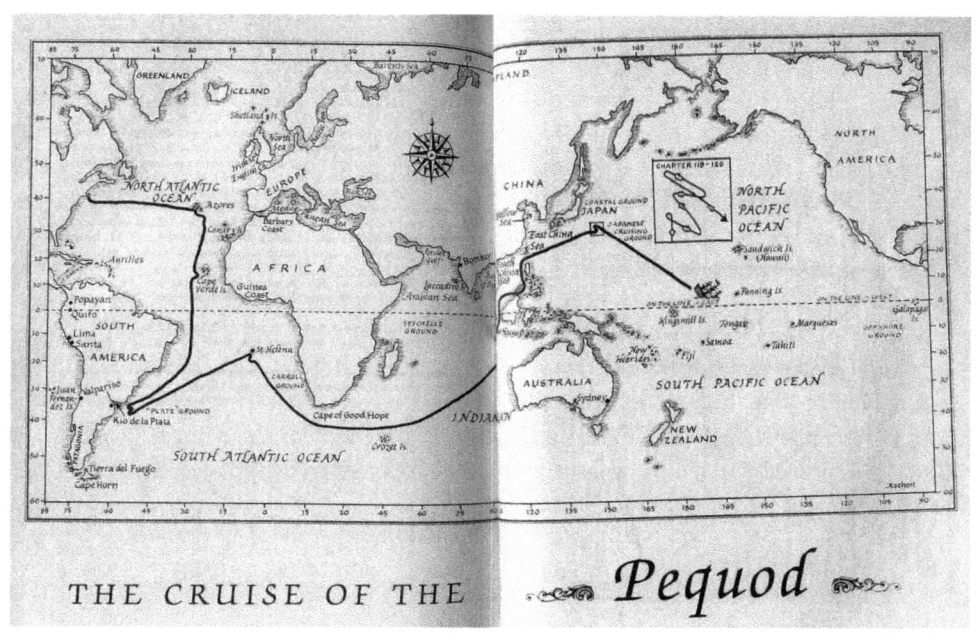

This illustration shows the voyage of the *Pequod* as Captain Ahab chases Moby Dick. In Melville's novel, the ship sets out from the New England coast, crossing the Atlantic until it meets the Indian Ocean. The vessel finally sinks in the Pacific Ocean, somewhere off the coast of New Guinea. (Library of Congress)

since Spanish explorer Ferdinand Magellan accomplished the feat in the 16th century. The world becomes the geography of *Moby Dick*. Melville the miniaturist had turned again into the great storyteller.

THE GEOGRAPHY OF EVIL

The far-flung exploits of Captain Ahab have a purpose. He is obsessed with killing a large white whale known as Moby Dick. This aspiration seems cruel, but Ahab regards it as essential. Years earlier the whale, lashing out against its attacker, destroyed Ahab's ship and deprived him of part of one leg. Now he seeks revenge. Meanwhile, an ambiguity has been brewing. Who or what is evil: Ahab for wanting to kill Moby Dick or the whale for having taken Ahab's leg? Melville never answers directly, but it is clear that Ahab puffs the whale into a gargantuan source of evil. The fate of the world, it seems, rests on whether Ahab can exterminate Moby Dick. Perhaps the job is too large for one person or one crew, but Ahab persists without thought of the difficulties of his undertaking.

THE NOBLE SAVAGE

Ahab has a polyglot crew, one composed of people of all nationalities. Among them is Queequeg, a Polynesian man who at first intimidates Ishmael the narrator.

But after the initial surprise Queequeg becomes a fearless and loyal companion. He is by appearances what Europeans once called a savage. This sentiment arose in the 16th and 17th centuries when Europeans branded anyone who did not look or behave like them as primitive and ungodly. This was the period when Europeans extirpated the Amerindians and abused Africans in horrific ways. In many ways, deplorable treatment of people of African descent continues today. Yet ideas began to change, at least in some circles. The Enlightenment of the 18th century opened a new chapter on ethnicity. The Enlightenment continued to classify these half-naked peoples as savages, but they were not inferior because of this status. They lived, it was thought, in a free society with the chance to indulge their passions and realize their ambitions. If they were savages, they were also noble, imbued with a quality that Europeans had lost in their ascent toward civilization and in their fall from grace in the opening chapters of Genesis. Put simply, Queequeg reflected Melville's respect for people of color, a lesson he may have learned from the more liberal Enlightenment thinkers.

THE BIBLE

Melville's attitudes toward religion are not easy to clarify. Parts of *Moby Dick* seem to be a polemic against the hell and brimstone approach of some clerics. Yet Melville knew the Bible well. Ahab, once a king of Israel, appears here as a ship's captain. Even though Moby Dick is not a fish, it seems to evoke the sense of powerlessness and terror that Jonah felt upon being taken by a large fish. In a larger sense, *Moby Dick* may be a commentary on the book of Job. Despite his innocence, Job suffers a series of disasters, exactly what befalls the crew. In the end Moby Dick smashes Ahab's ship and leaves only one person alive to tell the story, just as in Job, only one person remains alive after each disaster to inform Job what has befallen his family and property. Either God is inscrutable or we inhabit an inscrutable universe.

Christopher Cumo

Further Reading

Melville's *Moby Dick* is similar to other literary works whose authors develop characters who are obsessed by a singular pursuit, whether a quest for revenge or to win the love of a woman who has married someone else. In this respect, Miguel de Cervantes' classic *Don Quixote,* published in the early 1600s, is a good companion read to *Moby Dick* because it is about how a man refuses to give up on his fantasy of a more chivalric, more dignified world. Similarly, the main character of Fitzgerald's *The Great Gatsby* also chases after the woman he loves, refusing to give up, and his quest eventually costs him his life. Lastly, *Frankenstein,* by Mary Shelley, is about a singular-minded pursuit that also ends in the protagonist's demise.

Bibliography

Baker, Anne. *Heartless Immensity: Literature, Culture, and Geography in Antebellum America.* Ann Arbor: University of Michigan Press, 2006.

Carbaugh, Donal. "'The Mountain' and 'The Project': Dueling Depictions of a Natural Environment." In *Ecolinguistics Reader: Language, Ecology and Environment,* edited by Alwin Fill and Peter Mühlhäusler. London: Continuum, 2001.

de Villiers, Dawid W. "Crossing 'The Deadly Space Between': Moby-Dick and the Traversal of the Sea." *English Studies in Africa* 51, no. 2 (2008): 69–83.

Drown, Amber. "Islandscapes and Savages: Ecocriticism and Herman Melville's *Typee*." Master's thesis, Texas State University, 2011.

Fisher, Philip. "Democratic Social Space: Whitman, Melville, and the Promise of American Transparency." *Representations* 24 (1998): 60–101. doi:10.2307/2928476.

Gesler, Wil. "Using Herman Melville's *Moby-Dick* to Explore Geographic Themes." *Journal of Geography* 103, no. 1 (2004): 28–37. doi:10.1080/00221340408978569.

Graber, Samuel. "'Clouds Involved the Land': Melville, 'Donelson,' and the Transatlantic Aspects of National War News." *ESQ: A Journal of Nineteenth-Century American Literature and Culture* 63, no. 4 (2017): 515–60. doi:10.1353/esq.2017.0019.

Howarth, William. "Earth Islands: Darwin and Melville in the Galapagos." *The Iowa Review* 30, no. 3 (2000): 95–113. www.jstor.org/stable/20154883.

Hsu, Hsuan L. *Geography and the Production of Space in Nineteenth-Century American Literature*. Cambridge, UK: Cambridge University Press, 2010.

Kelley, Wyn. *Melville's City: Literary and Urban Form in Nineteenth-Century New York*. Cambridge, UK: Cambridge University Press, 1996.

Laloë, Anne-Flore. *The Geography of the Ocean: Knowing the Ocean as a Space*. London: Routledge, 2016.

Long, James W. "Plunging into the Atlantic: The Oceanic Order of Herman Melville's *Moby Dick*." *Atlantic Studies: Global Currents* 8, no. 1 (2011): 69–91. doi:10.1080/14788810.2011.539790.

Marx, Leo. "The Idea of Nature in America." *Daedalus* 137, no. 2 (2008): 8–21. www.jstor.org/stable/20028176.

Mentz, Steven. "Toward a Blue Cultural Studies: The Sea, Maritime Culture, and Early Modern English Literature." *Literature Compass* 6, no. 5 (2009): 997–1013. doi:10.1111/j.1741-4113.2009.00655.x.

Radford, Zachary Michael. "The Whale and the World in Melville's *Moby-Dick*: Early American Empire and Globalization." Master's thesis, University of Montana, 2012.

Satchell, Kim. "Reveries of the Solitary Islands: From Sensuous Geography to Ecological Sensibility." In *Landscapes of Exile: Once Perilous, Now Safe,* edited by Anna Haebich and Baden Offord. Oxford, UK: Peter Lang, 2006.

Schirmeister, Pamela. *The Consolations of Space: The Place of Romance in Hawthorne, Melville, and James*. Stanford, CA: Stanford University Press, 1990.

Schultz, Elizabeth. "From 'Sea of Grass' to 'Wire and Rail': Melville's Evolving Perspective on the Prairies." *American Studies* 52, no. 1 (2012): 31–47.

Steinberg, Philip E. *The Social Construction of the Ocean*. Cambridge, UK: Cambridge University Press, 2001.

Tally, Robert T., Jr. *Melville, Mapping and Globalization: Literary Cartography in the American Baroque Writer*. London: Continuum, 2009.

Thomas, Leah. "Cartographic and Literary Intersections: Digital Literary Cartographies, Digital Humanities, and Libraries and Archives." *Journal of Map & Geography Libraries: Advances in Geospatial Information, Collections & Archives* 9, no. 3 (2013): 335–49. doi:10.1080/15420353.2013.823901.

My Ántonia

Told to readers through a narrator who in turn gets the story from a friend named Jim Burden, My Ántonia recounts the story of a small Nebraska town and its

> As I looked about me I felt that the grass was the country, as the water is the sea. The red of the grass made all the great prairie the colour of wine-stains, or of certain seaweeds when they are first washed up. And there was so much motion in it; the whole country seemed, somehow, to be running.
>
> **Willa Cather, My Ántonia (1918)**

inhabitants, in particular the titular character, a Bohemian (Czech) immigrant girl. At age 10, the orphaned Jim moves to his grandparents' farm, where he first meets their neighbors, the Shimerdas. Ántonia Shimerda is four years older than Jim, and never a serious love interest, even though he predictably has a crush on this attractive, strong girl. When her father commits suicide, she takes over many of the farm duties, and so doesn't have the opportunity to attend school as Jim does. When Jim's grandparents move into the nearby town of Black Hawk, Ántonia becomes a "hired girl" in the houses of richer families to support her own.

Though by this point Jim is clearly in love with the "lower-class" Ántonia, he never admits it, and leaves for college. When he returns, Ántonia has been used by an unscrupulous man, leaving her penniless and with a child. Jim promises her that he'll come back after law school, but doesn't, perhaps rejecting Ántonia in the way he feels she rejected him. However, 20 years later, they reconcile.

THE GEOGRAPHY OF PLACE

Willa Cather herself spent her youth in Red Cloud, Nebraska, and so a strong feeling of nostalgia for that time and place is infused in the novel. The Nebraska prairie had only recently been settled after the "Indian Wars" had driven the tribes into reservations, with the last of the "pioneers" coming from northern and eastern Europe, from the ruins of the plantation system in the South, and from the crumbling mill towns of the Northeast. In the novel, Ántonia symbolizes the prairie itself, or perhaps mirrors it, a strong woman for a difficult land. As she tells Jim, "there wasn't a tree here when we first came." In many ways, the book is a swan song to that end-stage of building and growing, the final chapter of the "conquest" of the continent.

The concept of "land" was an integral part of Cather's world. Today, owning property is still part of what we consider the American dream, but it is not quite the same thing as the vision of land shared by pioneers from the 1600s through the end of the 1800s. Many of them immigrated from European countries where land was parceled out and owned by the aristocracy, and farmers worked for landlords rather than for themselves. On the American frontier, they had the chance to buy their own property, farm their own crops, and support their own families with the work of their minds and hands.

Of course, it was rarely that simple, but that was the dream, which Cather illuminates clearly in her novels. To Cather and her characters, "sunflower-bordered roads always seem to me the roads of freedom." In *My Ántonia,* we see that this dream is already fading, since Jim Burden has no interest in staying and farming the land, and becomes a lawyer for a railroad company instead. This job symbolizes his lack of connection to one place, contrasted with Ántonia's stable commitment to the farmland around Black Hawk. And yet, both the character of Jim and Cather herself long for the beauty they left behind: "I used to love to drift along the pale-yellow cornfields, looking for the damp spots one sometimes found at their edges, where the smartweed soon turned a rich copper colour and the narrow brown leaves hung curled like cocoons about the swollen joints of the stem."

THE LAND AS STRUGGLE

One of the themes in *My Ántonia* is the difficulty of the life of those who work the land. Agriculture is always a challenge, with long hours of labor between sunup and sunset, but out on the Highs Plains of America it was particularly harsh. "Winter comes down savagely over a little town on the prairie. The wind that sweeps in from the open country strips away all the leafy screens that hide one yard from another in summer, and the houses seem to draw closer together." The land itself is a merciless teacher in the novel, and never seems to give Ántonia's family any breathing space.

In our days of factory farming and chemical fertilizer, we have forgotten the early hardships of farming the Great Plains, now considered the breadbasket of the world. It is no accident that during the mid-1800s, this area was considered a "desert" by travelers, despite its tall grass. And as Cather often describes in her novels, sometimes the farmers themselves were their own worst enemy. The deep loam of the American Midwest and South had sustained and would sustain the abuse of various farming practices, but the Plains would not. Less than 40 years after the events described in *My Ántonia*, the dust bowls would sweep across these windy plateaus, forcing tens of thousands of families to abandon their farms. These were not a freak of nature, but partially the result of decades of unsustainable farming practices.

THE PASSING OF THE PIONEERS

At the end of the book, Jim Burden returns to the prairie, 20 years after he last saw Ántonia. She is married now, with a dozen children, and he is a successful lawyer back East. He marvels at the changes already wrought in the land, the work of one short generation that has brought the Great Plains from "desert" to productive farmland. He finds the "first road" from the settlement, now disappearing into the soil. "The rains had made channels of the wheel-ruts and washed them so deeply that the sod had never healed over them. They looked like gashes torn by a grizzly's claws, on the slopes where the farm-wagons used to lurch up out of the hollows with a pull that brought curling muscles on the smooth hips of the horses. . . . I had only to close my eyes to hear the rumbling of the wagons in the dark."

The wheels of those pioneer wagons had already gone silent by the time Cather wrote her sad and beautiful anthem to the prairie. But they remain a vital part of the American mythology, and as Cather puts it in the last line of *My Ántonia*, we will always share "the precious, the incommunicable past."

Eric D. Lehman

Further Reading

Sarah Orne Jewett captures a similar narrative style in *The Country of the Pointed Firs*. Both she and Cather provide glimpses into people's lives that can be considered as "sketches," rather than building intricate plots with complex character development. They are both very interested in how storytelling contributes to a person's appreciation of their local environment.

Although it has a swift-moving plot, James Fenimore Cooper's *The Prairie* tells a tale similar at its outset to Cather's. The novel is about a family looking to settle in the midwestern prairie. However, their plans are thwarted by their interactions with factions of warring natives.

Bibliography

Cayton, Andrew R. L., and Susan E. Gray, eds. *The American Midwest: Essays on Regional History*. Bloomington: Indiana University Press, 2001.

Christenson, Leah K. "Rethinking Human-Land Relations in the Work of Aldo Leopold and Willa Cather." Master's thesis, Western Illinois University, 2011.

Cody, James. "Willa Cather's Use of the Natural Environment as a Psychological Sanctuary in Her 'Novels of Feeling.'" PhD diss., Drew University, 2012.

Collins, Rachel. "'Where All the Ground Is Friendly': Subterranean Living and the Ethic of Cultivation in Willa Cather's *My Ántonia*." *ISLE: Interdisciplinary Studies in Literature and Environment* 19, no. 1 (2012): 43–61. doi:10.1093/isle/iss004.

Edwards, Thomas S., and Elizabeth A. DeWolfe, eds. *Such News of the Land: U.S. Women Nature Writers*. Hanover, NH: University Press of New England, 2001.

Hendel, Erica. "Unsettling Nature at the Frontier: Nature, Narrative, and Female Empowerment in Willa Cather's *O Pioneers!* and Mourning Dove's *Cogewea, the Half Blood*." Master's thesis, University of Montana, 2006.

Kirkland, Graham. "From Rivers to Gardens: The Ambivalent Role of Nature in *My Ántonia*, *O Pioneers!*, and *Death Comes to the Archbishop*." Master's thesis, Georgia State University, 2010.

Kristensen, Allan Juhl. "Making Plain/s Space: The Literary Geographies of Cather, Kroetsch, and Heat-Moon." PhD diss., Newcastle University, 2009. hdl.handle.net/10443/976.

La Force, Melanie Jean. "Life, Literature, and Land: Perspectives on Prairie Preservation." *Proceedings of the 14th Annual North American Prairie Conference* (1995): 251–57.

Ramirez, Karen E. "Narrative Mappings of the Land as Space and Place in Willa Cather's *O Pioneers!*" *Great Plains Quarterly* 30, no. 2 (2010): 97–115. www.jstor.org/stable/23534149.

Roskowski, Susan J. "Willa Cather and the Fatality of Place: *O Pioneers*, *My Ántonia*, and *A Lost Lady*." In *Geography and Literature: A Meeting of the Disciplines*, edited by William E. Mallory and Paul Simpson-Housley. Syracuse, NY: Syracuse University Press, 1987.

Rosowski, Susan J. "Willa Cather's Ecology of Place." *Western American Literature* 30, no. 1 (1995): 37–51. doi:10.1353/wal.1995.0050.

Ross, Patricia. *The Spell Cast By Remains: The Myth of Wilderness in Modern American Literature.* New York: Routledge, 2006.

Russell, Danielle. *Between the Angle and the Curve: Mapping Gender, Race, Space, and Identity in Willa Cather and Toni Morrison.* New York: Routledge, 2006.

Stout, Janis P. *Picturing a Different West: Vision, Illustration, and the Tradition of Austin and Cather.* Lubbock: Texas Tech University Press, 2007.

Strong, Justina Frances. "Landscapes of Memory: The Cartography of Longing." Master's thesis, University of Alabama, 2009.

Urgo, Joseph R. *Willa Cather and the Myth of American Migration.* Urbana: University of Illinois Press, 1995.

N

Nineteen Eighty-Four

Nineteen Eighty-Four, by British author George Orwell, is one of the best-known dystopian novels in the English language. It takes place in London, England, which has been renamed "Airstrip One," and has become a far outpost of Oceania, one of three superstates that dominate the world. Oceania includes much of the English-speaking world (what had been the United States, Canada, and Australia) as well as Latin America. The second superstate, Eurasia, combines the Soviet Union, Turkey, and what had been central and eastern Europe. Eurasia consistently shoots rocket bombs into London in a reprise of the German Blitz, which had just ended when Orwell was writing the book. The third superstate, Eastasia, is centered in China, and includes parts of India as well as Korea and Japan. China was undergoing its communist revolution when Orwell wrote the book, which was published in 1949.

In the book, the rest of the world (much of the Middle East as well as the northern two-thirds of Africa, Indochina, and Indonesia) has become subject to perpetual warfare as the boundaries of the three superstates change and their alliances shift. The main reward of conquest for the superstates is acquisition of slave labor in the "disputed areas." The three superstates may have been locked in endless war, but all were totalitarian dictatorships, with variations in ideology to suit local history and culture. Oceania's dominant ideology is Ingsoc (English socialism), which solidifies its dominance with pervasive surveillance, punishment of deviance, and manipulation of language. Eurasia's establishment professes neo-Bolshevism, and Eastasia proscribes a dominant ideology of Obliteration of the Self (that is, "Death Worship"), perhaps a variation of Buddhist fascism.

The book's major character, Winston Smith, is a mid-level party functionary in the Ministry of Truth, where he erases and recomposes records of "unpersons," including histories and media reports meant to reflect shifting alliances, erasing individuals who have fallen out of favor. These practices are modeled after those of the Soviet Union under Joseph Stalin, who was the head of state in the Soviet Union as Orwell wrote the book. "Big Brother," the personification of the omnipotent state, is also modeled on Stalinist mass-media images. Like much else in Oceania's geopolitics, Big Brother may not have existed, except as a screen image meant to galvanize support among the masses, and as a reminder that any deviation from acceptable behavior and belief would be tracked and punished. Real or not, Big Brother is always watching everybody.

SHIFTING BOUNDARIES OF LAND AND LANGUAGE

Oceania's ruling class reinforced its dominance by reconstituting the English language (as "Newspeak") to reduce the number of concepts that everyone except the ruling class may express by combining words and eliminating complexity and nuance. Thus, the acceptable lexicon (and the dictionary) became thinner over time. This applied to knowledge of geography as well, because most people were encouraged by Big Brother to ignore the fact that yesterday's enemies had become today's allies, and vice versa.

A forbidden text supposedly written for the dissident underground in Oceania (it actually was used by the ruling class to flush out dissidents), Emmanuel Goldstein's *The Theory and Practice of Oligarchical Collectivism,* said that a measure of ignorance among most people was necessary so they would routinely accept shifting geographical boundaries as well as the disappearance of people who had been purged. Only a tiny minority was allowed to remember how things had changed (the so-called "Inner Party"—2 percent of the population). Functionaries such as Smith (the "Outer Party"—13 percent of the people) changed their attitudes as dictated or faced arrest, torture, and brainwashing. Most of the society (proles—85 percent of the people) had no significant role in the shifting geopolitical world. The Ministry of Truth constructed mass-media propaganda expressed in periodic marches and chants ("Hate Weeks") of simple "truths," along with alcohol, a national lottery, and cheap pornography. The proles also were preoccupied by the daily struggle to survive in a world of scarcity.

The novel, which has been translated into at least 65 languages, has become enmeshed in political debates in many cultures around the world. Words such as "thoughtcrime," "Big Brother," "telescreen," and "memory hole" (down which yesterday's reality was dumped) have become part of world political discourse. The adjective "Orwellian" describes language that is the opposite of what it professes. In Oceania, the Ministry of Love oversaw hatred, torture, and brainwashing, as the Ministry of Truth manufactured lies. The Ministry of Peace made war, and the Ministry of Plenty kept all except the elite struggling for minimal rations. When rations were reduced, "Miniplenty" issued reports that the living standard had risen to new highs.

THE GEOPOLITICS OF WAR

With a large proportion of superstate resources consumed by the geopolitics that required worldwide perpetual war, consumption levels were kept low for everyone except the elite: ratty clothes, cheap gin, rancid cigarettes, and dirty housing, with very few luxuries. Abstinence from luxury and pleasure was held up as a virtue in a world of liquid maps and gung ho hatred against largely unseen enemies. Ideological conformity and universal surveillance (down to forbidden diaries) were part of daily life, as necessary security, under pretense of external threat. Independent thinking was prosecuted as "thoughtcrime," as helicopters peered into people's bedroom windows. Much of the book's plot traces Winston Smith's journey into thoughtcrime (as he begins to doubt how the maps are being redrawn and people "vaporized"). His doubts develop with a love affair (his partner turns out to be an informer), followed by his arrest and torture.

In Orwell's dystopian future, World War II never really ended, even though German fascism had been crushed. The Soviet Union advanced its power to the English Channel as Britain fell into civil war and revolution. A world atomic war reduced much of the world to poverty. However, after a spate of such all-out war, the leadership of the three superstates realized that such a level of conflict would destroy all of them, so they settled into an equilibrium of conflict that allowed all of them to maintain their domestic power by rallying their populations against each other. Similar geopolitics played out as a template for the Cold War that was setting in as *Nineteen Eighty-Four* was published.

Bruce E. Johansen

Further Reading

Many other works of dystopian literature were written in the 20th century. For example, Ursula K. Le Guin wrote *The Dispossessed,* Margaret Atwood wrote *The Handmaid's Tale,* and Aldous Huxley wrote *Brave New World,* all of which imagine different futures for our society based on the strengths and weaknesses they perceive in human nature.

Bibliography

Crispin, Aubrey, and Paul Chilton, eds. *Nineteen Eighty-four in 1984: Autonomy, Control, and Communication.* London: Comedia Publications Group, 1983.

Hillegas, Mark R. *The Future as Nightmare: H. G. Wells and the Anti-Utopians.* Carbondale: Southern Illinois University Press, 1967.

Lewis, Jonathan. "Big Brother Is Listening to You: The Space of Language in George Orwell's *Nineteen Eighty-Four.*" *E-TEALS: An Electronic Journal of Teacher Education and Applied Studies* no. 2 (2011): 27–53.

Madsen, Claus. "Iterative Mapping of Otherness: A Mapping Discussion of the Transforming Potential of the Other." In *Transforming Otherness,* edited by Jason Finch and Peter Nynas. New Brunswick, NJ: Transaction Publishers, 2011.

Shadow, Ben. "The Geography of 1984." Writing as I Please (blog). February 13, 2013. writingasiplease.wordpress.com/2013/02/28/1984-geography.

Walford, Rex. "Geography and the Future." *Geography* 69, no. 3 (1984): 193–208. www.jstor.org/stable/40570839.

Wegner, Phillip E. *Imaginary Communities: Utopia, the Nation, and the Spatial Histories of Modernity.* Berkeley: University of California Press, 2002.

No Country for Old Men

No Country for Old Men is one of Cormac McCarthy's most famous novels. Set near the Mexican-American border in 1980, the plot and character development play with the notion of "borderline" experiences and worldviews. The story centers around a hunter coming upon the remains of a drug deal gone wrong. His subsequent actions determine his fate and that of the rest of the characters. In this respect, the setting of the story is dangerous only because of the economic motives of the characters who are pitted against each other in a money chase. The Texas-Mexico border sits as a silent witness to human atrocity motivated by greed, guilt, and the love of violence.

While on a hunting trip, the novel's protagonist, Llewelyn Moss, comes across what appears to be the aftermath of a drug deal gone wrong. He takes a case that contains $2.4 million in cash and, at first, hides it under his bed. Much of the suspense involving place in this novel has to do with hiding places for this satchel of money. Moss hides it outside, at one point, near the Rio Grande, and then in an air duct in a motel room.

Two hit men, Carson Wells and Anton Chigurh, come after Moss to retrieve the stolen money. He and his wife have to flee. Wells offers to protect Moss in exchange for the money, but Chigurh kills the former. Moss tries to meet up at a motel in El Paso with his wife, Carla Jean, who had gone to stay with her family. However, Carla Jean calls Sheriff Ed Tom Bell and tells him about the money and asks for his help. Her call is traced, and her husband's location is revealed. He is killed by a group of Mexicans who are after the money. Chigurh finds the money in the motel room and returns it to its owner. Then he kills Carla Jean and is subsequently badly injured in a car accident, but he survives and escapes. Sheriff Bell retires out of frustration and disappointment.

THE GEOGRAPHY OF VIOLENCE ALONG THE BORDERLANDS

Amid a high body count of both the innocent and the guilty, McCarthy puts as a backdrop a stark but beautiful landscape. The natural landscape of the borderlands seems blessed in contrast to the cursed state of human affairs that he sets up. As in other McCarthy novels, the setting of the land here seems deeply inhospitable to humans. However, McCarthy's characters rarely wrestle with tragedy caused by nature's flora and fauna; instead, they find hell in each other (to paraphrase a line from Sartre's play *No Exit*). After the early scene in the novel where Llewelyn Moss stumbles on a massacre while hunting, much of the devastation of the novel happens inside seedy motel rooms and modest houses.

The title itself draws attention to place and suggests some hostility of the land toward the weak and aging. But it is not the countryside that wants to kill the human characters. It is almost as if human violence has become a location that is more place than the natural environment, taking it over or erasing it. The border between countries, this geopolitical divide (and all of its policing), does nothing to confine violence or promote rule of law. The most important border in this story is not the border between the United States and Mexico, but the border between violence and law, between life and death, and that border does not follow the contours of a river or any other geographical feature. The map of violence that McCarthy draws in this novel transcends nation-states.

THE LAYERED MAPPING OF WAR

Numerous historical layers of war are mapped onto McCarthy's American West. Sheriff Bell, for instance, is a veteran of World War II. He is haunted by his experiences there—he left his unit to die—and has spent his life attempting to atone for his cowardly act. This guilt fuels his resolve to save the Mosses. Additionally, Carson Wells was a lieutenant colonel in the Army, served during Vietnam, and is an ex-special forces officer. Moss is also a veteran of the Vietnam War. Chigurh is one of the few male protagonists who has no connection that we know of to an officially sanctioned war, but he is a psychopathic killer. A few critics point to these character backgrounds and to various comments about American involvement in war to suggest that McCarthy develops an antiwar theme in *No Country for Old Men*. However, it is possible that something more complex is going on: rather than favoring pacifism, *No Country for Old Men* speaks to a disillusionment with the reasons for American involvement in wars. McCarthy sets this historical data against a contemporary drug war in the Southwest. This is not an ideological war but an economic one, and the centrality of the chase—to hide or find the bag of money—underscores this message. The presence of a hit man, Carson Wells, who wants to turn security guard (that is, get paid by Moss to protect him) draws attention to the lack of ideological impetus behind this war (it's not about what's ethically right; it's about the money), just as the failure of the justice system draws attention to a lack of morality.

Lynn Marie Houston

Further Reading

Although set in an earlier time period, *True Grit* by Charles Portis captures many of the same sentiments as McCarthy, including the violence and lawlessness of the frontier. In Portis's novel, his protagonist, 14-year-old Mattie Ross, attempts to track down and seek revenge on the outlaws who killed her father.

Bibliography

Armstrong, Kayla M. "'If there be such space': Haunted Landscapes and Crises of Sonhood in Cormac McCarthy's Westerns." Honors thesis, College of William and Mary, 2017.

Beck, John. *Dirty Wars: Landscape, Power, and Waste in Western American Literature*. Lincoln: University of Nebraska Press, 2009.

Bruns, John. "The Map Is Not the Country: Cartography in Joel and Ethan Coen's *No Country for Old Men*." *Film Criticism* 36, no. 2 (2011): 2–21.

Ellis, Jay. *No Place for Home: Spatial Constraint and Character Flight in the Novels of Cormac McCarthy*. New York: Routledge, 2013.

Estes, Andrew Keller. *Cormac McCarthy and the Writing of American Spaces*. Amsterdam: Rodopi, 2013.

Jillett, Louise, ed. *Cormac McCarthy's Borders and Landscapes*. New York: Bloomsbury Publishing USA, 2016.

McFarland, Ron. "Mapping Cormac McCarthy's *No Country for Old Men*." *The Midwest Quarterly* 58, no. 4 (2017): 433.

McGilchrist, Megan Riley. *The Western Landscape in Cormac McCarthy and Wallace Stegner: Myths of the Frontier*. New York: Routledge, 2012.

Weiss, Daniel. "Cormac McCarthy, Violence, and Borders: The Map as Code for What Is Not Contained." *The Cormac McCarthy Journal* 8, no. 1 (2010): 73–89.

O

The Odyssey

The Odyssey is an epic Greek poem believed to date from the eighth century B.C.E. (before the Common Era). Along with *The Iliad,* which describes events in the Trojan War, it is credited to a poet named Homer. The poem follows the adventures of Greek warrior Odysseus (Ulysses in Latin) as he makes his way home after the war to the island of Ithaca. *The Odyssey* also describes the efforts of Odysseus' wife, Penelope, to forestall the prospective suitors who have gathered in her husband's long absence, and the attempts of the couple's son, Telemachus, to find his father.

THE AEGEAN AND BEYOND

Historians and archaeologists differ over whether the Greek stories connected with the Trojan War have a basis in historical fact. If they do, the conflict probably took place in the mid-13th century B.C.E. on the coast of Asia Minor. The city of Troy (or Ilios) lay at a strategic site near the southern entrance to the Dardanelles, a strait that forms part of the link between the Aegean Sea and the Black Sea to the northeast.

The first section of the route that Odysseus and his men followed after the Greek victory was relatively straightforward. After leaving the shores of Troy, they anchored off the nearby island of Tenedos before making a raid on Ismara, a city on the European coast northwest of Troy. Afterward their ships were blown south by a gale through the Aegean east of the Greek mainland.

Odysseus expected to reach Ithaca, one of the Ionian Islands off the western coast of Greece, by rounding the southern tip of Greece and proceeding northwest. Instead, winds and currents drove his ships southward to the Land of the Lotus-Eaters, whose inhabitants fed some of his crew fruit that lulled them into forgetfulness. After escaping, the Greeks beached their ships on an island inhabited by man-eating giants known as Cyclops. One of these savage creatures, Polyphemus, imprisoned Odysseus and a party of his men in a cave, but most escaped thanks to Odysseus' cunning.

DANGEROUS WATERS

The sailors next visited a floating island ruled by Aeolus, king of the winds. Before they departed, the king gave Odysseus a bag holding the winds, but Odysseus' men, thinking that it held treasure, surreptitiously opened the bag. The ships were blown back, but Aeolus refused further help. Instead, the hapless Greeks then

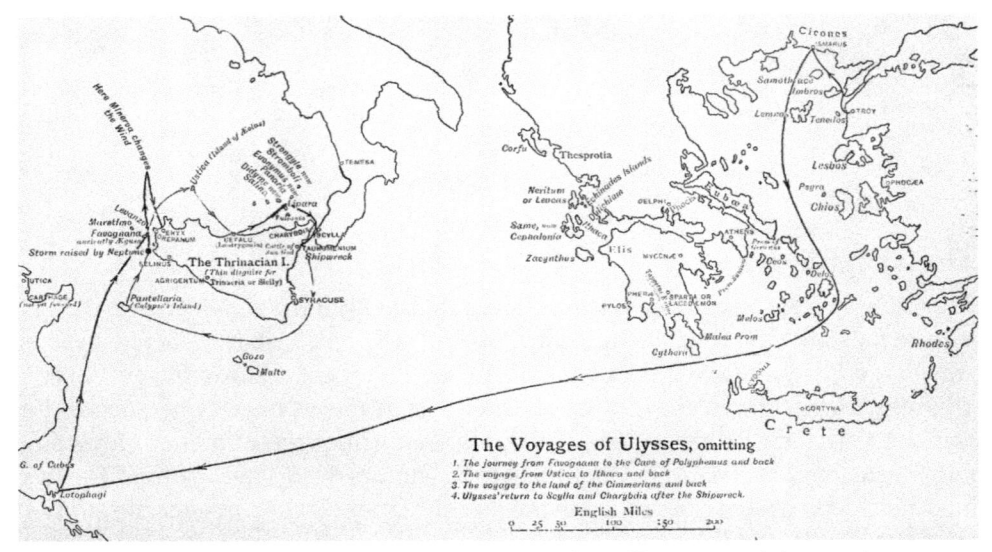

This map plots Ulysses's course on his sea voyage from Troy around the southern tip of Greece and then proceeding West and Northwest. His shipwreck is indicated just past the turbulent waters of Charybdis. (Archive.org)

came to the land of the Laestrygonians, cannibals who devoured most of them. Along with his remaining crew members, Odysseus managed to reach Aeaea, home of a witch named Circe who turned Odysseus' men into pigs. Thanks to help from the god Hermes, Odysseus was able to resist her magic and free his men.

Subsequently the Greeks sailed past rocks where birdlike nymphs known as Sirens attempted to lure the sailors to their death with their bewitching song, but Odysseus gave his men beeswax to seal their ears. The sailors' route then carried them between a whirlpool known as Scylla and a six-headed monster named Charybdis, the latter of which seized six of Odysseus' crew.

Upon reaching the land of Thrinacia, Odysseus' men slaughtered and ate cattle belonging to the sun god, Helios, and were punished with death. Now alone and clinging to his ship's wreckage, Odysseus was washed ashore on the island of Ogygia, where the nymph Calypso held him prisoner for seven years.

A REAL VOYAGE?

It took Odysseus 10 years to reach Ithaca. Although his experiences involved numerous supernatural figures, some researchers have concluded that his voyage may actually have taken place, or that its details are based on authentic geographical and seagoing knowledge. These writers cite similarities between the places Homer described and particular islands and seacoasts known to us today.

The Land of the Lotus-Eaters, for instance, is usually identified as North Africa, and the fruit that Odysseus' sailors sampled as dates. The Cyclops may have lived near Sicily in the Aegadian Islands and Aeolus in the Aeolian Islands, all of which are Italian. Or they may have inhabited the Balearic Islands of Spain, which are much farther to the west. The Greeks may have encountered the Laestrygonians near the southern tip of the large French island of Corsica.

Circe's home may have lain on the western shore of Italy, and perhaps Odysseus and his men encountered the Sirens among the rocky Galli Islands farther down the Italian coast. Scylla and Charybdis could have guarded the dangerous Strait of Messina between Sicily and mainland Italy, Thrinacia may have been Sicily itself, and Calypso may have lived in the Maltese archipelago south of Sicily.

THE ITHACA MYSTERY

Today's island of Ithaki does not bear much resemblance to Homer's Ithaca, and writers have puzzled over its identity for centuries. The poet probably lived far away on the eastern shores of the Aegean, and may simply have been ignorant of western Greece. However, Robert Bittlestone proposed a startling solution to the mystery in his 2005 book *Odysseus Unbound,* which he wrote with James Diggle and John Underhill. The book argues that the Paliki Peninsula, which is connected by an isthmus to the western coast of the island of Cephalonia, was once a separate island—Homer's Ithaca. The writers believe that earthquakes could have triggered landslides that filled the narrow channel since the time that the tales of Odysseus were created.

Although *Odysseus Unbound* was published by the respected Cambridge University Press and was positively reviewed by many authorities, others have raised serious questions about its thesis. As is the case with the many other locales in *The Odyssey,* the identification of Odysseus' home remains as fascinating to modern readers as it was to the ancient Greeks themselves.

Grove Koger

Further Reading
Other work about the heroes of ancient Greece and their relationship with the gods is *The Aeneid* by Virgil and *The Argonautica* by Apollonius. However, more modern versions of the hero's journey and subsequent homecoming are *Ulysses* by James Joyce and *The Penelopiad* by Margaret Atwood.

Bibliography
Bittlestone, Robert, James Diggle, and John Underhill. *Odysseus Unbound: The Search for Homer's Ithaca.* Cambridge, UK: Cambridge University Press, 2005.
Crang, Mike. "Time: Space." In *Spaces of Geographical Thought: Deconstructing Human Geography's Binaries,* edited by Paul Cloke and Ron Johnston. London: SAGE Publications, 2005.
Dueck, Daniela. *Geography in Classical Antiquity.* Cambridge, UK: Cambridge University Press, 2012.
Eisner, Robert. *Travelers to an Antique Land: The History and Literature of Travel to Greece.* Ann Arbor: University of Michigan Press, 1993.
Haller, Benjamin Stephen. "Landscape Description in Homer's *Odyssey.*" PhD diss., University of Pittsburgh, 2007.
Hartog, Francois. *Memories of Odysseus: Frontier Tales from Ancient Greece.* Chicago: University of Chicago Press, 2001.

Hegglund, Jon. "*Ulysses* and the Rhetoric of Cartography." *Twentieth Century Literature* 49, no. 2 (2003): 164–92. doi:10.2307/3176000.

Heise, Ursula K. "Journeys through the Offset World: Global Travel Narratives and Environmental Crisis." *SubStance* 41, no. 1 (2012): 61–76. www.jstor.org/stable/23261103.

Helms, Mary W. *Ulysses' Sail: An Ethnographic Odyssey of Power, Knowledge, and Geographical Distance.* Princeton, NJ: Princeton University Press, 1988.

Johnson, Scott Fitzgerald. *Literary Territories: Cartographical Thinking in Late Antiquity.* Oxford, UK: Oxford University Press, 2016.

Rennell, Lord. "The Ithaca of the Odyssey." *Annual of the British School at Athens* 33 (1933): 1–21. doi:10.1017/S0068245400011813.

Ricci, Gabriel R. "'If Peopled and Cultured': Bartram's Travels and *The Odyssey*." In *Travel, Discovery, Transformation.* New York: Routledge, 2017.

Schultz, Elizabeth. "Odysseus Comes to Know His Place: Reading *The Odyssey* Ecocritically." *Neohelicon* 36, no. 2 (2009). doi:10.1007/s11059-009-0001-9.

Skempis, Marios, and Ioannis Ziogas. *Geography, Topography, Landscape: Configurations of Space in Greek and Roman Epic.* Berlin: De Gruyter, 2014.

St. Onge, Joseph. "The Geography of Exploration: A Study in the Process of Physical Exploration and Geographical Discovery." Master's thesis, Utah State University, 2000.

Tally, Robert T., Jr., ed. *Geocritical Explorations: Space, Place, and Mapping in Literary and Cultural Studies.* New York: Palgrave Macmillan, 2011.

Turchi, Peter. *Maps of the Imagination: The Writer as Cartographer.* San Antonio: Trinity University Press, 2011.

Van Wijngaarden, Gert Jan. "Immaterial Landscapes: Homeric Geography and the Ionian Islands in Greece." *Quaternary International* 251 (2012): 136–41. doi: 10.1016/j.quaint.2011.02.020.

Vinci, Felice. *The Baltic Origins of Homer's Epic Tales:* The Iliad, The Odyssey, *and the Migration of Myth.* New York: Simon & Schuster, 2005.

Waterhouse, Helen. "From Ithaca to *The Odyssey*." *Annual of the British School at Athens* 91 (1996): 301–17. doi:1017/S0068245400016518.

Wright, John K. "Terrae Incognitae: The Place of the Imagination in Geography." *Annals of the Association of American Geographers* 37, no. 1 (1947): 1–15. doi:10.1080/00045604709351940.

Oedipus Rex

This play by Sophocles opens *in media res,* in the middle of the action. The ancient Greek city of Thebes is experiencing a terrible plague. King Oedipus sends his brother-in-law Creon to consult with the Oracle of Delphi. Creon returns to tell him that the Oracle has revealed that Thebes must bring a murderer to justice to end the plague. They realize that they must punish the person who killed Thebes' previous ruler, King Laius, but his murderer has never been found. The setting of Thebes is central to this text as Oedipus's relentless desire to free the city and its people from a plague will be his undoing by revealing the prophecy that cursed him from birth.

THE ANTIHERO TRAVELOGUE AND THE LIMITS OF THE RULING CLASS

King Laius and his Queen Jocasta have struggled to have children. Laius consults with the Oracle of Delphi to learn if he and his wife would ever conceive. The Oracle predicts that if they have a son, he would one day kill the king. When the couple goes on to have a son, they attempt to steer fate and avoid the prophecy by giving the child to a shepherd who is tasked with leaving the baby in the mountains to die. Incapable of condemning the child, the shepherd saves him. Young Oedipus, not knowing his true origin, is eventually brought to the court of King Polybus and Queen Merope of Corinth, who raise him.

As a young man, Oedipus consults the Oracle of Delphi and learns of the prophecy that he would kill his father and marry his mother. Taking matters into his own hands, he leaves the city of Corinth and heads to Thebes, thinking that this will save him from the horrific prophecy. On his journey, he has an altercation on the road with travelers from Thebes. Neither party is willing to step aside to allow the other to pass, and a scuffle ensues; Oedipus's anger gets the best of him: he kills the charioteer and the passenger (King Laius) and unknowingly brings to fruition the first part of the prophecy.

Prior to this event, this first part of the play employs many of the traits of the travelogue, which would normally set up Oedipus as the classical hero of an adventure tale. He is born to an aristocratic family but suffers a misfortune that he seems to not have merited as it has little to do with him as a character. The text initially elicits our empathy for Oedipus, as it is not clear whether the danger of the prophecy is worth the sacrifice of a baby's life. However, this changes as the prophecy comes true. Oedipus, then, is revealed not to be the hero of the travelogue, but one of the victims of prophecy. The play is steeped in ancient Greek customs of strong belief in prophecy and in making extreme sacrifices based on their advice. The only way to thwart the prophecy in the play was for Laius and Jocasta to not have an heir for the kingdom. Behind this play is a commentary on the periodic need for a new ruling class. If King Laius and Queen Jocasta had not conceived a son together to inherit the throne (such inheritance would not have passed to a daughter), then the position of king would have passed to a more distant member of the family, ushering in new blood to oversee the kingdom. The ancient Greeks cared greatly about the ethics of rulers and their responsiveness to the people they represented. Changing rulers periodically would keep them from growing too fond of their power.

MAPPING DISEASE AS FATE

As Oedipus continues his travel to Thebes, he encounters the Sphinx, who is wreaking havoc on the region by devastating the crops and killing those travelers who could not solve its riddle. Oedipus solves the Sphinx's riddle and the monster is so surprised that it loses its footing and falls from a rock ledge to its death below.

Reaching Thebes, Oedipus is celebrated for killing the Sphinx by being made king and marrying the recently widowed queen, Jocasta. In marrying Jocasta (his mother), the second half of the prophecy is fulfilled.

This brings us to present day in the story, as Thebes suffers from a plague. Scholars have traced the history of diseases in ancient Greece and have proposed that the plague referenced here as stemming from "religious pollution," brought on according to the narrative due to a failure to properly appease the gods, is possibly a highly contagious disease known to pass from infected cattle to humans. Details in the play state that the effects of the epidemic include dead livestock, failed crops, a high mortality rate among townspeople, and the inability of women in the area to become pregnant or to bring healthy fetuses to full term. A real disease with these effects had been documented since before about the fourth century B.C. We now understand better that its transmission is through infected meat and bodily secretions, but for the ancient Greeks who did not understand epidemiology the way we do today, it seemed as if the gods were cursing them for moral failures.

THE HUMAN GEOGRAPHY OF INCEST AND SUICIDE

King Oedipus asks the blind seer, Tiresias, to name the killer as a way to undo the plague. Tiresias claims that he, Oedipus, is the one who murdered King Laius. Jocasta is moved to reveal her part in the attempt to stop the prophecy from happening in having a son removed from their home.

A messenger then arrives with news of Oedipus's parents in Corinth. King Polybus has died of natural causes. This seems to be good news to Oedipus and everyone around the king as they believed Polybus was his real father and that the prophecy had failed to come true. Not wanting the other part of the prophecy to come to life, King Oedipus decides not to attend his father's funeral. The messenger from Corinth tells the king that he was in fact adopted, that Polybus and Merope were not his biological parents.

The realization that Oedipus had, in fact, killed King Laius years earlier sends Jocasta running into the palace, where she hangs herself. Overcome by grief, King Oedipus takes a brooch from Jocasta's gown and gouges out his eyes. Oedipus leaves Thebes accompanied by his daughter Antigone. The final scenes of the play are symbolic as Oedipus does not want to see the tragic results of his own existence. Simply by living into adulthood, his entire family was cursed by the gods. Here the Greeks show the abject nature of humankind's relationship to the gods. Living in ancient times without science to explain phenomena like disease and astronomical occurrences created stories like this play, in which humans seem to exist at the capricious will of the gods.

Lynn Marie Houston

Further Reading

Other ancient playwrights who explore concepts of fate in terms of humankind versus the will of the gods include Aristophanes, Aeschylus, and Euripedes. Whereas the first wrote comedies, the latter two—like Sophocles—are known especially for their masterful treatment of tragedy.

Bibliography

Cohen, Ada. "10: Mythic Landscapes of Greece." In *The Cambridge Companion to Greek Mythology,* edited by Roger D. Woodward, 305. Cambridge, UK: Cambridge University Press, 2007.

Kicey, Michael Andrew. "Road to Nowhere: The Mobility of Oedipus and the Task of Interpretation." *American Journal of Philology* 135, no. 1 (2014): 29–55.

Kousoulis, Antonis A., Konstantinos P. Economopoulos, Effie Poulakou-Rebelakou, George Androutsos, and Sotirios Tsiodras. "The Plague of Thebes, a Historical Epidemic in Sophocles' *Oedipus Rex*." *Emerging Infectious Diseases* 18, no. 1 (2012): 153.

McPhail, Cameron Kenrick. "The Roles of Geographical Concepts in the Construction of Ancient Greek Ethno-cultural Identities, from Homer to Herodotus: An Analysis of the Continents and the Mediterranean Sea." PhD diss., University of Otago, 2016.

Nast, Heidi J. "Mapping the 'Unconscious': Racism and the Oedipal Family." *Annals of the Association of American Geographers* 90, no. 2 (2000): 215–55.

Rehm, Rush. *The Play of Space: Spatial Transformation in Greek Tragedy*. Princeton, NJ: Princeton University Press, 2002.

Rodighiero, Andrea. "The Sense of Place: Oedipus at Colonus, 'Political' Geography, and the Defence of a Way of Life." In *Crisis on Stage: Tragedy and Comedy in Late Fifth-Century Athens*, edited by Andreas Markantonatos and Bernhard Zimmerman, 55–80. Berlin: De Gruyter, 2012.

Walter, Eugene Victor. *Placeways: A Theory of the Human Environment*. Chapel Hill: University of North Carolina Press, 1988.

Westgate, J. Chris. "Introduction: A Rhetoric of Sociospatial Drama." In *Urban Drama: The Metropolis in Contemporary North American Plays*, 1–15. New York: Palgrave Macmillan, 2011.

Of Mice and Men

Of Mice and Men, by John Steinbeck, is set during the Great Depression and is the story of two migrant workers, Lennie Small and George Milton. At the novel's opening, the two characters are walking to a nearby ranch. We learn that they recently left a farm near Weed, California, where Lennie, who has mental disabilities, was wrongly accused of rape when he touched a woman as he was trying to feel the soft texture of her dress. Steinbeck situates the events of the novel along the Salinas River near Soledad, California. This real place takes its name from the Spanish word for "loneliness" or "isolation." The characters in the novel are not able to successfully find their place over the course of the novel, and they end up alone. In fact, Steinbeck names the novel after a line from a Robert Burns poem in which the speaker admits that even if they have good intentions, living things (both mice and men) often encounter only despair in this life. The tragedy of this story lies in the loyalty and compassion exhibited by the men who are doomed by their own passions. The natural landscape in Steinbeck's novel fails to redeem or comfort them.

THE GREAT DEPRESSION: THE CULTURE OF SACRIFICE

As the two men make their way to the nearby ranch, George finds that Lennie, who loves petting soft things but often accidentally kills them, has been carrying and stroking a dead mouse. George gets rid of it, fearing that Lennie could catch a disease from the dead animal. He calms Lennie down with the story he often tells him about what life will be like when they have their own farm, where Lennie can keep rabbits.

This is just the first of many instances in the novel where the men wind up killing something they love. Next, Lennie plays too roughly with his new puppy and accidentally kills it. After that, a ranch hand named Candy is powerless to stop another ranch hand, Carlson, from shooting his beloved old dog, and afterward bemoans the fact that he didn't do it himself (as a kindness to the creature). Later, Lennie strokes Curley's wife's hair to feel how soft it is, but he is too forceful and causes her to scream. When he goes to cover her mouth, he accidentally snaps her neck. Finally, George has to shoot Lennie to save him from a horrible death at the hands of Curley and his men. Lennie has become a danger to other people.

These deaths become symbolic representations of the life of working-class people during the Great Depression, whose dreams of a better life are thwarted by a system that relies on their cheap labor. Although the novel shows the downtrodden and marginalized members of the working class as those who kill the things they love, in the economy of the Great Depression these members of society had little agency. They were kept poor by a system that enslaved them with false hope.

DREAM GEOGRAPHY

The imaginary place that George and Lennie continually map in their conversations represents the American dream of land ownership and self-possession. The two men dream of owning fertile land that they can farm, that will provide them with a comfortable life, and that will allow them the freedom to be in charge of themselves. Lennie's part of this fantasy includes having rabbits, as he loves soft things. Essentially, they dream of working less for more money, having nice things without having to work too hard for them. From the beginning, Steinbeck clues readers in to the unlikely reality of the scheme because Lennie manages to accidentally kill almost all the soft things he wants to touch, including mice, puppies, and women. Therefore, the message that is conveyed about this imaginary space is that it is invented as a representation of the things these men want but can never have. Their joint pursuit of this imaginary dreamscape is what gives them hope in an otherwise bleak world. However, their dream of abundance ends in death and loneliness.

The natural world reflects the brutality of human existence in *Of Mice and Men*. Steinbeck includes a description of a heron that dives into the water to kill a snake, exhibiting in this relationship between predator and prey, the harsh laws of survival in the world.

Lynn Marie Houston

Further Reading

The Grapes of Wrath is another novel by Steinbeck with many of the same themes. Also, many of Jack London's stories take place in the Pacific Northwest and involve characters who must sacrifice things they love to survive in the wild. Other authors who set some of their stories in Northern California are Bret Harte and John Muir.

Bibliography

Dickstein, Morris. "Steinbeck and the Great Depression." *The South Atlantic Quarterly* 103, no. 1 (2004): 111–31.

Ditsky, John M. "Music from a Dark Cave: Organic Form in Steinbeck's Fiction." *The Journal of Narrative Technique* 1, no. 1 (1971): 59–67.

Ferrell, Keith. *John Steinbeck: The Voice of the Land*. New York: Rowman & Littlefield, 2014.

Gladstein, Mimi Reisel. "Edenic Ironies: Steinbeck's Conflicted Vision." *The Steinbeck Review* 11, no. 1 (2014): 1–13.

Haugen, Hayley Mitchell. *The American Dream in John Steinbeck's* Of Mice and Men. Detroit: Greenhaven Press, 2010.

Marsden, John L. "California Dreamin': The Significance of 'A Coupla Acres' in Steinbeck's *Of Mice and Men*." *Western American Literature* 29, no. 4 (1995): 291–97.

Owens, Louis. "Deadly Kids, Stinking Dogs, and Heroes: The Best Laid Plans in Steinbeck's *Of Mice and Men*." *Western American Literature* 37, no. 3 (2002): 319–33.

Owens, Louis. *John Steinbeck's Re-Vision of America*. Athens: University of Georgia Press, 1985.

Steinbeck, Elaine. *Steinbeck and the Environment: Interdisciplinary Approaches*. Tuscaloosa: University of Alabama Press, 2007.

Wharton, Alexander. "'Live off the fatta the lan': Steinbeck's Salinas Valley." *Metaphor* 4 (2015): 33.

Willis, Lloyd. "Monstrous Ecology: John Steinbeck, Ecology, and American Cultural Politics." *The Journal of American Culture* 28, no. 4 (2005): 357–67.

The Old Man and the Sea

The Old Man and the Sea is among the late works of American author and Nobel laureate Ernest Hemingway. It is a novella that bears superficial similarity to American author Herman Melville's masterpiece *Moby Dick*. In both cases, men take to the sea in the most important quest of their lives. Captain Ahab seeks a great white whale whereas Santiago, the protagonist in *The Old Man and the Sea*, simply wants a large fish to sell so he can sustain himself. Santiago is poor and his luck has turned against him. He manages, however, to hook a large marlin. Now he must bring it back to shore. Luck is again against him because sharks devour large parts of the carcass. When Santiago reaches home, he has little to show for his efforts but the skeleton of a marlin.

THE GEOGRAPHY OF PLACE

The geography of *The Old Man and the Sea* is Cuba, Santiago's home country, and the Caribbean Sea in which he fishes. From an American perspective, Cuba

> The clouds were building up now for the trade wind and he looked ahead and saw a flight of wild ducks etching themselves against the sky over the water, then blurring, then etching again and he knew no man was ever alone on the sea.
> **Ernest Hemingway, *The Old Man and the Sea* (1952)**

Ernest Hemingway came up with the idea for his story *The Old Man and the Sea* after meeting Gregorio Fuentes, a Cuban fisherman. Here, the two men pose next to their catch. (Philippe Giraud/Sygma via Getty Images)

is possibly the most important Caribbean island. It is closest to the United States, being only about 90 miles south of Florida. For generations it produced the sugar that Americans ate and provided the slave model on which the antebellum southern economy was built. Yet, *The Old Man and the Sea* is not a geography of slavery. Santiago is free, though he is poor like the slaves who peopled Cuba before him. This is a Cuba that Hemingway knew, having lived sporadically in the capital Havana. The waters in which Santiago fishes are part of the Caribbean Sea and more mysterious perhaps than the island. Perhaps these are the waters that Italian Spanish explorer Christopher Columbus sailed in reaching Cuba during his first foray in the Americas. Perhaps these are the waters that the Portuguese and other Europeans delivered slaves to the sugar barons of Cuba. Perhaps these waters represent an unknown because Santiago is not certain why he has had a run of 84 consecutive days without catching a fish. Even the neighbors are spooked, thinking Santiago himself unlucky. For this reason, the parents of young Manolin will no longer let the youngster fish with Santiago. They want him to fish in a lucky boat with a lucky man. The restriction pains Manolin, who respects Santiago as a fine person. Despite his parents' wishes, Manolin remains loyal to Santiago, helping him unload his tackle when he returns to shore every evening. The two talk about American baseball, particularly the rivalry between the New York Yankees and the Cleveland Indians. Set in the 1950s, *The Old Man and the Sea* recollects a time when the two were among the best in Major League Baseball (MLB). In this way Santiago and Manolin forge a bond akin to friendship.

THE SEA AS A GEOGRAPHY OF MYSTERY

The Caribbean Sea is the site of the main action of the novella. On the 85th day, Santiago, feeling like his luck must change, decides to sail farther from shore than usual. It is as though he is transgressing a natural limit or boundary. His action demonstrates the dramaticism necessary to transform events and bring him luck. Although he cannot see it, Santiago is certain that the sea hides in its waters the fish he is destined to catch. His exploration farther from shore is his quest to find the luck that has so far eluded him. In this sense, though, mere luck does not quite capture the events. Luck implies randomness, but Santiago's actions are not random. He has calculated his actions on the reasonable supposition that if the waters he ordinarily searches have yielded nothing, he must find new waters to search. This commitment to the new brings upon Santiago the dramatic events of *The Old Man and the Sea*. In these waters, Santiago spots and then hooks a magnificent marlin. Here is the catch of a lifetime, but Santiago cannot control the fish because of its size and strength. The marlin pulls Santiago and his boat for two days before it begins to tire. During this time, Santiago's esteem for the fish and its desire for independence deepens. He knows the fish suffers from being hooked, just as he suffers from the fatigue of being awake two consecutive days.

Now that the marlin has tired, Santiago momentarily has the upper hand. He pulls the fish close enough to the boat so he can kill it with his harpoon. Fastening the fish to the side of the boat because it is too big to bring into the hull, Santiago steers his boat back to Cuba. Yet the decision to harpoon the fish, perhaps necessary, nonetheless puts the catch in danger. The marlin has left a trail of blood, though strictly speaking the trail should not be large because once the heart stops at death it cannot pump more blood through the wound. But sharks are sensitive. They need only a small amount of blood to detect a kill, and they come after the marlin. Santiago fights them off with a harpoon and then with an oar to which he has connected a knife. He kills several, but more appear to take the place of the dead sharks. Despite his efforts, Santiago is powerless to save the fish for the market. The sharks devour it, and he returns home with nothing but a large skeleton. The ordeal has exhausted him, and Santiago sleeps deeply. While he sleeps, the village comes to life, discovering the large skeleton attached to Santiago's boat. It is evident that his luck has changed, though not enough to bring a fish to market. Nonetheless, the community renews its respect for Santiago. He and Manolin forge a partnership once more.

Christopher Cumo

Further Reading

A few tales involving the sea would serve as adequate comparison texts to Hemingway's *Old Man and the Sea*. For instance, *Moby Dick* is set earlier and is a story of a much grander scope, but it also has to do with man's relationship to ocean creatures. Also, John Steinbeck's *The Pearl* is a novella about a poor fisherman who discovers a large pearl during a dive. However, like many of these other works that feature a seascape, what the main characters think will make them happy ultimately fails to do so.

Bibliography

Ammary, Sylvia. *The Influence of the European Culture on Hemingway's Fiction*. Lanham, MD: Lexington Books, 2015.

Anderson, Eric Gary, and Melanie Benson Taylor. "The Landscape of Disaster: Hemingway, Porter, and the Soundings of Indigenous Silence." *Texas Studies in Literature and Language* 59, no. 3 (2017). doi: 10.7560/TSLL59304.

Bharadwaj, Apoorva. *The Narcissism Conundrum: Mapping the Mindscape of Ernest Hemingway through an Enquiry into His Epistolary and Literary Corpus.* Newcastle upon Tyne: Cambridge Scholars Publishing, 2013.

Biggs, C. J. "Environmental Relationships and Our Changing Nature: A Study of Hemingway and Harrison's Northern Michigan Writings." Honors thesis, University of Michigan, 2016.

Freudenburg, William R., Scott Frickel, and Robert Gramling. "Beyond the Nature/Society Divide: Learning to Think about a Mountain." *Sociological Forum* 10, no. 3 (1995): 361–92. doi:10.1007/BF02095827.

Godfrey, Laura G. "Hemingway, the Preservation Impulse, and Cultural Geography." In *Hemingway's Geographies: Intimacy, Materiality, and Memory.* New York: Palgrave Macmillan, 2016. doi: 10.1057/978-1-137-58175-4.

Godfrey, Laura G. "Introduction: Ernest Hemingway's Intimate Geographies." In *Hemingway's Geographies: Intimacy, Materiality, and Memory.* New York: Palgrave Macmillan, 2016. doi: 10.1057/978-1-137-58175-4_1.

Godfrey, Laura G. "The Illusion of Remembered Places." In *Hemingway's Geographies: Intimacy, Materiality, and Memory.* New York: Palgrave Macmillan, 2016.

Scott, Camryn. "Ernest Hemingway: The Modern Transcendentalist." *Criterion: A Journal of Literary Criticism* 9, no. 1 (2016).

Oliver, Mary

Mary Oliver's poetry explores the human need for connection to the other living beings that inhabit the Earth. Yet in doing so, she underscores the distance between our civilized lives and the lives of those that inhabit wild spaces, which infuses her poetry with a sense of longing. Known as a very accessible poet, her work presents philosophical and spiritual concepts that are inclusive of a wide range of beliefs. Although Oliver spent her childhood and adolescence in Ohio, she has lived in Provincetown, Massachusetts, for most of her adult life, and her poetry concentrates on the features of a two-mile stretch of land on northwestern Cape Cod in a national park.

Mary Oliver's poetry is often set in the landscape around Provincetown, Massachusetts, which includes a woodland area with freshwater ponds that she frequently visits. It is no surprise, then, to find in her work the animals that frequent these waterways, especially waterfowl such as geese and swans. Some of her poems take specific, real pond names as their titles. However, more often, especially in her better-known poems, the hillsides and waterways remain unnamed—they could be anywhere. In those poems, she writes generally of trees, branches, flowers, mountains, rivers, snakes, and fish, choosing not to share more detail, such as species name. However, she has included enough place-names in her body of work that locals can map her walking routes as she gathers material for her poems. She especially loves recording in her poetry the cycle of the different seasons as they come to the ponds and woods to which she keeps returning.

Mary Oliver is firmly rooted in the Romantic tradition of nature poetry founded on private communion with the natural landscape, which the poet treats as a manifestation of secret truths about mortality, God, and/or what it means to be human.

Mary Oliver follows in the footsteps of many poets before her who have also tapped into this tradition. Like many of them, Oliver develops speakers in her poems that seek insight about human nature by observing our animal counterparts and by noting the ways we share (or fail to share) space with them. The images of the flora and fauna of her local landscape serve to establish that the creatures/beings that inhabit the natural world are purer than we are as humans, although the natural world as she presents it is not devoid of violence and suffering. For the most part, the natural spaces in her poems offer comfort for the human speakers that reflect on them. Usually tinged with longing from all the things that seek to keep us from time spent outdoors, her poems advocate that identity is best connected to local place.

Pulitzer Prize winner Mary Oliver was originally from Ohio, but lived most of her life in Provincetown, Massachusetts. As a young poet, she stayed briefly in the home of the poet Edna St. Vincent Millay as she helped her family organize Millay's papers. (Frederick M. Brown/Getty Images)

"Sleeping in the Forest" personifies the earth as a female host welcoming the poet. The speaker talks about how time spent in the natural world offers humans the ability to renew themselves and rejuvenate their energy. Place is where humans go to find themselves, to get in touch with their true identity, which for Mary Oliver means our animal nature, or kinship with nonhuman living things.

In "Wild Geese," she elaborates on what connects us as family to the animal inhabitants of natural spaces. For her, it is, in part, the fact of having a body. The poem claims that our bodies are what makes us animal and we should follow the instincts they communicate to us. However, to do that, one must listen to the body. Listening is immensely important in Oliver's interaction with the natural world. But by the end of the poem, readers are made to understand that although Oliver admits that our bodies make us animals, that as humans we have hang-ups about morality and identity. The poem teaches us that if we pay attention to what animals do, then we can let go of our grief and anxiety and feel a sense a connection and wonder. The beauty of the world around us is cause for hope and celebration.

The same acceptance of the animal part of human nature appears in her poem "August." In it, the speaker says that "all day my body / accepts what it is." Later, she talks about her hand, which had picked blackberries earlier in the day, as a "thick paw," likening herself to a bear.

"At Great Pond" is a good example in Oliver's work of how people morph into elements of the natural world and vice versa. At the beginning of the poem, she personifies the sun as an orange bird. Then she sees a white bird and claims that it could be a man meditating. The speaker claims that later, as she reflects on what she saw, that she will "almost" become the lily and the sun. Through the personification of nature and by morphing humans into flora and/or fauna, Oliver shows that the primary function of human interaction with place is of a kind of spiritual communion.

Numerous other poems of Oliver's position the natural world as healer and the human-centered world as dysfunctional. "Morning Poem" from *Dream Work* is one of her works that posits nature as the antidote or cure to the ways the human world wears us down. Just like in "Wild Geese," this poem, too, advocates getting in touch with our inner "beast," because it knows better than the human part what is good for us and what will spiritually fulfill us. Here, to the human observer, ponds are "prayer[s] heard and answered" even for those who don't know how to pray.

Not all of the images in Oliver's poetry are peaceful. Sometimes they accurately portray the violent scenes that are part of the lives of animals. This reflects a subtle undercurrent in Oliver's work that depicts love as sometimes violent. For instance, living creatures are willing to go to extreme lengths to protect their families, their loved ones, their young—this is common among both humans and other animals. One example of this is in her poem "Spring" from *House of Light*, where she describes a mother black bear as both "white teeth" and "perfect love."

Although the role of nature in her work seems to be a physical manifestation of rebirth, the geography of her local area also helps place humankind in context for her speakers. In Oliver's work, the natural world reminds us that there are forces outside of us that are larger than our problems, and this lesson should serve to minimize our suffering.

Lynn Marie Houston

Further Reading

Mary Oliver's plain-spoken truths about the human condition often prompt readers to compare her works to those of Maya Angelou, Rumi, and Hafez. The way in which her poetry fashions the natural world as a dynamic character creates an affinity between her work and that of Wendell Berry.

Bibliography

Anderson, Lorraine, ed. *Sisters of the Earth: Women's Prose and Poetry about Nature.* New York: Vintage Books, 2003.

Burton-Christie, Douglas. "Mapping the Sacred Landscape: Spirituality and the Contemporary Literature of Nature." *Horizons* 21, no. 1 (1994): 22–47. doi:10.1017/S0360966900027912.

Elder, John. *Imagining the Earth: Poetry and the Vision of Nature.* Athens: University of Georgia Press, 1996.

Riley, Jeannette E. "Finding One's Place in the 'Family of Things': Terry Tempest Williams and a Geography of Self." *Women's Studies: An Interdisciplinary Journal* 32, no. 5 (2003): 585–602. doi:10.1080/00497870390207121.

Oliver Twist

Charles Dickens's novel is set in England in the 1830s. Dickens tells the story of the young boy named Oliver Twist, whose mother dies shortly after his birth. Oliver grows up in an orphanage and, at nine, is sent to a workhouse for adults. He is then apprenticed to an undertaker, but he runs away and has to navigate the spaces and subcultures of London. His quest for self-preservation, stemming from his lack of financial means, ends as a happy tale of charity and a hopeful message about the strength of family bonds.

THE URBAN GEOGRAPHY OF LONDON

Outside London, Oliver meets a boy who goes by the name of the Artful Dodger. He offers Oliver a place to stay. However, the owner of the house, Fagin, leads a gang of orphan boys who steal for him. While Oliver is in the urban labyrinth of London, this criminal gang is one of the main subcultures he associates with. In this novel, the space of criminality is limited to the streets and to public, commercial spaces; the Victorian houses of the middle-class and upper-class families are mainly devoid of influence from criminal elements. In the one case where someone connected to Fagin's gang breeches that space—in other words, when Nancy communicates with Oliver's friends regarding Fagin's dastardly plans—she is punished for it. Sikes kills her but then dies himself as he tries to escape from justice. Other Dickens's novels represent the boundaries of these spaces as more fluid.

After a few days of training with Fagin and the others, Oliver is with two other boys when they steal a handkerchief from an elderly gentleman, Mr. Brownlow. Oliver feels great remorse, despite being nearly arrested for the crime. Instead, Mr. Brownlow brings Oliver to his home so that he can recover from his fever.

The gang of criminals that Oliver falls into have an uncanny knowledge of London's layout, knowing how to hide themselves from the authorities, and yet knowing how, where, and when to access the possessions and dwelling of the upper classes. The places where Fagin and his group dwell are hidden from the rest of the city, and without access to people outside the criminals, such as the upper-class family who eventually adopt him after a robbery gone wrong, Oliver becomes imprisoned in a life of crime, dependent on routes that others map out for him. This is one of the elements of the novel that prompts scholars to talk about how it fits

---

The public-houses, with gas-lights burning inside, were already open. By degrees, other shops began to be unclosed, and a few scattered people were met with. Then, came straggling groups of labourers going to their work; then, men and women with fish-baskets on their heads; donkey-carts laden with vegetables; chaise-carts filled with livestock or whole carcasses of meat; milk-women with pails; an unbroken concourse of people trudging out with various supplies to the eastern suburbs of the town. As they approached the City, the noise and traffic gradually increased; when they threaded the streets between Shoreditch and Smithfield, it had swelled into a roar of sound and bustle.

Charles Dickens, Oliver Twist (1837–1839)

into the Gothic tradition, one that explores the darker recesses of the human psyche and, in this case, the dark corners of the city.

THE RURAL/URBAN DICHOTOMY

Oliver enjoys being in Mr. Brownlow's home, and the latter notices that Oliver looks quite a bit like the portrait of an ancestor hanging on his wall. However, under orders from Fagin, Bill Sikes and his lover, Nancy, capture Oliver and take him back to his life of crime. In the next burglary, a servant shoots Oliver and the women who live in the house, Mrs. Maylie and her adopted niece Rose, take him in. As they all get along so well, they take Oliver with them when they spend the summer in the country.

When Oliver Twist first comes to the city of London, he is subconsciously looking for it to mother him. At first, he is gravely disappointed. As he enters the city through the suburbs of Islington, Pentonville, and Saffron Hill, Oliver's initial impression of London, the Field Lane neighborhood, is that it is a dirty, diseased, overcrowded place, where seemingly motherless children run rampant in the streets. Oliver is led by the Artful Dodger into Fagin's lair through a circuitous route that does not proceed along the most expedient route to their destination. The path they take points to their purpose: to conceal their presence, for which they also use the cover of night. They are not the only characters to use the physical layout of the city as a means of concealment. Nancy also takes a circuitous route on her way to the Maylies' so that her destination and purpose (to leak the news about Oliver) are not discovered by any members of Fagin's gang. Her courage in opposing the group's evil plans prompts her to bridge the two communities and classes. But alas, a member of the gang overhears her betrayal.

Fagin is set on recapturing Oliver, and when Sikes hears that Nancy has leaked information, he kills her. As he attempts to get away, he accidentally hangs himself. Eventually, Oliver finds out who his parents were and discovers that Rose is his aunt. Oliver is adopted by Mr. Brownlow, and together with the Maylies, they all move to the countryside.

The distinction between the descriptions, plot elements, and character development that take place in the country, as opposed to those that happen in the city, reflects a perspective that life in the countryside is more "natural" but also more rudimentary. Oliver is brought to the country by the Maylies to recuperate after being shot. There, he finds peace and healing in the sunshine and quiet solace of the natural landscape—taking in vistas on his walks in the countryside while he picks wildflowers. In the country, he begins his journey toward a new identity. The journey comes full circle when he discovers who his family is and moves out to the country to live peacefully with them after his tribulations in the city.

Oliver Twist presents a more corrupt version of the city than almost any other of his works. In *Oliver Twist,* the city is the place where one encounters criminality, but it is also the place where one is educated about the finer things, where one becomes "cultured." This is the case because the city places citizens in closer contact with each other and with the recorded history of human artistic and cultural production. As Oliver initially makes a place for himself within city life, Dickens seems to conclude that it is a natural progression of human civilization to move from an isolated, rural existence to an informed state of being afforded by residence in the city. However, the barriers to achieving this elevated state are the penchant toward crime and the erosion of family bonds that can happen in city life. Dickens's novel presents a narrative that overcomes these obstacles when morality triumphs over immorality. However, this is no easy or clear-cut dichotomy: the countryside continues to exist as a space of rejuvenation from the ills of finer society, which in Dickens's novels is prone to greed, hypocrisy, arrogance, and ostentation, and is where the majority of characters find happiness and community at the end of this novel.

Lynn Marie Houston

Further Reading

If you enjoyed reading *Oliver Twist,* you might like to read other authors who wrote about life in London in the 19th century: William Makepeace Thackeray and Anthony Trollope. Tobias Smollett lived in London during the mid-1800s and was a great influence on Charles Dickens.

Bibliography

Addison, Neil Matthew. "Dickens and the Literary City: A Study of London as Stage and Protagonist in Charles Dickens' Works." *Reitaku University Journal* 95 (2012): 1–31.

Baumgarten, Murray. "Fictions of the City." In *The Cambridge Companion to Charles Dickens*, edited by John O. Jordan, 106–19. Cambridge, UK: Cambridge University Press, 2001.

Baumgarten, Murray. "Reading Dickens Writing London." *Partial Answers: Journal of Literature and the History of Ideas* 9, no. 2 (2011): 219–31.

Boev, Hristo. "Walking the Streets of the Modern City: Reclaiming Street Space in Dickens's and Dos Passos's Representations of Women." *International Journal of Cross-Cultural Studies and Environmental Communication* 1 (2013): 55–69.

Boone, Troy. "Early Dickens and Ecocriticism: The Social Novelist and the Nonhuman." In *Victorian Writers and the Environment: Ecocritical Perspectives,* edited by Lawrence M. Mazzeno and Ronald D. Morrison, 105–21. London: Routledge, 2016.

Budrewicz-Beratan, Aleksandra. "Near the Riverbank: Women, Danger and Place in Dickens." In *Crossroads in Literature and Culture,* edited by J. Fabiszak, E. Urbaniak-Rybicka, and B. Wolski, 59–72. Berlin, Heidelberg: Springer, 2013.

Craig, David M. "The Interplay of City and Self in *Oliver Twist, David Copperfield,* and *Great Expectations.*" *Dickens Studies Annual* 16 (1987): 17–38.

Dubroc, Anita Michelle. "City as Prison: Negotiating Identity in the Urban Space in the Nineteenth-Century Novel." Master's thesis, Louisiana State University, 2009.

Eichenlaub, Justin. "The Infrastructural Uncanny: *Oliver Twist* in the Suburbs and Slums." *Dickens Studies Annual* (2013): 1–27.

Frost, Mark. "Journeys through Nature: Dickens, Anti-Pastoralism and the Country." *Representations* (June 2016): 53–71.

Gruß, Susanne. "Bleak London: (Neo-) Dickensian Psychogeographies." In *English Topographies in Literature and Culture: Space, Place, and Identity,* edited by Ina Habermann and Daniela Keller, 74. Leiden, Netherlands: Brill Rodopi, 2016.

Hanson, Julienne. "Presentiment, Contrast and Ambiguity in Fictional Space: The London Novels of Charles Dickens and Peter Ackroyd." *The Journal of Space Syntax* 3, no. 1 (2012): 81–124.

Kaufmann, Priscilla. "Urban Images of Nineteenth-Century London: The Literary Geography of Charles Dickens." Student work, University of Nebraska at Omaha, 1987.

Mancoff, Debra N., and Dale J. Trela. *Victorian Urban Settings: Essays on the Nineteenth-Century City and Its Contexts*. London: Routledge, 2013.

Mighall, Robert. "Gothic Cities." In *The Routledge Companion to Gothic,* edited by C. L. Spooner and E. McEvoy, 68–76. London: Routledge, 2007.

Miller, Joseph Hillis. *Charles Dickens: The World of His Novels*. Cambridge, MA: Harvard University Press, 1958.

Murail, Estelle, and Sara Thornton. "Dickensian Counter-Mapping, Overlaying, and Troping: Producing the Virtual City." In *Dickens and the Virtual City,* 3–32. Cham, Switzerland: Palgrave Macmillan, 2017.

Parrinder, Patrick. "'Turn Again, Dick Whittington!': Dickens, Wordsworth, and the Boundaries of the City." *Victorian Literature and Culture* 32, no. 2 (2004): 407–19.

Ridenhour, Jamieson. *In Darkest London: The Gothic Cityscape in Victorian Literature*. Lanham, MD: Scarecrow Press, 2012.

Robinson, Brian. "Charles Dickens and London: The Visible and the Opaque." *GeoJournal* 38, no. 1 (1996): 59–74.

Robles, Fanny. "Dickens and His Urban Museum: The City as Ethnological Spectacle." In *Dickens and the Virtual City,* edited by Estelle Murail and Sara Thornton, 133–53. Cham, Switzerland: Palgrave Macmillan, 2017.

Sen, Sambudha. "Hogarth, Egan, Dickens, and the Making of an Urban Aesthetic." *Representations* 103, no. 1 (2008): 84–106.

Tambling, Jeremy. *Dickens and the City*. London: Routledge, 2017.

Tambling, Jeremy. *Going Astray: Dickens and London*. London: Routledge, 2016.

Tambling, Jeremy. *Lost in the American City: Dickens, James, and Kafka*. New York: Springer, 2001.

Wilkes, David. "Dickens, Bakhtin, and the Neopastoral Shepherd in *Oliver Twist*." *Dickens Studies Annual* 24 (1996): 59–79.

Wolfreys, Julian. *Writing London: The Trace of the Urban Text from Blake to Dickens*. Basingstoke, UK: Palgrave, 1998.

On the Road

"The road is life" is the central assertion of *On the Road,* a novelized version of Jack Kerouac's experiences in late 1940s America. A young writer named Sal Paradise narrates his adventures with and without his "hero" Dean Moriarty (based on Neal Cassady), poet Carlo Marx (Allen Ginsberg), and heroin addict Old Bull Lee (William Burroughs). Sal leaves his somewhat stable life and hitchhikes around America, working as night watchman, cotton picker, and railroad brakeman to make enough money to get him to the next place. Between travels Dean shuttles between women, primarily the beautiful but underage Marylou and the patient, suffering Camille. At one point, Sal defends the "hipster angel" Dean to a group of women he has betrayed, unaware that eventually he will be given the same treatment.

THE GEOGRAPHY OF PLACE

The novel takes place in the great "triangle" between New York, San Francisco, and Mexico City: "all that raw land that rolls in one unbelievable huge bulge over to the West Coast, and all that road going, all the people dreaming in the immensity of it." From the beat streets of Denver to the mountains of North Carolina, we are taken from place to place, never stopping too long, never getting to know the floor of one apartment or the tabletops of one café, always moving to the next shining experience. In this way, rather than bring one or two places to life, as most books attempt to do, *On the Road* takes on the in-between spaces, the roads connecting place to place.

Kerouac's characters, too, are marginal figures, caught somehow "in-between" the bourgeois and working class, full of movement rather than stability. He puts it clearly near the beginning of the novel: "the only people for me are the mad ones, the ones who are mad to live, mad to talk, mad to be saved, desirous of everything at the same time, the ones who never yawn or say a commonplace thing, but burn, burn, burn like fabulous yellow roman candles exploding like spiders across the stars."

Perhaps Sal's happiest moment is when he becomes someone else, and has the life he imagined in these in-between spaces. He wakes up one morning, "and that was the one distinct time in my life, the strangest moment of all, when I didn't know who I was—I was far away from home, haunted and tired with travel, in a cheap hotel room I'd never seen, hearing the hiss of steam outside, and the creak of the old wood of the hotel, and footsteps upstairs, and all the sad sounds, and I looked at the cracked high ceiling and really didn't know who I was for about fifteen strange seconds. I wasn't scared; I was just somebody else, some stranger, and my whole life was a haunted life, the life of a ghost." Through the magic of geography, he has escaped from his past, from the "normal" life everyone else lives, and now exists in the marginal spaces as an alien phantom.

THE QUEST FOR "IT"

What are they searching for? Perhaps for "IT," as Dean Moriarty so often claims. But more concretely, both he and Sal Paradise often search for Dean's lost hobo father, "Old Dean Moriarty, the father we never found." Paradise has also lost his wife to divorce and father to death. These losses may symbolize the lost patriarchy, or the loss of stability that comes in a nomadic society. It becomes clearer and clearer as the novel progresses that Sal and Dean are searching for a home. The tragedy of the novel is that even when possible homes present themselves—Paradise's sojourn with his lover Terry, Moriarty's child with Camille—they continue on, believing that some place better exists. As Kerouac puts it, "Nothing behind me, everything ahead of me, as is ever so on the road."

At last, they leave the confines of the United States, and head to "the magical south," a Mexico that at first seems to answer all their dreams. They revel in cheap sex, free marijuana, and beautiful roads that wind high into strange mountain jungles. But in the heart of Mexico City, where Sal and Dean hope to find "it" at last, they find instead a bitter separation. Sal gets sick and Dean abandons him there, as he had done with countless others before, driving back in the car while Sal trembles and shakes with dysentery. Later, at the very end of the novel, Sal does the same, leaving his former friend on the New York streets despite Dean's "apology" of traveling across the entire country just to see him.

THE ROAD AS HOME

The characters in *On the Road* travel at breakneck speeds along the small, newly paved roads between towns and cities, roads that actually had two ends to them. But by the time this book was published, the interstate highway system had already changed the landscape of America forever, running huge swaths of concrete from city to city, allowing people to move faster and more safely across the entire country.

And yet, the highways also did great damage, dissecting neighborhoods, shattering and isolating urban areas. They encouraged the ruin of the cities they served, drawing residents into the suburbs and business and manufacturing into the countryside. And though today the highway system allows us to reach places in record time, it also keeps us away from the small towns along their edges, drying them up like tumbleweeds and sending the children of their inhabitants away. America is still adjusting to this great change, and may never get over it.

In that way, Kerouac's novel can act as both herald and cautionary tale. The wandering life that many Americans lead today allows for more flexibility, builds wealth, and promises freedom. Most people read this book when they are young and are invigorated by the life it describes, finding nomads like Dean Moriarty attractive and exciting. And *On the Road* surely presents a necessary antidote to the tired, received ideas of a stagnant past. But a nomad might leave you when the chips are down, and the carefree life of the road is probably just a search for home.

Eric D. Lehman

In his book *On the Road*, Jack Kerouac chronicles the ways in which the American landscape and culture were changed by the U.S. highway system. This vintage automobile pointed toward a long stretch of open road recalls the freedom his characters experience during most of their journey. (Spencer Platt/Getty Images)

Further Reading

Two other novels written by authors active during the same time period as Kerouac, which also involve drug-fueled travel are *Naked Lunch* by William Burroughs and *Fear and Loathing in Las Vegas* by Hunter S. Thompson. Moreover, these three novels all seem to be based on the authors' personal experiences. Another work that features an epic road trip is *Blue Highways* by William Least Heat-Moon. "Howl" by Allen Ginsberg is known as the poetic manifesto of the Beat generation, whereas *On the Road* is known as its classic novel.

Bibliography

Bennett, Robert. "Tract Homes on the Range: The Suburbanization of the American West." *Western American Literature* 46, no. 3 (2011): 281–301. doi:10.1353/wal.2011.0060.

Burd, Gene. "The Search for Natural Regional Space to Claim and Name Built Urban Place." *Journal of Architectural and Planning Research* 25, no. 2 (2008): 130–44. www.jstor.org/stable/43030828.

Cresswell, Tim. "Mobility as Resistance: A Geographical Reading of Kerouac's *On the Road*." *Transactions of the Institute of British Geographers* (1993): 249–62.

Gipko, Jesse. "Road Narratives as Cultural Critiques: Henry Miller, Jack Kerouac, John Steinbeck, and William Least Heat-Moon." PhD diss., Duquesne University, 2014.

Juarez, David Ryan. "Haunted by You: A Study of the Real and Psycho-Literary Space of Jack Kerouac's Lowell." Master's thesis, University of Texas at Austin, 2014. hdl.handle.net/2152/28516.

Larson, Lars Erik. "Routes and Roots: American Literature as a Means of Understanding Contemporary Space and Place." *Pursuits* 13, no. 1 (2015): 1–10.

Melehy, Hassan. "Literatures of Exile and Return: Jack Kerouac and Quebec." *American Literature* 84, no. 3 (2012): 589–615. doi: 10.1215/00029831-1664728.

Slethaug, Gordon. "Mapping the Trope: A Historical and Cultural Journey." In *Hit the Road, Jack: Essays on the Culture of the American Road,* edited by Gordon Slethaug and Stacilee Ford. Montreal & Kingston: McGill-Queens University Press, 2012.

Smith, Lee W. "A Specific Elsewhere: Locating Masculinity in Jack Kerouac's *On the Road*." Master's thesis, University of Essex, 2017.

Theroux, Paul. *The Tao of Travel: Enlightenments from Lives on the Road*. Boston: Houghton Mifflin Harcourt, 2011.

One Flew Over the Cuckoo's Nest

Ken Kesey's iconic tale of patients in a mental institution was intended as a political wake-up call to his generation. Featuring the rebellious Randle McMurphy, the story is told from the point of view of "Chief" Bromden, a Native American man who had been institutionalized in the mental hospital because he suffers from PTSD. The men in the hospital ward are terrorized by Nurse Ratched, also called Big Nurse, who attempts to dictate when and what the patients will watch on television, when and how many cigarettes they can smoke, and ultimately, for those who are under mandatory (not voluntary) confinement, when they will be released. McMurphy tries to champion the rest of the men by engaging Nurse Ratched in a battle of wills; however, she has him lobotomized for his resistance to her orders. Before successfully escaping the hospital, "Chief" puts McMurphy out of his misery by suffocating him.

THE POLITICAL LANDSCAPE OF THE 1960s

Ken Kesey's classic tale of man versus the state was written in 1962, during a time of social and political upheaval when American citizens began to question much of what the previous generation had accepted at face value. The consequences of the 1960s protests were increased rights, such as the right to vote and access to education, for women and marginalized ethnic and racial groups. Kesey's tale of institutional corruption comes out of the suspicion and dislike of the status quo that prompted the civil rights movement of the 1960s. McMurphy's death as a martyr for a larger cause fits within the historical contest of this era as a revolutionary one. Events where protestors died for their political beliefs, such as the Kent State shooting, are echoed in McMurphy's sacrifice.

THE CULTURE OF MENTAL ILLNESS

Kesey writes McMurphy as a savior who shows a group of the men in the ward that they are not truly sick and that they are capable of standing up against the corrupt power of the institution. The result is that "Chief" dares to escape, and the men who are there voluntarily have the courage to check themselves out of the hospital and return to their lives.

McMurphy's battle with Nurse Ratched is similar to a battle between God and Satan for the souls of the men. In the climax of the story, after Jimmy stands up for himself against Nurse Ratched, she pushes him too far, threatening to tell his mother that he slept with a prostitute whom McMurphy had introduced to the ward. Ratched knows that Jimmy can be controlled through his fear of his mother's disapproval, and she is trying to use that to make him comply (that is, refuse to support McMurphy's attempts to undermine her power) when she makes this threat. In response to being abused by her one too many times, he kills himself. The point of the plot and character development is to impart on readers that the "normal" people, like Nurse Ratched, are the ones who are ill.

The Chief describes the system of repression in American culture as "the Combine." He uses this analogy of an agricultural harvesting machine as a means to talk about how the system "uses" people for its malicious ends. Nurse Ratched is the ultimate manifestation of the combine in the mental hospital, but the reach of this machine extends well beyond its walls. According to the Chief's view of this cultural and political system, it is particularly damaging to people in marginalized groups, such as Native Americans and nonwhites. Kesey chooses a particularly apt metaphor here as the combine harvester is one of the technologies modern man has used to make nature do what man wills it to. The social machine as represented by Nurse Ratched enforces normality and accepted behavior, with the threat of death as the ultimate punishment.

THE FIGHT OVER NATIVE AMERICAN LAND

At the heart of this novel is the issue of the colonization of native land. The narrator, "Chief" Bromden, flashes back more than once to the trauma caused in his childhood by a visit from federal agents who were sent to force his tribe into selling their land. This and his father's manipulation by a white wife (whose name he takes to be able to get a Social Security card) is the beginning of his mental "illness," which is exacerbated by serving in World War II. Kesey's purpose for including this backstory further illustrates the ways in which an institutional power structure takes advantage of a marginalized group, just the way that Nurse Ratched abuses the patients in her ward. Kesey places the origins of this corruption at the very foundation of the United States: when newly arrived Europeans swindled natives out of their lands. The Combine tames what is natural, and therefore imposes false and artificial regulations about what is and is not acceptable.

THE DREAMSCAPE OF INSTITUTIONALIZATION

We can also look back at the handling of the Chief's PTSD as a similar institutional failure: he fought in combat for the American military but instead of offering him proper treatment, Kesey shows that he is relegated to a mental hospital. Chief speaks regularly of a fog that no other character sees. This fog can be seen as a symbolic representation of his disconnect from reality after witnessing the horrors of war. The fog machine is related to his concept of the Combine—both are mechanical and both speak to the great risks of conforming. This is also a way in which Kesey can make visible Chief's PTSD—he is in a fog of his own making, cut off from the reality that others share. The fog seems, sometimes, to be a protective buffer for him, but ultimately his survival relies on stepping out of the fog. As a representation of a mental disorder, the fog functions as a symbol that reveals the choice the Chief has: in choosing to fight both the fog and the Combine, he chooses recovery and survival.

Lynn Marie Houston

Further Reading

Other authors who also wrote about their disillusionment with the constraints American culture places on free thinking are John Dos Passos and Tom Wolfe. Be sure to look at *The Big Money* and *The Electric Kool-Aid Acid Test*, respectively. Norman Mailer, Philip Roth, Theodore Dreiser also investigate the dark underbelly of American culture in their works, much like Kesey does in *One Flew Over the Cuckoo's Nest* with regard to mental health care, in which the people making the rules are the ones who are the most dangerous.

Bibliography

Knapp, James F. "Tangled in the Language of the Past: Ken Kesey and Cultural Revolution." *Midwest Quarterly* 19 (1978): 398–412.

Martin, Terence. "*One Flew Over the Cuckoo's Nest* and the High Cost of Living." *Modern Fiction Studies* 19 (1973): 53–55.

Olderman, Raymond M. *Beyond the Waste Land: A Study of the American Novel in the Nineteen-Sixties*. New Haven, CT: Yale University Press, 1972.

Robinson, Daniel. "The Awakening of the Natural Men in *One Flew Over the Cuckoo's Nest*." *Notes on Contemporary Literature* 21, no. 1 (1991): 4–6.

Shaw, Patrick W. "The American West as Satiric Territory: Kesey's *One Flew Over the Cuckoo's Nest* and Berger's *Little Big Man*." *Studies in Contemporary Satire* 10 (1983): 1–8.

Sullivan, Ruth "Big Mama, Big Paper, and Little Sons in Ken Kesey's *One Flew Over the Cuckoo's Nest.*" *Literature and Psychology* 25 (1974): 33–44.

Vitkus, Daniel J. "Madness and Misogyny in Ken Kesey's *One Flew Over the Cuckoo's Nest.*" *Alif: Journal of Comparative Poetics* 14 (1994): 64–90.

One Hundred Years of Solitude

Colombian author Gabriel Garcia Marquez's masterpiece *Cien Anos de Soledad*, or in English, *One Hundred Years of Solitude*, tells the story of the Buendía family through several generations in a small town somewhere in South America. The patriarch of the family José Arcadio and his wife, Ursula Iguarán, settle in a swampy jungle between the mountains, intrepid pioneers of this particular unwanted portion of land. Their children are José Arcadio and Aureliano, who in turn have children whose names repeat, just as time itself seems to throughout the decades of births, marriages, and deaths. Each character is wrapped up in his or her particular solitude, which creates the tragic conditions for Marquez's heartbreaking elegy for the human race.

THE GEOGRAPHY OF PLACE

In one of the most striking opening lines in literature, Marquez sets the scene: "Many years later, as he faced the firing squad, Colonel Aureliano Buendía was to remember that distant afternoon when his father took him to discover ice." Not only does this set up the cyclic nature of time that the author plays with throughout the novel, it sets the geography of a place where ice must be "discovered." Marquez continues, describing Macondo as "a village of twenty adobe houses, built on the bank of a river of clear water that ran along a bed of polished stones, which were white and enormous, like prehistoric eggs." This vision of a world where "many things lacked names" is a vision of the beginning of time, of Eden.

However, Macondo is Eden as Marquez imagines it: a fetid swamp surrounded by wilderness, unable to connect with the rest of the world. José Arcadio Buendía has forgotten the route by which he brought these people into the mountains, and only the gypsies can find their way in and out. Everything has to be learned over again, from the beginning, and José Arcadio's desperate search for truth eventually leads him to be figuratively tied to the tree of knowledge, and literally tied to the tree in the courtyard of the Buendía house.

Over the years Macondo gradually finds the world, and the world finds it. The arrival of the railroad brings politics, wealth, and revolution. Colonel Aureliano Buendía becomes the leader of this revolution, a long, twilight struggle that takes place over many years, the instigator of "32 uprisings," all of which he loses. The growing town is visited by other horrors, too—an insomnia plague, a ravenous *norteamericano* banana company, and a massacre at the train station that the government promptly erases from history. And yet, connection to the outside world does not change the essential nature of the town or the Buendía family—they remain locked in the "solitudes" of their own making.

MAGICAL REALISM

Macondo is also a place where magic can happen, and does. However, the characters accept various "magical" events simply as another part of life. Marquez is working with the tradition of "magical realism," the term for which was coined in 1955 but which existed in literature long before that. In fact, *One Hundred Years of Solitude* is often credited with globally popularizing this method of storytelling. As Marquez himself put it, he "was destroying the line of demarcation that separates what seems real from what seems fantastic." When José Arcadio kills Prudencio Aguilar after an insult, he and other characters see Aguilar's ghost walking around in the courtyard. This is not a sign of madness, nor is it something that causes the characters to question their worldviews or the mundane, rational world itself. Nor is a priest or shaman called to interpret this strange episode. In Macondo, magic is a fact of life, but it is not life entire.

A LANDSCAPE OF CHILDHOOD

In blending the fantastic and the rational, Marquez re-created the geography of his childhood, and of the stories told to him in rural Colombia. He adds lush poetic language, with lines like this: "The men on the expedition felt overwhelmed by their most ancient memories in that paradise of dampness and silence, going back to before original sin, as their boots sank into pools of steaming oil and their machetes destroyed bloody lilies and golden salamanders." This poetic language, combined with the use of magical realism, creates a world of its own, a distinct literary landscape that has often been imitated, some might say, but never duplicated, even by Marquez himself.

In that sense, Macondo and the Buendía family are fictional. And even though it is in some ways a "fantasy" world, in which one of the Buendía daughters can be taken bodily to heaven, almost everyone in Latin America (and the rest of the world) who reads the book recognizes their own country's history somewhere in the endless, pointless revolutions, the exploitation by large capitalist companies, the terribly close family life that can bring great beauty or great horror.

END OF THE LINE

This family solitude leads finally to incest, to the "intricate labyrinths of blood" that causes the family's destruction, which is linked to the destruction of Macondo, perhaps of the entire world. The final members of the Buendía family, Amaranta Ursula and Aureliano Babilonia, engender "the mythological animal that was to bring the line to an end," actually just a child with a superfluous pig's tail. But as Babilonia finally translates the mysterious manuscripts of the gypsy Melquíades, brought to Macondo over a century earlier, a "biblical hurricane" wipes out the town.

In this ultimate act of geographical elimination, Marquez seems to have shown that time is not cyclical, but has a beginning and end. But we can posit that another family will settle this unwanted place between the mountains, and that the whole sordid history will repeat itself. Perhaps a new race, or a new species, will have better luck in breaking that cycle, Marquez seems to say. Because, as he writes in the last line, "races condemned to one hundred years of solitude did not have a second opportunity on earth."

Eric D. Lehman

Further Reading

Other Latin American authors who employ aspects of magical realism in their novels are Mario Vargas Llosa (*The Feast of the Goat*), Isabel Allende (*The House of the Spirits*), Alejo Carpentier (*The Chase*), Jorge Luis Borges (*Labyrinths*), and Julio Cortázar (*Hopscotch*).

Bibliography

Beecroft, Alexander. "On the Tropes of Literary Ecology: The Plot of Globalization." In *Globalizing Literary Genres: Literature, History, Modernity,* edited by Jernej Habjan and Fabienne Imlinger. New York: Routledge, 2016.

Deckard, Sharae. "The Political Ecology of Storms in Caribbean Literature." In *The Caribbean: Aesthetics, World-Ecology, Politics,* edited by Chris Campbell and Michael Niblett. Liverpool, UK: Liverpool University Press, 2016.

DeVries, Scott. *A History of Ecology and Environmentalism in Spanish American Literature.* Lanham, MD: Bucknell University Press, 2013.

Guest, Dorothy Glenda. "Magical Realism and Writing Place: A Novel and Exegesis." PhD diss., Griffith University, 2006.

Heise, Ursula K. "Local Rock and Global Plastic: World Ecology and the Experience of Place." *Comparative Literature Studies* 41, no. 1 (2004): 126–52. www.jstor.org/stable/40468106.

Madan, Aarti. "Writing the Earth, Writing the Nation: Latin American Narrative and the Language of Geography." PhD diss., University of Pittsburgh, 2010.

Mutis, Ana Maria. "The Death of the River and the River of Death: The Magdalena River in El amor en los tiempos del cólera and La novia oscura." *HIOL: Hispanic Issues On Line* 12 (2013): 145–62.

Reiss, Timothy J. "Imagining the Urban: Geographies against Histories in Some Caribbean and Latin-American Writing." *The Centennial Review* 42, no. 3 (1998): 437–56. www.jstor.org/stable/23740000.

P

The Plague

The Plague was a central work of existentialism, which in the 20th century was a philosophical and literary movement. There is controversy, however, because its author, Nobel laureate Albert Camus, denied he was an existentialist. This denial, in turn, is controversial because some scholars insist that Camus was emblematic of the movement, and *The Plague,* along with other works, a novel central to the movement. This is not the place for scrutinizing existentialism. It is enough here to say that Camus's quest to find meaning in a meaningless universe, rationality in an irrational world, and life amid the certainty of death all qualify him as an existentialist. In *The Plague,* Camus explores how the people of Oran, Algeria, try to cope with the plague, a symbol of evil and death, in the midst of the ordinary lives that they wish to pursue. In the tenor of existentialism, the novel does not end on an optimistic note. Although the plague finally abates, Camus wrote that it would return, if not to Oran, then somewhere else.

ORAN: THE GEOGRAPHY OF *THE PLAGUE*

Oran is a large city in Algeria, and the country deserves our immediate attention. In the 19th century, Algeria unhappily became a French colony. A large number of French citizens settled it in the 19th and 20th centuries, but they never outnumbered what one might call the native inhabitants. Yet, even these natives were not the original settlers, having been preceded by the Berbers. The Camus family settled Algeria, and Albert was born there. That is, Camus set the novel in a country he knew well. Yet, *The Plague* is less interested in the native Algerians. The drama instead involves the European inhabitants, not of Algeria at large, but of Oran.

Oran is in northwestern Algeria on the Mediterranean coast. Camus did not, of course, spend his entire life in Algeria, and seems never to have visited Oran. The port city is nonetheless a good choice of geography because Camus needed some way to introduce plague, by which, at the most literal level, the author seems to have meant primarily bubonic plague and secondarily pneumonic plague. A merchant ship brought rats to Oran. Rats, however, do not harbor the plague bacillus. The fleas that inhabit the rats do, and their bite infects a rat. In this sense, plague is primarily a disease of small mammals like rats and does not occur frequently among humans. The examples of plague throughout history, however, reveal incidents of appalling mortality.

The notorious case of the Black Death must have been on Camus's mind. Like the plague that afflicts Oran, the Black Death reached Europe, first Sicily and then mainland Italy, by the Mediterranean Sea. Also like the Black Death, the plague in

Oran kills large numbers of people. It is important to note that Camus wrote at a time when most scholars assumed that the Black Death was plague. Since then scientists and scholars have squared off so that there is no longer consensus about what erupted in Europe between 1347 and 1351. It is also important to note that Camus rejected this medieval background, preferring to set *The Plague* in modern Oran.

THE GEOGRAPHY OF WAR, NAZISM, AND EVIL

Camus had an enduring hatred of evil. His morality led him to join the French Resistance against the Nazi occupation of France during World War II. This experience shaped Camus and *The Plague,* which he wrote after the war. In this literary landscape, the plague emerges as more than a biological evil, though it is that. The plague emerges as a symbol of human evil and of the Nazism that sought to destroy Europe. The people enmeshed in *The Plague,* surrounded by the specters of death and evil, must make choices about how to respond to the evil that they must either confront or try to flee. Here again is a stark theme of existentialism, one that is evident in the writings of Camus's contemporaries: French novelist and art critic André Malraux, and French philosopher and author Jean-Paul Sartre. Put simply, humans are condemned to choose. The attempt to evade choice is itself a choice, though not a courageous one. Camus concentrates particular attention on the doctor and the atheist, the two men who feel the greatest compassion to comfort the suffering of those infected with the plague. One witnesses in the choices of these men that atheism does not simply reject morality. In this instance, it is the foundation for a Christlike morality, paradoxical as this may sound. Ethical atheism was a pillar of existentialism. One finds it in the characters that Camus and Malraux created. The geography of atheism was thus the geography of morality and so an antidote to the nihilism of Nazism. In *The Plague,* the atheist, like Jesus, pays for his morality with his life. He contracts and dies of the plague. This is not death with the promise of an eternity in paradise. If Camus did not relinquish the morality of Jesus, he could no longer believe the promise of immortality. Death means the eternal silence of the grave, a view that one finds in Malraux, Sartre, and several other existentialists. *The Plague* thus presents a single geography of life and death because all life ends in death.

Christopher Cumo

Further Reading

Other French writers whose works are inspired by philosophy and imbued with elements of nihilism, existentialism, or the avant-garde include Jean-Paul Sartre, André Gide, André Malraux, Jean Cocteau, and Simone de Beauvoir.

Bibliography

Garrett, Laurie. *The Coming Plague: Newly Emerging Diseases in a World Out of Balance.* New York: Farrar, Straus and Giroux, 1995.

Kasbarian, John Antranig. "Mapping Edward Said: Geography, Identity, and the Politics of Location." *Environment and Planning D: Society and Space* 14, no. 5 (1996): 529–57. doi:10.1068/d140529.

Pratt, Mary L. "Mapping Ideology: Gide, Camus, and Algeria." *College Literature* 8, no. 2 (1981): 158–74. www.jstor.org/stable/25111385.
Tally, Robert T., Jr., ed. *Geocritical Explorations: Space, Place, and Mapping in Literary and Cultural Studies.* New York: Palgrave Macmillan, 2011.
Twidle, Hedley. "The Sea Close By: The Coastal Diaries of Albert Camus, Athol Fugard and Stephen Watson." *Alternation,* Special Edition 6 (2013): 29–67.
West, John K. "Political or Personal: The Role of the Chenoua Landscape in Camus's La Mort Heureuse." *The French Review* 73, no. 5 (2000): 834–44. www.jstor.org/stable/398293.

Poe, Edgar Allan

Edgar Allan Poe was a 19th-century American writer who is considered a pioneer of the horror genre. Although Poe lived in many different cities in the United States (born in Boston, and lived in Richmond, Philadelphia, New York, and Baltimore, among others), his work rarely features settings that are recognizably American. Instead, the places where his plots happen often conjure up an aura of old Europe to underscore the ways in which older traditions are either falling away or are being revived in sometimes perverted ways in the New World. Some critics associate Poe generally with Romanticism, but he is perhaps better known in terms of the Gothic, which is a literary movement whose works explore mysticism, the supernatural, and the darker recesses of the human psyche. Many of his stories involve dark spaces underground, such as basements, tombs, or crypts, where his characters are often buried, sometimes while still alive. Poe is fascinated by the meeting point between life and death.

DEATH AND DUNGEONS IN POE'S SHORT STORIES

"The Pit and the Pendulum" is a short story set in Toledo, Spain, during the time of the Spanish Inquisition, a religious inquest to identify and punish heretics in

Edgar Allan Poe was born in Massachusetts, moved to Virginia, and lived for a brief time in Maryland. There are landmarks commemorating his legacy in Boston, Providence, Richmond, and Baltimore. (Library of Congress)

the Catholic religion, a type of "religious cleansing" that represented intolerance toward people of other faiths. Poe makes no attempt at any historical accuracy in this work, as nothing like the prison he describes existed at the time, but he takes liberties with the concrete details to convey to readers the emotional impact of being subject to torture during the Inquisition. The story opens with a man being falsely tried, convicted, and sentenced to death. Breaks in scenes occur every time the man faints. When he comes to, he thinks he is in a tomb but discovers that it is a cell. In exploring the confines of the dark space, the man nearly falls into a deep pit. After fainting, he wakes up strapped to a device. From the ceiling, a bladed pendulum is descending and swinging closer and closer to his body. The man manages to escape by smearing food onto the ropes that bind him and enticing rats to chew through the strands. Then, the walls become hot and begin moving in to force him to the center of the room and into the pit. However, French troops invade Spain and he is pulled out of his cell. This story is more straightforward than many of Poe's works as there is almost no supernatural element in it, with the exception of some of the coincidences in the story, which may suggest some supernatural element of protection over the protagonist (he is first saved from falling in the pit when he trips over the rags he is wearing and he is on the verge of again being jettisoned into the pit when a hand reaches out and saves him). However, the Gothic element that exists has to do with the minds that devised such torture devices as part of the Inquisition and the fear that others had been killed in that space by the same devices that were about to be used against him. Although these particular torture methods did not exist, many new ways of inflicting pain on the human body resulted as part of the trials during this dark period in history. The threat of pain in this story makes it compelling: the suspense of waiting as the pendulum slowly descends and our narrator continues telling us the minutiae of his situation. Poe crafts a narrator who is hyperaware of sensory input: he narrates in vivid detail every sound, the light and texture of the prison cell, and even the sensation of rats crawling over his body. Mapping the space of his cell in the dark is a gruesome endeavor that helps to catalog every sensory input that contributes to the protagonist's fear. The darkness and his fear give him an impression of the dungeon as being larger and more irregularly shaped than it is when he sees it in the light and notices that what he thought were wall angles were really chains and other metal accessories related to prisoner restraint.

Poe's short story "The Cask of Amontillado" achieves a similar step-by-step narration, like in "The Pit and the Pendulum," of an atrocity about to occur. "The Cask of Amontillado" is set in an Italian city during carnival, a yearly festival before the time of Lenten fasting. Montresor, the narrator, decides to enact revenge on one of his rivals, Fortunato. Like many of the victims in Poe's stories, Fortunato is buried alive by being walled up in catacombs after being lured underground with the promise of sampling a rare vintage of wine. In this story, the place of burial is not a tomb but an expansive wine cellar far beneath a house. The details of the exchange between the men center around Montresor's feelings of superiority over Fortunato in setting this trap for him, even though the latter has enjoyed greater success in society, perhaps because of his connections with the Masons. Montresor narrates feeling a slight pang of guilt after he finishes sealing up the wall, as if he were almost not sure that he could go through with his plan. Some of the most dynamic moments of this story involve moving through the dark, damp space of the catacombs underneath Montresor's house and his ability to leverage aspects of Fortunato's personality in such a way as to get the latter to voluntarily follow him to his death.

Many critics have debated how European settings function in the work of Edgar Allan Poe. Some believe that he set out to demonstrate the "skeletons in the closet" of our European ancestors, exposing the history of their aristocracies as filled with insanity and violence. He often portrays Americans as failing, despite trying, to distance themselves from such a tradition, as if he were worried that the sins of our forefathers followed them across the Atlantic as they immigrated to America.

Although there is no cellar crypt in "The Tell-Tale Heart," in this story a psychopath's victim is buried under the floorboards of a house. In recounting the methodical manner in which he murdered and dismembered the man he lived with (who is possibly an older male family member or an employer), the unnamed narrator's purpose is to prove that he is not insane. He hopes to accomplish this also through the logical and dispassionate manner in which he tells the story. He claims that he had to kill the man because of he had a deformed eye, with a film over it, making it resemble, he says, a vulture's eye. He goes into the man's bedroom seven nights in a row and shines a flashlight onto the eye. On the eighth night, the man wakes up to the flashlight and now, seeing the eye open, the narrator smothers him in his bed. After he hides the man's body under the floorboards, the police show up to ask him questions because a neighbor reported some noise. Confident that they do not suspect him, he offers the policemen seats over the spot where he has entombed his victim. However, as they chat pleasantly, the narrator begins to hear what he believes is the beating of the old man's heart. He cracks and confesses to the crime. This short story is a variation of Poe's favorite theme of burying someone alive: although the man is indeed dead, because of the narrator's insanity, he believes the man's heart is still beating.

"The Masque of the Red Death" is a highly symbolic tale that relies on the event of a masquerade ball to hide the identity of an intruder. Although the countryside is suffering a plague, Prince Prospero gathers the members of the nobility into his castle and seals it shut. There, thinking themselves safe, they eat and drink without worry. One night, Prince Prospero throws a masquerade ball to entertain his guests. He decorates seven rooms of his castle in different colors. Poe describes the castle's structure as particularly well fortified. In fact, after the guests are inside the gates, they weld all the bolts shut behind them. The layout of this castle conforms to Poe's fantastical—as opposed to realistic—approach to architecture throughout his writing. He is unconcerned with the details of history or design. Instead, his descriptions of the interior space of the castle in "The Masque of the Red Death" are of what he calls "irregular" and "bizarre" rooms that twist and turn like a maze. The seven rooms where the ball is being held are decorated with rich tapestries and stained-glass windows. Each chamber is color-coordinated as follows, moving in an east-to-west orientation: blue, purple, green, orange, white, violet, and black. Although the last room's draperies are black velvet, the stained-glass windows were red. None of the other rooms contain any furniture or fixtures, but the last room houses a large clock, whose hourly chimes interrupt the gaiety of the partygoers. Critics read this color symbolism as representative of the stages of life from infancy through old age, the black of the final room representing the darkness of the grave. Amid the revelry, Prince Prospero notices a masquerader who has dressed like someone dying from the Red Death. He is outraged and offended at the impropriety of such a costume. He follows the figure through the chambers and finally dies. When the rest of the partygoers grab the figure, there is nothing under the clothing. They all die of the Red Death they had thought they could cheat. The character of the Red Death here, in having no physical body, is a symbol, and the meaning of the story is that death comes for us all; there is no escape, no matter how much money or power one has. In this story, Poe is using an age-old idea in literature that death is the great equalizer: pauper and prince (and everyone in between) succumb to the grave.

HAUNTED INTERIOR SPACES

In his literary works, Poe sometimes features European settings, but these are not thriving environments. In "The Fall of the House of Usher," Roderick and Madeline Usher live in a house that is crumbling and that eventually is swallowed by the earth. As a part of the literary movement known as the American Renaissance, Poe's literary goals were to contribute to a sense of American literature as distinct from the European literary tradition. Poe's European settings are in line with these goals because they offer critiques of "ancient tradition" as unhealthy and passé.

"Ligeia" is a short story by Poe in which the main character's wife, Ligeia, dies. Prior to her death, she had asserted to her husband her belief that by willpower a human being could avoid death. The narrator notices strange occurrences after his wife's death, suggesting that her spirit lingers on. The narrator remarries, and his new wife, the Lady Rowena, shortly becomes gravely ill. It is difficult to discern, as the narrator admits to ingesting opium, but he thinks he witnesses a ghostly presence poisoning his new wife's drink. Lady Rowena dies, but as she is being preparing for burial she seems to come back to life. At one point, after the narrator has been trying to revive her, the formerly deceased Rowena stands up and walks. As her burial shroud drops, it is revealed to be Ligeia. This story traffics in the unreliable narrator, so the unfolding of the plot could easily be an opium-induced dream on the part of our protagonist. Because the majority of the action takes place only in one room in a house, the bridal chamber, the trappings of the room and our narrator's sensibility of it is very important. Many of Poe's stories are confined to a limited interior space, which helps increase the suspense of his fantastical plots. Like many of the other descriptions of interior architecture in his works, the room in Ligeia is irregular in shape ("pentagonal"), with vaulted ceilings, and is located in a high recess of a castle-like structure. His descriptions of the castle's exterior, with its ivy and trelliswork, are inspired by Romanticism. Poe's narrators sometimes doubt their senses when it comes to brushes with the supernatural: this can be due to drug or alcohol consumption, but it also has to do with the play of light around darkly lit interior spaces or the drafty nature of such spaces. Both in "The Fall of the House of Usher" and in "Ligeia," the narrators keep trying to assure themselves that all is well and that the movements of draperies are just from drafts and that the sense of a presence in the castle or the room is merely due to the way the light is reflecting off the angles of the walls. The poem "Annabel Lee" follows the same theme as in "Ligeia": the untimely death of a beautiful young woman. Poe's own wife died tragically at an early age from tuberculosis.

"The Raven" is one of Poe's most read and quoted works. In this poem, a young man is reading by firelight when a raven wanders into his room. Like in other works by Poe, the decorations of the room are described in great detail: there are heavy draperies, velvet cushions, and a bust of Pallas (the goddess of wisdom in the Greek pantheon). The young man's love, Lenore, has recently died, and he begins to suspect that the raven is a messenger from the afterlife. The trick is that, although the raven can speak, he seems to only know one word, "Nevermore." Therefore, it is very important what questions the narrator asks and how he asks them. Essentially, the narrator manifests his own message, which is that he believes he will never see Lenore again. Poe, who is known for his contributions to Gothic literature, explores the darker recesses of the human psyche by showing the narrator's devastation and loss of hope after his true love passed away. He infuses this work, as he does many of his works, with an element of the supernatural, but readers are left to ponder whether the bird is truly something supernatural or whether the narrator's sorrow has caused a complete descent into madness that causes him to have a skewed perspective on reality.

Lynn Marie Houston

Further Reading

H. P. Lovecraft is another author of horror, but his stories are often in the realm of science fiction. In his work *The Thing on the Doorstep,* he includes numerous fantastical tales, including one about a young man who shot his friend six times. Like may of Poe's narrators, this narrator is also unreliable. In fact, the young man in Lovecraft's work wants to tell his story with the purpose of proving his innocence, just like the narrator of Poe's "The Tell-Tale Heart." Arthur Conan Doyle's *The Adventures of Sherlock Holmes* also deals with noir subjects and plots that often include the same heightened suspense that Poe creates in his works.

Bibliography

Ascari, M., and S. Knight, eds. *From the Sublime to City Crime.* Monaco: Liberfaber, 2015.

Forbes, Erin E. "Edgar Allan Poe and the Great Dismal Swamp: Reading Race and Environment after the Aesthetic Turn." *Modern Philology* 114, no. 2 (2016): 359–87.

Garcia, Patrícia. "The Fantastic of Place and the Fantastic of Space: Two Models of Transgression." *Letras & Letras* 28, no. 2 (2013).

Grumberg, Karen. "Gothic Temporalities and Insecure Sanctuaries in Lea Goldberg's *The Lady of the Castle* and Edgar Allan Poe's 'Masque of the Red Death.'" *Comparative Literature* 68, no. 4 (2016): 408–26.

Hsu, Hsuan L. *Geography and the Production of Space in Nineteenth-Century American Literature.* Cambridge, UK: Cambridge University Press, 2010.

May, Whitney Shylee. "The Influence of Place on Identity in Poe's 'Morella' and 'William Wilson.'" *The Edgar Allan Poe Review* 18, no. 2 (2017): 218–33.

Riddel, Joseph N. "The 'Crypt' of Edgar Poe." *Boundary* 2 (1979): 117–44.

Rigal-Aragón, Margarita, and José Manuel Correoso-Rodenas. "Poe's Spaces and the Following." *Studia Neophilologica* 89, no. 1 (2017): 14–33.

Roeger, Tyler. "The Ocean and the Urban: Poe's 'The Oblong Box.'" *Atlantic Studies* 13, no. 2 (2016): 227–48.

Schueller, Malini Johar. "Harems, Orientalist Subversions, and the Crisis of Nationalism: The Case of Edgar Allan Poe and 'Ligeia.'" *Criticism* 37, no. 4 (1995): 601–23.

Senf, Carol. "The Evolution of Gothic Spaces: Ruins, Forests, Urban Jungles." In *Dracula*, edited by M. M. Crişan, 259–74. Cham, Switzerland: Palgrave Macmillan, 2017.

Szabo, Lucian-Vasile, and Marius-Mircea Crişan. "'Bloodthirsty and Remorseless Fangs': Representation of East-Central Europe in Edgar Allan Poe's Gothic Short Stories." In *Dracula*, edited by M. M. Crişan, 53–68. Cham, Switzerland: Palgrave Macmillan, 2017.

Tally, Robert T., Jr. "The Poetics of Descent: Irreversible Narrative in Poe's 'MS. Found in a Bottle.'" In *Studies in Irreversibility: Texts and Contexts*, edited by Benjamin Schreier, 83–98. Newcastle-upon-Tyne: Cambridge Scholars, 2007.

Taylor, Matthew A. "The Nature of Fear: Edgar Allan Poe and Posthuman Ecology." *American Literature* 84, no. 2 (2012): 353–79.

Vanderbilt, Kermit. "Art and Nature in 'The Masque of the Red Death.'" *Nineteenth-Century Fiction* 22, no. 4 (1968): 379–89.

Wisker, Gina. "Behind Locked Doors: Angela Carter, Horror and the Influence of Edgar Allan Poe." In *Re-visiting Angela Carter,* edited by R. Munford, 178–98. London: Palgrave Macmillan, 2006.

Wright, Tom F. "Edgar Allan Poe and the Southern Gothic." In *The Palgrave Handbook of the Southern Gothic,* edited by Susan Castillo Street and Charles Crow, 9–20. London: Palgrave Macmillan, 2016.

Zanger, Jules. "The City from the Inside: Poe's Urban Fiction." *Journal of the Fantastic in the Arts* 3, no. 2 (10) (1991): 29–36.

The Poisonwood Bible

Barbara Kingsolver conducted extensive research for her novel *The Poisonwood Bible,* which tells the story of the Price family—Nathan, Orleanna, and their four daughters Rachel, Leah, Adah, and Ruth May—as they leave the United States to live as missionaries in Africa, and become embroiled in the colonial politics of the Congo. She consulted numerous historical texts and literary works set in Zaire throughout various time periods. These sources, combined with her own experiences traveling in other African nations, helped her to write a novel that is critical of Western involvement in the Belgian-occupied Congo from the 1950s to the 1990s.

The novel contains seven different "books," many of which have biblical references in their titles. Events are narrated from different perspectives provided by the different characters in the story. In addition to being about the effects of past colonization on the trajectory of an African region, *The Poisonwood Bible* is also about how the Price family unravels as some of them come to understand that the Christian missionary work that sent them to that area serves as a neocolonial influence.

A BIBLICAL PLACE

In *The Poisonwood Bible,* the African country of Zaire becomes a modern-day Eden for a short time to the Price family. Like the Biblical landscape, Zaire is lush and fertile. Also, similar to the story in Genesis is the existence of evil in the garden in the form of a snake. The snake acts as a complex symbol in *The Poisonwood Bible*. It is the opposing force to Christianity, embodying the local spirituality, and a tool by which to counter colonialism. For instance, the local witch doctor attempts to gain back power in the story by placing venomous snakes in the huts of anyone who counters him and supports the new values brought by the Prices. This is how Ruth May dies, bitten by a green mamba.

Nathan Price, a Baptist preacher, enters a precarious position when he shows up as a missionary in Africa, just as the influence of the white colonizers and their religion wanes. The God of Christianity, as brought to the locals by Nathan Price, is a god of vengeance and destruction. However, the local view, as spoken by Brother Fowles, sees God in nature—the cycle of life and death, in which redemption is possible. The conflict between these two worldviews fuels the strife of the region, eventually making it unsafe.

COLONIALISM AND PLACE/MAPPING

The Price family is living in an area affected by Patrice Lumumba's revolution. The names of towns and countries (in the formerly Belgian-occupied Congo) were changed to indigenous words to reclaim local independence away from colonial influence. The names of towns derived from or given European rulers were changed. From the perspective of Leah Price, who knew these areas by their previous names, these places were erased from the map. The towns and waterways she used to use to orient herself in a place no longer existed.

After the girls go their separate ways and leave their father behind in Africa, the name "Congo" changes to Zaire. When the women of the Price family travel back to that region 30 years after they had initially arrived, they are told that there is no such town as "Kilanga." In Kingsolver's narrative, Ruth May's spirit lingers on after her death, and she continues to inhabit the land, blessing her mother and sisters when they travel back, despite the confusion of names or abandonment of the town. Even though the area may lack a name or have changed names, the fact that Kingsolver writes that Ruth May's consciousness persists in that space attests to the fact that the essential characteristics of place do not change, and that even Anglos who journey there remain a part of the landscape.

Anatole, one of the African locals whom Leah Price befriends (and later marries), has never seen a map of the whole world, let alone a globe, even though he is a schoolteacher. When Leah offers to teach the local students geography, he declines, stating that they would think she was lying about the Earth being round. Kingsolver's character development in relation to place points out many of the details of countries struggling to find their identity apart from colonialism and outside influence.

Other issues in the book relate to erroneous names. At one point, Reverend Price mistranslates the word *precious* into Kikongo when he is trying to communicate the centrality of Jesus and his teachings to Christian dogma. Instead, he tells the local natives that "Jesus is poisonwood." Poisonwood is a local tree that creates a rash on skin when touched. This mistranslation is eerily accurate for the natives because they feel that Christianity has poisoned much of their land and culture.

Reverend Price is just the latest version of colonizer. Early in the novel, we see him attempt to beat the wildness of Africa into submission by taking the jungle and making of it an ordered garden, but he fails when he ignores the advice of the locals to avoid the poisonwood tree and to plant his seeds in mounds so that they aren't washed away by the heavy rains.

THE HEART OF DARKNESS

Like in any literary work about Africa that positions it as a colonized place, Africa is the continent of darkness. It is featured as such in Conrad's classic novel *The Heart of Darkness,* and it is also portrayed in this manner in *The Poisonwood Bible*. Although the tendency is to see the continent as dark because of the skin color of its indigenous people, Kingsolver emphasizes that the darkness is related to the lushness and hostility of the landscape. Tree canopies of multiple layers will keep sunlight from touching the ground, creating an unnatural darkness even during the daytime. This is what is referred to as "the bush," and it can be dangerous, causing characters to lose their way, or it can be helpful if characters need to hide. Like Conrad's *Heart of Darkness,* much of this book is about understanding oneself in the world in terms of the haves or have-nots of the colonial power dynamic.

FLORA AND FAUNA

In *The Poisonwood Bible,* Kingsolver describes the environment as the meeting point of life and death that drives her plot and character development. From the opening paragraph of the novel, she asks readers to picture an overgrown forest "filled with life: delicate, poisonous frogs . . . seedlings . . . sucking life out of death." Many flora and fauna serve as powerful elements in the text. For example, at one point, the village is attacked by a massive ant horde. The ants sweep through, eating everything in their path. Kingsolver's description of their attack emphasizes both the horror and the beauty: their destruction is a like a forest wildfire that clears away the dead trees to make way for new growth.

Humans belong to this ecosystem, too. As the Price family struggles to live in the African environment, they squeeze each other like vines competing for sunlight. The ultimate sin in this novel is one that the Price family doesn't see until they have already come undone: the sin of pride, of hubris, their neocolonial determination to have "dominion over every creature that moved upon the earth." One of the specific scenes in which this is illustrated is when Nathan Price shows his ignorance of the hazards of the local environment by suggesting that, on Easter, they baptize the children of the village in the river. The townspeople reject the idea and think poorly of Price and his religion because he has not accounted for the dangerous crocodiles that live in the river and that would likely kill the children if they were brought there.

At least two competing views of nature exist in the novel: Adah's and Brother Fowles. Adah is the voice of hard science, who believes that nature needs to be studied and understood so that humans can stay safe against it. Fowles believes that nature is animated by a spiritual force. In his view, the natural world is proof of God's existence and proof that life wins out in the end over destruction. Orleanna is sympathetic to Fowles's worldview. Kingsolver demonstrates this by taking us along with Orleanna on her hikes around the African countryside and also through her passion for gardening. Here we see an embrace of pantheism that finds God in the forces of nature and celebration of local place.

THE PLACE OF WOMEN

Throughout the novel, Nathan Price attempts, and fails, to maintain control over the land of Africa, the people in his congregation, and the women in his home. Orleanna Price's time in Africa reveals to her a strength she didn't previously acknowledge she had. As her husband is more concerned with matters of his religion, particularly enforcing women's submission to men, he is often oblivious to the very real and physical danger that all of them are in. Mirroring the vote for African independence over colonial rule, Orleanna begins to assert more authority over her household to stand up and protect her daughter's lives; however, her rebellion against her husband happens too late to save Ruth May. It culminates in her taking her children away from Nathan and abandoning him, and eventually becoming active in the civil rights movement back in the United States. The three surviving daughters all grow into successful women: Rachel runs a hotel in the French Congo, Leah marries Anatole and starts a family with him (they are both part of a political resistance movement), and Adah attends medical school at Emory University.

COLONIALISM AND THE HAUNTED LANDSCAPE

In the last chapter of the novel, Ruth May becomes part of the landscape in a transformation brought about by death. Arriving in the African landscape prompted a desire in Ruth May to merge with the landscape. Kingsolver's plot fulfills this the way readers might expect of a magical realist novel.

She describes her perspective of the events that happen from a point of view that would situate her among the trees. One way to read the ending of the novel is that Kingsolver is using the soul's existence in the afterlife as a metaphor for a colonial relationship with the African environment. In her death, Ruth May is an unfortunate victim of the indigenous peoples' attempts to hold on to their land and culture. However, ultimately, she lives on in the landscape, which is accessible and welcoming. In some ways, this is a comforting way to animate the natural environment with human personality in a way that sustains it. In other ways, this is the colonizer's fantasy—he or she may not escape death in a faraway land, but the place welcome his or her spirit after death. By the end of the book, Leah Price admits that in emotional and symbolic ways, each member of the family, living or dead, left parts of themselves buried in the African soil.

Lynn Marie Houston

Further Reading

Other women writers who investigate the intersection between religion, patriarchy, and colonialism in their works are Toni Morrison, Ann Patchett, Anne Lamott, and Amy Tan. Another award-winning coming-of-age novel set in Africa is *Nervous Conditions* by Zimbabwean author Tsitsi Dangarembga.

Bibliography

Becker, Lindsey A. "'As Wide as the World': Examining and Overcoming American Neo-Imperialism in Three Novels." Antonian Scholars Honors Program, 10 (2012). sophia.stkate.edu/shas_honors/10.

Bodner, Kate H. "Journeys of Locatedness in *The Poisonwood Bible* and *A Thousand Acres*." Honors thesis, Wesleyan University, 2017.

Jacobs, J. U. "Translating the 'Heart of Darkness' Cross-Cultural Discourse in the Contemporary Congo Book." *Current Writing: Text and Reception in Southern Africa* 14, no. 2 (2002): 103–17.

Jacobson, Kristin J. "The Neodomestic American Novel: The Politics of Home in Barbara Kingsolver's *The Poisonwood Bible*." *Tulsa Studies in Women's Literature* 24, no. 1 (2005): 105–27.

Meire, Héloïse. "Women, a Dark Continent?: *The Poisonwood Bible* as a Feminist Response to Conrad's *Heart of Darkness*." In *Seeds of Change: Critical Essays on Barbara Kingsolver,* edited by Priscilla Gay Leder, 71–86. Knoxville: University of Tennessee Press, 2010.

Strehle, Susan. "Chosen People: American Exceptionalism in Kingsolver's *The Poisonwood Bible*." *Critique: Studies in Contemporary Fiction* 49, no. 4 (2008): 413–29.

Pride and Prejudice

Pride and Prejudice is a novel of manners in the "marriage plot" tradition of 19th-century women's literature. Written by Jane Austen, it chronicles the two love interests of Elizabeth Bennet and her attempts to decide which one is the better man. Wickham is a dashing military officer whose prospects seem unclear, while Darcy is the owner of a wealthy estate who seems to have few social skills. Given first impressions alone, Elizabeth favors Wickham over Darcy; however, over the course of the novel, she learns that judging people's characters too quickly can be a mistake.

Elizabeth's sisters also face their own romantic quandaries. Jane falls for a rich bachelor, Charles Bingley, but after Mrs. Bennet and the younger Bennet girls behave in an uncouth manner at a ball, he is persuaded by his family and Darcy to believe that Jane is too far beneath him and doesn't really care about him. To try to put her closer to fashionable society, the family sends her to visit her aunt and uncle in London. In the meanwhile, Darcy falls in love with Elizabeth, who rejects him when he proposes marriage. Darcy sets out to win Elizabeth over by correcting the ways in which he has injured her family, for instance, by convincing Bingley that Jane really does care for him. This leads Bingley to propose marriage to Jane, which she accepts. After Wickham runs off with Elizabeth's younger sister, Lydia, Elizabeth discovers that Wickham's story about Darcy ruining his prospects in life were a falsehood. Instead, Wickham had been trying to extort Darcy's family through various means. He finally accomplishes his scheme by requesting to be paid off for marrying Lydia so as to save the reputation of the other Bennet girls. Mr. Darcy contributes to this payment out of guilt for not being more transparent about the danger Wickham represented. Elizabeth realizes that she loves Darcy for who he is and is able to convince her father to let her accept his marriage proposal.

GENDERED LAWS REGARDING OWNERSHIP OF LAND

Mr. and Mrs. Bennet find themselves in dire circumstances to marry off their daughters to suitable spouses because of property laws in England at the time that dictated that women could not hold property. Because they had no sons, when Mr. Bennet dies, the house the women live in will pass to a male cousin, who, if he so desires, could turn the women out into the street. Therefore, to be truly secure, they must find homes of their own through marriage. In an attempt to retain control of the house, Mrs. Bennet tries to match Elizabeth and the cousin who will inherit the house, Mr. Collins. Elizabeth is appalled by his dull and demeaning character. She rejects the notion of marrying for financial security instead of love.

GENDERED SPACE

Elizabeth defies traditional gender notions in many ways for the time Austen was writing. Elizabeth refuses to see herself or other women as commodities in the marriage trade, a power grab for land and money. She also dares to cultivate her own opinions and express herself. She also insists on doing many things by herself and having her own intimate experiences of the world: for instance, she prefers to walk around the countryside rather than take a carriage.

Elizabeth's insistence on occupying an outdoor space without assistance is one of the most powerful commentaries on place in the novel. Women were seen as belonging to the interior spaces of the home, while men frequently cross the boundaries of the domestic space into the exterior world, whether for business or sport. Elizabeth's character is written as rebellious due to the ways in which she inhabits exterior space, the space of nature. She walks unaccompanied and is laughed at by Caroline Bingley when she shows up to their estate with mud on the hem of her dress from walking across the moors. Elizabeth, at least on one occasion, extols the virtues of pursuing a relationship with nature over pursuing romantic relationships with men.

THE BALLROOM AS CULTURAL SIGNIFIER

The interior space of the ballroom is a site of important events in the novel. This space is where courtship is conducted publically, and often a space that determines the ruin or salvation of whole families. During a set of dancing, couples would often have the opportunity to talk more intimately than anywhere else. But the rules of Victorian dancing culture were strict—after being formally introduced, men would invite a woman to dance and the woman could not turn him down unless she had already promised the dance to a partner ahead of time. It is in a ballroom at the Lucas's that Elizabeth first meets Mr. Darcy and is rejected by him. During another

In this 1894 line drawing, George Allen illustrates the scene at the ball in *Pride and Prejudice* where Elizabeth hears Mr. Darcy insult her while speaking to Mr. Bingley. Much of the plot conflict and character development in this Austen novel happens during social scenes in interior spaces. (Archive.org)

ball, one at Netherfield Hall, they finally dance together and realize a mutual attraction. At this latter dance, Mr. Bingley is swayed by his party to give up on Jane because of the bad behavior of her mother and sisters. Also at the Netherfield ball, we see Elizabeth upset with Mr. Collins who asks her to dance when she was hoping, instead, to dance with Mr. Wickham. The way men and women danced said much about their esteem in Victorian society. Mr. Collins is an embarrassment to Elizabeth because he dances so poorly. The ballroom is one of the most important interior spaces in the novel because it is the place where one's value and standing in the community is broadcast.

Lynn Marie Houston

Further Reading

Readers who enjoy *Pride and Prejudice* often enjoy novels written by the Brontë sisters, which often feature a plot where a female protagonist has to choose between two suitors: *Wuthering Heights* and *Jane Eyre* are two in particular. The Brontës were writing in England around the same time as Jane Austen.

Bibliography

Baker, Alan R. H., and Mark Billinge. "Cultural Constructions of England's Geography and History." In *Geographies of England: The North-South Divide, Material and Imagined.* Cambridge, UK: Cambridge University Press, 2004.

Barchas, Janine. *Matters of Fact in Jane Austen: History, Location, and Celebrity.* Baltimore: Johns Hopkins University Press, 2012.

Batey, Mavis. *Jane Austen and the English Landscape.* London: Barn Elms, 1996.

Bodenheimer, Rosemarie. "Looking at the Landscape in Jane Austen." *Studies in English Literature, 1500–1900* 21, no. 4 (1981): 605–23.

Brantlinger, Patrick. "Empire, Place, and the Victorians." In *The Oxford Handbook of Victorian Literary Culture,* edited by Juliet John. Oxford, UK: Oxford University Press, 2016.

Clark, Robert. *Jane Austen's Geographies.* New York: Routledge, 2017.

Crang, Mike. "Placing Stories, Performing Places: Spatiality in Joyce and Austen." *Anglia-Zeitschrift für englische Philologie* 126, no. 2 (2008): 312–29.

Curry, Mary Jane. "'Not a Day Went by without a Solitary Walk': Elizabeth's Pastoral World." *Persuasions: The Jane Austen Journal* 22 (2000): 175.

Gilligan, Kathleen E. "Jane Austen's Unnamed Character: Exploring Nature in *Pride and Prejudice* (2005)." *Inquiries Journal* 3, no. 12 (2011).

Handler, Richard, and Daniel Alan Segal. *Jane Austen and the Fiction of Culture: An Essay on the Narration of Social Realities.* Lanham, MD: Rowman & Littlefield, 1999.

Herbert, David. "Place and Society in Jane Austen's England." *Geography* 76, no. 3 (1991): 193–208.

Heydt, Jill. "First Impressions and Later Recollections: The Place of the Picturesque in *Pride and Prejudice*." *Studies in the Humanities* 12, no. 2 (1985).

Miller, Kathleen Ann. "Haunted Heroines: The Gothic Imagination and the Female Bildungsromane of Jane Austen, Charlotte Brontë, and LM Montgomery." *The Lion and the Unicorn* 34, no. 2 (2010): 125–47.

Shands, Kerstin W. "Embracing Space: Endings and Beginnings." In *Embracing Space: Spatial Metaphors in Feminist Discourse.* Westport, CT: Greenwood Press, 1999.

Vuong, Jennifer Michele. "Pride and Prejudice & the English Landscape-the Importance of the Picturesque to the Novel." PhD diss., Georgetown University, 2014.

Wenner, Barbara Britton. *Prospect and Refuge in the Landscape of Jane Austen.* London: Routledge, 2016.

Wilson, Cheryl A. "Dance, Physicality, and Social Mobility in Jane Austen's Persuasion." *Persuasions* 25 (2003): 55–75.

R

A Raisin in the Sun

A Raisin in the Sun by Lorraine Hansberry takes place in Chicago's South Side during the 1950s. The title is a line from a Langston Hughes poem, "Harlem," that asks what becomes of a dream that has to be given up. In Hansberry's play, an extended family dreams of leaving their small apartment to live in a house outside of the ghetto. Hansberry explores what it costs an African American family to dream of having a living space in which they can take pride and have room to grow and pursue the activities that are meaningful to them.

HOME AND THE CULTURAL GEOGRAPHY OF BELONGING

When Mama Lena's husband dies, she knows they will be getting a life insurance check for $10,000, enough money to help her family achieve some of their dreams. Her son, Walter, has no sense for business while her daughter-in-law works long hours as a housekeeper and is pregnant again with their second child. Their first born, Travis, lives with them, as does Mama Lena's other child, Beneatha. Three generations all occupy a small, two-bedroom apartment. Travis sleeps on the couch in the living room, a situation that often tires him out for school if anyone is in the living room late or comes home after his bedtime. The bathroom they use is located in the hall and is shared with a neighbor. In addition, Mama Lena tends to the plant she keeps outside over her sink, dreaming of a house with a yard in the sun so that she can garden.

The space of the apartment reflects the tension in the family. After Ruth finds out that she is pregnant again, she contemplates terminating the pregnancy because she doesn't see how they could fit another person in the apartment and she doesn't think they have enough money for a bigger place. This is the point in the drama when Mama Lena uses part of the life insurance money as a down payment on a house.

However, Walter's dream is to own his own business and become rich. He puts pressure on Mama to give him the money so that he can "be the man" of the house. She relents and gives him the rest of the money, but tells him to save $3,000 for Beneatha's education. He loses all of the money in a business transaction that goes wrong. The family thinks that their dreams of a better future are lost.

Meanwhile, a subplot to this larger quest for home is Beneatha's choice between two suitors: George and Joseph. George is from a wealthy African American family, and he looks down on Beneatha's family because of their class status. Joseph is from a village in Nigeria, and he tries to get Beneatha to understand and embrace her African heritage. Just as her family searches for a space to call home, Beneatha is searching for her cultural roots and a sense of belonging. She eventually accepts a marriage proposal from Joseph and makes plans to practice medicine with him in Nigeria.

RACE AND REAL ESTATE

A member of the homeowner's association pays the Younger family a visit. They are willing to pay them back all of the money that Walter lost, if they will agree not to move to the neighborhood, which we learn is all white. Mama Lena's decision to buy a house in a white neighborhood came from simple economics: it was the only house that had what she wanted at a price she could afford. At first, Walter pleads with Mama to accept the deal, but later changes his mind and finally becomes "a man" in the eyes of his family when he refuses to sell out to the racist organization that wants to keep them out of their neighborhood because of their race.

Although there was no such neighborhood as Clybourne Park, it is modeled after the Washington Park subdivision, the mostly white neighborhood where Hansberry's family moved when she was young. Members of the white community tried to force Hansberry's family out of their house through violence and also legal action. However, the Hansberrys won the right to stay in their home.

Lynn Marie Houston

Further Reading

If you enjoyed this play by Lorraine Hansberry, another play by an African American author you might like is *Fences* by August Wilson, which depicts the struggle of an African American man against racism and poverty. Bruce Norris has also written a play, called *Clybourne Park,* inspired by the setting of Hansberry's original work.

Bibliography

Avilez, GerShun. "Housing the Black Body: Value, Domestic Space, and Segregation Narratives." *African American Review* 42, no. 1 (2008): 135–47.

Gordon, Michelle. "'Somewhat Like War': The Aesthetics of Segregation, Black Liberation, and *A Raisin in the Sun.*" *African American Review* 42, no. 1 (2008): 121–33.

Gray, Leslie. "A Home You Can't Live in: Performances of the Black Body and Domestic Space in Contemporary Drama." Master's thesis, University of Oregon, 2015.

La'Nisa, S. Kitchiner. "Signifying Structures: Representations of the House in African-American and Black Southern African Women's Writing." PhD diss., Howard University, 2010.

Lipsitz, George. "The Racialization of Space and the Spatialization of Race Theorizing the Hidden Architecture of Landscape." *Landscape Journal* 26, no. 1 (2007): 10–23.

M'Baye, Babacar. "Discrimination and the American Dream in Lorraine Hansberry's *A Raisin in the Sun.*" In *The American Dream,* edited by Harold Bloom and Blake Hobby, 171–86. New York: Bloom's Literary Criticism, 2009.

Naick, Patrick Javaid. *Representations of the Black Metropolis: Place and African American Identity on Chicago's South Side.* Iowa City: University of Iowa, 2009.

Wright, Kristina. "Gaining Ground: The Politics of Place and Space in U.S. Women's Literature and U.S. Culture, 1959–2001." PhD diss., Tufts University, 2011.

The Red Badge of Courage

Stephen Crane's classic novel about the Civil War tells a realistic story about the psychological toll of war on military personnel. Although he never served, Crane gathered firsthand accounts to accurately describe the experience of combat. The details, along with the few place-names mentioned in the novel, have been enough to make military historians believe that Crane based *The Red Badge of Courage* off of the Battle of Chancellorsville (1863). Although the main character, Henry Fleming, is disabused of his romantic notions of war in the first half of the novel, by the end, his experiences of combat become the main inspiration for his sense of self. The natural imagery of the novel follows this double impulse, sometimes symbolizing condemnation of the war and other times affirmation of it.

NATURE'S INDIFFERENCE

The descriptions of the natural landscape often run counter to the plot and to the characters' thoughts and feelings. These images of nature help reinforce the concept, at the beginning of the novel, that war might not be everything that Henry Fleming thinks it will be. A teenage farm boy from upstate New York, Henry is inspired by the tales of war he reads in school to enlist in the 304th New York regiment of the Union Army. Henry soon begins to question his decision, fearing that he does not have the courage it takes to be a good soldier. In conversations with fellow soldiers as they march toward the front lines, none of the others will admit to fear, and Henry feels even worse about his cowardice. In the middle of this intense conflict in his soul, the young boy is surprised that the natural world seems indifferent to his suffering: "As he gazed around him the youth felt a flash of astonishment at the blue, pure sky and the sun gleamings on the trees and fields. It was surprising that Nature had gone tranquilly on with her golden process in the midst of so much devilment." Nature, here, seems to take a similar position as Henry's mother does in the first few pages of the novel: she's not buying into the hype and, instead, gives him a number of practical suggestions. Secretly, of course, Crane shows us that she is worried and perhaps even wishes her son had not decided to go to war. Henry is baffled that neither his mother nor the girls from school praise him for his decision or treat him like a hero.

NATURE'S INVOLVEMENT

Eventually, nature begins to be consumed by the machines of war. Crane's speaker narrates the regiment's first contact with Confederate gunfire, by first describing what it does to the trees around them: "Bullets began to whistle among the branches and nip at the trees. Twigs and leaves came sailing down. It was as if a thousand axes, wee and invisible, were being wielded." This is just moments before Henry deserts, as if Crane has developed his natural images to mimic Henry's experiences. At first, war is merely a hypothetical: will he run or will he fight? Here, for both nature and Henry, war becomes all too real as he witnesses its destruction of life. As he flees the battlefield, he looks to nature for a sign that he is doing the right thing, and he finds one: "This landscape gave him assurance. . . .

Nature had given him a sign. The squirrel, immediately upon recognizing danger, had taken to his legs without ado." Upon sensing danger, the squirrel runs, just like Henry did. After noticing this detail of the natural world, Henry feels momentarily better about his choice. He can tell himself that it was "instinct" and "natural."

NATURE'S REJECTION

However, in the next scene, nature begins to reject Henry's choice by glorifying the soldiers who die in war. As he wanders in the woods, he stumbles on a dead solider whose body is treated with reverence by the forest: "At length he reached a place where the high, arching boughs made a chapel. He softly pushed the green doors aside and entered. Pine needles were a gentle brown carpet. There was a religious half light." By choosing this description, Crane signals a major break in the parallel between Henry's wishes and nature's, where nature begins to put pressure on Henry to return to battle, perhaps speaking as his subconscious self which is plagued by guilt. In fact, when he joins a procession of wounded men, he looks at their wounds and wishes for one of his own, a "red badge of courage." The religious symbolism continues in Crane's depictions of nature. After Henry's friend Jim dies in a field, the narrator comments that "The red sun was pasted in the sky like a wafer." The sun's shape is compared to a Communion wafer, which means that Crane is linking Jim to Jesus, making a martyr out of the soldier who died from his battle wounds. Henry's guilt gets the better of him, and he returns to his regiment.

NATURE'S COMPLICITY

By the denouement of the plot, the natural images in the text seem to help glorify the war and Henry's renewed commitment to it. While watching the battle, Henry finds himself among a group of men retreating. He tries to stop one of the men to ask him a question, but the man hits Henry in the head with his rifle, injuring him. Henry finally has his battle wound, even though he was injured by a soldier from his own side. The wound enables Henry to rejoin his regiment without the loss of his pride.

In the next battle, Henry's regiment is ordered to defend the border of the woods. Finally, he finds his courage and fights hard, earning the respect and admiration of his fellow soldiers as well as his commanders. When Henry and Wilson are sent to get water, they overhear a general saying that the 304th regiment is fighting so poorly that it will be sacrificed, that they are going to put the men at the front of the next battle. Henry takes this as a challenge and vows to be even braver. When they are sent into the charge, Henry saves the regiment's banner after the color-bearer is shot. Many men die, leaving Henry and Wilson to become the noncommissioned leaders of the regiment. When they are charged by the Confederates, Henry's regiment forces them back, eventually taking their flag. Wilson and Henry are considered heroes by many.

After the battle, Henry contemplates his earlier actions. Accepting his earlier, cowardly actions rather than pretend they never happened, he sees himself as a real man who has survived "the red sickness of battle." The natural images seem to endorse this change in Henry's thinking, as the narrator states: "He turned now with a lover's thirst to images of tranquil skies, fresh meadows, cool brooks—an existence of soft and eternal peace . . . Over the river a golden ray of sun came through the hosts of leaden rain clouds." As Henry embraces his destiny and status as a war hero, nature seems to shower him with its bounty as a reward. The descriptions of the weather and the landscape at the end of the novel help to reinforce the romanticized notion that combat is a coming-of-age experience for men.

Lynn Marie Houston

Further Reading

If you enjoyed *The Red Badge of Courage,* you might enjoy other tales of war that aim to address the psychological devastation of combatants, such as Erich Maria Remarque's *All Quiet on the Western Front,* Joseph Heller's *Catch-22,* Kurt Vonnegut's *Slaughterhouse-Five,* or Ernest Hemingway's *A Farewell to Arms.*

Bibliography

Brown, Bill. *The Material Unconscious: American Amusement, Stephen Crane & the Economies of Play.* Cambridge, MA: Harvard University Press, 1996.

Casey, John Anthony, Jr. "Searching for a War of One's Own: Stephen Crane, *The Red Badge of Courage,* and the Glorious Burden of the Civil War Veteran." *American Literary Realism* 44, no. 1 (2011): 1–22.

Cox, James Trammell. "The Imagery of *The Red Badge of Courage.*" *Modern Fiction Studies* 5, no. 3 (1959): 209–19.

Halliburton, David. *The Color of the Sky: A Study of Stephen Crane.* Cambridge, UK: Cambridge University Press, 2008.

Kaplan, Amy. "The Spectacle of War in Crane's Revision of History." *Stephen Crane,* edited by Harold Bloom, 75–102. New York: Bloom's Literary Criticism, 2007.

Kent, Thomas L. "Epistemological Uncertainty in *The Red Badge of Courage.*" *Modern Fiction Studies* 27, no. 4 (1981): 621–28.

Lawson, Andrew. "The Red Badge of Class: Stephen Crane and the Industrial Army." *Literature & History* 14, no. 2 (2005): 53–68.

Marcus, Mordecai, and Erin Marcus. "Animal Imagery in *The Red Badge of Courage.*" *Modern Language Notes* 74, no. 2 (1959): 108–11.

Reynolds, Kirk M. "'The Red Badge of Courage': Private Henry's Mind as Sole Point of View." *South Atlantic Review* 52, no. 1 (1987): 59–69.

Seltzer, Mark. "Wound Culture: Trauma in the Pathological Public Sphere." *October* 80 (1997): 3–26.

Shulman, Robert. "Community, Perception, and the Development of Stephen Crane: From the Red Badge to 'the Open Boat.'" *American Literature* 50, no. 3 (1978): 441–60.

Shulman, Robert. "The Red Badge and Social Violence: Crane's Myth of His America." *Canadian Review of American Studies* 12, no. 1 (1981): 1–20.

Robinson Crusoe

Daniel Defoe's 1719 novel *Robinson Crusoe* is narrated by Crusoe himself, who opens his account with a summary of his early years as a restless and foolhardy young Englishman. Rejecting his father's advice to follow a safe life in business, he runs away to sea instead. Although his first voyage ends in shipwreck, he takes to the sea again on another eventful voyage, and after a long series of adventures finds himself shipwrecked and alone. The bulk of the book describes the physical and emotional struggles Crusoe undergoes as he makes a solitary life for himself far from civilization.

LAND AND SEA

Robinson Crusoe was born and grew up in York in the northeastern English county of Yorkshire, but upon visiting the port of Hull, he decides on the spur of the moment to join a friend aboard a ship bound for London. Much to his dismay, the ship is caught in a storm off the country's eastern coast near Yarmouth, and the crew must abandon ship, lucky to be alive.

After this frightening experience, Crusoe vows never to go to sea again. Yet he cannot resist temptation, and on a second voyage is captured by Turkish pirates and taken to the port of Sallee (today's Salé) on the Atlantic coast of Morocco, where he is held for two years. When he makes his escape in a small boat, Crusoe is picked up by a ship from Portugal sailing to that country's South American colony of Brazil. There his luck continues to improve, as he is able to establish himself as a planter growing sugarcane near the Brazilian port of Salvador. However, after setting out with a fellow planter on a voyage to Africa to buy slaves, his ship is caught in a storm and driven onto a reef. Crusoe is washed ashore, becoming the wreck's only survivor.

CRUSOE'S ISLAND

The following day Crusoe swims to the ship, which the tide has carried closer to dry land, and builds a raft from the ship's spars, allowing him to salvage food, wine, sailcloth, lumber, two "fowling pieces" (shotguns), a bag of shot, and some powder. Next, he climbs a hill and discovers to his "great affliction" that he is on an island. He sees

In this illustration for the text of *Robinson Crusoe*, Elmer Boyd's drawing depicts the protagonist hiding in the shade of a ridge line with his gun and dog. Based on a real account, Daniel Defoe's novel centers around the methods by which a shipwrecked sailor survives after he is stranded on a deserted island. (Library of Congress)

some rocks in the distance and two small islands that he estimates are about 10 miles away. As far as he can tell, "his" island is uninhabited.

Crusoe builds himself a tent on a hillside and surrounds it with a barricade of stakes, but is happy to discover a small cave in the hillside that he is able to enlarge and turn into a more secure home. He considers his situation, adding up the circumstances that are "evil"—that he has no hope of recue, for instance—and those that are "good," including the fact that God had "sent the ship in near enough to the shore." He feeds himself at first with birds that he has shot and makes furniture for his new home. In time, he builds another shelter on the other side of the island, grows grain from seed he was able to save from the wreck, and tames some of the wild goats he finds on the island.

Crusoe knows that his island is located near the mouth of the Orinoco River, which empties into the Atlantic Ocean on the northern coast of what is today the South American country of Venezuela. Since he has been able to salvage a writing quill and ink from the wrecked ship, he keeps a journal in which he calls his new home "The Island of Despair." However, in contemplating his own wicked and careless life, he comes to realize that God has "dealt bountifully" with him after all.

OTHER SAILORS AND OTHER ISLANDS

Daniel Defoe does not seem to have traveled outside Britain, and he based *Robinson Crusoe*—which he wrote in only four months—on the many printed accounts of real travelers that began to appear in the late 17th century. Defoe drew primarily upon the experiences of a quarrelsome Scottish sailor named Alexander Selkirk, who had been voluntarily marooned for more than four years on an uninhabited island in the South Pacific archipelago of Juan Fernández in 1704. Defoe may actually have met Selkirk, but he would also have had a chance to read about him in any of several sources, including Captain Edward Cooke's 1712 account *A Voyage to the South Seas, and Round the World*.

Another important source for *Robinson Crusoe* seems to have been British East India Company sailor Robert Knox, whose 1681 book *An Historical Relation of the Island Ceylon* described his 20-year captivity on the large island that lies south of India. Defoe owned a copy of the account, and drew upon it in writing his 1720 novel *Captain Singleton*.

Robinson Crusoe proved so popular that it went through four editions in its first year of publication. Since then it has been reprinted, translated, and adapted endlessly. Literary critics see the book as having given birth to the realistic novel, while readers in general enjoy it as an adventure story punctuated with thoughtful, sometimes repetitious, philosophical and religious ruminations. Defoe himself published two sequels, and although the first enjoyed some initial success, the second was a failure, and both are forgotten today. However, the original *Robinson Crusoe* gave rise to countless imitations, or "Robinsonades," and the name of its protagonist has become a byword for an individual abandoned on an island or in any other isolated location.

Grove Koger

Further Reading

Readers who enjoyed *Robinson Crusoe* would probably also enjoy other tales of how characters survive being shipwrecked. Two such works that have achieved widespread acclaim are William Golding's *Lord of the Flies* and Johann David Wyss' *The Swiss Family Robinson*. Lesser-known works, but those that still appeal to readers of young adult literature because of their theme of survival in tropical climates, are R. M. Ballantyne's *The Coral Island*, Kenneth Roberts' *Boon Island*, Jules Verne's *The Mysterious Island*, and Yann Martel's *Life of Pi*.

Bibliography

Balasopoulos, Antonis. "Nesologies: Island Form and Postcolonial Geopoetics." *Postcolonial Studies* 11, no. 1 (2008): 9–26. doi:10.1080/13688790801971555.

Baldacchino, Godfrey. "The Lure of the Island: A Spatial Analysis of Power Relations." *Journal of Marine and Island Cultures* 1, no. 2 (2012): 55–62. doi:10.1016/j.imic.2012.11.003.

Bayliss-Smith, Tim. "On Writing Goodbye." In *Contemporary Meanings in Physical Geography: From What to Why?*, edited by Andre Roy and Stephen Trudgill. New York: Routledge, 2014.

Beer, Gillian. "Discourses of the Island." In *Literature and Science as Modes of Expression*, edited by Frederick Amrine, 1–27. Dordrecht, Netherlands: Springer, 1989.

Carey, D. "Truth, Lies and Travel Writing." In *The Routledge Companion to Travel Writing*, edited by Carl Thompson. London: Routledge, 2016.

Carpenter, J. R. "A Topographical Approach to Re-Reading Books about Islands in Digital Literary Spaces." *MATLIT: Materialities of Literature* 4, no. 1 (2016): 81–94.

Daniels, Stephen, and Catherine Nash. "Lifepaths: Geography and Biography." *Journal of Historical Geography* 30, no. 3 (2004): 449–58. doi:10.1016/S0305-7488(03)00043-4.

DeGraff, Andrew, and Daniel Harmon. *Plotted: A Literary Atlas*. San Francisco: Pulp, 2015.

Dinerstein, Eric. "The Gift of Isolation." In *The Kingdom of Rarities*. Washington, DC: Island Press, 2013. doi:10.5822/978-1-61091-207-5_2.

Drake, George A. "The Dialectics of Inside and Outside: Dominated and Appropriated Space in Defoe's Historical Fictions." *Eighteenth-Century Fiction* 14, no. 2 (2002): 125–40. doi:10.1353/ecf.2002.0010.

Fallon, Ann Marie. *Global Crusoe: Comparative Literature, Postcolonial Theory and Transnational Aesthetics*. Burlington, VT: Ashgate, 2011.

Flynn, Christopher. "Nationalism, Commerce, and Imperial Anxiety in Defoe's Later Works." *Rocky Mountain Review of Language and Literature* 54, no. 2 (2000): 11–24.

Fuller, Jennifer. "From Robinson Crusoe to Dr. Moreau: Nineteenth Century Pacific Island Narratives and Their Contexts." PhD diss., University of Tulsa, 2013.

Goodwin, Craufurd D. "The First Globalization Debate: Crusoe vs. Gulliver." *QA Rivista dell'Associazione Rossi-Doria* (2011).

Gottlieb, Evan, and Juliet Shields, eds. *Representing Place in British Literature and Culture, 1660–1830: From Local to Global*. London: Routledge, 2013.

Howe, K. R. *Nature, Culture and History: The "Knowing" of Oceania*. Honolulu: University of Hawaii Press, 2000.

Jazeel, Tariq. "Reading the Geography of Sri Lankan Island-ness: Colonial Repetitions, Postcolonial Possibilities." *Contemporary South Asia* 17, no. 4 (2009): 399–414. doi:10.1080/09584930903324138.

Kim, Jeongoh. "A Sense of Place and the Uncertainty of the Self." PhD diss., Vanderbilt University, 2007.

Kincaid, Paul. "Islomania? Insularity? The Myth of the Island in British Science Fiction." *Extrapolation* 48, no. 3 (2007): 462–71.

Klinikowski, Autumn. "Geographers of Writing: The Authorship of Aphra Behn and Daniel Defoe in Oroonoko and Robinson Crusoe." Master's thesis, Oregon State University, 2001.

Kneale, James. "Islands: Literary Geographies of Possession, Separation, and Transformation." In *The Routledge Handbook of Literature and Space,* edited by Robert T. Tally Jr. New York: Routledge, 2017.

Kocabiyik, Orkun. "Representations Of the 'Self'and the 'Other' In Travel Narratives: Daniel Defoe's *Robinson Crusoe* and A. W. Kinglake's *Eothen*." *Acta Universitatis Danubius. Relationes Internationalis* 8, no. 2 (2015).

Le Juez, Brigitte, and Olga Springer. "Introduction: Shipwrecks and Islands as Multilayered, Timeless Metaphors of Human Existence." *DQR Studies in Literature* 57 (2015).

Lee, Sungho. "Mercantile Gentility Out of Reach: Moral Cartography and Rhetorical Guidance in Defoe's *Captain Singleton*." *The Modern Language Review* 112, no. 2 (2017): 299–319. doi:10.5699/modelangrevi.112.2.0299.

Madsen, Claus. "Iterative Mapping of Otherness: A Mapping Discussion of the Transforming Potential of the Other." In *Transforming Otherness,* edited by Jason Finch and Peter Nynas. New Brunswick, NJ: Transaction Publishers, 2011.

Marzec, Robert. *An Ecological and Postcolonial Study of Literature: From Daniel Defoe to Salman Rushdie*. New York: Springer, 2007.

Marzec, Robert P. "Enclosures, Colonization, and the Robinson Crusoe Syndrome: A Genealogy of Land in a Global Context." *boundary 2* 29, no. 2 (2002): 129–56.

O'Sullivan, Emer. "Imagined Geography: Strange Places and People in Children's Literature." *The Wenshan Review of Literature and Culture* 10, no. 2 (2017): 1.

Pearl, Jason H. "Desert Islands and Urban Solitudes in the 'Crusoe' Trilogy." *Studies in the Novel* 44, no. 2 (2012): 125–43. www.jstor.org/stable/23406594.

Pearl, Jason H. *Utopian Geographies and the Early English Novel*. Charlottesville: University of Virginia Press, 2014.

Peckham, Robert. "The Uncertain State of Islands: National Identity and the Discourse of Islands in Nineteenth-Century Britain and Greece." *Journal of Historical Geography* 29, no. 4 (2003): 499–515. doi:10.1006/jhge.2002.0407.

Peraldo, Emmanuelle. "'Two broad shining eyes': Optic Impressions and Landscape in Robinson Crusoe." *Digital Defoe: Studies in Defoe & His Contemporaries* 4 (2012): 17–30.

Phillips, Richard. "Politics of Reading: Decolonizing Children's Geographies." *Cultural Geographies* 8, no. 2 (2001): 125–50. doi:10.1177/096746080100800201.

Scott, Heidi. "Havens and Horrors: The Island Landscape." *ISLE: Interdisciplinary Studies in Literature and Environment* 21, no. 3 (2014) 636–57. doi:10.1093/isle/isu075.

Smethurst, Paul. *Travel Writing and the Natural World, 1768–1840*. New York: Palgrave Macmillan, 2012.

Theis, Mary E. "The Geography of Postmodern Meta-Utopian Spaces: 'Last Call for a Revolution?.'" In *Landscape, Seascape, and the Eco-Spatial Imagination,* edited by Simon C. Estok, Jonathan White, and I-Chun Wong. New York: Routledge, 2016.

Thomas, Leah. "Cartographic and Literary Intersections: Digital Literary Cartographies, Digital Humanities, and Libraries and Archives." *Journal of Map & Geography Libraries: Advances in Geospatial Information, Collections & Archives* 9, no. 3 (2013): 335–49. doi:10.1080/15420353.2013.823901.

Van Noy, Rick. "Surveying the Sublime: Literary Cartographers and the Spirit of Place." In *The Greening of Literary Scholarship: Literature, Theory, and the Environment*, edited by Steven Rosendale. Iowa City: University of Iowa Press, 2002.

Vandermeersche, Geert, and Ronald Soetaert. "Landscape, Culture, and Education in Defoe's *Robinson Crusoe*." *CLCWeb: Comparative Literature and Culture* 14, no. 3 (2012): 9.

Varney, Andrew. "Other Worlds—Narratives of Travel: *Robinson Crusoe* and *Gulliver's Travels*." In *Eighteenth-Century Writers in Their World*. London: Palgrave, 1999. doi:10.1007/978-1-349-27763-6_1.

Weaver-Hightwoer, Rebecca. *Empire Islands: Castaways, Cannibals, and Fantasies of Conquest*. Minneapolis: University of Minnesota Press, 2007.

Romeo and Juliet

The ongoing feud between the Montague and Capulet families establishes the crisis and tension for this play set in Verona, Italy, during the 14th century. The drama opens with a street fight between the members of the feuding families, which gains the attention of city officials, including Prince Escalus. Over the course of the play, Shakespeare employs spatial elements to reinforce the issues that divide the two families, particularly emphasizing those elements of urban geography on the boundary between two places, suggesting the nature of Romeo and Juliet as characters in between childhood and adulthood.

CULTURAL GEOGRAPHY AND YOUNG LOVE

Shakespeare himself was married at 18, and reports suggest that his marriage was not a happy one. His daughters, however, married later in life, one at 31 years old. In Elizabethan society, the culture out of which Shakespeare was writing, teen marriages were rare and frowned upon. Medical and folk advice circulated suggesting that marrying young was not healthy for a woman or for any children she might have. Even for the time and setting of the play, 14th-century Italy, it seems a marriage of teenagers would have gone against custom. Given the social norms of both the time of the play's setting and the time in which he was writing, Shakespeare wants his audience to be shocked when Juliet's father offers her in marriage to Paris. This removes some of the moral burden from the young couple themselves, as Juliet's father's impropriety is seen as the cause of the tragedy rather than it being their overly passionate and naïve love. Ultimately, however, the two characters possess a sense that they are exceptional, that to love in the face of hate is exceptional, and therefore they feel justified in breaching natural and social customs. They, too, then, break from what is considered decent by their society, just as Juliet's father does. However, at their young age, they could hardly have known better, whereas Juliet's mother, father, and older suitor would have known that what they were doing betrayed decency.

Romeo's credibility as a lover and the depths of his feelings for Juliet are called into question by what precedes the play: his declaration of love for Rosaline, who cannot love him due to her vow of lifelong chastity. At the opening of the play, Romeo pines for her, suffering from her refusal. When he discovers that she will be attending a ball at the Capulets' house, he and his cousin Benvolio decide to attend the party wearing masks so that nobody will recognize him as a Montague. Readers often wonder how Romeo is a lover to be taken seriously when he can so quickly switch the object of his affection for another. Romeo arrives at the Capulets' party and falls in love with Juliet after seeing her for the first time. Shakespeare includes little of substance to prompt Romeo's feelings. In fact, he intends for the frivolity of the connection to underscore that Romeo is looking to love, and it matters little who is the object of his desire. Shakespeare sets up a rather weak and capricious love story to underscore how silly the rivalry is between the two houses. Even a schoolboy's fleeting crush is stronger than the kill pact between the Montagues and Capulets. The play is not so much about the foolishness of love as it is about the foolishness of hate.

INSIDE/OUTSIDE

Because of the setting and story of the play, outside spaces are associated with the violence of toxic masculinity, whereas romantic love is confined to mostly secret, indoor spaces: the Friar's cell, the bedroom, and the tomb.

At the party, inside Juliet's family's house, Romeo expresses his love for her. The next evening, Romeo scales the wall into the garden outside Juliet's room just as she walks out onto her balcony and speaks out loud her wish that she could be with Romeo, even though he is a Montague. Romeo shows himself and again declares his love. They make plans to meet later that morning and are secretly married by Friar Lawrence in his cell.

The balcony scene is important to the narrative because it is a much different play if Juliet is just halfheartedly going along with Romeo's advances; rather, when Juliet returns his feelings through her own will, she is not merely being swayed by some false charm. The position of the balcony as a space between the interior and exterior is important. In an interior setting, most male actors would stand taller than their female counterparts (although in Shakespeare's day, female roles were played by boys), but the balcony places Juliet physically above Romeo, a position of power appropriate for the expression of her will in that relationship.

The play then switches to an exterior scene of bravado and death. Tybalt finds Romeo in the street and challenges him, but Mercutio jumps in. Tybalt kills Mercutio, and then Romeo kills him. Prince Escalus subsequently banishes Romeo from Verona forever. Juliet is brokenhearted, but consoled by the thought that Tybalt would have killed Romeo if he had refused to fight. As Romeo and Juliet spend the night together, Shakespeare brings us back to an interior scene of romantic love.

After Romeo travels to Mantua to wait for news from Juliet, Lord and Lady Capulet tell Juliet she must marry Paris, but she refuses. Desperate to stay true to Romeo, she goes to see Friar Lawrence, who comes up with a plan that involves

Juliet taking a potion that will make her seem dead so that he can get her away from her family and reunite the two lovers. The Friar is supposed to inform Romeo about their plan.

Juliet drinks the potion in her room, the same interior space where she consummated her love with Romeo. The next morning, the day of her wedding to Paris, she is found lifeless. She is interred in the family vault, but Romeo has not received the letter the Friar sent. After his servant reports that Juliet has died, Romeo goes to the Capulet vault. Paris, also there, challenges him to a duel. After Romeo kills Paris, he drinks a poison and dies next to Juliet. In this final scene, the violence of men's fighting, which has up until now been reserved for the public outdoor space of the street, encroaches into the interior scene of romantic love by taking place inside a tomb. Perhaps this reveals Shakespeare's interest in showing how the two strands of the narrative—extremes of hatred and love—have led to this place of death.

This poster advertising a New York theater's 1879 performance of *Romeo and Juliet* draws attention to the Italian setting through the use of Tuscan style columns in the background. It is most likely a depiction of the famous balcony scene, where Juliet expresses her love for Romeo. (Library of Congress)

Juliet wakes to find Romeo's dead body and then kills herself with his dagger. The townspeople begin to gather at the tomb, and Friar Lawrence tells them what happened. Too late to save the dead, the two families agree to end their feud. Shakespeare uses the distinction between exterior and interior spaces to mark the two opposite poles of human emotion that drive the outcome of this play.

THE URBAN GEOGRAPHY AND ARCHITECTURE OF FORBIDDEN LOVE

Romeo and Juliet involves a stage with five different setting locations, but none of them specify anything that is inherently Italian. Critics have noted that Shakespeare's Italian settings could be England. No place descriptions distinguish them as belonging to Italy. In Romeo and Juliet, we have very general directions on place: "A public place" for duels, and when Romeo is in Mantua, the stage directions simply read "Mantua. A Street." No additional elements place us on a seemingly real street or even on a particular kind of street. Because Shakespeare spared details on these places, directors have been able to adapt the play to a variety of different settings and even other historical times. The lack of specificity in the original has given way to great imagination on the part of directors. *Romeo and Juliet* has been adapted to cultures as diverse as Japan and India. Shakespeare's sparse use of the Italian setting also functions in another way: he uses elements of the Italian city that translate to the English city of the time. Italy is not so much real Italy as an Italian-decorated England.

Staging the balcony scene is one of the most challenging parts of the set design. The setup is a rich space used by Shakespeare as both access to the interior of the Capulets' house and to the exterior world. Shakespeare's Italian settings abound with these in-between places inherent to urban geography.

That the Prince happens to frequent public or semipublic places emphasizes his humanity over his status as ruler. The Prince shows up three times, twice in public, where he witnessed the aftermaths of the duels between the feuding houses, and again at the end of the play, in the graveyard, where he finds the dead bodies of Paris, Romeo, and Juliet, and chastises the two families for their hate. In this less public scene, not a bustling street but the family's tomb, the Prince admits that he has lost something, too, as he mourns the loss of his kinsmen (Mercutio and Paris). Again, his appearance in this space, outside of his court, emphasizes that he is connected to his people. Shakespeare places the Prince in these settings as a kind of choral figure (similar to the choruses employed in ancient Greek drama) who is able to covey to the audience the larger picture because he is both a voice of authority and also a true representative of the town's citizens. This is one of the ways that Shakespeare injects some amount of peaceful stability into the play's otherwise tragic structure.

Lynn Marie Houston

Further Reading

West Side Story is a musical made by adapting the plot of *Romeo and Juliet* to the culture of 1950s New York City. *The Hunchback of Notre Dame* by Victor Hugo is another tragic love story, but this novel is about unrequited love; however, it features a single grave shared between the protagonists, much like the ending of *Romero and Juliet*. The 12th-century Legend of *Tristan & Isolde* also features a pair of star-crossed lovers.

Bibliography

Baker, Christopher. "The Persistence of the Sacred in Baz Luhrmann's Romeo + Juliet." *Journal of Religion & Film* 11, no. 2 (2016): 15.

Bassi, Shaul. "The Grave and the Ghetto: Shakespearean Places as Adaptations." In *Shakespeare's Italy and Italy's Shakespeare: Place, "Race," Politics*, 139–57. New York: Palgrave Macmillan, 2016.

Clark, Glenn. "The Civil Mutinies of Romeo and Juliet." *English Literary Renaissance* 41, no. 2 (2011): 280–300.

Emmerichs, Sharon. "Playing God: The Landscape of Resurrection in Romeo and Juliet." *Cahiers Élisabéthains* 83, no. 1 (2013): 11–21.

Eriksen, Roy. "Embedded Urbanism: Shakespeare in the City." *Actes des congrès de la Société française Shakespeare* 28 (2011): 67–80.

Henke, Robert. "2 Private and Public Spheres and the 'Civic Turn' in Da Porto, Bandello, and Shakespeare's Romeo and Juliet." In *Shakespeare, Romeo and Juliet, and Civic Life: The Boundaries of Civic Space*, edited by Silvia Bigliazzi and Lisanna Calvi, 66. London: Routledge, 2015.

Kermode, Lloyd Edward. "Experiencing the Space and Place of Early Modern Theater." *Journal of Medieval and Early Modern Studies* 43, no. 1 (2013): 1–24.

Raber, Karen. "Vermin and Parasites: Shakespeare's Animal Architectures." In *Ecocritical Shakespeare,* edited by Lynne Bruckner and Dan Brayton, 37–56. London: Routledge, 2016.

Rasmus, Agnieszka, and Magdalena Cieślak, eds. *Images of the City.* Newcastle upon Tyne: Cambridge Scholars Publishing, 2009.

Shaughnessy, Robert. "Stage, Screen, and Nation: Hamlet and the Space of History." In *A Concise Companion to Shakespeare on Screen,* edited by Diana E. Henderson. Oxford, UK: Wiley-Blackwell, 2006.

Sillars, Stuart. "Defining Spaces in Eighteenth-Century Shakespeare Illustration." *Shakespeare* 9, no. 2 (2013): 149–67.

Smith, Sabine H. "The Urban Residential Balcony as Interstitial Site." In *Resistance and the City: Negotiating Urban Identities: Race, Class, and Gender*, edited by Christopher Ehland and Pascal Fischer, 168–84. Leiden, Netherlands: Brill, 2018.

Vela, Richard. "Post-Apocalyptic Spaces in Baz Luhrmann's William Shakespeare's Romeo + Juliet." In *Apocalyptic Shakespeare: Essays on Visions of Chaos and Revelation in Recent Film Adaptations,* edited by Melissa Croteau and Carolyn Jess-Cooke, 90. Jefferson, NC: McFarland & Co., 2009.

S

The Scarlet Letter

The Scarlet Letter is Nathaniel Hawthorne's 1850 novel about a romance between a married Puritan woman and her religious minister and the subsequent fallout to their affair. It is set in Massachusetts in the 1640s during the time of early colonization. The book opens with Hester Prynne's public punishment for her affair, which has been discovered due to her pregnancy. For the rest of her life, she is required to wear a scarlet letter "A," signifying her status as an "adulteress." However, her lover, Arthur Dimmesdale, a clergyman, remains silent about her guilt. In fact, he finds himself in the hypocritical position of publically leading the charge to attempt to determine who the father of her child is. Place functions in the novel as a way to delineate the boundaries of Puritan moral law. Hawthorne uses nature, specifically the woods on the outside of town and a wild rosebush that grows outside the prison door, to reveal the flaws and hypocrisy of Puritan society.

Hester gives birth to a daughter, Pearl, and refuses to tell anyone who the father is. When her husband returns from his travels abroad, he assumes a new identity, Roger Chillingworth, so that he can find out who the child's father is and seek revenge on him. Hester takes Pearl and sets up residency in a cottage outside of town, where she earns money from her sewing. Arthur Dimmesdale, Hester's lover and the town's minister, becomes increasingly ill, seemingly from guilt over his sin. His strained conscience is worsened by Roger Chillingworth, who rightly suspects Dimmesdale to be Pearl's father. Dimmesdale mounts the scaffold where Hester was punished, declares his sin to the town, and then passes away. Some witnesses claim that on his chest was burned or carved a letter "A." The story uses an element of the supernatural to highlight how important this place of public spectacle was to the Puritan notion of moral order and just punishment for sins.

NATURE AND THE CULTURAL GEOGRAPHY OF PURITANISM

The Puritans were greatly suspicious of the woods and forests of New England because the wilderness represented a threat to their idea of the order they wanted to impose in the Americas: after all, in the woods are natives as well as some flora and fauna they had never seen before. The woods represented the evil of paganism, and the Puritans invented many stories about the misdeeds that occur in the woods, such as satanic cabals and rituals of witchcraft. However, the Puritan distrust of the woods was not all about xenophobia or religious intolerance. The first settlers in the colonies, like the first members of the Massachusetts Bay Colony, were a small number with limited supplies, and they had to overcome starvation and harsh winters.

Hawthorne was not a Puritan, although he was related to one of the judges who condemned innocent women to death during the Salem witch trials. Hawthorne was writing in the Romantic tradition, which views nature as purer than the corruption found in towns. The space in between town and wilderness that Hester occupies once she moves into her cottage to raise her daughter Pearl is a space where Hester can heal and gather strength.

Hester meets up with Dimmesdale during one of his walks in the woods. The forest is a fitting meeting spot for them because it exists outside of the control of the Puritan settlement and both Hester and Dimmesdale were willing to shirk the morals of their society to pursue their affair. Hawthorne's description of the woodland setting, especially the play of light in the woods, are highly sensual but also tinged with symbolism linked to a fight between good and evil. Here, Hester feels free to take off the scarlet letter that she is forced to wear in town and as she does, clouds move away to allow sunlight to shine on her, signifying a righteousness to her action. Puritan laws cannot oppress her in the dense forest. However, ultimately, Pearl, who is closely aligned with the natural world in Hawthorne's descriptions, reacts poorly to seeing Hester with Dimmesdale. Even though the woods offers a temporary reprieve from Puritan judgment, the couple feels they have no place in either the Puritan world or in nature.

PUNISHMENT AS A PLACE: THE SCAFFOLD AND PRISON AT THE TOWN CENTER

The scaffold spatially represents the punishment that was at the heart of the Puritan community, and in *The Scarlet Letter* it is situated right next to the prison. As a raised wooden stage, it represents the Puritan understanding of the shame related to being looked at on display as a form of humiliation. Scaffolds often worked along with pillories (whipping posts) and stocks in Puritan society to make a public demonstration of punishment for sins, and often all of the townspeople were encouraged to join in the spectacle by shouting (as they do in Hawthorne's novel), name-calling, and throwing garbage at sinners. Hester first appears on the scaffolding as she is being punished for her affair. Later, Dimmesdale dies on the scaffolding, possibly of self-inflicted wounds, psychological deterioration stemming from his guilt, or from a supernatural effect.

An image that counters the public humiliation of the scaffold is the wild rosebush outside the prison. This is not just an image that expresses the Puritan notion that there is beauty in suffering because it brings us closer to God. No, here is something wild that has escaped the attention of the order-loving Puritans, and Hawthorne describes it in great detail. It is often talked about as a symbol for Hester herself, who is "wild" in that she is willing to step outside the bounds of the Puritan world's moral order, and in doing so, flourishes and finds a way to coexist with those in a society that has wronged her. Hester Prynne, in finding love outside of the constraints of Christian marriage, became an outcast but, in many ways, lived a life truer to her own sense of herself. The rose outside the prison symbolizes not the beauty in punishment, but the beauty to be had in living true to oneself in a repressive environment.

Lynn Marie Houston

Further Reading

Other writers of the American Renaissance whose works exhibit similar themes are Washington Irving, who mainly wrote short stories; the members of the transcendentalist movement—Ralph Waldo Emerson and Henry David Thoreau—who wrote nonfiction and poetry; Walt Whitman, who wrote poetry; and Herman Melville, who, like Hawthorne, wrote novels. The latter's classic *Moby Dick* would be a good choice for further reading after *The Scarlet Letter* because it is set in the same geographic location of Massachusetts. Although Arthur Miller was writing in the 20th century, his play *The Crucible,* about the Salem witch trials, is set during the same time period and location.

After reading Hawthorne's masterpiece, two good works to read next are the short stories "The Legend of Sleepy Hollow" or "Rip Van Winkle" by Washington Irving, as they involve the theme of the individual versus the community.

Although writing a couple of decades after Hawthorne, Henry James often picks up the same theme of women as unfortunate but proud victims of a patriarchal society. Specifically, James wrote *Daisy Miller* about this theme, even though it is set in Europe and Hawthorne's setting is colonial America.

Bibliography

Bowden, Martyn J. "Invented Tradition and Academic Convention in Geographical Thought About New England." In *Nature and Identity in Cross-Cultural Perspective,* edited by A. Buttimer and L. Wallin, 235–50. Dordrecht, Netherlands: Springer, 1999.

Estes, Andrew Keller. "A Debate in American Literature: The Nature of US Spaces." *Spatial Practices* 16 (2013): 57.

Faiq, Tatheer Assim. "Allegorical and Cultural Landscapes in the Novels of Nathaniel Hawthorne and Al-Nahda Arab Writers." PhD diss., Griffith College, 2015.

Finn, Margaret L. *Immanent Nature: Environment, Women, and Sacrifice in the Nature Writing of Nathaniel Hawthorne, Catharine Maria Sedgwick, and Sarah Orne Jewett.* Philadelphia: Temple University, 2010.

Gersdorf, Catrin. "Nature in the Grid: American Literature, Urbanism, and Ecocriticism." *Real-Yearbook of Research in English and American Literature* 24 (2008).

Goodenough, Elizabeth. "Grandfather's Chair: Hawthorne's 'Deeper History' of New England." *The Lion and the Unicorn* 15, no. 1 (1991): 27–42.

Hannah, Daniel. "(Un)settling Desires: Erotics and Ecologies in Nathaniel Hawthorne's Transatlantic Romances." In *Transatlantic Literary Ecologies,* edited by Kevin Hutchings and John Miller. New York: Routledge, 2016.

McGrath, Derek. "'Is the World, Then, So Narrow?' Simultaneous Need for Home and Travel in Hawthorne's The Scarlet Letter." Honors thesis, Florida Atlantic University, 2007.

Murphy, Bernice. *The Rural Gothic in American Popular Culture: Backwoods Horror and Terror in the Wilderness.* London: Palgrave Macmillan, 2013.

Scheper, George L. "'Where Is Our Home?': The Ambiguity of Biblical and Euro-American Imaging of Wilderness and Garden as Sacred Place." In *The Elemental Passion for Place in the Ontopoiesis of Life,* edited by Anna-Teresa Tymieniecka, 321–38. Dordrecht, Netherlands: Springer, 1995.

Schirmeister, Pamela. *The Consolations of Space: The Place of Romance in Hawthorne, Melville, and James.* Stanford, CA: Stanford University Press, 1990.

Sears, John F. *Sacred Places: American Tourist Attractions in the Nineteenth Century.* Amherst: University of Massachusetts Press, 1998.

Takao, Naochika. "Sex and the City: The Reconstruction of Middle-Class Urban Consciousness in The Scarlet Letter." *The Japanese Journal of American Studies* 19 (2008): 25–41.

Tanner, Tony. *Scenes of Nature, Signs of Men: Essays on 19th and 20th Century American Literature.* Cambridge, UK: Cambridge University Press, 1989.

Wood, Joseph S. "'Build, Therefore, Your Own World': The New England Village as Settlement Ideal." *Annals of the Association of American Geographers* 81, no. 1 (1991): 32–50.

Slaughterhouse-Five

Slaughterhouse-Five, or The Children's Crusade: A Duty-Dance with Death is a 1969 novel by U.S. author Kurt Vonnegut Jr. The novel derives its name from the underground meat locker in Dresden, Germany, where the author as well as the novel's fictional protagonist, Billy Pilgrim, took shelter as prisoners of war during the ferocious firebombing of Dresden by combined U.S. and U.K. air forces in February 1945. When Billy and his fellow prisoners of war emerge from their shelter, they find very few survivors in a devastated landscape that resembles the surface of the moon. Perhaps as a result of his World War II experiences, Billy becomes "unstuck in time," which causes him to jump back and forth between different moments in his life—past, present, and future. While working as an optometrist in Ilium, New York, after the war, Billy believes that on the night of his daughter's wedding in 1967 he is kidnapped by aliens from the distant planet Tralfamadore, where (in a time warp) he shares zoo-like living quarters with Montana Wildhack, a Hollywood starlet similarly abducted. Time becomes a kind of place for the narrator, as places lose their distinguishing qualities in the blur of war and travel.

CONTEMPORARY AND HISTORICAL POLITICS

Because Billy Pilgrim has become unstuck in time, he moves rapidly from year to year and from place to place. As Vonnegut explains in Chapter 2, "Billy has gone to sleep a senile widower and awakened on his wedding day. He has walked through a door in 1955 and come out another one in 1941. He has gone back through that door to find himself in 1963." As a result, *Slaughterhouse-Five* contains many different geographic locations from Billy's life, but focuses on four distinct settings—Ilium, Luxembourg, Dresden, and Tralfamadore—to shape the story, albeit in fragmented form. Aside from Tralfamadore, the novel's literary landscape is taken largely from Vonnegut's own life and thus reflects the historical and cultural contexts of the mid-20th century. The fragmentation of place in the novel serves to reveal the lessening importance of "the local" and of place-based identities in a posthuman era.

Billy was born in Ilium, graduated from Ilium High School, and attended the Ilium School of Optometry for one semester before being drafted into the U.S. Army for military service in World War II. Following his honorable discharge, Billy resumes his studies at the optometry school and during his senior year proposes marriage to Valencia Merble, the daughter of the school's founder. Staying in Ilium, Billy and Valencia raise two children and live in "a lovely Georgian home." Although Ilium is a fictional place-name, it is what the Romans called the ancient city of Troy—and thus by extension Troy, New York, near Schenectady, where Vonnegut himself worked for General Electric from 1947 to 1951. Billy owns several optometry offices in Ilium's shopping plazas, but other parts of the city (like many industrial towns in upstate New York during the 1960s) are in decline. Ilium has a "black ghetto," which was so deeply "hated" by its residents that "they had burned down a lot of it.... It was all they had, and they'd wrecked it." In that historical period, black neighborhoods in Los Angeles, Newark, Detroit, and Washington, D.C., also burned.

In December 1944, Billy (like Vonnegut) saw action in the Battle of the Bulge, which was the last major German offensive of World War II. Lost behind enemy lines, Billy wanders in a Luxembourg forest, which Vonnegut describes as "dark and old. The pines were planted in ranks and files. There was no undergrowth. Four inches of unmarked snow blanketed the ground." Billy joins three other soldiers attempting to find their way back to their units. Two of the soldiers are shot by Germans; the other two (including Billy) are taken prisoner.

VIOLENCE AGAINST PLACE

Packed into boxcars, Billy and other American POWs are transferred by train to Dresden, the capital of Saxony and a city without military significance. "Every other big city in Germany had been bombed and burned ferociously," Vonnegut explains, but "Dresden had not suffered so much as a cracked windowpane." As a result, when Billy arrives, he looks out on "the loveliest city that most of the Americans had ever seen. The skyline was intricate and voluptuous and enchanted and absurd. It looked like a Sunday school picture of Heaven." When another soldier in the boxcar refers to Dresden as "Oz," the author identifies himself as that soldier: "That was me. The only other city I'd ever seen was Indianapolis, Indiana," which is where Vonnegut was born and raised. However, when attacked by Allied aircraft, Dresden turns into "one big flame," which "ate everything organic, everything that would burn.... When the Americans and their guards did come out, the sky was black with smoke.... Dresden was like the moon now, nothing but minerals.... Everything else in the neighborhood was dead." In this way, Vonnegut explores what is violence against place, one that strips it of its identifying features and life-sustaining qualities.

ALIEN ABDUCTION

Haunted by these memories, Billy finds some solace when he is captured by aliens from the planet Tralfamadore, which is 446,120,000,000,000,000 miles from Earth. For their amusement and edification, the Tralfamadorians place Billy in a zoo that is "a simulated Earthling habitat. Most of the furnishings had been stolen from the Sears & Roebuck warehouse in Iowa City, Iowa" (which Vonnegut would have known from his years teaching at the Iowa Writers' Workshop there). Because Tralfamadorians see everything in four dimensions—including the dimension of time—they never try to explain events (such as the destruction of Dresden), as Earthlings might. Tralfamadorians accept the way things are. "Ignore the awful times, and concentrate on the good ones," is their advice to Billy.

POSTWAR TRAUMA

Like Billy Pilgrim, Vonnegut was haunted by what he had experienced in Dresden in 1945. After many years of trying to write a more conventional novel that would express his outrage about those events, Vonnegut finally found his voice in a wholly original work that is part autobiography, part science fiction, part absurdist comedy in the face of tragedy, and part antiwar protest (at a time when the United States was fighting an unpopular war in Vietnam). Thanks in part to the importance of its landscapes, *Slaughterhouse-Five* succeeds in balancing its different parts to create a masterpiece that established Vonnegut's reputation as one of the great writers of the postwar period.

James I. Deutsch

Further Reading
Norman Mailer's *The Naked and the Dead* also captures, in a similar tone as Vonnegut, the devastation of World War II. Erich Maria Remarque does something parallel for the First World War in *All Quiet on the Western Front*.

Bibliography
Grove, Jairus Victor. "Becoming War: Ecology, Ethics and the Globalization of Violence." PhD diss., Johns Hopkins University, 2011.
Hammond, Thomas. "Transforming the History Curriculum with Geospatial Tools." *Contemporary Issues in Technology and Teacher Education* 14, no. 3 (2014): 266–87.
Hobbins, Peter. "Venom, Visibility and the Imagined Histories of Arthropods." In *Rethinking Invasion Ecologies from the Environmental Humanities,* edited by Jodi Frawley and Iain McCalman. New York: Routledge, 2014.
Leeds, Marc, and Peter J. Reed, eds. *Kurt Vonnegut: Images and Representations.* Westport, CT: Greenwood Press, 2000.
Marvin, Thomas F. *Kurt Vonnegut: A Critical Companion.* Westport, CT: Greenwood Publishing Group, 2002.
Morse, Donald E. *The Novels of Kurt Vonnegut: Imagining Being an American.* Westport, CT: Praeger, 2003.
Mustazza, Leonard. *Forever Pursuing Genesis: The Myth of Eden in the Novels of Kurt Vonnegut.* Lewisburg, PA: Bucknell University Press, 1990.
Öjehag-Pettersson, Andreas. "Space Craft: Globalization and Governmentality in Regional Development." PhD diss., Karlstads Universitet, 2015.

Weiner, Jesse. "Mapping Hubris: Vonnegut's Cat's Cradle and Odysseus' Apologoi." *International Journal of the Classical Tradition* 22, no. 1 (2015): 116–37. doi:10.1007/s12138-014-0358-7.

Yaeger, Patricia. "Introduction: Dreaming of Infrastructure." *PMLA* 122, no. 1 (2007): 9–26. doi:10.1632/pmla.2007.122.1.9.

Snyder, Gary

Gary Snyder is a writer associated with San Francisco and the Pacific Northwest. His work grew in fame from his association with the Beat generation of the 1950s. He is known for the way that he blends tenets of Buddhism into his literary work to express the need for humans to feel more connected to the natural world. Doing so, he feels, will heal us and help us experience the divine.

THE GEOGRAPHY OF GRACE

Gary Snyder's poetry alternates between wanting to capture the unique details of a place and making the case that a particular place is part of a larger ecological system. Specific places are usually conduits for Snyder to access something grander; named places in his works stand in for the quality of "earthness" and come to represent the whole planet, the connectedness of all of its spaces and living things.

Snyder's poetics of place is buttressed by an Eastern spirituality that asks readers to be more conscious of their body and its connection to mind. By cultivating an awareness of our mortal bodies, Snyder argues, we can stay in touch with the Earth. In this way, his poetry is greatly inspired by the poetic project of Walt Whitman. For example, much like Whitman's idea that the body of someone engaged in physical work can bring that person closer to an understanding of the divine current running through living things, Snyder feels that working in an agricultural setting can do the same. He reveals in some of his work (for instance, the poem "Hunting") that doing the work of procuring our own food brings us closer to the sacredness of human origins. Gathering our own food helps us be present and relive a time before civilization corrupted us and threw us into an imbalanced relationship by cutting us off from the life force. For Snyder, the "old ways" are better because they encourage us to slow down and have an immediate relationship to nature as unfiltered as possible through elaborate human technology.

Tracking an animal through the woods is not the only way that his speakers connect with the natural world. His poem "Things to Do Around Portland" suggests more modest activities that can be spiritually rewarding when interacting with a place: getting out into nature, walking, hiking, and eating the fresh bounty of the Earth. Through these activities, Snyder emphasizes the value of the senses and of the pastoral pursuit. He describes a human body alive with the taste, touch, sight, smell, and sounds in a way that connects to other living beings through our mortality and impermanence.

The speakers in Snyder's poems often disdain the trappings of civilization and favor a life of want and wandering. They frequently eschew the concept of private property and argue for the communal nature of our experience on this Earth. The natural spaces in his poems are usually utopian spaces that thrive without human intervention. In many poems that feature speakers in nature, Snyder sometimes refuses to include "I," opting for sentence fragments that do not assert the human ego over the landscape's presence. In fact, readers can feel his desire for humans to have as little impact as possible on their natural environment. He writes about the negative consequences that can result when humans intervene too much in the natural world. The poems "Logging 14" and "Logging 15" from his book *Myths and Texts* feature the degradation of nature by various forces of civilization. Snyder's point is that distancing ourselves from nature has caused various illnesses and spiritual dysfunction.

The concept of place in Snyder's work is often represented through the metaphor of a trail. "The Trail Is not a Trail" is a good example. Snyder's speakers often "become one" with the trail in various ways. His line breaks and dashes sometimes confuse whether reference is being made to the speaker or the trail, his use of the pronoun "it" is purposefully vague so that it could refer to either, and the speaker's spiritual or philosophical trajectory is discussed in terms of a path (a synonym for a trail). A similar transformation happens in "By Frazier Creek Falls" from his collection *Turtle Island,* where the human speaker feels a part of all that is, which Snyder names the "living flowing land." The speaker also becomes a conduit for the creek and the landscape: "We *are* it / it sings through us."

Although there are moments of this kind of grace and connection in Snyder's poetry, he also draws our attention in a realistic way to the impossibility of human comprehension to take in the totality of the mystical cosmos. However, Snyder might argue, it is the attempt that counts. In attempting to access the sacred and divine within natural spaces, his human speakers break down the barriers that keep them from the peace that can be found in wildness and communion with nature. They often find creative ways to disengage from the demands of a capitalist society that keeps us constantly in a state of panic and unfilled want. By eroding the false boundaries we set up between self and other, between self and the rest of the world, Snyder believes we can connect with the life spark that exists in all living things. Place functions in his writing to make humans aware of their position within a wider ecology.

Lynn Marie Houston

Further Reading

Gary Snyder's poetry is rooted in the physical body and its sensory perceptions, very much like the poetry of Walt Whitman who also encouraged readers to cultivate a closer relationship with the Earth by valuing the movements and processes of the human body. Another poet who likes to compare the course of a human life to a trail or path is Robert Frost, such as in his poem "The Road Not Travelled." Similar to the poetry of Mary Oliver, Gary Snyder's work often reminds humans that they are just one small part of the wider world of living things. Other works by the authors involved in the Beat movement (such as Jack Kerouac and Allen Ginsberg) would pair well with Snyder's work, as he was associated with the origins of that movement.

Bibliography

Akamine, Reiko. "Places and Mythopoesis: A Cross-Cultural Study of Gary Snyder and Michiko Ishimure." *Studies in the Humanities* 26, no. 1 (1999): 81.

Barnhill, David Landis. "An Interwoven World: Gary Snyder's Cultural Ecosystem." *Worldviews: Global Religions, Culture, and Ecology* 6, no. 2 (2002): 111–44.

Dean, Tim. *Gary Snyder and the American Unconscious: Inhabiting the Ground.* London: Springer, 1991.

Gray, Timothy. "Gary Snyder: Poet-Geographer of the Pacific Rim." *Studies in the Humanities* 26, no. 1 (1999): 18–40.

Gray, Timothy G. "Semiotic Shepherds: Gary Snyder, Frank O'Hara, and the Embodiment of an Urban Pastoral." *Contemporary Literature* 39, no. 4 (1998): 523–59.

Hertz, Jason T. "Re-Inhabiting the Islands: Senses of Place in the Poetry of Gary Snyder and Derek Walcott." Master's thesis, Western Carolina University, 2011.

Hönnighausen, Lothar. "'By Division, Out of Wonder': Gary Snyder, Wendell Berry, and Ecopoetics." *Soundings* 78, no. 2 (1995): 279–91.

Kern, Robert. "'Mountains and rivers are us': Gary Snyder and the Nature of the Nature of Nature." *College Literature* 27, no. 1 (2000): 119–38.

McClintock, James I. *Nature's Kindred Spirits: Aldo Leopold, Joseph Wood Krutch, Edward Abbey, Annie Dillard, and Gary Snyder.* Madison: University of Wisconsin Press, 1994.

Norton, Jody, and Gary Snyder. "The Importance of Nothing: Absence and Its Origins in the Poetry of Gary Snyder." *Contemporary Literature* 28, no. 1 (1987): 41–66.

Scigaj, Leonard M. *Sustainable Poetry: Four American Ecopoets.* Lexington: University Press of Kentucky, 2015.

Strain, Charles B. "The Pacific Buddha's Wild Practice: Gary Snyder's Environmental Ethic." In *American Buddhism: Methods and Findings in Recent Scholarship*, edited by Christopher Queen and Duncan Ryuken Williams, 143. London: Taylor & Francis, 2013.

Wrighton, John. "Environmental Ethics in the Poetry of Gary Snyder." In *Ethics and Politics in Modern American Poetry,* 64–90. London: Routledge, 2012.

The Sound and the Fury

The Sound and the Fury, a novel by American author and Nobel laureate William Faulkner, derives its title from part of the speech by Macbeth, a Shakespearean character: "It [Life] is a tale told by an idiot, full of sound and fury, signifying nothing." Perhaps English playwright William Shakespeare was the first to give voice to nihilism, though Faulkner put this nihilism in an American context. This was not his first novel. After his first two novels sold poorly and received little critical acclaim, Faulkner vowed to write his guts out. Free from the need to please critics or readers, Faulkner concentrated on satisfying his own inner convictions of what constituted good fiction. The result, *The Sound and the Fury,* was among the groundbreaking works of American literature. The theme, a family in decline, is the novel's subject. Faulkner manages to make the subject riveting through the use of novel literary techniques much admired but poorly imitated.

THE GEOGRAPHY OF PLACE

Like American playwright Tennessee Williams, William Faulkner focuses on the South, but not in any amorphous sense. He grounds *The Sound and the Fury* and other novels in the Mississippi of his birth. This is not a transcendent

Mississippi but a Mississippi that had lost the Civil War and participated in the failed Confederacy. The Mississippians of *The Sound and the Fury* were sometimes inarticulate and their education threadbare. One of the characters, Benjy, has severe mental deficits. The African Americans who people the novel are the products of segregated schools, at a time when white schools had the better budgets. These characters, too, have not mastered English. Faulkner's Mississippi and its people have fallen on hard times.

THE LITERARY LANDSCAPE OF MEMORY

The 20th century was a time of literary experimentation. Faulkner participated in this experimentation with great vigor. *The Sound and the Fury* is, at one level, a novel of memories. Sometimes, as in the case of Benjy, these memories are confused and the level of disorder appalling. His memories are not all his own because he appears to carry with him the memories of other characters, particularly Candace Compson, "Caddy" to everyone. The gleaning of memories from other memories is not novel. One finds Greek philosopher Plato employing the technique more than 2,000 years ago at the beginning of the *Phaedo*. What is a departure, however, is the attempt to enlighten readers with a torrent of seemingly disordered memories. Probably on purpose, Faulkner displays none of the logic that is central to Plato's prose. In fact, Faulkner creates a universe very different from the one that Plato's characters inhabited.

William Faulkner is one of the most celebrated Southern writers. He received a Nobel Prize and two Pulitzer Prizes for his work, which is set primarily in Mississippi. (Library of Congress)

THE DISSOLUTION OF TIME

Faulkner treats time in a radical way. On the day Quentin Compson, brother to Benjy and Caddy, commits suicide, he breaks his watch and removes the hands, evidently on purpose. Thereafter, his watch ticks but cannot reckon time. Faulkner has thrust Quentin outside time, where he must face alone the primal decision of whether or not life is worth living. Time ceases, sharpening the mandate to decide one's fate. French existentialist and Nobel laureate Albert Camus once remarked that philosophy has only one important issue: suicide. Here Faulkner has made suicide the essential issue of literature. Although Faulkner might not have considered himself an existentialist, *The Sound and the Fury* poses the same questions, and echoes the angst at the core of existentialism.

THE UNSPOKEN NARRATIVE

The Sound and the Fury contains four sections, each narrated by a separate character. Each covers essentially the same events. But the retelling of these events is disjointed and often out of order. *The Sound and the Fury* dispenses with the ordinary chronology of events that is normally necessary for narration. Benjy narrates the first section. Through minimal command of English, the absence of chronology, and the sense of immediacy and fear, Benjy tells us little, though we learn from him that Caddy is the protagonist. Yet, Faulkner does not give Caddy a section of her own. One can tell from the sections that Caddy is intelligent, though she has dropped out of the family and the novel in a significant way. Caught cheating in school, she was expelled, eloped with a man, had his child, and exists somewhere as a single mother. Whatever chance she might have had for success has bypassed her. In fact, the only section to cohere to any extent is that narrated by Dilsey, an African American servant. By the time one gets to her perspective, it is clear that the Compson family is in decline, not in any theoretical sense, but in the concrete way that Caddy failed to develop her intellectual promise and that Quentin has committed suicide.

INARTICULATENESS AND STREAM OF CONSCIOUSNESS

Many of the characters in *The Sound and the Fury* may be inarticulate, but when they try to express themselves, readers receive no respite from them. Faulkner provides readers the detritus of their thoughts, all of them. One receives an outpouring of emotions, instincts, and impulses, fear being basic to them. It is as though Faulkner has planted the id in Mississippi. Normal sexual yearnings are twisted in Benjy's mind to a preoccupation with sheep. It seems obvious as well that Benjy desires Caddy and that Caddy is aware of these incestuous feelings. In such cases, one wishes for inarticulateness rather than stream of consciousness.

Christopher Cumo

Further Reading

Other American novels that helped define Modernist literature include John Dos Passos' *U.S.A. Trilogy* (*The Big Money* being the most famous) and Henry Roth's *Call It Sleep*. Modernist novels that also employ a similar stream of consciousness technique are Virginia Woolf's *Mrs. Dalloway* and James Joyce's *Ulysses*.

Bibliography

Aiken, Charles Shelton. *William Faulkner and the Southern Landscape*. Athens: University of Georgia Press, 2009.

Baldwin, Marc D. "Faulkner's Cartographic Method: Producing the 'Land' through Cognitive Mapping." *The Faulkner Journal* 7, no. 1 (1991): 193.

Casemore, Brian. *The Autobiographical Demand of Place: Curriculum Inquiry in the American South*. New York: Peter Lang, 2008.

Cleland, Lucy. "'A Mystical Estate': Paternity and Inheritance in *Absalom, Absalom!, The Sound and the Fury,* and *Ulysses*." Honors thesis, Wellesley College, 2013.

Clere, Sarah. "Faulkner's Appropriation of 'The Legend of Sleepy Hollow' in *The Hamlet*." *The Mississippi Quarterly* 62, no. 3/4 (2009): 443.

Clough, Edward. "Building Yoknapatawpha: Reading Space and the Plantation in William Faulkner." PhD diss., University of East Anglia, 2014.

Doyle, Don Harrison. *Faulkner's County: The Historical Roots of Yoknapatawpha*. Chapel Hill: University of North Carolina Press, 2001.

Hagood, Taylor. "Taking Money Right Out of an American's Pockets: Faulkner's South and the International Cotton Market." *European Journal of American Culture* 26, no. 2 (2007): 83–95.

Kartiganer, Donald M., and Ann J. Abadie, eds. *Faulkner and the Natural World*. Jackson: University Press of Mississippi, 1999.

Kirby, Jack Temple. *Mockingbird Song: Ecological Landscapes of the South*. Chapel Hill: University of North Carolina Press, 2006.

Millgate, Michael. *Faulkner's Place*. Athens: University of Georgia Press, 2009.

Miner, Ward L. *The World of William Faulkner*. Durham, NC: Duke University Press, 1963.

Nicolaisen, Peter. "'The dark land talking the voiceless speech': Faulkner and 'Native Soil.'" *Mississippi Quarterly* 45, no. 3 (1992): 253.

Owens, Margaret R. "Faulknerian Social Strata Meridians in Yoknapatawpha County: A Study in Literary Geography." Honors thesis, University of North Georgia, 2018.

Parrish, Susan Scott. "Faulkner and the Outer Weather of 1927." *American Literary History* 24, no. 1 (2012): 34–58.

Putzel, Max. *Genius of Place: William Faulkner's Triumphant Beginnings*. Baton Rouge: Louisiana State University Press, 1985.

Rabbetts, John. *From Hardy to Faulkner: Wessex to Yoknapatawpha*. New York: Palgrave Macmillan, 1989.

Rabbetts, John. "'Novels of Character and Environment': The Sense of Place and the Folk-Historical Perspective." In *From Hardy to Faulkner*. London: Palgrave Macmillan, 1989.

Ryden, Kent C. *Mapping the Invisible Landscape: Folklore, Writing, and the Sense of Place*. Iowa City: University of Iowa Press, 1993.

Seymour, Betty Jean. "The Individual and the Problem of Self-Definition in Faulkner: Isolation and Gesture in *Light in August, The Sound and the Fury, Absalom, Absalom!,* and *As I Lay Dying*." Master's thesis, University of Richmond, 1967.

Urgo, Joseph R., and Ann J. Abadie, eds. *Faulkner and the Ecology of the South*. Jackson: University Press of Mississippi, 2009.

Urgo, Joseph R. "The Yoknapatawpha Project: The Map of a Deeper Existence." *The Mississippi Quarterly* 57, no. 4 (2004): 639.

Wall, Joshua Logan. "Sound and Fury: Accent and Identity in Faulkner's Immigration Novel." *MELUS: Multi-Ethnic Literature of the United States* 42, no. 1 (2017): 94–115.

Watson, Jay, and Ann J. Abadie, eds. *Faulkner's Geographies*. Jackson: University Press of Mississippi, 2015.

Weinstein, Philip M. *Faulkner's Subject: A Cosmos No One Owns*. Cambridge, UK: Cambridge University Press, 1992.

Stevens, Wallace

Wallace Stevens wrote many poems set in Connecticut, where he lived for the latter half of his life. However, the relationship of these poems to the places in Connecticut is complicated. Although Stevens might name streets, neighborhoods, cities (like Hartford or New Haven), and other geographical markers, his poems rarely cultivate a sensory-rich experience of place that helps readers feel embodied in a landscape. Instead, he emphasizes mindscapes, a map of thoughts as they parade through the mind of a speaker, who could be situated anywhere. For example, in his poem "An Ordinary Evening in New Haven," the town of New Haven is as prominent as the other places he names in rapid succession: Bergamo, Rome, Sweden, Salzburg, and Paris. He does not delve into deep place-based description but instead writes poems about the train of thinking in the mind of his speaker, and how confrontation with the reality in front of him prompts certain thoughts and (less often) feelings.

Other poems by Stevens similarly deal with how imagination can alter reality, or at least the human perception of it. His poem "Thirteen Ways of Looking at a Blackbird" is about how one looks at a landscape and either becomes or fails to become part of the identity of that landscape. Many of his poems are about how the processes of coming to know and coming to be are intimately linked. His speaker in "Thirteen Ways of Looking at a Blackbird" admonishes others to turn away from imaginary concepts toward real, concrete objects. Similarly, too, in "The Snow Man," he explores a winter landscape that brings with it a melancholy that suggests to his speaker that nothingness can take on a presence, but that also imagines how what appears to be hardship to one person may be another person's status quo; it all depends one one's perspective.

NATURE VERSUS TECHNOLOGY

One of Stevens's poems that presents a treatise on space is "Anecdote of the Jar." The title tells readers much about the nature of this poem. Much like Jesus' anecdotes to his disciplines, this anecdote is meant to teach an important concept about the changing rules regarding the relationship between humankind and the rest of the world. The introduction of a human-made artifact into the natural environment has the power to change our perception of the environment. There is a Zen-like quality to this poem that asks readers to reflect on the constructed nature of our reality and on how we can best live our lives given this new insight.

At first, the jar seems neutral, along with the place descriptions. Stevens's speaker refers to the location, the state of Tennessee, without any adjective. He also does not include any description when referring to the "hill" where the jar was set down. Yet, once the jar is laid on the hill, the wilderness suddenly becomes "slovenly," which means "disordered" or "unkempt." Nothing else had changed in that space except the introduction of the human-made jar. Humans often look on the technology they have created as if it is sacred or holy, as if a drive to better technology will necessarily make our lives better (instead of admitting the many new problems it might also create). In this case, the piece of human technology he refers to is empty; he never tells us that there is anything in the jar and later calls it "bare," which would suggest that it is plain and unfilled. The artifact symbolizes humanity's empty pursuit of the next greatest technological invention, which inevitably changes the way we see ourselves and the world around us.

As soon as the jar is introduced to the landscape, Stevens tells us the effect is that now the hill becomes something different, something other, because it contains something unlike what is around it. Before, the land here was just land. Now it is land with jar and land without jar, one area graced by human ingenuity and the rest of the area not similarly graced. This is how the speaker comes to note that introducing the jar makes the wilderness "surround" the hill. The trees haven't moved, but suddenly there is a shift in the speaker's perception. He sees the forest is forest because of the existence of the jar. Before, the forest was just part of what was, not any different from anything else. Now, the forest is something other than the jar, which marks a dividing line between the two areas. The totality of this space, however, suffers a loss: the presence of the jar causes it to lose its wildness.

Finally, the human-made artifact of the jar asserts it "dominion," which means it takes over. Stevens's speaker does not necessarily see this as a good thing because of what he asserts in the final two lines of the poem. He returns to the place of Tennessee and mentions its birds and bushes. These are references to the lush flora and fauna of the state, living things that reproduce. The jar does not reproduce like these living things that make the state so beautiful and green in the warmer months. The jar is sterile, and yet it is the jar that has "dominion." This poem uses the dynamics of place to express a distrust of human technology and a worldview that does not embrace the changes being introduced into the world by new technologies.

The famous linguist Ferdinand de Saussure taught his students about how language shapes our reality by dividing it into categories that are represented by different words. The famous example most people cite is how some cultures have more terms for precipitation than others do: some have different words for a heavy rain versus a light rain; some use different words to denote a fluffy snow as opposed to a dense snow, whereas English simply has "rain" or "snow." De Saussure used proximal categories of words that help divide our reality into separate concepts: we know that a shrub is a shrub because it is not a tree or a flower. We make distinctions in language to order our perception of the world. In "Anecdote of the Jar," Wallace Stevens tackles this very concept.

Lynn Marie Houston

Further Reading

Other poets who write with Wallace Stevens's philosophical sensibilities include John Ashbery, Mark Strand, and Timothy Donnelly. Jorie Graham has a distinct interest in perception, and her poems are also of a contemplative nature.

Bibliography

Burt, Stephen. "Wallace Stevens: Where He Lived." *ELH* 77, no. 2 (2010): 325–52.

Cocola, Jim. *Places in the Making: A Cultural Geography of American Poetry.* Iowa City: University of Iowa Press, 2016.

Cresswell, Tim. "Towards Topopoetics: Space, Place and the Poem." In *Place, Space and Hermeneutics,* edited by Bruce Janz, 319–31. Cham, Switzerland: Springer, 2017.

Deshmane, Chetan. "The Place of Place in Stevens." *IUP Journal of English Studies* 5 (2010): 86–96.

Doreski, William. "Wallace Stevens in Connecticut." *Twentieth Century Literature* 39, no. 2 (1993): 152–65.

Eeckhout, Bart. "The Invisible Skyscraper: Stevens and Urban Architecture." In *Wallace Stevens, New York, and Modernism*, edited by Lisa Goldfarb and Bart Eeckhout, 101–20. London: Routledge, 2012.

Han, Gül Bilge. "The Poetics of Relational Place-Making and Autonomy in Stevens." *Wallace Stevens Journal* 40, no. 2 (2016): 143–71.

Nolan, Sarah A. *Ecopoetry and Ecocentrism: The Poetics of Wallace Stevens and William Carlos Williams*. Master's thesis, California State University, Long Beach, 2010.

Schwarz, Daniel. *Narrative and Representation in the Poetry of Wallace Stevens: A Tune Beyond Us, Yet Ourselves*. New York: Springer, 1993.

Spurr, David. "Architecture in Frost and Stevens." *Journal of Modern Literature* 28, no. 3 (2005): 72–86.

Voros, Gyorgyi. *Notations of The Wild: Ecology Poetry Wallace Stevens*. Iowa City: University of Iowa Press, 1997.

Watson, Douglas Frank. "A Sense of Place in the Poetry of Robert Frost, William Carlos Williams, and Wallace Stevens." PhD diss., Texas Tech University, 1980.

A Streetcar Named Desire

This Tennessee Williams play is set in the French Quarter of New Orleans. The play opens as Blanche DuBois arrives at her sister Stella's home, a first-floor apartment next to the train tracks. The setting is confined to one small apartment that offers no easy escape or solution to the situation these two sisters find themselves in, trapped in a world dominated by men. Each sister deals with this world in a different way: Stella by embracing and accepting it as her destiny, and Blanche by inventing an imaginary place where her life is better.

THE SPATIAL IMAGINARY OF GRIEF

Although Blanche tells her sister that she is visiting on vacation, she has actually lost her job and the family mansion, Belle Reve, which translates as "the beautiful dream." Blanche is stuck in the past and becomes more so as her mental condition deteriorates over the course of the play. When Blanche was newly married, she found her young husband in bed with another man. As a result of being exposed as gay, he committed suicide. Blanche then began sleeping with young men who reminded her of her late husband. She lost her teaching job for sleeping with a 17-year-old boy.

Stella's husband Stanley suspects from the beginning that Blanche's manners are a façade, and he is angered by Blanche's constant insults about his low-class manners. Stella is caught in the middle, trying to satisfy both her sister and her husband. Stanley is more concerned about financial gain than he is about Blanche's weak mental state. He is convinced that Blanche sold the family plantation for a profit and that he is entitled to a percentage. Blanche gradually loses touch with reality as she realizes that her sister's apartment is not a safe space for her, and she has nowhere else to go.

THE SPACE OF MALE POWER

Tennessee Williams sets this explosive drama in a tiny apartment, which adds to the tension and intensity of these interpersonal relationships. Stella and Blanche go out for the night so that Stanley can have the apartment to play cards with his friends. When Stella and Blanche come home, Stanley is at first dismissive of them, but as the game drags on, he becomes more openly hostile. Blanche is attracted to one of the men there, Mitch, and asks Stella about him. She learns during this conversation that Stella actually likes Stanley for the powerful drive he possesses to succeed. Mitch strikes up a conversation with Blanche, and she turns on the radio. Stanley flies into a rage, throwing the radio out the window. When Stella reproaches him, he hits her, and his male friends have to subdue him. Stella runs upstairs to her neighbor Eunice's apartment. In this now iconic scene, Stanley begs his wife to come back by screaming her name. In this moment, Stanley owns the space of the entire neighborhood with his voice. Williams uses space to paint a picture of unbridled male power that will beat everything weaker than it into submission. He controls the space of the apartment and he controls the entire space of the city. Stella has no choice but to come back to him.

The next day Blanche tries to reason with her sister, calling Stanley an animal and asking her to leave him. Stella refuses, defending his actions. Meanwhile, Stanley does some digging into Blanche's affairs and tells her that his friend Shaw knows her from the Hotel Flamingo, a place where prostitutes are known to work. Blanche denies his accusations.

Stella throws a birthday party for Blanche during which Stanley goes into a rage. At the height of their argument, Stella goes into labor. Mitch shows up and confronts Blanche about her past. She admits that she has been promiscuous. He attempts to force himself on her, but she throws him out.

KINDNESS FROM STRANGERS IS PREFERABLE

Blanche cannot handle what her reality has become, so she changes into her finest evening gown, puts on a tiara, and talks to her dead husband, pretending she is once again a young southern belle with a promising future. Stanley returns to the apartment drunk. After a verbal argument, he rapes her.

This causes Blanche to further detach from reality. As the play ends, Blanche answers the door thinking a former lover is coming to take her away to the Caribbean, but instead it is a doctor who has come to take her to the asylum. The last scene is of Stella holding her newborn while the abusive Stanley puts his arm around her in their tiny powder keg of an apartment.

Ostensibly, Stanley is the villain of this play; however, the villain wins in the end as he gets to express his animal urges against both sisters, beating and raping with impunity. Under other circumstances, the reversal of normal class privilege might gain admiration from viewers, but the gender commentary in the play is too bleak to permit approval of Stanley's coup against the supposed "upper-class" sisters by putting them in their place. Although it seems that Williams meant for viewers to pity Blanche, the other imaginary world that she inhabits actually seems much more appealing than the one that Stella occupies. Even the reality of the insane asylum seems like a safer space than Stella's situation. In the end, every character in this play is doomed (as if a streetcar had run over them) by their own desires.

Lynn Marie Houston

Further Reading

If you liked *A Streetcar Named Desire,* you might like Edward Albee's play *Who's Afraid of Virginia Woolf,* as it examines a night of verbal sparring between a married couple that results in a shocking revelation.

Bibliography

Corrigan, Mary Ann. "Realism and Theatricalism in *A Streetcar Named Desire*." *Modern Drama* 19, no. 4 (1976): 385–96.

Crandell, George. "Misrepresentation and Miscegenation: Reading the Racialized Discourse of Tennessee Williams's *A Streetcar Named Desire*." *Modern Drama* 40, no. 3 (1997): 337–46.

Fleche, Anne. "The Space of Madness and Desire: Tennessee Williams and Streetcar." *Modern Drama* 38, no. 4 (1995): 496–509.

Holditch, W. Kenneth. "The Broken World: Romanticism, Realism, Naturalism in *A Streetcar Named Desire*." In *Confronting Tennessee Williams's* A Streetcar Named Desire: *Essays in Critical Pluralism,* edited by C. Kolin, 147–66. Westport, CT: Greenwood, 1993.

Holditch, W. Kenneth, and Richard F. Leavitt. *Tennessee Williams and the South.* Jackson: University Press of Mississippi, 2002.

Jackson, Esther Merle. *The Broken World of Tennessee Williams.* Madison: University of Wisconsin Press, 1965.

Koprince, Susan. "Domestic Violence in *A Streetcar Named Desire*." In *Tennessee Williams's* A Streetcar Named Desire, edited by Harold Bloom. New York: Bloom's Literary Criticism, 2009.

Ribkoff, Fred, and Paul Tyndall. "On the Dialectics of Trauma in Tennessee Williams' *A Streetcar Named Desire*." *Journal of Medical Humanities* 32, no. 4 (2011): 325–37.

Van Duyvenbode, Rachel. "Darkness Made Visible: Miscegenation, Masquerade and the Signified Racial Other in Tennessee Williams' *Baby Doll* and *A Streetcar Named Desire*." *Journal of American Studies* 35, no. 2 (2001): 203–15.

Vlasopolos, Anca. "Authorizing History: Victimization in *A Streetcar Named Desire*." *Theatre Journal* 38, no. 3 (1986): 322–38.

Sula

Toni Morrison's novel *Sula* examines how place is shaped by the people who live there and how, with their passing, the landscape changes. The story opens with the danger brought on by a proposal for land traditionally occupied by a black community to be developed into a golf course. This would represent its appropriation by upper-class white culture, epitomized by the neighboring town of Medallion. Originally, this hilly land in Ohio, known as Bottom, was given as a gift to a slave by his master because the owner thought it was worthless in terms of agricultural production, not as fertile as the soil of the valley it surrounds. The slave owner told his slave that the land was the "bottom of heaven" because it was so beautiful. However, with time, the surrounding rich, white community came to realize the commercial value of land with such views. The story that Morrison tells about the history of this community focuses on the lives of its residents, primarily two women, Nel and Sula, who started off as friends, but then had a disagreement and grew apart. Sula was very unconventional and misunderstood during her lifetime, but after she passes, Nel and the other townspeople come to realize her worth, much like the eventual appreciation by white neighbors of the land occupied by the black community of Bottom.

NEL VERSUS SULA: MAPPING SOCIAL MORES ONTO DIFFERENT FAMILY STRUCTURES

On the surface, it appears that Morrison categorizes the families Nel and Sula come from as socially acceptable and socially unacceptable, respectively. However, both families are responding to behaviors of the past generation. Here, Morrison reveals a sense of history that is reactionary and dialectical, meaning it continues to swing from side to side like a pendulum in response to the values of the previous generation. In addition, Morrison's development of the family cultures is rooted in conflicting ideas of femininity, where traditional morals are shown to be limiting and often founded on lies and hypocrisy.

Scholars note that Morrison develops Nel's family as concerned with proper moral upbringing and acceptance of social norms. As a child, she travels with her mother to New Orleans to see her great-grandmother Cecile, who is sick. On the train ride to New Orleans, Helene is harassed by a white train conductor. Instead of standing up for herself, she tries to win him over with a smile. When the other black passengers scorn Helene for her politeness, Nel decides that she will never react the way her mother did. By the time they arrive in New Orleans, Cecile has already passed. Instead, they are greeted indifferently by Rochelle, who is Helene's mother, Nel's grandmother, and a former prostitute. Nel has doubts about the straitlaced life her mother encourages.

Sula's family, on the contrary, embraces a loose lifestyle. Sula is being raised by two unconventional women: her grandmother, Eva, and her mother, Hannah. She lives with three informally adopted boys. Their family history is plagued by violence and loss. Her grandmother, Eva Peace, was abandoned by her husband after the birth of their three children: Hannah, Pearl, and Plum. One winter, Eva left town, too, but came back a few months later with only one of her legs and plenty of money. (The town gossip is that Eva lost her limb by having a train run over it for the insurance money.) When Eva's son, Plum, returns from World War I, he suffers from a heroin addiction. Because she wants to end his misery, Eva pours kerosene on Plum while he is asleep and sets him on fire, killing him.

The relationship between the two female characters is the heart of the novel and is the vehicle by which Morrison critiques an ideology that restricts women's life experiences. As preteens, Sula and Nel develop a close friendship built around a shared loneliness. One afternoon, Sula and Nel find a young neighbor, named Chicken Little down by the river. Sula plays a game with Chicken Little, swinging him around as he laughs. However, the young boy disappears into the river after she loses her grip on him. Both Sula and Nel fear they will be held accountable for his death. This traumatic event forms the seed of guilt that eventually catapults Nel back into a life of conventional morality. In contrast, it is what allows Sula, who processes her guilt and accepts the totality of her personhood (both the good and the bad), to break free of the narrow worldview imposed on her by life in the small town.

The tragedies continue throughout the story. Hannah questions Eva about Plum's death. While Eva admits to killing him, she justifies it through motherly love by saying that she couldn't stand to see him suffer. A few days later, Hannah's dress catches fire. In an effort to reach her to put out the fire, Eva leaps out of the window on the second floor. They are both taken to the hospital, where Hannah dies. During the crisis, Eva noticed that Sula had been on the porch quietly watching her mother burn. From Eva's perspective, of course, Morrison wants us to see Sula as perverse, but throughout the narrative the author attempts to show us how this is not the case, that in fact Sula embraces the totality of life—its joys and sorrows, the sacred and the profane.

After high school, Nel marries Jude Greene, and Sula goes away for 10 years. During that time, Nel embraces a traditional role. In contrast, Sula lives unconventionally, having affairs, even with some white men. However, after finding the same scripted routines of human behavior everywhere she goes, she returns home.

A few weeks after her return, Sula has Eva moved to a nursing home. She and Nel reunite, and Jude is quite taken with her. They end up having an affair, which prompts Jude to leave Nel and move to Detroit by himself. Nel ends her friendship with Sula.

Years pass, and Nel learns that Sula is seriously ill. She visits, but they exchange heated words and fail to reconcile. Shortly afterward, Sula dies, and the cohesiveness of the community dissolves, as if there were a supernatural connection between Sula's spirit and the well-being of the town. Because she put Eva in a nursing home and had an affair with Jude, the townspeople didn't like Sula very much. Yet, somehow Sula's presence in the community gave them the impetus to live harmoniously with one another. Morrison uses these two different women from opposite family situations to draw attention to the need for a healthy balance between piety and freedom and to the message that one loses its meaning without the other.

THE GEOGRAPHY OF SUFFERING AND ITS ERASURE

The story of Nel and Sula's friendship is set against the backdrop of the land and its conflicted history, but also against that of the secondary characters. One of them, Shadrack, allows Morrison to inject a note of nihilism into the novel. Shadrack fought in WWI and has returned with post-traumatic stress disorder (PTSD). Morrison doesn't develop this illness in a clinical fashion, but rather in an imaginative way: to deal with all of the death he has witnessed, Shadrack organizes a National Suicide Day, a day where he marches through town ringing a bell and calling attention to the suffering that is part of existence. Initially the townspeople tried ignoring it, but eventually the event became a yearly occasion in the community. In response to the lingering effects of the Great Depression, one year a group of townspeople actually join Shadrack on his National Suicide Day march. Ironically, as they pass through the tunnel being constructed to connect Bottom to the neighboring communities, it collapses and most of them are crushed to death.

After Sula's death, the community of Bottom is plagued by disaster and disease. One day after visiting Eva in the nursing home, Nel realizes that after Chicken Little's death she had turned to social norms as a way to define herself as "good." Nel runs to find Sula's grave. She realizes that it was Sula she had missed these years, not her husband. She calls out for her friend and what she lost by clinging to rigid notions of proper behavior and failing to embrace the totality of existence. By the conclusion of the story in 1965, the entire community is about to be razed for the construction of a golf course, and all of its history lost. Morrison asserts that for some populations, such as African Americans, their history might be full of suffering, but it is all they have as history to preserve, and it is intimately linked to local geographies.

Lynn Marie Houston

Further Reading

If you enjoyed *Sula,* you should make sure to read other novels by Toni Morrison, such as *The Bluest Eye,* a novel about a young African American girl living in the 1930s who develops a hatred for her skin and eye color, praying for blue eyes. The story also deals with rape, incest, and racism. Also, you might like *Beloved,* a novel that explores how an ex-slave is haunted by what she does to try to protect her children from slavery.

Alice Walker also explores similar characters and their struggles in *The Color Purple*. Lastly, Zora Neale Hurston writes, like Morrison does, about the conditions of African Americans post-slavery. Although Hurston was writing a few generations earlier than Morrison, many critics compare the work of these two women as having much in common in terms of the African American fight for identity and voice.

Bibliography

Anderson, Pauline P. "Earth, Water, and Black Bodies: Elements at Work in Toni." *Environment* 3 (1996): 155–82.

Bjork, Patrick Bryce. *The Novels of Toni Morrison the Search for Self and Place Within the Community.* New York: P. Lang, 1992.

Christian, Barbara. "Community and Nature: The Novels of Toni Morrison." *The Journal of Ethnic Studies* 7, no. 4 (1980): 65.

Dixon, Melvin. *Ride Out the Wilderness: Geography and Identity in Afro-American Literature.* Urbana: University of Illinois Press, 1987.

Jones, Carolyn M. "Southern Landscape as Psychic Landscape in Toni Morrison's Fiction." *Studies in the Literary Imagination* 31, no. 2 (1998): 37.

Lounsberry, Barbara, and Grace Ann Hovet. "Principles of Perception in Toni Morrison's *Sula.*" In *Black American Literature Forum* 13, no. 1 (1979): 126–29.

McKee, Patricia. "Spacing and Placing in Toni Morrison's *Sula.*" *MFS Modern Fiction Studies* 42, no. 1 (1996): 1–30.

Russell, Danielle. *Between the Angle and the Curve: Mapping Gender, Race, Space, and Identity in Willa Cather and Toni Morrison.* New York: Routledge, 2006.

Terry, Jennifer Ann. "'Shuttles in the rocking loom of history': Dislocation in Toni Morrison's Fiction." PhD diss., University of Warwick, 2003.

Wallace, Kathleen R., and Karla Armbruster. "The Novels of Toni Morrison: 'Wild Wilderness Where There Was None.'" *Armbruster and Wallace* (2001): 211–30.

The Sun Also Rises

Ernest Hemingway's first novel tells the story of Jake Barnes and his friends in 1920s Paris, as they try unsuccessfully to connect emotionally and philosophically to the world around them. Many of the characters were wounded in some way during World War I, symbolized by Jake's possibly literal and definitely emotional castration. Robert Cohn, a "former middleweight boxer" and budding author, is one of the only characters not wounded by the war, and he falls head over heels in love with Lady Brett Ashley, a beautiful but promiscuous British divorcée whom Jake and nearly everyone else is also in love with. On a trip to Spain to see the running of the bulls in Pamplona, everything "explodes" when Lady Brett becomes infatuated with the bullfighter Pedro Romero. Robert Cohn beats up Romero, as well as Jake, and the fiesta ends. Lady Brett eventually loses Romero and calls Jake for help. He goes to her aid, but this is not a happy ending. Hemingway leaves these two emotionally sterile human beings with only their fantasies to keep them alive.

THE GEOGRAPHY OF PLACE

One of the central features of *The Sun Also Rises* is the contrast between the "civilized" world of Paris and the "natural" world of rural Spain. Hemingway describes sitting "at a table on the terrace of the Napolitain . . . watching it get dark and the electric signs come on, and the red and green stop-and-go traffic-signal, and the crowd going by, and the horse-cabs clippety-clopping along at the edge of the solid taxi traffic, and the *poules* going by, singly and in pairs, looking for the evening meal." In this city-world, Jake Barnes and his friends go from party to party in a desultory way, looking for something they cannot describe.

The broken people who populate the book remain in this self-destructive cycle in all the landscapes they visit but one. We get a brief respite in Spain, where Jake and his friend Bill find peace fishing the Irati River. On the way: "We walked on the road between the thick trunks of the old beeches and sunlight came through

> Then we crossed a wide plain, and there was a big river off on the right shining in the sun from between the line of trees, and away off you could see the plateau of Pamplona rising out of the plain, and the walls of the city, and the great brown cathedral, and the broken skyline of the other churches.
>
> **Ernest Hemingway, *The Sun Also Rises* (1926)**

the leaves in light patches on the grass. The trees were big, and the foliage was thick but it was not gloomy. There was no undergrowth, only the smooth grass, very green and fresh, and the big gray trees well-spaced as though it were a park. 'This is country,' Bill said.'" A time of tranquility and simple pleasures is ruined by the arrival of their "friends" and the beginning of the fiesta of San Fermin in Pamplona, where the climax of the novel takes place.

THE FIESTA AT PAMPLONA

Pamplona is the perfect place for the final blowup between the characters, a place of blood and sweat and primal feelings, where the group of friends can take a fiesta approach to life, drowning the self in alcohol, sex, and excitement. This is why the festival of San Fermin appeals so much to the characters—because the way they try to live every day in Paris is the norm during this time. A rocket goes up to announce the beginning of the fiesta, and "By the time the second rocket had burst there were so many people in the arcade, that had been empty a minute before, that the waiter, holding the bottle high up over his head, could hardly get through the crowd to our table. People were coming into the square from all sides, and down the street we heard the pipes and the fifes and drums coming. They were playing the *riau-riau* music, the pipes shrill and the drums pounding, and behind them came the men and boys dancing." This party keeps going for seven days, and the characters barely sleep, going from the events in the cafés to the bullring.

As Hemingway describes the fiesta (also the original title of the book), readers can interpret whether this party life is heaven or hell. "It was like certain dinners I remember from the war. There was much wine, an ignored tension, and a feeling of things coming that you could not prevent happening." As Jake tries to escape the physical and emotional wounds of the war, he unintentionally or subconsciously re-creates the war in various ways. Perhaps this means that the only escape is death.

THE BULLRING

Hemingway describes the geography of the bullring itself as no English or American writer had ever done before, as a place of ritualized death, for edification, not entertainment. It is not a sport, but an aesthetic experience, and any ugliness is caused not by the death that occurs there, but by a lack of excellence on the part of the bullfighters. Pedro Romero embodies the qualities necessary to make the ritual work, and furthermore he believes in and represents a set of values. Even though Jake and several of the other characters admire these values, they remain foreign and brutal. But we might say that some values are better than none.

The landscape of the bullring becomes a microcosm for the events of the novel, and Hemingway speaks of the "terrain" of the bull and the bullfighter, bringing the geography of place that has dominated the book down to the human level. In the energetic space between the bullfighter and the bull, Hemingway shows the seductive dance between life and death. Robert Cohn is unable to appreciate the fights, preferring illusion to reality in all things, including his fantasy of romantic love for Lady Brett. As a passionate man himself, Jake also prefers the symbol rather than the reality, but then again, he has no choice. Readers might see him as one of the steers during the running of the bulls, guiding and calming the more powerful animals, but unable and unwilling to compete in the ring.

Eric D. Lehman

Further Reading

If you liked *The Sun Also Rises,* you may also like Hemingway's *A Moveable Feast, Death in the Afternoon, The Dangerous Summer, A Farewell to Arms,* and *For Whom the Bell Tolls.* Another author writing at the same time as Hemingway was F. Scott Fitzgerald. If you liked the postwar romance and socializing in Hemingway's work, try Fitzgerald's *The Great Gatsby* or *Tales of the Jazz Age.*

Bibliography

Borcău, Mădălina. "The Geography of Self-Representation: Orientalism in Ernest Hemingway's *The Sun Also Rises.*" *Romanian Journal of English Studies* 11, no. 1 (2014): 65–70.

Godfrey, Laura Gruber. "Hemingway, the Preservation Impulse, and Cultural Geography." In *Hemingway's Geographies: Intimacy, Materiality, and Memory.* New York: Palgrave Macmillan, 2016.

Godfrey, Laura Gruber. "Introduction: Ernest Hemingway's Intimate Geographies." In *Hemingway's Geographies: Intimacy, Materiality, and Memory.* New York: Palgrave Macmillan, 2016.

Jeffrey, Herlihy-Mera. "When Hemingway Hated Paris: Divorce Proceedings, Contemplations of Suicide, and the Deleted Chapters of *The Sun Also Rises.*" *Studies in The Novel* 44, no. 1 (2012): 49–61.

Kack, Elin. "Troubling Space: Dispersal of Place in *The Sun Also Rises* and *The Garden of Eden.*" *The Hemingway Review* 37, no. 2 (2018): 6–22.

Kevin, Maier. "Old Worlds, New Travels: Jack London's *People of the Abyss,* Ernest Hemingway's *The Sun Also Rises,* and the Cultural Politics of Travel." *Studies in American Naturalism* 11, no. 1 (2017): 43–54.

Keyser, Catherine. "An All-Too-Moveable Feast: Ernest Hemingway and the Stakes of Terroir." *Resilience: A Journal of the Environmental Humanities* 2, no. 1 (2015).

Larson, Kelli A. "On Safari with Hemingway: Tracking the Most Recent Scholarship." In *Hemingway and Africa,* edited by Miriam B. Mandel, 323–84. Rochester, NY: Camden House, 2011.

Mellette, Justin. "'Floating I saw only the sky': Leisure and Self-Fulfillment in Hemingway's *The Sun Also Rises.*" *The Hemingway Review* 34, no. 1 (2014): 61–75.

Northrop, Rachel. "Bodies on the Line: Border Crossing in the Fiction of Ernest Hemingway and Salman Rushdie." Master's thesis, City University of New York (CUNY), 2016.

Rodriguez-Pazos, Gabriel. "Bulls, Bullfights, and Bullfighters in Hemingway's *The Sun Also Rises.*" *The Hemingway Review* 34, no. 1 (2014): 82–96.

Sindelar, Nancy W. *Influencing Hemingway: People and Places That Shaped His Life and Work.* Lanham, MD: Rowman & Littlefield Publishers, 2014.

Tomkins, David. "The 'Lost Generation' and the Generation of Loss: Ernest Hemingway's Materiality of Absence and *The Sun Also Rises.*" *Modern Fiction Studies* 54, no. 4 (2008): 744–65.

Vernon, Alex. "The Rites of War and Hemingway's *The Sun Also Rises.*" *The Hemingway Review* 35, no. 1 (Fall 2015): 13–35.

Their Eyes Were Watching God

Their Eyes Were Watching God by Zora Neale Hurston tells the life story of the African American character Janie Crawford, who lives in various places in Florida during the early 20th century. Janie is the product of a rape, as was her mother before her, who was a slave. She is raised by her grandmother, who tries to set her up for a better life by marrying her off to an older man who can provide for her. However, Janie believes that one should marry for love. She eventually runs off with Joe Starks, who becomes the first mayor of Eatonville, the first black-only town in Florida. Starks quickly becomes jealous and controlling, and Janie's life is miserable as she runs the general store for him. Starks dies of a kidney disease and Janie achieves a state of independence for the first time in her life. Despite having many well-to-do suitors, Janie meets a young gambler named Tea Cake and falls in love. They move to Southern Florida and work on a farm, where they are happy. However, as they try to survive the flooding after a hurricane, Tea Cake is bitten by a rabid dog and gets rabies. In a delirious state, he threatens to shoot Janie, and she has to kill him in self-defense. When she returns to Eatonville after being acquitted of murder, the townspeople gossip about her but ultimately accept her again among their community.

THE PEAR TREE

In a key passage in *Their Eyes Were Watching God,* Janie sits under a blooming pear tree. She is 16 and blossoming, too, in terms of an awakening sexuality. As she sits under the tree, she sees a bee gathering pollen, and she is inspired to desire a relationship. However, she doesn't want to marry for money or security, which is what her grandmother wants for her; she wants true compatibility and a sense of connection with her partner. In the pear tree scene, Hurston described Janie's vision of love as much more romantic than her grandmother's perspective on marriage. When her grandmother arranges a marriage for Janie with Logan Killicks, a middle-aged farmer who can provide for her, Janie is heartbroken because the relationship does not live up to the image she conjured while sitting under the pear tree. Neither does her marriage to Joe Starks, who is very controlling and possessive. Sitting under the pear tree, Janie had imagined a relationship of equals. She finally finds that when she meets Tea Cake, although she loses him after a fatal brush with a rabid dog. Here, early in the novel, the image of the pear tree foreshadows that relationship, which is the outcome of Janie's lifelong quest for the love she first imagined while watching the bee and feeling connected to the cycles of nature. Like the loss of blossoms in the fall, Janie eventually realizes that even love is part of the cycle of life and death.

EATONVILLE, FLORIDA

Zora Neale Hurston grew up just north of Orlando in Eatonville, Florida, one of the first all-black municipalities in the United States. The town holds an annual festival in honor of Hurston. Hurston seems to have been inspired by real people in the town, such as Joe Clarke, who was the first mayor of the town and owner of a popular store, which she frequented. In her novel, she features the store as a center of the community's life, not bound together by commercialism, but by the gossip exchanged as citizens sat on the front porch and talked or played checkers. The novel begins and ends with the talk of townsfolk.

Hurston was deeply invested in the culture of this region of Florida. As an anthropologist with the Works Progress Administration, she returned to Eatonville and captured audio recordings of interviews, folk tales, and songs. The everyday speech of this community is a feature of her work. It was because of her heavy use of dialect that other African American authors sometimes had a problem with her representation of black people: they thought she showed them as "too common," but Hurston saw the beauty in black, working-class culture of early 20th-century Florida.

Lynn Marie Houston

This photo, taken in the 1950s, features Zora Neale Hurston in profile as she listens to a friend play guitar. Readers can image she had such a setting in mind when she wrote in *Their Eyes Were Watching God* about the group of men who would play cards and music on the porch outside of Joe Stark's store. (Fotosearch/Getty Images)

Further Reading
Other authors wrote about African American culture at the same time as Hurston and are also members of the Harlem Renaissance—you may enjoy Langston Hughes, Claude McKay, Nella Larsen, and Jean Toomer.

Bibliography
Ashland, Alex. "Off the Grid: Zora Neale Hurston's Racial Geography in *Their Eyes Were Watching God*." *Iowa Journal of Cultural Studies* 17, no. 1 (2017): 76–90.

Bullard, Robert D. "Differential Vulnerabilities: Environmental and Economic Inequality and Government Response to Unnatural Disasters." *Social Research* 75, no. 3 (2008): 753–84.

Cassidy, Thomas. "Janie's Rage: The Dog and the Storm in *Their Eyes Were Watching God*." *CLA Journal* 36, no. 3 (1993): 260–69.

Dixon, Melvin. *Ride Out the Wilderness: Geography and Identity in Afro-American Literature*. Champaign: University of Illinois Press, 1987.

Friedman, Susan Stanford. *Mappings: Feminism and the Cultural Geographies of Encounter*. Princeton, NJ: Princeton University Press, 1998.

Hicks, Scott. "Rethinking King Cotton: George W. Lee, Zora Neale Hurston, and Global/Local Revisions of the South and the Nation." *Arizona Quarterly: A Journal of American Literature, Culture, and Theory* 65, no. 4 (2009): 63–91.

King, Sigrid. "Naming and Power in Zora Neale Hurston's *Their Eyes Were Watching God*." *Black American Literature Forum* 24, no. 4 (1990): 683–96.

Larson, Lars Erik. "Routes and Roots: American Literature as a Means of Understanding Contemporary Space and Place." *English Faculty Publications and Presentations* 9 (2015).

Lillios, Anna. "'The Monstropolous Beast': The Hurricane in Zora Neale Hurston's *Their Eyes Were Watching God*." *Southern Quarterly* 36, no. 3 (1998): 89.

Penate, Patricia Coloma. "Foot Tracks on the Ocean: Zora Neale Hurston and the Creation of an African-American Transcultural Identity." *Foot* 8 (2012): 7.

Rieger, Christopher B. "Clear-Cutting Eden: Representations of Nature in Southern fiction, 1930–1950." Doctoral thesis, Louisiana State University, 2002.

Roberts, Brian Russell. "Archipelagic Diaspora, Geographical Form, and Hurston's *Their Eyes Were Watching God*." *American Literature* 85, no. 1 (2013): 121–49.

Stein, Rachel. *Shifting the Ground: American Women Writers' Revisions of Nature, Gender, and Race*. Charlottesville: University of Virginia Press, 1997.

The Things They Carried

The Things They Carried (1990) is a groundbreaking work of creative nonfiction by veteran author Tim O'Brien. In this work, O'Brien writes about his time in Vietnam, where he served in the Army after being drafted. His loose fictionalization of autobiographical events created a new genre that attempts to get at the truth of war through the repetition of key scenes, often with variations as to how they happened. This style accurately portrays the way memory works in victims of trauma.

In the beginning of this series of linked stories, O'Brien reveals many of the things soldiers in Vietnam carried, not only their gear, but also all of the emotional burdens as well. One of the emotional items carried by their platoon leader, Jimmy

Cross, is his love of a woman back home named Martha, who writes letters to him but does not return his romantic feelings. After one of his men dies, Lieutenant Cross decides that his love for Martha is keeping him from being an effective leader, so he burns all of her letters.

O'Brien narrates the story of being drafted and having thoughts about fleeing to Canada. He makes a trip to the border, where he goes fishing only 15 feet away from the safety of the Canadian shore. However, afraid of being labeled a coward and of not living up to other's expectations of him, he cannot do it. He returns home and makes preparations to go to war in Vietnam.

O'Brien details much of the brutality of war, including the senseless loss of Curt Lemon, who stepped on a land mine while playing a game of catch with another soldier. He also tells about how he killed an enemy soldier. This story also captures the tragedy of war, as O'Brien goes through the man's things and finds a photograph of his family and a journal he'd kept.

The Things They Carried also follows some of the characters home to the United States after their return. Norman Bowker, for instance, has a hard time readjusting to civilian life and ends up hanging himself. O'Brien reflects on the ways it is hard for Vietnam veterans to live with the memories they have of the war, especially their feelings of guilt over the deaths of their fellow soldiers. Many of the stories deal with the emotional toll of trying to prove one's masculinity by being brave in the face of intensely traumatic events.

THE JUNGLES OF VIETNAM

The heavily forested areas of Vietnam provided numerous challenges for the U.S. military and prompted them to develop chemical weapons of deforestation, namely Agent Orange, an herbicide that proved extremely toxic to the Vietnamese population and also to the U.S. soldiers in close proximity to it. However, with less leaf cover, the enemy had less chance to hide their movements and operations, especially their practices of guerilla warfare. This chemical also served to destroy the fertility of the land so that the enemy could not sustain themselves through agricultural production. O'Brien mentions Agent Orange specifically as one of the many things that U.S. soldiers carried with them as they marched through Vietnam, and that would possibly haunt them later on with various kinds of cancers.

THE VETERAN'S TROUBLED NOTION OF HOME

When the veteran characters in *The Things They Carried* return home, many have problems readjusting to their lives as civilians. In Norman Bowker's case, many of his friends have moved away or their lives have changed significantly because they got married and had kids. It is difficult for him to relate to them after his experiences and he is plagued by the sense that the world has moved on and forgotten about the war while he is still struggling with the experiences he had in Vietnam. O'Brien illuminates how there is no one to listen to the stories Norman needs to tell, as he drives around his town on the Fourth of July trying and failing to reach out to someone who will listen to him. Like many veterans coming home from an unpopular war, Norman is unsure of how to relate to those back home, who might be judgmental about his actions or perspective. He ends up driving in circles around a lake, not really engaged with the setting, but lost in his memories of Vietnam. Bowker finally wades into the lake and commits suicide. Here, the lake fails to act as a symbol of hope and renewal. Instead of baptism, Bowker finds oblivion as his past follows him home and makes it impossible for him to return to the life he knew.

Lynn Marie Houston

Further Reading

O'Brien's novel is a fictionalized account based loosely around his time serving in Vietnam. Another work that is an actual memoir written about the author's deployment in Vietnam is Philip Caputo's *A Rumor of War*. Another work with the same setting but written from a journalist's perspective is *Dispatches* by Michael Herr. Robert Olen Butler also served in Vietnam and has written a number of works that feature Vietnamese characters. Be sure to read his collection of short stories *A Good Scent from a Strange Mountain* as well as his novels *Perfume River, They Whisper,* and *The Deep Green Sea*.

Bibliography

Bates, Milton J. *The Wars We Took to Vietnam: Cultural Conflict and Storytelling*. Berkeley: University of California Press, 1996

Lewis, Lloyd B. *The Tainted War: Culture and Identity in Vietnam War Narratives*. Westport, CT: Greenwood, 1985.

Chen, Tina. "'Unraveling the Deeper Meaning': Exile and the Embodied Poetics of Displacement in Tim O'Brien's *The Things They Carried*." *Contemporary Literature* 39, no. 1 (Spring 1998): 77–98.

Kim, Na Rae. "A Transnational Perspective on Vietnam War Narratives of the US and South Korea." Master's thesis, Georgia State University, 2015.

Kitchen, Judith. "Out of Place: Reading O'Brien and O'Brien." *The Georgia Review* 50, no. 3 (1996): 477–94.

McMullan, Paloma. "Corporeal Territories: The Body in American Narratives of the Vietnam War." PhD diss., University of Nottingham, 2004.

Owens, David M. "The Devil's Topographer: Ambrose Bierce and the American War Story." PhD diss., Purdue University, 2001.

Silbergleid, Robin. "Making Things Present: Tim O'Brien's Autobiographical Metafiction." *Contemporary Literature* 50, no. 1 (Spring 2009): 129–55.

Smith, Patrick A., ed. *Conversations with Tim O'Brien*. Jackson: University Press of Mississippi, 2012.

Uchmanowicz, Pauline. "Vanishing Vietnam: Whiteness and the Technology of Memory." *Historical Memory and Representations of the Vietnam War* 6 (2000): 168.

Vernon, Alex. "Salvation, Storytelling, and Pilgrimage in Tim O'Brien's *The Things They Carried*." *Mosaic: An Interdisciplinary Critical Journal* 36, no. 4 (2003): 171–88.

Wesley, Marilyn. "Truth and Fiction in Tim O'Brien's *If I Die in a Combat Zone* and *The Things They Carried*." *College Literature* 29, no. 2 (2002): 1–18.

To Kill a Mockingbird

Harper Lee sets her novel *To Kill a Mockingbird* in Maycomb, Alabama, during the Depression era. The story is narrated by Jean Louise "Scout" Finch, whose father is a prominent lawyer in the town. The narrative pits the high moral standards of Atticus Finch and his family against the closed-mindedness of the rest of its citizens. The environment of racism and prejudice lingers in the minds of an older generation in the South who lived through slavery and the Civil War.

THE CULTURAL ENVIRONMENT OF THE DEPRESSION

A number of characters in the story are disenfranchised for various reasons. Whites from the lower socioeconomic class behave much like the protagonist of the William Faulkner short story "Barn Burning." The father in that story is frustrated by the fact that former slaves are being given prestigious positions, such as being asked to wear fine linen coats as butlers inside mansions, when he is working the fields and living in a shack. He turns to violence against the plantation system that has not so much abolished slavery as it has inserted poor white migrant workers into the position once occupied by African Americans. The economic downturn following emancipation and the Civil War hit the South extremely hard and caused resentment toward black people Northerners, and the wealthy.

Boo Radley is also a marginalized character in the novel, held seemingly hostage in his house by his brother due to a possible mental and emotional development disorder. Scout, her brother Jem, and their friend Dill are intrigued by rumors about him. The children then sneak over to the house at night but are scared away when Boo's brother, Nathan Radley, fires his gun. Lee uses techniques of character development throughout the novel to show people at their best and worst within short time frames. Her novel parallels how progressive cultural developments upended life in the South. For instance, Boo Radley was feared by the children, but he was ultimately shown to be a valuable member of society when he saved Scout from being killed by Bob Ewell.

Another example is Mr. Cunningham, who leads a mob to the county jail with the intent of killing Tom Robinson, a black man who was falsely accused of raping a white woman. Scout appeals to Cunningham by speaking in a heartfelt manner about his son, his family, and his financial situation. Although he was prepared to murder an innocent man merely because he was black, Mr. Cunningham has a conscience, and is able to be brought to reason through an appeal to his humanity. Harper Lee's novel simultaneously captures both the darkness and light within human nature. Both of these extremes vacillated wildly in the confusing times after Reconstruction and during the Depression.

MAPPING RACISM

When Atticus Finch takes Tom Robinson's case, he knows the chances are slim that he can save him, but he believes it is important to try to see that Tom gets a fair trial. Atticus is a mouthpiece in the novel for the importance of rejecting negative social norms in favor of one's individual sense of justice. The Finch family is attacked in many ways because of their "unpopular" views of racial equality, bringing the fight against bigotry into their home. Scout and Jem, when they find themselves whispered about and taunted, have trouble keeping their tempers. At a family Christmas gathering, Scout beats up her cousin Francis when he accuses Atticus of ruining the family name by being a "n****r-lover." Jem cuts off the tops of a neighbor's flower bushes after the old woman, Mrs. Dubose, speaks ill of Atticus. As his punishment, Jem is forced by Atticus to read out loud to her every day. Jem does not realize it at the time, but later he understands that he was helping Mrs. Dubose break her morphine addiction. Atticus holds this old woman up as an example of true courage: the will to keep fighting even when you know you cannot win. She is a foil for Atticus who takes on Tom's case to fight for racial justice, even though he cannot win.

Throughout the trial, Atticus presents solid evidence that Tom is not responsible for the crime and that the true abuser is actually Mayella's father, Bob Ewell. According to the sheriff's testimony, Mayella's bruises were on the right side of her face, which means she was most likely punched with a left hand. Tom Robinson's left arm is useless due to an old accident, whereas Mr. Ewell leads with his left. Given the evidence of reasonable doubt, Tom should go free. However, the jury of all white men ultimately finds Tom Robinson guilty of the crime despite all the evidence to the contrary. Lee's point is that racism exists systematically in the legal institutions of our country, and that even though families like the Finches may fight against it at a local and interpersonal level, they are up against larger structures—legal precedent and tradition—which many white people, at the time, were reluctant to abolish.

Lee permits a small victory in how long it takes the jury to decide, a sign that she has some hope for the future and that she believes change is happening in small increments. Atticus says that normally a decision like this would be made in minutes, because a black man's word would not be trusted. His hopes for an appeal are dashed when Tom tries to escape from prison and is shot to death in the process. Jem has trouble handling the results of the trial, feeling that his trust in the goodness and rationality of humanity has been betrayed.

After the trial concludes, Bob Ewell accuses Atticus of ruining his honor and vows to get revenge. He attacks Scout and Jem with a large kitchen knife while they walk home after a school Halloween pageant. During the attack, Boo Radley stabs Mr. Ewell and saves the children. The sheriff declares that Mr. Ewell fell on his own knife so that Boo won't have to be tried for murder. This lie is deemed acceptable because it serves a larger good. The sheriff's response dialogues directly with Jem's disappointment, showing that sometimes the law does protect the innocent.

Lee's novel maps the way that people cling to past ways of being as part of their identities. She charts the difficulty they have developing their thinking, despite having role models like Atticus Finch to show them the way. Even Boo Radley, with his possible developmental issues, knows right from wrong, just as the Finch children, although young, already know that many of the townspeople are wrong in their views. Much like Faulkner's story, "A Rose for Emily," *To Kill a*

Mockingbird critiques the Southern inability to let go of the past and embrace a more progressive identity. In the novel, the physical and symbolic spaces of the town of Maycomb serve as a microcosm of the region to demonstrate how deeply rooted, and yet wrong, the old values are.

Lynn Marie Houston

Further Reading

If you enjoyed *To Kill a Mockingbird,* you might enjoy another story that tells of a black man falsely accused of a crime, and how one person tries to make a difference in the mindset of a small Southern town: Ernest J. Gaines's *A Lesson Before Dying* continues Harper Lee's interest in justice and equality. If Scout's development in the novel interests you, then you should like Betty Smith's *A Tree Grows in Brooklyn,* which narrates a young woman's coming-of-age in Brooklyn at the beginning of the 20th century.

Bibliography

Best, Rebecca H. "Panopticism and the Use of 'the Other' in To Kill a Mockingbird." *The Mississippi Quarterly* 62, no. 3/4 (2009): 541–52.

Hobbs, Steven H. "The Tribes of Maycomb County: The Continuing Quest to Transcend Our Differences." *Cumberland Law Review* 47 (2016): 61.

Johnson, Claudia. "The Secret Courts of Men's Hearts: Code and Law in Harper Lee's *To Kill a Mockingbird*." *Studies in American Fiction* 19, no. 2 (1991): 129–39.

Kreyling, Michael. *The South That Wasn't There: Postsouthern Memory and History.* Baton Rouge: Louisiana State University Press, 2010.

Phelps, Theresa Godwin. "The Margins of Maycomb: A Rereading of *To Kill a Mockingbird*." *Alabama Law Review* 45 (1993): 511–29.

Watson, Rachel. "The View from the Porch: Race and the Limits of Empathy in the Film *To Kill a Mockingbird*." *The Mississippi Quarterly* 63, no. 3/4 (2010): 419–43.

U

Uncle Tom's Cabin

Harriet Beecher Stowe crafted the characters and plot of her novel from historical events and from interviews that she conducted with former slaves. President Abraham Lincoln credited her with influencing the Civil War because she educated readers about the evils of slavery in this best-selling work. The geography of *Uncle Tom's Cabin* vacillates between the hostile world of plantation life and the safe sites of the Underground Railroad, the secret network of people helping to take slaves to freedom. Stowe's representations of geographical features give a sentimental tone to this book, as aspects of the landscape align with Christian ideals to aid the cause of abolition and escaping slaves.

THE PHYSICAL AND CULTURAL GEOGRAPHY OF SLAVERY

The Mason-Dixon Line, the geographical division between the Northern and Southern states in the United States, is a prominent distinction in this novel as the narrative follows two families of slaves through their saga to escape the brutality of slavery and reunite as a family.

Uncle Tom, his wife, and children, are slaves on a plantation owned by the Shelby family. Arthur Shelby and his wife, Emily, try to be kindhearted toward their slaves. However, when the Shelbys' debts mount, they decide to sell two slaves—Uncle Tom and a young boy named Harry—to Mr. Haley, a notoriously harsh slave trader.

Tom is well liked by his owners, and everyone on the plantation because of his gentle nature and positive temperament. He lives his life without complaint, with his wife and their children in their own cabin, which has been provided. Although he is heartbroken, he says he will not run away before the sale, as that would only increase the debt owed by his master, thus forcing additional sales of slaves on the plantation. As Tom is being taken away, Mrs. Shelby tells him that she will buy him back as soon as she can. During the boat ride to the slave market, Tom meets a young white girl named Eva and they become friends. Eva falls overboard, but Tom jumps into the river and saves her. Subsequently, her father, Augustine St. Clare, purchases Tom out of gratitude.

The sale of the young boy Harry, son of Eliza, who serves as Emily Shelby's personal servant, does not go as planned for the Shelbys. Arthur's wife is reluctant to sell Eliza's son. After overhearing the Shelbys debate his sale, she flees north with Harry, trying to plot a course for Canada. Although she is chased by Haley, she is able to escape from Kentucky by jumping onto ice blocks floating in the Ohio River and successfully reaching the other shore. A slave hunter named Loker is

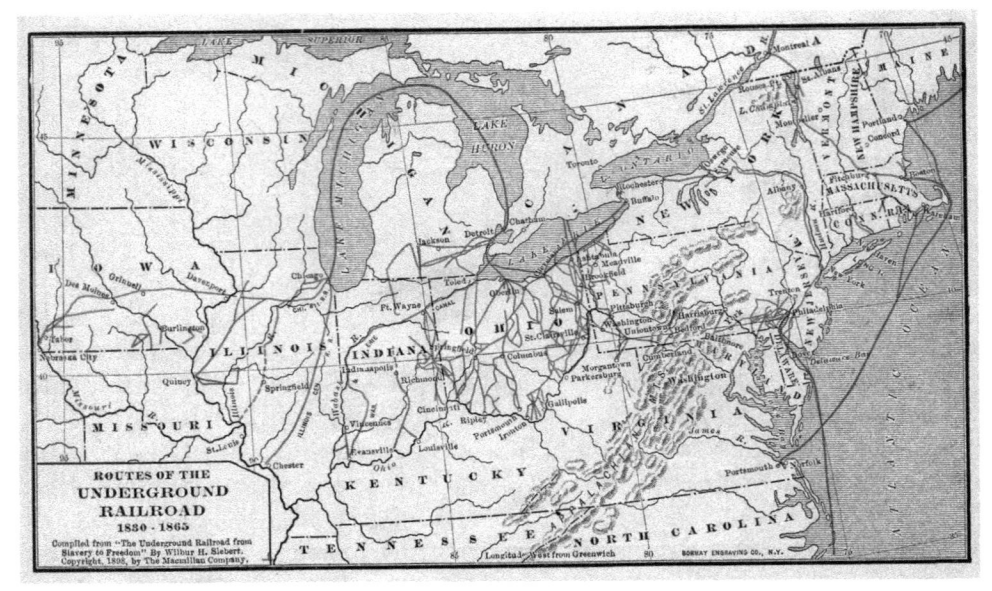

This map from 1920 shows routes that were used between 1830 and 1865 to help deliver slaves to freedom in the northern United States and Canada. Note the heavy concentration of routes passing through Ohio, which is where Eliza in *Uncle Tom's Cabin* crosses north from Kentucky. (Interim Archives/Getty Images)

now pursuing Eliza and Harry. In a Quaker village, Eliza finds refuge with a kind family. She also finds her husband George there: he had escaped from a harsh master on a plantation near the Shelbys'. The Quakers are connected with the Underground Railroad and help the family escape.

The bulk of the narrative in this novel is related to the day-to-day lives of slaves whose work assignments are in the interior of houses. In this respect, Stowe gives us a privileged look into the daily work of slaves. She does not include as much description of what life is like working outside in the fields. However, what she does well is to detail the voyage of escape, which involves unknown terrain and help from strangers. The river, for instance, is a prominent symbol in Eliza's frantic journey north and is based on a true story. Other elements of the natural landscape help to conceal the escaped slaves. In Stowe's description, the agency seems to be on the part of the environment more so than on the part of the African American characters seeking freedom. They are traveling through areas they do not know, relying on the goodwill and decency of other people as well as on the bounty of the Earth.

Many scholars note that the literary work is based on the real-life story of Josiah Henson who fled his life as a slave and made it to freedom in Canada in 1830. The homestead where he settled, married, and opened a school, is now a historic site and museum in Dresden, Ontario.

Much of what motivates the characters in Stowe's novel is not the notion of freedom in the abstract so much as the particular freedom of private property: they long for a land where they can be free, where they have the resources to build their own house and cultivate their own crops. In this respect, having land means a place to keep families together.

THE ROLE OF CHRISTIAN SENTIMENTALISM

Much of the novel pursues an indictment of slavery from a Christian perspective, which involves slaves finding strength in God to be kind and forgiving to the whites who do them wrong. For example, Tom develops a good relationship with his new master and his daughter, Eva, partly because he and Eva have similar beliefs about faith and morals. When Eva falls gravely ill, she soliloquizes from her bed, telling her family that she does not fear death and will be happy in heaven where the types of injustices she deplores, like slavery, do not exist. In another example, as George and Eliza are on their journey north toward freedom, the slave hunter Loker and his men are on their trail. As they close in, George shoots Loker in his side, but they deliver him to the nearby village so his wound can be tended.

The Christian principles of "loving one's neighbor" and "turning the other cheek" are what defines many of the slave characters in the novel, certainly Uncle Tom, whose name has come to be used in a derogatory manner in contemporary references. These Christian notions do not offer the kind of solace they did to previous generations. Instead, such practices now seem weak; in fact, many readers of the novel since the 20th century read Uncle Tom as a figure who participates in his own oppression by internalizing it and failing to speak out or act out against it. Stowe's point obviously was about trying to retain one's dignity and the sanctity of one's soul in a situation that strips everything else away from a person. However, many passages of her text are seen as heavy-handed in terms of their sentimentality, meaning that they blatantly and self-consciously seek to elicit from readers a scripted emotional response.

The St. Clare family is one of Stowe's primary vehicles for this sentimentality. When Mr. St. Clare, for example, discusses slavery with his cousin Ophelia, she voices her opposition to it at the institutional level, but admits that she views blacks through the eyes of prejudice. St. Clare shares that, on the contrary, he does not harbor prejudice toward blacks but is frustrated because he feels he cannot do anything to get rid of the institution of slavery. He then buys Topsy, a young black girl, so that Ophelia can witness the humanity of slaves. After Eva's death, St. Clare vows to set Tom free. However, in another plot twist that emphasizes how unfair life was for African Americans at the time, and how capricious their fate, St. Clare is killed while attempting to break up a fight, before he can put into motion his plan to set Tom free. This leaves Tom's future up to St. Clare's wife, Marie, who is self-centered and unfeeling. Miss Ophelia urges Marie to carry out St. Clare's wish that Tom be freed, but Marie refuses to do so.

Even when Tom is faced with one of the worst examples of desperation caused by the brutality of slavery—when a female slave tells him about how she killed her newborn baby rather than give up another child to slavery—his suggestion to her is that she turn toward God.

Tom becomes a martyr when he refuses to follow orders to beat his fellow slaves and then is beaten himself by his violent new master, Simon Legree. Legree is determined to crush Tom's faith in God and nearly succeeds, until one night Tom has a dream about heaven. He has spiritual visions of Christ and Eva that help him regain his determination to endure Legree's torture. When two slaves escape, Legree takes it out on Tom, who is fatally beaten. At that moment, George Shelby arrives to pay for Tom's freedom, but Tom is on his deathbed. He dies a few days later, but before he does, he forgives Legree and the overseers.

All of the plot points converge at the end so that families are reunited and the escaped slaves find freedom, but Uncle Tom remains a casualty to the cause of Stowe's Christian sensibilities and sentimental style.

THE CABIN IN *UNCLE TOM'S CABIN*

Harriet Beecher Stowe subscribed to the 19th-century idea of the home as the cultural center of family life. The characters of Tom, Chloe, and their three children may have lived in a glorified shack in Kentucky, but Stowe imbues it with the love she imagines the family felt there in that space. She talks about Chloe beautifying the space by keeping it clean and planting flowers. Although it is modest, made of hewn logs, it is big enough for everything the family could want. In fact, although Tom's cabin pales in comparison with the Shelby mansion, in many ways Stowe sees it as an ideal dwelling place, unlike the typical slave quarters and unlike the rootlessness of the life of a free slave, who was never really free, but always on the run from slave hunters, especially after the Congress passed the Fugitive Slave Act in 1793, a pair of laws that made it easier for owners to reclaim runaway slaves. Stowe imagines this space as a hideaway—a space of communal worship and of racial harmony, where slaves came together in faith and socialized and even broke bread with their white master when he dropped by for visit. The cabin is also a space of learning, where George Shelby first teaches Tom to read. This initial idyllic setting is contrasted to every other place that Tom is forced to call home, spaces that grow progressively worse as the novel advances.

Lynn Marie Houston

Further Reading

If you enjoyed reading *Uncle Tom's Cabin,* you might enjoy other works of African American literature that address questions of freedom and autonomy, such as Zora Neale Hurston's *The Eyes Were Watching God,* or the slave narratives written by both Frederick Douglass and Olaudah Equiano.

Bibliography

Askeland, Lori. "Remodeling the Model Home in *Uncle Tom's Cabin* and *Beloved*." *American Literature* 64, no. 4 (1992): 785–805.

Bennett, Zachary M. "Improving Slavery's Border: Nature, Navigation, and Regionalism on the Ohio River." *Register of the Kentucky Historical Society* 116, no. 1 (2018): 1–28.

Burduck, Michael L. "Early-19th-Century Literature." *American Literary Scholarship* 2010, no. 1 (2010): 249–72.

Carpenter, Cari M. "Bleeding Feet and Failing Knees: The Ecogothic in *Uncle Tom's Cabin* and *Chasing Ice*." In *Ecogothic in Nineteenth-Century American Literature*, edited by Dawn Keetley and Matthew Wynn Sivils, 147–60. New York: Routledge, 2017.

Cowa, William Tynes. *The Slave in the Swamp: Disrupting the Plantation Narrative.* New York: Routledge, 2013.

Dixon, Melvin. *Ride Out the Wilderness: Geography and Identity in Afro-American Literature.* Urbana: University of Illinois Press, 1987.

Jaudon, Toni. "The Geography of Feeling: Christianity, the Nation-State, and the Labor of Love in Nineteenth-Century United States Literature." PhD diss., Cornell University, 2009.

Oh, Canaan. "Following the North Star to Canada." *Uncle Tom's Cabins: The Transnational History of America's Most Mutable Book,* edited by Tracy C. Davis and Stefka Mihaylova, 33. Ann Arbor: University of Michigan Press, 2018.

Sheley, Nancy Strow. "The Language of Flowers in Harriet Beecher Stowe's *Uncle Tom's Cabin* and Other Nineteenth-Century American Works." *Resources for American Literary Study* 30 (2005): 76–103.

Vlach, John Michael, Leslie King-Hammond, and Roberta Sokolitz. *Landscape of Slavery: The Plantation in American Art.* Columbia: University of South Carolina Press, 2008.

W

Waiting for Godot

Samuel Beckett was an Irish-French playwright, novelist, and poet who received a Nobel Prize for literature in 1969 for his oeuvre, which testifies to the human struggle for meaningfulness within a moment of life that begins and ends in oblivion. That moment is filled with pressing uncertainty that can lead to apathy and inertia, and induce feelings of despair. *Waiting for Godot* exemplifies Beckett's perspective in a way that makes it most accessible. For this reason, it is an unparalleled masterpiece of absurdist theater and classic 20th-century avant-garde literature.

The play is a tragicomedy in two acts. It begins in a mysterious world with an empty road, barren tree, sitting rock, and humdrum sky. Enter the tramps—Vladimir ("Didi") and Estragon ("Gogo")—who are waiting for a man name Godot. They bide their time by putzing about, but, above all, by talking. Much of that is given to debates that seem to be speeding toward resolution, but end up in a swirl of zappy-zany dialogue. At times, their words reach an impasse as ideas are inconclusive. Then comes the fleeting awareness of the inevitable failure to grasp control of their own lives: "nothing to be done," says Estragon. So, they continue waiting for Godot.

Two strangers appear on the road. First, comes Lucky, a deranged slave carrying suitcases, with a rope around his neck. This unusually long rope leads to Pozzo, an aristocratic landowner, who has been driving this slave for 60 years. Didi and Gogo turn to investigate and are put off by Pozzo's bullying and his total control of and merciless disregard for Lucky. Pozzo, however, turns out to be an articulate optimist, whereas Lucky, when ordered to speak, seems erudite at first, but utters phrases in a jumbled repetition. These intellectual residuals, once the lifeblood of this inspiring teacher, are now sapped of brilliance. The pair eventually moves on. Then, suddenly, a boy turns up to deliver a message: "Mr. Godot told me to tell you he won't come this evening, but surely to-morrow." The tramps question the boy about Mr. Godot of whom they know little. They decide to abandon the endeavor of waiting, but they never get around to it.

For Act II—same dismal place, time of day, but the tree now has a leaf. Didi and Gogo are again going about their routine. Pozzo and Lucky reappear, the former blind and now driven by the latter who is mute. They collide, fall over each other, and become helpless. Pozzo moans and groans about his fate and condition. Eventually, they gain their composure and depart but not before Pozzo, whose attitude seems to have softened with empathy, casts a note of gloom: "They give birth astride of a grave, the light gleams an instant, then it's gone once more. On!"

As Gogo naps, the boy from before comes by to repeat the message to Didi about Godot not arriving today but certainly tomorrow. Didi begins to notices that his experiences are repetitive and his life has become stagnant. Like his partner, he has been unable to think or move in any meaningful way. For them waiting is involuntary; they cannot make a conscious choice and see it through with persistent action. When Gogo awakes, they decide (again) once and for-all to commit suicide by hanging themselves if Godot fails to arrive the following day. But they will need a suitable piece of rope, so they agree to leave for the night and return with proper rigging to the tree by morning. Again, the idea gets lost in the yackity-yack, and they fail to make a move. Habit is "the great deadener," as one character has said.

THEATRE OF THE ABSURD

Although Samuel Beckett was born in Dublin, he made his home in Paris and wrote his greatest works in French. The production of *Waiting for Godot* in 1953 at the Left Bank Theatre De Babylone was the beginning of Beckett's involvement in all matters of stagecraft. *Godot* inspired a theatrical revolution that challenged audiences' conventional notions of stage performance. That challenge came from the philosophy of absurdism, which embraces uncertainty, relativism, and nothingness. Satire, dark comedy, and existential fiction are examples of literary genres that find their place in the theatre of the absurd.

Absurdists rejected 19th-century naturalism or realism, an art movement that began in France during the 1850s. For realists, the aim of art was the production of truthful representation of the actual, verified through experience. But, for absurdists, words and language fail to effectively communicate objective reality simply because the physicality of words do not inherently match anything beyond them. Any correspondence is arbitrary and intentional. Because we are then alienated from our surroundings, words become all we know, language an end in itself.

Artists associated with early 20th-century art movements such as symbolism, expressionism, and surrealism critiqued realist representations that they saw as portrayals of surficial experience. Things more definitive of reality—psychological structures that shape experience—were reserved for the human mind. Artists could draw on these through a more spontaneous approach to creativity combined with standard forms of artistic representation. Thus, objective reality became less significant to the artistic endeavor. But, absurdists questioned the integrity of not only objective but also subjective experiences. They saw no deep structures in the human mind directing experience. Thus, there could be no uniform composite of human behavior. This is why fictional characters of absurdist literature, such as Didi and Gogo, have little if any psychological depth; they simply are as they appear. They are often ambiguous, disconnected, contradictory, and gloomy. The same can be said for dialogue and plot, and of the scenes in which these occur.

THE GEOGRAPHY OF PLACE

Waiting for Godot is a story not about a historical event nor a geographical place, nor is it about anyone nor everyone in particular. The waiting takes place in a barren, hostile but all-too-familiar landscape. Nature and culture are also missing in the details of the scene. The setting—with its nonspecific road, tree, rock, sky—has become the most notable in modern theater, probably because it lacks the conventional props of contemporary productions. There is, however, one very significant reference to place coming from Gogo who puts the scene within the stretch of the known universe: "Look at this muckheap! I've never stirred from it."

Neither man has a personal connection to the landscape. Yet, each one manifests tendencies that skew them toward specific elements and orientation. Didi, who aligns with tree and sky, is more thoughtful, lighter on his feet, troubled by his hat, and dispenses food. Gogo belongs to the stone and earth. He is troubled by his feet, concerned about food, and often daydreams and sleeps. Here, the landscape does not reflect the characters' consciousness but rather sustains their awareness. Didi and Gogo's antithetical positions (like the mind/body, subject/object dualisms tormenting modern philosophy) never get resolved in the play, therefore the ultimate significance of the scene's geography eludes them. Its bareness and their forgetfulness compel the characters to focus on the basics of human experience: eating, urinating, defecating, hurting, bickering, outfitting, and so on and so on.

Ken Whalen and Dalilah Nabilah Laidin

Further Reading

Other European playwrights who write out of Modernist traditions associated with nihilism, existentialism, surrealism, avant-garde, or "theatre of the absurd" are Eugene Ionesco, Jean Genet, Federico Garcia Lorca, and Jean-Paul Sartre. The latter's play *No Exit,* is very similar to *Waiting for Godot* because it is about a small group of characters waiting in a space that they discover is their own personal hell.

Bibliography

Chaudhuri, Una. *Staging Place: The Geography of Modern Drama.* Ann Arbor: University of Michigan Press, 1997.

Cless, Downing. *Ecology and Environment in European Drama.* New York: Routledge, 2010.

Cohn, Ruby. *Just Play: Beckett's Theater.* Princeton, NJ: Princeton University Press, 1980.

Fuchs, Elinor, and Una Chaudhuri. *Land/Scape/Theater.* Ann Arbor: University of Michigan Press, 2002.

Kenner, Hugh. *A Reader's Guide to Beckett.* Syracuse, NY: Syracuse University Press, 1996.

May, Theresa J. "Greening the Theater: Taking Ecocriticism from Page to Stage." *Interdisciplinary Literary Studies* 7, no. 1 (2005): 84–103.

McMullan, Anna. *Performing Embodiment in Samuel Beckett's Drama.* New York: Routledge, 2010.

Noh, Aegyung. "A Cultural Geography of 'the Sweet Old Style': Samuel Beckett's *Happy Days.*" *The Journal of Modern English Drama* 26, no. 1 (2013): 293–312.

Walcott, Derek

THE GEOGRAPHY OF PARADISE: DEREK WALCOTT'S ISLAND

In awarding Derek Walcott the Nobel Prize for Literature in 1992, the Swedish Academy cited the "melodious" language of his poetry and plays as well, and the numerous authors who influenced his work, the earliest being Homer. Both factors—his resonant language and Homeric resources—derive from the geography of his origin in the small volcanic island of St. Lucia in the Eastern Caribbean. Walcott frequently throughout his writing life pointed out the parallel between the archipelagos of Greek islands and Caribbean islands. The former many centuries ago gave birth to a civilization that formed the Western world; the latter during Walcott's lifetime was the crucible of another culture, formed from the heritage of colonialism, combining the cultural forms and forces of Europe, Africa, as well as Asia.

As a biracial man in a multicultural island nation, Walcott's relation to historical Europe and Africa are contested in his own work (as in "A Far Cry from Africa"), but the places themselves—be they the islands of Homer's Greece or of the Caribbean, or continental North America and Europe—find their place in his 28 volumes of poetry, notable from *In a Green Night: Poems 1948–1960* (1962) to *The Fortunate Traveller* (1981) to *White Egrets* (2010) and *Morning, Paramin* (2013). His masterwork *Omeros* (meaning "Homer," 1990) calibrates the contemporary story of St. Lucian characters named Hector, Helen, and Achille, against the epic precedent in Homer's *Iliad,* in its ocean and island-born rivalries. In 1993, he published *The Odyssey,* a stage version of the epic set in island after island. The Nobel Committee called him an "assiduous" traveler, noting that his first and unwavering source of his inspiration was his home island of St. Lucia.

Walcott recounts his childhood and youth in St. Lucia in the biographical epic *Another Life* (1973), patterned after Wordsworth's *The Prelude*. His Wordsworthian sense of the glories of childhood are realized in being "blest with a virginal, unpainted world / with Adam's task of giving things their names." Coming into his vocation as artist, he realized that no one had considered the landscape of his home worthy of rendition into paint and poetry. In this place, he found a life that he felt almost predated geography. The Adamic situation of the poet emerged from the Eden-like place, where the natural had its own history and issued its own languages: his speakers listen to the dialects of trees, inlets, marshes, mountains, and volcanoes.

The island, then, is capable of utterance, or speech that the poet strains to comprehend and imitate in the sonorities of his lines. Critical response to his work has always praised its music, a music that derives not only from the languages and literature of his heritage (English and French Creole, both written and oral), but also from the sounds and rhythms of the sea and of the island's vitality. Walcott's emotive response to the landscape and seascape of his island is always tinged with awe and wonder at the sublime power of their natural forces, which to the indigenous inhabitants begat deities and forces that surely obeyed a will inscrutable, yet evident to humans. The volcano's vent in the south, the great forms of the Pitons, mountains precipitous from their summit plunging below the water to depths beyond vision, the sorcery of the clouds and mists among the echoing forests drenched and dried by rains—these features are the fundament of the geographies of Walcott's Caribbean poetry. Wonder and awe are the poet's enduring response to his island. Walcott's sense of the Adamic is not that of romantic self-generated genius, forgetful of its origin in tradition. He does not reject the colonial inheritance of literature but, however painfully, assimilates it, making it serve the wonder that remains his motive.

The young poet wanted those natural languages to inflect his own. The poet-child in *Another Life* scratched words in sand and hoped for the sea's voice to emanate from his pen. Every place is articulate, and can teach the poet its speech. Years later, he wrote about a scene by a highway through the Catskill Mountains of New York, where the speaker desires to river rocks in his mouth "to learn her language, / to talk like birch or aspen confidently" ("Upstate"). The paradise of his childhood in the island had already fallen, however, through the predatory history of colonialism, slavery, and the new imperialism of tourism. Place, in Walcott's work, incorporates both the paradisal state of innocence and the disfigurements of centuries of wars, oppression, and domination; of indigenous peoples eradicated, of imported peoples enslaved, of the freed peoples dispossessed of their lands and resources. From the glimpses of paradisal childhood, the poet as a young man is exiled to survive as a writer for decades in the metropolitan countries. "Home" for him is a vexed issue in the island he returns to as a prodigal, estranged ("Homecoming: Anse la Ray," "The Light of the World"). His alter-ego character named Shabine, fleeing Trinidad ahead of the law, asks, "Where is my rest place, Jesus? . . . / Where is the pillow I will not have to pay for" ("The Schooner *Flight*"). In "North and South," Walcott calls himself, "a single, circling, homeless satellite." Whether he goes as exile or guest, Walcott's poetic world is wide, from the Caribbean to the Greek archipelago, from New England to Italy, and his first love and his greatest is for his homeland islands.

Robert R. Bensen

Further Reading
Other poets who write about the politics of race in the Americas, particularly with regard to the geography of the Caribbean islands, are Aimé Césaire, Lucille Clifton, and Yusef Komunyakaa.

Bibliography
Bergam, Marija. "Transplantations: Vegetation Imagery in the Poetry of Derek Walcott and Lorna Goodison." *European Journal of English Studies* 16, no. 2 (2012): 113–24.

Bishop, Karen Elizabeth. "Introduction: The Cartographical Necessity of Exile." In *Cartographies of Exile: A New Spatial Literacy*. New York: Routledge, 2016.

Cahill-Booth, Lara. "Walcott's Sea and Caribbean Geomythography." *Journal of Postcolonial Writing* 49, no. 3 (2013): 347–58.

Carter, Paul. "Sea Level: Towards a Poetic Geography." In *From International Relations to Relations International: Postcolonial Essays*, edited by Philip Darby. London: Routledge, 2015.

Chamberlin, J. Edward. *Come Back to Me My Language: Poetry and the West Indies*. Champaign: University of Illinois Press, 1993.

Hambuch, Doris. "Geo-and Ecocritical Considerations of Derek Walcott's Multitasking, Omnipresent Sea." *International Journal of Applied Linguistics and English Literature* 4, no. 6 (2015): 196–203.

Handley, George B. *New World Poetics: Nature and the Adamic Imagination of Whitman, Neruda, and Walcott*. Athens: University of Georgia Press, 2010.

Heise, Ursula K. "Poetry and the Natures of the New World." *Twentieth Century Literature* 56, no. 1 (2010): 116–21. www.jstor.org/stable/25733449.

Hertz, Jason T. *Re-inhabiting the Islands: Senses of Place in the Poetry of Gary Snyder and Derek Walcott.* Master's thesis, Western Carolina University, 2011.

Jefferson, Ben. "Contesting Knowledge, Contested Space: Language, Place, and Power in Derek Walcott's Colonial Schoolhouse." *Teorie vědy/Theory of Science* 36, no. 1 (2014): 77–103.

Meryan, Dania. "Sites of (Post) Colonial Becomings: Body, Land and Text in the Writings of Wilson Harris, Derek Walcott, Mahmoud Darwish and Ghassan Kanafani." PhD diss., University of Leicester, 2013.

Posmentier, Sonya. *Cultivation and Catastrophe: The Lyric Ecology of Modern Black Literature.* Baltimore: Johns Hopkins University Press, 2017.

Rauscher, Judith. "Toward an Environmental Imagination of Displacement in Contemporary Transnational American Poetry." In *Ecocriticism and Geocriticism,* edited by Robert T. Tally Jr. and Christine Battista. New York: Palgrave Macmillan, 2016.

Soosaar, Susanna. "The Experience of Places in Derek Walcott's *The Prodigal*." PhD diss., Tartu Ülikool, 2017.

Tally, Robert T., Jr., ed. *Geocritical Explorations: Space, Place, and Mapping in Literary and Cultural Studies.* New York: Palgrave Macmillan, 2011.

Tally, Robert T., Jr., and Christine M. Battista. "Introduction: Ecocritical Geographies, Geocritical Ecologies, and the Spaces of Modernity." In *Ecocriticism and Geocriticism.* New York: Palgrave Macmillan, 2016.

Whitman, Walt

Walt Whitman was heavily influenced by the places he lived and the reasons he lived there. Originally from Brooklyn, he worked in New Orleans, where he was appalled to see how slaves were treated. After his brother suffered injuries in the Civil War and was sent to a Washington, D.C. hospital, Whitman moved there to be near him. Finally, he traveled to Camden, New Jersey, to pay his last respects to his mother, who was dying. Soon after, he had a stroke. Instead of returning to Washington, he bought a house in New Jersey, where he remained until he died. Whitman's poetic project throughout most of his poems was to find a way to undo the mind/body split that had plagued Western cultures since at least the Enlightenment. In fact, Whitman was interested in eroding all distinctions in societal hierarchies, such as race, class, and gender divisions. He was also greatly interested in capturing a truly American voice through the depiction of the bodies of the American people as they engaged in their work. All of these major themes in his oeuvre involve sensory-rich depictions of bodies as they occupy space.

THE UNIFYING LANDSCAPE OF THE BODY

The lack of distinctions between people is at the heart of his "Song of Myself" poems, which are invocations of the mind and body to join together and become one in the present moment. He begins in "Song of Myself I" by grounding the body's experience of existence in a local geography—"every atom . . . form'd from this soil, this air"—and by claiming an organic kinship to every other human being: "every atom belonging to me as good belongs to you." He is interested in bringing us back to the organic chemical matter of the universe, of which our bodies are composed, to help us understand that the physical realities uniting humans are greater than the political concepts dividing them at the time of the Civil War. In the first section of this poem, he includes one of his key symbols: the blade or "spear" of grass. He comes back to this image time and again, and titles the collection *Leaves of Grass* to further promote its symbolic connotation as a unifying device to remind us of our organic origins and the fact that we all share the conditions that come with having a mortal body.

The purpose of unifying mind and body in Whitman's poetry is to create an authentic self that, similar to what the transcendentalists (Ralph Waldo Emerson and Henry David Thoreau) advocated, does not rely on anyone else's determinations of reality. Whitman states explicitly in "Song of Myself II" that he wants his readers to go outside and experience the natural world firsthand: "You shall no longer take things at second or third hand." Whitman is attempting to undo what he sees as a crisis of identity: the ways in which Western culture has privileged the mind and soul over the body. This idea can be traced back at least to the Enlightenment, where a philosopher like René Descartes coined the slogan for this enterprise: "I think; therefore, I am." If Whitman had been able to revise this famous saying, he might have proposed something more like "I eat; therefore, I am" or "I am mortal; therefore, I am," an indication that, for him, identity is rooted in being both body and mind. The American tradition prior to Whitman participated in the separation of these two facets of being from the origins of the country in Puritan settlement of the East Coast. The Puritans embraced a religious philosophy of turning away from the desires of the flesh and focusing on one's soul to gain entry to the afterlife. Whitman takes a more scientific approach in the sense that he feels spiritual presence lives on in the recycling of the organic matter of which we are made and which knows no boundaries between the various cultural distinctions we make between races, classes, or genders.

"Song of Myself VI" centers on the image of the grass as a unifier of people. Whitman's speaker notes that the grass covers the earth in which we bury people: it is the "beautiful uncut hair of graves." In growing over the graves of all the dead, the grass unites everyone, whether white or black, man or woman, rich or poor. Whitman is tapping into an ancient literary symbol of death as the great equalizer—king or peasant, the grave waits for us all. By reminding us of this, he brings us back to our bodies and to the senses, which is how the body knows the world. The grass also gives hope that something about us lives on. Whitman's speaker imagines what happens to him (and to us, too, as we all share the same mortal condition) after death: "I bequeath myself to the dirt to grow from the grass I love, / If you want me again look for me under your boot-soles." The organic matter that makes up our bodies returns to the Earth when we die and then allows new life to grow—for instance, in the form of grass or other vegetation.

THE PHYSICAL GEOGRAPHY OF EQUALITY

Beyond being conceptually interested in the philosophical rift between mind and body, Whitman is specifically interested in the bodies of Americans. Through representing the bodies of American working-class people in his poem, Whitman believes that his poetry can serve a democratic project. He wants to create work that embodies the American identity and he feels that portraying the bodies of workers in their tasks can help convey it. He compiles the voices of workers into a kind of musical round in at least two of his poems, "I Hear America Singing" and "I Sing the Body Electric." In each of these poems, he catalogs numerous different trades to capture the spirit and diversity of democracy. In "I Sing the Body Electric," he also includes pleas on behalf of equality for women and slaves, two disenfranchised groups within America at the time.

Lynn Marie Houston

Further Reading

Many poets have written tributes to Walt Whitman because they admired and emulated his style. Some of these poets include Federico Garcia Lorca, Pablo Neruda, and Allen Ginsberg.

As the founder of the transcendentalist movement, Ralph Waldo Emerson's work is often compared to that of Walt Whitman who was on the fringes of that literary platform.

Bibliography

Beer, Samuel H. "III. Liberty and Union: Walt Whitman's Idea of the Nation." *Political Theory* 12, no. 3 (1984): 361–86.

Buell, Lawrence. *The Environmental Imagination: Thoreau, Nature Writing, and the Formation of American Culture.* Cambridge, MA: Harvard University Press, 1995.

Chiarappa, Michael J. "Affirmed Objects in Affirmed Places: History, Geographic Sentiment and a Region's Crafts." *Journal of Design History* 10, no. 4 (1997): 399–415.

Felstiner, John. *Can Poetry Save the Earth?: A Field Guide to Nature Poems.* New Haven, CT: Yale University Press, 2009.

Gerhardt, Christine. *A Place for Humility: Whitman, Dickinson, and the Natural World.* Iowa City: University of Iowa Press, 2014.

Gerhardt, Christine. "Managing the Wilderness: Walt Whitman's Southern Landscapes." *Forum for Modern Language Studies* 40, no. 2 (2004): 225–35.

Hsu, Hsuan L. *Geography and the Production of Space in Nineteenth-Century American Literature.* Cambridge, UK: Cambridge University Press, 2010.

Killingsworth, Jimmie M. *Walt Whitman and the Earth: A Study of Ecopoetics.* Iowa City: University of Iowa Press, 2009.

Najdek, Carl M. "'The Earth to be Spann'd, Connected by Net-Work': Walt Whitman's Industrial Internationalism." *American Political Thought* 3, no. 1 (2014): 95–113.

Payne, Daniel G. *Voices in the Wilderness: American Nature Writing and Environmental Politics.* Hanover, NH: University Press of New England, 1996.

Roche, John F. "Democratic Space: The Ecstatic Geography of Walt Whitman and Frank Lloyd Wright." *Walt Whitman Quarterly Review* 6, no. 1 (1988): 3.

Shivers, Lynne, Joan Tracy, and Debra White. *Jottings in the Woods: Walt Whitman's Nature Prose and a Study of Old Pine Farm.* Indianapolis: Dog Ear Publishing, 2007.

Williams, William Carlos

In the early 20th century when Williams was writing his poetry, Americans began moving toward spending more time in interior spaces rather than in agricultural work, thanks to the outcomes of the Industrial Revolution and increased use of machinery in agricultural production. Williams chronicles both the beauties and horrors humans find in these interior spaces of homes and offices. One of the poems that describes the beauty of inhabiting the architecture of the home is "Danse Russe." In this short poem, the speaker first established a somewhat lonely scene—although he lives with his wife and children, they are all sleeping, and he is drawn to look at the sunset, a time typically symbolic of a contemplation of mortality because sundown often serves as a metaphor for death. He physically shares an architectural space with his family, but is unable to share the emotions of this moment with them. He has to embrace it by himself, and he does so by dancing around his room wearing no clothes. It is ultimately a joyful scene about the labyrinths of emotions our homes become.

One of Williams's poems that explores an uneasy disconnect between interior and exterior spaces, between what happens inside the home and out in the street, is "The Young Housewife." The housewife's space, by definition, is going to mainly be the home, but her duties would have also included interactions with salespeople and delivery personnel. The first stanza presents an unusual perspective of space because the first-person narrator seems to see through the walls of the house; he seems to know or imagine intimate details of how the housewife occupies this space—for example, that she has slept in and at 10 in the morning is still wearing her nightgown. The next stanza presents an image of her leaving the house and venturing into the street to buy goods from various vendors, but she does so in a self-conscious way. The speaker uses the image of a "fallen leaf" to describe the housewife. Leaves then appear again as "dried leaves" under the wheels of his car. Although the poem is enigmatic, there is a progression of time implied by the two different leaf images, and it invokes the aging process. Just as a leaf desiccates after it falls from the tree, a young housewife will age into an older housewife, and that transition might happen quickly if her days are spent in isolation.

The backstory to "The Red Wheelbarrow" is difficult for readers to discern, but any interpretation of the poem has to be rooted in agrarian, working-class culture. Wheelbarrows are used as tools to haul debris. This one is sitting near chickens. In the 1920s when this was written, American farmers were among the first to feel the coming economic depression as prices of crops fell at the same time that costs rose for necessary machinery. Eventually, small family farms would give way to large agribusiness. Even though the scene in "The Red Wheelbarrow" seems simple, the first line emphasizes its importance. Rain feeds the crops and is needed for them to grow. The red wheelbarrow seems to have been abandoned, perhaps just momentarily, by the human that would use it, as it seems stationary and there is no mention of the human hands and feet that move it. In this moment of rest, the rain has "glazed" it. What or who depends on crops doing well and nourishment from chickens? The answer to this is all of society. In a few very short lines, Williams has evoked the land of the people who work to produce our food.

Williams's most poignant statement about place and human geography comes in his poem "Dedication for a Plot of Ground." In it, he gives tribute to his grandmother, Emily Dickinson Wellcome, and chronicles key moments from her life that involved fighting for others, standing up for her own independence, and working the land. He ends the poem with the following admonition, welcoming onto the land that is being dedicated only other people who had spirits similar to his grandmother: "If you can bring nothing to this place / but your carcass, keep out." In a larger sense, he clearly means these last two lines as descriptions of the kinds of humans he welcomes on Earth, people who contribute their sense of morals and generous hearts. The poem establishes legacy of the spirit that lives on in the land, drawing other like-minded humans to that place through the speaking of this poem-prayer.

The collection *Paterson* (1946–1958) comprises five volumes and is meant to represent both the poet and a city he knew well, Paterson, New Jersey, along the Passaic River, upstream of Rutherford, his hometown. In this deep and extended meditation on place as it embodies human qualities and humans as they embody the characteristics of the space where they live, Williams maps out the inclusive geography of the town—from neighborhoods, foliage, river, and the quality of sky. In the final volume in the collection, the protagonist of the collection, named Paterson, readies for death. Taken as a whole, the five volumes are a love letter to the town and its surroundings as they existed in the mid-20th century. This collection is the fullest expression of Williams's motto "no ideas but in things," an outlook that makes the concrete details of place very important to his work.

In many ways, Williams Carlos Williams was inspired by T.S. Eliot's *The Waste Land* and sought to contribute his own version of what a wasteland looks like in the daily life he knew. The difference between Williams's wasteland and Eliot's is that Williams's is able to find slivers of hope and beauty in his. In "Between Walls," the speaker of the poem looks out onto the courtyard or back portion of a hospital. He muses on the lack of vegetation, but sees something else that is a kind of manmade beauty—slivers of glass from a bottle that glint in the sunlight. They appear among cinder blocks. The scene evokes a kind of wasteland, but just as the speaker notes that nothing will grow, he sees the green of the glass, which stands in for the vegetation. There is still something out there in this space to catch his eye. The scene vacillates between the absence of life and something that resembles growth, appropriate for its proximity to the hospital, symbolically a place of both birth and death.

The same dynamic happens in a more famous poem of his, "Young Sycamore," where the speaker observes a sycamore growing defiantly in an urban space between "pavement and the gutter." The tree is probably in danger, as the speaker notes in passing that it is infested with caterpillar cocoons, which in large numbers can kill a tree. However, in this moment, the speaker takes in the tree's great strength and beauty. Its precariousness in time and place make it even more beautiful.

As a Modernist, Williams Carlos Williams was engaging with the increasing ways that humans felt alienated from each other. That isolation finds its way into the way he writes about space and place in his poetry, but yet he finds innovative ways to highlight hope and beauty in the most unexpected scenes.

Lynn Marie Houston

Further Reading

If you enjoy reading the poetry of William Carlos Williams, you may also enjoy reading other Modernist poets with aesthetics similar to Williams. They include H. D., Marianne Moore, Ezra Pound, and Wallace Stevens.

Bibliography

Axelrod, Rise B., and Steven Gould Axelrod. "The Metropoetics of Paterson." *William Carlos Williams Review* 29, no. 2 (2009): 121–35.

Burke, Daniel Edmund. "From Pastorals to Paterson: Ecology in the Poetry and Poetics of William Carlos Williams." PhD diss., Marquette University, 2014.

Cahalan, James M. "Teaching Hometown Literature: A Pedagogy of Place." *College English* 70, no. 3 (2008): 249–74.

Cocola, Jim. *Places in the Making: A Cultural Geography of American Poetry*. Iowa City: University of Iowa Press, 2016.

Conrad, Bryce. *Refiguring America: A Study of William Carlos Williams' In the American Grain*. Urbana: University of Illinois Press, 1990.

Derksen, Jeff. "Poetry and Globalized Cities: A Material Poetics of Canadian Urban Space." In *Material Cultures in Canada,* edited by Thomas Allen and Jennifer Blair. Waterloo, Ontario: Wilfrid Laurier University Press, 2015.

Giles, Paul. *The Global Remapping of American Literature*. Princeton, NJ: Princeton University Press, 2011.

Hahn, Stephen. "'It was . . . civilization I was after': George Tice, William Carlos Williams, and the Archaeology of Paterson." *Literary Review* 50, no. 4 (2007): 62.

Koopman, Adrian, and Elwyn Jenkins. "Toponyms in Poetry." *Journal of Literary Studies* 32, no. 2 (2016): 37–60.

Lee, James Kyung-Jin. "The City as Region." In *A Companion to the Regional Literatures of America*, edited by Charles L. Crow. Malden, MA: Blackwell Publishing, 2003.

Newmann, Alba Rebecca. "'Language is not a vague province': Mapping and Twentieth-century American Poetry." PhD diss., University of Texas at Austin, 2006.

Quinn, Bernetta. "'Paterson': Landscape and Dream." *Journal of Modern Literature* 1, no. 4 (1971): 523–48.

Raine, Anne. "Ecocriticism and Modernism." In *The Oxford Handbook of Ecocriticism*, edited by Greg Garrard. Oxford, UK: Oxford University Press, 2014.

Ramazani, Jahan. "The Local Poem in a Global Age." *Critical Inquiry* 43, no. 3 (2017): 670–96.

Ramos, Peter. "Cultural Identity, Translation, and William Carlos Williams." *Multi-Ethnic Literature of the United States* 38, no. 2 (2013): 89–110.

Rauscher, Judith. "Toward an Environmental Imagination of Displacement in Contemporary Transnational American Poetry." In *Ecocriticism and Geocriticism*, edited by Robert T. Tally Jr. and Christine Battista. New York: Palgrave Macmillan, 2016.

Santos, M. Irene Ramalho. "Narcissus in the Desert: A New Cartography for the American Lyric." *Journal of Romance Studies* 11, no. 1 (2011): 21–36.

Selby, Nick. "Ecopoetries in America." *The Cambridge Companion to American Poetry Since 1945* (2013): 127–42.

Šuvaković, Miško, and Dubravka Đuric. "The Spatial Turn: A Comparative Analysis of the Functions of Place in Experimental Poetry and Visual Arts." *Zivot Umjetnosti* 96 (2015).

Tarlo, Harriet, and Judith Tucker. "Place as Pause: The Value of Collaborative, Cross-Disciplinary Practices in Place." *Landscape Values* (2016): 358.
Tashjian, Dickran, and William Carlos Williams. *William Carlos Williams and the American Scene, 1920–1940: Whitney Museum of American Art . . . December 12, 1978–February 4, 1979.* Berkeley: University of California Press, 1978.
Watson, Douglas Frank. "A Sense of Place in the Poetry of Robert Frost, William Carlos Williams, and Wallace Stevens." PhD diss., Texas Tech University, 1980.
White, Eric B. "William Carlos Williams and the Local." In *The Cambridge Companion to William Carlos Williams,* edited by C. MacGowan, 8–23. New York: Cambridge University Press, 2016.

The Wizard of Oz

Without a doubt, L. Frank Baum's Land of Oz was located in Omaha, Nebraska. Omaha's geographic footprints are all over the first Oz book, as Dorothy's destination, and as the home of the legendary Wizard. The first clue is provided by the tornado that transports Dorothy and Toto out of Kansas. Tornadoes usually move southwest to northeast, and if Dorothy, Toto, and their house were "not in Kansas anymore," and transport was by tornado, they very probably came to rest in Nebraska.

Before he is unmasked, the Wonderful Wizard exists mainly as an enigma, unseen by residents of the Emerald City, appearing as a giant head, a beautiful fairy, or a monster, all by sleight of hand. The Wizard grants an interview to Dorothy and her traveling party with great reluctance, appearing at first as a disembodied voice. Once all of his many forms have been dropped, the Wizard turns out to be Oscar Zoroaster Phadrig Isaac Norman Henkle Emmannuel Ambroise Diggs ("OZ" is the first initial from his first two names), a former salesman from Omaha, who developed all of his facades while he was a circus magician. While living in Omaha, the Wizard first worked as a ventriloquist's apprentice and later as a balloonist. All of these details appear in Baum's several dozen Oz books, although not in the 1939 movie that popularized them.

THE MIDWEST

At the end of the Oz story, the Wizard departs the Emerald City in the gondola of a great balloon with a sign that reads "State Fair, Omaha." (The annual Nebraska State Fair has long been held in Lincoln, not Omaha.) At every turn, the great and grand wizard turns out to be a very ordinary (although creative) working person.

L. Frank Baum, author of the Oz books, was a resident of the Midwest who lived in the very late 19th and early 20th centuries, in 1898, the same time that the Trans-Mississippi Exposition, which hosted exhibits from 28 of the 45 states was held in Omaha. As Baum wrote the first of many Oz books, published in 1900, the exposition ran for six months, attracting 2.6 million visitors, including President William McKinley, who spoke October 12, 1898, to an audience liberally estimated at 99,000 people.

RACISM

Before Baum authored the Oz books, he edited the Aberdeen, South Dakota *Saturday Pioneer* from 1888 to 1891. During this time, he penned two vitriolic editorials, disparaging American Indians, which fanned racial hatred in the area. On December 20, 1890, days after the assassination of Sitting Bull and slightly more than a week before the Wounded Knee massacre, he suggested the deliberate destruction of American Indian people (Stannard 1992, 126).

A week after the Wounded Knee massacre, the demand for annihilation was repeated in Baum's newspaper. Ironically, in our time, Baum, once an advocate of genocide, has been restyled as an advocate of multiculturalism, with Oz's riot of different characters presented as a paradigm of diversity.

CHARACTER SYMBOLISM

Objects and characters in the Oz stories also have been said to carry symbolic freight corresponding to political and social fissures in the Gilded Age as political populism challenged its emphasis on wealth. The yellow brick road has been characterized as symbolic of the gold standard, and the silver slippers as support for coinage of silver. Dorothy is said to represent the honest and openhearted nature of common people in the Midwest. The Tin Man is the much-exploited eastern industrial worker, and the Scarecrow the Midwestern farmer. The Wicked Witch of the East has been styled as representing eastern bankers, and the Wicked Witch of the West as symbolic of railroad barons.

This image illustrates the scene in *The Wizard of Oz* where Dorothy and her entourage meet the Cowardly Lion. When the lion first jumps out of the woods, he scares them, but when Dorothy admonishes the lion, he begins to cry. (Library of Congress)

POLITICS

The Wizard of Oz may be an allegory for William Jennings Bryan, a candidate for U.S. president at the time that Baum was writing the first Oz book. Bryan also hailed from Omaha. He was a crusader for "free silver," a populist issue, as opposed to the elites' advocacy of a gold standard. At the time that Baum was writing the first Oz book, Omaha was a center of activism on behalf of populism, which spread through the upper Midwest as farmers' and workers' reactions to the ostentatious wealth of the Gilded Age.

The Knights of Labor, Prohibition Party, Socialists, Farmers' Alliance, and others gathered under the populist banner as the People's Party, holding its 1892 national convention in Omaha, and adopting the "Omaha platform," its major manifesto. The People's Party received 8.5 percent of the national vote that year. Dorothy donned her silver slippers and made her way to Omaha (the Land of Oz) just as Bryan was advancing the coinage of silver, yet another possible reminder that Baum's fanciful story was firmly rooted in the political geography of his time and place.

Bruce E. Johansen

Further Reading

Other stories that appeal to young adult readers interested in the genre of fantasy and messages about character building include *Mary Poppins* by P. L. Travers, *The Chronicles of Narnia* by C. S. Lewis, and *The Snow Queen* by Hans Christian Andersen.

Bibliography

Algeo, John. "The Toponymy of Middle–Earth." *Names* 33, no. 1–2 (1985): 80–95.

Chaston, Joel. "The Wizard of Oz: The Shaping of an Imaginary World, and: Oz and Beyond: The Fantasy World of L. Frank Baum." *The Lion and the Unicorn* 25, no. 1 (2001): 157–60.

Dosi, Mohamed A. M., Leonce Rushubirwa, and Garth A. Myers. "Tanzanians in the Land of Oz: Diaspora and Transnationality in Wichita, Kansas." *Social & Cultural Geography* 8, no. 5 (2007): 657–71.

Ekman, Stefan. *Here Be Dragons: Exploring Fantasy Maps and Settings*. Middletown, CT: Wesleyan University Press, 2013.

Hollingsworth, Zachary Hez. "'A Modernized Fairy Tale': Speculations on Technology, Labor, Politics, and Gender in the Oz Series." PhD diss., University of Mississippi, 2018.

Kirch, Claire. "The Wizard of Omaha: Timothy Schaffert." *Publishers Weekly,* January 31, 2014.

Nathanson, Paul. *Over the Rainbow: The Wizard of Oz as a Secular Myth of America*. Albany: State University of New York Press, 1991.

O'Keefe, Deborah. *Readers in Wonderland: The Liberating Worlds of Fantasy Fiction*. New York: Continuum, 2004.

O'Reilly, M. *Oz and Beyond: The Fantasy World of L. Frank Baum*. Lawrence: University Press of Kansas, 1997.

Peterson, Amanda Marie. "Orphanhood and the Search for Home in L. Frank Baum's *The Wonderful Wizard of Oz* and Boris Pasternak's *Doctor Zhivago*." Master's thesis, University of Montana, 2011.

Schwartz, Evan I. *Finding Oz: How L. Frank Baum Discovered the Great American Story*. Boston: Houghton Mifflin Harcourt, 2009.

Sergeant, Alexander. "Scrutinising the Rainbow: Fantastic Space in *The Wizard of Oz*." PhD diss., University College Cork, 2011.

Stannard, David E. *American Holocaust: Columbus and the Conquest of the New World*. New York: Oxford University Press, 1992, 261–68.

Young, Donna E. "To the Stars through Difficulties: The Legal Construction of Private Space and the Wizard of Oz." *Southern California Interdisciplinary Law Journal* 20 (2010): 135.

Wordsworth, William

William Wordsworth is one of the Romantic poets most studied for his relationship to place. A poet in the Romantic tradition, Wordsworth lived in the picturesque Lake District of England. That region shaped the ways that he thought and wrote about the natural landscape. The concept of nature as it appears in his poetry is one that helps form human subjects through its ability to heal and renew.

NATURE: MAP AND MUSE

One of Wordsworth's most quoted theories of poetry comes from his observation of nature and was laid out in his "Preface to the Lyrical Ballads." He believed that poetry was a "spontaneous overflow of powerful feelings" and "emotion recollected in tranquility." The natural landscape evoked these "powerful feelings" for Wordsworth at the same time that it allowed him to be at peace. He writes that observing nature allows him to feel "[a] presence that disturbs me with the joy / Of elevated thoughts, a sense sublime" and to "hear [. . .] / The still, sad music of humanity" ("Tintern Abbey").

Although Wordsworth felt that science was important, he felt that maps made by geographic surveyors failed to capture the emotional and sacred aspects of the land. He writes in "Upon a stone on the side of Black Comb" about such a surveyor making a map, a "geographic Labourer," who camps on the mountain called Black Comb with all of the scientific equipment. At the end of the poem, the surveyor's view is described as being eclipsed or as if the surveyor himself has been blinded. Many scholars read this as a symbol for how the scientific mapping of a landscape fails to take in its spiritual message. This story is used in the poem (which Wordsworth claims to have carved in rock on the mountainside) to encourage visitors to the mountain to stop their hike to take in the view and find the true meaning in the vista.

Wordsworth's most famous poem about place was his "Lines Composed a Few Miles above Tintern Abbey, On Revisiting the Banks of the Wye during a Tour July 13, 1798," often abbreviated as "Tintern Abbey." The impetus for the poem was a walk he took along the banks of the River Wye that runs along the border between England and Wales. What's noticeable about the poem is the absence both of people that inhabit the landscape and also the building referred to in the title, the abbey. The poem "Tintern Abbey" depicts the space of natural world through a private relationship with an observer. This one-on-one relationship to a landscape became a distinct feature of Wordsworth's poetry as he believed that nature could renew human beings by providing access to divinity. He writes about how the "round ocean[. . .], the living air [. . .] and the blue sky" suggest to the observer "[a] motion and a spirit that [. . .] rolls through all things." The human purpose, then, is to preserve these natural spaces because they are sacred. In Romantic tradition, he mourns the loss of lands to the development and outgrowth of cities as well as the loss of traditional ways of life that depended on an intimacy with the land.

Like "Tintern Abbey," Wordsworth's "Michael: A Pastoral Poem" was also inspired by a walk the poet took through a real landscape. The poem tells a story about a family of sheepherders who lose their land in a bad business deal and is based on a real piece of property near Greenhead Gill, east of the town of Grasmere, which is situated in northwest England, part of the Lake District that was Wordsworth's home. However, all that remained there was the dilapidated sheepfold, a stone enclosure used to keep sheep. The family and the cottage Wordsworth describes were imaginative inventions.

The geographical location of Wordsworth's home had a profound effect on his work. The Lake District even inspired Wordsworth to write a guide to the region. For Wordsworth, nature can put humans in touch with their origins because the landscape of one's childhood shapes one's identity. In his poetry, he expresses the belief that nature possesses a natural goodness and wants to grant abundance to humankind, like a steadfast lover: "[n]ature never did betray / The heart that loved her" ("Tintern Abbey"). People who live in the countryside, like farmers and shepherds, take on nature's good characteristics. Consequently, the details of regional topography create a monument to the hopes and dreams of the people who have lived there.

In addition to experiencing a kind of ecstasy by looking out onto a landscape, Wordsworth believes that the human relationship with nature has a didactic quality: the natural world can be a good moral influence because it transmits sacred messages. He expresses this notion clearly in his Duddon sonnets, poems dedicated to the River Duddon, which winds its way through his homeland, as well as his poem about the River Derwent, also located in the same region: he writes that the "beauteous stream" did shape his thinking so that "[a]mong the fretful dwellings of mankind" he could attain "[a] knowledge, a dim earnest, of the calm / That Nature breathes among the hills and groves" (excerpt from *The Prelude*). Even in poems in which Wordsworth describes traveling abroad, the new landscapes tend to bring back his memories of the Lake District, whether through comparison or contrast. It becomes a touchstone geography for him whose resemblance he searches for in all other lands.

To receive this wisdom or these messages, however, one must separate oneself from the rest of the world. Wordsworth was one of the first modern poets to fully explore as a major project in poetry the revelatory nature of the landscape, as a source of messages from the Divine. In this respect, his poems transmit his beliefs that nature has a consciousness and that it desires to be a source of inspiration for humankind.

Lynn Marie Houston

Further Reading

Many other British poets in the Romantic tradition are known for the frequent inclusion of nature in their works. John Keats writes about the sensuality of natural scenery. Percy Bysshe Shelley often personifies nature as a majestic force but (unlike Wordsworth) one that is separate and distant from the lives of humans. Alfred, Lord Tennyson emphasizes the awe-inspiring destructive power of nature. Similarly, Lord Byron tends to write about the savage and severe elements of nature. Perhaps the closest Romantic poet to Wordsworth in terms of natural imagery, Samuel Taylor Coleridge portrays nature as a kind of mirror that reflects human loss; however, for him, nature inhabits a distinct world apart from the observer. In slight contrast, Wordsworth's poems suggest that his observers access a world of moral truths when gazing upon a natural landscape.

Bibliography

Bergren, Katherine. "Localism Unrooted: Gardening in the Prose of Jamaica Kincaid and William Wordsworth." *Interdisciplinary Studies in Literature and Environment* 22, no. 2 (2014): 303–25.

Fernández, María Antonia Mezquita. "Literary Spaces: Visions of Nature and Sense of Place in the Poetry of William Wordsworth and Claudio Rodríguez." *Castilla: Estudios de Literatura* 9 (2018): 237–62.

Matless, David. "Nature, the Modern and the Mystic: Tales from Early Twentieth Century Geography." *Transactions of the Institute of British Geographers* (1991): 272–86.

Matley, Ian M. "Literary Geography and the Writer's Country." *Scottish Geographical Magazine* 103, no. 3 (1987): 122–31.

Ottum, Lisa. "Discriminating Vision: Rereading Place in Wordsworth's *Guide to the Lakes*." *Prose Studies* 34, no. 3 (2012): 167–84.

Simpson, David. *Wordsworth's Historical Imagination: The Poetry of Displacement*. London: Routledge, 2014.

Squire, Shelach J. "Wordsworth and Lake District Tourism: Romantic Reshaping of Landscape." *Canadian Geographer/Le Géographe Canadien* 32, no. 3 (1988): 237–47.

Stewart, Suzanne. "Roads, Rivers, Railways and Pedestrian Rambles: The Space and Place of Travel in William Wordsworth's Poems and JMW Turner's Paintings." *Nineteenth-Century Contexts* 34, no. 2 (2012): 159–84.

Whyte, Ian. "William Wordsworth's *Guide to the Lakes* and the Geographical Tradition." *Area* 32, no. 1 (2000): 101–6.

Wiley, Michael. *Romantic Geography: Wordsworth and Anglo-European Spaces*. London: Springer, 1998.

Wuthering Heights

This epic tale of an intergenerational feud and cyclical romance between two houses was written by Emily Brontë and published in 1847. It chronicles two generations of families who live in a remote area of Yorkshire. Heathcliff and Catherine are the two main characters of the first generation and their story is what sets the plot in motion.

Heathcliff and Catherine grow up together after her father brings Heathcliff back with him from a trip to the city, where he had found the young boy starving on the street. As close as they are, Catherine's older brother Hindley never accepts Heathcliff because of jealousy that he has usurped his place in the household. Heathcliff is also at odds with the wealthier family across the moors, the Lintons.

As she grows up, Catherine becomes closer with the Lintons, especially Edgar. They eventually become engaged, and Heathcliff runs away because he is enraged that Catherine would marry someone other than him. Catherine does not love Edgar the way she loves Heathcliff, but Edgar can offer her a better life. However, when Heathcliff disappears, Catherine is so upset that she falls very ill. When Heathcliff

> My love for Linton is like the foliage in the woods: time will change it, I'm well aware, as winter changes the trees—my love for Heathcliff resembles the eternal rocks beneath—a source of little visible delight, but necessary.
> **Emily Brontë, *Wuthering Heights* (1847)**

returns three years later, Edgar's sister Isabella falls in love with him. Although he does not care for her, he courts her as a way to enact revenge on Edgar and Catherine for marrying. This upsets Catherine so much that she begins to fall ill again. Heathcliff and Isabella elope. When they return, Catherine dies after giving birth to a daughter named Cathy. Hindley dies six months later, leaving Heathcliff as owner of Wuthering Heights. Isabella gives birth to a son, Linton. As they enter young adulthood, Heathcliff attempts to orchestrate a marriage between Linton and Cathy. However, Linton dies and Cathy becomes close with Hindley, who greatly resembles the uncouth Heathcliff. After Heathcliff passes, they marry. With their union, it seems that the romance between Heathcliff and Catherine lives on.

THE TWO FEUDING HOUSES

The architecture and location of Wuthering Heights and Thrushcross Grange are most likely inspired by real residences that Emily Brontë would have known. Although scholars have not pinpointed the exact ones, theories of the architectural model for the Wuthering Heights estate include houses called Top Withens and High Sunderland Hall. The real-life Thrushcross Grange is thought to be either Ponden Hall or Shibden Hall. Brontë's architectural representation in the novel is most likely a collage of multiple structures in and around West Yorkshire, close to Haworth, the hometown of the Brontë sisters. Specifically, scholars have noted that the walk from Liverpool to Wuthering Heights is about the same distance between Liverpool and the Gimmerton Valley. Several geographical and architectural elements from this region are noted in the text: Penistone Crags and the Gimmerton chapel and its bells. Nature in the work of the Brontë sisters is based on more remote rural areas than is the work of Jane Austen, for instance, which is often set in more polished settings—planned gardens, for example.

THE CULTURAL GEOGRAPHY OF PASSION

The word *wuthering* from the title of Brontë's novel refers to the name of a house, but it is a word that situates the house and its inhabitants in the stormy English moors. The word means "stormy weather," Brontë's narrator tells us in Chapter 1 of the book, particularly the fierce wind that accompanies storms in that part of West Yorkshire, England. The severe weather in that locale is an appropriate setting for the tumultuous relationships chronicled in the book.

The landscape of the moors as a setting reflects the stormy nature of the relationships between people in the novel. Like the tempers of the humans who occupy this space, the weather changes abruptly and severely. Storms arise suddenly in all

This photo of the North Yorkshire moors was taken in 1955. Centered in the frame is Top Withins, one of the estates thought to be the inspiration for the setting of *Wuthering Heights*. (Topical Press Agency/Getty Images)

seasons. Due to fairly steep changes in topography, much of the moors is not conducive to settlement and building as there are few flat spaces for houses and roadways. The ups and downs of life in the moors is a symbol for the passion between Heathcliff and Catherine, as is their desire to channel the savagery of such a landscape. In it, they find power and strength and a connection that survives after death due in part to the haunting nature of the landscape. These are characters who are portrayed as living closer to nature than to civilized society, which is why Heathcliff feels Catherine's betrayal by marrying Edgar is a tragic denial of their shared nature.

THE MOORS OF ENGLAND AS THE PLACE OF THE SUPERNATURAL

The story begins and ends with a framed narrative, the impressions of a young man named Lockwood who has rented Thrushcross Grange for a brief stay. He visits Wuthering Heights and is forced to stay overnight due to a snowstorm. During the night, he believes that a ghost tries to get in through the window. Heathcliff believes it is the ghost of Catherine. The next day, the visitor asks Nelly Dean, a servant, about the strange events, and she tells him the history of the place and its inhabitants, ending with the present-day, a time when Cathy and Hindley are growing closer in their relationship and Heathcliff is falling increasingly ill. This narrative frame is important because it provides the perspective of an outsider looking in. Lockwood's interactions with the landscape and its people are fresh and unbiased by the generational feud between the two families of the region. Brontë harnesses this outsider's perspective to draw out the supernatural elements of the text, showing that even newcomers are affected by ghosts of the past, and that the landscape has an inherently spiritual nature, observed even by those who are new to it.

Lynn Marie Houston

Further Reading

Emily Brontë's sister wrote *Jane Eyre,* a novel that explores two lovers separated by class, as is the case for Catherine and Heathcliff, the protagonists of *Wuthering Heights.* Jane Austen's works, such as *Pride and Prejudice,* are also frequently compared to the work of the Brontës.

Bibliography

Austin, Linda M. "Emily Bronte's Homesickness." *Victorian Studies* 44, no. 4 (2002): 573–96.

Baker, Alan R. H., and Mark Billinge. "Cultural Constructions of England's Geography and History." *Cambridge Studies in Historical Geography* 37 (2004): 175–83.

Broome, Sean. "*Wuthering Heights* and the Othering of the Rural." PhD diss., University of Derby, 2015.

Chitham, Edward. *Western Winds: The Brontë Irish Heritage.* Stroud, UK: The History Press, 2015.

Cook, Susan E. "Mapping Hardy and Brontë." In *Literary Cartographies: Spatiality, Representation, and Narrative,* edited by Robert T. Tally Jr. New York: Palgrave Macmillan, 2014.

Defant, Ivonne. "Inhabiting Nature in Emily Brontë's Wuthering Heights." *Brontë Studies* 42, no. 1 (2017): 37–47.

Duthie, Enid L. *The Brontës and Nature.* New York: Palgrave Macmillan, 1986.

Gilroy, Amanda, ed. *Green and Pleasant Land: English Culture and the Romantic Countryside.* Leuven, Belgium: Peeters Publishers, 2004.

Godfrey, Laura Gruber. "'That Quiet Earth': Tourism, Cultural Geography, and the Misreading of Landscape in *Wuthering Heights.*" *Interdisciplinary Literary Studies* 12, no. 2 (2011): 1–15.

Habermann, Ina, and Daniela Keller. "English Topographies: Introduction." In *English Topographies in Literature and Culture: Space, Place, and Identity,* edited by Ina Habermann and Daniela Keller, 1. Leiden, Netherlands: Brill, 2016.

Helsinger, Elizabeth K. *Rural Scenes and National Representation: Britain, 1815–1850.* Princeton, NJ: Princeton University Press, 2014.

Homans, Margaret. "Repression and Sublimation of Nature in *Wuthering Heights.*" *Publications of the Modern Language Association of America* 93, no. 1 (1978): 9–19.

Jakubowski, Zuzanna. *Moors, Mansions, and Museums: Transgressing Gendered Spaces in Novels of the Brontë Sisters.* Frankfurt, Germany: Peter Lang, 2010.

Kennedy, Margaret. "Protecting the 'House Beautiful': Eco-Consciousness in the Victorian Novel." PhD diss., Stony Brook University, 2013.

Matley, Ian M. "Literary Geography and the Writer's Country." *Scottish Geographical Magazine* 103, no. 3 (1987): 122–31.

Mazzeno, Laurence W., and Ronald D. Morrison. "Dark Nature: A Critical Return to Brontë Country Deirdre D'Albertis." In *Victorian Writers and the Environment: Ecocritical Perspectives,* edited by Laurence W. Mazzeno and Ronald D. Morrison. London: Routledge, 2016.

Perriam, Geraldine. "'Impudent Scribblers': Place and the Unlikely Heroines of the Interwar Years." PhD diss., University of Glasgow, 2011.

Rotherham, Ian D. "A Fear of Nature: Images and Perceptions of Heath, Moor, Bog and Fen in England." In *Between the Atlantic and the Mediterranean: Responses to Climate and Weather Conditions Throughout History*, edited by Cristina Joanaz de Melo, Ana Isabel Queiroz, Luis Espinha da Silveira, and Ian D. Rotherham. Sheffield, UK: Wildtrack Publishing, 2013.

Simmons, Ian G. "The Moorlands of England and Wales: Histories and Narratives." In *Presenting and Representing Environments,* edited by Graham Humphrys and Michael Williams. Dordrecht, Netherlands: Springer, 2005.

Smith, Andrew, and William Hughes. *Ecogothic*. Manchester, UK: Manchester University Press, 2018.

Tenen, Dennis Yi. "Toward a Computational Archaeology of Fictional Space." *New Literary History* 49, no. 1 (2018): 119–47.

Tetley, Sarah, and Bill Bramwell. "Tourists and the Cultural Construction of Haworth's Literary Landscape." In *Literature and Tourism: Essays in the Reading and Writing of Tourism,* edited by Mike Robinson and Hans Christian Anderson, 155–70. London: Thomson, 2002.

Thornham, Sue. "'Not a Country at All': Landscape and Wuthering Heights." *Journal of British Cinema and Television* 13, no. 1 (2016): 214–31.

Wegner, Phillip E. "Space and Place in Critical Reading." In *Introducing Criticism in the 21st Century,* edited by Julian Wolfreys. Edinburgh: Edinburgh University Press, 2015.

Y

"The Yellow Wallpaper"

In the short story "The Yellow Wallpaper," Charlotte Perkins Gilman explores a woman's relationship with the interior of one room in their rented "vacation" home after her husband, a doctor, confines her there as a "rest cure" for her depression. The story is written by the protagonist, Jane, in the form of a journal she begins as the family moves into the remote, rented house, hoping that some time away would help lift her spirits. Her husband fears she is suffering from "nervous depression," but she has recently given birth and is probably experiencing postpartum depression, a condition yet undiscovered by male doctors at the time. As part of her "cure," her husband forbids her to write, but she secretly defies him by hiding the journal and writing while he is away or at night while he is sleeping. Left alone for days while her husband travels for work, the protagonist begins to see curious movement among the patterns in the wallpaper. Eventually, she comes to believe that a woman is trapped in it. She begins to tear down the wallpaper in an effort to free this woman, and gives in to a mental breakdown. In this way, although the setting doesn't change, the protagonist does. Gilman emphasized the character's descent into madness by contrasting the changes in her mental state and the stability of the location. Although she doesn't leave the room, she gradually gives way to her mental decline, which we witness through her perceptions and voice as the story is in the form of a journal. The space of this bedroom room is an important metaphor for the power dynamics of women's oppression.

A GOTHIC DOPPELGÄNGER

The story can be read as adhering to a setting appropriate for a piece of Gothic literature: a mysterious, isolated estate, where a female character spends a lot of time alone. The house that the family has rented has a presence about it, and otherwise benign architectural elements begin to take on a sinister appearance. For instance, the room where they sleep used to be a nursery and the windows have bars over them. The psychology of this protagonist becomes the central landscape of the story as the oppression by her husband strips her of her sanity. In this case, the well-intentioned husband is actually the Gothic villain who keeps our protagonist imprisoned against her will.

Gilman also creates a double identity by placing a doppelgänger (or twin figure) in the story. As the female protagonist begins to lose her sanity, she starts seeing a woman imprisoned in the wallpaper, a psychological manifestation of her own situation. By the end of the story, the woman starts tearing off the wallpaper while her use of pronoun shifts from "her" to "me" to describe the woman in the wallpaper. She has now become the woman she imagined was imprisoned there. This was foreshadowed earlier with statements she makes, such as that she has to go back to hiding in the wallpaper when John comes home. At first, such statements might seem metaphorical, pertaining to how she has to hide her true self and her true wants and desires, but by the conclusion of the story it becomes clear that Gilman is constructing a plot in which the protagonist's confinement and lack of human interaction has pushed her over the brink into insanity.

THE GEOGRAPHY OF DOMESTICITY

In this short story, Gilman has turned the 19th-century language of domesticity on its head. She exposes the institution of marriage and the interior spaces of homes for what they often were: prisons for women. The location of the property is far from other dwellings, which serves to isolate the wife and distance her from anyone who might see the problem with how she is being treated and attempt to intervene. Psychologists study this technique used by abusers where they will isolate their victims from their friends and family so that they have no possibility of receiving support or help from the outside.

Many of the details the narrator shares about the house's architecture emphasize captivity, such as the bars on the windows and the garden gates that lock. This confinement is linked to women's infantilization, as many of these restraints, such as the locked barrier at the top of the stairs (to prevent children from falling) and the bed that is nailed down to the floor, exist because the room they are using as a bedroom used to be a nursery. Although the narrator requests to make modifications to the room, her husband refuses on the grounds that if he agrees, it will ultimately teach her the wrong lesson, and she will feel empowered to request additional changes when he thinks these requests are just distractions from her recovery. He wants her to turn her attention inward instead of outward to the furnishings of the house. He sees her desire to renovate the room as her wish to be a good wife and to do her duty by beautifying their surroundings, but her requests are rooted in her need to have a safe space. Instead, she feels that she has to control, rather than express her emotions to reassure her husband. Their conflict over the nature of this interior space mirrors the larger power dynamic of oppression in their relationship.

WOMEN'S ART AND A ROOM OF ONE'S OWN

Many women writers in the 19th century already advocated for the "room of one's own" that Virginia Woolf would write about in her 1929 manifesto. However, the seclusion here of being forced to live in one room works against the narrator and any desires or ambitions she might have. She lacks a sense of community and the purpose of being given meaningful and intellectually stimulating work. The story points out that, ultimately, it is not the physical space that is important to women, but the ability to a do a certain kind of work in that space. The fact that the narrator's mental health seems to be triggered by or wrapped up in the details of the furnishings is particularly symbolic, as furnishing a home is the only productive work that she is allowed to do, and, in this case, she is denied even that small contribution. She isn't involved in the preparation of meals, and John's sister, Jennie, is taking care of the baby and other household matters. However, in this case, the home furnishings, specifically the wallpaper, are transformed into something much more than decoration: they become a secret code that only our protagonist can read. A room of one's own means nothing if it is a space in which one is confined by a patriarchal system of judgment. The space that Virginia Woolf advocates is a space in which women are allowed autonomy and the means to pursue their own self-identity. Because he is her husband, John can control her access to space, denying her permission, as one example, to even visit relatives when she asks. Because he is a doctor, he can lay claim to controlling her body by prescribing the bed rest cure. In writing about her protagonist's mental decline, which Gilman has admitted is based around true events of her life when she was put on "bed rest" after the birth of her child, Gilman suggests that this is the last arena the protagonist has to herself, which she allows to run free, and stops attempting to control. The protagonist seeks to project her own situation onto her surroundings, in effect creating art, even though she is not allowed to write.

SURVEILLANCE, GENDER, AND THE HOME INTERIOR

At first, the protagonist believes she sees eyes in the wallpaper's pattern, but these individual body parts then add up to what she believes is a woman in the wallpaper. It is significant that she first sees eyes because of the way her confinement is accompanied by surveillance. One of the disconcerting elements of the story is how the protagonist describes Jennie as being used by John as a spy. She reports to him on the protagonist's activities and health. Gilman is demonstrating how other women are co-opted by the patriarchy into turning on other women. Our protagonist engages in the opposite behavior. The protagonist's desire to free the woman in the wallpaper is the desire to create a kind of community and to grant another human being the independence she has been denied. It is a motherly kind of act, seeking to make someone else's situation better than one's own. Eventually the protagonist imagines that the one woman in the wallpaper turns into an army—she sees them all outside her window, creeping among the hedges.

Because the protagonist's issue is most likely related to the changes in hormones that follow giving birth, she is a prisoner of her own body. John's profession allows Gilman to exacerbate the situation that 19th-century women found themselves in: their husbands got to make decisions about their bodies, where they went, who they saw, what they had for meals, and so on. The protagonist eventually takes control by prohibiting John and Jennie from accessing her room. She locks the door and throws the key out the window. Even though at this point in the story she now believes she is the woman in the wallpaper and has been "freed" from the pattern, the irony is that she is now in a locked room. Gilman underscores that it is not the space itself, which she seems triumphant to be locked in by herself, but the presence of those who seek to control the protagonist that is the real conflict in the story. In the absence of any solution to her crisis, the protagonist uses the space of her prison to invent a narrative in which she can be free. This is meant to be read as having a kind of logic as Gilman explains in her essay "Why I Wrote the Yellow Wallpaper" that she intended to try to change the medical practices at the time that caused women to suffer and that ran counter to women's true needs.

Lynn Marie Houston

Further Reading

Another story that deals with a woman hidden away by her husband because he believes her to have mental health issues is *Jane Eyre* by Charlotte Brontë. Much has been written about the gendered and postcolonial politics of "the mad woman in the attic" in 19th-century literature. Critics like Sandra Gilbert and Susan Gubar, in their study *The Madwoman in the Attic: The Woman Writer and the Nineteenth-Century Literary Imagination,* address many other literary works from that time period that develop this same theme. Kate Chopin is another 19th-century woman writer who explores the subtle power dynamics of marriages, especially in *The Awakening* and "The Story of an Hour."

Bibliography

Allen, Polly Wynn. *Building Domestic Liberty: Charlotte Perkins Gilman's Architectural Feminism.* Amherst: University of Massachusetts Press, 1988.

Betjemann, Peter. "Charlotte Perkins Gilman's Grammar of Ornament: Stylistic Tagging and the Politics of Figuration in 'The Yellow Wallpaper' and 'The Unexpected.'" *Word & Image* 24, no. 4 (2008): 393–402.

Brown, Gillian. "The Empire of Agoraphobia." *Representations* 20 (1987): 134–57.

Davis, Cynthia J. "'The World Was Home for Me': Charlotte Perkins Gilman and the Sentimental Public Sphere." *Arizona Quarterly: A Journal of American Literature, Culture, and Theory* 66, no. 1 (2010): 63–86.

Davison, Carol Margaret. "Haunted House/Haunted Heroine: Female Gothic Closets in 'The Yellow Wallpaper.'" *Women's Studies* 33, no. 1 (2004): 47–75.

Donaldson, Laura E. "The Eve of De-struction: Charlotte Perkins Gilman and the Feminist Recreation of Paradise." *Women's Studies: An Interdisciplinary Journal* 16, no. 3–4 (1989): 373–87.

Egan, Kristen R. "Conservation and Cleanliness: Racial and Environmental Purity in Ellen Richards and Charlotte Perkins Gilman." *Women's Studies Quarterly* 39, no. 3/4 (2011): 77–92.

Gaudelius, Yvonne. "Kitchenless Houses and Homes Charlotte Perkins Gilman and the Reform." *Charlotte Perkins Gilman: Optimist Reformer,* edited by Jill Rudd and Val Gough, 111. Iowa City: University of Iowa Press, 1999.

Golden, Catherine. "The Writing of 'The Yellow Wallpaper': A Double Palimpsest." *Studies in American Fiction* 17, no. 2 (1989): 193.

Herndl, Diane Price. "The Writing Cure: Charlotte Perkins Gilman, Anna O., and 'Hysterical' Writing." *NWSA Journal* 1, no. 1 (1988): 52–74.

Horowitz, Helen Lefkowitz. *Wild Unrest: Charlotte Perkins Gilman and the Making of "The Yellow Wall-Paper."* New York: Oxford University Press, 2010.

MacPike, Loralee. "Environment as Psychopathological Symbolism in 'The Yellow Wallpaper.'" *American Literary Realism, 1870–1910* 8, no. 3 (1975): 286–88.

Notaro, Anna, and Hélène Cixous. "Space and Domesticity in 'The Yellow Wallpaper' by Charlotte Perkins Gilman." *Journal of American Studies of Turkey* 10 (1999): 59–68.

Rosenman, Ellen Bayuk. "Sexual Identity and 'A Room of One's Own': 'Secret Economies' in Virginia Woolf's Feminist Discourse." *Signs: Journal of Women in Culture and Society* 14, no. 3 (1989): 634–50.

Schweninger, Lee. "Reading the Garden in Gilman's 'The Yellow Wallpaper.'" *Interdisciplinary Studies in Literature and Environment* 2, no. 2 (1996): 25–44.

Scott, Heidi. "Crazed Nature: Ecology in the Yellow Wall-Paper." *The Explicator* 67, no. 3 (2009): 198–203.

Vertinsky, Patricia. "A Militant Madonna: Charlotte Perkins Gilman-Feminism and Physical Culture." *The International Journal of the History of Sport* 18, no. 1 (2001): 55–72.

Appendix: Literary Landscapes and Capital Cities

GENEVA

Geneva, Switzerland, is famous for what seem like contradictory impulses: Calvinism, commerce, chocolate, and clocks. A sculpture in the English Garden on the shore of Lake Geneva epitomizes this split: a large clock keeps perfect time, but it is made out of flowers. This tug-of-war between scientific precision and artistic, natural beauty draws numerous travelers to visit the city. Although it is the home of three international humanitarian organizations, the Red Cross, the World Health Organization, and the United Nations, Geneva has also been home to many writers.

Jean-Jacques Rousseau (1712–1778) was born in Geneva. His political and social ideas, especially those in *The Social Contract,* were influential in shaping the French and American Revolutions and the time period known as the age of Enlightenment. Remembered more for his philosophical writing than his small collection of literary works, Rousseau penned an autobiography of his life, *Confessions,* that helped to shape the future of that genre as it developed into modern times. He spent his childhood at 40 Grand Rue, Geneva, but for much of his adult life, Rousseau traveled between European countries because he had been exiled from Geneva due to his beliefs. His birthplace is a now a museum dedicated to his life and ideas.

Less than two decades after Rousseau's death, the city of his birth hosted an extraordinary writing retreat for some of the most brilliant writers of the Romantic time period: Lord Byron, Mary Shelley, and Percy Shelley. These three authors rented houses just north of Geneva one summer and spent their time sailing on the lake, riding horses in the mountains, and trying to outdo each other in coming up with frightening stories. The famous works that resulted from this sojourn were various poems by Byron, including "The Prisoner of Chillon," and *Frankenstein* by Mary Shelley, as well as a short story about vampires written by Byron's personal physician. The latter would go on to inspire Bram Stoker's masterpiece *Dracula*. The group went on various sightseeing trips during their time in Switzerland, including the Chateau de Chillon, a 16th-century prison for political dissidents, which sparked Byron's poem and is also featured as a setting in Henry James's short story *Daisy Miller*.

Other writers who spent time in Geneva and whose works include descriptions inspired by the city are Charles Dickens, W. Somerset Maugham, Ian Fleming, Vladimir Nabokov, Sir Arthur Conan Doyle, Mark Twain, F. Scott Fitzgerald, J. R. R. Tolkien, and John le Carré. Argentinian author Jorge Luis Borges is buried there.

Geneva's influence on literary history seems to have been greatly subjective, depending on the author. Although Rousseau embraced liberal views on religion and human nature, the Romantic authors who visited during the 19th century began exploring in their works the tragic flaws in humankind. Later authors have taken away vastly differing impressions of the city. Over the centuries, Geneva has maintained the independent spirit that prompted it to remain a city-state for so long, rebuking attempts by neighboring France (the Savoyards) to annex it. The wall surrounding Geneva's old town section is a reminder of the city's history of fighting to maintain an independent space, just as the famous water fountain landmark (the *Jet d'Eau*) shooting up from the lake represents the city's power and charisma.

PARIS

One cannot traverse Europe end to end without passing through the Hexagon, the affectionate name that the French give their country. Located in the north of the shape used by architects and honeybees alike, Paris is the city through which all major thoroughfares pass. Paris may be able to claim residency by some of history's greatest writers simply because it is a natural crossroads. However, these writers were also certainly drawn to Paris for more intangible reasons: its culture, people, or the legacy of other writers who went before them. This legacy is very evident in the Père Lachaise Cemetery.

The cemetery, near the heart of the city, is the final resting place of Honoré de Balzac, born about 150 miles away in Tours, France. The playwright and novelist Oscar Wilde, born almost 500 miles away in Dublin, Ireland, is also interred there. Gertrude Stein, born a continent away in Pittsburgh, Pennsylvania, and living in California before she moved to Paris, will also spend eternity in Père Lachaise Cemetery. They are joined there by two locally produced writers, Marcel Proust and Molière. Proust, the 20th century novelist, was born in Auteuil, near the capital city. Molière, the 17th-century playwright and poet, was born, lived, and died in Paris.

Père Lachaise Cemetery is located in Paris's 20th arrondissement, or administrative district, about a 35- or 40-minute walk east of the Notre Dame Cathedral. The formal name of this cemetery is Cimetiere de l'Est, "Cemetery of the East." Today, the sculptures and tombs provide a visual feast of pyramids, obelisks, rectangular structures called "ziggurats," domed basilicas, miniature Gothic cathedrals, and tall upright stones called "menhirs," interspersed with and accented by simple flat headstones and thousands of trees. The walking paths are paved with stone that will outlast, perhaps, the memories of the writers buried there.

Balzac's tomb is topped with a bust of the author. He wrote *Eugenie Grandet, Lost Illusions, Old Man Goriot,* and other novels and short stories that comprise *The Human Comedy.* Balzac went to Paris with his family when he was a young teenager. Just across the river from the Eiffel Tower is the Maison de Balzac. This is the last of Balzac's homes in Paris to survive the demands of the city for building space. Unlike the author himself, the house is curiously modest, but it is also roomy and comfortable. Balzac wrote *The Human Comedy* in this house, famously writing in his rapid longhand throughout the night. Behind the house is a pleasant garden just a stone's throw from the banks of the River Seine.

Oscar Wilde's journey to his final resting place in Paris was neither as short nor as comfortable as Balzac's. In 1897 Wilde, then in his early 40s and just released from prison, left the United Kingdom and crossed the English Channel to stay with friends in Normandy, France. The irresistible pull of Paris caught Wilde and he moved into the Hôtel d'Alsace on Rue des Beaux-Arts where he hoped to revive his career. The hotel that he made his residence is just a short walk from the Louvre art museum. Although approaching death, Wilde would have walked across the Pont des Arts pedestrian bridge to visit the world's largest and internationally famous museum. In Wilde's final days, this cast-iron bridge provided him with magnificent views of the city he chose to call home. Looking a short distance up river, Wilde saw the Pont Neuf, the oldest stone bridge in Paris. This stone bridge and its 12 arches consists of two spans. One span connects Ile de la Cité, an island in the River Seine on which the ancient city of Paris was founded, to one side of the river. The bridge continues straight across the island, then the bridge's second span connects the island to the other riverbank. From Wilde's perspective on the Pont des Arts, the Pont Neuf is divided in the middle by the trees of the Square du Vert-Galant, a green park on the sharp point of Ile de la Cité. Cerebral meningitis claimed the life of Dublin's famous son, and then Paris resident Wilde, as he rested in the Hôtel d'Alsace on November 30, 1900, aged 46. Today the five-star hotel offers guests a stay in its "Oscar Wilde Suite."

Three years after Wilde's death, Gertrude Stein, the author of *Three Lives* and *Tender Buttons,* arrived in Paris. Twenty-nine at the time, she had spent a great deal of her youth vacationing in Europe with her family. Her father was a wealthy merchant and could indulge her and her family in these trips. When Stein returned at age 29, her brother accompanied her. They purchased artwork and established a literary salon in her apartment home. It is located on the small side street of rue de Fleurus, near a large garden called Le Jardin du Luxembourg about a 15-minute walk from Wilde's Hôtel d'Alsace on Paris's south bank. From 1903 until 1938, Stein hosted gatherings of artists and authors in her salon. The list of authors who regularly met there is impressive. American novelists Ernest Hemingway and F. Scott Fitzgerald visited frequently, perhaps drawn by the companionship of a fellow American. American poet Ezra Pound also called during the get-togethers Saturday evenings. The topics of their conversations in room number 27 Rue de Fleurus are lost to history. A photograph of an aging Stein in the apartment shows the large fireplace decorated with ceramics and figurines on the hearth. The walls are covered with large and small paintings, the smaller ones stacked vertically, one on top of another.

Hemingway, while still in Chicago, corresponded with Stein by letter. Later, in September 1921, he married and moved to Paris as the *Toronto Daily Star* newspaper's European correspondent. Upon his arrival, he was forced to move into a primitive apartment without running water, but rented a room nearby so he could have a quiet place to work. His time in Paris was tumultuous but productive. His marriage ended in divorce but not before producing a son. He remarried shortly after that divorce, and a second son was born with his second wife. During these Paris years, he developed his unique literary style and wrote some of his finest work, including *The Sun Also Rises* and a book of short stories entitled *Men Without Women.*

French author Marguerite Duras, who died in 1996 and is interred about a half mile from Rue de Fleurus in Montparnasse Cemetery, arrived in Paris about seven years before Stein's famous Saturday evening gatherings came to an end in 1938. Among Duras's widely read and discussed later novels are *The Ravishing of Lol Stein*, published in 1964, and *The Lover*, which was published in 1984 when Duras was 70. This latter novel tells of a 15-year-old French girl in French Indochina who has an affair with a 27-year-old Chinese man.

Although French, Duras was born in 1914 in Gia Dinh province, French Indochina. Today we call her birthplace Vietnam. She left the French colony in 1931 to study law, mathematics, and political science at the prestigious University of Paris, also known as "the Sorbonne." After graduation, Duras worked for the Minister of the Colonies, the French government official responsible for administrating the country's many overseas colonies, until her world forever changed in June 1940. Germany overran French defenses and began its occupation of Paris that would last the entire war. Duras actively participated in the Resistance during the German occupation. She would write of those wrenching, horrific years for herself, her fellow Parisians, and her fellow French in *The War: A Memoir*. She wrote this in 1944, and it was published in 1985. Duras said the memoir was based on a diary she found in the cupboards of Neauphle-le-Chateau.

Today, the Musée d'Orsay occupies the former train station through which prisoners of that war and survivors of the concentration camps were returned home. The fantastic, palatial façade of the *gare,* or train station, and its intricately detailed interior were undoubtedly a marvelous site to the French who arrived at the station. The museum is located just across the Seine from Jardin des Tuileries and a short walk from Oscar Wilde's Hôtel d'Alsace.

EDINBURGH

Edinburgh is the capital city of Scotland. It surrounds Castle Rock, a massive and ancient rock formation that is visible for miles around. Outside the city to the south are the Pentland Hills. These gently rolling hills are covered in miles and miles of green, with no trees in sight. On the other side of the city, the battleship gray water of the Firth of Forth gives the city vital access to the sea. *Firth* is the Scottish word for a wide inlet to a river. The city, the hills, and the firth are often all shrouded in cold, misty fog.

Built atop Castle Rock in the center of the city is Edinburgh Castle, rising above everything else as an easy landmark. The same would have been true 800 years ago, when it was first built. It is a timeless reminder of the hardworking, intelligent, and creative Scots who built it. It is also a memorial to the brave, hard-fighting Scots who defended this castle, again and again, from invading English soldiers—a ready reminder of the sacrifices of the countless Scots who died defending it.

Walking among these weathered stone buildings of Edinburgh around 1800, bundled up in warm wool, was a young Walter Scott. He wrote narrative poems and novels that are still read and reread by people around the world. As he passed along the streets of Edinburgh, with the castle never out of sight, did he imagine the warder call "To arms! the foemen storm the wall"? Edinburgh was rightly proud of Walter Scott, author of *The Lady in the Lake,* and in the 1840s an ornate memorial to him was built along a wide, cobblestoned street just below the castle in the "Old Town" section of Edinburgh.

Just a few years after this Sir Walter Scott memorial appeared, a young boy named Robert Louis Stevenson may have been sent on an errand to the Old Town. This son of Edinburgh would later write of a murderous Dr. Jekyll. Although the story of Dr. Jekyll and Mr. Hyde takes place in London, the character was probably modeled after a respected 18th-century Edinburgh citizen named William Brodie. By day, Brodie was a tradesman, president of a city tradesmen's guild, and city councillor. At night, this figure of late 18th-century Edinburgh society led a double life as a burglar and leader of a ring of thieves. He was hanged until dead near St. Giles' Cathedral, which is just around the corner from today's Edinburgh Waverly train station.

A little over a century after Stevenson published *The Strange Case of Dr. Jekyll and Mr. Hyde,* single mom J. K. Rowling pulled into Edinburgh with her young daughter in tow and the first three chapters of *Harry Potter,* written in longhand, in her suitcase. Although well traveled by then, and English by birth, it was in Edinburgh where she wrote the popular tale during her free time when she wasn't teaching. After years of imagining and writing, Rowling's *Harry Potter and the Philosopher's Stone* was published in 1997.

Twenty-five years before real-life schoolteacher Rowling taught in Edinburgh's schools, author Muriel Spark published her novel about a fictitious Edinburgh schoolteacher named Jean Brodie, the main character in her 1961 novel *The Prime of Miss Jean Brodie.* Spark was born in the Scottish city in 1918 and lived with her family in Bruntsfield Place, southwest of the castle and Old Town. In 1936, she took a job in one of the city's premier department store on Princes Street. She was just 18 years old at the time. While studying the department store's patrons, she undoubtedly gathered material for the many novels she would write later in life. The department store, called "Small's," was a short walk down Princes Street from the Sir Walter Scott Memorial and just across the street from the Princes Street Gardens, which frame the castle above. *The Prime of Miss Jean Brodie* takes place in an all-girls school in Edinburgh. This is a topic that Spark knew well, having herself attended James Gillespie's High School for Girls in Edinburgh.

To reach the red sandstone Gillespie's High School building from her home on Bruntsfield Place, Spark walked across the western end of an open parkland called Bruntsfield Links. "Links" is the Scottish name for the game of golf, and Bruntsfield Links is one the earliest golf links in Scotland. To honor one of the city's most accomplished writers, Edinburgh renamed a path that Spark took to reach the school as the "Muriel Spark Walk." Spark's high school alma mater is now used by University of Edinburgh as a residence hall for students.

Although a talented writer at a young age, Spark become a novelist only after a circuitous 20-year detour through life. She married in 1937, followed her husband to Africa, and in 1944 returned to England, where she worked in intelligence in World War II. After the war, in 1947, she became editor of the *Poetry Review*. Finally, in 1957, her first novel, *The Comforters,* was published.

LONDON

As a young man, William Shakespeare first entered London through a gate in the old stone wall that was built by the Romans around A.D. 100. By the time young Shakespeare made his entrance, the wall had stood for 1,500 years. Shakespeare, a young aspiring actor, was probably in his late teens or early 20s at the time. Each of the gates in the wall was actually a pair of smaller arches, one for incoming traffic and one for outgoing traffic. There were probably about seven of them in the wall. The city at that time was located on the north side of the River Thames. People also entered and left the city on boats, and also across the single bridge that spanned the river. Shakespeare, however, was from Stratford-upon-Avon, which is about 100 miles to the north, so he very likely approached the city over land. His hometown was a small market town of just a few inhabitants along the River Avon and a main road in the area. London, on the other hand, was worlds away and probably had as many as 200,000 inhabitants. These inhabitants were packed into a 330-acre area ringed by the Roman wall and the river, and Shakespeare instantly blended in with the throngs of people on the narrow, crowded streets. Homes in London at the time were built in the Tudor style. This means they had big oak beams that were visible on the exterior. The area between the beams was filled with what they called wattle and daub, laths and plaster, or bricks in sometimes intricate and decorative patterns. Wattle and daub involves upright branches interwoven by smaller branches and covered by a thick coat of clay mud. The second story of these homes usually had an overhang that Shakespeare could duck under to get out of the frequent rains of southeastern England. Sometimes a third floor extended over the second floor, and sometimes even a fourth floor extended over the third. This design protected the lower floors but it also made it convenient for tenants to dump their waste out the windows and directly onto the streets below. The streets themselves were usually narrow and surfaced with cobblestones. The wider streets usually had a gutter on each side. The narrow streets usually had a single gutter running down the center. These gutters drained rainwater and wastewater. Shakespeare's streets were usually busy and pungent.

Some think that Shakespeare first entered London as a young actor who had to support himself by working in a theater's horse stables, while some think he first entered the city as a member of a traveling acting troupe. These were common in 16th-century England. Regardless of his early circumstances, in just a few years he had settled into a successful acting career in the city full of people who wanted to be distracted from their sometimes miserable, often dangerous lives. A writer who lived in London at the same time Shakespeare did, Thomas Dekker, described the city this way:

> Carts and coaches make such a thundering din as if the world ran on wheels; at every corner men, women, and children meet in such shoals that posts are set up to strengthen the houses lest with jostling with one another they should shoulder them down. Besides, hammers are beating in one place, tubs hooping in another [the noise made by coopers or barrel makers], pots clinking in a third, water-tankards running at tilt in a fourth. . . . It was noisy, crowded, bawdy, bustling and busy. Trades of every kind and description! Churches, inns, houses, workshops, stalls, stables and theatres! Animals—cats, dogs, pigs, horses and sheep! Bull baiting, bear baiting and cock-fighting! Inns, taverns and bawdy houses! Actors, courtiers, churchmen, merchants, shoppers, apprentices, money lenders, bawds, beggars and thieves! (Dekker 1606)

In 1593, another wave of the bubonic plague spread through the crowded city quickly, carried by fleas that infested rats that coexisted with the people indoors and outdoors. The plague forced Shakespeare and his acting troupe off the stage because theaters were forced to close, but he survived the killer disease. Just a couple years later, in 1595, he reached great success as the leading London playwright. The following year, 1596, Shakespeare's son died at age 11, probably from the plague, a terrible disease that killed about one-third of all people on the British isle in the 1340s and kept returning generation after generation. London authorities banned the public presentation of plays within the city limits so Shakespeare's company of actors moved across the river to stay in business. He still lived north of the river, which means the London Bridge became an integral lifeline for the playwright. This bridge, built at the site of the Roman's first bridge across the river, was a surreal microcosm of the strange and grotesque scenes that Shakespeare saw every day on his daily commute to the south bank and his theater.

A German attorney visiting London in 1598, Paul Hentzner, wrote this about this strange stretch of London life:

> On the south is a bridge of stone eight hundred feet in length, of wonderful work; it is supported upon twenty piers of square stone, sixty feet high and thirty broad, joined by arches of about twenty feet diameter. The whole is covered on each side with houses so disposed as to have the appearance of a continued street, not at all of a bridge. Upon this is built a tower, on whose top the heads of such as have been executed for high treason are placed on iron spikes: we counted above thirty. This visitor did not mention the public latrine that was a permanent fixture on the bridge. There were many public latrines in Shakespeare's London. Like the one on London Bridge, they hung over the Thames and waste dropped straight down into the river. (Hentzner 1797)

The wealthy Shakespeare probably lived in a home with richly wood-paneled interior walls decorated with lavish molded plasterwork, and had a private or semi-private latrine.

Two centuries after Shakespeare dodged the merchants and thieves and diseased souls of London's streets, a young Charles Dickens was taken to the Camden Town neighborhood of London from Portsmouth, one of England's main port cities along the southern coast. When Charles was just 12, in 1824, his father was imprisoned for debt. He left school so he could work at a boot-blacking factory along the

Thames. By then the city had grown to around a million people and its homes and factories had swallowed up the old Roman wall. The location of Shakespeare's theater was absorbed by the city, and several other bridges were added across the river. The city streets, however, remained overcrowded and dirty. The growth of the city could not keep up with the constant stream of people moving to London to feed the Industrial Revolution. People crowded into already crowded houses. But it was the jarring transition from the educated son of a relatively well-paid office worker in Portsmouth, with two servants to help around the house, to a child laborer in a London factory that scarred teenage Charles. His job involved pasting labels to bottles of shoe polish. Rather than live with his family in a debtors' prison, he lived in a boardinghouse and later a back attic.

A "back-to-back" in London in Dickens's day were houses that backed up to each other, one entrance on one street and another entrance on another street. This left little space for windows, and ventilation was a luxury. These were built as cheaply as possible. Rooms were rented to accommodate those impoverished working-class adults, orphaned children, and working young teenagers like Dickens. Tenants collected their water at a common well in the street. Common "privies," the name for outhouses in the city, served as their bathrooms but it was common for "night soils" to be collected indoors and later disposed of using any means necessary.

In Dickens's lifetime, he saw the population of London grow from around 1 million to more than 3 million. This explosive population growth and lack of building regulations resulted in collections of poor people in narrow streets lined by impromptu factories, such as the boot-blacking factory where Dickens worked, and poorly kept lodging houses. It also encouraged unscrupulous builders to construct shoddy hovels on otherwise worthless or unused parcels to turn a quick profit. These structures were built without foundations, with dirt floors and narrow walls along unpaved streets. They provided a roof for their tenants and a profit for their owners and managers, but added to the squalor that developed in some parts of Dickens's London.

Hampstead Heath, in the north part of London, was a short ride by Hansom cab from central London, but for Dickens it was a lifetime away from the boot-blacking factory of his youth. Londoners who could afford the fare, as Dickens could when his writing career took hold later in his life, escaped the crowded city for the heath. A heath is an open, natural space. Hampstead Heath sits on one of the highest spots in the city and provides lord-of-the-manor views to the capital city to the south. It was in Victorian times, and remains today, a popular place to walk for city dwellers.

The Spaniards Inn sits just off the northern edge of the heath. For centuries, it has attracted writers taking a break from their country ambles. The white, three-story building was built in 1585 as a toll collection point and inn for travelers. The inn sits on one side of the road, and the single-story tollhouse on the other side narrows the road down to one lane.

The ground floor, paneled in warm, darkly stained wood, was a good spot to rest and get a pint of ale or a cup of tea. A restaurant on the second floor is equally warm and inviting. On warmer days, patrons sat in the expansive garden out the back door. And so, on a warm spring or summer day in 1819, young Londoner John

Appendix

Keats relaxed in the garden and wrote these words, from his poem "An Ode to a Nightingale":

> Adieu! adieu! thy plaintive anthem fades
> Past the near meadows, over the still stream,
> Up the hill-side; and now 'tis buried deep
> In the next valley-glades:
> Was it a vision, or a waking dream?
> Fled is that music:—Do I wake or sleep?

Other inns and other gardens also lay claim to be the spot where Keats wrote this poem, but the Spaniards Inn will not relinquish its claim easily. A paper posted on the wall inside says, "John Keats reportedly wrote 'An Ode to a Nightingale' in the pub's expansive garden one fine summer afternoon." Also, a wooden bench in the garden has these words carved into the back rest: "Keats enjoyed many an ale here."

The back rest of a second bench at the Spaniards Inn says, "Charles Dickens found inspiration right here. . . ." Dickens immortalized the inn in the best way he could. In his novel *The Pickwick Papers,* he wrote the following:

> Mrs. Raddle smiled sweetly, Mr. Raddle bowed, and Mrs. Cluppins said, "she was sure she was very happy to have an opportunity of being known to a lady which she had heerd so much in favour of, as Mrs. Rogers." A compliment which the last-named lady acknowledged with graceful condescension.
> "Well, Mr. Raddle," said Mrs. Bardell; "I'm sure you ought to feel very much honoured at you and Tommy being the only gentlemen to escort so many ladies all the way to the Spaniards, at Hampstead."

Later that same day, wrote Dickens, "the party walked forth in quest of a Hampstead stage. This was soon found, and in a couple of hours they all arrived safely in the Spaniards Tea-gardens. . . ." The inn has also been frequented by other great English and Scottish writers, including William Blake, Robert Louis Stevenson, Mary Shelley, and Lord Byron.

The Spaniards Inn claims to be home to ghosts that have taken up residence in its more than 400 years of existence. Perhaps this claim is helped by its appearance in the 1897 novel *Dracula* by Bram Stoker. In the novel, Lucy Westenra was interred in family tombs in a church near what Stoker calls "Hampstead Hill." Dr. John Seward, "the lunatic-asylum man" as Lucy describes him, and Professor Van Helsing, pursue her there, and find one of vampire Lucy's intended victims, a young child, near her tomb.

In one of the novel's chapters written from Seward's perspective, he says, "A little way off, beyond a line of scattered juniper-trees, which marked the pathway to the church, a white, dim figure flitted in the direction of the tomb. The tomb itself was hidden by trees, and I could not see where the figure disappeared. I heard the rustle of actual movement where I had first seen the white figure, and coming over, found the Professor holding in his arms a tiny child." They leave the child on the heath for a policeman to find, then "By good chance we got a cab near the 'Spaniards,' and drove to town."

ENGLAND'S LAKE DISTRICT

The large house in the small village of Cockermouth in England's Lake District doesn't have the swagger it once did. Today, most drivers pass the two-story red house at the intersection of Crown and Sullart Streets without a glance. But in 1770, this house was a crown jewel in the small market town that grew at the junction of the two most important rivers in the area, the River Cocker and the River Derwent. This house was, more importantly, the birthplace of a poet who would change the way English words sound in the birthplace of the English language. William Wordsworth was born in the house that was originally built for the High Sheriff of Cumberland and later purchased by one of the wealthiest men in the area, James Lowther, 1st Earl of Lonsdale. William's father, the earl's legal agent, was allowed to live and raise his family there.

The two-story red home, with a row of nine partitioned windows running end to end on the second floor and two single-story pillars supporting a small roof over the entrance, backed up onto the River Derwent. The space between the house and river was filled with a classic English garden, with vegetables, fruit, herbs, and flowers growing between practical, perpendicular garden paths. An author of a series of books about buildings in England would later say about it, "Quite a swagger house for such a town" (Pevsner, 1979). Good thing, too, because despite the world growing all around it, it holds its own as the destination of visitors from around the world who stop during their tour of the Lake District. Wordsworth lived in the house for the first 14 years of his life. It is generally agreed that William learned his love of nature while playing in the garden and swimming in the river.

Of course, life was not all about playing in the garden and swimming. He also attended the well-regarded Old Grammar School in the faraway village of Hawkshead. This school, still standing, was about 200 years old when young William attended. The two-story building is built on a gentle slope, which gives the house a slightly off-kilter look from the street.

During Wordsworth's celebrated life, he would roam the Lake District and write of what he saw. As a man of about 32, William and his sister Dorothy passed a strip of land on the shore of Ullswater lake. This is the second largest lake in the Lake District. As our luck would have it, the daffodils were in bloom then and one of England's greatest poets was stopping to rest there. In her diary later, Dorothy wrote, "I never saw daffodils so beautiful they grew among the mossy stones about and about them, some rested their heads upon these stones as on a pillow for weariness and the rest tossed and reeled and danced and seemed as if they verily laughed with the wind that blew upon them over the lake, they looked so gay ever dancing ever changing" (Wordsworth 1802). Although it is not recorded, it is almost certain that this gave William the inspiration to write his most famous poem, "I Wandered Lonely as a Cloud (Daffodils)."

He was also inspired by a narrow but tall waterfall hidden in the woods surrounding Ullswater. The little waterfall, called Aria Force, cuts through the rocks as it tumbles quickly to the lake, about three-quarters of a mile downstream. After a walk along that part of the Ullswater, he wrote "Airey-Force Valley" in 1836: "Wild stream of Aira, hold thy course." Fittingly, Wordsworth is buried in the

St. Oswald's Churchyard, in the center of Grasmere village, which itself is in the center of his beloved Lake District.

Down away from Ullswater, between the larger Windermere lake and smaller Esthwaite Water lake, painted sheep keep the grass trim on Hill Top farm. The meadows enclosed by stone fence walls were home to Peter Rabbit. The sturdy farm buildings, made of the same locally quarried material as the fences, were home to the author who imagined Peter to life, Beatrix Potter. She was born to a wealthy family in the pricey South Kensington section of London, just south of Hyde Park, and first visited the Lake District when she was 16. She and her family took frequent vacations to the area, during which Beatrix would sketch the local wildlife. Back in London as a young woman, she wrote and illustrated her first book, *The Tale of Peter Rabbit* in 1902. Using money earned from the sale of this book, she bought a field in Near Sawrey, near where she and her family vacationed the following year. In the following years, as her book sales grew, she bought Hill Top farm and a second farm nearby. The 17th-century two-story stone Hill Top house and other farm buildings are still as they were then, although a parking lot has been added to accommodate visitors. The roofs are slate, a material quarried locally that is very common in the Lake District and supplied to roof homes throughout England. Eventually, Potter would write seven books based in or around Hill Top.

The area around Potter's home, like all of the Lake District's rolling green hills, are crossed by meandering stone fences and grazing sheep. The narrow two-lane roads are kept on course by hedges, but mostly by waist-high stone walls topped with thin slices of slate propped at 45 degrees. Lay-bys, little pull-offs that allow cars to pass on the narrow roads, occasionally put a dent in the bordering meadows. Because the area draws so many visitors, in Potter's time and today, many of the homes also rent rooms. To find one, just look for the hanging wooden sign, or the freestanding sign advertising "teas, coffees, cakes." Later in her life, in addition to becoming an accomplished sheep farmer, Potter donated land that served as the cornerstone of what became the Lake District National Park.

Although Charlotte Brontë and her family were primarily associated with West Yorkshire, several miles to the southeast of the Lake District, she was naturally drawn to the area. At a young age, one of her pencil drawings, based on an engraving of the same subject, depicts Derwentwater, a lake in the Lake District. Later, as a woman in her early 20s, she sent some poems to Robert Southey in 1837. He was England's Poet laureate from 1813 until his death in 1843. Like his friend and brother-in-law Samuel Taylor Coleridge, he lived in the Lake District. Southey wanted her to visit him if she visited the area. Brontë also apparently wrote to Wordsworth and Coleridge. Brontë's *Jane Eyre* was published in 1847, then *Shirley* was published in 1849. One year on, in 1850, she made her first visit. In August of that year, she stayed in the Lake District, where she met the novelist Elizabeth Gaskell. Gaskell would later write the first biography of Charlotte Brontë.

Coleridge was drawn to there by his friend and Lake District native son Wordsworth. These two poets were neighbors in Somerset, about 200 miles south. That was in 1797 and 1798, during which time they collaborated on the collection of poems called *Lyrical Ballads*. Coleridge's "The Rime of the Ancyent Marinere," or "The Rime of the Ancient Mariner" as it is called today, first appeared in this compilation. Coleridge left Somerset for the continent of Europe, but returned to England in 1800 and settled in Keswick. This is a small village in the very heart of the district near the northern tip of Derwentwater, the subject of young Charlotte Brontë's pencil drawing. He and his family lived in a new, very large home called "Greta Hall," and were joined in 1803 by Southey and his family. Coleridge left Keswick in 1804 for Malta, an island in the center of the Mediterranean about a 50-mile sail south of Sicily. Southey lived in the hall until his death in 1834. During Coleridge's relatively brief residence, and Southey's much longer residence, this hall was the gathering place for some of the United Kingdom's most accomplished writers at the time. Of course, Wordsworth visited, as did Charles Lamb, William Hazlitt, Percy Bysshe Shelley, and Walter Scott.

Lamb is best known for his *Essays of Elia* and for the children's book *Tales from Shakespeare,* which he coauthored with his sister, Mary Lamb. Hazlitt authored numerous essays and is also known as a painter, social commentator, and philosopher. Shelley was a prolific author of poetry and prose. Scott, of Edinburgh, Scotland, was author of narrative poems and novels and is remembered today as an innovator of the historical novel.

Greta Hall is situated just above the River Greta and overlooks the rolling hills that surround the village. It rests on a low hilltop with a view over the village to Derwentwater just in the distance. On its front, it has three rows of windows on each of its three floors. Around the right side, extending off the main structure, is an unusual two-floor curved exterior. The bedrooms inside this clever wing of the hall reflect the exterior's gentle curve. In the winter, the grounds that slope gently away from the home, as well as the surrounding hills, are covered in snow. It is a two-minute walk to the center of Keswick, and Coleridge would walk through the village on his long walks through the surrounding countryside. Greta Hall today is renovated and offers a bed-and-breakfast for up to 16 guests in 10 bedrooms. Guests today sit on the ground floor warmed by the large fireplace, just as those great writers did 200 years ago.

NEW ENGLAND

The New England region of the United States has been the site of numerous important historical events that have inspired authors, especially during the colonial period: Plymouth Landing, the Boston Tea Party, and Paul Revere's Ride, to name just a few. This region was where some of the first colonies were established by a sect of Puritans, known as the Pilgrims, who were looking for freedom to practice their version of the Protestant religion. They arrived at Plymouth in 1620, after first landing their ship in present-day Cape Cod. The Puritans and the history of their settlements provided fodder for the writings of Nathaniel Hawthorne. Their persecution of witches led to the infamous Salem witch trials, a topic taken up by many American authors, including Arthur Miller in *The Crucible.*

One of the first poets in the American colonies was a Puritan. Anne Bradstreet helped found a few towns in Massachusetts, moving as her husband's work in colonial government required. Her first book, *The Tenth Muse Lately Sprung Up in America,* was published in 1650 in both England and America.

The Merrimack River Valley, where Bradstreet lived, is now known as the "Valley of the Poets." Henry David Thoreau canoed the Merrimack River with his brother and wrote about his journey in his book *A Week on the Concord and Merrimack Rivers.* John Greenleaf Whittier also lived in the Merrimack River Valley, as did Robert Frost as a teenager. Frost's poetry became famous for its depictions of typical New England, working-class scenes, such as the details of the rural lives of farmers. The house where he wrote the majority of his canonical poems still stands in South Shaftsbury, Vermont. Other houses where he lived—in Ripton, Vermont; Cambridge, Massachusetts; and the New Hampshire towns of Franconia and Derry—have also been turned into museums.

Many other literary luminaries wrote some of their greatest works while living in Massachusetts: Nathaniel Hawthorne, as mentioned previously, was actually born in Salem and wrote about the Puritans in some of his classics: *The Scarlet Letter* and "Young Goodman Brown." Hawthorne was related to one of the judges in the Salem Witch Trials and often agonized over the deaths caused by his ancestor. He writes about the way that these feelings of guilt haunted the town of Salem in his novel *The House of the Seven Gables,* whose setting is the Turner-Ingersoll Mansion. Later in his life, Hawthorne moved to Concord, Massachusetts. He lived in that town at the same time as the transcendentalists Ralph Waldo Emerson and Henry David Thoreau.

Emerson and Thoreau influenced a wide range of thinkers in New England. Their beliefs were embraced by a large group of writers in Massachusetts at the time, including Amos Bronson Alcott, Orestes Brownson, William Henry Channing, Margaret Fuller, Frederic Henry Hedge, Charles Lane, Theodore Parker, Elizabeth Palmer Peabody, and George Ripley. Some of them participated in various projects spearheaded by Emerson and Thoreau. For instance, Ripley used ideas from Emerson and Thoreau to start Brook Farm, an experiment in communal living, while Amos Bronson Alcott and Charles Lane formed their own commune called Fruitlands. Others helped Thoreau build the cabin he lived in on Emerson's land bordering Walden Pond, where he conducted an experiment in living "spartanlike" and close to the land. Visitors can still swim in the pond that sparked his work *Walden* and see where his cabin stood, along with a complete replica of it closer to the parking lot.

Herman Melville was on the fringes of the transcendentalist movement. Although his short story "Bartleby, the Scrivener" takes place in New York City, his hometown, the messages it conveys about the negative consequences of technological reliance, the Puritan work ethic, and private ownership of property are properly aligned with the beliefs Emerson and Thoreau expressed, especially their anti-Industrial Revolution sentiments. Melville eventually moved to Pittsfield, Massachusetts, where he wrote his masterpiece *Moby Dick.*

Many say that the idea for Melville's novel was sparked by his view of the sloping, snow-covered peaks of Mount Greylock as it towers above the rest of the Taconic and Berkshire mountain ranges. Greylock is a magnet for visitors and authors alike: Thoreau camped there in 1844, and Hawthorne wrote his short story "Ethan Brand," after hiking the mountain's trails. Oliver Wendell Holmes, another Massachusetts native, describes it as a "purple throne" in his poem "A Berkshire Summer Morning."

The New England region technically includes Connecticut and Rhode Island, although most associate it with Massachusetts and the neighboring states of Connecticut and New Hampshire, as well as Vermont and Maine farther north. Mark Twain lived in Hartford, Connecticut, not far from where Harriet Beecher Stowe wrote *Uncle Tom's Cabin*. Wallace Stevens also lived in Hartford.

Surprisingly, the literary history of the New England region includes very few famous authors from Boston, although the city figures prominently as a setting in many works, including one of the most intimate descriptions of its culture in *The Bostonians* by Henry James, who was from New York City. More recently Nick Flynn addresses his childhood in the Boston suburbs in his memoir *Another Bullshit Night in Suck City*.

New England authors range in their genres and styles, but include a number of talented writers. Elizabeth Bishop was born in Worcester, Massachusetts. Stephen King was born in Portland, Maine. Although John Updike and Mary Oliver were born in Pennsylvania and Ohio, respectively, they both moved to Massachusetts and write about the landscape there.

NEW YORK CITY

Herman Melville was born in 1819 about a football field away from the lower Manhattan docks, and he lived much of his life along the edges of Manhattan Island. Growing up so close to the docks, it was only natural he found work there also. The idea for the whaler *Pequod* and Captain Ahab, and the ultimate encounter with the white whale were born when Melville worked on a wooden sailing ship as a young man. Melville's book *Moby Dick, or, The Whale* was published in 1851.

On the other end of Manhattan Island, a century later, the poet and writer Langston Hughes helped establish the literary and artistic movement known as the Harlem Renaissance, a blossoming of black American culture in the early 1900s. The streets in Harlem are laid out in a grid pattern, unlike the tangled streets of Melville's lower Manhattan. Hughes was born in Missouri and grew up in Illinois and Ohio. Columbia University, which is located very close to Harlem, first drew Hughes to New York but he soon left to work on a freighter making runs to Africa and Europe. Just a few years later, he returned to Harlem, though, and continued to write, but was only discovered after he moved to Washington, D.C. The remainder of his life involved travel and advocacy around the country, but Harlem will always be remembered as his home. His residence at 20 East 127th Street in Harlem has been given landmark status by the New York City Landmarks Preservation Commission, and East 127th Street has been renamed "Langston Hughes Place." This is a pleasant, tree-lined street with brown sandstone residences. No. 20 is a narrow four-story row house, covered in vine, with 11 steps leading to the sedate second-floor entrance.

Wallace Thurman and Zora Neale Hurston, among many others, also contributed to the richness of this Harlem voice. At a time when black voices were seldom heard in American culture and writing, theirs broke through.

Around 80 blocks to the south of Harlem is the Broadway theater district, a noisy, bright part of Manhattan. Entering a Broadway theater from the busy street can be exciting: the Majestic, the Imperial, the Schoenfeld, the Shubert, or the Richard Rodgers. You walk past the street-level ticket booth into the ornate, carpeted lobby. There is another set of doors opposite the entrance protected by ushers in uniforms. Step through the doors into the theater itself. The ceiling is low, too low for a theater. But you're just under the balcony. Keep walking forward and suddenly you are in a massive indoor space with chandeliers hanging from the sky-high ceiling.

On December 3, 1947, *A Streetcar Named Desire* opened in the Ethel Barrymore Theater, just around the corner from Times Square. This play by Tennessee Williams was set in New Orleans. Eight years later, in 1955, *Cat on a Hot Tin Roof* opened in another theater a couple city blocks away. It was also set in the South, in a plantation home on the Mississippi River. In 1959, Lorraine Hansberry's play set in Chicago, *A Raisin in the Sun,* opened in the Barrymore to great reviews. So many plays that have appeared in Broadway theaters were written elsewhere, take place elsewhere, by writers born elsewhere, but they reach the widest audience and meet the widest acclaim when they open in a Broadway theater. These theaters are scattered in a cluster around Times Square, the center of the theater universe. This has been true since the early 1900s, when New York's status as the theater capital was solidified, and remains true today.

New York City is also a magnet for all other sorts of writers struggling to make their way to the top, and struggling to prevent their fall back down. In "Only in New York" fashion, the Hotel Chelsea is where many of these struggles converged into a single, infamous story in a single, infamous lodging house with lacy High Victorian cast-iron balconies and a big vertical sign that screams, in all capital letters, "HOTEL."

North Carolina native Thomas Wolfe spent the last years of his life sleeping in the Chelsea, and the books he wrote there, *The Web and the Rock* and *You Can't Go Home Again,* were only published after he died in 1938.

Arthur Miller's play *Death of a Salesman* opened on Broadway in 1949, and a few years later *The Crucible* opened at the Martin Beck Theatre on Broadway. Around this time, Miller visited Dylan Thomas at Hotel Chelsea. Miller was on top of the world. Two Tony Awards and a Pulitzer in four years. Thomas was nigh on the bottom of his fall, and would be dead within months, probably killed by his own lifestyle and neglect for his health.

Thirteen years after that encounter, in 1962, Miller found himself back at the Hotel Chelsea. This time the hotel welcomed Miller's own struggle near the bottom. His disastrous marriage to Marilyn Monroe had ended, and she had committed suicide. The play he wrote while he lived there, *After the Fall,* bombed.

Jack Kerouac, in Jack Kerouac fashion, neither on his way up nor on his way down, but definitely on the road to somewhere, breezed through Hotel Chelsea four years before the publication of his breakthrough *On the Road.*

THE SOUTH

Southerners are particularly proud of their cultural heritage and celebrate its presence in literature and other art forms. Although other states would surely make the case in favor of one of their own cities, Louisiana's New Orleans ranks as one of the most famous literary cities in the South. It boasts residency by George Washington Cable, William Faulkner (who visited from his native Mississippi), Walker Percy, Tennessee Williams, and Eudora Welty. Many of these authors frequented the Hotel Monteleone on Royal Street in the French Quarter, whose Carousel Bar served as a meeting spot for writers and which is mentioned in numerous literary works (Ernest Hemingway's "Night Before Battle," Eudora Welty's "A Curtain of Green," and Tennessee Williams's *The Rose Tattoo* and *Orpheus Descending*, among others). Truman Capote spent his childhood living in the hotel before being sent to live with family in Alabama.

Other parts of the neighborhood are commemorated in Tennessee Williams's plays. One of them is titled with the French word for this "old neighborhood": his play *Vieux Carré*.

Although Williams came from Missouri, he lived in a few different houses in the French Quarter and frequented a number of popular restaurants: Brennan's, Galatoire's, and Marti's. He was living on Royal Street when the streetcar line was called "Desire" because its final stop was on Desire Street. His Pulitzer Prize–winning play *A Streetcar Named Desire* captures some of the atmosphere of New Orleans' French Quarter. The city hosts the Tennessee Williams Literary Festival in honor of one of its greatest playwrights.

Also located in the French Quarter, on Canal Street between Dauphine and Bourbon Streets, is another literary monument of note: a statue erected to Ignatius Reilly, the protagonist of J. K. Toole's *A Confederacy of Dunces*. This treasured work of Louisiana literature was discovered by Walker Percy and published after its author passed away. Percy is, himself, a powerful figure in the history of Southern literature. Although he grew up in Mississippi, he lived most of his adult life in Covington, Louisiana, which is just across Lake Pontchartrain from New Orleans. His novel, *The Moviegoer,* is considered by many to be a classic depiction of quintessential New Orleans culture.

The literary heritage of Louisiana extends well beyond the borders of the famous Crescent City, however. Kate Chopin lived for a handful of years in the town of Cloutierville located in the parish of Natchitoches. The house, originally built by Alexic Cloutier, inspired the setting of a number of Chopin's works, including *The Awakening*. Chopin only began writing about life in the bayou when she returned to her hometown of St. Louis, Missouri, after the death of her husband.

Writers who lived in one of the most southern U.S. states, Florida, include Zora Neale Hurston and Ernest Hemingway, both of whom traveled in the Caribbean islands while they wrote. Hurston's work captures the folk life of working-class

---

To understand the world, you must first understand a place like Mississippi.
William Faulkner, quote

people, while much of Hemingway's work from his time in the Florida Keys is about the sport of fishing.

A famous literary character from the South loved to fish: Huckleberry Finn, the creation of Mark Twain (otherwise known as Samuel Clemens). Although Twain wrote *The Adventures of Huckleberry Finn* in Connecticut, he was born in Missouri and raised along the Mississippi River, much like his main character.

The South has produced a number of extraordinary women writers. From Kate Chopin, Margaret Mitchell, and Harper Lee, to Flannery O'Connor, Eudora Welty, and Ann Patchett (born in California, but raised in Tennessee), Southern women have written about historical and cultural concerns related to gender in the Bible Belt. A common them found throughout literary works by Southern women is the unrealistic gender expectations that traditional Southern culture holds for men and women.

Many literary works have been set in the South, even if their authors have spent little time there. For example, *Uncle Tom's Cabin*, a famous novel written Southern slavery, was written by Harriet Beecher Stowe, who lived and died in Connecticut but conducted research about the Southern plantation system and the lives of its slaves. Perhaps the earliest genre of Southern literature, after the documents and letters of European colonials, is the slave narrative. Frequently taught examples of this genre were written by Olaudah Equiano, Harriet Tubman, Frederick Douglass, and Harriet Jacobs.

THE SOUTHWEST

The streets are generously wide in the six villages of Pueblo of Laguna Reservation, thanks to the generosity of the land that provides miles and miles of open space in northern New Mexico. But flat open space would be monotonous so the land provides low rolling hills, spaced out to maximize their beauty and dotted with sage to hold them in place. Look closer and see that the land has also provided the building materials for the squat one-floor dwellings that are scattered naturally, organically around the village. The sky, too, is generous. Blue from horizon to horizon, accented occasionally with wispy white. Here a young Leslie Marmon Silko, born in 1948, became aware of what the land and skies offer. She attended Bureau of Indian Affairs schools and outgrew the half-million-acre reservation, moving to the big city 45 miles down the road, Albuquerque, to study English and then law. But she outgrew that too, and left to devote her full attentions to the creation of words that explored how a Laguna Pueblo, or other Native American, can retain that identity in a land that has been settled so comprehensively by white Europeans and their descendants. After achieving widespread success, she also settled into a teaching job on the Navajo Nation in tiny Tsaile, Arizona. The college is located about an hour's hike from the source of an ancient canyon, Canyon de Chelly, that has provided its generosity to the Navajo for centuries, and to the ancient Puebloans before them.

One of those descendants of European settlers in America, Tony Hillerman, was born 700 miles due east in rural Oklahoma. He taught journalism from 1966 to 1987 in Leslie Marmon Silko's alma mater, and set many of his novels on the Navajo

Nation. The nation is a majestic spread of land nearly the size of South Carolina. Most of the nation is situated in the northeastern corner of Arizona but tumbles over into Utah and New Mexico. To a South Carolinian, the nation probably appears dry and barren, but the Navajo may not find it so. Like the Pueblo of Laguna, the land can be generous to those who live there, and who represent hundreds and hundreds of generations to whom the land has provided.

The Navajo Nation is an independent nation with a president, legislature, and court system. Those who have read Hillerman's *Leaphorn & Chee* series of novels will also know the nation has a police force. Six police districts cover the entire nation, headquartered in six villages throughout its 27,413 square miles: Chinle, Crownpoint, Dilkon, Kayenta, Shiprock, and Tuba City. The low, nearly flat-roofed police headquarters are a part of the landscape. In Kayenta, the building unwittingly mirrors the flat-topped Black Mesa just to the south.

The American Southwest is a unique melting pot. There are the native people who have always lived there, the white Americans who moved in from the east, but also Mexicans who, through the centuries, moved up from the south. Their native language is Spanish but represents a melting together of Spanish and native cultures that took place much farther south in what we now call Mexico. This is the heritage of another of the Southwest's acclaimed writers, Rudolfo Anaya. He was born in middle-of-nowhere Pastura, northern New Mexico, about 100 miles east of Albuquerque. His trilogy *Bless Me, Ultima, Heart of Aztlan,* and *Tortuga* explore the complex mix of influences in the lives of people of Mexican descent living in the United States. The second in the series, *Heart of Aztlan,* plays out in a "barrio" in Albuquerque, a microscopic melting pot of its own where urban and poor rural Mexican Americans settle into the same few city blocks. It is not clear but the barrio may have been located in modern-day Barelas and the South Valley section of Albuquerque. This area has through the decades maintained close ties to Albuquerque's Hispanic roots. It is located along the slow, muddy Rio Grande as it leaves the city on its way to Pueblo of Isleta, the permanent home of native people of the area just to the south. The Catholic influence, brought first to the Southwest by Spanish and their descendants to the South, provides the bones of the area to today. The first hint of this influence along the Rio Grande south of Albuquerque was the St. Augustine Mission, established in 1613. The white fortresslike church, built of thick windowless walls and topped by three modest crosses, still holds Mass daily, twice on Sundays.

Albuquerque's Barelas section, both during the time in which *Heart of Aztlan* is set and presently, is a residential area of single-family homes sandwiched between the Albuquerque Rail Yards and the river. Today, it is home to the National Hispanic Cultural Center, a 20-acre campus of modern buildings shaped to reflect the Mesoamerican, Spanish, Mexican, and New Mexican roots of the Southwest.

The Southwest region is defined as encompassing the border states of Arizona, New Mexico, and Texas. Sharing a border with Mexico often defines the culture of these states and is a major theme in the literature produced either by authors from those areas or in works set in those areas. Although Cormac McCarthy, born in Rhode Island, is not from the Southwest originally, he relocated to Tennessee as a young boy, and has since lived in Texas and New Mexico. Many of his novels are situated along the border between the United States and Mexico. Another writer who is known for her groundbreaking perspectives on culture along the border is Gloria Anzaldúa, who was born and raised in southern Texas before moving to California later in life.

CALIFORNIA AND THE SAN FRANCISCO BAY AREA

California's coast has long been viewed as a destination for dreamers and for those in the history of the nation's founding who had the tenacity to build America westward, surviving the frontier to arrive in the port towns of the Pacific West and Northwest. Many literary works of the 20th century seek to disrupt these historical myths and to reveal that the West Coast is just as flawed as any other place in terms of what it offers as "the American dream." The task of authors in exposing these myths has been difficult, given the majesty and fertility of the landscape, which leads people to want to believe in an abundance of social equality, as well. Many prominent immigrant writers from the West Coast have found audiences receptive to countercultural narratives about the people who thrive and relationships that flourish in neighborhoods like San Francisco's Chinatown (Maxine Hong Kingston and Amy Tan) or the barrios of Los Angeles (Helena Maria Viramontes and Dagoberto Gilb).

Joan Didion's memoir *Where I Was From* is considered by many literary scholars to be one of the best texts on the social, cultural, and political history of California. Didion has written numerous works set in California, both fiction and nonfiction. Even her fictional works draw on her life experiences there and her career in journalism during the 1960s, when she worked as a political reporter.

In contrast to Didion's settings, which are often the interior of political offices and parties of Hollywood stars, nature writer John Muir has made vast contributions to the preservation of large areas in the Sierra Nevada Mountains. Although he was born in Scotland, Muir hiked and camped his way through many of the wilderness areas in California and its surrounding states. He is the founder of the Sierra Club, a well-known conservation group. He also wrote about these lands in numerous works, among them *Studies in the Sierra, Picturesque California, The Mountains of California, My First Summer in the Sierra,* and *The Yosemite.*

San Francisco is the home to many literary landmarks associated with the Beats, a literary movement from the 1960s that advocated for "dropping out" of the repressive and conservative mainstream culture of the 1950s. Vesuvio Café is perhaps one of its most famous institutions. Here, writers involved in the Beat movement exchanged ideas and hosted readings. The City Lights Bookstore is also part of the

---

Once I knew the City very well, spent my attic days there, while others were being a lost generation in Paris, I fledged in San Francisco, climbed its hills, slept in its parks, worked on its docks, marched and shouted in its revolts.... It had been kind to me in the days of my poverty and it did not resent my temporary solvency.
John Steinbeck, *Travels with Charley: In Search of America* (1962)

famed history of the Beat generation as it runs the publishing company that first published Allen Ginsberg's poem "Howl."

Although the Beats valued travel and fought against consumerism, without a place to congregate and call "home," the movement would likely not have successfully coalesced around a core set of ideals and mutual inspiration. However, like many of their philosophies, the Beats' conception of home was avant-garde and took into account the emerging identities possible through the ease of commercial air travel. At least three locations are cited as origins for the Beat movement: the North Beach area of San Francisco, Venice West in Los Angeles, and Greenwich Village in New York City. William Burroughs, Allen Ginsberg, and Jack Kerouac originally met at Columbia University in New York. However, San Francisco became perhaps the place best associated with them after they relocated there. It is the city where they successfully fought their legal battle against an attempt to censor Ginsberg's poem "Howl" for obscenity after City Lights Bookstore owner Lawrence Ferlinghetti was arrested for publishing it.

However, San Francisco has other claims to fame besides the Beats. Jack London was born in San Francisco and lived in Oakland when he wasn't traveling to areas farther north in the Pacific Northwest and Canada, where most of his literary works are set. Additionally, a number of poets were bred in the city by the Bay. For example, Gary Snyder and Robert Hass, two key Western poets whose work tackles the human relationship to the natural world.

Although San Francisco is the heart of California's literary history for many, other equally important authors came from other cities in the Golden State. John Steinbeck, for instance, was born in Salinas, which is located 100 miles south of San Francisco and known as "the salad bowl of America" due to its agricultural production. Lastly, T. C. Boyle is a contemporary author who has achieved the distinctive honor of writing critically acclaimed stories that span the entire coastline, not just concentrated in one city or region. He writes about concerns spanning from immigration problems in Southern California to tensions related to marijuana farming in Northern California and everything in between.

Thomas B. Porter and Lynn Marie Houston

FURTHER READING

Dekker, Thomas. "The Seven Deadly sins of London, Drawn in Seven Several Coaches, through the Seven Several Gates of the City: Bringing the Plague with Them." London: E. Arber, 1606. archive.org/details/sevendeadlysinso00dekkuoft/page/n1.
Dickens, Charles. *The Pickwick Papers.* London: Chapman and Hall, 1906.
Didion, Joan. *Where I Was From.* New York: Vintage Books, 2013.
Hentzner, Paul. *Paul Hentzner's Travels in England, during the Reign of Queen Elizabeth.* Strawberry Hill, UK: Paul Hentzner, 1797.
Keats, John, and John Barnard. *John Keats.* Oxford, UK: Oxford University Press, 2017.
Pevsner, Nikolaus. *The Buildings of England.* Harmondsworth, UK: Penguin Books, 1979.
Wordsworth, Dorothy. "Grasmere Journal, 15 April 1802." *Journals of Dorothy Wordsworth: The Alfoxden Journal 1798, The Grasmere Journals 1800–1803,* edited by Mary Moorman. New York: Oxford University Press, 1971.

Bibliography

Aiken, Charles S. "Humanistic Geography and Literature: Essays on the Experience of Place." *Geographical Review* 73, no. 2 (1983): 232–34.

Alves, Daniel, and Ana Isabel Queiroz. "Exploring Literary Landscapes: From Texts to Spatiotemporal Analysis through Collaborative Work and GIS." *International Journal of Humanities and Arts Computing* 9, no. 1 (2015): 57–73.

Ameel, Lieven. "Review of *Narrating Space/Spatializing Narrative: Where Narrative Theory and Geography Meet,* by Marie-Laure Ryan, Kenneth Foote, and Maoz Azaryahu." *Social & Cultural Geography* 18, no. 7 (2017): 1062–64.

Anderson, Jon. "Towards an Assemblage Approach to Literary Geography." *Literary Geographies* 1, no. 2 (2016): 120–37.

Azizi, Kyoumars, and Shahram Afrougheh. "Space, Geography and Literature: 'A Geocritical Perspective.'" *International Research Journal of Applied and Basic Sciences* 6, no. 5 (2013): 641–43.

Brooker-Gross, Susan R. "Teaching about Race, Gender, Class and Geography through Fiction." *Journal of Geography in Higher Education* 15, no. 1 (1991): 35–47.

Brosseau, Marc. "In, of, out, with, and through: New Perspectives in Literary Geography." In *The Routledge Handbook of Literature and Space,* edited by Robert T. Tally Jr., 9–27. London: Routledge, 2017.

Buell, L. "American Literature and the American Environment: There Never Was an 'Is' without a 'Where.'" *The Harvard Sampler: Liberal Education for the Twenty-First Century*, edited by Jennifer M. Shephard, Stephen M. Kosslyn, and Evelynn M. Hammonds, 32–56. Cambridge, MA: Harvard University Press, 2011.

Buell, Lawrence. *The Future of Environmental Criticism: Environmental Crisis and Literary Imagination.* Oxford, UK: John Wiley & Sons, 2009.

Bushell, Sally. "The Slipperiness of Literary Maps: Critical Cartography and Literary Cartography." *Cartographica: The International Journal for Geographic Information and Geovisualization* 47, no. 3 (2012): 149–60.

Chaudhuri, Una. *Staging Place: The Geography of Modern Drama.* Ann Arbor: University of Michigan Press, 1997.

Eagle, Dorothy. "Review of *Humanistic Geography and Literature: Essays on the Experience of Place,* by Douglas Pocock." *The Modern Language Review* 79, no. 1 (1984): 142–44.

Flaim, Mary L., and John J. Chiodo. "A Novel Approach to Geographic Education: Using Literature in the Social Studies." *The Social Studies* 85, no. 5 (1994): 225–27.

Gatta, John. *Making Nature Sacred: Literature, Religion, and Environment in America from the Puritans to the Present.* New York: Oxford University Press, 2004.

Gesler, Wilbert M. "Therapeutic Landscapes: Medical Issues in Light of the New Cultural Geography." *Social Science & Medicine* 34, no. 7 (1992): 735–46.

Guerin, Caroline A., and Davi Thornton. "Review of *Narrating Space/Spatializing Narrative: Where Narrative Theory and Geography Meet,* by Marie-Laure Ryan, Kenneth Foote, and Maoz Azaryahu." *Quarterly Journal of Speech* 103, no. 3 (2017): 304–7.

Harvey, David. "Between Space and Time: Reflections on the Geographical Imagination." *Annals of the Association of American Geographers* 80, no. 3 (1990): 418–34.

Hever, Hannah. "We Have Not Arrived from the Sea: A Mizrahi Literary Geography." *Social Identities* 10, no. 1 (2004): 31–51.

Hones, Sheila. "Humanistic Geography and Literary Text: Problems and Possibilities." *Keisen Jogakuen College Bulletin* 4 (1992): 136–12.

Hones, Sheila. "Literary Geography and the Short Story: Setting and Narrative Style." *Cultural Geographies* 17, no. 4 (2010): 473–85.

Hones, Sheila. "Literary Geography: Setting and Narrative Space." *Social & Cultural Geography* 12, no. 7 (2011): 685–99.

Hones, Sheila. "Text as It Happens: Literary Geography." *Geography Compass* 2, no. 5 (2008): 1301–17.

Hsu, Hsuan L. *Geography and the Production of Space in Nineteenth-Century American Literature.* Cambridge, UK: Cambridge University Press, 2010.

Huggan, Graham, and Helen Tiffin. *Postcolonial Ecocriticism: Literature, Animals, Environment.* New York: Routledge, 2015.

King, Russell, John Connell, and Paul E. White, eds. *Writing across Worlds: Literature and Migration.* London: Psychology Press, 1995.

Lando, Fabio. "Fact and Fiction: Geography and Literature." *GeoJournal* 38, no. 1 (1996): 3–18.

Lau, Lisa, and Margaret Pasquini. "'Jack of All Trades'? The Negotiation of Interdisciplinarity within Geography." *Geoforum* 39, no. 2 (2008): 552–60.

Leander, Kevin M., and Margaret Sheehy. *Spatializing Literacy Research and Practice.* New York: Peter Lang, 2004.

Ley, David, and Marwyn S. Samuels, eds. *Humanistic Geography.* London: Croom Helm, 1978.

Lutwack, Leonard. *The Role of Place in Literature.* Syracuse, NY: Syracuse University Press, 1984.

Matley, Ian M. "Literary Geography and the Writer's Country." *Scottish Geographical Magazine* 103, no. 3 (1987): 122–31.

Moslund, Sten. *Literature's Sensuous Geographies: Postcolonial Matters of Place*. London: Springer, 2015.

Noble, Allen G., and Ramesh Dhussa. "Image and Substance: A Review of Literary Geography." *Journal of Cultural Geography* 10, no. 2 (1990): 49–65.

Philips, R. S. "The Language of Images in Geography." *Progress in Human Geography* 17, no. 2 (1993): 180–94.

Piatti, Barbara, and Lorenz Hurni. "Mapping the Ontologically Unreal–Counterfactual Spaces in Literature and Cartography." *The Cartographic Journal* 46, no. 4 (2009): 333–42.

Pocock, Douglas C. D. "Geography and Literature." *Progress in Human Geography* 12, no. 1 (1988): 87–102.

Pocock, Douglas C. D., ed. *Humanistic Geography and Literature (RLE Social & Cultural Geography): Essays on the Experience of Place*. London: Routledge, 2014.

Prieto, Eric. *Literature, Geography, and the Postmodern Poetics of Place*. New York: Springer, 2012.

Racine, Félix. *Literary Geography in Late Antiquity*. New Haven, CT: Yale University, 2009.

Rao, Eleonora. "Mapping the Imagination: Literary Geography." *Literary Geographies* 3, no. 2 (2017): 115–24.

Reynolds, Nedra. *Geographies of Writing: Inhabiting Places and Encountering Difference*. Carbondale: Southern Illinois University Press, 2007.

Ridanpää, Juha. *Geography and Literature*. New York: Oxford University Press, 2013.

Robinson, Brian. "The Geography of a Crossroads: Modernism, Surrealism, and Geography." In *Geography and Literature: A Meeting of the Disciplines*, edited by Paul Simpson-Housley and William Mallory, 185–98. Syracuse, NY: Syracuse University Press, 1987.

Rossetto, Tania. "Theorizing Maps with Literature." *Progress in Human Geography* 38, no. 4 (2014): 513–30.

Ryan, Marie-Laure. "Narrative Cartography: Toward a Visual Narratology." In *What Is Narratology?*, edited by Tom Kindt and Hans-Harald Müller, 333–64. Berlin: Walter de Gruyter, 2003.

Sandberg, L. Anders, and John S. Marsh. "Focus: Literary Landscapes—Geography and Literature." *Canadian Geographer/Le Géographe Canadien* 32, no. 3 (1988): 266–76.

Saunders, Angharad. "Literary Geography: Reforging the Connections." *Progress in Human Geography* 34, no. 4 (2010): 436–52.

Schilling, Derek. "On and Off the Map: Literary Narrative as Critique of Cartographic Reason." In *Literary Cartographies*, edited by Robert T. Tally Jr., 215–28. New York: Palgrave Macmillan, 2014.

Selberg, Torunn, and Nevena Škrbić Alempijević. "Turning Fiction into Reality: The Making of Two Places within Literary Geography." *Studia Ethnologica Croatica* 25 (2013): 183–206.

Silk, John. "Beyond Geography and Literature." *Environment and Planning D: Society and Space* 2, no. 2 (1984): 151–78.

Squire, Shelagh J. "The Cultural Values of Literary Tourism." *Annals of Tourism Research* 21, no. 1 (1994): 103–20.
Tally, Robert T., Jr., ed. *Geocritical Explorations: Space, Place, and Mapping in Literary and Cultural Studies*. New York: Springer, 2011.
Tuan, Yi-Fu. "Space and Place: Humanistic Perspective." In *Philosophy in Geography*, edited by Stephen Gale and Gunnar Olsson, 387–427. Dordrecht, Netherlands: Springer, 1979.
Tuan, Yi-Fu. "Language and the Making of Place: A Narrative-Descriptive Approach." *Annals of the Association of American Geographers* 81, no. 4 (1991): 684–96.
Tuathail, Gearóid Ó., and Gerard Toal. *Critical Geopolitics: The Politics of Writing Global Space*. Minneapolis: University of Minnesota Press, 1996.
Wason-Ellam, Linda. "Children's Literature as a Springboard to Place-Based Embodied Learning." *Environmental Education Research* 16, no. 3–4 (2010): 279–94.
Wright, John K. "Terrae Incognitae: The Place of the Imagination in Geography." *Annals of the Association of American Geographers* 37, no. 1 (1947): 1–15.
Yap, Erica X. Y. "Readers-in-Conversations: A Politics of Reading in Literary Geographies." *Social & Cultural Geography* 12, no. 7 (2011): 793–807.

About the Editor and Contributors

EDITOR

LYNN MARIE HOUSTON has taught university-level English courses since 1998. Prior to beginning her teaching career, she was a John Christopher Hartwick scholar and a triple major (BA summa cum laude with honors program distinction in art history, English, and Spanish) at Hartwick College in Oneonta, New York. Post-baccalaureate, she received a Fulbright grant in comparative literature and studied in Geneva, Switzerland, completing an independent research project in Swiss poetry, a *licence es lettres* at the University of Geneva, and a master's-level thesis on John Updike.

In 1998, she entered the doctoral program at Arizona State University, where she researched 19th- and 20th-century American literature while teaching courses in composition and early American literature. Her dissertation involved conducting ethnographic interviews with ranchers along the U.S.-Mexico border and reading poetry, fiction, and memoir by cancer survivors to explore how a phenomenon like mad cow disease is emblematic of the new realities humans have to account for when thinking about the relationship between our bodies and the food we produce and consume, as well as the land we use for its production. Chapters of her dissertation have appeared in peer-reviewed scholarly journals, including *Multi-ethnic Literature of the U.S. Association (MELUS)* and *South Atlantic Quarterly*, published by Duke University.

After completing her PhD, she held teaching positions at universities from the East Coast to the West Coast and stops in between, ranging from positions where she mentored graduate students and undergraduate English majors, to a position where she taught developmental English at the community college level, and finally to a position in the writing center of a private, Catholic university. She co-authored two books with two of her graduate students from California State University, Chico: *Reading Joan Didion* with William Lombardi and *Reading Barbara Kingsolver* with Jennifer Warren, both published by Greenwood Press.

After nearly dying from taking one sting too many while keeping honeybees, she left a full-time teaching job to pursue her passion for creative writing. In 2017, she graduated with an MFA from Southern Connecticut State University. Her poetry has received awards from the following organizations: the Eric Hoffer Society, Able Muse Press, the New England Book Festival, Main Street Rag Publishing, the National Federation of Press Women, *Cultural Weekly, The Heartland Review,* the Connecticut Press Club, the National Indie Excellence Awards, Brain Mill Press, *Broad River Review,* Whispering Prairie Press, the National Federation of State Poetry Societies (Arizona State), and *Prime Number Magazine.* She currently enjoys a wide variety of writing and editing activities as the editor in chief of a small press, as the Online Writing Lab Coordinator for Sacred Heart University in Connecticut, and as a writer-editor in avionics and military history. Stay updated on her activities at lynnmhouston.com.

CONTRIBUTORS

ROBERT R. BENSEN's poetry and literary essays have been widely published in *The Paris Review, Callaloo, The Caribbean Writer, Native Realities, Jamaica Journal, AGNI, Akwe:kon, Poetry Wales, The Thomas Hardy Review, The Journal of Commonwealth Literature (India), Ploughshares,* and many other journals. Among his books of poetry, published in collaboration with artists, are *In the Dream Museum* (with Lebbeus Woods, Red Herring Press), *Scriptures of Venus* (with Hyde Meissner, Swamp Press), *Day Labor* (with Phil Young, Serpent & Eagle Press), *Two Dancers* (with Charles Bremer, Woodland Arts Editions), and *Orenoque, Wetumka and Other Poems* (with Phil Young, Bright Hill Press). His poetry has been awarded a fellowship from the National Endowment for the Arts and the Robert Penn Warren Award. He has also won several fellowships from the National Endowment for the Humanities and the Newberry Library, and teaching and research awards from Hartwick College. He has written numerous essays on Caribbean and Native American literature, and edited anthologies of those literatures, most recently *Children of the Dragonfly: Native American Voices on Child Custody and Education* (University of Arizona Press). A major bibliographic study, *Native American and Aboriginal Canadian Childhood Studies,* was commissioned by Oxford University Press online. He taught at the University of Illinois at Urbana-Champaign (1968–74), and was professor of English and director of writing at Hartwick College, Oneonta, New York (1978–2017). He now teaches at the State University of New York at Oneonta, and is a docent at the Fenimore Art Museum, Cooperstown, New York. He is married to Dr. Mary Lynn Bensen, librarian and head of reference and instruction at Milne Library, SUNY-Oneonta. Their daughter, Annalee Lucia Bensen, is a dancer residing in Brooklyn.

MARCI L. CARRASQUILLO received her BA from the University of Connecticut, her MA and PhD from the University of Oregon, and is currently an associate professor of English at Rowan University. A two-time Ford Foundation Fellowship recipient, she is currently at work on a book project titled *Chueco Roads: Remapping the American Road Trip,* which traces the figure of the road in Latina/o literature since the liberation movements of the 1960s. She has published articles on the novels of Oscar "Zeta" Acosta and the coquí (a tree frog) as a critical symbol of Puerto Rican nationalism. She teaches U.S. Latina/o literature, as well as all periods of U.S. literature.

CHRISTOPHER CUMO focuses primarily on the histories of agriculture and the natural sciences and is the author of eight books, an encyclopedia, and numerous short pieces.

JAMES I. DEUTSCH is a curator and editor at the Center for Folklife and Cultural Heritage at the Smithsonian Institution, where he has helped plan and develop public programs on California, China, Hungary, Peace Corps, Apollo Theater, Circus Arts, National Aeronautics and Space Administration, Mekong River, U.S. Forest Service, World War II, Silk Road, and White House workers. In addition, he serves as an adjunct professor—teaching courses on American film history and folklore—in the American Studies Department at George Washington University. Deutsch has also taught American Studies classes at universities in Armenia, Belarus, Bulgaria, Germany, Kyrgyzstan, Norway, Poland, and Turkey.

BRUCE E. JOHANSEN is Frederick W. Kayser Professor of communication and Native American studies at the University of Nebraska at Omaha, where he has been teaching and writing since 1982. He has authored 47 published books, most recently a three-volume set, *Climate Change: An Encyclopedia of Science, Society, and Solutions* (2017). Johansen holds the University of Nebraska award for Outstanding Research and Creative Activity (ORCA), the state system's highest faculty recognition.

AMANDA LOUISE JOHNSON teaches hemispheric American literature at Rice University, where she researches the survival of the romance genre in the early Southern and Caribbean regions, and has published essays on Thomas Jefferson's Anglophilia and other transnational topics.

GROVE KOGER is the author of *When the Going Was Good: A Guide to the 99 Best Narratives of Travel, Exploration, and Adventure* (Scarecrow Press, 2002) and assistant editor of *Laguna Beach Art Patron Magazine, Palm Springs Art Patron Magazine,* and *Deus Loci: The Lawrence Durrell Journal.* He blogs at worldenoughblog.wordpress.com.

DALILAH NABILAH LAIDIN earned a master's in geography from Universiti Brunei Darussalam. Her thesis entitled "*Makam Raja Ayang:* Keeping the Myth Alive through Heritage Tourism" is an interpretation of a difficult-heritage landscape in Bandar Seri Begawan. She recently published a book chapter describing society and culture in Brunei Darussalam.

ERIC D. LEHMAN is the author of 16 books of history, travel, and fiction, including *The Quotable New Englander, Great Pan Is Dead,* and *Homegrown Terror: Benedict Arnold and the Burning of New London.* His biography of Charles

Stratton, *Becoming Tom Thumb,* won the Henry-Russell Hitchcock Award from the Victorian Society of America, and was chosen as one of the American Library Association's outstanding university press books of the year. His novella, *Shadows of Paris,* was awarded the Novella of the Year from the Next Generation Indie Book Awards, won a Silver Medal for Romance from the Foreword Review Indie Book Awards, and was a finalist for the Connecticut Book Award. He teaches creative writing and literature at the University of Bridgeport, and lives in Connecticut with his wife, poet Amy Nawrocki, and their two cats.

LACAR MUSGROVE is a writer, editor, historian, and educator from New Orleans. She graduated from the Louisiana School for Math, Science, and the Arts before going on to study literature at Boston University. She holds an MFA in creative writing and an MA in history from the University of New Orleans and is published in the field of cultural history. To find out more and read her work, visit www.LacarMusgroveEditor.com.

SALVADOR OROPESA is a professor of Spanish and Department Chair of Languages at Clemson University. His teaching and research areas of specialization are peninsular and Mexican literature. He received his PhD from Arizona State University and his Licenciatura en Filología Hispánica from the Universidad de Granada. His more recent book is *Literatura y comercio en España: las tiendas (1868–1952)* published by the Universidad de Málaga, and with Maureen Ihrie, he edited *World Literature in Spanish: An Encyclopedia* in three volumes with ABC-CLIO.

CHRIS PETERS is a writer, programmer, designer, and geographer who has worked in Colorado and central Illinois.

THOMAS B. PORTER holds journalism degrees from the State University of New York at Morrisville and St. John Fisher College and has worked in a daily newspaper newsroom. Currently serving as a senior technical writer and team leader at the Communications-Electronics Life Cycle Sustainment Command, he is an avid reader, traveler, and lover of literary podcasts.

ÁNDREA LAURENCELL SHERIDAN is an associate professor of English and interdisciplinary studies at SUNY Orange in the Hudson Valley region of New York. She has been awarded the President's Award for Excellence in Teaching and the SUNY Chancellor's Award for Excellence in Teaching (2018). She earned an MA in English from SUNY New Paltz (2017), an MA in humanities and social thought concentrating in literary cultures from New York University (2008), and a BA in English from Russell Sage College, minoring in Spanish and women's studies (2005). Ándrea currently serves as the diversity coordinator and blog editor for the International David Foster Wallace Society, and frequently presents at national and international conferences on Wallace and other postmodern literature as well as popular culture. She is currently working on her first essay collection on the postmodern novel.

About the Editor and Contributors

RACHELANNE SMITH is a scholar with an MA in English literature from Sacramento State University. She is a writer, a fanatical reader, and a teacher.

KEN WHALEN holds an MA from the University of Maryland, College Park, and a PhD in geography from the University of Florida. He has published essays on a variety of topics including environmentalism, difficult heritage, political violence, and geographical representation. He is an assistant professor at the American University of Kurdistan.

VICTORIA WILLIAMS, PhD, is an independent writer and researcher living in London, England. She is author of ABC-CLIO's *Weird Sports and Wacky Games Around the World: From Buzkashi to Zorbing,* and has written on a variety of subjects, including Hollywood film (for ABC-CLIO's *Movies in American History: An Encyclopedia*), human sacrifice and Mesoamerican mythology (for ABC-CLIO's *Conflict in the Early Americas*), British folk customs (for ABC-CLIO's *They Do What? A Cultural Encyclopedia of Extraordinary and Exotic Customs from Around the World),* and other topics. Williams wrote her doctoral thesis (King's College, London) on European fairy tales in 19th-century British art and literature and on film, with special reference to the Brothers Grimm.

Index

Page numbers for main entries are indicated in **bold** type.

Aberdeen, South Dakota, 300
Absalom, Absalom! (Faulkner), **1–4**
   cultural geography of Mississippi, 1–2
   Mississippi and New Orleans, 2
Absurdism, 289
An Account of the Principalities of Wallachia and Moldavia (Wilkinson), 84
Adams, Douglas
   The Hitchhiker's Guide to the Galaxy, 138–140
   The Restaurant at the End of the Universe, 139
"The Adventure of the Final Problem" (Doyle), 8
"The Adventure of the Lion's Mane" (Doyle), 9
Adventures of Huckleberry Finn (Twain), **4–7**
   fishing in, 331
   moral law of the river, 6
   nature versus civilization, 4–5
   racism, 5–6
Adventures of Sherlock Holmes (Doyle), **7–10**
   the detective abroad, 8
   excerpt, 7
   Holmes in southern England, 8–9
   in London, 7–8
   space as mystery, 9
Aeaea (mythical island), Greece, 198
Aegadian Islands, Italy, 198
Aegean region, 197
Aeolian Islands, Italy, 198
Affairs. *See* Infidelity
Afghan immigrants, 164–165
Afghanistan
   The Kite Runner (Hosseini), 163–165
   Soviet invasion, 163, 164
   Taliban regime, 163–164
Africa
   European colonization, 135–137
   as heart of darkness, 136, 232
   mapping in imagination of colonizers, 135–136
   The Odyssey (Homer), 198
African Americans
   ghettos (1960s), burning of, 256
   Harlem Renaissance, 143–145, 328–329
   housing and land ownership, 238–239, 268–269, 271
   post-Civil War South, 28
   in *The Sound and the Fury* (Faulkner), 261, 262
   Their Eyes Were Watching God (Hurston), 275–276
   trauma of slavery, 34–36
   See also Race issues; Slavery
African diaspora, geography of, 143–144
After the Fall (Miller), 329
Afterlife, mapping of, 76–77
Agent Orange, 81, 278
Agriculture. *See* Rural life
Air, as symbol of freedom, 31–32
"Airey-Force Valley" (Wordsworth), 324
Airstrip One (fictional place), 192
Alabama
   To Kill a Mockingbird (Lee), 280–282
Alaska
   The Call of the Wild (London), 56–59
Albuquerque, New Mexico, 332
Alcott, Amos Bronson, 327
Algeria
   colonization, 223
   Oran, 223–224
Alien abduction, 255, 256–257

Alien invasions, 86–88
Alienation
   landscape of, 112, 180
   Modernist sense of, 104
All Quiet on the Western Front (Remarque), **10–14**
   war and the physical geography of mortality, 12–13
All the Pretty Horses (McCarthy), **14–17**
   awards, 14
   excerpt, 14
   geography of place, 14–15
   polyglossia, 15
Allen, George, 236
Almanac of the Dead (Silko), **17–19**
   geography of the Southwest, 18–19
America, Las Vegas as symbol for, 97–98
American dream
   freedom and self-possession, 98, 114, 204
   immigrant hopes for, 156
   property ownership, 74, 140–141, 188, 204
American exceptionalism, 98
American Indians. *See* Native Americans
American Renaissance movement, 150, 228
American Revolution, 151
Amerindians. *See* Native Americans
Amherst, Massachusetts, 75–76
Amper River, Germany, 48
Anaya, Rudolfo
   Bless Me, Ultima, 45–47, 332
   Heart of Aztlan, 332
   in Southwest (region), 332
   Tortuga, 332
Andaman Islands, 8
"Anecdote of the Jar" (Stevens), 264–265
Animals. *See* Fauna
"Annabel Lee" (Poe), 229
Another Bullshit Night in Suck City (Flynn), 328
Another Life (Walcott), 291–292
Antigone (Sophocles), **20–22**
   distance of time and place, 21
   geography of burial, 21–22
   place and values of the *polis,* 21
Antiheroes, 73–74, 116, 201
Anzaldúa, Gloria, **22–25**
   Borderlands/La Frontera, 23
   Chicana third space feminism, 23–24
   hybridity and the border, 23
   "El otro Mexico," 23
   in Southwest (region), 333
   "To Live in the Borderlands," 23
Apocalypse Now (movie), 81
Architecture
   castles, 120, 121, 227
   of forbidden love, 249–250
   of human mind, 77–78
   of surveillance, 86
Arctic regions, 100
Aristotle (Greek philosopher), 170
Arizona
   Almanac of the Dead (Silko), 17–19
   Dust Bowl border control, 109
   Navajo Nation, 331–332
Arkansas, Dust Bowl in, 108
Arranged marriage, 182
"Arrival at Santos" (Bishop), 42
Art, women's, 310–311
Arthurian tales, **25–28**
   British geography, 25–26
As I Lay Dying (Faulkner), **28–30**
   geography of death and decay, 29
   physical and cultural geography of Mississippi, 28
As You Like It (Shakespeare), 182
"At Great Pond" (Oliver), 210
Atheism, 64–65, 170, 224
Athens, Greece, 21, 181–184
Atomic bombs, 51, 90
Atwood, Margaret
   The Handmaid's Tale, 122–127
"August" (Oliver), 209–210
Austen, Jane
   country house novels, 54
   Pride and Prejudice, 234–237
   settings for her works, 305
Australia
   Gulliver's Travels (Swift), 118
Austria
   Styria, 84
Austro-Hungarian Empire
   Transylvania, 83–84
Authentic, search for, 60–61
Automobiles, as extension of persona, 98
Avalon (fictional place), 25
The Awakening (Chopin), **30–33**
   New Orleans, Esplanade Avenue, 30–32
   repressive space of domestic life, 31
   setting, 330
   water and air as symbols of freedom, 31–32

Index

Balearic Islands, Spain, 198–199
Ballroom, as cultural signifier, 235–236
Baltimore, Maryland, 225
Balzac, Honoré de
   The Human Comedy, 316–317
   in Paris, 316–317
"Barn Burning" (Faulkner), 280
Barrio as identity, 141
"Bartleby, the Scrivener" (H. Melville), 327
Basements, 49–50, 95–96
Baum, L. Frank
   background, 299–300
   Oz books, 299
   racism, 300
   The Wizard of Oz, 299–301
"Bear Paw" (Hugo), 146–147
Beardsley, Aubrey, 26
Beat generation, 214–217, 258, 333–334
"Because I Could Not Stop for Death" (Dickinson), 76
Beckett, Samuel
   background, 289
   Nobel Prize, 288
   Waiting for Godot, 288–290
Belonging, home and cultural geography of, 238–239
Beloved (Morrison), **34–37**
   ghostly geography of trauma, 35–36
Berbers, 223
"A Berkshire Summer Morning" (Holmes), 328
Berry, Wendell, **37–39**
   "XI," 38
   The Farm, 38
   "History," 37, 38
   "The Long-Legged House," 37
   sacred geography, 38
   scarred geography, 38
   This Day, 38
   "2008, XI," 38
"Between Walls" (W. Williams), 297
Bewick, Thomas
   History of British Birds, 153
Bible
   creation of life, 101
   fall from grace, 171, 172
   flat earth, 174
   The Handmaid's Tale (Atwood), 123
   Job, 186
   Jonah, 186
   The Poisonwood Bible (Kingsolver), 230–231
   Revelation, 51, 174
"Big Brother," 192–193
Bildungsroman (novel of education)
   Bless Me, Ultima (Anaya), 45–47
   The Catcher in the Rye (Salinger), 59–61
   defined, 112
   Great Expectations (Dickens), 111–114
   Harry Potter series (Rowling), 127–130
   The House on Mango Street (Cisneros), 140–143
Billy Budd (H. Melville), **39–42**
   cultural space of capital punishment, 41
   mapping the morality of chance, 40–41
   mutiny and ocean travel, 40
"Birches" (Frost), 103–104
Birds, as symbols for freedom, 32
Bishop, Elizabeth, **42–45**
   "Arrival at Santos," 42
   "Brazil, January 1, 1502," 43–44
   "Cape Breton," 42, 43
   "Casablanca," 42
   A Cold Spring, 42
   "First Death in Nova Scotia," 42
   "Florida," 42
   "From the Country to the City," 42
   Geography III, 42
   geography of travel: Elizabeth Bishop's North and South America, 42–44
   "The Map," 42
   in New England, 328
   "North Haven," 42
   North & South, 42
   "Over 2,000 Illustrations and a Complete Concordance," 42
   "Paris, 7 A.M.," 42
   "Quai d'Orléans," 42
   Questions of Travel, 42
   "Questions of Travel," 44
   "Santarém," 42
   "Seascape," 42
   "Varick Street," 42
Bittlestone, Robert
   Odysseus Unbound (with Diggle and Underhill), 199
Black culture. *See* African Americans; Race issues
Black Death, 223–224
Black Hawk, Nebraska, 188–189
Blackfeet, 146

Blake, William, 323
Bless Me, Ultima (Anaya), **45–47**
   Chicano movement, 45
   land as a source of healing, 45–46
   setting, 332
Blindness, borders and, 161
Body. *See* Human body
Bohemian (Czech) immigrants, 188
The Book Thief (Zusak), **47–50**
   basements as shelters, 49–50
   geography of fascism, 47–49
   sky, 49
   theft and the landscape, 49
Border Trilogy (McCarthy), 14
Borderlands/La Frontera (Anzaldúa), 23
Borders
   blindness and, 161
   between civilization and wilderness, 58
   contact zones, 15
   crossings, 14–15
   as cultural crossroads, 23
   Dust Bowl border control, 109
   geography of violence, 195
   hybridity and, 23
   identity and, 23
   shifting boundaries of land and language, 192–193
   as third country, 23–24
   U.S./Mexico, 14–15, 22–24, 194–196, 332–333
Borges, Jorge Luis, 316
Boston, Massachusetts, 123, 225, 328
The Bostonians (James), 328
Botany. *See* Flora
Bottom, Ohio, 269, 271
Boundaries. *See* Borders
Boyd, Elmer, 243
Boyle, T. C., 334
Bradstreet, Anne
   in New England, 326–327
   The Tenth Muse Lately Sprung Up in America, 327
Brain. *See* Human mind
"Brass Spittoons" (Hughes), 143–144
Brave New World (Huxley), **50–52**
   landscape of dystopia, 50–51
   landscape of totalitarianism, 51–52
   science and technology, 51
Brazil
   in Bishop's poetry, 43–44
   Robinson Crusoe (Defoe), 243
"Brazil, January 1, 1502" (Bishop), 43–44

Brideshead Revisited (Waugh), **52–55**
   country house tradition, 54
   excerpt, 53
   idyllic settings, 53
   real and fictional geography, 53–54
Britain. *See* England; Great Britain; Scotland; Wales
British East India Company, 244
British Empire, threats to, 85
Brobdingnag (fictional place), 117–118
Brod, Max, 179
Brodie, William, 319
Brontë, Charlotte
   Jane Eyre, 153–156, 325
   in Lake District, England, 325
   Shirley, 325
   visit to North Lees Hall, 154
Brontë, Emily
   Wuthering Heights, 304–308
Brooklyn, New York, 73–75
The Brothers Karamazov (Dostoyevsky), 64
Brownson, Orestes, 327
Bryan, William Jennings, 300–301
Bubonic plague, 223–224, 321
Buddhism, in Snyder's works, 258
Bulge, Battle of the (1944–1945), 256
Bullring, 273–274
Burial
   ancient Greek rituals, 20, 21–22
   in Dickinson's poetry, 76–77
   "The Fall of the House of Usher" (Poe), 95–96
   geography of, 21–22, 28–29
   grass growing over, 294
   while alive, 95–96, 226–227
Burns, Robert, 59, 203
Burroughs, William, 214
"By Frazier Creek Falls" (Snyder), 259
Byron, Lord
   in London, 323
   "The Prisoner of Chillon," 315
   Romanticism, 315
   "year without a summer," 100, 101

Cable, George Washington, 330
California
   Afghan immigrant community, 164–165
   border with Mexico, 23
   The Call of the Wild (London), 56–59
   early exploration, 117
   Frost in, 102

The Grapes of Wrath (Steinbeck), 108, 109–110
   in Hass's poetry, 130–131
   literary landscape, 333–334
   Los Angeles, 98, 256
   Of Mice and Men (Steinbeck), 203–205
   San Francisco, 97, 258, 333–334
The Call of the Wild (London), **56–59**
   cultural border between civilization and wilderness, 58
   excerpt, 56
   geography of mushing, 56–57
"Camas Prairie School" (Hugo), 146
Camden, New Jersey, 293
Camelot (fictional place), 25
Camus, Albert
   background, 223
   existentialism, 180, 223, 261–262
   in French Resistance, 224
   morality, 224
   nihilism in works by, 178
   Nobel Prize, 180, 223
   The Plague, 223–225
   on suicide, 261–262
Canada
   The Call of the Wild (London), 56–59
   Underground Railroad, 284
"Cape Breton" (Bishop), 42, 43
Cape Cod, Massachusetts, 208, 326
Capital punishment, 40, 41
Capitalism
   basis for, 38
   encouraging greed and waste, 37
   mistrust of, 156
   shifting modes of, 73–74
Capote, Truman
   In Cold Blood, 80
   in New Orleans, 330
Captain Singleton (Defoe), 244
Card, Orson Scott
   Ender's Game, 86–88
Cardiff, Wales, 25
Caribbean region
   British colonialism, 154
   European colonization, 172
   The Old Man and the Sea (Hemingway), 205–208
   parallels with Greek islands, 291
   South as part of, 1
Carlisle, England, 25
Carmilla (Le Fanu), 84
"Casablanca" (Bishop), 42

"The Cask of Amontillado" (Poe), 226–227
Cassady, Neal, 214
The Castle (Kafka), 179
Castles
   architecture, 120, 121, 227
   Arthurian tales, 25–28
   Edinburgh, Scotland, 318–319
   Elsinore, 120–121
Cat on a Hot Tin Roof (T. Williams), 105, 329
The Catcher in the Rye (Salinger), **59–61**
   Central Park epiphany, 60–61
   excerpt, 59
   New York City, 59–60
   postmodernism, 59, 92
   sex, nuns, and the city, 60
Cather, Willa
   background, 188
   My Ántonia, 187–191
Catholicism
   Brideshead Revisited (Waugh), 54
   Long Day's Journey into Night (O'Neill), 170
   sex, nuns, and New York City, 54
   in Southwest (region), 332
   Spanish conquest and, 45
   Spanish Inquisition, 225–226
   Waugh's conversion to, 54
Catskill Mountains, New York, 150–151, 292
Central Park, New York City, 60–61
Ceremony (Silko), **61–64**
   geography of recovery, 62–63
   war and homecoming, 62
Chance, mapping the morality of, 40–41
Chancellorsville, Battle of (1863), 240
Channing, William Henry, 327
Chaos, war and, 79–80
Characters
   places and, 139
   symbolism, 300
Charybdis, 198, 199
Le Chevalier de la Charrette (The Knight of the Cart) (Troyes), 25
Chicago, Illinois
   The House on Mango Street (Cisneros), 140–142
   The Jungle (Sinclair), 156–158
   A Raisin in the Sun (Hansberry), 238–239

Chicano culture
  Amerindian heritage, 46
  barrio as identity, 141
  Chicana third space feminism, 23–24
  Chicano movement, 45
  disenfranchisement of Latinas, 140
  gender and repression, 141–142
  The House on Mango Street (Cisneros), 140–143
  race and class issues, 140–141
Chickasaw Amerindians, 28
Childhood, landscape of, 221
China, communist revolution in, 192
Chopin, Kate
  The Awakening, 30–33, 330
  in South (region), 330, 331
Christianity
  geography of death, 29
  The Handmaid's Tale (Atwood), 123
  herd mentality, 65
  as impediment to progress, 64
  missionaries, 230–233
  morality, 65
  Mormons, 8
  slavery and Christian sentimentalism, 285–286
  slavery's abolition and, 283
  as target of intellectuals, 64
  toxicity and, 123–124
  See also Catholicism; Puritans
Church of Jesus Christ of Latter-day Saints, 8
"Ci Vediamo" *(The Triggering Town)* (Hugo), 146
Cien Anos de Soledad (Garcia Marquez). *See One Hundred Years of Solitude* (Garcia Marquez)
Cincinnati, Ohio, 34–36
Circe (witch), 198
Cisneros, Sandra
  The House on Mango Street, 140–143
Cities
  versus forest in the battle for souls, 66–67
  urban geography and architecture of forbidden love, 249–250
  urban geography of London, 211–212
  urban/rural dichotomy, 37, 112–113, 212–213
Cities of the Plain (McCarthy), 14
Civil War, U.S.
  economic downturn following emancipation, 280
  Missouri, 106
  The Red Badge of Courage (Crane), 240–242
  Stowe's influence on, 283
Civilization
  border with wilderness, 58
  degrading nature, 259
  versus nature, 4–5, 272
  town versus forest in the battle for souls, 66–67
Clark, William, 106
Clarke, Joe, 276
Class issues
  cross-class friendships, 163
  cultural geography of class equality, 154–155
  death as great equalizer, 228, 294
  democracy, 145
  disadvantaged people helping one another, 110
  England, 160
  expected behavior, 70–72
  gender and, 30–32, 70
  geography and wealth distribution, 148
  The Handmaid's Tale (Atwood), 123, 126
  housing and land ownership, 140–141, 268–269, 271
  Industrial Revolution, 112
  lower-class coup, 266, 267–268
  "old money" versus "new money," 114–115
  race and, 1–2, 144
  theft, 49
Clybourne Park (fictional neighborhood), Chicago, Illinois, 239
Coahuila, Mexico, 14–15
Cockermouth, England, 324
Cod, Cape, Massachusetts, 208, 326
A Cold Spring (Bishop), 42
Cold War, 194
Coleridge, Samuel Taylor
  in Lake District, England, 325–326
  Lyrical Ballads (with W. Wordsworth), 325–326
  "The Rime of the Ancient Mariner," 325–326
Collins, Suzanne
  The Hunger Games, 147–149

Colombia, Garcia Marquez in, 221
Colonialism
    Africa, 135–136
    Algeria, 223
    brutality, 135, 136–137
    Caribbean region, 154, 172
    haunted landscape and, 233
    Indochina, 81
    missionary work as neocolonialism, 230, 231–232
    moral landscape of, 136–137
    place/mapping and, 231–232
    slavery in American colonies, 1
    Southwest (region), U.S., 18–19
Color symbolism, 227–228
Colorado, Dust Bowl in, 108
Columbus, Christopher, 206
Comanches, 15
The Comforters (Spark), 320
Communism
    denouncing religion, 64
    McCarthy era, 66
    Russia, 51
    as totalitarianism, 51
    Vietnam War, 81
Communist Manifesto (Engels and Marx), 51, 64
Conan Doyle, Sir Arthur. *See* Doyle, Sir Arthur Conan
Concentration camps, 47–50
Concho River, Texas, 14–15
A Confederacy of Dunces (Toole), 330
Confessions (Rousseau), 315
Congo region, Africa, 135–136, 230–233
Congo River, Africa, 143
Connecticut, in Stevens's poetry, 264
Conrad, Joseph
    Heart of Darkness, 135–138, 232
    travel to Congo region, 136–137
Consumer culture, 97–99
Cooke, Edward
    A Voyage to the South Seas, and Round the World, 244
Cooper, James Fenimore
    American Renaissance movement, 150
    The Last of the Mohicans, 166–168
Corsica (island), 199
Country house novels, 54
Countryside, versus cities, 112–113
Cowardice, 163–164, 195, 240–242
Crane, Stephen

The Red Badge of Courage, 240–242
Crime and Punishment (Dostoyevsky), **64–66**
    geography of atheism, 64–65
    geography of guilt, 65
Criminology, 7
The Crossing (McCarthy), 14
Crossroads, 103
The Crucible (Miller), **66–69**
    geography of hypocrisy: puritan greed and infidelity, 67–68
    productions of, 329
    town versus forest in the battle for souls, 66–67
The Crying of Lot 49 (Pynchon), 92
Cuatro Ciénagas, Coahuila, Mexico, 14–15
Cuba
    The Old Man and the Sea (Hemingway), 205–208
Cultural geography
    of belonging, 238–239
    border between civilization and wilderness, 58
    of capital punishment, 41
    of class equality, 154–155
    contrasts between European and American culture, 71–72
    cultural landscape of masculinity, 74
    of industrial production, 156–157
    of military-industrial complex, 87–88
    Mississippi, 1–2, 28
    nature and cultural geography of Puritanism, 252–253
    of passion, 305–306
    of slavery, 283–285
    young love and, 247–248
Curanderismo (traditional folk medicine), 45–46
"A Curtain of Green" (Welty), 330
Czech immigrants, 188

Dachau concentration camp, 47–49
"Daffodils (I Wandered Lonely as a Cloud)" (W. Wordsworth), 324
Daisy Miller (James), **70–72**
    Chateau de Chillon as setting in, 315
    contrasts between European and American culture, 71–72
    figure of the expatriate, 71
    geography of flirtation, 70–71
Dancing, 235–236

Dangerous waters, 197–198
Dante
   Inferno, 76, 133
Darkness
   Africa as heart of, 136, 232
   as evil, 136, 137
Dartmoor, England, 9
Darwin, Charles, 100
Darwinism, 51
De Saussure, Ferdinand, 265
Death
   accidental, 204
   in bullring, 273
   capital punishment, 40, 41
   Christian ideals, 29
   by drowning, 30, 32, 270
   earth and, 103–105
   geography of death and decay, 29
   as great equalizer, 228, 294
   Holocaust, 47–50
   Irish potato famine, 170
   lingering presence after, 9
   mapping the afterlife, 76–77
   mercy killings, 204, 217, 269, 270, 285
   from plagues, 223–224, 227–228
   in Poe's short stories, 225–229
   reanimation, 101, 228
   seasonal associations, 77, 103–104
   self-defense killings, 275
   spatial imaginary of grief, 266–267
   sundown as metaphor for, 296
   in war, 10–13, 241
   See also Burial; Murder; Suicide
Death of a Salesman (Miller), **73–75**
   cultural landscape of masculinity, 74
   land and the American dream, 74
   productions of, 329
   shifting modes of capitalism, 73–74
Death (personified), 47, 48
"Dedication for a Plot of Ground" (W. Williams), 297
Defoe, Daniel
   Captain Singleton, 244
   research, 244
   Robinson Crusoe, 242–247
Dekker, Thomas, 321
Del Rio, Texas, 15
Delaware tribe, 168
Delphi, Oracle of, 200–201
Democracy, 21, 145
Denmark

Hamlet (Shakespeare), 92, 120–122
Depression. *See* Great Depression
Descartes, René, 294
Desert, 98–99
Detective stories, 7–10
Detroit, Michigan, 256
Devil, tempting faithful, 66–67
Devon, England, 9
Diagon Alley (fictional place), 128
Dickens, Charles
   in Geneva, 316
   Great Expectations, 111–114
   in London, 321–322, 323
   Oliver Twist, 211–214
   The Pickwick Papers, 323
Dickinson, Emily, **75–79**
   architecture and geography of the human mind, 77–78
   "Because I Could Not Stop for Death," 76
   "I Died for Beauty," 76
   "I Felt a Funeral, in my Brain," 77
   "I Heard a Fly Buzz—When I Died," 76
   mapping the afterlife, 76–77
   pastoral tradition, 75–76
   "Perhaps I asked too large," 77
   "There's a Certain Slant of Light," 77
Didion, Joan
   new journalism, 79, 80
   Slouching towards Bethlehem, 80
   Where I Was From, 333
"Digging" (Heaney), 133
Diggle, James
   Odysseus Unbound (with Bittlestone and Underhill), 199
Disease, as fate, 201–202
Dispatches (Herr), **79–83**
   at the movies, 81
   new journalism, 80
   Vietnam landscape, 81–82
   war and chaos, 79–80
   war and witness, 80–81
Dmitry (Russian sailing ship), 84
Dogsledding, 56–57
Domestic life. *See* Home
Doppelgängers (twin figures), 309–310
Dostoyevsky, Fyodor
   The Brothers Karamazov, 64
   Crime and Punishment, 64–66
Douglass, Frederick, 331
Dover, England, 160–161

Downton Abbey (television series), 54
Doyle, Sir Arthur Conan
   "The Adventure of the Final Problem," 8
   "The Adventure of the Lion's Mane," 9
   Adventures of Sherlock Holmes, 7–10
   in Geneva, 316
   "His Last Bow," 9
   The Hound of the Baskervilles, 9
   The Sign of the Four, 8
   A Study in Scarlet, 8
Dracula (Stoker), **83–85**
   abroad and at home, 83–84
   creating a Transylvanian monster, 84
   excerpt, 83
   inspiration for, 315
   London in, 323
   a threat to the empire, 85
   train transportation, 94
Drake, Sir Francis, 117
Dream Work (Oliver), 210
Dreams
   failed, 115–116
   geography of, 204
   institutionalization dreamscape, 219
   See also American dream
Dresden, Germany, 90, 255, 256
Dresden, Ontario, 284
Drought. *See* Dust Bowl
Drowning, 30, 32, 270
Drug deals, 194–195
Drug use
   Fear and Loathing in Las Vegas (Thompson), 97–99
   heroin addiction in World War I veterans, 269
   "Ligeia" (Poe), 228
   Long Day's Journey into Night (O'Neill), 169
   surreal landscape of, 99
Drug war, 196
Duddon sonnets (W. Wordsworth), 303
Duncan, King (Scotland), 177
Dungeons, in Poe's short stories, 225–229
Duras, Marguerite
   The Lover, 318
   in Paris, 318
   The Ravishing of Lol Stein, 318
   The War, 318
Dust Bowl, 107–109, 189

Dystopia
   The Handmaid's Tale (Atwood), 122–127
   The Hunger Games (Collins), 147–149
   landscape of, 50–51
   Nineteen Eighty-Four (Orwell), 192–194

Earth
   antecedents, 138–139
   flat earth geography, 174–175
   The Hitchhiker's Guide to the Galaxy (Adams), 138–139
East Egg (fictional place), New York, 114–115
Eastasia (fictional superstate), 192
Eatonville, Florida, 276
Ecological disaster, geography of, 108–109
Economics
   cultural geography of industrial production, 156–157
   profit conflict with environmental safety, 88–89
   shifting modes of capitalism, 73–74
Ecopoetry, defined, 146
Edinburgh, Scotland, 318–320
Egypt
   Hamlet (Shakespeare), 121
El Paso, Texas, 195
Electricity, 100–101
"XI" (Berry), 38
Eliot, T.S.
   The Waste Land, 297
Elizabeth I, Queen (England), 160
Elizabethan society, 247. *See also* Shakespeare, William
Elsinore, Denmark, 120–121
Elsinore (castle), 120–121
Emerson, Ralph Waldo, 150, 294, 327
Ender's Game (Card), **86–88**
   architecture of surveillance, 86
   cultural geography of the military-industrial complex, 87–88
An Enemy of the People (Ibsen), **88–90**
   pollution of land and politics: role of science, 89–90
Engels, Friedrich
   Communist Manifesto (with Marx), 51, 64

England
- *Adventures of Sherlock Holmes* (Doyle), 7–10
- Arthurian tales, 25–28
- *Brideshead Revisited* (Waugh), 52–55
- colonialism, 136, 154
- country house novels, 54
- countryside versus London, 112–113
- *Dracula* (Stoker), 83–85
- fairies, 182
- French and Indian War, 166–168
- Frost in, 102, 103
- gendered land ownership laws, 235
- geography, 25–26
- *Great Expectations* (Dickens), 112–114
- *Hamlet* (Shakespeare), 121
- *Harry Potter* series (Rowling), 127–130
- *Jane Eyre* (C. Brontë), 153–156
- *King Lear* (Shakespeare), 160–163
- Lake District, 302–303, 324–326
- Middle-earth as, 175
- moors, 154, 306–307
- *Nineteen Eighty-Four* (Orwell), 51, 192–194
- *Oliver Twist* (Dickens), 211–214
- *Pride and Prejudice* (Austen), 234–237
- rejection of "the Other," 85
- *Robinson Crusoe* (Defoe), 242–243
- southern England, 8–9
- *See also* Great Britain; London, England

"Englands of the Mind" (Heaney), 133
Enlightenment, 100, 172–173, 186, 294
Environmental safety, 88–89
Equality, physical geography of, 295
Equiano, Olaudah, 331
Erdrich, Louise, 146
Erosion. *See* Dust Bowl
Esplanade Avenue, New Orleans, Louisiana, 30–31
Esquire magazine, 79, 80
Essays of Elia (C. Lamb), 326
"Ethan Brand" (Hawthorne), 328
Ethnicity, 163–164. *See also* African Americans; Chicano culture; Immigrants; Race issues
Ethnography, 117–118
Euphrates River, Asia, 143
Eurasia (fictional superstate), 192
Europe
- contrasts between European and American culture, 71–72
- as setting in Poe's works, 225–228
- social customs, 70–72

Everything Is Illuminated (Foer), 90
Evil
- *The Crucible* (Miller), 66–69
- darkness as, 136, 137
- geography of, 95–96, 185, 224
- good versus, 40
- *The Lord of the Rings* (Tolkien), 175
- plague as symbol of, 224
- snake as, 231

Existentialism
- *The Catcher in the Rye* (Salinger), 59
- ethical atheism, 224
- Faulkner and, 29, 261–262
- forerunner, 180
- humans are condemned to choose, 224
- Kafka and, 180
- nihilism and, 178
- *The Plague* (Camus), 223, 224
- *The Sound and the Fury* (Faulkner), 261–262

Exorcism, 35
Expatriates, 71
Extremely Loud & Incredibly Close (Foer), **90–93**
- New York City: before and after 9/11, 91
- place of family, 91–92
- post-postmodern redemption, 92

Eye, as window, 78

Fairies, 181–182
Fall from grace, 171, 172
"The Fall of the House of Usher" (Poe), **94–97**
- geography of place, 94
- geography of the house of Usher, 94–96
- haunted interior space, 228–229

Fall (season), association with death, 77
Family
- decline of, as theme, 105, 260
- feuds, 6, 247–251, 305
- place of, 91–92
- social mores and family structure, 269–270
- violence in, 1

Fantasy genre. *See Harry Potter* series (Rowling); *The Lord of the Rings* (Tolkien)
"A Far Cry from Africa" (Walcott), 291
Faraday, Michael, 100
The Farm (Berry), 38

Farming. *See* Rural life
Fascism
   architecture of surveillance, 86
   geography of, 47–49
   The Handmaid's Tale (Atwood), 122–127
Fate, disease as, 201–202
Faulkner, William
   Absalom, Absalom!, 1–4
   "Barn Burning," 280
   decline of family, as theme, 105, 260
   existentialism, 261–262
   focus on South, 260
   As I Lay Dying, 28–30
   literary experimentation, 261
   on Mississippi, 330
   in New Orleans, 330
   nihilism, 260
   Nobel Prize, 28, 168, 260, 261
   Pulitzer Prizes, 261
   "A Rose for Emily," 281–282
   The Sound and the Fury, 260–263
   stream of consciousness, 28
Fauna
   in Bishop's poetry, 43
   in Hass's poetry, 131
   in Oliver's poetry, 208–210
   The Poisonwood Bible (Kingsolver), 232–233
Fear and Loathing in Las Vegas (Thompson), **97–99**
   excerpt, 97
   Las Vegas as symbol for America, 97–98
   road travel and settlement of the West, 98
   surreal landscape of hallucinogenic drugs, 99
Feminism, Chicana third space feminism, 23–24
Fences, 102–103
Ferlinghetti, Lawrence, 334
Feuds
   Adventures of Huckleberry Finn (Twain), 6
   Romeo and Juliet (Shakespeare), 247–251
   Wuthering Heights (E. Brontë), 305
Fez, French Morocco, 53
Fictional geography, 53–54, 138
Field Guide (Hass), 130–131
Fielding, Henry, 54

"First Death in Nova Scotia" (Bishop), 42
First Nations, 57–58
Fishing, 205–208
Fitzgerald, F. Scott
   in Geneva, 316
   The Great Gatsby, 114–116
   in "Lost Generation," 114
   in Paris, 317
Flat earth geography, 174–175
Fleming, Ian, 316
Flirtation, geography of, 70–71
Flora
   Agent Orange, 81
   in Dickinson's writing, 75–76
   indigenous knowledge of, 231–232
   nurturing, in place of children, 124–125
   in Oliver's poetry, 208–209
   pear trees, 275–276
   The Poisonwood Bible (Kingsolver), 232–233
   "The Problem of Describing Trees" (Hass), 131
   symbolizing living outside moral order, 253–254
Florida
   literary landscape, 330–331
   Their Eyes Were Watching God (Hurston), 275–276
"Florida" (Bishop), 42
Flowers. *See* Flora
Flynn, Nick
   Another Bullshit Night in Suck City, 328
Foer, Jonathan Safran
   Everything Is Illuminated, 90
   Extremely Loud & Incredibly Close, 90–93
En folkefiende (Ibsen). *See An Enemy of the People* (Ibsen)
Folklore, mythology and, 183
Food production, horrors of, 156–157
Fools Crow (Welch), 146
Forest
   encroaching forest as covenant, 38
   jungles of Vietnam, 278
   as meeting point of life and death, 232
   A Midsummer Night's Dream (Shakespeare), 182–183
   supernatural mischief, 182
   as threat to order, 252
   town versus forest in the battle for souls, 66–67
   See also Wilderness

Fort Edward, New York, 166
Fort William Henry, New York, 166
The Fortunate Traveller (Walcott), 291
France
    Arthurian tales, 25–28
    attempts to annex Geneva, 316
    colonialism, 81
    Corsica, 199
    French and Indian War, 166–168
    Paris, 272–274, 289, 316–318
    realism, 289
    Sherlock Holmes in, 8
    World War II, 224
Frankenstein (M. Shelley), **100–102**
    compared to *Brave New World* (A. Huxley), 51
    Geneva writing retreat, 315
    geography of horror, 101
    geography of place, 100
    science and the literary landscape, 100–101
Free will, 179–180
Freedom
    in American dream, 98, 114, 204
    water and air as symbols of, 31–32
French and Indian War, 166–168
French Indochina, 81, 318
French Morocco
    Brideshead Revisited (Waugh), 53
French Quarter, New Orleans, Louisiana, 266–268, 330
French Resistance, 224
Freud, Sigmund, 173
Frogstar (fictional planet), 139
"From the Country to the City" (Bishop), 42
La Frontera/Borderlands (Anzaldúa), 23
Frost, Robert, **102–104**
    "Birches," 103–104
    earth and death, 103–104
    "Mending Wall," 102–103
    in New England, 104, 327
    Pulitzer Prize, 102
    "The Road Not Taken," 103
    self-identity, 103
    "Stopping by Woods on a Snowy Evening," 103
    tradition and the changing landscape, 102–103
Fuca, Juan de, 117
Fuentes, Gregorio, 206
Fugitive Slave Act (1793), 286

Full Metal Jacket (movie), 81
Fuller, Margaret, 327
Funerals. *See* Burial

Galli Islands, Italy, 199
Galvani, Luigi, 100–101
Garcia Marquez, Gabriel
    background, 221
    One Hundred Years of Solitude, 220–222
Gardens. *See* Flora
Gaskell, Elizabeth, 325
Gender
    class and, 30–32
    gendered space, 235, 248, 296
    land ownership laws, 235
    repression and, 141–142
    surveillance, gender, and the home interior, 311–312
    witchcraft and, 178
    See also Men; Women
Genesis, book of
    creation of life, 101
    evil in, 231
    fall from grace, 171, 172
    The Handmaid's Tale (Atwood), 123
Geneva, Switzerland, 315–316
Geography
    of African diaspora, 143–144
    of atheism, 64–65
    British geography, 25–26
    burial, 21–22
    of death and decay, 28–29
    of domesticity, 310
    of dreams, 204
    of ecological disaster, 108–109
    of evil, 185, 224
    of fascism, 47–49
    of flirtation, 70–71
    of grace, 258–259
    of guilt, 65
    of home (Ireland), 132–134
    of horror, 101
    House of Usher, 94–96
    of human mind, 77–78
    of hypocrisy, 67–68
    of ideas, 170
    identity and, 160
    of memory and resistance, 125–126
    of misogyny, 124–125
    of mushing, 56–57
    of mystery, 206–207

of Nazism, 224
of nihilism, 177–178
North America, 42–44
Oran: geography of *The Plague* (Camus), 223–224
of paradise, 290–292
real and fictional, 53–54
of recovery, 62–63
sacred geography, 38
scarred geography, 38
semifictional, 117–118
South America, 42–44
Southwest, 18–19
of suffering, 270–271
of then and now: Western space, 146–147
time and, 175
of totalitarianism, 149
of trauma, 35–36
of travel, 42–44
of upstate New York, 166–167
of violence, along borderlands, 195
war and the physical geography of mortality, 12–13
wealth distribution and, 148
See also Cultural geography; Geography of place; Human geography; Landscape; Physical geography
Geography III (Bishop), 42
Geography of place
  All the Pretty Horses (McCarthy), 14–15
  "The Fall of the House of Usher" (Poe), 94
  Frankenstein (M. Shelley), 100
  The Glass Menagerie (T. Williams), 105–106
  Long Day's Journey into Night (O'Neill), 169–170
  Lord of the Flies (Golding), 171–172
  The Lord of the Rings (Tolkien), 174–175
  Macbeth (Shakespeare), 177
  "The Metamorphosis" (Kafka), 180
  Moby Dick (H. Melville), 184–185
  My Ántonia (Cather), 188–189
  The Old Man and the Sea (Hemingway), 205–206
  One Hundred Years of Solitude (Garcia Marquez), 220
  On the Road (Kerouac), 214–215

The Sound and the Fury (Faulkner), 260–261
The Sun Also Rises (Hemingway), 272–273
Waiting for Godot (Beckett), 289–290
Geopolitics of war, 193–194
George, Lake, New York, 166
Gerard, Emily
  The Land beyond the Forest, 84
  "Transylvanian Superstitions," 84
Germany
  The Book Thief (Zusak), 47–50
  Hitler's consolidation of power, 51–52
  World War I, 10–14
  World War II, 90, 255–258, 318
Ghosts and ghostly geography
  colonialism and, 233
  gothic manors, 153, 154
  Hamlet (Shakespeare), 120
  interior spaces in Poe's works, 228–229
  natural spaces, 150–151
  slavery and, 34–36
  of trauma, 35–36
Gibson, Wilfrid, 103
Gide, André, 64
Gilded Age, 300–301
Gilead, Republic of, 123–126
Gilman, Charlotte Perkins
  "Why I Wrote the Yellow Wallpaper," 312
  "The Yellow Wallpaper," 309–313
Ginsberg, Allen
  "Howl," 334
  in *On the Road* (Kerouac), 214
The Glass Menagerie (T. Williams), **105–107**
  fragile landscape of Laura's psyche, 106
  geography of place, 105–106
  literary landscape of memory, 105
God. *See* Religion
Golding, William
  Lord of the Flies, 171–174
  Nobel Prize, 171
Goldstein, Emmanuel
  The Theory and Practice of Oligarchical Collectivism, 193
Good versus evil, 40
Gothic literature
  doppelgänger, 309–310
  exploring darker recesses of human psyche, 211–212
  Poe, Edgar Allan, 225, 226, 229

Gothic manors, haunted space of, 154
Grace
    fall from, 171, 172
    geography of, 258–259
Grand Isle, Louisiana, 30–32
The Grapes of Wrath (Steinbeck), **107–111**
    dust storms and geography of ecological disaster, 108–109
    mapping migration during "dirty thirties," 109–110
Grasmere, England, 303
Great Britain
    Arthurian tales, 25–28
    geography, 25–26
    See also England
Great Depression
    cultural environment of, 280
    culture of sacrifice, 203–204
    Dust Bowl, 107–109
    To Kill a Mockingbird (Lee), 280–282
Great Expectations (Dickens), **111–114**
    autobiographical aspects, 112
    British countryside versus London, 112–113
The Great Gatsby (Fitzgerald), **114–116**
    antihero, 116
    failed dream, 115–116
    geographical landscape, 114–115
Great Neck, Long Island, New York, 114
Great Plains, 187–191
Greece, ancient
    Antigone (Sophocles), 20–22
    belief in prophecy, 201
    earth as a globe, 174
    The Iliad (Homer), 21, 197
    A Midsummer Night's Dream (Shakespeare), 181–184
    The Odyssey (Homer), 197–200
    Oedipus Rex (Sophocles), 20, 200–203
    The Republic (Plato), 50–51
    static electricity, knowledge of, 100
Greed, 67–68
Greek islands, parallels with Caribbean islands, 291
Greenhead Gill, England, 303
Grief, spatial imaginary of, 266–267
Guadalupe, New Mexico, 45–46
Guardian, 79
Guilt
    geography of, 65
    impact on worldview and morality, 270
    physical and psychological impact of, 252, 253
Gulliver's Travels (Swift), **117–119**
    catalog of virtue and vice, 118
    semifictional geography and ethnography, 117–118
    travel narrative genre, 117

Haiti
    Absalom, Absalom! (Faulkner), 1
Half Moon (ship), 150
Hallucinogenic drugs, 98–99
Hamlet (Shakespeare), **120–122**
    castle architecture, intrigue of, 121
    outside the walls of Elsinore, 120–121
    productions of, 92, 121
The Handmaid's Tale (Atwood), **122–127**
    geography of memory and resistance, 125–126
    geography of misogyny, 124–125
    toxicity and Christian culture, 123–124
The Handmaid's Tale (television series), 123
Hansberry, Lorraine
    A Raisin in the Sun, 145, 238–239, 329
"Harlem" (Hughes), 145, 238
Harlem Renaissance, 143–145, 328–329
Harper's magazine, 80
Harry Potter and the Chamber of Secrets (Rowling), 129
Harry Potter and the Deathly Hallows (Rowling), 129
Harry Potter and the Philosopher's Stone (Rowling), 127, 319
Harry Potter and the Sorcerer's Stone (Rowling), 127
Harry Potter series (Rowling), **127–130**
    place of magic in growing up, 129–130
    three realms, 128–129
    written in Edinburgh, 319
Hass, Robert, **130–132**
    in California, 334
    Field Guide, 130–131
    "Iowa City: Early April," 131
    "Measure," 132
    "Meditation at Lagunitas," 131
    "Misery and Splendor," 131–132
    "The Problem of Describing Trees," 131
    Rivers of Words (nonprofit organization), 132
    "San Pedro Road," 131

Index

Hauntings. *See* Ghosts and ghostly geography
Hawthorne, Nathaniel
  American Renaissance movement, 150
  "Ethan Brand," 328
  The House of the Seven Gables, 327
  in New England, 327, 328
  Puritan history and, 326, 327
  Romanticism, 253
  The Scarlet Letter, 252–255, 327
  "Young Goodman Brown," 67, 327
Hayford, Harrison, 39
Hazaras, 163–165
Hazlitt, William, 326
Health and medicine
  Agent Orange and, 278
  disease as fate, 201–202
  "dust pneumonia," 109
  environmental toxins, 123
  land as source of healing, 45–46
  mental illness, 217–219
  traditional folk medicine, 45–46, 62
  treatment of women, 309–312
  tuberculosis, 170, 229
Heaney, Seamus, **132–135**
  "Digging," 133
  "Englands of the Mind," 133
  geography of home (Ireland), 132–134
  Nobel Prize, 132
  "Place and Displacement," 133
  "The Place of Writing," 133
  "The Placeless Heaven," 133
  Preoccupations, 133
  "Sandstone Keepsake," 133–134
  "The Sense of Place," 133
  "Through-Other Places, Through-Other Times," 133
Heart of Aztlan (Anaya), 332
Heart of darkness, Africa as, 136, 232
Heart of Darkness (Conrad), **135–138**
  Africa as continent of darkness, 136, 232
  mapping Africa in the imagination of colonizers, 135–136
  moral landscape of colonialism, 136–137
The Heart of Gold (starship), 138–139
Hedge, Frederic Henry, 327
Helicopters, 81, 82
Hell's Angels (Thompson), 80
Hemingway, Ernest
  in Cuba, 206
  in Florida, 330–331
  in "Lost Generation," 114
  Men Without Women, 318
  "Night Before Battle," 330
  Nobel Prize, 168
  The Old Man and the Sea, 205–208
  in Paris, 317–318
  Stein and, 317–318
  The Sun Also Rises, 272–274, 318
Henson, Josiah, 284
Hentzner, Paul, 321
Hermes (god), 198
Herr, Michael
  Apocalypse Now, 81
  Dispatches, 79–83
  Full Metal Jacket, 81
Hessian soldiers, 151
Heyward, Duncan, 166
Highway 66, 109
Hillerman, Tony
  Leaphorn & Chee series, 332
  Navajo Nation and, 331–332
Hiroshima, Japan, 90
"His Last Bow" (Doyle), 9
An Historical Relation of the Island Ceylon (Knox), 244
"History" (Berry), 37, 38
History of British Birds (Bewick), 153
The Hitchhiker's Guide to the Galaxy (Adams), **138–140**
  characters and places, 139
  earth and its antecedents, 138–139
  perspectives, 139
Hitler, Adolf, 51–52. *See also* Nazism
Hobbes, Thomas, 173
The Hobbit (Tolkien), 174, 175
Hogsmeade (fictional place), 129
Hogwarts Express (train), 127, 129
Holmes, Oliver Wendell
  "A Berkshire Summer Morning," 328
Holocaust, 47–50, 90
Home
  art and a room of one's own, 310–311
  basements as shelters, 49–50
  basements as sources of evil, 95–96
  bed as safe haven, 180
  cabin in *Uncle Tom's Cabin* (Stowe), 286
  as celebration of woman's love for family, 78

Home (cont.)
   country house novels, 54
   as cultural center of family life, 286
   cultural geography of belonging and, 238–239
   eye is a window, 78
   "The Fall of the House of Usher" (Poe), 94–96
   family and relationships as, 34, 35
   feuding houses, 6, 247–251, 305
   geography of domesticity, 310
   geography of (Ireland), 132–134
   haunted space of gothic manor, 154
   immigrant housing, 157–158
   internal tensions, 266–267
   as prison, 180, 309–312
   race and class issues in housing, 140–141, 238–239, 268–269, 271
   repressive space of domestic life, 31, 40
   road as, 216
   safety of, 128–129
   search for, 215
   surveillance, gender, and the home interior, 311–312
   veteran's troubled notion of, 278–279
   war and homecoming, 62
   See also Land ownership
"Homecoming: Anse la Ray" (Walcott), 292
Homer
   The Iliad, 21, 197, 291
   influence on Walcott, 291
   The Odyssey, 197–200
Horror, geography of, 101
Horror genre. *See Dracula* (Stoker); *Frankenstein* (M. Shelley); "The Metamorphosis" (Kafka); Poe, Edgar Allan
Hosseini, Khaled
   background, 164
   The Kite Runner, 163–165
The Hound of the Baskervilles (Doyle), 9
House of Light (Oliver), 210
The House of the Seven Gables (Hawthorne), 327
The House on Mango Street (Cisneros), **140–143**
   barrio as identity, 141
   gender and repression, 141–142
   race and class issues, 140–141
Housing. *See* Home
Houyhnhnms (wise, talking horses), 117, 118

"Howl" (Ginsberg), 334
Huckleberry Finn. See Adventures of Huckleberry Finn (Twain)
Hudson, Henry, 150–151
Hughes, Langston, **143–145**
   "Brass Spittoons," 143–144
   geography of African diaspora, 143–144
   "Harlem," 145, 238
   Harlem Renaissance, 144–145, 328
   "I, Too," 145
   "Let America be America Again," 145
   "The Negro Speaks of Rivers," 143
   in New York City, 328
Hugo, Richard, **146–147**
   "Bear Paw," 146–147
   "Camas Prairie School," 146
   "Ci Vediamo" (The Triggering Town), 146
   geography of then and now: Western space, 146–147
   "Indian Girl," 146
   "Indian Graves at Jocko," 146
   "The Lady in Kicking Horse Reservoir," 146
   "Landscapes," 146
   "A Map of Montana in Italy," 146
   "A Night at the Napi in Browning," 146
   "Pishkun," 146
   "2433 Agnes, First Home, Last House in Missoula," 146
Hull, England, 243
Human-animal relationships, 56–58
Human body
   connecting us as family to animals, 209
   connection to mind, 258
   unifying landscape of the body, 293–294
The Human Comedy (Balzac), 316–317
Human geography
   of immigrant experience, 157–158
   of incest and suicide, 202
Human mind
   architecture and geography of, 77–78
   connection to body, 258
   landscape of psyche, 106
   madness, 160–161
   See also Memory
The Hunger Games (Collins), **147–149**
   the Capitol, 147–149
   changing geography of totalitarianism, 149
   districts, 147–149

the games, 147–149
geography and wealth distribution, 148
"Hunting" (Snyder), 258
Hurons, 166–167
Hurston, Zora Neale
   background, 276
   in Florida, 330–331
   Harlem Renaissance, 329
   Their Eyes Were Watching God, 275–277
Huxley, Aldous
   Brave New World, 50–52
Huxley, Thomas Henry, 51
Hybridity, 23, 45
Hypocrisy, 10, 67–68

"I, Too" (Hughes), 145
"I Died for Beauty" (Dickinson), 76
"I Felt a Funeral, in my Brain" (Dickinson), 77
"I Hear America Singing" (Whitman), 295
"I Heard a Fly Buzz—When I Died" (Dickinson), 76
"I Sing the Body Electric" (Whitman), 295
"I Wandered Lonely as a Cloud (Daffodils)" (W. Wordsworth), 324
Ibsen, Henrik
   An Enemy of the People, 88–90
Ideas, geography of, 170
Identity
   barrio as, 141
   borderlands and, 23
   country identity after colonialism, 231
   geography and, 160
   Harlem Renaissance and black identity, 143
   mystery of self, 131
   relationship to place, 140
   self-identity, 103
   Whitman on, 294
The Iliad (Homer), 21, 197, 291
Ilium (fictional city), New York, 255–256
Illinois
   as free state, 5
   The House on Mango Street (Cisneros), 140–142
   The Jungle (Sinclair), 156–158
   A Raisin in the Sun (Hansberry), 238–239
Imagination, altering reality, 264
Imaginative geography, defined, 156

Immigrants
   Afghan immigrants, California, 164
   housing, 157–158
   human geography of immigrant experience, 157–158
   My Ántonia (Cather), 188
In a Green Night (Walcott), 291
In Cold Blood (Capote), 80
Inarticulateness, 262
Incest, 2, 202, 221
India
   Gulliver's Travels (Swift), 117, 118
   The Sign of the Four (Doyle), 8
"Indian Girl" (Hugo), 146
"Indian Graves at Jocko" (Hugo), 146
Indianapolis, Indiana, 256
Indians. *See* Native Americans
Indigenous people
   assimilatory pressures on, 45–46
   first encounter with European invaders, 43
   loss of lands and the space of interracial relations, 167–168
   noble savage, 185–186
   religion, 45, 46
   See also Colonialism; Native Americans
Indochina, French colonialism, 81, 318
Indonesia
   Tambora, Mount, 100
Industrial food system, horrors of, 156–157
Industrial Revolution, 112
Infanticide, 35
Inferno (Dante), 76, 133
Infidelity
   The Awakening (Chopin), 30–31
   The Crucible (Miller), 67–68
   Death of a Salesman (Miller), 73
   The Scarlet Letter (Hawthorne), 252–255
   A Streetcar Named Desire (T. Williams), 266
   Sula (Morrison), 270
Inishowen peninsula, Ireland, 133–134
Insects, transformation into, 179–180
Inside/outside, 235, 248–249, 296
Inspiration. *See* Muse
Institutionalization, 217–219, 267–268
Ionian Islands, Greece, 197
Iowa City, Iowa, 257
"Iowa City: Early April" (Hass), 131
Iran, Sherlock Holmes in, 8

Irati River, Spain, 273
Ireland
   Arthurian tales, 25–28
   Heaney, Seamus, 132–134
   potato famine, 170
   Troubles (1968–1998), 133
Irving, Henry, 84
Irving, Washington, **150–152**
   American Renaissance movement, 150
   haunted natural spaces, 150–151
   "The Legend of Sleepy Hollow," 150, 151
   "Rip Van Winkle," 150–151
Ismara, Greece, 197
Isolation. *See* Alienation
"IT," quest for, 215
Italy
   Brideshead Revisited (Waugh), 53, 54
   "The Cask of Amontillado" (Poe), 226–227
   Daisy Miller (James), 70–72
   in Hugo's poetry, 146
   The Odyssey (Homer), 198, 199
   Romeo and Juliet (Shakespeare), 247–251
   World War II, 52
Ithaca (island), Greece, 197, 198, 199

Jacobs, Harriet, 331
Jalalabad, Afghanistan, 164
James, Henry
   The Bostonians, 328
   Daisy Miller, 70–72, 315
James I, King (England and Scotland), 177
Jane Eyre (C. Brontë), **153–156**
   British colonialism, 154
   British moors, 154
   cultural geography of class equality, 154–155
   haunted space of the gothic manor, 154
   publication of, 325
Japan
   Gulliver's Travels (Swift), 118
   World War II, 51, 90
Jefferson (fictional city), Mississippi
   Absalom, Absalom! (Faulkner), 1–4
   As I Lay Dying (Faulkner), 28–30
Jews: Holocaust, 47–50
Job, book of, 186
Journalism
   Fear and Loathing in Las Vegas (Thompson), 97–99
   muckraking investigations, 156–158
   new journalism, 79, 80
Joyce, James, 28
Juan Fernández archipelago, South Pacific Ocean, 244
The Jungle (Sinclair), **156–159**
   cultural geography of industrial production, 156–157
   human geography of the immigrant experience, 157–158
Jungles, 278. *See also* Forest

Kabul, Afghanistan, 163–165
Kafka, Franz
   background, 179
   The Castle, 179
   as closet existentialist, 180
   "The Metamorphosis," 179–181
   Salinger comparisons, 179
   The Trial, 179
Kansas
   Dust Bowl, 108
   The Wizard of Oz (Baum), 299
Kaup, Monika, 141
Keats, John
   in London, 322–323
   "An Ode to a Nightingale," 323
Kemmler, William, 41
Kent, England, 112
Kentucky
   Adventures of Huckleberry Finn (Twain), 6
   Beloved (Morrison), 34–36
   in Berry's verse, 37
   The Great Gatsby (Fitzgerald), 115
   Uncle Tom's Cabin (Stowe), 283–284, 286
Kerouac, Jack
   in New York City, 329
   On the Road, 214–217
Kesey, Ken
   One Flew Over the Cuckoo's Nest, 217–220
Keswick, England, 326
Khyber Pass, Afghanistan, 164
Kilanga, Zaire, 231
Kindness from strangers, 267–268
King, Stephen, 328
King Lear (Shakespeare), **160–163**
   blindness and borders, 161
   geography and identity, 160
   wilderness and wild weather, 160–161

Kingsolver, Barbara
   The Poisonwood Bible, 230–234
Kiowas, displacement of, 15
The Kite Runner (Hosseini), **163–165**
   ethnicity, 163–164
   sense of place, 164–165
Klondike region, Canada, 56–59
Knickerbocker, Texas, 15
The Knight of the Cart (Le Chevalier de la Charrette) (Troyes), 25
Knox, Robert
   An Historical Relation of the Island Ceylon, 244
Künstlerroman (novel of artistic development), 140–143

La Encantada, Mexico, 14–15
Labor movement, 110
"The Lady in Kicking Horse Reservoir" (Hugo), 146
Laguna Puebla, 18, 62–63, 331
Lake District, England, 302–303, 324–326
Lamb, Charles
   Essays of Elia, 326
   in Lake District, England, 326
   Tales from Shakespeare (with M. Lamb), 326
Lamb, Mary
   Tales from Shakespeare (with C. Lamb), 326
Land
   farmers' relationship with, 37–38
   healing of, 38
   pollution of land and politics, 89–90
   shifting boundaries, 192–193
   as source of healing, 45–46
   as struggle, 189
The Land beyond the Forest (Gerard), 84
Land ownership
   American dream, 74, 140–141, 188, 204
   fight over Native American land, 218–219
   gendered laws regarding, 235
   race issues, 140–141, 238–239, 268–269, 271
   See also Home
Landscape
   of childhood, 221
   colonialism and haunted landscape, 233
   cultural landscape of masculinity, 74
   of dystopia, 50–51
   gendered landscape of witchcraft, 178
   geographical, 114–115
   literary landscape and free will, 179–180
   literary landscape of alienation, 180
   literary landscape of memory, 105, 261
   moral landscape of colonialism, 136–137
   political landscape of the 1960s, 218
   of psyche, 106
   science and the literary landscape, 100–101
   sky as, 49
   surreal landscape of hallucinogenic drugs, 99
   theft and, 49
   of totalitarianism, 51–52
   tradition and changing landscape, 102–103
   unifying landscape of the body, 293–294
   Vietnam, 81–82
"Landscapes" (Hugo), 146
Lane, Charles, 327
Langtry, Texas, 15
Language
   dialects, 276
   mistranslations, 231
   Newspeak, 192–193
   problems in accurately representing world, 131
   racist, 4
   shaping reality, 265
   shifting boundaries, 192–193
Laputa (fictional place), 117
Las Pasturas, New Mexico, 45–46
Las Vegas, Nevada, as symbol for America, 97–98
The Last of the Mohicans (Cooper), **166–168**
   geography of upstate New York, 166–167
   loss of indigenous lands and the space of interracial relations, 167–168
Latino culture. *See* Chicano culture
Law and order
   Athenian law, 182
   Dust Bowl migrant camps, 110
   gendered laws regarding land ownership, 235
   punishment as place, 253–254
   slavery, 6
Le Carré, John, 316

Le Fanu, J. Sheridan
  Carmilla, 84
Leaphorn & Chee series (Hillerman), 332
Leaves of Grass (Whitman), 294
Lee, Harper
  To Kill a Mockingbird, 280–282
  in South (region), 331
"The Legend of Sleepy Hollow" (W. Irving), 150, 151
"Let America be America Again" (Hughes), 145
Lewis, Meriwether, 106
Lewis and Clark expedition, 106
"Ligeia" (Poe), 228–229
"The Light of the World" (Walcott), 292
Lilliput (fictional place), 117, 118
Lincoln, Abraham, 283
Lincoln, Nebraska, 299
"Lines Composed a Few Miles above Tintern Abbey" (W. Wordsworth), 302, 303
Literary landscape
  of alienation, 180
  free will and, 179–180
  of memory, 105, 261
  science and, 100–101
Lithuanian immigrants, 156
Little Neck, Long Island, New York, 114
"Logging 14" (Snyder), 259
"Logging 15" (Snyder), 259
London, England
  Adventures of Sherlock Holmes (Doyle), 7–8
  Brideshead Revisited (Waugh), 53
  versus British countryside, 112–113
  Dracula (Stoker), 84
  Great Expectations (Dickens), 112–113
  Harry Potter series (Rowling), 129
  literary landscape, 320–323
  Nineteen Eighty-Four (Orwell), 51, 192–194
  Oliver Twist (Dickens), 211–214
  Robinson Crusoe (Defoe), 243
  The Strange Case of Dr. Jekyll and Mr. Hyde (Stevenson), 319
  urban geography, 211–212
London, Jack
  in California, 334
  Call of the Wild, 56–59
Long Day's Journey into Night (O'Neill), **168–171**
  as autobiographical, 169–170

geography of ideas, 170
geography of place, 169–170
Long Island, New York, 114–116
"The Long-Legged House" (Berry), 37
Lonsdale, Earl of, 324
Lord of the Flies (Golding), **171–174**
  fall from grace, 171, 172
  geography of place, 171–172
  state of nature, 172–173
The Lord of the Rings (Tolkien), **174–176**
  geography of place, 174–175
  morality and mythology, 175
  time and geography, 175
Los Angeles, California, 98, 256, 334
Los Angeles Times, 79
"Lost Generation," 114
"Lost generation" theme, 11
Louisiana
  literary landscape, 330
  See also New Orleans, Louisiana
Louisville, Kentucky, 115
Love
  cultural geography and young love, 247–248
  cultural geography of passion, 305–306
  forbidden love, 249–250, 252–253
  impossibility of, 15
  "marriage plot" literature tradition, 234–236
  Pride and Prejudice (Austen), 234–236
  Romeo and Juliet (Shakespeare), 247–251
The Lover (Duras), 318
Lowther, James, 1st Earl of Lonsdale, 324
Lumumba, Patrice, 231
Luxembourg
  Slaughterhouse-Five (Vonnegut), 255, 256
Lyrical Ballads (Coleridge and W. Wordsworth), 325–326

Macbeth, King (Scotland), 177
Macbeth (Shakespeare), **177–179**
  gendered landscape of witchcraft, 178
  geography of nihilism, 177–178, 260
  geography of place, 177
Machiavelli, Niccolò
  The Prince, 175
Macondo (fictional town), 220–221
Madness, 160–161
Magic
  Harry Potter series, 127–130

The Lord of the Rings (Tolkien), 174, 175
magical realism, 221, 233
place in growing up, 129–130
Magrathea (fictional planet), 138
Malory, Thomas
   Le Morte d'Arthur, 25
Malraux, André, 178, 224
Malvern, England, 54
Mango Street, Chicago, Illinois, 140–142
Mantua, Italy, 248–249
"The Map" (Bishop), 42
"A Map of Montana in Italy" (Hugo), 146
Mapping
   Africa in imagination of colonizers, 135–136
   the afterlife, 76–77
   colonialism and place/mapping, 231–232
   disease as fate, 201–202
   migration during 1930s, 109–110
   morality of chance, 40–41
   racism, 280–282
   social mores onto different family structures, 269–270
   of war, 195–196
Maps
   in *Gulliver's Travels* (Swift), 117, 118
   nature as, 302–303
   Ulysses's voyage, 198
   Vietnam War, 81–82
   voyage of *Pequod,* 185
Marquez, Gabriel Garcia. *See* Garcia Marquez, Gabriel
Marriage
   arranged, 182, 275
   Elizabethan society, 247
   for love, 275
   "marriage plot" literature tradition, 234–236
   as prison, 310
   teenage, 247–248
Marx, Karl
   Communist Manifesto (with Engels), 51, 64
Maryland, Poe in, 225
Masculinity, cultural landscape of, 74, 248
Mason-Dixon Line, 283
"The Masque of the Red Death" (Poe), 227–228
Massachusetts
   The Crucible (Miller), 66–69

Dickinson in, 75–76
The Handmaid's Tale (Atwood), 123
literary landscape, 326–328
in Oliver's poetry, 208
Poe in, 225
The Scarlet Letter (Hawthorne), 252–255, 327
Maya almanacs, 17–18
Maycomb, Alabama, 280–282
McCarthy, Cormac
   All the Pretty Horses, 14–17
   Border Trilogy, 14
   Cities of the Plain, 14
   The Crossing, 14
   No Country for Old Men, 194–196
   in Southwest (region), 332–333
McCarthyism, 66
McKinley, William, 299
"Measure" (Hass), 132
Meat industry, 156–158
Medallion, Ohio, 269
"Mediated" texts, 39
Medicine. *See* Health and medicine
Medieval times, 175
"Meditation at Lagunitas" (Hass), 131
Melville, Elizabeth, 39
Melville, Herman
   American Renaissance movement, 150
   "Bartleby, the Scrivener," 327
   Billy Budd, 39–42
   Moby Dick, 184–187, 327, 328
   in New England, 327–328
   in New York City, 328
Memory
   geography of, 125–126
   literary landscape of, 105, 261
   portals to, 131
   in trauma victims, 277
Men
   cultural landscape of masculinity, 74, 248
   space of male power, 267
   See also Gender
Men Without Women (Hemingway), 318
"Mending Wall" (Frost), 102–103
Mental illness
   culture of, 218
   One Flew Over the Cuckoo's Nest (Kesey), 217–220
   A Streetcar Named Desire (T. Williams), 266–268
   "The Yellow Wallpaper" (Gilman), 309–312

Mestizaje ('hybridity'). *See* Hybridity
"The Metamorphosis" (Kafka), **179–181**
    free will and Kafka's literary landscape, 179–180
    geography of place, 180
    Kafka as closet existentialist, 180
    literary landscape of alienation, 180
Mexico
    All the Pretty Horses (McCarthy), 14–17
    border with U.S., 14–15, 22–24, 194–196, 332–333
    On the Road (Kerouac), 215
Mexico City, Mexico, 215
"Michael" (W. Wordsworth), 303
Middle Ages, 175
Middle-earth (fictional place), 174–175
A Midsummer Night's Dream (Shakespeare), **181–184**
    forest setting, 182–183
    mythology and folklore, 183
    place of law and order, 182
Midwest (region), U.S., 299, 300
Migration, 109–110. *See also* Immigrants
Military-industrial complex, 87–88
Millay, Edna St. Vincent, 209
Miller, Arthur
    After the Fall, 329
    The Crucible, 66–69, 326, 329
    Death of a Salesman, 73–75, 329
    in New York City, 329
    Puritan history and, 326
Mind. *See* Human mind
"Misery and Splendor" (Hass), 131–132
Misogyny, 124–125, 178
Missionaries, 230–233
Mississippi
    cultural geography, 1–2, 28
    history, 1–2
    physical geography, 28
    The Sound and the Fury (Faulkner), 260–263
Mississippi River, U.S., 4–6, 143
Missoula, Montana, 146
Missouri
    Adventures of Huckleberry Finn (Twain), 4–6
    Dust Bowl, 108
    relationship to South, 106
    St. Louis, 106
Mitchell, Margaret, 331
Moby Dick (H. Melville), **184–187**
    Bible, 186
    excerpt, 184
    geography of evil, 185
    geography of place, 184–185
    inspiration for, 328
    noble savage, 185–186
    written in New England, 327
Modernism, 104, 143, 297
Mohicans, 166–168
Molching (fictional city), Germany, 47–50
Moldavia, 84
Molière, 316
Monroe, Marilyn, 329
Montana, in Hugo's poetry, 146
Montcalm, Louis-Joseph de, 166
Moore, Thomas, 50
Moors, England, 154, 306–307
Morales, Joseph, 46
Morality
    American exceptionalism, 98
    Arthurian tales, 25–26
    catalog of virtue and vice, 118–119
    colonialism, 136–137
    Death of a Salesman (Miller), 73, 74
    guilt and, 65
    human nature, 118
    To Kill a Mockingbird (Lee), 280–282
    law of the river, 6
    mapping social mores onto different family structures, 269–270
    mapping the morality of chance, 40–41
    morality tales, 174–176
    mythology and, 175
    overconsumption, 98
    Puritan-inspired, 98
    Puritans, 252, 253–254
    See also Religion
Mormons, 8
Morning, Paramin (Walcott), 291
"Morning Poem" (Oliver), 210
Morocco
    Brideshead Revisited (Waugh), 53
    Robinson Crusoe (Defoe), 243
Morrison, Toni
    Beloved, 34–37
    Nobel Prize, 34
    Pulitzer Prize, 34
    Sula, 268–272
Le Morte d'Arthur (Malory), 25
Motorcycle races, 97–99
The Moviegoer (Percy), 330
Movies, Vietnam War in, 81
"Muggle" realm (fictional place), 128

Index

Muir, John, 333
Munich, Germany, 47–48
Munro, George, 166–167
Murder
   Beloved (Morrison), 35
   Billy Budd (H. Melville), 40–41
   Crime and Punishment (Dostoyevsky), 64–66
   Hamlet (Shakespeare), 120
   Macbeth (Shakespeare), 177, 178
   One Hundred Years of Solitude (Garcia Marquez), 221
   in Poe's works, 226–227
Muse, nature as, 302–303
Mushing, geography of, 56–57
Muslims, 163
Mussolini, Benito, 52
Mutiny, 40
My Àntonia (Cather), **187–191**
   excerpt, 188
   geography of place, 188–189
   land as struggle, 189
   passing of the pioneers, 189–190
Mystery
   Adventures of Sherlock Holmes (Doyle), 7–10
   geography of, 206–207
Mythology, 174, 175, 183
Myths and Texts (Snyder), 259

Nabokov, Vladimir, 316
Narrative, unspoken, 262
Native Americans
   Caribbean region, 172
   Chicano heritage, 46
   Chickasaws, 28
   conflicts with Anglo Americans, 17–19
   displacement, 15
   forced land sales, 218–219
   French and Indian War, 166–168
   in Hugo's poetry, 146–147
   loss of lands and the space of interracial relations, 167–168
   Navajo medicine men, 62
   Puritans and, 67
   racism against, 300
   time as circular, 18
   Yeehats, 57–58
Nature
   versus civilization, 4–5, 272
   complicity, 241–242
   conflict with economic profit, 88–89
   cultural geography of Puritanism and, 252–253
   as cure to human world, 210
   degradation by civilization, 259
   God in, 231
   hard science view of, 232–233
   harsh laws of survival, 204
   in Hass's poetry, 131–132
   haunted spaces, 150–151
   human impact on, 264–265
   indifference of, 240
   involvement of, 240–241
   as map and muse, 302–303
   in Oliver's poetry, 208–210
   rejection by, 241
   Romantic connection to, 104
   spiritual force in, 232–233
   spiritually and, 258
   state of, 171, 172–173
   versus technology, 264–265
   as threat to order, 252
   See also Fauna; Flora; Pastoral tradition
Navajo medicine men, 62
Navajo Nation, 331–332
Nazism
   birthplace of, 48
   The Book Thief (Zusak), 47–50
   French Resistance, 224
   geography of, 224
   Hitler's consolidation of power, 51–52
Nebraska
   Dust Bowl, 108
   My Àntonia (Cather), 187–191
   The Wizard of Oz (Baum), 299
"The Negro Speaks of Rivers" (Hughes), 143
Neocolonialism, 230, 231–232
Nevada
   Fear and Loathing in Las Vegas (Thompson), 97–99
New Albion. *See* California
New American Review, 79
New England
   Frost and, 102–104
   literary landscape, 326–328
   Moby Dick (H. Melville), 184–187, 327
   O'Neill's plays set in, 169
New Hampshire, Frost in, 102
New Haven, Connecticut, 264
New Jersey, Whitman in, 293
New journalism, 79, 80

New Mexico
  Almanac of the Dead (Silko), 18
  Bless Me, Ultima (Anaya), 45–47
  Ceremony (Silko), 61–64
  Dust Bowl, 108
  literary landscape, 331–332
New Orleans, Louisiana
  The Awakening (Chopin), 30–33
  Esplanade Avenue, 30–31
  literary landscape, 330
  sexual desire in, 2
  A Streetcar Named Desire (T. Williams), 266–268
  in *Sula* (Morrison), 269
New York City
  as amoral, 115, 116
  "Bartleby, the Scrivener" (H. Melville), 327
  Beat movement, 334
  Brideshead Revisited (Waugh), 53
  The Catcher in the Rye (Salinger), 59–61
  Central Park, 60–61
  Death of a Salesman (Miller), 73–75
  The Great Gatsby (Fitzgerald), 114–116
  Harlem Renaissance, 143–145, 328–329
  literary landscape, 328–329
  9/11 terrorist attack, 90–92
  On the Road (Kerouac), 215
  theater, 169, 329
New York State
  capital punishment debate, 41
  Catskill Mountains, 150–151, 292
  Civil War regiments, 240
  geography of upstate New York, 166–167
  The Last of the Mohicans (Cooper), 166–168
  Slaughterhouse-Five (Vonnegut), 255–256
New Yorker magazine, 80
Newark, New Jersey, 256
Newspeak, 192–193
Nietzsche, Friedrich, 29, 64, 170, 178
"A Night at the Napi in Browning" (Hugo), 146
"Night Before Battle" (Hemingway), 330
Nihilism, 170, 177–178, 260, 270–271
9/11 terrorist attacks, 90–92
Nineteen Eighty-Four (Orwell), **192–194**
  "Big Brother," 192–193
  evils of totalitarianism, 51

  geopolitics of war, 193–194
  Newspeak, 192–193
  shifting boundaries of land and language, 192–193
No Country for Old Men (McCarthy), **194–196**
  geography of violence along borderlands, 195
  layered mapping of war, 195–196
No Exit (Sartre), 195
Nobel laureates in literature, 168–169. *See also specific laureates*
Noble savage, 166–168, 185–186
Nore, England, 40
Norse mythology, 174
North America
  contrasts between European and American culture, 71–72
  geography of travel, 42–44
"North and South" (Walcott), 292
North Dakota, Dust Bowl in, 108
"North Haven" (Bishop), 42
North Kent, England, 112
North & South (Bishop), 42
Northwest Passage, 151
Norway
  An Enemy of the People (Ibsen), 88–90
Nova Scotia, 43
Nuns, 60

Oates, Joyce Carol, 90
Obliteration of the Self (ideology), 192
O'Brien, Tim
  The Things They Carried, 277–279
Oceania (fictional superstate), 192–193
Oceans and seas
  Aegean and beyond, 197
  dangerous waters, 197–198
  as geography of mystery, 206–207
  Ithaca mystery, 199
  mutiny and ocean travel, 40
  real or mythical voyage?, 198–199
  Robinson Crusoe (Defoe), 242–247
  suicide by drowning, 30, 32
O'Connor, Flannery, 331
"An Ode to a Nightingale" (Keats), 323
Odysseus Unbound (Bittlestone, Diggle, and Underhill), 199
The Odyssey (Homer), **197–200**
  Aegean and beyond, 197
  dangerous waters, 197–198
  Ithaca mystery, 199

as real voyage?, 198–199
The Odyssey (Walcott), 291
Oedipus at Colonus (Sophocles), 20
Oedipus Rex (Sophocles), **200–203**
  antihero travelogue, 201
  human geography of incest and suicide, 202
  limits of the ruling class, 201
  mapping disease as fate, 201–202
  in trilogy of Theban plays, 20
Of Mice and Men (Steinbeck), **203–205**
  dream geography, 204
  Great Depression: culture of sacrifice, 203–204
Ogygia (fictional island), 198
Ohio
  Beloved (Morrison), 34–36
  Sula (Morrison), 268–271
  Underground Railroad, 284
Oklahoma, Dust Bowl in, 108, 109
Olching (fictional city), Germany, 47–49
The Old Man and the Sea (Hemingway), **205–208**
  excerpt, 205
  geography of place, 205–206
  sea as geography of mystery, 206–207
Oliver, Mary, **208–210**
  "At Great Pond," 210
  "August," 209–210
  Dream Work, 210
  House of Light, 210
  "Morning Poem," 210
  in New England, 328
  Pulitzer Prize, 209
  Romantic tradition, 208–210
  "Sleeping in the Forest," 209
  "Spring," 210
  "Wild Geese," 209, 210
Oliver Twist (Dickens), **211–214**
  excerpt, 211
  rural/urban dichotomy, 212–213
  urban geography of London, 211–212
Omaha, Nebraska, 299, 300–301
Omeros (Walcott), 291
On the Road (Kerouac), **214–217**
  geography of place, 214–215
  quest for "IT," 215
  road as home, 216
One Flew Over the Cuckoo's Nest (Kesey), **217–220**
  culture of mental illness, 218
  dreamscape of institutionalization, 219

fight over Native American land, 218–219
  political landscape of the 1960s, 218
One Hundred Years of Solitude (Garcia Marquez), **220–222**
  end of the line, 221–222
  geography of place, 220
  landscape of childhood, 221
  magical realism, 221
O'Neill, Ella Quinlan, 169
O'Neill, Eugene Gladstone
  background, 169–170
  decline of family, as theme, 105
  family of, 169
  Long Day's Journey into Night, 168–171
  Nobel Prize, 168–169
O'Neill, James, 169
O'Neill, Jamie, 169
Oracle of Delphi, 200–201
Oran, Algeria, 223–224
"An Ordinary Evening in New Haven" (Stevens), 264
Oregon, Dust Bowl border control, 109
Orientalism, 85
Orinoco River, Venezuela, 244
Orpheus Descending (T. Williams), 330
Orwell, George
  Nineteen Eighty-Four, 51, 192–194
"Other"
  rejection of, 85
  "us versus them" worldview, 86, 88
"El otro Mexico" (Anzaldúa), 23
Outside/inside, 235, 248–249
"Over 2,000 Illustrations and a Complete Concordance" (Bishop), 42
Oxford, England, 53
Ozona, Texas, 15

Pacific islands
  Juan Fernández archipelago, 244
  Lord of the Flies (Golding), 171–174
Pacific Northwest, 117, 258
Paghman, Afghanistan, 165
Paliki Peninsula, Greece, 199
Pamplona, Spain, 272, 273–274
Panem (fictional country), 147–149
Paradise, geography of, 290–292
Paris, France, 272–274, 289, 316–318
"Paris, 7 A.M." (Bishop), 42
Parker, Theodore, 327
Pascal, Blaise, 180
Pashtuns, 163–165

Pasing, Germany, 48
Passion, cultural geography of, 305–306
Pastoral tradition
   All the Pretty Horses (McCarthy), 15
   Berry's poetry, 37–38
   defined, 75–76
   Dickinson's poetry, 75–76
Patchett, Ann, 331
Paterson, New Jersey, 297
Paterson (W. Williams), 297
Peabody, Elizabeth Palmer, 327
Pear trees, 275–276
People's Party, 301
Pequod (whaling ship), 185, 328
Percy, Walker
   The Moviegoer, 330
   in New Orleans, 330
Père Lachaise Cemetery, Paris, France, 316–317
"Perhaps I asked too large" (Dickinson), 77
Persia, Sherlock Holmes in, 8
Peter the Great, Czar (Russia), 64
Phaedo (Plato), 105, 106, 261
Phoniness, 60
Physical geography
   of equality, 295
   Mississippi, 28
   of slavery, 283–285
   war and mortality and, 12–13
Picasso, Pablo, 114
The Pickwick Papers (Dickens), 323
Pioneers, 188, 189–190
"Pishkun" (Hugo), 146
"The Pit and the Pendulum" (Poe), 225–226
Place
   characters and, 139
   colonialism and place/mapping, 231–232
   of family, 91–92
   identity and, 140
   of law and order, 182
   punishment as, 253–254
   sense of, 164–165
   shaped by people who live there, 268
   of supernatural, 306–307
   time as, 255
   trail metaphor, 259
   violence against, 256
   See also Geography of place
"Place and Displacement" (Heaney), 133
Place names, changes in, 231
"The Place of Writing" (Heaney), 133
"The Placeless Heaven" (Heaney), 133
The Plague (Camus), **223–225**
   geography of war, Nazism, and evil, 224
   Oran: the geography of *The Plague,* 223–224
Plagues, 200, 202, 223–224, 227–228, 321
Plants. *See* Flora
Plato (Greek philosopher)
   Phaedo, 105, 106, 261
   The Republic, 50–51
Plymouth, England, 9
Plymouth, Massachusetts, 326
Pneumonic plague, 223–224
Poe, Edgar Allan, **225–230**
   American Renaissance movement, 150, 228
   "Annabel Lee," 229
   "The Cask of Amontillado," 226–227
   death and dungeons in Poe's short stories, 225–229
   European settings in his works, 225–228
   "The Fall of the House of Usher," 94–97, 228–229
   Gothic tradition, 225, 226, 229
   haunted interior spaces, 228–229
   "Ligeia," 228–229
   "The Masque of the Red Death," 227–228
   "The Pit and the Pendulum," 225–226
   "The Premature Burial," 101
   "The Raven," 229
   Romanticism, 225, 228
   supernatural elements in his works, 225, 226, 228–229
   "The Tell-Tale Heart," 94, 227
Poetry
   defined, 44
   technical terminology, origins in agriculture, 133
   Wordsworth's theories about, 302
The Poisonwood Bible (Kingsolver), **230–234**
   Africa as heart of darkness, 232
   colonialism and place/mapping, 231–232
   colonialism and the haunted landscape, 233
   flora and fauna, 232–233
   place of women, 233

Zaire as Biblical place, 230–231
Polidori, John William (physician), 100, 101, 315
Polis (Greek city-state), 21
Politics
   geopolitics of war, 193–194
   The Handmaid's Tale (Atwood), 123
   political landscape (1960s), 218
   pollution of land and politics, 89–90
   Slaughterhouse-Five (Vonnegut), 255–256
   The Wizard of Oz (Baum), 300–301
Pollution, 88–90, 123
Polyglossia, 15
Porter, Cole, 114
Post-postmodernism, 92
Post-traumatic stress disorder (PTSD), 270–271
   causes, 87
   Ender's Game (Card), 87
   One Flew Over the Cuckoo's Nest (Kesey), 217, 218–219
Postmodernism, 59, 92
Postpartum depression, 309–312
Potter, Beatrix
   in Lake District, England, 325
   The Tale of Peter Rabbit, 325
Pound, Ezra, 317
Prairies, 187–191
Pratt, Mary Louise, 15
"Preface to the Lyrical Ballads" (W. Wordsworth), 302
The Prelude (W. Wordsworth), 291, 303
"The Premature Burial" (Poe), 101
Preoccupations (Heaney), 133
Pride and Prejudice (Austen), **234–237**
   ballroom as cultural signifier, 235–236
   gendered laws regarding land ownership, 235
   gendered space, 235
The Prime of Miss Jean Brodie (Spark), 319
The Prince (Machiavelli), 175
Prison, 253–254
   home as, 180, 309–312
   life of crime as, 211–212
   marriage as, 310
"The Prisoner of Chillon" (Byron), 315
Prisoners of war (POWs)
   World War I, 11, 12–13
   World War II, 255, 256
Prisons, 14, 15

"The Problem of Describing Trees" (Hass), 131
Prostitution, 60, 65, 123–124, 169
Proust, Marcel, 316
Providence, Rhode Island, 225
Provincetown, Massachusetts, 208
Psyche, landscape of, 106
PTSD. *See* Post-traumatic stress disorder
Pueblo Indians, 62–63, 331
Puget, Peter, 117
Pulitzer Prize winners. *See specific authors and works*
Punishment, as place, 253–254
Pure Food and Drug Act, 157
Puritans
   The Crucible (Miller), 66–69
   history in New England, 326–327
   moral order and just punishment, 252, 253–254
   morality inspired by, 98
   nature and cultural geography of Puritanism, 252–253
   religious philosophy, 294
   The Scarlet Letter (Hawthorne), 252–255, 327
   writers, 326–327
Pynchon, Thomas
   The Crying of Lot 49, 92

"Quai d'Orléans" (Bishop), 42
Quakers, 284
Questions of Travel (Bishop), 42
"Questions of Travel" (Bishop), 44

Race issues
   class and, 1–2, 144
   democracy, 145
   housing and land ownership, 140–141, 238–239, 268–269, 271
   institutional racism, 281
   To Kill a Mockingbird (Lee), 280–282
   loss of indigenous lands and the space of interracial relations, 167–168
   mapping racism, 280–282
   pejorative language, 4
   race and real estate, 239
   racial mixing, 1–2
   racism, 5–6, 300
   social order and, 1–2, 5
   white supremacy, 1–2, 167–168
   See also African Americans; Chicano culture; Immigrants

Rackham, Arthur, 95
Railroads, 127, 129
A Raisin in the Sun (Hansberry), **238–239**
   home and the cultural geography of belonging, 238–239
   productions of, 329
   race and real estate, 239
   title, 145, 238
Rape and attempted rape
   Beloved (Morrison), 35
   false accusations, 203, 280–281
   A Streetcar Named Desire (T. Williams), 267
   Their Eyes Were Watching God (Hurston), 275
"The Raven" (Poe), 229
The Ravishing of Lol Stein (Duras), 318
Real estate. *See* Home; Land ownership
Realism, 221, 289
Reanimation, 101, 228
Recovery, geography of, 62–63
The Red Badge of Courage (Crane), **240–242**
   nature's complicity, 241–242
   nature's indifference, 240
   nature's involvement, 240–241
   nature's rejection, 241
Red Cloud, Nebraska, 188
Red Death, 228
"The Red Wheelbarrow" (W. Williams), 296
Redemption, in post-postmodernism, 92
Religion
   atheism, 64–65, 170, 224
   Biblical places, 230–231
   Brideshead Revisited (Waugh), 53, 54
   Catholicism, 45, 54, 170, 225–226
   creation of life, 101
   The Crucible (Miller), 66–69
   geography of death, 29
   God in nature, 76
   Holocaust against Jews, 47–50
   hypocrisy, 67–68
   indigenous, 45, 46
   mapping the afterlife, 76–77
   Mormons, 8
   Muslims, 163
   as "opiate of the masses," 64
   sex, nuns, and New York City, 60
   symbolism, 241
   town versus forest in the battle for souls, 66–67
   See also Bible; Christianity; Morality; Puritans
Remarque, Erich Maria
   All Quiet on the Western Front, 10–14
Repression, gender and, 31, 40, 141–142
The Republic (Plato), 50–51
Resistance, geography of, 125–126
The Restaurant at the End of the Universe (Adams), 139
Revelation, book of, 51, 174
Revolutionary War, 151
Rhode Island, Poe in, 225
Rhys, Jean
   Wide Sargasso Sea, 154
Richmond, Virginia, 225
"The Rime of the Ancient Mariner" (Coleridge), 325–326
The Ring of the Nibelung (Wagner), 174
Rio Grande, U.S.-Mexico, 15
"Rip Van Winkle" (W. Irving), 150–151
Ripley, George, 327
River Derwent, England, 303, 324
River Duddon, England, 303
River Wye, England-Wales, 302
Rivers
   as blood of African people, 143
   moral law of, 6
Rivers of Words (nonprofit organization), 132
"The Road Not Taken" (Frost), 103
Road travel
   crossroads as symbolic of life decisions, 103
   Dust Bowl migrants, 109–110
   road as home, 216
   On the Road (Kerouac), 214–217
   settlement of the West and, 98
Robinson Crusoe (Defoe), **242–247**
   Crusoe's island, 243–244
   Defoe's sources, 244
   land and sea, 243
Rolling Stone magazine, 79, 97
Roman Catholicism. *See* Catholicism
Romania
   Transylvania, 83–84
Romanticism
   connection to nature, 104, 208–209
   Geneva retreat, 315
   Hawthorne, Nathaniel, 253
   Oliver, Mary, 208–209
   Poe, Edgar Allan, 225, 228
   tragic flaws in humankind, 104

Wordsworth, William, 302
Rome, Italy, 70–72
Romeo and Juliet (Shakespeare), **247–251**
  cultural geography and young love, 247–248
  inside/outside, 248–249
  productions of, 249–250
  urban geography and architecture of forbidden love, 249–250
Roosevelt, Theodore, 157
"A Rose for Emily" (Faulkner), 281–282
The Rose Tattoo (T. Williams), 330
Rousseau, Jean-Jacques
  Confessions, 315
  in Geneva, 315, 316
  The Social Contract, 315
  on state of nature, 172–173
Route 66, U.S., 109
Rowling, J. K.
  in Edinburgh, 319
  Harry Potter and the Chamber of Secrets, 129
  Harry Potter and the Deathly Hallows, 129
  Harry Potter and the Philosopher's Stone, 127, 319
  Harry Potter and the Sorcerer's Stone, 127
  Harry Potter series, 127–130, 319
Royal Navy, 39–41
Ruling class, limits of, 201
Rural life
  in Berry's works, 37–38
  fences, 102–103
  in Frost's poetry, 102–104
  The Grapes of Wrath (Steinbeck), 107–111
  land as struggle, 189
  Of Mice and Men (Steinbeck), 203–205
  "The Red Wheelbarrow" (W. Williams), 296
  rural/urban dichotomy, 212–213
  in Snyder's works, 258
Russia
  communist takeover, 51
  Crime and Punishment (Dostoyevsky), 64–66
  Orthodox Christianity, 64
  See also Soviet Union

Sacred geography, 38
Sacrifice, culture of, 203–204
Saint-Domingue (French colony), 1
Saint Petersburg, Russia, 64–66
Salem, Massachusetts, 66–68, 326, 327
Salinger, J. D.
  Catcher in the Rye, 59–61, 92
  Kafka comparisons, 179
Sallee (now Salé), Morocco, 243
Saltillo, Mexico, 14–15
Salvador, Brazil, 243
San Angelo, Texas, 14–15
San Diego, California, 23
San Francisco, California, 97, 258, 333–334
San Jose, California, 164
"San Pedro Road" (Hass), 131
"Sandstone Keepsake" (Heaney), 133–134
"Santarém" (Bishop), 42
Sartre, Jean-Paul
  existentialism, 180, 224
  No Exit, 195
  Nobel Prize, 180
Saturday Pioneer (Aberdeen, South Dakota), 300
Saudi Arabia, Sherlock Holmes in, 8
Scaffolds, 253–254
The Scarlet Letter (Hawthorne), **252–255**
  nature and the cultural geography of Puritanism, 252–253
  punishment as a place: the scaffold and prison at the town center, 253–254
  Puritanism in, 327
Scarred geography, 38
Schenectady, New York, 256
"The Schooner Flight" (Walcott), 292
Schopenhauer, Arthur, 64
Science
  amoral use of, 51
  criminology, 7
  Frankenstein (M. Shelley), 51, 100–102
  literary landscape and, 100–101
  nature versus technology, 264–265
  pollution, 89–90
Science fiction
  Ender's Game (Card), 86–88
  The Hitchhiker's Guide to the Galaxy (Adams), 138–140
Scotland
  Edinburgh, 318–320
  Harry Potter series (Rowling), 128, 129
  Macbeth (Shakespeare), 177–179
Scott, Walter, 319, 326
Sealts, Merton M., Jr., 39

Seas. *See* Oceans and seas
"Seascape" (Bishop), 42
Self-identity, 103
Selkirk, Alexander, 244
Semifictional geography, 117–118
Sense of place, 164–165
"The Sense of Place" (Heaney), 133
September 11 terrorist attacks, 91
Settlement, road travel and, 98
Sex
   forced (*See* Rape and attempted rape)
   geography of flirtation, 70–71
   The Handmaid's Tale (Atwood),
      123–124
   incest, 2, 202, 221
   nuns, New York City, and, 60
   A Streetcar Named Desire
      (T. Williams), 266
   See also Gender; Infidelity; Men;
      Women
Sexual harassment, 156
Shakespeare, William
   Hamlet, 92, 120–122
   King Lear, 160–163
   in London, 320–321
   Macbeth, 177–179, 260
   marriage, 247
   A Midsummer Night's Dream, 181–184
   misogyny, 178
   nihilism, 260
   Romeo and Juliet, 247–251
   Tales from Shakespeare (C. Lamb and
      M. Lamb), 326
   The Two Gentlemen of Verona, 182
   As You Like It, 182
Shelley, Mary Wollstonecraft
   Frankenstein, 51, 100–102
   Geneva writing retreat, 315
   in London, 323
   Romanticism, 315
Shelley, Percy, 315, 326
Shelter. *See* Home
Shiite Muslims, 163
Shipwrecks, 242–245
Shirley (C. Brontë), 325
Sicily (island), Italy, 199
Sierra Nevada Mountains, California, 333
The Sign of the Four (Doyle), 8
Silko, Leslie Marmon
   Almanac of the Dead, 17–19
   Ceremony, 61–64
   in New Mexico, 331

Sinclair, Upton
   The Jungle, 156–159
Sir Gawain and the Green Knight
   (Arthurian tale), 26
Sitting Bull, 300
Sky
   in Dickinson's poetry, 77–78
   as landscape during war, 49
   as symbol for freedom, 31–32
Slaughterhouse-Five (Vonnegut), **255–258**
   alien abduction, 255, 256–257
   contemporary and historical politics,
      255–256
   postwar trauma, 257
   violence against place, 256
Slaughterhouses, 156
Slavery
   Christian sentimentalism and, 285–286
   daily life, 284
   escaped slaves, 4–6, 34–35, 283–286
   land ownership, 269
   Nineteen Eighty-Four (Orwell), 192
   physical and cultural geography of,
      283–285
   plantation owners' fears of resistance,
      125
   sale of slaves, 283–284
   slave narrative, 331
   slave ships, 243
   South's dependence on, 1
   trauma of, 34–36
   Uncle Tom's Cabin (Stowe), 283–286
   Waiting for Godot (Beckett), 288
   West Indies, 1, 172
   Whitman's pleas for equality for, 295
Sled dogs, 56–57
"Sleeping in the Forest" (Oliver), 209
Slouching towards Bethlehem (Didion), 80
Slovenia
   Styria, 84
Snakes, as evil, 231
"The Snow Man" (Stevens), 264
Snyder, Gary, **258–260**
   "By Frazier Creek Falls," 259
   in California, 334
   geography of grace, 258–259
   "Hunting," 258
   "Logging 14," 259
   "Logging 15," 259
   Myths and Texts, 259
   "Things to Do Around Portland," 258
   "The Trail Is not a Trail," 259

Turtle Island, 259
    Whitman as inspiration for, 258
Social class. *See* Class issues
The Social Contract (Rousseau), 315
Social mores. *See* Morality
Socialism, 156, 192
Socrates, 105
Soledad, California, 203
Somerset, England, 325–326
"Song of Myself" poems (Whitman), 293–294
"Song of Myself I" (Whitman), 294
"Song of Myself II" (Whitman), 294
"Song of Myself VI" (Whitman), 294
Sophocles
    Antigone, 20–22
    Oedipus at Colonus, 20
    Oedipus Rex, 20, 200–203
The Sound and the Fury (Faulkner), **260–263**
    dissolution of time, 261–262
    existentialism, 261–262
    geography of place, 260–261
    inarticulateness and stream of consciousness, 262
    literary landscape of memory, 261
    nihilism, 260
    title, 260
    unspoken narrative, 262
South America
    geography of travel, 42–44
    One Hundred Years of Solitude (Garcia Marquez), 220–222
South Dakota
    Aberdeen newspaper, 300
    Dust Bowl, 108
South (region), U.S.
    African Americans post-Civil War, 28
    Anglo-Saxon self-image, 1
    Caribbean past, 1–2
    economic downturn following emancipation, 280
    literary landscape, 330–331
    racial separation, 2
    in Williams, Tennessee's works, 105–106
Southey, Robert, 325, 326
Southwest (region), U.S.
    All the Pretty Horses (McCarthy), 14–17
    Almanac of the Dead (Silko), 17–19
    conflicts between natives and Anglo Americans, 17–19
    drug war, 196
    geography, 18–19
    literary landscape, 331–333
Soviet Union
    invasion of Afghanistan, 163, 164
    Stalinism, 192
    World War II, 194
    See also Russia
Space
    gendered space, 235, 248, 296
    of male power, 267
    as mystery, 9
    private versus public, 76
    ship as confined space, 40–41
    spatial imaginary of grief, 266–267
Spain
    The Odyssey (Homer), 198–199
    "The Pit and the Pendulum" (Poe), 225–226
    The Sun Also Rises (Hemingway), 272–273
Spanish Inquisition, 225–226
Spark, Muriel
    The Comforters, 320
    in Edinburgh, 319–320
    as *Poetry Review* editor, 320
    The Prime of Miss Jean Brodie, 319
Spithead, England, 40
"Spring" (Oliver), 210
St. Louis, Missouri, 106
St. Lucia, 291–292
St. Petersburg (fictional town), Missouri, 4–5
Stalin, Joseph, 192
Star Trek (television series), 138
State of nature, 171, 172–173
Stein, Gertrude, 114, 316, 317
Steinbeck, John
    in California, 334
    The Grapes of Wrath, 107–111
    Of Mice and Men, 203–205
    Travels with Charley, 333
Stevens, Wallace, **264–266**
    "Anecdote of the Jar," 264–265
    nature versus technology, 264–265
    in New England, 328
    "An Ordinary Evening in New Haven," 264
    "The Snow Man," 264
    "Thirteen Ways of Looking at a Blackbird," 264

Stevenson, Robert Louis
   in Edinburgh, 319
   in London, 323
   The Strange Case of Dr. Jekyll and Mr. Hyde, 319
Stoker, Bram
   Dracula, 83–85, 94, 315, 323
   in England, 84
"Stopping by Woods on a Snowy Evening" (Frost), 103
Stowe, Harriet Beecher
   in New England, 328
   Uncle Tom's Cabin, 283–287, 328, 331
The Strange Case of Dr. Jekyll and Mr. Hyde (Stevenson), 319
Strangers, kindness from, 267–268
Stream of consciousness, 28–29, 262
A Streetcar Named Desire (T. Williams), **266–268**
   American South as setting for, 105
   kindness from strangers is preferable, 267–268
   New Orleans settings in, 330
   productions of, 329
   space of male power, 267
   spatial imaginary of grief, 266–267
Strikes. *See* Labor movement
A Study in Scarlet (Doyle), 8
Styria, Austria-Slovenia, 84
Sudan, Sherlock Holmes in, 8
Suffering, geography of, 270–271
Suicide and attempted suicide
   Antigone (Sophocles), 20
   The Awakening (Chopin), 30, 32
   Death of a Salesman (Miller), 73–75
   The Handmaid's Tale (Atwood), 124
   human geography of, 202
   King Lear (Shakespeare), 161
   My Ántonia (Cather), 188
   National Suicide Day, 271
   Oedipus Rex (Sophocles), 202
   One Flew Over the Cuckoo's Nest (Kesey), 218
   The Sound and the Fury (Faulkner), 261–262
   A Streetcar Named Desire (T. Williams), 266
   The Things They Carried (O'Brien), 279
   Waiting for Godot (Beckett), 289
Sula (Morrison), **268–272**
   geography of suffering and its erasure, 270–271
   Nel versus Sula: mapping social mores onto different family structures, 269–270
Sumatra
   Gulliver's Travels (Swift), 118
The Sun Also Rises (Hemingway), **272–274**
   bullring, 273–274
   excerpt, 272
   fiesta at Pamplona, 273
   geography of place, 272–273
   written in Paris, 318
Sunni Muslims, 163
Supernatural
   in Arthurian tales, 26
   in Irving, Washington's works, 150
   A Midsummer Night's Dream (Shakespeare), 182
   moors of England as place of, 306–307
   in Poe's works, 225, 226, 228–229
   See also Vampires
Supernatural novels. *See Dracula* (Stoker)
Surrealism, 99
Surveillance
   Adventures of Sherlock Holmes (Doyle), 9
   architecture of, 86
   Ender's Game (Card), 86
   gender and, 311–312
   The Handmaid's Tale (Atwood), 124–125
   Nineteen Eighty-Four (Orwell), 193
   "The Yellow Wallpaper" (Gilman), 311–312
Survival
   harsh laws of nature, 204
   sled dogs, 56–57
   during war, 11
Sussex, England, 9
Swift, Jonathan
   Gulliver's Travels, 117–119
Switzerland
   Daisy Miller (James), 70–72
   Geneva, 315–316
   Sherlock Holmes in, 8
Symbolism
   characters in *The Wizard of Oz* (Baum), 300
   color symbolism, 227–228
   crossroads as symbolic of life decisions, 103
   Las Vegas as symbol for America, 97–98

plague as symbol of evil, 224
religious symbolism, 241
water and air as symbols of freedom, 31–32
wild rosebush as symbol of living outside moral oral, 253–254

The Tale of Peter Rabbit (Potter), 325
Tales from Shakespeare (C. Lamb and M. Lamb), 326
Taliban regime, 163–164
Tambora, Mount, Indonesia, 100
Tarrytown, New York, 150
Tasmania, Australia, 118
Technology. *See* Science
"The Tell-Tale Heart" (Poe), 94, 227
Tenedos (island), 197
Tennessee, in Stevens's poetry, 264–265
The Tenth Muse Lately Sprung Up in America (Bradstreet), 327
Texas
  All the Pretty Horses (McCarthy), 14–17
  border with Mexico, 194
  Dust Bowl, 108
Thebes, Greece
  Antigone (Sophocles), 20–22
  civil war, 20–22
  Oedipus Rex (Sophocles), 20, 200–203
Theft, landscape and, 49
Their Eyes Were Watching God (Hurston), **275–277**
  Eatonville, Florida, 276
  the pear tree, 275–276
The Theory and Practice of Oligarchical Collectivism (Goldstein), 193
"There's a Certain Slant of Light" (Dickinson), 77
The Things They Carried (O'Brien), **277–279**
  jungles of Vietnam, 278
  veteran's troubled notion of home, 278–279
"Things to Do Around Portland" (Snyder), 258
Third space feminism, 23–24
"Thirteen Ways of Looking at a Blackbird" (Stevens), 264
This Day (Berry), 38
Thomas, Dylan, 329
Thompson, Hunter S.
  Fear and Loathing in Las Vegas, 97–99
  Hell's Angels, 80

new journalism, 80
Thoreau, Henry David
  American Renaissance movement, 150
  in New England, 327, 328
  transcendentalism, 294
  Walden, 327
  A Week on the Concord and Merrimack Rivers, 327
Thrinacia, land of, 198
"Through-Other Places, Through-Other Times" (Heaney), 133
Thurman, Wallace, 329
Tibet, Sherlock Holmes in, 8
Tijuana, Mexico, 23
Time
  as circular, 18
  dissolution of, 261–262
  distance of time and place, 21
  geography and, 175
  having a beginning and end, 221
  as place, 255
  "unstuck in time," 255
"Tintern Abbey" (W. Wordsworth), 302, 303
To Kill a Mockingbird (Lee), **280–282**
  cultural environment of the Depression, 280
  mapping racism, 280–282
"To Live in the Borderlands" (Anzaldúa), 23
Toledo, Spain, 225–226
Tolkien, John Ronald Reuel
  in Geneva, 316
  The Hobbit, 174, 175
  The Lord of the Rings, 174–176
Toole, J. K.
  A Confederacy of Dunces, 330
Tornadoes, 299
Toronto Daily Star, 317–318
Tortuga (Anaya), 332
Totalitarianism
  changing geography of, 149
  The Hunger Games (Collins), 147–149
  isolation of populace, 148
  landscape of, 51–52
  Nineteen Eighty-Four (Orwell), 192
Town. *See* Cities; Civilization
Toxic masculinity, 248
Toxicity, Christian culture and, 123–124
Tradition, changing landscape and, 102–103
"The Trail Is not a Trail" (Snyder), 259

Train travel, 127, 129
Tralfamadore (fictional planet), 255, 256–257
Trans-Mississippi Exposition (1898), 299
Transcendentalism, 294
Transnationalism, 18
Transylvania, 83–84
"Transylvanian Superstitions" (Gerard), 84
Trauma
  geography of, 35–36
  memory and, 277
  postwar trauma, 11, 62, 257 (*See also* Post-traumatic stress disorder)
  of slavery, 34–36
Travel
  geography of travel, 42–44
  Hamlet (Shakespeare), 120–121
  North America, 42–44
  ocean travel, 40
  South America, 42–44
  See also Oceans and seas; Road travel
Travel narrative, as genre, 117
Travels with Charley (Steinbeck), 333
Trees. *See* Flora; Forest
The Trial (Kafka), 179
The Triggering Town ("Ci Vediamo") (Hugo), 146
Trojan War, 21, 197
Troubles (1968–1998), 133
Troy, New York, 256
Troy (Ilios), 197, 198
Troyes, Chrétien de
  Le Chevalier de la Charrette (The Knight of the Cart), 25
Truth, 79, 80, 220
Tuberculosis, 170, 229
Tubman, Harriet, 331
Tucson, Arizona, 18
Turtle Island (Snyder), 259
Twain, Mark
  Adventures of Huckleberry Finn, 4–7, 331
  in Geneva, 316
  in New England, 328
  in South (region), 331
"2433 Agnes, First Home, Last House in Missoula" (Hugo), 146
The Two Gentlemen of Verona (Shakespeare), 182
"2008, XI" (Berry), 38

Ukraine, Sherlock Holmes in, 8
Uncle Tom's Cabin (Stowe), **283–287**
  the cabin, 286
  physical and cultural geography of slavery, 283–285
  role of Christian sentimentalism, 285–286
  setting, 331
  written in New England, 328
Underground Railroad, 283, 284
Underhill, John
  Odysseus Unbound (with Bittlestone and Diggle), 199
Unions, 110
United States, border with Mexico, 14–15, 22–24, 194–196, 332–333
Unspoken narrative, 262
Updike, John, 328
"Upon a stone on the side of Black Comb" (W. Wordsworth), 302
Upstate New York, geography of, 166–167
Urban geography. *See* Cities
"Us versus them" worldview. *See* "Other"
Utah, Mormons in, 8
Utopia, 50

Vampires
  Carmilla (Le Fanu), 84
  Dracula (Stoker), 83–85
  Polidori's tale, 101
Vancouver, George, 117
Vancouver Island, 117
"Varick Street" (Bishop), 42
Venezuela
  Orinoco River, 244
Venice, Italy, 53, 54
Verona, Italy, 247–251
Vevey, Switzerland, 70–72
Vice, 118–119
Vietnam War
  difficulty of readjusting to civilian life, 278
  Dispatches (Herr), 79–83
  jungles, 278
  landscape, 81–82
  in movies, 81
  The Things They Carried (O'Brien), 277–279
  veterans, 195
Vieux Carré (T. Williams), 330
Violence
  geography of, along borderlands, 195
  Lord of the Flies (Golding), 171–174
  against place, 256

Virginia, Poe in, 225
Virtue. *See* Morality
Visual perception, 78
Vlad II (Wallachian nobleman), 84
Vlad III "the Impale" (Wallachian nobleman), 84
Volcanoes, 100
Volta, Alessandro, 100–101
Vonnegut, Kurt, Jr.
  background, 256, 257
  Slaughterhouse-Five, 255–258
A Voyage to the South Seas, and Round the World (Cooke), 244
Voyages. *See* Oceans and seas

Wagner, Richard
  The Ring of the Nibelung, 174
Waiting for Godot (Beckett), **288–290**
  geography of place, 289–290
  productions of, 289
  theatre of the absurd, 289
Walcott, Derek, **290–293**
  Another Life, 291–292
  "A Far Cry from Africa," 291
  The Fortunate Traveller, 291
  geography of paradise: Derek Walcott's island, 290–292
  "Homecoming: Anse la Ray," 292
  In a Green Night, 291
  influences on, 291
  "The Light of the World," 292
  Morning, Paramin, 291
  Nobel Prize, 290–291
  "North and South," 292
  The Odyssey, 291
  Omeros, 291
  "The Schooner Flight," 292
  St. Lucia, 291
  White Egrets, 291
Walden (Thoreau), 327
Wales, Arthurian tales set in, 25
Wallachia, 84
War
  chaos and, 79–80
  Civil War, U.S., 106, 240–242
  cultural geography of military-industrial complex, 87–88
  detachment between veterans and civilians, 11
  on drugs, 196
  Ender's Game (Card), 86–88
  French and Indian War, 166–168

geography of, 224
geopolitics of, 193–194
homecoming and, 62, 278
layered mapping of, 195–196
in movies, 81
physical geography of mortality and, 12–13
postwar trauma, 11, 219, 257
psychological toll, 240
Revolutionary War, 151
in science fiction, 86–88
survival, 11
Theban civil war, 20–22
Trojan War, 21, 197
veteran's troubled notion of home, 278–279
witness and, 80–81
See also Post-traumatic stress disorder; Vietnam War; World War I; World War II
The War (Duras), 318
Washington, D.C., 256, 293
Washington Park, Chicago, Illinois, 239
Washington State, early exploration, 117
The Waste Land (Eliot), 297
Water
  dangerous waters, 197–198
  as symbol of freedom, 31–32
  See also Oceans and seas; Rivers
Waugh, Evelyn
  Brideshead Revisited, 52–55
Wealth distribution, geography and, 148
Weather, wilderness and, 160–161
Weaver, Raymond, 39
The Web and the Rock (Thomas Wolfe), 329
Webb, Daniel, 166
Weed, California, 203
A Week on the Concord and Merrimack Rivers (Thoreau), 327
Welch, James
  Fools Crow, 146
Wellcome, Emily Dickinson, 297
Welty, Eudora
  "A Curtain of Green," 330
  in South (region), 330, 331
West Egg (fictional place), New York, 114–115
West (region), U.S.
  geography of then and now, 146–147
  in Hugo's poetry, 146–147
  morality in Wild West, 74

West (region), U.S. (*cont.*)
  road travel and settlement of, 98
  San Francisco, 333–334
  See also Pacific Northwest; Southwest (region), U.S.
Western novels, 14–17
Whales, 184–187
Where I Was From (Didion), 333
Whitby, England, 84
White Egrets (Walcott), 291
White supremacy, 1–2, 167–168
Whitman, Walt, **293–295**
  on death, 294
  "I Hear America Singing," 295
  "I Sing the Body Electric," 295
  on identity, 294
  Leaves of Grass, 294
  Snyder inspired by, 258
  "Song of Myself I," 294
  "Song of Myself II," 294
  "Song of Myself" poems, 293–294
  "Song of Myself VI," 294
  travels, 293
  unifying landscape of the body, 293–294
Whittier, John Greenleaf, 327
"Why I Wrote the Yellow Wallpaper" (Gilman), 312
Wide Sargasso Sea (Rhys), 154
"Wild Geese" (Oliver), 209, 210
Wild West, morality, 74
Wilde, Oscar, 316, 317
Wilderness
  border with civilization, 58
  flora and fauna, 232–233
  as place of dread, 112–113
  wild weather and, 160–161
  See also Forest
Wilkinson, William
  An Account of the Principalities of Wallachia and Moldavia, 84
Williams, Thomas Lanier "Tennessee"
  Cat on a Hot Tin Roof, 105, 329
  focus on South, 260
  The Glass Menagerie, 105–107
  in New Orleans, 330
  Orpheus Descending, 330
  The Rose Tattoo, 330
  A Streetcar Named Desire, 105, 266–268, 329, 330
  Vieux Carré, 330
Williams, William Carlos, **296–299**
  "Between Walls," 297
  "Danse Russe," 296
  "Dedication for a Plot of Ground," 297
  influences on, 297
  as Modernist, 297
  "no ideas but in things" motto, 297
  Paterson, 297
  "The Red Wheelbarrow," 296
  "The Young Housewife," 296
  "Young Sycamore," 297
Wiltshire, England, 54
Windows, eye as, 78
Winter, 77, 103–104, 264
Witchcraft
  gendered landscape of, 178
  Harry Potter series (Rowling), 127–130
  Macbeth (Shakespeare), 178
  Salem, Massachusetts, 66–68
  traditional medicine, 46
Witness, war and, 80–81
The Wizard of Oz (Baum), **299–301**
  character symbolism, 300
  Midwest, 299
  politics, 300–301
  racism, 300
Wolfe, Thomas (novelist)
  in New York City, 329
  The Web and the Rock, 329
  You Can't Go Home Again, 329
Wolfe, Tom (new journalist), 79
Women
  ancient Greece, 21
  art and a room of one's own, 310–311
  Chicano culture, 140
  geography of misogyny, 124–125
  The Handmaid's Tale (Atwood), 122–127
  indigenous women, 44
  "marriage plot" literature tradition, 234–236
  The Poisonwood Bible (Kingsolver), 233
  Southern writers, 330–331
  Whitman's pleas for equality for, 295
  See also Gender
Woolf, Virginia, 310
Worcestershire, England, 54
Wordsworth, Dorothy, 324
Wordsworth, William, **302–304**
  "Airey-Force Valley," 324
  correspondence from Brontë, Charlotte, 325
  Duddon sonnets, 303

"I Wandered Lonely as a Cloud
(Daffodils)," 324
in Lake District, England, 324–326
"Lines Composed a Few Miles above
Tintern Abbey," 302, 303
Lyrical Ballads (with Coleridge),
325–326
"Michael," 303
nature: map and muse, 302–303
"Preface to the Lyrical Ballads," 302
The Prelude, 291, 303
Romanticism, 302
theories of poetry, 302
"Upon a stone on the side of Black
Comb," 302
Works Progress Administration (WPA),
276
World War I
All Quiet on the Western Front
(Remarque), 10–14
The Great Gatsby (Fitzgerald), 115
heroin addiction in veterans, 269
physical and emotional wounds, 272,
273
PTSD, 270–271
World War II
atomic bomb, 51, 90
The Book Thief (Zusak), 47–50
Brideshead Revisited (Waugh), 52–55
cowardice, 195
Dresden bombings, 90, 255
French Resistance, 224
German occupation of Paris, 318
Holocaust, 47–50, 90
in Hugo's poetry, 146
Nineteen Eighty-Four (Orwell),
194–195
PTSD, 219
Slaughterhouse-Five (Vonnegut),
255–258
totalitarianism, 51–52

war and homecoming, 62
Wounded Knee massacre, 300
WPA (Works Progress Administration),
276
Wuthering Heights (E. Brontë), **304–308**
architectural model for, 305, 306
cultural geography of passion, 305–306
excerpt, 305
moors of England as place of
supernatural, 306–307
two feuding houses, 305

Yahoos (base humanity), 117
Yeats, William Butler, 44
Yeehat Indians, 57–58
"The Yellow Wallpaper" (Gilman),
309–313
geography of domesticity, 310
Gothic doppelgänger, 309–310
surveillance, gender, and the home
interior, 311–312
women's art and a room of one's own,
310–311
Yoknapatawpha (fictional) County,
Mississippi, 1–4, 28–30
Yorkshire, England, 243, 304–306
You Can't Go Home Again (Thomas
Wolfe), 329
"Young Goodman Brown" (Hawthorne),
67, 327
"The Young Housewife" (W. Williams),
296
"Young Sycamore" (W. Williams), 297

Zacatecas, Mexico, 15
Zaire
independence, 231
The Poisonwood Bible (Kingsolver),
230–233
Zusak, Markus
The Book Thief, 47–50